D1368271

# E-Business

## A Management Perspective

Jonathan Reynolds

# E-Business
## A Management Perspective

**OXFORD**

UNIVERSITY PRESS

# OXFORD
### UNIVERSITY PRESS

Great Clarendon Street, Oxford OX2 6DP

Oxford University Press is a department of the University of Oxford.
It furthers the University's objective of excellence in research, scholarship,
and education by publishing worldwide in

Oxford New York

Auckland Cape Town Dar es Salaam Hong Kong Karachi
Kuala Lumpur Madrid Melbourne Mexico City Nairobi
New Delhi Shanghai Taipei Toronto

With offices in

Argentina Austria Brazil Chile Czech Republic France Greece
Guatemala Hungary Italy Japan Poland Portugal Singapore
South Korea Switzerland Thailand Turkey Ukraine Vietnam

Oxford is a registered trade mark of Oxford University Press
in the UK and in certain other countries

Published in the United States
by Oxford University Press Inc., New York

© Oxford University Press 2010

British Library Cataloguing in Publication Data

Data available

Library of Congress Cataloging in Publication Data

Data available

Typeset by MPS Limited, A Macmillan Company
Printed in Italy
on acid-free paper by
L.E.G.O. S.p.A

ISBN 978-0-19-921648-2

1 3 5 7 9 10 8 6 4 2

Dedicated to
HLA and TJR

# Preface

## About this volume

An enormous range of e-business frameworks and models, alongside fragmented empirical literature and technologically driven 'how-to' books, has made it difficult for either students or practitioners to make sense of what they see in the real world and to relate this to the evolving underlying conceptualizations of e-business. This text provides readers with authoritative insight into e-business issues integrated across a range of management and non-management related disciplines.

This volume seeks to draw together a widely varied range of conceptual models and frameworks, existing empirical research, statistical and case study material to provide a coherent insight into e-business from a management perspective. It uses these to:

- define the nature and scope of e-business technologies and the brief history of their development and implementation;

- review the environmental drivers facilitating and constraining the application and growth of e-business technologies;

- evaluate the ways in which e-business technologies can be applied within firms to achieve new business development and process improvements;

- consider the organizational dimension of e-business implementation within firms, from project management, skills and cultural perspectives; and

- reflect upon the likely nature of future challenges and opportunities from e-business technologies

It makes use of over sixty-five case studies and vignettes designed specifically for this book and derived from a wide range of organizations in commercial as well as public and not-for-profit contexts drawn from a number of geographical markets. Over 150 review and discussion questions will seek to probe your understanding both of the issues presented and the evolving challenges faced by users and practitioners. There are sixty specific activities designed to allow the reader to explore their own understanding of these topics.

The text focuses primarily upon the contribution of e-business technologies to the effectiveness and efficiency of for-profit firms, with insights drawn, where relevant, for not-for-profit and public sector organizations. It includes the application of e-business technologies to both large and small firms in both developed and emerging economies. The scope of what the text includes in a definition of e-business technologies naturally extends beyond PC-based web channels to mobile and other platforms, including store-based kiosks and emerging, pervasive technologies, such as digital TV, SMS, social networking platforms and location-based commerce.

## Part one: The changing environment for e-business

Following an introductory chapter which defines the nature and explores the scope and economic and social impact of e-business technologies, four chapters review interrelated sets of drivers which provide the context for the application of e-business technologies by organizations.

### Chapter 2: Economics of e-business

This chapter examines the economic arguments for the particular contribution that e-business makes to growth and productivity. It considers the potential contribution of e-business technologies to economic growth, market competitiveness and productivity. It examines the difficulties in measuring the net economic benefits of e-business, the effects of e-business on the location of economic activities and critically assesses the potential for efficiency gains and growth in consumer power from e-business technologies for individuals.

### Chapter 3: Technological issues

This chapter reviews the e-business technologies that have had the most lasting impact upon the corporate environment and seeks to understand the importance of security and privacy in e-business, as well as its role in standardization. It examines the ways in which ICT costs, benefits, and risks can be evaluated.

### Chapter 4: Social and behavioural issues

This chapter discusses the effects which digital technologies have had on the behaviour of individuals and groups within in society and how e-business technologies fit into the consumer decision-making process, and it assesses the likely consequences of e-business technologies for change at a societal level.

### Chapter 5: Ethical and regulatory issues

This chapter explores the legal and ethical issues facing users, firms, and regulators in relation to privacy, the increasingly complex and contested intellectual property rights environment, and implications that e-business technologies bring with them for fraudulent and criminal activity, and increasing scrutiny of the Internet by regulators.

## Part two: The application of e-business technologies

Four chapters review specific aspects of the application and operationalization of e-business technologies, focusing upon strategic and marketing issues, followed by discussions of product and service innovation, and the reshaping of business processes.

## Chapter 6: The strategy of e-business

This chapter examines the effects of e-business on industry structure, and considers how value is created in firms and how e-business influences the value chain. It explores the ways in which firms involved in e-business can compete, critically assesses whether the concept of a business model is relevant to e-business firms, and finally seeks to understand what e-business strategy means for public sector organizations.

## Chapter 7: Digital marketing

This chapter reviews the extent to which digital marketing both complements and changes contemporary marketing practice and explores attitudes towards the adoption of digital marketing techniques by firms. It sets out the particular challenges for organizations in developing an integrated multi-channel marketing strategy, distinguishing between first- and second-generation digital marketing techniques.

## Chapter 8: Product and service innovation

This chapter reviews the circumstances surrounding successful e-business innovation. It seeks to develop the reader's insight into the theoretical foundations of innovation and identifies different types of innovation involving e-business, including e-product innovation, e-service innovation, and open innovation. It considers the role of users and user communities in open innovation for e-businesses as well as the characteristics and challenges of e-business innovation in the public sector.

## Chapter 9: Reshaping business processes

This chapter sets out the main principles underlying efficient operational processes, supply chains, and networks, and their relevance to an organization's overall business performance. It examines the ways in which such processes can be supported, developed and restructured by the Internet. It provides specific insights into the features of electronic procurement and trends in the sourcing of goods and services by firms, alongside the growing importance of information sharing and collaboration as a means of driving supply chain integration. Finally, it analyses the characteristics and consequences of both outsourcing and off-shoring of business processes by firms.

---

# Part three: The organization of e-business

Recognizing that successful e-business implementation goes beyond simple investment, two chapters examine the organizational dimensions of e-business technology adoption. This resolves into the challenges posed by e-business project design and management, the associated skills required to manage e-business investment, and the overarching cultural creativity or transformation which must often accompany new or redesigned business models.

## Chapter 10: E-business project management

This chapter sets out the differences between e-business and conventional project management. It also differentiates between project management and systems development. It describes the environment of the entrepreneurial or start-up e-business and how that relates to the development of a project management approach. Finally, it articulates the variety and uses of the various tools, techniques, and methodologies available to an e-business project manager.

## Chapter 11: E-business skills and culture

The chapter focuses on the human resource requirements of e-business, defining what is meant by e-business skills, distinguishing between e-business skills shortages, gaps, and mismatches, and outlining trends in demand for and supply of such skills. It seeks to raise the reader's awareness of the recruitment practices of e-businesses. Finally, it sets out selected behavioural and cultural dimensions of e-business organization and entrepreneurship.

# Part four: Conclusions

## Chapter 12: Future Challenges and Opportunities

This chapter concludes the text by examining the nature and scale of challenges in the business environment that will affect the future development of e-business technologies. It focuses on specific developments in economic, technological, social, and regulatory environments. It considers the strengths and weaknesses of forecasting and scenario-planning tools for gaining insight into e-business futures before reviewing the nature and implications of future scenarios for e-business.

# Acknowledgements

The editor and authors would like to thank Alexandra Lazarus-Priestley, Angela Butterworth, Fiona Goodall and Hannah Brannon at Oxford University Press for their advice, guidance, and support throughout the publication of this text. The continued encouragement of Angela Adams, formerly of OUP and now of the Saïd Business School, has also been much appreciated.

In addition, the editor is personally indebted to Spyros Gkinos for his tireless, but always courteous, pursuit of the very many permission holders involved.

In listing those whom OUP would like to thank, we include the many reviewers who made a direct contribution to the way this book was put together.

The editor and the publisher are grateful to those who granted permission to reproduce copyright material.

Crown Copyright is reproduced under Class License Number C2006010631.

Every effort has been made to trace and contact copyright holders but this has not been possible in every case. If notified, the publisher will undertake to rectify any errors or omissions at the earliest opportunity.

# How to use this book

There are many specific features included in the chapters of *e-Business: A Management Perspective* that are designed to help you both to learn, and to organize information. Some of these features emphasize how theory is applied in real organizations, and others help you to gain a deeper understanding of how this links to practice, in order to ground your theoretical understanding of e-Business in a management perspective.

## Chapter Learning Outcomes

Each chapter opens with a bulleted outline of the main concepts and ideas. These serve as helpful signposts to what you can expect to learn from each chapter.

## Short cases

The book is packed with examples that link the topics to real-life organizations to help you gain an understanding of e-Business in action.

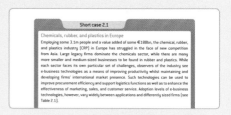

## Long cases

Longer case studies provide an opportunity to apply what you have learnt and analyse a real-life example.

## Activity Boxes

These are short questions and examples, which give you the opportunity to relate the topic to your own experience.

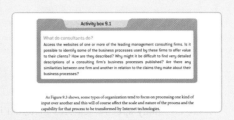

## Chapter Summary

Each chapter ends with a précis that summarizes the most important arguments developed within that chapter.

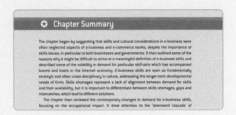

## End of chapter Review and Discussion questions

Two sets of questions have been included at the end of every chapter to check that you have grasped the key concepts and provide you with an opportunity for discussion.

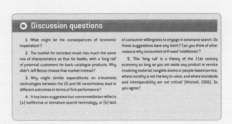

## Further Reading

An annotated list of recommended reading on each subject will help guide you further into the literature on a particular subject area.

# How to use the Online Resource Centre

There is a wide range of web-based content for tutors and students to support this text. Students can go to the Online Resource Centre to find web links, chapter summaries and an author blog. Tutors will be able to access a suite of customizable PowerPoint slides, which can be used in lectures and seminars, alongside a bank of additional case studies and exercises.

All of these resources can be incorporated into your institution's existing virtual learning environment.

## For students

### Author blog

To complement this text we are launching an author blog discussing a number of up-to-date issues, from the perspective of eBusiness.

### Annotated web links

Links to websites relevant to each chapter, direct students towards valuable sources of information and professional associations.

### Flashcard glossary

Glossary terms presented in an interactive flashcard format to help revise key terms and concepts. Downloadable to MP4 players.

## Oxford NewsNow

The latest news relevant to e-Business from a variety of publications, brought direct to this Online Resource Centre, and always up to date.

# For lecturers

## PowerPoint® lecture slides

A suite of chapter-by-chapter PowerPoint® slides has been included for use in your lecture presentations. They are fully customizable so you can tailor them to match your own presentation style.

## A bank of additional case studies

In addition to the many case studies included in the text, a further collection of relevant and engaging case studies are available for use in group tutorial work and assignments.

## Additional exercises and questions with solutions

A suite of additional student activities, together with answers to all end-of-chapter review and discussion questions, provide you with a wide range of seminar resources.

## Suggested answers to the end-of-chapter self-assessment questions

Suggested answers to all of the end-of-chapter questions provide the opportunity to discover how well students have understood the key topics.

# Contents in brief

# Contents in full

## Part two  The application of e-business technologies

## Part three    The organization of e-business

## Part four    Conclusions

# List of cases

## Short cases

# Long cases

# 1

# Introduction

## Learning outcomes

Completing this Chapter will enable you to:

- Define the nature and explore the scope and economic and social impact of e-business technologies
- Place the recent developments of e-business technologies into context
- Review the different levels of adoption of and readiness for e-business worldwide
- Understand the roles e-business technologies play for public and not-for-profit as well as for commercial sector organizations

## The nature, scope, and impact of e-business technologies

It is hard today for many of us to think of our individual lives, our communities, or indeed a world without e-business technologies. These technologies range from hardware to software, from web browsers to email and social networks, from mobile web to location-based services and from e-procurement hubs to enterprise resource planning systems. But it is what such technologies make possible, rather than what they are in their own right, which is important and it is this that provides the fundamental focus of this book. Think about how natural it is now to carry around an MP3 player the size of a business card with one's entire recorded music collection on it. If we were to think back to the 1980s, it would have been almost inconceivable for individuals to consider this to be possible, although miniaturization of technology was well in hand. However, whilst the devices themselves are suitably impressive, it is the transformational effect which they, the social networks which have grown up around them and the Internet on which they rely, have had on the ways and places in which we discover, share, and enjoy music and video that is so significant. Similarly, the growth of e-procurement and collaboration systems, ranging from public platforms like eBay and Alibaba.com to bespoke sectoral or company supply chain systems such as the aerospace industry's Exostar or Wal-Mart's Retail Link, have been instrumental in enabling not just large, but small and medium-sized enterprises (SMEs) to obtain access to international markets in ways that would have been difficult and prohibitively expensive as little as ten years ago..

E-business technologies have therefore become recognized internationally as transformational drivers of social and economic growth, when effectively implemented. For individuals and organizations of all kinds, as well as for nations and regions, economic transformation can be achieved in two broad ways, through:

- *Doing new and better things*: developing products and services which are either wholly innovative, or which are more effective substitutes for existing products and services; and
- *Doing things better*: applying efficiency improvements to existing tasks and processes for both organizations and end users.

The Information and Communications Technology (ICT) sector alone, within which the Internet and digital content segments have been the most dynamic, contributed nearly a quarter of GDP growth in North America and Europe between 1999 and 2004 (European Commission, 2006). In terms of doing things better, the widespread adoption of information and communications technology more generally is seen as contributing to half the productivity improvements achieved by European enterprises during a similar period—and an even higher proportion in the US, although as we shall see, actually unpicking cause and effect to demonstrate the unequivocal effects of technology on business efficiency let alone national productivity is a complex task. But whilst much of the discussion and debate about e-business technologies has been focused on the attributes and characteristics of the technologies themselves and their economic impact, many of the challenges posed by e-business for organizations are in practice as much managerial in nature as they are economic, as much societal and behavioural as they are technological.

In terms of social transformation, e-business technologies have changed the scale, style, and mechanisms of communication between individuals and groups or networks of individuals. They have affected consumer behaviour not just in relation to the consumption of physical goods but also in relation to consumption of digitized products (such as downloadable music, video, and software) as well as services and information goods. Whilst we might think that the most prominent consumption effects of e-business have been the direct substitution effects of e-commerce upon retail sales through conventional channels of consumption, it is actually the indirect effects upon the consumer's decision-making process, for example in relation to search strategies, that have greater social significance. At a societal level, the issues may be even more complex. On the one hand, the Internet has been seen as a force for good—providing opportunities for social cohesion, enriching the quality of life and promoting diversity and inclusiveness. But it has also been seen as a harmful force: raising concerns over the extent and consequences of 'digital divides' opening up between groups within society or between countries which exacerbate economic polarization, the possibilities of social exclusion, as well as fear of the undesirable results of mass participation in fields as diverse as commerce, newsgathering and politics.

One particularly critical challenge has been to distinguish, from all the technological possibilities arising from e-business innovation, genuine and clear-cut opportunities for improvements in efficiency or effectiveness from those which simply add to the cost base, provide no net benefits, or may even serve to reduce efficiency. Why is this? Firstly, it is because managers and policy-makers often make assumptions about the inevitability of benefits accruing from a new technology (so-called technological determinism). For example, the introduction of interactive whiteboards in schools and colleges was assumed to be of *prima facie* benefit to the ways in which pupils and students learned. But only after substantial roll-out programmes by governments in a number of developed economies was any work actually done on the nature of these benefits, whether they were additional to or similar to those derived from existing teaching techniques, and how they might be properly exploited (Becta, 2003).

Secondly, the process of understanding both the nature and the consequences of these opportunities can be complex. For example, studies show that issuing handheld devices to employees of commercial enterprises, with the explicit objective of improving communications and productivity, are likely to cause a wide variety of perhaps unanticipated process and behavioural changes, both positive and negative. For example, one piece of research demonstrated a 45 per cent decline in laptop usage and an average increase of an hour a day in employees' available working time (Goldman Sachs, 2001). Other studies have indicated that uncontrolled email interruptions can lead to inefficient information processing and to employees engaging in types of coping behaviour which serve to reduce productivity, whilst themselves becoming 'overwhelmed, frustrated and detached' (Denning, 2006). Even when productivity objectives are met, however, the use of handhelds also gave rise to issues in relation to employees' work/life balance (Tiemann, 2007).

The issues and developments discussed in this book continue to be fast-moving in their nature and often unpredictable in their consequences. And whilst judging the appropriateness of these kinds of investments at the best of times can be difficult, undertaking the same kind of evaluation during a period of economic downturn can be particularly challenging. In the first quarter of 2009, research company Gartner suggested that global ICT spending would have declined by 3.8 per cent by the end of that year—a larger and more broad-based percentage drop since the dot.com collapse of 2001. But even those actively involved in e-business on a day-to-day basis, find it difficult to maintain a coherent understanding of current developments. For example, Google runs an annual Zeitgeist event bringing together the best and most influential minds within North America and Europe to consider the future implications of e-business technologies, but whilst 'Zeitgeist is the very best forward thinking event in the corporate world, even

> **Technological Determinism** A view that technology determines behaviour. Attributed to sociologist and economist Thorstein Veblen in 1921. Critics suggest that it is technology working within a complex social structure which determines change in behaviour.

> **Zeitgeist** The intellectual, moral, and cultural characteristics of a particular period of time.

### Activity box 1.1

#### Tracking the spirit of the times

The Google Zeitgeist is more than just a corporate event. Take a look at Google Trends on the Google Zeitgeist site at http://www.google.com/intl/en/press/zeitgeist/index.html. What is exercising the minds of individuals and businesses at present? Select a range of popular e-business terms and examine the search volumes by region and over time. What are the implications of your conclusions?

Zeitgeist is struggling to keep up to speed' (Thwaites, 2007). For managers and decision-makers removed from the cutting edge of innovation in e-business technologies, the challenge can seem overwhelming.

Existing commercial organizations also face the challenge of integration. They need to understand whether innovation in and implementation of e-business can profitably complement current business models (and, if so, how their integration can be achieved) or whether such technologies can—alternatively—lead to new, potentially more effective, but also commercially sustainable ways of doing business, which might require moving away from an existing model. For example, using the Internet, mobile, and conventional telephones, UK catalogue retailer Argos (http://www.argos.co.uk) has been able to provide a 'Check and Reserve' service for its products (to allow customers to check availability and secure an item for in-store pickup or home delivery). This superficially simple innovation required it to implement a single stock-monitoring system across channels without adding to costs and to make significantly more intensive use of its existing supply chain.

Longer term, the effective implementation of e-business technologies must also be seen in the context of complex economic and social, as well as legal and regulatory, change, in addition to providing considerable technical and operational challenges for firms and other organizations. Nowhere better can this be seen than in the case of digital downloading of music, an area to which we have already referred. Digital music downloads generated $3.7bn of trade revenues worldwide in 2008, amounting to 20 per cent of total recorded music sales (http://www.ifpi.org) (IFPI, 2009) (see Table 1.1). The rapid growth and ready availability of digitized music has had a variety of consequences in addition to availability of the music itself in this form, amongst which have been:

- The creation of a new market for physical products (such as portable music players);
- The creation of new, information-based services such as Internet radio and other music search and download systems (for example, Pandora, http://www.pandora.com and Last FM http://www.last.fm);

### Table 1.1  Selected characteristics of the global digital music market, 2005–2008

| Characteristic | 2005 | 2008 | % change |
|---|---|---|---|
| 1. Record company revenues * | $22bn | $18.5bn | -15.9% |
| 2. Broadband lines | 209m | 382m | 82.7% |
| 3. Digital platform sales * | $1.1bn | $3.7bn | 263% |
| 4. Single tracks downloaded | 420m | 1.46bn | 280% |
| 5. Illegal swaps/downloads | 20bn | 40bn | 100% |
| 6. Mobile subscriptions | 1.8bn | 4.1bn | 127% |
| 7. 3G mobile subscriptions | 90m | 409m | 354% |
| 8. Portable music player sales | 84m | 140m** | 66.6% |

Note: * = trade sales; ** = 2007 data

- Changed consumer buying behaviour for music products overall, including declining purchases of conventional music products, the growth of new ways for artists to obtain direct access to consumers (such as by means of http://www.youtube.com and http://www.myspace.com); and

- Debate over ethical issues in relation to intellectual property rights and the extent of unauthorized downloading and sharing of content (see the discussion in IFPI, 2009 and the case of Pirate Bay in Short Case 5.3).

As a consequence, for example, music publishers, retailers, trade associations, and software companies have had to invest (often after the event) in the development of digital rights management tools. Governments have had to move to develop policy to regulate this new area, but not only has this process tended to lag behind user and company behaviour in the market, it has also tended to vary by jurisdiction. For example, not all countries have implemented the World Intellectual Property Organization (WIPO) Copyright Treaty of 1996—and it is argued that the treaty may even be inappropriate for some countries at differing stages of economic development (Commission on Intellectual Property Rights, 2002).

Appropriate human resource strategies involving education, training, and organizational change are also prerequisites for effective and, for commercial firms, profitable exploitation of e-business technologies. For example, there is a shortage of e-skills on a worldwide basis, which has led organizations to become much more actively involved in longer-term strategies for education, training, and development.

Finally, as the example of digital downloading above reminds us, it is important to remember that it is not just commercial firms which can make use of or which are affected by e-business technologies. Non-commercial organizations—as diverse in nature as charities, not-for-profit services, trade associations, social communities, and political parties—can also employ e-business technologies to improve their effectiveness and efficiency. For example, we deliberately use the example of Oxfam as a case in this chapter to demonstrate the ways in which third-sector organizations can exploit e-business technologies and their associated economic and social characteristics. At the local, national, and international levels, governments too have sought to benefit, with varying degrees of success, from the application of e-business technologies, as well as—in their role as policy-making bodies—creating the right kind of conditions in which e-business potential can flourish within their respective jurisdictions. (See the example of Canada, discussed in Long Case 1.1 in this chapter.) Throughout this book we seek to discuss some of the similarities and difference between public and private sector organizations in their exploitation of the e-business toolkit.

Ultimately, though, it is the individual end user who has witnessed some of the most profound changes in their capabilities and potential. Developments in user-created content, social networking, citizen journalism, information search, and mobility in communications and service access have empowered those individuals able to exploit online resources (and are increasingly disenfranchising those who are not). The consequences of this have been to create secondary feedback effects for the strategies of businesses and other organizations, as well as to increase the potential for significant independent peer-to-peer activity, both potentially cutting out conventional intermediaries altogether, as well as creating opportunities for new kinds of business. For example, in addition to its 86mn active users, eBay's Stores allow individual sellers to amalgamate their listings in customized pages. In 2008, nearly 725,000 individuals in the US and 178,000 in the UK were estimated to use eBay as their primary or secondary source of income. Such changes and their consequences are, therefore, also within the remit of this book.

---

**Activity box 1.2**

The evolution of eBay
Look at the 'fast facts' available about eBay on the website (news.ebay.com/fastfacts. cfm). Evaluate and give examples of the ways in which the acquisition of PayPal and Skype—and the subsequent sale of a majority stake of Skype—has transformed the growth opportunities and synergies available to eBay.

---

This introductory chapter continues by considering the origins, changing definition and evolution of e-commerce and e-business technologies; the growth of interest in e-business from the early rhetoric, through subsequent disillusionment and the reasons for it, to the growing contemporary accommodation of Internet and related technologies into commercial innovation and business processes. It discusses current trends in the levels of adoption of e-business technologies by businesses and governments, drawing upon international surveys of usage, and highlights the priorities and concerns of managers, investors and policy-makers in relation to e-business. It outlines the drivers and barriers to adoption and critically evaluates some of the most popularly used concepts.

## Defining e-business

'When I use a word', Humpty Dumpty said in rather a scornful tone, 'it means just what I choose it to mean—neither more nor less.'

'The question is', said Alice, 'whether you *can* make words mean so many different things.' Through the Looking Glass (And What Alice Found There)    *Lewis Carroll, 1872*

The terms 'e-commerce', 'e-business', and associated terms such as 'e-government', have proved elusive and ambiguous in their nature and scope. In large part, this is because just as the activities the words seek to describe continue rapidly to evolve, so the terminology itself has also had to evolve. And it is often several years before the definition of a new phenomenon is generally accepted by those involved in its use or study. Finally, there is also a degree of fashion in using modern terminology; by labelling particular activities with up-to-date business language. (Phrases such as 'information superhighway' and 'teleshopping', for example, seem dated and quaint to today's way of thinking.) And, as ever, there is a professional mystique to be developed and maintained by using language and labels to discriminate between those who know and those who do not. Interestingly, e-business innovation and the development of the Internet more generally have spawned

**Figure 1.1** E-This and E-That.

a new generation of users: digital natives who coin terminology 'on the fly' and in a much more open and democratic manner than conventional professionals and academics. But there is also the danger of getting caught up in semantics when discussing the labels attached to emerging kinds of e-business activities and the changing meanings attached to them.

Electronic commerce, or e-commerce, has been the most popularly used—or abused— term in this context. It was originally coined to describe the kinds of transaction handling enabled by electronic funds transfer systems (EFTS) and electronic data interchange (EDI) developed in the late 1960s. However, the lack of common standards for EDI until the mid-1980s led to fragmented computer systems and ways of working, and only some, mainly large, organizations could benefit, by agreement one with another. Once common standards emerged, electronic payment systems began to transform the way in which businesses operated:

> 'The beauty of EDI is it's largely unseen, but it is an incredibly efficient vehicle for the transfer of information between organizations and trading partners. It's sort of an invisible technology. It's really at the core of most productivity improvements of the last half of the century.'  *Kerry Stackpole, President and CEO of the Data Interchange Standards Association, quoted in Weisman, 2000*

These tightly focused interbusiness considerations predated definitions of e-commerce coined in the late 1990s, but increasing open computer technology and the Internet paved the way for the term to evolve. Applegate et al. (1996) were amongst the first to identify three classes of e-commerce applications: business-to-customer (sell-side e-commerce), business-to-business (buy-side e-commerce), and intra-organizational. At that point, 'e-commerce' began to be adopted as a portmanteau word by practitioners, used to describe 'doing business online', when this only comprised specific activities to do with buying and selling undertaken either by entirely Internet-based firms as well as by a small number of traditional firms, notably to consumers. Indeed, the origins of the re-use of the term at that stage are supposed to date to the first advertising banner being displayed on a web page in 1994. This narrow definition was noted by researchers:

> 'managers may view e-commerce too narrowly and may not consider the strategic importance of e-commerce technologies.'  *Riggins and Rhee, 1998*

**Digital Natives** A term applied to individuals who have grown up immersed in digital technologies. Attributed to US writer and game designer Marc Prensky.

**EDI** Electronic Data Interchange—a pre-Internet set of standards defining the electronic exchange of information relevant to business.

It was first important to recognize the wide variety of pre-sale and post-sale activities to which companies might apply e-business technologies, hence:

> 'the distributing, buying, selling, marketing and servicing of products or services over electronic systems such as the Internet and other computer networks.'

Note that the definition above had moved away from a purely transactional one: e-commerce as web commerce now included marketing and servicing activities. Whilst there were frameworks to guide managers in choosing which Internet applications were most suitable to their particular situation, or how they might use Internet technology to gain competitive advantage, few were sufficiently farsighted or comprehensive to encompass the consequences of what we have now come to term e-business, including the importance of the effects of e-business technologies on the nature of all kinds of organizations and on the relationships between them as well as between consumers and other consumers.

E-business, a term originally attributed to former IBM Chairman Louis Gerstner, tended once to be regarded as synonymous with e-commerce in focusing on the commercial transactions that take place between buyers and sellers. It is clear that a much broader and more holistic definition of this term has come into common acceptance, which incorporates whole value chains and value networks between suppliers, intermediaries, and consumers, and is as focused as much upon the potential for economic transformation within and between businesses as it is upon the opportunities that specifically present themselves for the use of different buying and selling methods by those businesses, hence:

> 'the automation of the entire spectrum of interactions between enterprises and their distributed employees, trading partners, suppliers and customers.' *Aberdeen Group website, 2001*

Such automation also involves the use of networked resources and a business process-oriented focus has been widely recognised, hence according to another definition, e-business is:

> 'the transformation of key business processes through the use of Internet technologies.' *IBM*

or

> 'automated business processes (both intra- and inter-firm) over computer-mediated networks.' *OECD*

In addition, the OECD has proposed that e-business processes should be involved with integrating tasks and therefore extend beyond a simple standalone or individual application. So this evolving, broad concept of e-business also includes the digitization of internal business processes, as well as cooperative or collaborative processes between companies which are not necessarily transaction-focused. A typical example of this might be collaborative e-design processes between business partners within industrial engineering firms or development project partnerships.

As the application of e-business technologies in some markets and industries becomes apparently ubiquitous, the introduction to this chapter reminded us that the practical scope of the term 'e-business' should also include organizations which may share the characteristics of businesses with the exception of the profit motive. Indeed, to some extent there is the potential for us all as individuals to be businesses—or at least to be able to use network resources to market ourselves, our news, views, and opinions, and our second-hand goods more widely than ever before: *we are all marketers now.*

The potential benefit to public sector organizations, especially governments, of investment in e-business technologies may in principle be even more significant than that for businesses (although they also share in the challenges facing conventional businesses). In most developed and some developing economies the state has established e-government activities. E-government has been defined as:

> 'The use of technology to enhance the access to and delivery of government services to benefit citizens, business partners and employees.' *Deloitte and Touche, 2003*

It has become a common expressed goal for governments to use networked technologies to increase transparency of government activity to citizens, reducing the costs of government activity and increasing government's effectiveness. For example, European government administrations exchange over 6bn documents annually. One key objective of e-government is to replace as much of this as possible with electronic exchange. However, as chapter 5 will point out, not all such applications are benign: it has also been a common goal for some governments to use e-business technologies to enhance surveillance and regulation of their citizens.

E-government 'The use of technology to enhance the access to and delivery of government services to benefit citizens, business partners and employees' (Deloitte and Touche, 2003).

# The history and development of e-business

> 'Despite all the attention that Internet companies get these days, it's just a transitory phase, because in five years' time there won't be any "Internet companies". They'll all be Internet companies.' *Andy Grove, Chairman, Intel, 1999*

So began a now familiar period in the history of technology development which—broadly between 1995 and 2001—encompassed the dot.com boom and bust, and from aspects of which the ICT sector has only recently emerged, only to be plunged into a global economic slowdown in 2008–2009. It is not the intention of this section to dwell extensively either on the facts or on the myths surrounding this period. It was not the first and will not be the last economic bubble to have burst (Kindleberger, 2005) and there are available some excellent histories of this most recent manifestation written by those who directly experienced it (for example, Cassidy, 2002; Malmsten, Portanger, and Drazin, 2002). But some object lessons can be learned from the experience of users, investors, and organizations which are of relevance to readers of this text. And of course the history of e-business did not in practice begin in 1995, even though the visibility of the topic was considerably higher from that point onwards. For example, there was considerable speculation as to the commercial viability of 'electronic marketing' and 'teleshopping' in the 1970s and 1980s, and the way in which these approaches might challenge existing business models (see, for example, Rosenberg and Hirschman, 1981; Business Week, 1986; and Davies and Reynolds, 1988).

Part of the excitement surrounding the dot.com boom was the sense that the technologies involved offered the potential for new entrants to be potentially disruptive of

Disruptive Innovation A technological innovation, product, or service that eventually overturns the prevailing status quo in the market. Attributed to Christensen (1997).

Sustaining Innovation Incremental investments in products and services involving more conventional technology. Attributed to Christensen (1997).

established ways of conducting business. Indeed, a key concept relevant to e-business, and one that is too good to keep to a later chapter that explicitly addresses product and service innovation in e-business, is that of disruptive innovation. The term was introduced by Bower and Christensen as 'disruptive technology' in 1995 and was refined by Christensen in 1997 and 2002. Companies engaging in disruptive innovation target customers who find existing value propositions too expensive or too complicated. They offer solutions that are 'good enough' at a lower price. Such innovations offer considerably higher potential for growth than do incremental investments involving more conventional technology, referred to as sustaining innovation by Christensen (Bower and Christensen, 1995; Christensen, 1997).

'I started off thinking it was a technological problem, that disruptions occurred when a new company with deeper expertise entered the market. I've come to recognise that the technology is simply the enabler, while the disruption is caused by the strategy or new business model deployed. The best disruptions are brought about when an entirely new business model is introduced to an industry. This makes it difficult to copy.'    *Clayton Christensen, quoted in Planting, 2006*

Radical Innovation High-risk innovation involving significant change 'at a stroke' in markets, products, or services, with a higher degree of uncertainty over likely outcomes.

A major premise of disruptive innovations is that they work much more slowly and methodically through an industry than radical innovations. Rather than transforming markets 'at a stroke', disruptive innovations are more insidious, eroding the value of established ways of doing business by attracting customers from the bottom of the value chain. Indeed, early manifestations of the service are often poorly crafted and only attractive to 'low-end' customers. As the new proposition gets more proficient, however, so higher-end customers are tempted to switch to it. A related consequence of disruptive innovations in relation to business is that existing incumbents tend to discount their relevance or impact, often until it is too late. The growth of Skype and voice over Internet protocol (VoIP) is an excellent example of this.

## Activity box 1.3

### Identifying disruptive innovations
Is it possible to identify prospective disruptive innovations before they become fully active? Take some time to think about some of the many e-business innovations to which you have been exposed over the past year. Which of them have the potential to be disruptive and why?

Understanding the motivations of innovators and investors during such times is also important. During the dot.com boom, venture capitalist John Doerr sought to distinguish between two kinds of Internet entrepreneurs: what he called the 'missionaries and the mercenaries'. Mercenaries, he felt, were characterized by paranoia, thought opportunistically, focused on their competitors and were motivated by the lust for making money; while missionaries were driven by passion, thought strategically, focused on their customers, and were motivated by the desire to make meaning (Doerr, 2000). The best

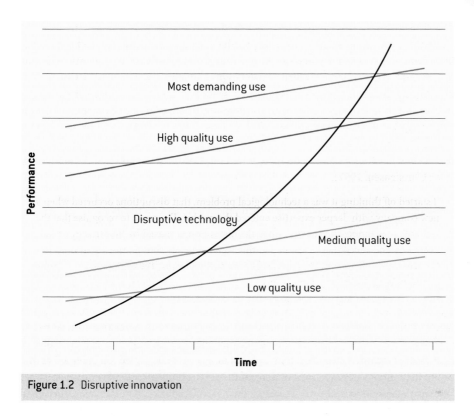

**Figure 1.2** Disruptive innovation

entrepreneurs, he suggested, were the missionaries, although it may well have been the mercenaries who benefited most from opportunism at the time. This is confirmed when we examine the popular perception of the causes of the dot.com downturn (Table 1.2), which are seen as being derived from a mixture of greed and inexperience.

As dot.com ventures became what IBM's Louis Gerstner had termed 'dot.toast', it also became clear that there was no one single way to exploit e-business technologies:

> 'there is an intrinsic irony in the mad rush to "discover" the dominant Internet business model. What awaits us is the perhaps deflating realisation that e-commerce is just another kind of business. There are countless "right" answers, endless combinations of business models and infinite permutations of key themes and approaches. There will be no magic bullet.'  *Rayport, 2000*

**Table 1.2  Causes of the dot.com shakeout**

| Factor | A major reason | A minor reason | Not a reason |
|---|---|---|---|
| Risk-taking investors looking for the fast money | 67% | 21% | 5% |
| Poor business plans | 56% | 27% | 9% |
| Youthful and inexperienced management | 39% | 38% | 15% |

Note: Sample drawn from those Americans aware of the trouble with the Internet

This is an idea which we will pick up in our discussion of e-business strategy in chapter 6.

On the heels of the business-to-consumer bubble emerged other online enthusiasms. For example, particular business-to-business applications—such as B2B marketplaces or exchanges—generated unrealistic expectations and attracted extensive attention from investors (White et al., 2007). Defined as 'web-based systems that link multiple businesses together for the purposes of trading or collaboration', there were at one point in 2001 over 2,200 e-marketplaces registered worldwide (Laseter et al., 2001). Forecasts suggested that $4.5trillion of e-trading could be conducted annually by organizations by 2005 (Business 2.0, 2000). However, by mid-2006 there were only 756 active e-marketplaces remaining. It again appears that reasons for failure centred on unrealistic assumptions in relation to the application of technology: that, in this case, it would change the preferences and behaviours of businesses in respect of procurement practices. In reality:

> 'the B2B.com bubble was based on naïve and simplistic models of how organizations really buy and sell things. Contrary to the claims made by the pundits, B2B does not fundamentally change the way purchasing and selling works. For example, selling firms do not want to trade in an automated environment driven by prices alone; buying firms still require traditional purchasing specialists.'  *New, 2006*

One consistent feature of the history and development of e-business, therefore, is hyperbole, particularly over emerging technologies. Technology insight consultancy Gartner first captured this idea in its concept of a hype cycle in 1995 (Figure 1.3 shows one of the more recent iterations of the cycle). New technologies, the firm suggested, get excessive attention at the early stages of their development. They then unsurprisingly disappoint and fall from favour. By the time they are quietly adopted into the mainstream they are often no longer newsworthy.

**B2B Marketplace/Exchange** Web-based systems that link multiple businesses together for the purposes of trading or collaboration.

**Hype Cycle** A concept seeking to describe the stages in the maturity, adoption, and business application of specific technologies. Attributed to technology consultancy Gartner, Inc. in 1995.

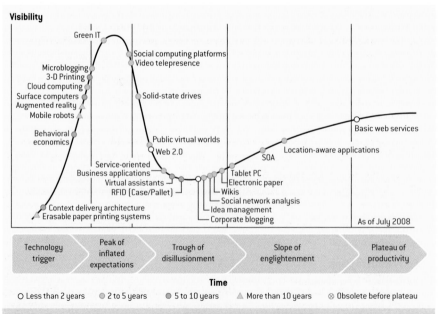

**Figure 1.3** Gartner's 'hype cycle' for emerging technologies, 2008.

Gartner's hype cycle is a useful graphical representation of the maturity, adoption and business application of specific technologies and comprises five stages:

1) *Technology trigger*: A breakthrough, product launch or other event that generates significant press attention and interest. In 1995, Gartner's examples included biometrics and e-cash; in 2006, quantum computing and telepresence; and in 2008, mobile robots and cloud computing.

2) *Peak of inflated expectations*: In the second phase, excessive visibility leads to over-enthusiastic and unrealistic expectations. In 1995, examples included netcasting and smart cards; in 2006, digital paper and Web 2.0; and in 2008, green IT and social computing platforms. Successful applications of the technology are outweighed by the failures.

3) *Trough of disillusionment*: Unsurprisingly, the failure to meet unrealistic expectations leads to the abandonment of the technology by the press and other commentators, who move on to the 'next big thing'. In 1995, examples included personal digital assistants; in 2006, wikis and the tablet PC; and in 2008, Web 2.0, virtual worlds, and corporate blogging.

4) *Slope of enlightenment*: In this stage, quiet experimentation takes place amongst organizations still wishing to understand the benefits and practical application of the technology. Here in 1995, we could find speech recognition and desktop videoconferencing; and in 2006, location-aware applications; whilst in 2008, the tablet PC and—still—location-aware applications.

5) *Plateau of productivity*: Finally, provided the technology has not become obsolete or superseded, it reaches a point at which its benefits become once again widely demonstrated and accepted. Such stability allows for further evolution. In 1995, examples included database mining and imaging; in 2006, Gartner suggested that VoIP and internal web services were at this final stage; and in 2008, basic web services.

It has been suggested that it was Gartner's hype cycle model, when applied to e-business, which predicted the dot.com crash:

> 'E-business is set to fall into a period of disillusionment by 2001, before successful organizations move through the "hype cycle" and emerge fully transformed so that they can be referred to as just plain "businesses" again.'     *Drobik, 1999*

This may have been a lucky guess, since cyclical models of this kind—of which marketing's product lifecycle model is another example—often suffer from having no clear criteria on where the inflection points on the curves are likely to be and, without further interpretation, remain at best descriptive models, and can be—at worst—self-fulfilling prophecies (Dhalla and Yuspeh, 1976). Gartner's 'priority matrix' seeks to provide some additional judgement to help determine the importance and timing of potential investments based on benefit rather than hype.

It is interesting to observe the recent bout of excitement over Web 2.0, social media, and the investments being made by media verticals in start-up businesses in this space. Parallels with the dot.com investments of the late 1990s suggest themselves. Indeed, citing the original acquisition of Skype by eBay, the *Economist* has referred to Web 2.0 as 'Bubble 2.0' (*Economist*, 2005). Gartner itself commented in 2008:

'Although Web 2.0 is now entering the Trough of Disillusionment, it will emerge within two years to have transformational impact, as companies steadily gain more experience and success with both the technologies and the cultural implications.'    *Gartner, 2008*

How do firms accommodate the scope for disruptive innovation which these eras have brought about? Christensen and Anthony suggest that disruptive innovators must 'fumble forward' with new strategies, continually adapting themselves to make the innovation work (Christensen and Anthony, 2007): 'Google ... didn't have it right from the beginning. It had to fundamentally rethink its business three times before it built the model that now powers its success.' This approach is not unrelated to the concept of logical incrementalism coined by Quinn in the 1970s (Quinn, 1978) and Mintzberg's (1992) notion of emergent strategy (where companies' strategies emerge in the absence of intentions).

> **Logical Incrementalism** An approach to strategy formulation which involves a non-linear mixture of strategic planning and spontaneous change. Attributed to James Quinn (1978).

> **Emergent Strategy** A situation where companies' strategies emerge, rather than being deliberately planned. Attributed to Henry Mintzberg (1992).

## Adoption of e-business

'e-Business has gained new momentum in the EU and in other advanced economies of the world.'    *European Commission, 2007)*

How significant are e-business and e-commerce activities amongst organizations around the world? Much but not all of this capability will be linked to the market context within which the organization operates. The Economist Intelligence Unit has published an annual e-readiness ranking of the word's largest economies since 2000 (see Activity 1.4). Currently sixty-five countries are assessed on their ability to promote and support e-business and information and communications technology (ICT) services. A country's e-readiness is essentially a measure of its e-business environment, a collection of factors that indicate how amenable a market is to Internet-based opportunities. E-readiness is a relative rather than an absolute target. Because the opportunities afforded by e-business technologies evolve, and individual countries do not always develop their capabilities to keep pace, they can fall in the rankings. Hence, Western European countries—including

### Activity box 1.4

#### Assessing the state of e-readiness

'The importance of e-readiness cannot be gauged by technology or average Internet access speeds. Returns from e-readiness are realised when countries use information technology to boost economic and social development'    *Economist Intelligence Unit, 2006*

Examine the 2008 e-readiness ranking produced by the Economist Intelligence Unit in association with IBM at tinyurl.com/3uydpc and compare this with the 2000 ranking, to be found at tinyurl.com/lz74fy. In addition to the trends discussed in the text, what are the major differences that you can detect in the extent of e-readiness between countries? What might explain some of these changes?

France, Germany, Italy, and to a lesser extent the UK—have fallen back in recent years to the benefit of a number of Asian countries.

However, a market-based ranking by geographical location or at the country level is not necessarily the only or the best indicator of the adoption level of e-business activity by individual firms. For example, it is necessary to consider the structure of industry in a country, since the extent of small- and medium-sized enterprises will depress country averages. In particular, there is a pronounced and persistent gap in e-business adoption between small firms and large ones (Figure 1.4). It is also important to recognize that leading companies in some countries may be able to rise above the collection of factors affecting the national market as a whole.

At the level of the firm, it is also possible to think about e-business adoption in terms of a number of component indicators which, when aggregated, can generate a balanced 'scorecard' of elements. The European Commission's 'e-business scorecard' has been developed to view an organization from four broad, but complementary, perspectives, within which certain measurable indicators can be identified:

A. Use of ICT networks

  A-1    Internet connectivity (covers internet access + bandwidth)

  A-2    Use of a LAN

  A-3    Use of a Wireless LAN

  A-4    Remote access to the company's computer network

B. e-integration of internal business processes

  B-1    Use of an intranet

  B-2    Use of an ERP (enterprise resource planning) system

  B-3    Companies tracking production time/working hours online

  B-4    Companies sending or receiving e-invoices

C. e-procurement and supply chain integration

  C-1    Companies placing above a certain proportion of their orders to suppliers online

  C-2    Companies using specific ICT solutions to support sourcing and procurement processes

  C-3    Companies linking their ICT system with suppliers

  C-4    Online management of capacity/inventory

D. e-Marketing and Sales

  D-1    Use of a CRM (Customer Relationship Management) system

  D-2    Companies receiving above a certain proportion of orders from customers online

  D-3    Companies using specific ICT solutions to support marketing and sales processes

  D-4    Companies linking their ICT system with customers

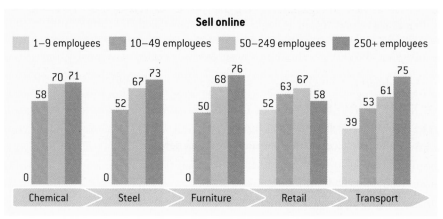

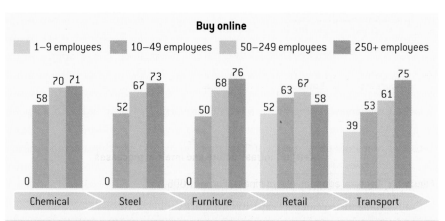

**Figure 1.4** European E-business index, by firm size

Note: This figure reflects Gartner's view of the market in summer 2008.

There will also be substantial differences in e-business adoption visible by sector. As Figure 1.5 shows in its summary of just ten European sectors using the EC e-business definitions, differential adoption is apparent between manufacturing and service sectors, as well as between those sectors which are primarily business-to-business and those which are business-to-consumer. For example, the footwear industry is dominated by small-scale trade firms who do not see e-business as a useful tool for their sector; whilst within the ICT industries themselves (ICT manufacturing and telecommunications) firms—even small ones—make intensive use of e-business technologies. In other sectors, such as tourism, the benefits of e-business in sales and marketing areas are particularly pronounced. We discuss other indices of e-business readiness and development potential in chapter 4.

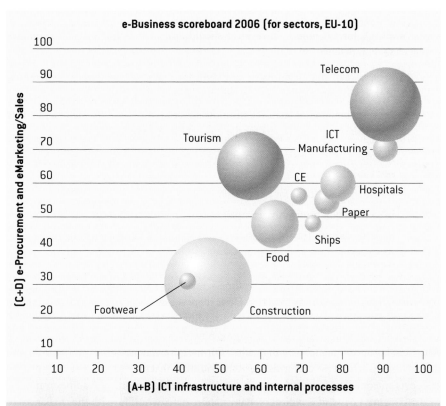

**Figure 1.5** Sectoral adoption of e-business, Europe 2006.

Notes:

1. The Commission's 'scoreboard' comprises 16 component indicators grouped in four categories. Categories A and B & C and D are grouped together for the purposes of this figure. See text for a detailed discussion of the component indicators.

2. The size of the bubbles is indicative of the size of the sector by employment

3. CE = Consumer Electronics

# Adoption of e-government

Finally, whilst we can think about public services in terms of e-business adoption in a not dissimilar way from commercial organizations (perhaps deliberately seeking to emulate good practice in the private sector), the example of e-government also shows how the particular approach to e-business technology applications may be different in some respects. Therefore, according to consultancy Accenture, best practice in e-government does indeed comprise the introduction of services on a par with the best of the private sector (for example, using text messages for 'amber alerts' on missing children; or vehicle licence renewal), and moving away from a one-size-fits-all approach to more customized strategies based on their own unique challenges and value propositions (as in the case of the government of Singapore's, SinGov (http://www.gov.sg) and Singapore Infomap portal (http://www.sg), for example). However, it should also increasingly exhibit distinctive public sector competences, by:

- Evolving away from an infrastructure built for a monolithic, government-centric view of service into shared services, simplification and new organizational designs;

- Using a combination of tactics to promote adoption of service strategies and create real enthusiasm amongst users for the most effective channels:

  – the stick (strong pressure or mandatory use of more efficient channels for some services);

  – the carrot (incentives for online use);

  – marketing pull (innovative campaigns to increase awareness);

  – high touch push (providing individual support for complex or highly personal services).

Figure 1.6 shows the e-government readiness rankings which have been produced to accompany a discussion of best practice. Here, there is a much clearer regional distinction to be observed than in the case of the EIU e-readiness rankings discussed in association with Activity 1.4: with North American governments well ahead of a mixture of leading Asian and European states, but with much of Europe governments some way behind—and indeed lagging behind the performance of the countries that they govern. For example, the UK government fell to 'follower' status in the Accenture e-government readiness rankings in 2006 (Figure 1.6)—but is typical of many nation-states wrestling with the challenges of transforming complex bureaucracies and is seen as being on the verge of more dramatic change. Long Case 1.1 discusses the specific case of Canada.

E-government can be seen as evolving through a series of basic stages of development:

- Building the initial infrastructure (involving the establishment of a web presence);

- Putting government services online (involving the provision of information and relatively simple transactional services, such a passport or licence applications);

- Transforming structures and processes (involving much back office restructuring and integration of service delivery across departments as well as between government and the private sector); and

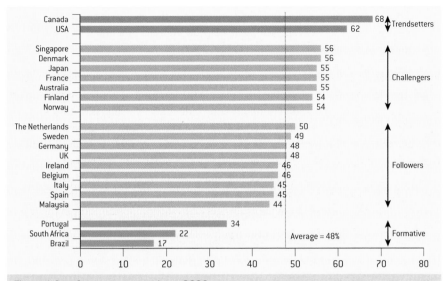

**Figure 1.6** e-Government rankings, 2006

Note: Countries selected based on the location of Accenture's government practice worldwide.

- Integrating and rationalizing the main service delivery channels (involving an extension of the third stage into the provision of an increasingly seamless and channel neutral interface between government and its citizens and other stakeholders).

Governments have sought to use technology to support their activities for many years. For example, the UK government set up a Technical Support Unit as early as 1957 to advise on the use of computers in government. In the 1990s, attention shifted from efficiencies in hardware procurement to focus on the efficiency and transparency of government processes. In 1997, the UK prime minister set a target that 25 per cent of all dealings with government should be capable of being carried out electronically by 2002, using telephone, television, or PC. Subsequent initiatives included an online portal for businesses (http://www.businesslink.co.uk, 2003), an online portal for citizens (http://www.direct.gov.uk, 2004), and in organizational terms an Office of the E-Envoy (2000), replaced by an e-government unit in the Cabinet Office in 2004, together with a Chief Information Officer Council (CIOC) in 2005, to bring together thirty CIOs from central and local government alongside public sector agencies. In line with the four-stage model outlined above, one of the UK's most recent policy pronouncements on 'transformational government' had three recognizable themes:

- Customer-centric services ('providing government with the knowledge, tools and techniques for establishing the wants, needs and preferences of both citizens and businesses'. Interestingly, this included the closure of over 550 government websites 'to make access to information easier for citizens and businesses');
- Shared services (with nine sectors of government planning to share corporate services by 2016, which may be delivered by outsourced professional service firms);

- Professionalism (recognizing and obtaining the skills required to deliver e-government services and putting in place appropriate procurement, training, and assessment frameworks) (Cabinet Office, 2007).

But this initiative must also be seen in the context of the UK government's 'Digital Britain' policy agenda: seeking 'to secure the UK's place at the forefront of innovation, investment and quality in the digital and communications industries'. Notably, this 2008 initiative makes it clear that the approach straddles both public and private sectors of the UK economy and that e-business technologies are seen as having a role in leading economic recovery:

> 'The Government is determined that the UK will strengthen its place as a world leader in the communications and digital technology sectors. For the present financial and banking crisis, Britain must get through the worst and prepare for the upturn. The digital economy will be central to this. The digital Britain report will lead the way.' *DCMS, 2008*

## Long case 1.1

### Canada

For five consecutive years, growth in the Canadian ICT sector has exceeded the growth of the overall economy. In 2007, the share of ICT in Canadian GDP was 4.7 per cent and it was estimated that some 8.3 per cent of the growth in the overall economy from 2002 to 2007 could be attributed to the sector. Of the 30,000 companies involved in the sector, those such as Research in Motion (RIM) and Nortel Networks are most prominent. But it is Canada's own government which has received some of the highest plaudits as one of the world's top-tier performers in terms of e-government. For six years in a row, Canada topped the e-government rankings developed by consultancy Accenture, and, although its leading position has most recently been successfully challenged by Singapore, it has remained within the 'trendsetters' group. The Canadian experience tallies very much with the stage model outlined in this chapter, but also highlights some of the difficulties experienced by even the leading governments in pursuing an electronic agenda. The motivation for Canada's e-government drive, in the context of a mission of public sector renewal, is clear:

> 'By defining approaches to act more as a single enterprise, the view is that we will be more efficient, more effective and obviously spend our taxpayer dollars better, and ultimately improve services to Canadians. Improving and modernizing internal services is essential to delivering improved citizen services.' *Ken Cochrane, former government of Canada CIO*

Canada's Government On Line (GOL) strategy was threefold:

1. Tier one: online presence.
2. Tier two: electronic federal service delivery.
3. Tier three: seamless government.

Of the most commonly used services, 130 are now online. By the beginning of 2008, there were over a hundred funded projects seeking to provide joined-up  ≫

services at the various levels of government. In addition, Government of Canada departments and agencies are grouping their electronic information and services according to topic or target audience. For example, Seniors Canada (http://www.seniors.gc.ca) was established to provide citizens aged fifty-five plus with easy electronic access to seniors-related services, including:

- Care facilities;
- Community services;
- Computers and learning;
- End of life;
- Finances and pension;
- Health and wellness;
- Housing;
- Legal matters; and
- Seniors' networks across the country.

Achieving 'seamless e-government' is not just a technical issue, but also a human one. If those delivering the service to citizens are not engaged and supportive then citizens are unlikely to be satisfied and trust in e-government will not be engendered. One part of Canada's public service renewal policy has been about developing talent. It established the Canada School of Public Service in 2004 from several disparate training organizations. The school provides specialist skills, but also emphasizes training that develops administrators' sense of their role as 'public servants and stewards of the public trust'.

How successful have these initiatives been? Canada has operated a citizens' Internet feedback panel since 2001. More than 50,000 Canadian Internet users provided feedback on service delivery, policy, and programme issues. The government is therefore able to keep track of citizens' attitudes towards e-government. Recent findings suggest that:

- 86 per cent of Canadian Internet users feel that the Internet has made it easier to find information about government programs and services;
- 74 per cent of Canadian Internet users had visited a Government of Canada website in the past twelve months; and, interestingly,
- 90 per cent of Canadians think federal government websites are as good or better than those created by the private sector.

But Canadian e-government has also faced several challenges in developing its strategy. These included working across several jurisdictions and levels of government, across departments which had hitherto developed standalone systems and processes, and a general lack of technical standardization. While the government had put in place several standardization initiatives to systematize the capture, description, organization, and dissemination of data and information, these projects had not always been successful:

'There still seems to be no central organization in Canadian government to support overall metadata management or to ensure compliance. Specific policies and services, such as namespaces designation, registries, repositories, and other tools that would provide  ≫

this support across government agencies are under consideration, but have yet to be implemented.' *Park et al., 2009*

Moreover, the motives for moving from tier two to tier three also have to be considered alongside the changing economic context of the country:

'We're digging ourselves into a very deep deficit and we'll want to dig ourselves out. It will be extremely logical to invest now in things that will make the government more efficient in the future.' *Bernard Courtois, President of the Information Technology Association of Canada, 2009*

*Questions*

1. Are there undesirable consequences that arise from the single 'citizen-centric' view of e-government? Is it driven more, for example, by the need to save money than for reasons of improving the customer experience of government?

2. In 2008, Ken Cochrane, Canada's CIO and champion of the Canadian e-government initiative, retired. A replacement was appointed in April 2009. What will be the challenges she faces?

## Long case 1.2

### Oxfam

Founded in 1942, Oxfam GB has an income of £300m annually which is used to combat global poverty, hunger, and social injustice around the world. Of this, 35 per cent comes from donations and 26 per cent from trading sales of donated or purchased goods. The organization's Internet presence has become very important for raising awareness of campaigns, as well as developing into a means of collecting donations and selling products. In terms of raising awareness, Oxfam's programmes and campaigns are publicized online and with a level of detail on projects which could not be easily matched through other media. Users can join Oxfam campaigns such as Make Trade Fair, Arms Control, and events such as Trailwalker, an annual sponsored walk in five countries. Online donations to charities have outstripped telephone giving, particularly for national disasters. Online giving can be spontaneous and requires little effort. The Asian tsunami in December 2004 marked a turning point in online giving. Forty-four million US dollars was donated online to the Disasters Emergency Committee appeal (15 per cent of total funds raised) and on New Year's Eve $10m in twenty-four hours. But,

'in terms of fundraising we've got a long way to go. I think the sector as a whole is still too reticent about asking people to donate online. In this digital climate this needs to change.' *Lindsay Boswell, CEO, Institute of Fundraising*

Oxfam is a retailer, with 750 shops in the UK alone. But it also uses its shops to sell a wide range of products on eBay varying from clothing to books, china to CDs (http://www.oxfam.org.uk/applications/ebayshop/index.php). All of the products listed have been donated to Oxfam and are selected by shop volunteers across the country, who list the »

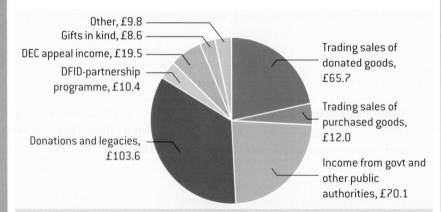

**Figure 1.7** Origins of Oxfam's income

items on eBay Stores and mail them out to purchasers. One hundred per cent of the profits from every sale go directly to Oxfam. Charities pay standard listing fees, but eBay donates any 'final value fees' back to Oxfam.

*Questions*

1. To what extent is Oxfam an 'e-business'?

2. 'More than ever charities have to deal with fragmented audiences who all demand different types of information at different times and through different media.' How might Oxfam improve the effectiveness of its online presence and activities?

## ✪ Chapter Summary

The chapter began by setting out the distinctive contributions which e-business technologies could make to both economies and societies, at the level of the individual as well as that of the organization, through doing new and better things, or through doing things better. It stressed both the fast-moving and complex nature of the transformational change being experienced by all stakeholders in this area and the difficulties being experience in keeping track of developments. It highlighted the importance of distinguishing between the 'hype' of inflated expectations and the clear-cut opportunities facing organizations.

The chapter then reflected on the nature and scope of e-business, including the origins and definitions of some of the key terminology—before putting recent developments in the context of the short but sometimes painful history of e-business as a potentially disruptive form of innovation. Finally, the chapter examined the characteristics of adoption of e-business by organizations around the world and by countries, as well as by governments themselves. It emphasized that e-readiness is not just a function of technology or Internet access speeds, but of the genuine use of technology to boost economic and social development.

## ❷ Review questions

1. What are the differences between e-commerce and e-business?

2. What are the strengths and weaknesses of the different definitions of e-business?

3. What is meant by 'disruptive innovation'? Give three examples.

4. Review the relative strengths and weaknesses of Gartner's 'hype cycle'.

5. What constitutes 'e-readiness'?

6. What were the main causes of the dot.com crash?

7. What constitutes current 'best practice' in e-government? Think of examples from your own experience of how this kind of best practice might affect you as a citizen.

8. Elaborate upon the four stages in the development of effective e-government.

## Q Discussion questions

1. Why is it so difficult to demonstrate the effects of e-business technologies on economic performance?

2. Compare the websites created for the leader of the UK Conservative Party (http://www.webcameron.org.uk) with the sites for the US Republican Party (http://www.gop.com) and the French Front National (http://www.frontnational.com/). What kinds of innovations have been enabled through the use of e-business technologies? Evaluate the relative effectiveness of each example.

3. Think of contemporary examples of e-business 'hype' (at the 'peak of inflated expectations'). Can you identify the evidence which will lead to them falling into the 'trough of disillusionment'?

4. What are the similarities and differences in the challenges faced in e-business and e-government?

5. Compare the rankings produced for e-business readiness by country with those for e-government readiness. What can you conclude?

## → Suggestions for further reading

Accenture, (2007), *Leadership in Customer Service: Delivering on the Promise*, Accenture.
A helpful tour d'horizon of the journeys being made by governments worldwide in their development of electronic technologies in the service of their citizens.

Department of Culture, Media and Sport, (2009), *Digital Britain: The Future of Communications*, Interim Report.
The UK government's latest statement on the plans to secure Britain's place 'at the forefront of the global digital economy'.

European Commission, (2008), *The European e-Business Report 2007-8 edition*, e-Business w@tch.
The latest e-business report for Europe, produced by the e-business observatory set up by the Commission, e-business w@tch. Contains specialist sectoral case studies as well as an overview of developments.

OECD, (2009), *Information Technology Outlook*, 2008. OECD.
The ninth in a biennial series designed to provide member countries with a broad overview of trends and near-term prospects in the information technology (IT) industry, analysis of the growing impact of IT on the economy and society, developments and emerging applications in selected areas of information technology, and a review of IT policies and new policy directions.

Hafner, K. and Lyon, M., (2003), *Where Wizards Stay Up Late: The Origins of the Internet*, Free Press
A readable history of everything from packet-switching exchanges to ARPAnet. For those who prefer more academic fare, then try the 'first significant philosopher of cyberspace':

Castells, M., (2009), *The Rise of the Network Society: Information Age: Economy, Society, and Culture v. 1*, 2$^{nd}$ Edition, WileyBlackwell

## → References

Accenture, (2005), *Leadership in Customer Service: New Expectations, New Experiences*, Accenture.

Accenture, (2006), *Leadership in Customer Service: Building the Trust*, Accenture.

Accenture, (2007), *Leadership in Customer Service: Delivering on the Promise*, Accenture.

Applegate, L.M., Holsapple, C.W., Kalakota, R., Radermacher, F.J., and Whinston, A.B. (1996), 'Electronic Commerce: Building blocks of New Business Opportunity', *Journal of Organizational Computing and Electronic Commerce*, 6(1), pp. 1–10.

Becta, (2003), *Educational Research on Interactive Whiteboards—a Selection of Abstracts and Further Sources*, Evidence and Research Team, http://www.becta.org.uk/page_documents/research/wtrs_bibs_whiteboards.pdf.

Bower, J.L. and Christensen C.M., (1995), 'Disruptive Technologies: Catching the Wave', *Harvard Business Review*, 73(1), pp. 43–53.

Business 2.0, (2000), 'B2B Blasts Off', *Business 2.0*, September, p. 91.

Business Week, (1983), 'Home Shopping: Is It a Revolution in Retailing or Just a Fad?', *Business Week*, 15 December, p. 68.

Business Week, (1986), 'Home Shopping: Is It a Revolution in Retailing or Just a Fad?', *Business Week*, 15 December, p. 62.

Cabinet Office, (2007), *Transformation Government Enabled by Technology, Annual Report 2006*, CM6970, http://www.cio.gov.uk/transformational_government/annual_report2006/index.asp.

Cassidy, J., (2002), *Dot.con: How America Lost its Mind and Its Money in the Internet Era*, HarperCollins.

Christensen, C.M., (1997), *The Innovator's Dilemma: When New Technologies Cause Great Firms to Fail*, Harvard Business School Press.

Christensen, C.M. and Anthony, S.D., (2007), 'How to be a Disrupter', *Forbes*, 23 January, http://www.forbes.com/2007/01/22/leadership disrupter-christensen-lead-innovation-cx_hc_0122christensen.html.

Commission on Intellectual Property Rights, (2002), *Integrating Intellectual Property Rights and Development Policy*, London, http://www.iprcommission.org/papers/pdfs/final_report/CIPRfullfinal.pdf.

Davies, R.L. and Reynolds, J., (1988), *Teleshopping and Teleservices*, Longman.

Denning, P.J., (2006), 'Infoglut', *Communications of the ACM*, 49(7), p. 15.

Department of Culture, Media and Sport, (2008), Digital Britain—the Future of Communications, Press Release, 28 October, http://www.culture.gov.uk/reference_library/media_releases/5548.aspx/

Dhalla, N.K. and Yuspeh, J., (1976), 'Forget the Product Life Cycle Concept', *Harvard Business Review*, 54(1), pp. 102–10.

Doerr, J., (2000), 'Mercenaries vs. Missionaries: John Doerr Sees Two Kinds of Internet Entrepreneurs', *Knowledge@Wharton*, 13 April, knowledge.wharton.upenn.edu/article.cfm?articleid=170.

Drobik, A., (1999), 'The End of E-Business', *Research Note*, 9 November, Stamford: Gartner.

Economist Intelligence Unit, (2006), *The 2006 e-Readiness Rankings*, IBM Institute for Business Value.

Economist Intelligence Unit, (2008), *The 2008 e-Readiness Rankings*, IBM Institute for Business Value.

*Economist*, (2005), 'Bubble 2.0', *The Economist*, 22 September.

European Commission, (2006), 'Effects of ICT Capital on Economic Growth', *Staff Papers*, 30 June, Enterprise and Industry Directorate General.

European Commission, (2007), *The European e-Business Report 2006–7 edition*, e-Business w@tch.

European Commission, (2008), *The European e-Business Report 2007–8 edition*, e-Business w@tch.

Gartner, (2008), 'Gartner Highlights 27 Technologies in the 2008 Hype Cycle for Emerging Technologies', press release, 11 August, http://www.gartner.com/it/page.jsp?id=739613.

Goldman Sachs, (2001), *Goldman Sachs Mobile Device Usage Study*, GS Research Ltd.

IFPI, (2009), *Digital Music Report 2009*, http://www.ifpi.com/content/library/DMR2009.pdf.

Kelly, A., (2006), 'Fundraisers Widen the Net', *Guardian*, 10 July, media.guardian.co.uk/mediaguardian/story/0,,1816519,00.html.

Kindleberger, C.P. (2005), *Manias, Panics, and Crashes: A History of Financial Crises*, Wiley.

Laseter, T., Long B., and Capers, C., (2001), *B2B Benchmark: The State of Electronic Exchanges*, Booz Allen Hamilton.

Malmsten, E., Portanger, E., and Drazin, C., (2002), *Boo Hoo: A Dot Com Story*, Random House.

Mintzberg, H., (1992), 'Opening up the Definition of Strategy', in Quinn, J.B., Mintzberg, H., and James, R.M. (eds), *The Strategy Process—Concepts, Contexts and Cases*, Prentice-Hall International.

New, S., Meakin T., and Southworth, R., (2002), *Understanding the E-marketspace: Making sense of B2B*, Saïd Business School, University of Oxford.

Park, E.G., Lamontagne, M., Perez, A., Melikhova, I. and Bartlett, G., (2009), 'Running ahead Toward Interoperable e-Government: The Government of Canada Metadata Framework', *International Journal of Information Management*, 29, April, pp. 145–50.

Planting, S., (2006), 'Disruptive Innovation a Surprising Solution', *Financial Mail*, 5 May, p. 12.

Quinn, J.B., (1978), 'Strategic Change: Logical Incrementalism', *Sloan Management Review*, 20(1), pp. 7–21.

Rayport, J.F., (2000), 'The Truth about Internet Business Models', *Strategy+Business*, http://www.strategy-business.com/press/16635507/19334.

Riggins, F.J. and Rhee, H.-S., (1998), 'Towards a Unified View of Electronic Commerce', *Communications of the ACM*, October, 41(10), pp. 88–95

Rosenberg, L.J., and Hirschman, E.C., (1981), 'Retailing without Stores', *Harvard Business Review*, 56, September, p. 81

Thwaites, D., (2007), 'Google Zeitgeist, Europe', *Latitude: Leaders in Search*, weblog entry, May 21st, http://www.latitudegroup.com/index.php?/weblog/permalink/google_zeigeist/.

Tiemann, R., (2007), 'At Work, at Rest, at Play', *Financial Times Digital Business Supplement*, 14 March, p. 1.

Weisman, J., (2000), 'The Making of e-Commerce: Ten Key Moments', *E-Commerce Times*, 22 August, http://www.ectnews.com/story/4085.html.

White, A., Daniel, E., Ward, J., and H. Wilson, (2007), 'The Adoption of Consortium B2B e-Marketplaces: An Exploratory Study', *The Journal of Strategic Information Systems*, 16(1), March, pp. 71–103

## ⊗ Weblinks

Economist Intelligence Unit, e-Readiness data. Current data and analysis can be found here: http://www.eiu.com/site_info.asp?info_name=ibm_ereadiness&page=noads&rf=0.

European Commission E-Government Observatory. A reference and information tool on eGovernment issues and developments across Europe: ec.europa.eu/idabc/en/Chapter/140.

IFPI. Representing the music industry worldwide. Statistics, analysis, and policy documents here: http://www.ifpi.org.

The European e-Business MarketW@tch. The European Union's sectoral e-business observatory: http://www.ebusiness-watch.org/.

The Wayback Machine: A look back at the history of the Internet, as seen through the various incarnations of websites. 85bn web pages are available from 1996 to the present day: http://www.archive.org/web/web.php. See also the Internet Timeline: http://www.zakon.org/robert/internet/timeline/.

# Part one

# The changing environment for e-business

# 2

# Economics of e-business

## Learning outcomes

Completing this chapter will enable you to:

- Consider the potential contribution of e-business technologies to economic growth, market competitiveness, and productivity
- Appreciate the difficulties in measuring the net economic benefits of e-business
- Examine the effects of e-business on the location of economic activities
- Critically assess the potential for efficiency gains and growth in consumer power from e-business technologies for individuals
- Reach conclusions over the economic rhetoric attached to e-business technologies

## Introduction

The economic effects of e-business technologies have been profound and, in some cases, unexpected. They have ranged from improvements in a country's productivity and competitiveness through to the personal efficiencies gained by individual consumers in comparing prices or product specifications. They can be unexpected: as in the unforeseen growth in the central importance of search technology to the effective exploitation of the Internet. Why should these broader effects be important to organizations and why do we devote an entire chapter to them? Organizations need to have an accurate appreciation of the extent to which technologies such as the Internet can transform the marketplaces in which they operate. For example, the design and development of digitized products in sectors such as prerecorded music, movies, and entertainment has had a transformational effect on an existing market structure hitherto dominated by physical goods. Our focus in this Chapter is on some of the economic implications for industries, organizations and individuals.

Often, these implications are hidden and the means of measuring the attendant changes are poorly developed. For example, we have little real idea as to the ways in which the availability of e-books will affect levels of demand for their hard-copy equivalents, nor how the adoption of e-business technologies such as broadband, customized web portals or e-procurement platforms might influence the long-term productivity growth of firms or nations, although some tentative evidence is now starting to emerge. Economists have developed useful ways of thinking about the production, distribution, and consumption of goods and services by individuals and firms (microeconomics). They also seek to explain how economies work and evolve (macroeconomics). In both these instances, economists have recognized that e-business technologies can play a powerful role. But in many cases the rhetoric has occasionally outweighed the reality. Writing for the *Business Week* news magazine in 1998, distinguished academic and economic commentator Robert Kuttner felt that the potential for e-business technologies was clear:

> 'The Internet is a nearly perfect market because information is instantaneous and buyers can compare the offerings of sellers worldwide. The result is fierce price competition, dwindling product differentiation, and vanishing brand loyalty.'
> *Robert Kuttner, 1998*

Why is this rhetorical—at least so far? Well, even today, when, for example, many consumers in developed markets shop online, there is still price variability, product differentiation, and brand loyalty to be found; and physical stores still trade profitably in High Streets and malls. We will see the so-called 'efficient markets hypothesis' (EMH), emerging in a number of forms again and again throughout this book (notably in chapter 6), applied to markets between businesses as well as between businesses and consumers. We will also see counter-arguments and empirical evidence which seek to show that reality may be more socially and culturally determined than economists often allow for. Some have coined the phrase 'economic imperialism' to denote the way in which economics strays into other disciplines such as sociology and psychology (see, for example, the work of Gary Becker and Edward Lazear). Understanding the tension that can exist between different academic disciplines is important in interpreting what different writers have to say about the effects of e-business. Indeed, chapters 4 and 5 consider the environment for e-business from two other alternative and distinct perspectives. And finally it is also important to recognize that many of these fundamental questions are still largely unresolved. Whilst we are now considerably wiser than we were in 2001, the Internet is still far too recent a phenomenon, and it continues to evolve, which makes reaching wholly definitive conclusions as to its consequences for organizations and individuals difficult.

Nevertheless, sometimes commentators and analysts (and even company directors) subscribe to a form of technological determinism in which technologies such as the Internet are held to be unstoppable transforming forces. Often changes are anticipated which have not yet come about and claims for new technologies made which have little empirical evidence to support them. Those who claim that ICT and e-business technologies are less than utopian (such as writer Nicholas Carr) are commonly derided (Carr, 2003).

This chapter reviews the economic arguments for the particular contribution that e-business makes to growth and productivity. It explores the consequences of e-business

**Economic Imperialism** The extension of economics beyond the classical scope of the subject. Some economists claim to be able to explain all social behaviour by using the tools of economics.

technologies for the global economy. It identifies some of the microeconomic issues generated by e-business and the consequences for businesses and individuals.

# The contribution of e-business technologies to economic growth, market competitiveness, and productivity

It has been consistently suggested that the benefits of appropriate ICT investment in general are potentially huge, leading to lower transaction costs, higher productivity, and the enhanced capability for innovation and revenue growth (for example, BERR/DCMS, 2009). Some of the economic evidence for the more general scale and contribution of e-business technologies and ICT more generally within the UK as at 2007 is shown in Figure 2.1. But the precise process is still relatively poorly understood and the appropriate measurements difficult to make. In addition, different countries have invested in ICT and e-business technologies at different rates and this may have affected the extent of any benefits they are able to achieve. For example, research by economists continues to show that there has been greater investment in and diffusion of e-business technologies through the US economy than through many European economies. Chapter 1 demonstrated this in terms of the differing 'e-readiness' of particular countries.

We can see the statistical evidence of country differences in Figure 2.2, which shows the proportion of total domestic fixed capital investment relating to ICT in the US compared to the UK. Look at the consequences of the dot.com boom and bust in the figures for both countries. But also see the extent to which the US is consistently ahead of the UK in this respect, although the UK appears to be converging in total ICT investment terms by the end of the reporting period. As chapter 3 discusses, the technology required to deliver e-business requires constant re-evaluation for upgrading or replacement as the power of ICT increases. This implies that continuing investment is required to maintain, let alone enhance, an economy's ICT capital. At the same time, the cost of technology is falling

- Firms in the UK ICT sector contribute around 10% of GDP

- Computer and related activities alone contribute £58bn to UK GDP

- The IT industry employs 1.1mn in the UK

- The telecommunications industry has annual revenues of £52bn per annum

- The information industry that provides business services enabled by IT and communications employs around 4mn and generates exports of £20bn per annum

**Figure 2.1** The contribution of ICT and e-Business technologies to the UK economy

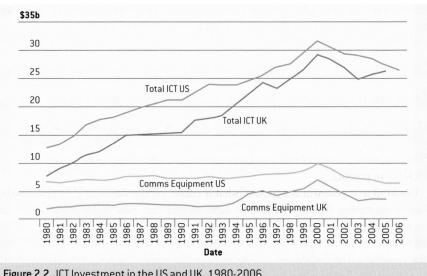

**Figure 2.2**  ICT Investment in the US and UK, 1980-2006

and organizations may be able to achieve a better 'bang for their buck' than was the case twenty years ago. The second most important contribution to the labour productivity of US firms between 1995 and 2003 was investment in ICT capital, accounting for 75 per cent of labour productivity growth (Inklaar et al., 2007). As early as 2002, the Net Impact Study sought to show that US firms had experienced some $155bn of cost savings from the adoption of e-business solutions (Varian et al., 2002).

For example, whilst rudimentary forms of email were available to some computer users in the early 1960s, there were few in the network and the economic benefits were relatively limited (van Vleck, 2001). The economic benefits of email today are perceived to be considerable. For a commercial business, these benefits can be derived from:

- improved communications;
- better access to information;
- lower costs than compared to conventional methods of communication;
- improved efficiency in the workplace;
- the easier finding of new business opportunities; and
- the ability to work more closely with customers and suppliers.

Lower transaction costs improve an economy's productivity and a higher capability for innovation can improve competitiveness. But the *net* economic effects of email may be less clear-cut. As the amount of email in circulation has increased, some have seen potentially substantial economic costs being incurred by organizations. Knowledge management research firm Basex estimated in 2007 that interruptions from email and other forms of communication (from what they termed information overload) cost the US economy $650bn annually in lowered productivity and stifled innovation.

> 'A typical worker gets 200 e-mails, dozens of instant messages, multiple phone calls (office phone and mobile phone), and several text messages, not to mention the vast amount of content that he/she has to contend with. It's not unlike the game of Tetris, where the goal is to keep the blocks from piling up. You barely align one and another is ready to take its place.' *BASEX, 2007*

And so, as the quotation above suggests, and as chapter 4 discusses in more depth, extensive reliance on email may also carry a social cost which may serve further to reduce efficiency in practice.

This kind of investment is a form of what is called 'capital deepening' by economists. Capital deepening through e-business technologies can have a beneficial effect on productivity, in particular improving the potential for increasing the efficiency of labour utilization. By increasing the amount of technology that is available to each employee, employees' efficiency might be expected to increase and, as a result, the output of firms can grow faster than would otherwise be possible.

> **Capital Deepening** An increase in the intensity of capital employed by an economy.

---

### Activity box 2.1

**Personal email productivity**

Can you think of ways in which you might measure the net effect of email on your personal productivity during the day? What steps might you take to improve that productivity?

---

Research undertaken in the UK in 2005 also showed that there were apparently measurable effects of e-business not just in terms of productivity but in respect of value added for sales and purchases by manufacturing firms as well (Clayton, 2005). A positive 4 per cent increase in value added for e-buying firms was partially offset by a 3 per cent reduction for firms involved in e-selling. This net effect makes sense if we assume that e-business makes markets more transparent, so that e-buying firms in particular benefit commercially from better pricing information:

> 'The essential feature of e-commerce, the electronic transaction, can be completed for a much lower cost than a face-to-face transaction or processing of voice orders over the phone or written orders sent by email or fax. Switching to e-commerce has cut average transaction costs for BT from $113 to $8.' *Phillips and Meeker, quoted in Willis, 2004*

But, as the discussion in relation to email shows, working out the net economic effects of e-business is difficult, even at the firm level, let alone at the international level, between countries. One of the major features of US economic growth in the last few years has been an extraordinary growth in labour productivity, following an earlier period of relatively slower growth. This most recent spurt has apparently been unaccompanied by any capital deepening. Major recent productivity gains have been focused on services, especially retailing. Explaining the resolution of this apparent paradox (often called the 'Solow paradox'[1]) is one of the key components in explaining any apparent gap in productivity growth between the US and Europe, since we know that capital substitution for labour has an important effect on productivity, and ICT-using firms, notably retailers, have made significant ICT investments in both regions.

There are three reasons in particular why we may find it especially difficult to establish the real economic benefits of e-business:

- Problems in actually measuring the benefits (Triplett, 1999; Pilat, 2002).

  Problems face both statisticians and firms in understanding the way in which e-business investment feeds through to benefits and ensuring that measurement and analysis can keep up with the pace of change. Take software, for example. Software investment may be categorized and accounted for in different ways—as 'consultancy', or as the rental of a service, or the purchase of a product. We discuss the notion of 'software as a service' in chapter 3. Countries and companies have different methods for estimating the amount spent on their own software: one recent US productivity study had to multiply by a factor of 3 the official level of software investment to reflect this (Basu et al., 2003). Secondly, economic analysis tends to lag behind e-business developments and tends to focus on larger legacy firms, which tend to be easier to analyse and measure: 'this area is one in which economists are still assembling a picture of rapid change' (Farooqui, 2005). Thirdly, whilst firms themselves are keen to put in place performance indicators to judge e-business effectiveness, they are 'often reluctant to embark on major overhauls of existing performance measurement systems' (Barnes and Hinton, 2006).

- The invisibility of some of these investments.

  We can think of e-business and ICT investment as an iceberg—with a visible part that is measured by the statisticians or the accountants, but a hidden part under water consisting of 'intangible' activities which nevertheless improve productivity. These will include: reorganising and reinventing business practices, such as outsourcing, and both formal and informal training. (Brynjolfsson et al., 2002). Indeed, we can think about the intangible knowledge derived from e-business technologies being one of the new factors of production for some organizations.

- The time taken for the benefits of e-business investment to emerge (Anon, 2003).

  Most commentators tend to assume that the impact of investment in e-business technologies takes place instantly at the point of production or use. But the benefits (as well as some of the hidden costs) may actually be arriving years after the money has been spent. Indeed, there may be a negative, downward, effect on efficiency in the period immediately following investment. In some cases, it may be two to three years before productivity improvements are seen and there may be a 'long and variable lag of between 5 and 15 years' before real changes in output can be identified and this time lag may be different in different countries.

E-business technologies can also affect different kinds of organization in unexpected ways. We might expect that levels of capital investment and economic rewards would be

---

1  Named after economist Robert Solow, who remarked that computers could be found everywhere other than in the productivity statistics.

linked to firm size: that is, the larger the firm, the larger the investment and the larger the benefit. We might also expect, other things being equal, for manufacturing firms to be able to benefit more from capital investment in production technologies than those in other sectors, since they can use e-business technologies to optimize both value chains and operational processes. Short case 2.1 provides an example of the chemicals, rubber, and plastics industry.

## Short case 2.1

### Chemicals, rubber, and plastics in Europe

Employing some 3.1m people and a value added of some €188bn, the chemical, rubber, and plastics industry (CRP) in Europe has struggled in the face of new competition from Asia. Large legacy firms dominate the chemicals sector, while there are many more smaller and medium-sized businesses to be found in rubber and plastics. While each sector faces its own particular set of challenges, observers of the industry see e-business technologies as a means of improving productivity whilst maintaining and developing firms' international market presence. Such technologies can be used to improve procurement efficiency and support logistics functions as well as to enhance the effectiveness of marketing, sales, and customer service. Adoption levels of e-business technologies, however, vary widely between applications and differently sized firms (see Table 2.1).

**Table 2.1  Adoption of e-business technologies by European chemical firms, 2007**

| Category | ERP | SCM | CRM | RFID |
|---|---|---|---|---|
| All firms | 68% | 39 | 40 | 13 |
| Small (10–49) | 27 | 12 | 18 | 1 |
| Medium (50–249) | 61 | 24 | 30 | 6 |
| Large (250+) | 80 | 52 | 53 | 18 |

ERP = Enterprise Resource Planning
SCM = Supply Chain Management
CRM = Customer Relationship Management
RFID = Radio Frequency Identification

>>

Research undertaken by the European Commission shows, in particular, that there is still a gap between the practices of larger firms and those of smaller. 'There is a "chicken and egg problem": [small firms] asked why they do not use e-business more intensively . . . say "because their customers and suppliers are not prepared for it"' (E-Business W@tch, 2008). However, even amongst larger firms, dependence upon legacy systems is still extensive. For example, 50 per cent of large firms and 30 per cent of medium-sized firms still rely to some extent upon electronic data interchange (EDI). Only 10 per cent of large firms in 2007 reported using XML-based e-procurement exchange formats, mainly the chemical industry's own CIDX data exchange, now transitioned to the American ChemITC (http://www.americanchemistry.com).

### Question

How can firms make progress with standardized data exchange, given the 'chicken and egg' problem described above?

In certain business-to-business markets, e-procurement processes have indeed made buyers and sellers much more sensitive to price, because the processes themselves can become more competitive. Chapter 9 discusses broad trends in process improvements through e-business, but the economic evidence appears clear. For example, Figure 2.3 shows that UK mechanical engineering firms which used e-business technologies had generally lower prices than those that did not—and the gap appeared to be increasing towards the middle of the decade (Criscuolo and Walden, 2003). The same analysis also

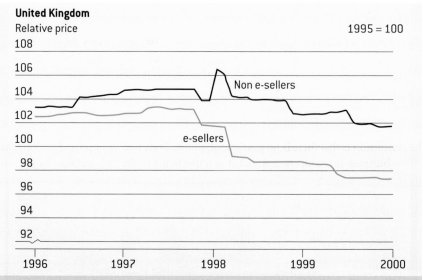

**Figure 2.3** Prices in mechanical engineering: e-sellers vs non-e-sellers

demonstrated that manufacturing firms employing more networked and integrated processes also tended to be able to achieve higher levels of labour productivity.

However, the leverage that firms can potentially receive from e-business investment would seem not always to be advantageous to larger firms. We know anecdotally that much new e-business activity has historically been concentrated amongst start-ups and initially small and medium-sized organizations, and this has now been demonstrated through micro-level analysis of firm data. Indeed, the apparent success of some Internet start-ups has been one of the defining characteristics of e-business development. What we can say is that younger firms are generally more flexible and more willing to adopt and implement e-business technologies, which in turn permits them to undertake more experimentation. Adopting e-business technologies may therefore allow small firms to redress some of the imbalance that can normally be found as a result of economies of scale. The productivity effects of, for example, e-buying and e-selling were reported to be almost equally strong between large and small firms in the UK, whilst we would normally have expected the benefits to be more significant for larger firms (Criscuolo and Waldren, 2003).

Recent UK research also suggests that service firms can appear to be able to benefit most from e-business investments:

'Our results show differences in impact of IT investment across sectors, with the strongest gains in the services industry. In manufacturing, we find that younger firms are able to get more out of their IT investment than older firms. In young manufacturing firms, enabling employees with computers and Internet is a more significant driver of productivity than investment on its own. In contrast, we find a degree of learning involved in the service sector where IT capital and networks are primarily used to build up client and service provision knowledge bases.' *Farooqui, 2005*

## Activity box 2.2

### Variations in e-business effects on firms

Research suggests that young service firms are most likely to obtain economic benefits from e-business. Think about Farooqui's explanation of how this can be achieved and relate this to a service firm or sector with which you are familiar.

The conclusion is that there is no guaranteed 'productivity win' or improved performance from e-business investments and that it is important to take into account the size and sector of firm, the kinds of e-business investments firms make, and how they are used. Research undertaken at the level of the firm in particular suggests that there is a close link between the e-business technology employed and the skills of those employed to make use of it, a dimension often neglected in e-business texts. We talk about the importance of e-business skills and culture in chapter 11.

'Firms that enjoy better performance will be those that select appropriate technology, integrate the processes most relevant to their operation and implement the organizational change to make it work.' *Goodridge and Clayton, 2004*

## Short case 2.2

### Alamy: an online marketplace for commercial photography

One of the biggest challenges facing news content providers worldwide is sourcing appropriate and innovative digital imagery to accompany stories. Similar problems beset advertising agencies and corporate communications firms. There are a number of large-scale competitors in this market, providing stock imagery. Getty Images, based in Seattle, operates in 100 countries, generated $850m in sales in 2007 (http://www.gettyimages.com). Corbis, also based in the US, is privately owned by Bill Gates and generates over $250m in sales (http://www.corbis.com). But on a small industrial estate in Oxfordshire in the UK is based a small commercial photography firm with a growing reputation for innovation and a customer-centric approach. Unlike Getty, Alamy, founded in 1999, relies upon an unedited collection of images supplied by amateur as well as professional photographers worldwide (http://www.alamy.com). It has, in effect, created a marketplace for photographers of all backgrounds: 'we do not edit our collection based on composition of an image, as we do not assume we know what the clients want'. Although it is still a relatively small business, Alamy's contractual arrangements are seen as especially fair, with contributors receiving the majority share of the fees generated by each sale.

'Alamy has built an exceptional reputation amongst photographers.' *Dudnick-Stern, 2008*

But it is also clear that the company 'punches above its weight' in its use of e-business technologies to enhance its market reach and performance:

'Solving problems through innovation is at the heart of our business. With so many images of every subject to choose from, we are constantly improving our search technology to bring the best results to our users. We are obsessed with the speed of our website, providing fast and first class customer service, and developing new tools to help photographers manage their commercial portfolios online.' *http://www.alamy.com*

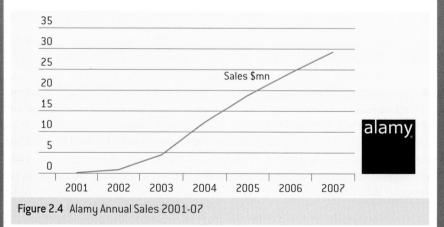

**Figure 2.4** Alamy Annual Sales 2001-07

»

For example, one of the biggest difficulties faced by customers of stock photo libraries lies in undertaking successful searches for imagery. The company's *AlamyRank* records all the images that are seen in search results by customers—so-called 'views'. The system also records when customers click on, and purchase, images they are interested in. Images that are seen but rarely clicked move down the results. Images with a greater

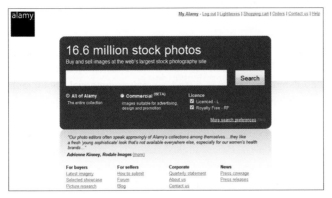

proportion of clicks to views are moved further up the results. This creates a strong incentive for contributors to describe their pictures accurately. Contributors who over-keyword or incorrectly keyword their images will be penalized, whereas those who are more accurate will gain greater visibility—and are therefore more likely to gain a greater financial benefit.

As the market for commercial stock photography evolves, the application of e-business technologies means smaller firms like Alamy are well placed to achieve economic benefits from the changing market; even one hitherto dominated by traditional agencies.

## Question

What are the biggest threats facing stock photography sites such as Alamy? How might they be overcome?

# Disintermediation and reintermediation

One of the leading economic principles associated with the growth of the Internet, which has profound implications for firms, is that of **disintermediation**. In conventional markets, intermediaries smooth the flow of transactions between buyers and sellers. Such intermediaries include wholesalers, retailers, travel agents, and brokers. They play and have played an important role in serving the markets on whose behalf they buy. Intermediaries save the end customer or consumer having to search for, compare, co-ordinate, and source products and services from a myriad of potential suppliers. Disintermediation, it has been argued, is a direct consequence of the Internet's capabilities to make a wide range of information efficiently available to the end user. Commentators proposed in the late 1990s that we would book our holidays directly with hotels, buy electrical goods directly from suppliers, and purchase industrial goods by cutting out the middleman. Such transactions would be conducted at a lower cost.

**Disintermediation**
Occurs when an intermediary is ejected from a conventional market niche between buyer and seller by a change in market conditions leading to buyer and seller dealing directly.

However, many markets created under the auspices of e-business will still have intermediation needs of their own, at least at present. As early as 1997, economists Joseph Bailey and Yannis Bakos proposed that there were four particular features of intermediation which might still be as relevant in online markets as offline, and which could be provided by new incumbents or by existing firms (Bailey & Bakos, 1997). These are:

- *Aggregation*: although searching for suppliers becomes easier online, a great many more possible sources of supply are revealed. There may therefore still be opportunities for intermediaries who aggregate or re-package content—particularly digital content—to prosper. For example, news-gathering portals like Google News have been very successful in making sense of the vast increase in accessibility of individual news stories on particular topics.

- *Providing trust*: despite the Internet's increasing maturity, users still require electronic intermediaries to play a role in providing trust and trusted payment services. This may favour established intermediaries, such as financial service providers and retailers. For example, leading UK grocery retailer brand Tesco has recently launched a successful price comparison site, Tescocompare.com.

- *Providing inter-organizational market information*: electronic markets can create the demand for the exchange of large amounts of information between buyers and sellers. Under these circumstances, firms may prefer to stick with an intermediary to handle the complexity. For example, a growing number of business service firms now provide advanced data management for clients (see Long case 9.2).

- *Matching suppliers and customers through filtering*: although the Internet reduces search costs, the proliferation of search results may favour the emergence of intermediaries that are able more efficiently to match buyers with sellers than can the two parties individually. (Short case 2.3 discusses the example of moneysupermarket.com).

The notion of e-business giving rise to new forms of intermediation, because of its continuing relevance even to electronic markets, was further developed by Alina Chircu and Robert Kauffman. They argued that, in practice, we were more likely to see an 'intermediation-disintermediation-reintermediation' (IDR) cycle developing. As value chains disintermediated, new, electronic, intermediaries would be established to satisfy buyer needs where intermediation was still relevant. Should so-called 'legacy' firms not be in a position to fill this niche, then new firms might spring up to seize the opportunity.

Think of the residential real estate market. The growth of the Internet has not generated a significant increase in one-to-one house sales as buyers and sellers negotiate directly. Instead, the availability of new ways of presenting house price information to prospective buyers has led to a number of innovative intermediaries being established. For example, On One Map (http://www.ononemap.com) was the UK's first property search engine, launched in 2005. Based on a Google mashup, the search engine displays on a map all the properties for sale that it can find in the user's selected location, and provides a summary of property details. This took the existing residential real estate industry by surprise and it was some time before the industry itself generated a response, because of the difficulties in organizing collaboration over market information. As generic property information has become more widely available, so On One Map has extended its services to reporting on the locations of schools, mobile phone masts, and supermarkets.

**Mashup** A web application which combines data from more than one source.

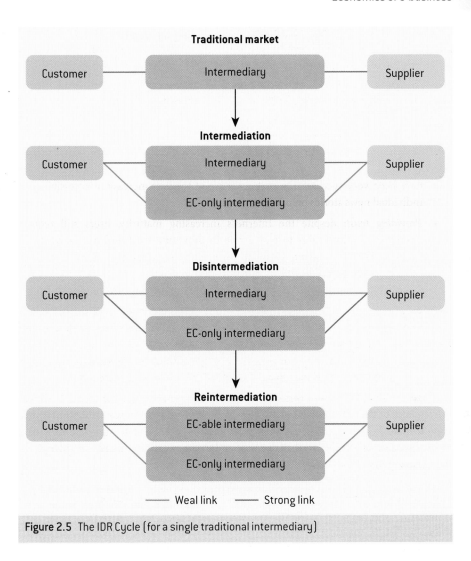

**Figure 2.5** The IDR Cycle (for a single traditional intermediary)

# E-business and its effects on the location of economic activities

The concept that the growth of the Internet would bring about the 'death of distance' has become a popular proposition. The suggestion is that communications are now so global that the additional cost of sending a message an extra hundred kilometres is effectively zero. According to economist Frances Cairncross, who coined the term in 1997, the consequence is 'a frictionless realm of social and economic interaction in which distance loses its meaning' (Cairncross, 2001). Figure 2.6 shows very clearly the downward

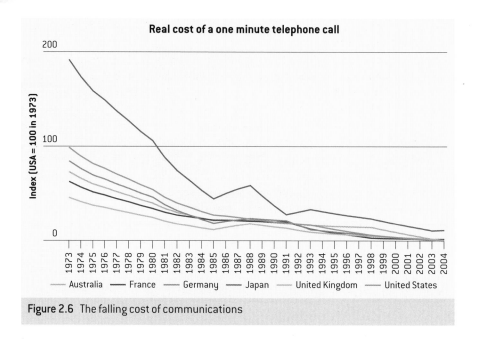

**Figure 2.6**  The falling cost of communications

convergence of telecommunications costs, which provides an indicator in support of this argument.

The consequences of the 'death of distance' and the implications for firms are potentially significant, argue economists:

> 'Just as steam gave British consumers access to cheap food in the nineteenth century, ICT is giving British business access to cheap labour today. However, whilst globalization then was about trade in goods, now the novel aspect is much more trade in business services.' *Crafts, 2005*

By this is meant, for example, the growth in offshoring of certain kinds of service activities, such as customer call centres and infrastructure support services to lower wage economies. We discuss this phenomenon in more detail in chapter 9. But Cairncross also cites the example of networking technology business Cisco (http://www.cisco.com), which calculates it saved itself 250,000 telephone calls and 17 per cent of its operating costs by setting up a website to provide its customers with technical back-up. Input to the website content and enquiries made of it can come from anywhere in the world. Such 'self-service' activities are supremely efficient and are often more than just Frequently Asked Questions pages. Take the example of Netcomposites, a small UK business in the composites industry (http://www.netcomposites.com). NetComposites' core business is in creating knowledge for the composites community, through research, consultancy, and technology transfer. The company's website, the leading online portal for the sector, contains some 12,000 pages of free information on composite materials, ranging from weekly news stories and general articles on composites through to very specific technical advice. It attracts over 200,000 user sessions each month and provides the basis for the firm's work in research, consultancy, and project management.

Provided that the underlying Internet infrastructure is in place, small businesses such as Netcomposites can establish themselves in rural areas (in this case, on the edge of Chesterfield) and, through Internet connectivity, make their goods and especially services available, in principle, to a global market. Short case 2.2 provided another excellent example. But although we might believe that the impact of e-business technologies is to disperse economic activities (as in the example of offshoring) the important phrase here is 'in principle'. The small business may still have to source raw materials, perhaps labour, and certainly incur transportation costs if it is product-oriented. Total dispersion of economic activities seems unlikely for other reasons: think of the number of activities that still require closeness and personal contact. For example, the City of London, for all its offshoring activity, still provides an important physical place for people to meet for those activities to which personal contact is critical. And of course, whilst we talk in this chapter of a knowledge economy, where intangible assets whiz between computers great distances apart, a substantial proportion of the global economy remains physical. And in this world, there are economic pressures working the other way:

> 'In a world of triple-digit oil prices, distance costs money. And while trade liberalization and technology may well have flattened the world, rising transport prices will once again make it rounder.' *Rubin and Tal, 2008*

---

### Activity box 2.3

#### Distance decay

Consider the last six purchases you made online. Where were the sellers based geographically? Did this affect your buying experience? If there were shipping costs, do you think this fully represented the transportation cost attached to your purchases?

---

# E-Business and its effects on the economic behaviour of individuals

There are a number of potentially powerful economic phenomena arising out of e-business applications which have significant implications for individuals, not just as customers or consumers, but as economic agents in their own right. These largely arise as a consequence of the greater visibility and interconnectedness of markets enhanced through e-business technologies. Along the way, they can create economic opportunities for individuals, too.

# Network effects and e-business

Network Effect  The idea that a service becomes more valuable as more people utilize it, thereby encouraging increasing numbers of users. Classic examples can be found in the communications market and include the telephone, fax machine, email, and of course the Internet itself.

As an e-business service is perceived to be more valuable, so more people will tend to use it. This phenomenon is termed a network effect and, although the concept is not a new one, it has particular resonance in e-business. Metcalfe's Law proposed that 'the value of a network is proportional to the square of the number of users of the system'. When a market reaches a critical mass, or tipping point, network effects take over and growth can become exponential. Its direct application to e-business has been questioned (Odlyzko and Tilly, 2005). This is because Metcalfe's Law presupposes that the value is a rational economic one. Calculating the value that an individual might see in having access to a social networking account is difficult and involves more than just economics. For example, the law assumes that all network connections and all groups are equally valuable. Think of your own friends on Facebook. In other areas, the notion of value is less complex. For example, the free Voice over Internet Protocol (VoIP) service Skype reached a landmark 1bn downloads of its software in September 2008, after only five years in existence. Clearly, Skype only becomes useful to any individual if there are sufficient concurrent users online or contactable. Take a look at Long case 2.1, which examines the evolving role of Skype from an economic perspective, and consider the questions posed in Activity 2.4, below.

## Activity box 2.4

### Understanding network effects: added value?

It has been suggested that social networking sites such as Bebo and Facebook rely upon network effects for their success. What does this mean in practice for you and your friends, if you are users of such sites? In other words, what is the value that is important to you that is generated through your use of them? Can you think of e-businesses in other sectors that are similarly dependent on such effects?

# The long tail

Long Tail  An interpretation of the Pareto law applied to the stimulation of consumer demand possible in electronic markets, developed by journalist Chris Anderson. Refers to the ability of firms to obtain significant profits from the sale of small amounts of previously hard-to-find items to many customers, rather than selling only large amounts of a smaller number of popular items.

One of the most enticing economic concepts to have been applied in the context of e-business is what has become known as the 'long tail'. Popularized in the context of the Internet by journalist and author Chris Anderson, although dating back to the development of Pareto, or power law, distributions by statisticians in the 1940s, the long tail refers to the profitable selling of small volumes of difficult-to-find products to many customers (who comprise the 'tail' of the distribution), instead of only selling large volumes of a smaller number of popular items to customers (who comprise the best selling 'head') (Anderson, 2004). (A typical long tail is shown in Figure 2.7.) Hitherto, it has been argued, the imperfections of markets, the nature of conventional marketing channels, and the poor levels of knowledge amongst consumers and customers has meant that only a limited range of products and services could be profitably sold.

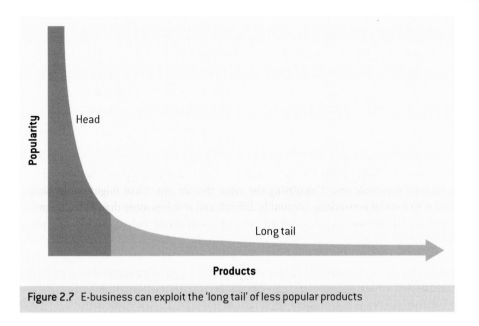

**Figure 2.7** E-business can exploit the 'long tail' of less popular products

Think about buying books in the pre-Internet era: the customer was reliant upon the bricks and mortar bookstores, the academics providing reading lists, and the magazines and newspapers featuring and reviewing titles which in turn would determine the stock of titles from which the general buyer would normally have to choose. Bestselling lists would be generated from this subset of all books available. While bookstores themselves could order any title in print, for example through a physical directory such as *British Books in Print* with 1.6m titles as at 2007, the typical High Street bookstore only stocks between 30,000 to 50,000 titles (Whitaker, 2007). Even one of the UK's biggest booksellers, Blackwell, only offers 160,000 titles in its massive Oxford store—just 10 per cent of all English-language books in print. It would be uneconomic (and well nigh impossible) for bookstores to stock every book in print. It would be similarly time-consuming and expensive for consumers to order up and scour book publishers' hard copy catalogues themselves for niche titles.

Making this information available online to the end user, realizing—in other words— the sales potential of the 'back catalogue' of hitherto small circulation titles, could transform the economics of book selection and buying. One person saw this opportunity and the rest, as they say, is history. We examine other aspects of the resultant Amazon. com business model in chapter 6, but this principle represents the foundation of Amazon's success. It is interesting here to note that founder Jeff Bezos was not originally wedded to books:

'Looking for the best product that could be sold on the Web, Bezos compiled a list of twenty possibilities, including computer software, office supplies, apparel and music. In the course of his research he was surprised to find that books rocketed from being almost at the bottom of the list to the very top, with music following in second place.' *Spector, 2000*

What made the market for books such an attractive 'long tail' proposition? Here are five reasons—and you may be able to think of some more:

- Books are *known value items*—everybody understands what a book is—and there is minimal product variability (really only hardback versus paperback for an individual title for example).
- The US book publishing and retailing industries were very fragmented and the potential for an aggregator was significant.
- Book titles are easily available from publishers.
- Book sales were highly concentrated: in 1994, only seventeen titles sold more than 1m copies, and only another eighty-three titles sold more than 400,000.
- A bounded universe of available titles was available from existing inventory lists and directories.

It is the final two characteristics which provide both the measure of and the key to one of the commercial opportunities generated by the Internet. Since it seems unlikely that there were only seventeen good quality books out of the 1.3m English titles available in 1994, this high concentration of 'bestselling titles' would seem to be an expression of the market's inefficiency—making the remainder of titles available would create new opportunities for profit. And the availability of a detailed inventory of a finite list of products would mean that this could be done by creating a searchable database online. Amazon demonstrated this by making 30–40 per cent of their sales revenue from books that would not normally be found in book stores (Brynjolfsson, Hu and Smith, 2006).

> 'our research suggests that search tools can also be very effective in allowing consumers to discover and purchase products they otherwise would not have considered, resulting in changes in sales distribution among a company's products.' *Brynjolfsson, Hu and Smith, 2006*

This is attractive, allowing producers such as publishers to work in response to much more reliable 'signals of demand' than publishing what they think people will want to read (so-called 'push' models of marketing).

The book market is inevitably used when demonstrating the way the long tail principle works. Indeed, the number of books in print pales into insignificance by comparison with the number of used, rare and out-of-print titles, where the principle also applies. AbeBooks, discussed in chapter 10, brings together 13,500 secondhand and antiquarian booksellers through five international websites which, between them, have inventories of over 110m titles, selling over 30,000 books per day to customers who would otherwise be unable to source rare or obscure titles (http://www.abebooks.com). Booksellers pay a subscription fee to list their titles, ranging from $25 to $500, depending on the number of titles.

However, Chris Anderson's argument is that the long tail principle applies to many markets. Indeed, he calls it 'the theory of the 21st century' (Anderson, 2006). But are there problems with long tails applied indiscriminately? Marketing writer Alan Mitchell thinks there are:

> 'The "long tail" is a theory of the 21st century economy so long as you set aside any product or service involving material, tangible atoms or people-based service, where

novelty is not the key to value, and where standards and interoperability are not critical.'
*Mitchell, 2006*

By this, he means that:

- The 'long tail' only really applies to 100 per cent digital products and services (the costs of marketing, sales, inventory, and distribution can otherwise intervene to make the long tail more costly than economists allow for).

- The 'long tail' is particularly powerful in market contexts where customers are constantly seeking variety—in clothing, in music, in books, for example.

- Conversely, customers do not always want, or appreciate, a potentially endless variety of all kinds of goods. How many types of baked beans can the consumer market support, for example? A smaller number of more standardised products may be preferred.

This debate is a continuing one. If you are interested in reading more about the long tail and its critics, then Chris Anderson's blog (http://www.longtail.com) contains links to the current discussion.

---

### Activity box 2.5

**Long tails or short?**

Can you think of 'tails' which are short and unlikely to benefit from e-business transformation?

More often than not, the 'long tail' concept is applied to new products and services. But are the 'long tails' for used and scarce products (such as those found in businesses like eBay) likely to be more extensive and potentially profitable?

---

## Search, search costs, and consumer power

It is popularly supposed that e-business technologies increase the power that individuals have as economic agents in relation to suppliers and markets. But consumer power is a complex phenomenon and has social as well as economic characteristics (French and Raven, 1959). One research team has recently proposed that consumer power in the Internet economy can be considered to have three components (Rezabakhsh et al., 2006):

- *Expert power*: reflects the ability the consumer now has to accumulate information on quality and prices in markets, independently of companies. Previously, so-called information asymmetries worked in the favour of companies. Think of the degree of expertise now accumulating with individuals that can now be shared through discussion fora and social networking sites such as TripAdvisor.

**Information Asymmetry**
A situation (negotiation or transaction) where one party has more, or higher quality, information about the other.

- *Sanction power*: reflects the consumer's ability to reward a supplier—through continued loyalty—or punish them—through withdrawing their patronage, or through engaging in negative word of mouth. Think, for example, of Facebook pages promoting boycotts of a company's products or services.

- *Legitimate power*: reflects the way in which consumers are increasingly able to shape prices and goods to their individual preferences. At the most extreme, this can extend to 'crowdsourcing', the outsourcing of a task or an activity to an unspecified, but generally large, group of people. A good example of this is news broadcaster CNN's iReport service, soliciting newsgathering from the general public. We discuss crowdsourcing in the context of value creation in chapter 6.

> Crowdsourcing the outsourcing of a task or activity to an unspecified, but generally large, group of people.

One of the economic features of e-business that we now take for granted (and indeed that has provided the basis for the growth of arguably the Internet's biggest brand, Google) is that of search. Efficient search should provide a basis for the mechanism by which the economist's 'perfect market' can be achieved and provides the theoretical basis for consumers' expert power. But does decreased online search cost in principle really lead to increased search in practice by consumers? Consumers in general face three types of online search cost:

- the cost of locating an appropriate seller;
- the cost of obtaining price information; and
- the cost of obtaining product information.

In practice, we now know that the amount of search that individuals conduct is much less than had been previously anticipated (Johnson et al., 2004). Different users conducting the same searches often have varied goals and perceive value in different ways. Indeed, the way in which individuals conduct searches and evaluate the perceived or actual search costs that they incur may in fact work against the concept of the long tail. Research examining the way in which consumers search for both books and MP3 players, for example, shows that price search and non-price product information search activities increase when cross-site search and in-site searching are made easier (Su, 2008).

Having said this, growing consumer power in this respect can be seen to be increasingly exhibited in the proliferation of price comparison services, which act as intermediaries. Originally developed in respect of consumer products such as electrical goods and entertainment products, such services take a commission from the supplier when the end user clicks through or makes a purchase. But such services work best in markets which are especially imperfect or confusing, or where there is lack of consumer expertise. In sectors such as mobile phone subscriptions, financial services, travel, and utilities such as gas and electricity it is difficult for consumers to assess propositions efficiently. It is estimated that nearly one-third of Europeans researching financial services make use of financial comparison sites. In other sectors, price comparisons have had some unexpected consequences:

> 'Many economists expected online price comparisons to drive down prices, but retailers are deadlocked, resulting in fluctuating prices, which vary each day' *Gatti et al., 2004*

## Short case 2.3

### Moneysupermarket.com

More than two dozen financial services comparison sites were estimated to be operating in the UK in 2008. The market is currently dominated by two main providers—Confused.com (http://www.confused.com) and Moneysupermarket.com (http://www.moneysupermarket.com)—although barriers to entry are low and the market is still immature. The market leader, Moneysupermarket.com, was founded by current CEO Simon Nixon as an offline intermediary business providing mortgage sourcing information in 1993. It went public through an IPO in 2007. The company operates two principal websites: moneysupermarket.com and travelsupermarket.com. Although still an independent company, it has received a lot of interest from potential acquirers. It generated revenues of £99m in the first half of 2008 with profits doubling to £14.4m. Its Internet business operates across four industry sectors: money (50 per cent of Internet revenues), insurance (30 per cent), travel (7 per cent), and home services (4 per cent). The fastest growing vertical of the four in 2008 has been homes services, where comparison of broadband, mobile phones, shopping, and utilities pushed revenues up by 78 per cent. Some 64m visitors used the sites during 2007.

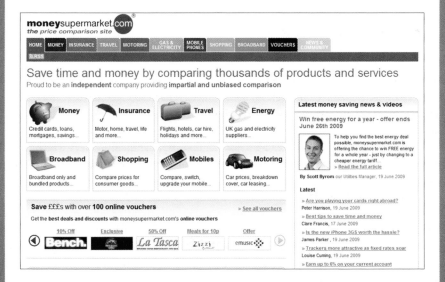

For example, comparing and contrasting car insurance deals can be complex. The company has eighty-nine motor insurance providers live on the site and offers user reviews and in-depth product comparisons based on a detailed set of questionnaire responses provided by the user. Quotes can be stored for up to thirty days. Moneysupermarket seeks to reassure prospective customers with its 'customer promise':

»

- best price—even if the user goes direct to the insurer's site;
- most comprehensive—including listing companies which do not pay Moneysupermarket.com to appear and explaining notable absences from the site;
- clear and impartial—no fees or commissions are charged;
- trustworthy;
- supportive.

The significant financial uncertainties of recent years have favoured sites like Moneysupermarket.com. CEO Simon Nixon observes that:

> 'People are going to the website as they are basically tightening their belts. Customers are also reviewing what they pay in insurance and utility bills rather than automatically renewing . . . but customers are more savvy now than they were maybe 12 months ago. They are looking at perhaps two or three price comparison sites. But the market is not very mature and I would say most people will be looking at comparison sites online within the next three to five years.'

In the face of growing competition in this space, moneysupermarket.com is increasing its spend on brand promotion and is planning to expand by launching a shopping channel as well as a service in Germany.

### Question

In the face of increasing competition for price comparison services, what strategy should moneysupermarket.com adopt?

Work undertaken on the markets for books and CDs has also suggested that consumers, in these markets at least, do not always choose the supplier with the lowest price, as economists might have expected, because of the inherent heterogeneity of many of the propositions offered by marketers who, for example, bundle them in ways which make comparisons difficult. For example, think how difficult it is to make effective comparisons of mobile phone tariffs.

However, the majority of consumers for both search and experience goods still effectively often short circuit this process by going directly to an intermediary—often their preferred sellers' website or store brand website: brands that they trust. Rather than use Internet-based search engines, they may also often resort to more conventional word of mouth in finding information. Electronic word of mouth is the second most used source of finding websites in the US—and for youth markets, the most important. This has important implications for the way in which e-business marketing is conducted, an area that we explore in more detail in chapter 7.

## Long case 2.1

### Skype

Skype could be said to have become synonymous with Internet telephony, in much the same way as Biros became synonymous with pens. Founded in 2003 by Niklas Zennström and Janus Friis, the company originally pursued an alternative technical model to commercial VoIP, which drew on the founders' experience with the file-sharing network Kazaa (http://www.kazaa.com) by replacing a client-server model of Internet telephony with a peer-to-peer approach. Downloaded software allows Skype users to have unlimited, free voice, video, and instant messaging communications with each other. The business generates revenue through value added services including the making and receiving of calls by these users to and from landlines and mobile phones (SkypeIn and SkypeOut), voicemail, SMS, call forwarding and personalization, including the sale of ringtones and avatars. Its 2008 revenues were in the order of $8bn. By the third quarter of 2008, Skype had claimed over 1bn downloads of its software and had 338m registered users, although the number of 'real' users is smaller—conservative estimates putting this at 34m at the end of 2008 (Figure 2.8) (Barton, 2008). Indeed, at any one time only some 13m concurrent users are online. Whilst as at the beginning of 2008 there were an estimated 1,400 commercial international VoIP services (http://www.myvoipprovider.com), Skype retained a strong lead in the consumer market.

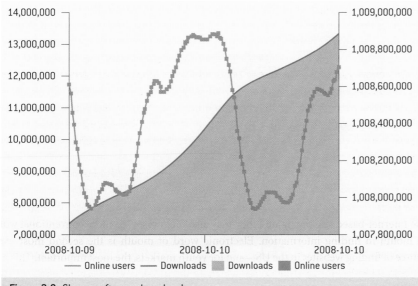

**Figure 2.8** Skype software downloads

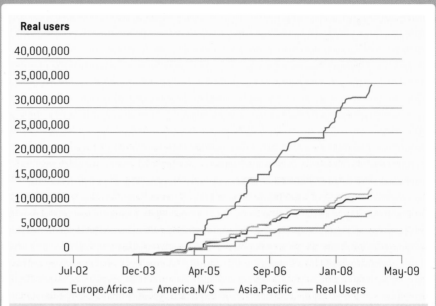

**Figure 2.9** 'Real users' of Skype

Note : the definition of 'real users' when associated with Skype is © Hudson Barton.

Barton (2006) summarizes Skype's distinctive features:

- integrated voice, text, video, file sharing, and screen sharing;
- software for every platform;
- service everywhere there is an Internet connection, especially if it is broadband; »

- full voice interface with PSTN;
- low cost client-based point-to-point service;
- encryption capability;
- firewall breaching agility;
- independent partners in hardware, software, and IP networks.

Skype is an excellent example of 'disruptive innovation' affecting established business models and one that has survived the hype of potentially unrealistic expectations. Its early success alerted conventional telecommunications providers to the potential impact from a share decline in retail voice telephony—particularly from long distance calls—on their longstanding revenue and profit streams. (A greater impact on profitability is a result of the generally higher margins being charged on voice compared to other products.) Whilst European carriers were more at risk than North American because of higher voice tariffs, nearly two-thirds of active residential US VoIP users reported that they had discontinued or replaced a traditional (non-VoIP) phone service when they acquired their VoIP service in 2006, and nearly one-third have Skype. Commercial VoIP offerings from conventional telecoms providers—developed as a means of competing with Skype and other free peer-to-peer services—have not been wholly successful, although the bundling of VoIP with broadband service is starting to make some inroads into the market. The provision of voice telephony within businesses is also contested, as firms seek to reduce their cost base and as 'enterprise' editions of VoIP appear. Skype began testing an Enterprise version of its service in early 2007 and 30 per cent of users now use Skype for business.

Skype's own growth has not been trouble-free, according to commentators. It was the first to point out that it was not a telephony replacement service and could not be used for contacting the emergency services; also that its service could clearly not be sustained through power failures. However, regulatory authorities in—for example—Norway, the US, and the UK have imposed requirements for service access which reflect the increasingly mainstream nature of the service and the growing proportion of users reliant upon it (Williams, 2007).

Skype was purchased by eBay in 2005 for $2.6bn. Skype founder Janus Friis commented: 'together we feel we can really change the way that people communicate, shop and do business online.' (Skype, 2005) Perspectives on this acquisition have been mixed. Positive commentary suggests the creation of a 'Skype-eBay ecosystem' which will create the scope for new types of services, applications software and content (Tauli, 2005). Others have been more sanguine:

> '"The Skype deal is absolutely a return to the 1999 mentality," says Pip Coburn of Coburn Ventures, a technology-strategy firm. It and many of the other recent and mooted internet deals seem to be based on little more than the belief of management that everything is going to change dramatically in the next few years, in highly unpredictable ways, and so all options need to be covered.' *Economist, 2005*

Ebay sold a 65% stake in Skype to private investors in September 2009.     »

## Long case 2.2

### EBay shops

EBay has been described disparagingly by some as an 'electronic yard sale' (http://www.ebay.com). But it is hard to criticize a business which generates $5.3bn in sales from 84m active users worldwide in its marketplace activities alone (the company also owns Paypal), selling a pair of shoes every four seconds, a major electrical appliance every two minutes, and a Ford Mustang every 26 minutes. Indeed, if eBay were classed as a retailer, it would be the world's sixth largest. It is also the world's biggest recycler, generating $100bn annually from sales between individuals of second-hand items. Yet one of the most intriguing economic consequences of eBay's business is not the realization of the potential of millions of attics, basements, and garages filled with second-hand goods; nor the benefits to be gained by re-selling cleverly acquired tickets or celebrity memorabilia. It lies in the role eBay has played in new business creation and entrepreneurship. In the UK alone, eBay has been responsible for the creation of 178,000 full-time and hobby businesses, which between them generated some £2bn in sales during 2007. According to a 2005 Gallup study commissioned by eBay, more than 700,000 Americans rely on eBay as a primary or secondary source of income.

Jack Sheng from El Monte, California (ID: eforcity) started selling cell phone chargers on eBay in 2000 and now claims to be 'a global entrepreneur'. 'My friends and I just started selling stuff on eBay to make some extra money. Today, we employ 180 people and our business is approaching $40 million.' But not all eBay traders conform to the classic stereotype of the entrepreneur:

> 'At 73 years old, George Crudgington is a counter-intuitive example of the new Ebay trader. Based in Chesterfield, Derbyshire, he sells about £100,000 of goods via Ebay every year. He needs to. He was made redundant from a job in engineering in his 50s without an adequate pension. Mr Crudgington now makes a living selling ceramic collectibles and antique fishing gear on Ebay. He has even bought a retirement home in France with the profits.' *Guthrie, 2008*

»

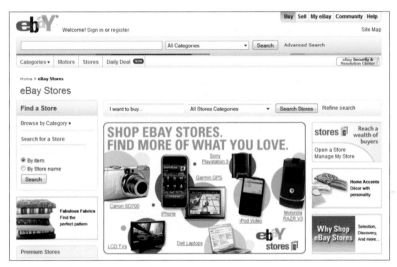

The company facilitates the growth of these businesses by providing e-business tools and applications to individuals. Subscribers can opt for a Basic, Premium, or Anchor Store, from between $16 to $300 per month. Internal tools such as Selling Manager monitor active listings and shipping status, generate bulk feedback, and print invoices and labels. eBay's ProStores subsidiary provides a professional front end for businesses. Opportunities are there, too, for new intermediaries. Recently, third-party application software writers have been allowed to supplement eBay's existing efforts and provide front ends for so-called 'power sellers' (power-sellers bring in over $1 billion per month in gross merchandise value in the US alone.) One example is Vancouver-based Auctomatic (http://www.auctomatic. com) which provides auction management software, including inventory management and picture storage facilities which interface with the eBay application program interface (API). Well over half eBay's listings now come through the API (that is, via third parties).

The level of conventional costs incurred by eBay traders are low, when compared to trading from a physical outlet, or in creating and maintaining an independent website. But in a marketplace of 84m active users, where barriers to entry are so low ('click here to create your store') competition can be fierce and margins can quickly be put under pressure. Network effects can have negative as well as positive consequences. »

*Questions*

1. 'eBay is to online auctions and trading what Biros are to pens.' Do you agree?
2. What measures can eBay traders put into place to minimize the competitive threats from 'a marketplace of 84m users'?

## ⊛ Chapter Summary

This chapter distinguished between the focus on how economies work and evolve and the focus on the production, distribution, and consumption of goods and services by organizations and individuals. Early claims by economists suggested that the development of the Internet would herald the arrival of the 'perfect market'. The chapter began by examining the possible contribution of e-business technologies to economic growth by summarizing statistical evidence of national differences in e-business investment between the US and the UK, and the differential consequences. It then sought evidence to demonstrate the productivity and performance effects of e-business on organizations. It concluded that the firms that enjoy better performance have (1) selected appropriate technology, (2) integrated the most relevant e-business processes, and (3) implemented organizational change in parallel. Particular advantages appear to accrue to younger firms and service-sector businesses. However, it also sought to show that establishing the net economic benefits of e-business is not straightforward and set out three main barriers to understanding: measurement, intangibility of investment, and timing.

The chapter then sought to assess critically two economic concepts relevant to organizations: the role of intermediation and so-called 'death of distance'. It demonstrated that new forms of intermediary in electronic markets had emerged. It also attempted to show that the effect of e-business technologies on the location of economic activities was more equivocal than commentators had initially expected.

The chapter finally addressed the effects of e-business technologies on the economic behaviour of individuals. It introduced the notion of network effects in the context of e-business applications and their consequences for demand. It noted that the notion of added value, so important in creating a 'tipping point' for such effects, was more complex and ambiguous than had been anticipated from the point of view of e-business It also reviewed the concept of the 'long tail' in relation to the creation and nature of likely future consumer demand. It concluded that the concept was helpful in exploiting hitherto uneconomic niches of demand, but that it was not universally applicable: especially for standardized, bespoke, or many forms of non-digital products. This led to a discussion of the notions of search, search costs, and consumer power. The chapter showed that consumer power was a complex phenomenon, with social as well as economic characteristics. It also pointed to the unexpected ways in which consumers evaluate search costs which can lead them to rely upon intermediaries that they trust, or—increasingly—specialized price comparison services, especially in markets which are particularly imperfect or confusing.

# ❓ Review questions

1. Why might the impact of e-business technologies upon economic performance be a poorly understood process?

2. What are the economic benefits of network email? Why are the potential gains hard to realize?

3. What do we know about the differential effectiveness of e-business investment by large vs small firms and by pre-existing against start-up companies? What might account for these differences?

4. What are the consequences of greater price sensitivity for the behaviour of (a) organizations and (b) individuals?

5. Give examples of two sectors in which the intermediation-disintermediation-reintermediation cycle can be observed.

6. What are the pros and cons of the 'death of distance' hypothesis?

7. What are the characteristics of markets with 'long tails'? Identify three contrasting examples to illustrate your answer.

8. Why might the amount of search that individuals conduct be less than had previously been anticipated?

# ❓ Discussion questions

1. What might be the consequences of 'economic imperialism'?

2. The market for recorded music has much the same mix of characteristics as that for books, with a 'long tail' of potential customers for back catalogue products. Why didn't Jeff Bezos choose that market instead?

3. Why might similar expenditures on e-business technologies between the US and UK nevertheless lead to different outcomes in terms of firm performance?

4. It has been suggested that reintermediation reflects (a) ineffective or immature search technology, or (b) lack of consumer willingness to engage in extensive search. Do these suggestions have any merit? Can you think of other reasons why consumers still need 'middlemen'?

5. 'The 'long tail' is a theory of the 21st century economy so long as you set aside any product or service involving material, tangible atoms or people-based service, where novelty is not the key to value, and where standards and interoperability are not critical' (Mitchell, 2006). Do you agree?

# ➡ Suggestions for further reading

BIS/DCMS, (2009), *Digital Britain: the Final Report*, http://www.culture.gov.uk/what_we_do/broadcasting/6216.aspx.
A report which sets out the UK Government's vision of the economic contribution which can be made by appropriate investments in e-business technologies.

Carr, N., (2003), 'IT Doesn't Matter', *Harvard Business Review*, 5, pp. 41–9. See also Carr's blog, 'Rough Type', http://www.roughtype.com/.
This is a classic article by unorthodox journalist, author and consultant Nicholas Carr. It argues, based on historical precedent, that while new technologies initially provide firms with opportunities to create competitive advantages, in the longer term they become invisible, ubiquitous commodities.

Anderson, C., (2006), *The Long Tail: How Endless Choice is Creating Unlimited Demand*, Random House.
This is a classic example of the way in which a longstanding economic idea can be popularized. The power law describes a mathematical relationship between the size and frequency of events. It has previously been applied to phenomena as diverse as earthquakes and

mortality; Anderson's bestselling book examines its characteristics and consequences in e-business.

Elberse, A., (2008), 'Should You Invest in the Long Tail?', *Harvard Business Review*, 86 (7/8), pp. 88–96.
Focusing on the music and home video industries, Harvard Professor Anita Elberse seeks to test the claims made by Chris Anderson's 'long tail' theory and finds it wanting: she concludes that there are more blockbusters and consumers don't like niches much. This has led to a spirited debate between the various protagonists, which can be followed on Chris Anderson's own blog, listed under Weblinks below.

Johnson, P. F., Klassena, R.D., Leendersa, M.R. and Awaysheha, A., (2007), 'Utilizing e-Business Technologies in Supply Chains: The Impact of Firm Characteristics and Teams', *Journal of Operations Management*, 25(6), November, pp. 1255–74.
Moving from the rational to the relational, this article presents a synthesis of related literatures—transaction cost economics and the relational view of the supply chain—which allows it to generate a two-dimensional framework for e-business technology with both transactional and relational dimensions. The study draws on both case study interviews and survey data.

# ➡ References

Anderson, C., (2004), 'The Long Tail', *Wired*, October.

Anderson, C., (2006), *The Long Tail: How Endless Choice is Creating Unlimited Demand*, Random House.

Anon, (2003), 'The New "New Economy"—American productivity—America's extraordinary gains in productivity.' *The Economist*,13 September.

Bailey, J.P. and Bakos, Y., (1997), 'An Exploratory Study of the Emerging Role of Electronic Intermediaries', *International Journal of Electronic Commerce*, 1(3), pp. 7–20.

Barnes, D. and Hinton, M., (2006), 'Searching for e-Business Performance Measurement Systems', *The Electronic Journal of Information Systems Evaluation*, 10(1), pp. 1–8.

Barton, H., (2006), *Skype Growth: Analysis and Forecast for 2007*, http://idisk.mac.com/hhbv-Public/Blogs/skypegrowth/skypegrowth.html.

Barton, H., (2008), 'Skype is Poised for Strong Fall Growth', *Borderless Blog*, http://idisk.mac.com/hhbv-Public/Blogs/25321657.html.

Basex, (2007), *Information Overload: We Have Met the Enemy and He Is Us*, http://www.basex.com.

Basu, S., et al., (2003), 'The Case of the Missing Productivity Growth: Or, Does Information Technology Explain why Productivity Accelerated in the US but not the UK?', *NBER Working Paper* no. w10010.

Becker, G.S. and Murphy, K.M., (2001), *Social Economics: Market Behavior in a Social Environment*, Harvard University Press.

BERR/DCMS, (2009), *Digital Britain: The Interim Report*, http://www.culture.gov.uk/images/publications/digital_britain_interimreportjan09.pdf.

Brynjolfsson, E., Hu, Y., and Smith, M.D., (2006), 'From Niches to Riches: Anatomy of the Long Tail', *MIT Sloan Management Review*, 47(4), Summer, pp. 67–71.

Brynjolfsson, E.H., Lorin M., and Shinkyu, Y., (2002), 'Intangible Assets: Computers and Organizational Capital', in *Brookings Papers on Economic Activity*, Brookings Institution Press, p. 137.

Cairncross, F., (2001), *The Death of Distance 2.0. How the Communications Revolution will Change our Lives*, Texere Publishing (2nd edn).

Carr, N. (2003), 'IT Doesn' Matter, *Harvard Business Review*, 5, pp. 41–9. See also Carr's blog, 'Rough Type', http://www.roughtype.com/.

Clayton, T., (2005), *IT Investment, ICT Use and UK Firm Productivity*, National Statistics, http://www.statistics.gov.uk/articles/economic_trends/ET625_Clayton.pdf.

Crafts, N., (2005), 'The "Death of Distance": What Does it Mean for Economic Development?', *World Economics*, 6(3), July–Sept, pp. 1–14.

Criscuolo, C. and Waldron, K., (2003), 'E-commerce and Productivity', *Economic Trends*, 600, pp. 52–7, http://www.statistics.gov.uk/downloads/theme_economy/ET_Nov03.pdf.

Dudnik Stern, J., (2008), 'Crowd Sourcing to Crowd Pleasing: New Agency Dynamics', *Selling Stock*, 17 June.

E-Business W@tch, (2008), 'ICT and e-Business Impact in the Chemical, Rubber and Plastics Industry', *Impact Study # 01/2008*, Empirica GmbH, http://www.ebusiness-watch.org/studies/sectors/chemicals_generic/documents/Study_01-2008_Chemical.pdf.

*Economist*, (2005), 'Bubble 2.0', *The Economist*, 22 September 22.

Farooqui, S., (2005), 'Information and Communication Technology Use and Productivity', *Economic Trends*, 625, December, pp. 65–73, http://www.statistics.gov.uk/articles/economic_trends/ET625_Farooqui.pdf.

French, Jr, J.R.P. and Raven, B. (1959), 'THE bases of Social Power', in D. Cartwright (ed.), *Studies in Social Power*, pp. 150–67, University of Michigan, Institute for Social Research.

Gatti, R., Chirmiciu, A., Kattuman, P., and Morgan, J., (2004), 'Price vs. Location: Determinants of Demand at an Online Price Comparison Site', *Trust and Triviality: Where is the Internet Going?* Conference at University College London, 12 November.

Goodridge, P. and Clayton, T., (2004), 'E-business and Labour Productivity in Manufacturing and Services', *Economic Trends*, 609, August, pp. 47–53, http://www.statistics.gov.uk/articles/economic_trends/ET609Good.pdf.

Guthrie, J., (2008), 'Ebay's Enduring Appeal', *Financial Times*, 12 February.

Inklaar, R., Timmer, M., and van Ark, B., (2007), '"Mind the gap!" International comparisons of productivity in services and goods production', *German Economic Review*, 8(2), pp. 281–307.

Johnson, J. et al., (2004), 'On the Depth and Dynamics of Online Search Behavior', *Management Science*, 50(3), pp. 299–308.

Kuttner, R., (1998), 'The Net: A Market too Perfect for Profits', *Business Week*, 11 May, http://www.businessweek.com/archives/1998/b3577045.arc.htm.

Lazear, E.P., (2000), 'Economic Imperialism', *Quarterly Journal of Economics*, 115(1), pp. 99–146.

Mitchell, A., (2006), 'Long Tails, Tall Stories', *Right Side Up*, 19 July, http://rightsideup.blogs.com/my_weblog/2006/07/long_tails_tall.html.

Odlyzko, A. and Tilly, B., (2005), 'A Refutation of Metcalfe's Law and a Better Estimate for the Value of Networks and Network Interconnections', *Working Paper,* University of Minnesota Digital Technology Center, http://www.dtc.umn.edu/ffodlyzko/doc/metcalfe.pdf.

Pilat, D., (2002), 'International Comparisons of Productivity—Key Findings and Measurement Issues', in *ONS/DTI Productivity Workshop*.

Rezabakhsh, B., Bornemann, D., Hansen, U., and Schrader, U., (2006), 'Consumer Power: A Comparison of the Old Economy and the Internet Economy', *Journal of Consumer Policy*, 23, pp. 3–36.

Rubin, J. and Tal, B., (2008), 'Will Soaring Transport Costs Reverse Globalization?', *StrategEcon*, 27 May, pp. 4–7, http://research.cibcwm.com/economic_public/download/smay08.pdf.

Skype, (2005), *eBay to Acquire Skype*, 12 September, http://www.skype.com/company/news/2005/skype_ebay.html.

Spector, R., (2000), *Amazon.com. Get Big Fast*, Random House, p. 33.

Su, Bo-chiuan, (2008), 'Characteristics of Consumer Search On-Line: How Much Do We Search?', *International Journal of Electronic Commerce*, 13(1), pp. 109–29.

Tauli, T., (2005), 'The New Skype-EBay Ecosystem', *Forbes*, 12 October, http://www.forbes.com/entrepreneurstechnology/2005/10/11/telecom-skype-ebay-cx_tt_1012straightup.html.

Triplett, J.E., (1999), 'Economic Statistics, the New Economy, and the Productivity Slowdown'. in *Business Economics* 1999, National Association of Business Economics, p. 13.

Van Vleck, T., (2001), *The History of Electronic Mail*, http://www.multicians.org/thvv/mail-history.html.

Varian, H. et al., (2002), *The Net Impact Study: The Projected Economic Benefits of the Internet in the United States, United Kingdom, France and Germany*, http://www.netimpactstudy.com/NetImpact_Study_Report.pdf.

Whitaker, J. and Sons, (2007), *British Books in Print*, 2007, http://library.dialog.com/bluesheets/pdf/bl0430.pdf.

Williams, C., (2007), 'VoIP Providers Reined in by Regulator', *The Register*, 29 March, http://www.theregister.co.uk/2007/03/29/ofcom_voip/.

Willis, J.L., (2004), 'What Impact will E-Commerce Have on the US Economy?', *Federal Reserve Bank of Kansas City Economic Review*, Q2, pp. 53–71.

## ⊘ Weblinks

**E-Business W@tch.** The European e-business Sectoral Market Watch supports the European Commission's Directorate General for Enterprise in studying the impact of ICT and e-business technologies on firms, industries, and economies. Its case studies and data are available free of charge: http://www.ebusiness-watch.org/.

**Focus on the Digital Age.** The UK Office of National Statistics has brought together a whole series of analyses on ICT use within the UK, ranging from e-business to e-education and the use of ICT at home: http://www.statistics.gov.uk/focuson/digitalage/.

**The Future of the Internet Economy.** The OECD's 2008 conference on the Future of the Internet Economy commissioned several useful analyses of the economic implications of e-business, which are available online: http://www.oecd.org/FutureInternet.

**The Long Tail.** Author of 'The Long Tail', Chris Anderson is also Editor-in-Chief of *Wired* magazine and hosts a blog where he discusses the implications of his ideas: http://longtail.typepad.com/.

# 3

# Technology in e-business

*by Wojciech Piotrowicz*

## Learning outcomes

Completing this chapter will enable you to:

- Understand the role of technology in e-business and trace its evolution
- Gain insight into data, application, and process integration, both internal and inter-organizational
- Become familiar with emerging trends in e-business technology, such as web-based services and service-oriented architecture (SOA)
- Recognize the importance of security and privacy in e-business, as well as its role in standardization
- Understand the ways in which ICT costs, benefits, and risks can be evaluated.

## Introduction

Developments in information and communications technology (ICT) have created opportunities to build new business models and to better integrate organizations with customers and suppliers. Technology serves both as a driver of change, as well as an enabler supporting new business concepts. For example, there is a strong correlation between an increase in the penetration of domestic broadband access to the Internet and levels of online consumption by consumers. Similarly, the development of search software has enabled the growth of a number of profitable business models, driven by advertising revenues. However, changes in technology are rapid, with new hardware and software solutions emerging almost on a weekly basis. New ideas are announced as leading edge and promising, but chapter 1 reminded us to be cautious about the 'hype cycle' of new technologies. While some of them might well soon become commonly used, others may be rejected by businesses and users, or may be evidently premature. The purpose of this chapter is not to describe in painstaking detail which technologies are currently used, list those which are at an emerging stage of development, nor to place bets on which e-business technologies will prove to be the critical ones to determine business success, but rather to think in a more measured way about how we might classify e-business technologies, how they have developed over time, and to provide an outline of some of the main issues affecting their application within organizations. In particular, this chapter therefore also provides an overview of e-business security and standardization issues, as well as those related to technology evaluation.

## E-business technologies

A first and very obvious way of classifying IT technology in e-business is to distinguish between hardware and software. The second way is to look at technology maturity. Several business technologies and standards can already be perceived as well established, such as EDI (introduced in chapter 1 and discussed in terms of process applications in chapter 9), bar codes, material requirements planning (MRP), or the HTTP protocol. However, not all such technologies are able to fulfil current or emerging requirements. Over a decade ago the major existing technologies, such as electronic data interchange (EDI) and MRP, were already being criticized for their shortcomings, which included:

- lack of alignment between operational and functional buying requirements;
- lack of support for document flows;
- processing which included only structured data, such as price and quantity;
- concentration on internal automation, rather than extension of market possibilities;
- no support of group work; and
- insufficient support of business-to-business (B2B) communication (Brenner and Hamm, 1996).

Since then, software providers and other organizations have been working to improve applications. As systems have developed, some of the weak points have been eliminated, others reduced. Some of the new kinds of web-based technologies that we will discuss later in this chapter were proposed, such as web services and service-oriented architecture (SOA). However, it is important to understand that technology is not static. Some of the apparently 'final' solutions can really only be considered to be at an early stage in their development and are likely to undergo further constant evolution. This presents problems for organizations seeking to invest in e-business technology. Some technology perceived as 'leading' can be turn out to be a dead end in terms of development, and so selecting the right tools and applications is critical for long-term profitable growth.

MRP Materials Requirements Planning—a software-based production planning and inventory control system.

HTTP HyperText Transfer Protocol—a standard governing the transfer of hypertext between servers and browsers.

SOA Service-Oriented Architecture. Concept of flexible IT architecture design.

# Hardware

Hardware is both the backbone and the engine of e-business. Hardware, except for computers and other equipment with user interfaces, is in many cases not visible to system users, but it nevertheless creates the physical layer for e-business. It is obvious that without physical infrastructure, software applications cannot run. Hardware includes various computers, from large mainframe solutions through to server farms, servers dedicated to certain tasks through to desktop and laptop computers, small mobile handhelds, PDAs, and even mobile phones. A variety of peripheral equipment for the back and front offices of organizations is also employed (such as printers, card readers, and bar code scanners). Computers and other equipment may be connected through complex networks, perhaps composed of fibre optic cabling, between and within locations, local area network cabling within buildings, as well as wireless connection, mainly for mobile equipment (connected by satellite, radio or wi-fi). There is also the obvious, but sometimes forgotten, fact that to run computers a supply of energy is also needed, and that therefore in cases of supply uncertainty alternative emergency energy sources will need to be provided (UPS, electricity generators). Whilst computer capability develops very fast—new models are introduced almost on a weekly basis—the development of network infrastructure is more stable. Rapid development of computer capabilities and their wide usage and connection through networks provides an opportunity to build world-wide business solutions. However, hardware is just the backbone of e-business. Various software applications are required to link companies together and to automate business processes. Hardware and software interlinked together in a structured way comprise IT architecture. Figure 3.1 shows a visualization of this architecture for a large financial services company.

### Short case 3.1

## The iPhone in e-business

Following Apple's introduction of the iPod in 2005, over 175 million iPods in various models have been sold. The iPhone was launched in 2007 and a 3G version was launched in 2008. More than 17m of all versions have so far been sold. While iPod models are dedicated to entertainment, the functionality of the iPhone and, to some extent, the iTouch, substantially overlap with those provided by PDAs, mobile phones, and portable computers. The iPhone allows Internet browsing, access to mapping and GPS, and permits the user to run an increasing variety of applications (which in early 2009 numbered in the order of 25,000). Software creation is supported by the iPhone Developer Program, which encourages the creation, testing and distribution of iPhone applications. The iPhone, now compatible with MS Exchange and other corporate email systems, allows the viewing of company emails, and the management of calendar events and contacts. Data transmission uses an encrypted SSL 128-bit connection. The iPhone can now be managed remotely, while access can be authenticated via password, two-factor token or digital certificate. Various enterprise applications have already been developed for the iPhone, including Oracle Business Indicators, which allows access business performance data for Oracle users. SAP has developed Sales Force Automation software, while Salesforce.com Mobile has proposed Customer Relationship Management (CRM) software.

> GPS Global Positioning System—satellite system to determine location of the GPS device.

*Question*

What other opportunities can you think of for using the iPhone for e-business (both B2B and B2C)?

# E-business software applications

While we can all witness the development of much user-oriented hardware, the evolution of software is less visible, with only usually changes in the user interface being noted. But, just as with hardware, software can develop rapidly. Often, alongside established technologies such as EDI, new mainly web-based concepts are being created.

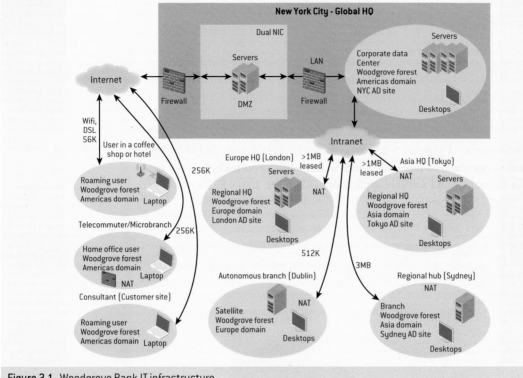

**Figure 3.1** Woodgrove Bank IT infrastructure

Vickery et al. (2003) categorized integrative information technologies into three groups:

- computerized productions systems (such as MRP, MRPII, and ERP (enterprise resource planning)) which integrate manufacturing activities, especially joint production planning, tracking, scheduling, and ordering from suppliers;

- integrated information systems, which create the possibility of transmitting and sharing information within the organization, both horizontally and vertically; and finally

- integrated electronic data interchange (such as EDI) which allows the sending and automation of electronic documents flow within and between organizations, as well as to and from customers and suppliers, providing vertical integration.

Software applications began to evolve in the 1960s and 1970s as companies started to integrate their internal operations with the main purpose of serving their customers. This marked the introduction of the earliest types of material requirements planning (MRP I) systems. In the 1970s and 1980s, increasing competition between Japan and the USA resulted in the development of just in time (JIT) implementations, and marked the main period of growth in electronic document interchange (EDI) applications (Chou et al., 2004), with the main goal of coordinating repeatable tasks between two partners (Sherer,

**ERP** Enterprise Resource-based Planning. Software packages providing a suite of systems to manage and co-ordinate operational processes across a wide range of internal business activities.

**JIT** Just in Time—a concept developed in manufacturing which aims at reducing inventory levels.

2005). From the 1990s the growth in Internet usage and in the technologies based on it, gave organizations the chance to further reduce the costs of communication. It was at this stage that concepts such as e-business and e-commerce were introduced.

It was widely assumed that web-based technologies would improve such areas as supply chain effectiveness (Chou et al., 2004). Companies started to redesign their internal processes, to improve effectiveness, and overcome functional barriers (Kirchmer, 2004). Applications to coordinate cooperation between partners were created, and planning capabilities were added. However, in most cases, cooperation only extended as far as linear relationships between two partners (Sherer, 2005). Developments from 2000 onwards were characterized by a growing integration between organizations and linkages by means of inter-organizational processes, which in turn were supported by Internet-based information technology and software applications (Kirchmer, 2004). ERP systems were initially developed to improve inter-organizational performance and cooperation between different functions and divisions within company, but later on the core ERP functions were extended by front-office applications, such as customer relationship management modules (CRM), while the back office was supported by supply chain management (SCM) solutions implemented as ERP modules or separately. As a result, consolidated so-called enterprise systems were created (Turner and Chung, 2005); examples of such integrated solutions are the kind of applications offered by SAP, Oracle, or PeopleSoft. The extension of ERP creates opportunities to increase cooperation with suppliers (SCM systems) and customers (CRM). However this traditional ERP-based approach is currently being challenged by the new concept of web services. Distinct from earlier solutions built around ERP, the new systems will likely be based on Internet-oriented web-based enterprise systems, which will link not only internal but also inter-organizational processes and will be accessed through the Internet. The introduction of web services is perceived as a solution to major problems related to ERP, such as their high cost and the long timescale required for their implementation in certain organizations, as well as their lack of flexibility. (It is often hard to change the system once it is implemented.) Their interconnectivity with other systems can also be problematic. Interconnectivity problems are especially important for 'legacy' software—applications developed several years ago using an older and in some cases discontinued technology. Recent web-based concepts, such as web services and SOA, which are presented in the next section, are both aiming at creating a flexible, modular IT architecture which can be modified to reflect changes in organizational and inter-organizational process design. Chapter 9 looks in more detail at the kinds of improvement in business processes which such mechanisms can permit.

According to Gammelgård (Gammelgård et al., 2007), e-business systems must meet certain general quality attributes:

- availability: the time during which the system is accessible and available to use;
- reliability: the extent to which the system can perform required functions, under defined conditions and during specific periods;
- data quality: the extent to which data is accurate, complete, available, etc.;
- functional fit: the minimization of the gap between IT system function and business requirements;
- information security: the extent to which information is protected;
- interoperability: the ability to integrate systems and components;

CRM Customer Relationship Management.

- modifiability: the ability to incorporate changes into the system;
- performance;
- safety: ensuring that the system does not cause death, injury, or have a negative impact on the environment;
- usability and user productivity: ensuring a positive impact on user performance as well as upon levels of user satisfaction.

# B2B integration

The nature of the integration possible between two independent business partners—in this instance using an example of integration between two supply chain partners—can be divided into three levels (Kotzab et al., 2003):

1. Technical integration, which is on a data integration level and concentrates on the data exchange between companies.
2. Application integration: the physical integration of software and hardware.
3. Business integration: the extent of cooperation between organizations. Sharing plans, schedules and inventory information, or perhaps undertaking joint work on product development and customer service. To achieve business integration, companies need to be integrated on both technical and application levels.

The process of integration adopted by organizations, beyond just simple information exchange, was initially summarized by Gosain et al. (2005). At first, they suggested, companies would standardize their processes and content interfaces, which would result in an agreement as to which technical specification would be used (for example, the desired information exchange format, data repository, or interface). The next step involved companies defining modular interconnected processes: that is, processes are divided into separate modules, sub-processes, or tasks, allowing each module to be executed by different organizations independently, avoiding overlapping phases and perhaps performing tasks simultaneously. A final important element is the requirement for structured data connectivity, which requires data standardization to allow the sharing of data in electronic format.

Recent integration concepts are based on connections through the Internet. Web-based integration is often referred to as collaborative-commerce (c-commerce). Chen et al. defined c-commerce as:

> 'The set of technologies and business practices that allows companies to build stronger relationships with their trading partners through integrating complex and cross-enterprise processes governed by business logic and rules, as well as workflows.' *Chen et al., 2007*

This definition goes well beyond the initial idea of EDI, which focused on data and information exchange, while cross-organizational process integration was hard to achieve. It also extends ERP-based integration into web-based integration, which is perceived as an approach to establishing collaboration across the whole supply/value chain, an idea which we pick up in more detail in chapter 9.

The most promising solution which can be used for supply/value chain collaboration and integration is web services. They can support integration (1) between companies, via a standard interface to customers and business partners, (2) within the company—reducing time and the cost required to integrate internal systems, and finally, (3) between the company and end users (internal and external) by delivering a better user experience (Huang and Chung, 2003). Figure 3.2 shows how web services integration can work in practice.

## Data standardization and integration

Data standardization is necessary for data exchange between companies and applications. Without common data standards, or the possibility of 'translating' data into a format recognized by another application, it is impossible to use electronic communication. Instead of automated data exchange between applications, time-consuming manual data entry is required. This used to get ludicrously repetitive: in some circumstances, there might be situations in which data was printed out from one computer system only to be entered into another system because of the lack of data integration. Data standardization was one of the first initiatives developed by organizations seeking to exchange information electronically. EDI-based standards were among the earliest such standards. In addition bespoke EDI-based standards were developed and used by certain companies and industries. Due to the high cost of EDI implementation and the specific document format required, these are mainly used by large organizations, and are almost absent from small and medium-sized firms. Another shortcoming of EDI is related to its

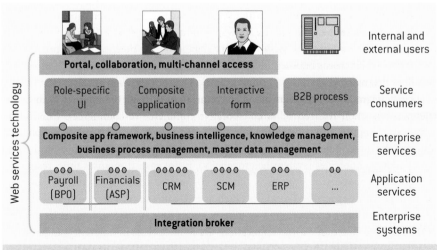

**Figure 3.2** Web Services integration

inability to support real-time information exchange and application integration (Gosain et al, 2005). As an alternative to EDI, XML (extensible markup language) was created by the World Wide Web Consortium in 1996. XML is the data interchange standard which allows the integration of inter-enterprise applications. XML was incorporated into various e-business frameworks dedicated to specific industries (vertical standards) or cross-industrial consortia. XML is also widely used in web services. Among various initiatives are the HR-XML Consortium (which works on development in the human resources area) and other more industry-specific groups, including the Alliance for Telecommunications Industry Solutions (ATIS), the Mortgage Industry Standards Maintenance Organization (MISMO), the Open Financial Exchange (OFX) Consortium, the OpenTravel Alliance (OTA) and the International Financial eXchange Forum (IFX Forum).

XML eXtensible Markup Language, data interchange standard.

## System/application integration

Integration goes beyond data, information, and message exchange. Companies increasingly integrate their applications, through a further step of process integration. Initially integration is mainly internal, between functions, divisions, and business units within countries, or between various locations of the company. The next step is integration with business partners, customers, and suppliers; while at the final stage the whole supply/value chain can be interconnected.

## Internal integration

Organizational e-business applications (such as ERP, CRM, and SCM) are interconnected in ways that seek to incorporate principles of flexibility, integration, and modularity. *Flexibilty* may mean the ability to use software modules delivered by different companies, or the ability to modify the system to reflect changes in the business environment. The *integration* in this case is between different applications, front- and back-office processes, as well as that achieved by process standardization. Finally *modularity* allows the linking of all the separate components (both software and hardware components) into one enterprise system (Turner and Chung, 2005).

However, in practice the creation of an integrated ERP-based system is a complicated process. The integration of different modules, from various software vendors and based on different technologies (system heterogeneity), is not easy. It requires time, resources, and project management skills (see chapter 10) and as result is often very costly. A plethora of highly specialized modules (such as HR, call-centre, warehousing) dedicated to certain functions and developed by different companies create additional integration problems. Data stored in various applications are in most cases in different standards and formats, which creates problem of data integration. Data transformation is required to allow communication between applications.

To facilitate and simplify system integration between various systems and modules within an organization, a dedicated solution such as enterprise application integration (EAI) has been used. This acts as a link between two or more different systems. The need to use a variety of applications has resulted in the creation of the application portfolio (AP) concept, which incorporates all applications used within a single organization that should be managed as an integrated system (Riempp and Gieffers-Ankel, 2007). Recently new functions that allow web integration through web services have been added into ERP and other packages. Figure 3.3 provides an illustration of how complex and multi-layered such interdependencies can become, even within organizations.

Beyond application integration, the organization's internal process integration is supported by workflow and document management systems. Workflow management systems (WfMS) are concentrated on managing process logic: process flow is captured

**AP** Application Portfolio-the integrated management of all company IT applications.

**EAI** Enterprise Application Integration. Systems used to integrate' various IT applications.

**WfMS** Workflow Management Systems used to visualize and model processes

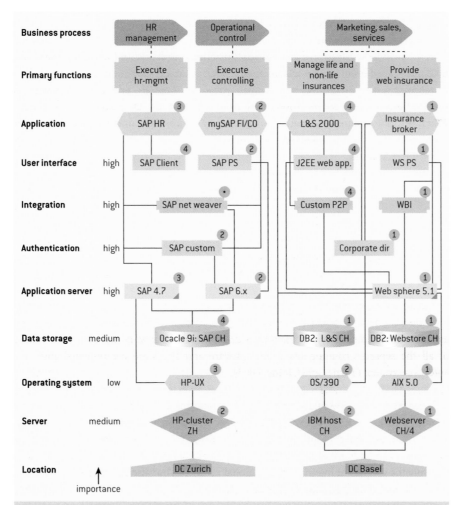

**Figure 3.3** Interdependencies between IT within organizational information systems

and visualized. WfMS allows presenting in graphical form, as well as the modelling and simulation of organizational processes. Function logic, systems and application, data and people are incorporated into it. Process flows can be created within the company from nothing, or can be built from predefined templates. Workflows can include employees, or can be fully automated. Even though there are WfMS applications which can be implemented separately from ERP, WfMS elements are incorporated into ERP CRM or SCM solutions and this process continues (Carsodo, 2004). Weske et al. defined all business process management (BPM) systems, including WfMS, EAI, ERP, and CRM as:

> 'A generic software system that is driven by explicit process design to enact and manage operational business.' *Weske et al., 2004*

Associated with business activity monitoring (BAM) is business process modelling (BPM). BPM aims to create flexible tools which allow the changing of organizational processes in real-time by modifying the application without any break. BAM can be used to monitor organizational process performance in real-time. There is also work in progress aimed at creating autonomic WfMS which will be able automatically to adapt to changing external and internal environments based on built-in logic. Such intelligent workflows might be able to include self-learning and self-optimization mechanisms (Strohmaier and Yu, 2006). So-called event-driven architecture is also built upon the similar idea of being able to respond fast to environmental changes. However, there are problems in integrating process flows between different organizations, as they often use different workflow systems which are not compatible (owing to different software, data, and process description standards). Web services and SOA, described below, are perceived as solutions which will allow the redesigning of processes, between as well as within organizations, in as flexible a manner as required, to respond to business changes and without waiting months—as is currently necessary in traditional workflow systems.

## Business and process integration

'no process integration, no collaboration.' *Chen et al., 2007*

Web services are defined by the World Wide Web Consortium (W3C) as 'a software system designed to support machine-to-machine interaction'. Web services are perceived as a major approach to integrating applications and processes. They are composed of independent modules which can be used to build IT applications. Such independent blocks can be used as required. Web services include standards that support the integration of business processes. Examples include: BPEL4WS (Business Process Execution Language for Web Services), BPML (Business Process Modelling Language), RosettaNet, ebXML, and UBL. These new e-business standards are different from EDI. They look beyond data exchange, and allow not only the support of internal organizational processes, but also the integration of inter-organizational processes between partners (Xia et al., 2003). When widely adopted, they facilitate integration of the supply/value chain, beyond simple two-partner organizations. Additionally, they serve to remedy the lack of flexibility and agility, as well as the inability to

---

**BPM [1]** Business Process Management systems

**BAM** Business Activity Monitoring.

**BPM [2]** Business Process Modelling

**W3C** World Wide Web Consortium.

**BPEL4WS** Business Process Execution Language for Web Services.

**BPML Business Process Modelling Language—a meta-language for modelling business processes.**

**ebXML** E-business XML, undertaking electronic business using eXtensible Markup Language. XML-based infrastructure.

**UBL** Universal Business Language—a library of XML documents.

cope with real-time data associated with traditional IT systems. Short case 3.2 illustrates the way in which chip-maker Intel has developed internal and external integration.

New e-business frameworks support interoperability between partners offering standard interfaces and scalability benefits (Nurmilaakso et al., 2006). Such standards are also referred to as XML-based B2B standards, B2B interaction standards or open e-business standards. Interoperability is possible to achieve by defining common ontology, syntax, message exchange, and cross-organizational infractions (Sayal, 2001). Web services are playing an increasingly important role in BPM development. BPM takes into account all processes across all companies up to the final customer (Zhang, 2005).

## Short case 3.2

### Intel, the integrated e-corporation

Intel Corporation is one of the leaders in hi-tech manufacturing and in semiconductor chip making. Its two largest customers are Dell and HP, which account for 19 per cent and 16 per cent of revenue respectively. Intel's mission is:

> 'To do a great job for our customers, employees, and stockholders by being the preeminent building block supplier to the worldwide digital economy' as well as 'to be a worldwide, 100 percent e-Corporation that maximizes profitability, responsiveness and innovation.'

Over 60 per cent of materials transactions and 85 per cent of customer orders are processed electronically. The earliest versions of e-procurement applications date back to 1998, when the first web-based system to procure travel was implemented. In 2002, the company's 'e-procurement' initiative was started. It aimed at improvements in » the procurement of indirect materials, which then comprised 60 per cent of Intel's total procurement value. After implementation of the e-procurement system in 2004, Intel increased spending visibility and reduced the number of requisition-to-pay processes from over sixty-five in 2002 to fewer than ten in 2004, and fewer than five in 2005. In 2004, strategic sourcing, ERP integration, and spend analysis implementation was completed, but implementation of the central ERP system continued. By 2005, 14,000 suppliers were linked with Intel via various IT systems, including the RosettaNet standard. In 2005 the Order Management module of the ERP system was migrated into a new ERP platform, and a new supplier relationship management (SRM) system was developed, jointly with SAP. By 2006, 100 per cent of indirect materials purchasing was moved to the e-procurement system and 98 per cent of the procurement volume was captured by the reporting system.

SRM Supplier Relationship Management.

*Question*

To what extent can the model of a 100 per cent e-corporation be realistically applied in different companies and sectors?

## Activity box 3.3

### Achieving process and application integration

There are certainly benefits to be derived from process and application integration with business partners. But what are the potential dangers for the organizations concerned?

## Service-oriented architecture

According to the definition provided by Sun, service-oriented architecture (SOA) is:

'an architectural style that emphasizes well-defined, loosely coupled, coarse-grained, business-centric, reusable shared services.' *Sun, 2004*

SOA is a concept in software architecture. The term service-oriented computing (SOC) is also common. SOA uses open standards, among them web services and XML. While the SOA concept is not new, web services provide an opportunity to bring the concept to greater maturity. The core idea of SOA is the development of a set of services which communicate with each other. Service is requested by a service consumer (requester) from a service provider. A SOA is built from components (modules) that can be used and reused as required, allowing fast response to changes in environment. Using SOA it is possible to design, model, assemble, integrate, deploy, and manage services that are application and platform neutral. SOA allows reusing existing application and modifying them in a flexible way. Services are associated with roles and a service can be an element of the process such as: customer search, inquiry handling, customer credit verification, and the product availability check. Services are accessed via the Internet using standard protocols. We can summarize SOA fundamentals as follows:

- Loosely coupled interactions: services are invoked independently of their technology and location.

- One-to-one communication: one specific service is invoked by one consumer at a time. Communication is bi-directional.

- Consumer-based trigger: the flow is initiated by the client (service consumer).

- Synchronous: Replies are sent back to the consumer in a synchronous way (Sun, 2004)

The creation of the kind of SOA shown in Figure 3.4 may require the incorporation of other extended capabilities such as application-to-application (A2A) and B2B integration, workflow, and BPM, BAM, complex event processing, single customer view, and various other functionalities.

One idea which serves to extend the concept of SOA is that of cloud computing. Cloud computing assumes that not only will software be available as a service (SaaS: software as a service), but the whole infrastructure as well. So-called 'hardware as a service' (HaaS) is accessible via the Internet—and includes such elements as electronic storage space and data centres. Users pay the computing provider for access to and use of the software and infrastructure, instead of paying up front for their own internal IT system. Companies such as Microsoft, Google, Amazon, and Salesforce are actively promoting this concept.

SaaS  Software as a Service.

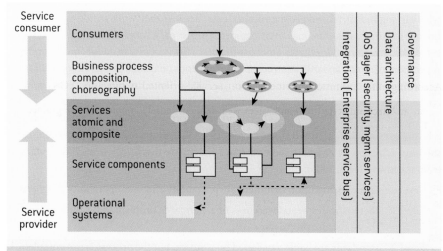

**Figure 3.4**  Service Oriented Architecture

# Technology standards

Technology standards in e-business allow cooperation between organizations. Standards also create opportunities to use solutions developed by different software companies, and may allow easier integration of applications and modules. Further, standardization can have an impact on knowledge and staff training requirements as it is easier to develop expertise in one particular and well-defined area.

Standards can be both *regulative* and *coordinative*. Regulative standards serve to reduce negative impacts (such as any effects on the environment) and will mostly be mandatory within any jurisdiction area. Coordinative standards, on the other hand, are created to promote interpretability, compatibility, reduce transaction costs, and create positive impacts. In e-business, coordinative standards dominate (Werle and Iverson, 2006). However, there are also legal requirements such as the EU WEEE directive which requires the recycling of old IT equipment. There are several different classifications of technology standards, and standards-like initiatives. This is inevitable in a fast-moving technological environment, but can create significant challenges for organizations.

Standards can be internally derived and used within an organization and externally, or can be created by standards development bodies (Sherif, 2005). In addition to formal standards development bodies (such as the National Institute of Standards and Technology, http://www.nist.gov), there are also less formal standardization organizations or consortia, or standards which are created by solution providers (vendors). Examples of such informal bodies include OASIS (Organization for the Advancement of Structured Information Systems, http://www.oasis-open.org), the W3C (World Wide Web Consortium, http://www.w3.org), and RosettaNet (http://www.rosettanet.org). (RosettaNet forms the basis of the discussion in Short case 3.3.) Formal standards are developed by national bodies (such as the British Standards Institute), at the European level (such as by the European Committee for Standardization: CEN, http://www.cen.eu) and finally at the international level (one example would be the International Standards Organization (ISO, http://www.iso.org) (Blind and Gauch, 2008).

Informal standards bodies often involve consortia, committees, fora, and working groups with varying industrial and geographical extents. Because they work as non-governmental bodies, in some cases they may even compete against each other. Companies involved in standards creation are inevitably amongst the first organizations to adopt those standards. A decision to join a standardization consortium depends on company size, IT sophistication, and size of the business partners (Zhia et al., 2003). There are dedicated intra-industry consortia, in a range of different sectors (including chemicals, banking, and insurance.)

As standards are often at various development stages, particularly in a rapidly evolving e-business context, a standards maturity model (SMM) allows organizations to determine the level achieved by any particular standard. There are five levels in the SMM, starting from the lowest (Sun, 2006):

Level 0    lack of recognition that there are portability and interoperability problems.

Level 1    there is widespread awareness of a standards problem, but solutions, even if they exist, are proprietary.

Level 2    standards are being developed by vendors, but the process is not complete. It may be submitted in draft form for consideration by a formal standards body.

---

**WEEE** Waste Electrical and Electronic Equipment directive—legislation which requires the reuse and recycling of certain types of electrical waste.

**OASIS** Organization for the Advancement of Structured Information Systems.

**ISO** International Standards Organization.

**SMM** Standards Maturity Model.

Level 3    standards are modified, revised but technically complete.

Level 4    most of the new tools and applications within the market use the standards.

Level 5    standards are at full maturity level: most applications and platforms support them.

Currently most web services standards are at level 3 (standards that are technically complete) and 4 (most applications support the standards). However there are already some standards completed at level 5 (where standard maturity has been achieved). Examples are the SOA-related informal standards developed by OASIS, such as ebXML which is formally recognized by ISO (Sun 2006).

**TCP/IP** Transmission Control Protocol (TCP) and the Internet Protocol (IP).

---

### Table 3.1    Examples of standards in the SMM model

Level 5 – TCP/IP, HTTP, SSL

Level 4 – XML, SOAP, WSDL, UDDI

Level 3 – BPEL, WS-security, WSRP

Level 2 – WS-reliability, Reliable Messaging, Reliable Exchange

Level 1 – Data semantic standards

Level 0 – Transactional semantic standards

**SSL** Secure Sockets Layer—a secure communications protocol.

**WSDL** Web Services Description Language.

**UDDI** Universal Description, Discovery and Integration.

**BPEL  Business Process Execution Language.**

**WSRP** Web Services for Remote Portlets.

---

## Short case 3.3

### RosettaNet

RosettaNet was created in 1998 as a voluntary industry organization to develop and deploy Internet-based business standards, and common language and open e-business processes to support the evolution of global trading networks (http://www.rosettanet. com). Initially created by forty companies, RosettaNet presently has over 500 members. Some companies act as *developers*, providing the resources necessary to continue work on the standards, while other companies are only standards *users*. Most developers are also users. Companies that participate actively in development are able to influence standards and their characteristics.

ROSETTANET
POWERED BY GS1 US

RosettaNet provides vertical (industrial) standards. Consortium participants are mainly from the semiconductor, electronic components, high-tech, and IT industries. »

The creation of the consortium was an answer to the growing recognition within the industry that the standards available were not able to fulfil business requirements. Nowadays, the standards cover not only internal aspects of business activity, but also inter-organizational cooperation and shared business processes between two RosettaNet adopters. There is also the possibility of linking RosettaNet with other selected XML-based standards. However RosettaNet documentation and processes are developed as specific to the industry

RosettaNet standards are composed of three levels: partner interface processes (PIPs), data dictionaries, and implementation frameworks (RNIF). PIPs describe activities, decisions, structures, and formats of business documents for the high-tech industry. There are seven PIPs modules: partner profile management, product information, order management, inventory management, marketing and support, service and support, and manufacturing.

*Question*
What are the advantages and disadvantages of industry-specific standardization?

PIP  Partner Interface Processes.

RNIF  RosettaNet Implementation Framework.

# E-business security

One of the major issues to have emerged in association with web services is that of security. As services are accessed via the Internet, secure access to web services and secure data transmission are critical. This section is designed to raise your awareness of some of the ways in which security in e-business and web services can be assured.

The six major issues affecting e-business security are:

- confidentiality/disclosure: ensuring that data cannot be accessed inappropriately by a third party when in transit;
- data integrity: ensuring that data cannot be modified between sender and receiver;
- authentication (identification): confirming that the identity of those sending documents or performing operations is known and that only authorized users can access the system;
- non-repudiability: making sure that the sender cannot deny that a document has been received;
- privacy: preventing either sender or receiver from being identified by an unauthorized person; and
- anonymity: respecting user anonymity—especially important in respect of micro-payments.

Several techniques exist to fulfil such requirements. The secure socket layer (SSL) protocol is a commonly accepted standard and is used to protect data sent via the Internet. Data are encrypted using public key cryptography. The protocol also provides authentication and data integrity protection. The HTTP protocol protected using SSL is referred as HTTPS.

Public key infrastructure (PKI) provides management of authentication services and the distribution of certificates. PKI supports data encryption, integrity, and non-repudiability. PKI is based on asymmetric key cryptography in which two keys are used for data encryption and decryption—public and private key. Public key is provided by a central authority.

Smart cards can be used for user authentication, for example employed in banking applications. Smart cards can be based on symmetrical (DES) and asymmetrical (RSA) cryptography. Most of the smart cards, in a similar way to credit cards, use chips for authentication purposes (earlier cards used a magnetic stripe only). Some banks have gone further: Barclays Bank has introduced PINsentry, which, together with the credit card or the authentication card, allows customers to identify themselves as the account holder and to access the account to perform banking transactions (http://www.barclays. co.uk/pinsentry/).

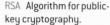

PKI  Public Key Infrastructure.

DES  Data Encryption Standard.

RSA  Algorithm for public-key cryptography.

For authentication purpose biometric methods can also be used—for example, fingerprint, eye, hand geometry, or voice identification—there is ongoing work on authentication using DNA. The simplest methods of authentication are passwords, but they do not guarantee high levels of security.

However, in relation to security it is not enough to rely on technology alone. Companies need to develop, implement, and review internal security policies. Additionally, physical security and access restriction plays an important role.

For SOA several security layers can be defined (IBM, 2006). Such service layers include: authentication, identity federation, session management, authorization, auditing, security tokens, and policy.

One of the most serious issues for every e-business is of course the threat of viruses and other forms of malware. These can adversely affect company operations, resulting in systems failure, fraudulent data capture ranging from password to data theft, or even hijacking of the computer itself. Security issues are also of concern to both suppliers and customers, and have significant ethical and regulatory dimensions. These are addressed in chapter 5. Security, due to its importance, is one of the issues which is standardized in the first instance, both by consortia and public bodies.

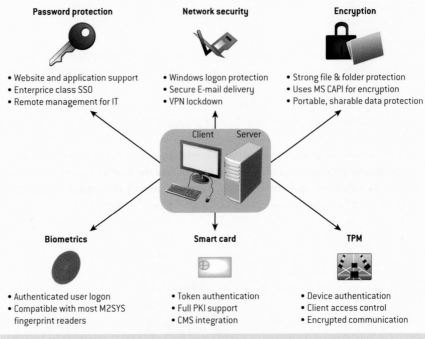

**Figure 3.5** Authentication framework for Windows-based personal computers.

## Activity box 3.4

A selective history of recent data theft and loss

- January 2008: computer gadgets company Geeks.com was hacked; customer data including credit card details were stolen.

- March 2008: up to 4.2 millions credit card details were stolen from Hannaford Bros supermarkets (New England) from access to the authorization system.

- April 2008: tapes which included personal data of 34,000 members of Boots Dental Plan were stolen from a car.

- November 2008: in a pub car park, a memory stick with passwords to tax and child benefit systems of 12m people was found. It had been lost by an employee of the subcontracting company which worked for the British government.

- January 2009: personal data of up to 4.5m people were stolen by hackers from the job website http://www.monster.co.uk.

Can you categorize the kinds of security risks an organization might face? How might it work to mitigate such risks?

# Online payment technology

Payment is one of the most sensitive security-related technologies, especially in business-to-consumer (B2C) interactions where trust in security and privacy levels plays a key role in consumer confidence in online transactions. Online payment is of course not limited just to B2C transitions, as users (buyers and sellers) can be both individuals and organizations. Indeed, several parties are involved in Internet payment: the seller (sometimes also called the merchant), the buyer, often a third party (the issuer), who provided payment services, as well as banks. Issuers, can be banks or other financial institutions, and provide a technical means to complete the transaction, involving such processes as validation and authorization. However, not all the organizations which provide a means for online payments are banks: we discuss the example of PayPal in Long case 3.2 (http://www.paypal.com). The transactions and e-payment framework designed by any organization must also reflect legal requirements.

Apart from the technology-related security issues discussed in the previous section, there are also social considerations which influence online payments, such as anonymity, privacy, and acceptance by sellers. Chapters 4 and 5 explore these issues in more detail. From a technical point of view, there is a need to differentiate between online payments with small-value amounts (so-called micro-payments) and those larger than 10–15 USD/Euro), so-called macro-payments. As the values transferred are lower, different levels of security and privacy are used. Micro-payments can often be completed using mobile technologies. Payments via mobile phone by means of such intermediaries as PayPal, or via the existing credit card/debit card system, can be added to the monthly phone bill. For example, mobile phone top-up payments can be made using pre-authorized credit card details held in an encrypted form by firms themselves or by third-party payment services, such as PayPal or WorldPay (http://www.worldpay.com). For example, payment for parking fees via mobile phone was introduced in many cities and towns. One system, used in over seventy locations in the UK, USA, Australia, and Canada is offered by Verrus (http://www.verrus.com). Among the cities which adopted the system are: San Francisco, Miami, Vancouver, Sydney, and Manchester. After setting up the account, online or by phone, the system allows users to pay their parking fee by sending a text message that includes the parking zone number and time of stay. Payment can be also used for taxi and tickets.

As we mentioned in the previous section, smart cards can be also used for electronic payment. Such a solution was employed in London, where the Oyster contactless smart card can be used to pay for transportation. The maximum amount stored on the card is £90 and the card can be topped up online. Several standards exist that regulate online payments: examples include XMLPay, W3C Ecommerce/Micro payment, and E-wallet by CEN/ISSS.

**CEN/ISSS** European Committee for Standardization (Comité Européen de Normalisation in French).

## Activity box 3.5

### Assessing the security of micropayments

Do you use micro-payments via mobile technology? Think about bus, cinema tickets, fees for music download, or parking charges? What are the advantages and disadvantages of such solutions?

## IT/IS Evaluation and e-business

When certain technology is selected to support organizational and inter-organizational processes there is a question of how to evaluate its impact on the organization and its performance. IT/IS evaluation is an area that uses different methods and tools to assess costs, risks, and benefits associated with a selected technology. Such an evaluation is also called a *justification*, or in case of post-implementation evaluation, an *assessment* or *appraisal*. There various terms are still in widespread use. From some points of view, an evaluation can be understood as a process to determine whether to continue or abandon an e-business project. (See chapter 10 for a discussion of the elements of e-business project management.) Another aspect of the evaluation process can be a post-implementation analysis of the benefits achieved (Farbey et al., 1999). A emerging issue in IT evaluation is analysis of a technology's impact on the natural environment and society, both directly, as well as through the support of different business models (Piotrowicz and Cuthbertson, 2009). Some of these ideas are further developed in chapter 12.

Smithson and Hirschheim (1998) defined information systems evaluation as: 'the assessment or appraisal of the value, worth and usefulness of an information system'. The role of IS evaluation is growing. The reasons are linked to the changing role of information systems. With the growth in e-business, investment in information technology is now a large part of an organization's costs, so there is a concern about obtaining and demonstrating value for money. Managers want to know what value is delivered after spending an increasing amount of money on IT, especially when returns are not clearly visible (Farbey et al., 1999) and the promised benefits are not achieved (Irani and Love, 2001).

The most common periods for evaluation are:

- before system implementation;
- when a system is selected and its expected impact can be assessed; and
- after system implementation, to evaluate the benefits achieved.

Evaluation can also be performed during the whole system lifecycle. According to Irani (2002) there are several problems with IS evaluation, which go beyond technological factors. There are difficulties in:

1. Understanding the human and organizational mechanism of investment decision making.
2. Understanding what the 'value' is and how it is defined.
3. Enabling system integration and 'technology fit'.
4. Including political issues related to capital budgeting and the decision-making process.
5. Including all the costs of an investment.
6. Appreciating a portfolio of evaluation methods and tools.
7. Taking into consideration risks related to different investment strategies.
8. Understanding the scope and impact of developing an IT infrastructure.
9. Appreciating a complexity of evaluating incremental system development, integration and upgrades.
10. Defining stakeholders and their involvement.

**Table 3.2  Common methods of IS evaluation**

| Financial methods | Non-financial methods |
|---|---|
| Return On Investment | Process measurement |
| Economic Value Added | Process estimation |
| Cost-benefit analysis | Workflow analysis |
| Benchmarking (financial aspects only) | Pilot implementation results |
| | Benchmarking |
| | Informal evaluation: |
| |    Opinions of managers |
| |    Opinions of users |
| |    Common sense |
| |    Informal benchmarking |

The problems measuring benefits include the common conclusion that IS evaluation is ineffective or inefficient and also that it is perceived as long and costly with little return (Irani and Love, 2001). Financial methods (return on investment (ROI), net present value (NPV), cost benefits analysis) still have a dominant position as IS evaluation tools. However, there are a variety of different evaluation methods, which often go beyond traditional financial measurement (see Table 3.2).

When new systems are considered for implementation, evaluation includes analysis of costs, benefits and risks.

ROI  Return on Investment.

NPV  Net Present Value.

## Costs

According to Love et al. (2006) the main cost categories are:

- direct and indirect costs;
- financial and non-financial costs; and
- initial investments and ongoing costs.

Direct costs include categories such as: hardware, hardware accessories, software, system development, training, maintenance, network security, consultancy support, increase in processing power installation engineers, networking hardware and software, and overheads (Love et al., 2004b; 2005). Direct costs can also be separated into cost groups such as:

- environmental operating costs;
- initial hardware and software costs;
- installation and configuration;
- system development;
- project management;
- project overheads;

- training;
- maintenance;
- unexpected hardware and software costs;
- security; and
- consumables.

Indirect implementation costs can often be higher than direct ones (Irani et al., 1997). Moreover, they are much harder to identify and companies often fail to identify and calculate them all (Gunasekaran et al., 2006). For example, in the case of an analysis of e-procurement by BAE Systems, the company found that there were many hidden costs, such as initial software and hardware investment, ongoing reconfigurations and upgrades necessary to invest in an enterprise solution. Another option might have been to use SaaS and to employ web-based access, as described in the Exostar case study in Long Case 3.1.

## Benefits

The evaluation of benefits can be separated into *strategic*, *tactical*, and *operational*. In each category benefits can be financial and non-financial as well as partially or totally intangible. In a situation where benefits are achieved at the operational level these are more often tangible and financial, whilst at the strategic level non-financial and intangible benefits dominate (Irani and Love, 2001). (Farbey et al., 1995) presented a *benefit evaluation ladder* that is composed of stages such as: mandatory changes, automation, direct value added systems, management information systems (MIS) and data and information systems (DIS), infrastructure, inter-organizational systems, strategic systems, and business transformation. Companies, however, have not always been climbing the ladder step by step. Whilst on the first steps of the ladder the benefits and costs are relatively straightforward to quantify; later this becomes much harder, as the complexity of the systems grows and their strategic importance increases. E-business benefits can also be classified according to the dimensions drawn from a balanced scorecard. An example of e-procurement benefits identified in four IT companies is shown in Table 3.3.

## Risks

Risk can be related to different investment strategies that might influence organizational competitive advantage, such as a decision not to invest in information technology. Another group of concerns related to risks is security (Irani, 2002), something we discussed earlier in this chapter. Risk appraisal concentrates on identifying the main risks associated with the project, as well as their possible impact (Serafeimidis and Smithson, 1999). These are twofold:

- Benefits delivery risks: factors that may influence the realization of business benefits.
- Technological delivery risks: factors that may influence system delivery according to issues of time, quality, and budget. This kind of delivery risk can be reduced by effective use of the kind of project management tools and techniques that are presented in the chapter 10.

**Table 3.3   A Balanced Scorecard Perspective on Evaluating e-Procurement Benefits**

| Level | Balance Scorecard perspectives | | | |
| --- | --- | --- | --- | --- |
| | Customer | Business process | Learning and growth | Financial |
| Strategic | Increased customer service (INT) | Eliminate/reduce problems with suppliers (INT) Eliminate 'unwanted' suppliers (INT) | Increased control (corporate level) (INT) Increased competitive advantage (INT) Improved cooperation and communication with other business units (INT) | Fraud prevention (INT) |
| Operational | | Increased efficiency (INT) Process transparency (INT) Improved supplier searching process (INT) | Improved monitoring and control (INT) Increased reporting capabilities (INT) Provide better information about suppliers (INT) Increased staff transferability (T) | Improved financial results (faster payment) (INT) Reduced buying costs (T-F) Reduced service costs (T-F) Reduced cost of procured goods and services (T-F) Reduced transaction costs (T-F) Reduced employment (or keep the same despite higher workload) (T-NF) |
| Tactical | | Improved order processing (T-NF) Improved order creation (T-NF) Improved procurement process (T-NF) Improved order approval (T-NF) Elimination of non-value-added activities (T-NF) Eliminate exceptions in the processes (INT) Eliminate problems with paper documents (INT) | Improved access to information (T-NF) | Reduced bank transfer costs (T-F) Reduced warehousing and transport costs (T-F) |

Notes:

INT = intangible benefits

T-F = tangible, financial

T-NF = Tangible, non-financial

## Long case 3.1

### Exostar: online cooperation in the aerospace industry

Exostar was created in 2000 by four aerospace and defence (A&D) industry leaders (BAE Systems, Boeing, Lockheed Martin, and Raytheon, later joined by Rolls-Royce) (http://www.exostar.com). Exostar operates as an independently incorporated company and was designed both to increase the efficiency of the A&D supply chain as well as to increase cooperation between business partners within the industry. Exostar considers itself as 'the leading provider of multi-enterprise solutions for secure information sharing, collaboration and business process integration throughout the extended value chain'.

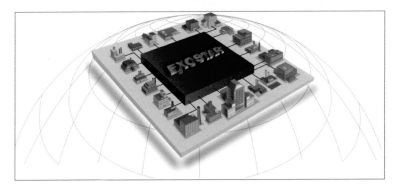

By 2004 the Exostar SaaS platform included four main products: ForumPass, designed to improve collaboration; SourcePass, used for sourcing (including supplier directory, request for information (RFI), request for quotation (RFQ), online auctions tools); and ProcurePass, a hosted procurement, order management with online catalogues, and SupplyPass for basic supply chain transactions (PO, invoicing, etc.). After eighteen months of planning, testing, and preparations, the SupplyPass application was closed as it did not meet more demanding customer requirements. In 2008, all SupplyPass users migrated to a new Supply Chain Platform, based on the E2open solution. Migration was a very complex process, as it required the transfer of all documents, data, and customer profiles to the new application without halting operations. The SaaS concept is used so that Exostar members need only use the Internet to use the application and pay an annual fee for such usage. Access to the application is through a single sign-on (SSO) Managed Access Gateway (MAG).

Currently Exostar offers:

- Supply Chain Platform: enabling visibility of operations and supply chain performance throughout multiple partner tiers, with Order Lifecycle Management, Demand/Supply Synchronization, Inventory Management, Logistics Management, and Multi-Tier Supply Chain Visibility modules.

- Supplier Integration (MachineLink): created to improve communication between Exostar members. (MachineLink creates a direct connection for high volume suppliers to the Supply Chain Platform and their back end systems)

- SourcePass, used for sourcing, by allowing requests for information, quotations and proposal to be sent, and creating and monitoring online auctions and    » analysing online bids. It provides access to a B2B supplier network of over 40,000 registered companies worldwide.

- ProcurePass: electronic procurement product designed to automate, improve, and control procurement processes through a catalogue-based shopping cart.
- ForumPass: based on Microsoft SharePoint technology, and used for secure collaboration, joint product design, net meetings, and document and file sharing.
- Secure Business Process Management (SecureForms): used to create digital process flows, which include process modelling and digital signature.

According to Accenture (2004) and the Aberdeen Group (2006), evaluation of participation in the Exostar platforms generated benefits such as:

- lower transaction costs and faster cycle times (Rolls-Royce, for example, reduced the cost of its procured goods by 20% per cent);
- increased transaction volumes and revenue with access to global markets.
- reduced inventory levels through improved information access and demand forecasting;
- easy identification of qualified supplier sources, availability, and pricing.
- secure exchange of proprietary and sensitive information among trading partners;
- improved integration of systems for future mergers and acquisitions;
- reduction of errors by eliminating manual data re-entry;
- paper-based and fax processes are almost fully eliminated;
- improved relationships with suppliers, as they also benefit from reduced transaction costs and improved efficiency.

More than 40,000 suppliers and close to 95,000 users are registered with the platform. In addition, some 500 new companies were joining every month at the end of 2008.

The workspace supports over 1m transactions per month and links more than 300 global procurement systems. Some 40–50 per cent of the global A&D sales volume is processed through Exostar.

For Exostar the key issue is security. Exostar's federated Identity Management (IdM) Service identifies and grants permission to perform certain actions (such as access data), and offers multiple authentication methods to access the Trusted Workspace. The Federated Identity Service (FIS) offers on-demand, managed PKI digital certificates. The MAG provides access to Exostar and for authentication purposes, supports a variety of user credentials, such as username and password, RSA token, or PKI certificate. Customers can deploy the Enterprise Identification Solution (EIS) to implement and manage PKI infrastructure and certificates. Exostar is a co-founder of CertiPath, an organization which concentrates on providing information security processes and policies in the A&D sector.

*Questions*
1. Why did so many companies decide to join Exostar?
2. Can you list and classify the benefits likely to have been generated by Exostar? Which of them are strategic and which tactical and operational?

## Long case 3.2

### PayPal: the online payment system

PayPal is a payment system used for P2P (Person-to-Person), B2B and B2C transactions, allowing the sending and receipt of money electronically (http://www.paypal.com). The system was developed in 1998, and in 2002 PayPal was bought by eBay. PayPal has 184mn registered users, of whom 73mn have been active within the past year. In addition to its site in the US, PayPal has created 18 national websites in Europe and Asia in local languages. In 2008 PayPal processed $USD 60bn in payments - a 27% increase on the previous year. It is estimated that almost 9% of global e-commerce transactions were completed via PayPal in 2007.

Person to Person services allow the transfer of money between individuals (for example, as payment for goods acquired at online auctions), whilst B2B and B2C services are offered to businesses and target in particular small businesses and online traders. There are three types of accounts: personal, premier and business. The basic way of payment is by e-mail, allowing transfers between two registered users who have each provided their bank account details or registered credit/debit cards. PayPal Mobile allows use of the system via web enabled mobile phone. To complete online payment only an e-mail address is needed, whilst financial data are not shared with or visible to participants. PayPal payment can be also used in e-commerce, as the last step of the web checkout.

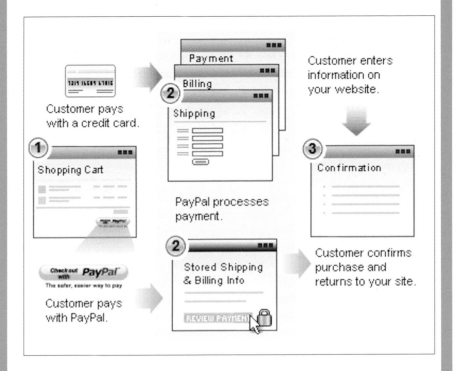

The PayPal system accepts all major credit and debit cards, so payment can be completed using the card directly at the webpage. For international trade, multiple  »

currencies are accepted—currently nineteen. Companies which use PayPal pay fees which depend on their monthly sales volume. Several levels of services are offered, which are a function of user's technical capability, but include complex solutions permitting integration with internal company applications.

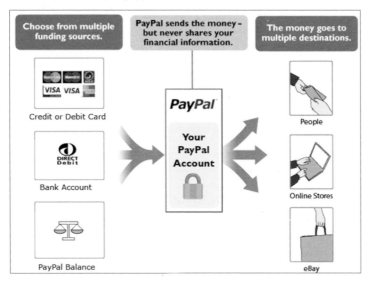

PayPal applies the standards and regulations of PCI DSS (payment card industry data security standards) developed by card credit issuers. For data encryption SSL 3.0 protocol, with 128bit key length, is used, while fraud detection models are incorporated in the system and monitor user activity. PayPal members are verified to confirm their address and identity. There is the opportunity (although not in all countries) to use the PayPal Security Key to confirm the transaction. This can be by means of a Security Key Token, which generates a security code every thirty seconds, or by sending temporary security codes to the mobile phone as text messages, for an additional charge. Further, to protect service users, PayPal employs over 2,000 staff members, often former law enforcement officers, who are responsible for fraud prevention. As result there is a reportedly low loss rate (0.29 per cent of transaction volumes) attributed to fraudulent activities. Companies are able to add PayPal as one of the payment methods by simply adding basket creation and payment buttons to their web pages. At the same time there are widely available tools and applications designed to create online shops of different levels of complexity, using a PayPal-based solution or integrating a third-party solution with it. PayPal payment is not only used by individual sellers on eBay, and small online shops, but also by large traditional and online retailers such Boots or Pixmania.com. (You can see a full list of shops that accept PayPal here: http://www.shopsthatusepaypal.co.uk )

*Questions*

1. Do you use PayPal or other online payment technologies? If yes, what are your experiences? If not, why not?

2. What are the advantages, disadvantages, and threats of online payment technologies for the various stakeholders involved?

## ✪ Chapter Summary

The purpose of this chapter has been to present the main issues related to technology in e-business. Technology covers much more than just hardware. Software applications and standards play an important role in integrating internal and inter-organizational data exchange and processes. In this chapter, current and major trends in systems availability, such as web services and SOA were introduced and summarized, as both aim to create flexible IT systems which can be modified as and when required. In IT development for e-business, selection standards are important, both formal as well as those developed by informal groups such as consortia. Payment in e-business is one of the areas where standardization is needed to provide secure financial transfers. Finally, this chapter introduced the concept of IT evaluation, indicating the importance of looking at the benefits, costs, and risks associated with system selection and implementation.

## ❓ Review questions

1. What are the some of the pre-existing shortcomings of current technologies for e-business? What have been the consequences of these for emerging ways of working within organizations?

2. What are the goals of B2B integration?

3. What are the main requirements for e-business security systems?

4. Outline the main characteristics of the SOA and web services concepts.

5. How are e-payment systems designed?

6. How can you classify the benefits derived from e-business technologies?

7. What is the role and impact of standardization in e-business technology?

8. What kinds of indirect costs are incurred by e-business technology implementation?

## ◯ Discussion questions

1. Is it possible to create fully secure e-business technologies? If not, why not?

2. Why is the flexibility and modularity of IT architecture important?

3. Is national and organizational culture influencing e-business technology selection and usage?

4. Should online transactions be fully anonymous?

5. Is it possible to quantify and measure e-business technology impacts on organizations?

# ➔ Suggestions for further reading

Ince, D., (2004), *Developing Distributed and E-commerce Applications*, Addison-Wesley.
A technical but accessible book which deals with applications design.

Shostack, A. and Stewart, A., (2008), *The New School of Information Security*, Addison-Wesley.
An easy-to-read book, which deals with the security issues beyond technology and techniques.

Schaeffer, M., (2007), *New Payment World*, Wiley.
A good guide for managers. It includes discussion of electronic payment tools as well as advice on how to design payment systems.

Papazoglou, M., (2008), *Web Services: Principles and Technology*, Prentice Hall
This book covers topics such as XML, SOA, standards, and security.

Irani, Z., and Love, P. (2008), *Evaluating Information Systems: Public and Private Sector*, Butterworth-Heinemann.
For those who would like to learn more about IT/IS evaluation.

# ➔ References

Aberdeen Group, (2006), 'Rolls-Royce Uses e-Procurement to Transform Procurement', *Business Success Case Study*.

Accenture, (2004), *Exostar: Electronic B-to-B Marketplace Development*.

Blind, K. and Gauch, S., (2008), 'Trends in ICT Standards: The Relationship Between European Standardisation Bodies and Standards Consortia', *Telecommunications Policy*, 32(7), pp. 503–13.

Brenner, W. and Hamm, V., (1996), 'Information Technology for Purchasing in Process Environment', *European Journal of Purchasing and Supply Management*, 2(4), pp. 211–19.

Cardoso, J., Bostrom, R.P., and Sheth, A. (2004), 'Workflow Management Systems and ERP Systems: Differences, Commonalities, and Applications', *Information Technology and Management*, 5(3–4), pp. 319–38.

Chen, M., Zhang, D., and Zhou, L., (2007), 'Empowering Collaborative Commerce with Web Services Enabled Business Process Management Systems', *Decision Support Systems*, 43(2), pp. 530–46.

Chou, D.C., Tan, X., and Yen, D.C., (2004), 'Web Technology and Supply Chain Management', *Information Management & Computer Security*, 12(4), pp. 338–49.

Draper, C., (2006), *Combine Autonomic Computing and SOA to Improve IT Management*, IBM, http://www.ibm.com/developerworks/library/ac-mgmtsoa/index.html.

Farbey, B., Land, F., and Targett, D., (1999), 'Moving IS Evaluation Forward: Learning Themes and Research Issues', *Journal of Strategic Information Systems*, 8(2), pp. 189–207.

Gammelgård, M., Simonsson, M., and Lindström, Å., (2007), 'An IT Management Assessment Framework: Evaluating Enterprise Architecture Scenarios', *Information Systems and E-Business Management*, 5(4), pp. 415–35.

Ghiya, K. and Powers, M., (2005), 'e-Procurement—Strengthening the Indirect Supply Chain Through Technology Globalization', *Intel Technology Journal*, 9(3), pp. 203–10.

Gosain, S., Malhotra, A., and El Sawy, O.A., (2005), 'Coordinating for Flexibility in e-Business Supply Chains', *Journal of Management Information Systems* 21(3) pp. 7–45.

Gunasekaran, A., Ngai, E.W.T., and McGaughey, R.E., (2006), 'Information Technology and Systems Justification: A Review for Research and Applications', *European Journal of Operational Research*, 173(3,) pp. 957–83.

Huang, Y. and Chung, J.-Y., (2003), 'A Web Services-Based Framework for Business Integration Solutions', *Electronic Commerce Research and Applications*, 2(1), pp. 15–26.

IBM, (2006), *Infrastructure Considerations for Service Oriented Architecture*, IBM.

Irani, Z., (2002), 'Information Systems Evaluation: Navigating through the Problem Domain', *Information & Management*, 40(1), pp. 11–24.

Irani, Z. and Love, P.E.D., (2001), 'Information Systems Evaluation: Past, Present and Future', *European Journal of Information Systems*, 10(4), pp. 183–8.

Irani, Z., Ezingeard, J.N., and Grieve, R.J., (1997), 'Integrating the Costs of a Manufacturing IT/IS Infrastructure into the Investment Decision Making Process', *Technovation*, 17(11/12), pp. 695–706.

Kirchmer, M., (2004), 'E-business Process Network—Successful Value Chains through Standards', *Journal of Enterprise Information Management*, 17(1), pp. 20–30.

Kotzab, H., Skjoldager, N., and Vinum, T., (2003), 'The Development and Empirical Validation of an e-Based Supply Chain Strategy Optimization Model', *Industrial Management & Data Systems*, 103(5), pp. 347–60.

Love, P.E.D., Ghoneim, A., and Irani, Z., (2004a), 'Information Technology Evaluation: Classifying Indirect Costs Using Structured Case Method', *Journal of Enterprise Information Management*, 17(4), pp. 312–25.

Love, P.E.D., Irani, Z., and Edwards, D.J., (2004b), 'Industry-Centric Benchmarking of Information Technology Benefits, Costs and Risks for Small-to-Medium Sized Enterprises in Construction', *Automation in Construction*, 13(4), pp. 507–24.

Love, P.E.D., Irani, Z., Ghoneim, A., and Themistocleous, M., (2006), 'An Exploratory Study of Indirect ICT Costs Using the Structured Case Method', *International Journal of Information Management*, 26(2), pp. 167–77.

Love, P.E.D., Irani, Z., Standing, C., Lin, C., and Burn, J.M., (2005), 'The Enigma of Evaluation: Benefits, Costs and Risks of IT in Australian

Small-Medium-Sized Enterprises', *Information & Management*, 42(7), pp. 947–64.

Marechaux, J.-L., (2006), 'Combining Service-Oriented Architecture and Event-Driven Architecture Using an Enterprise Service Bus', *IBM Developworks*.

Microsoft, (2007), 'Microsoft Deployment Woodgrove Bank Business Case', http://technet.microsoft.com/en-us/library/bb978389.aspx.

Nurmilaakso, J.-M., Kotinurmi, P., and Laesvuori, H. (2006), 'XML-Based e-Business Frameworks and Standardization', *Computer Standards & Interfaces*, 28(5), pp. 585–99.

Piotrowicz, W., (2008), 'Electronic Procurement Evaluation'. unpublished PhD theses, Brunel University.

Piotrowicz, W. and Cuthbertson, R., (2009), 'Sustainability—new dimension in information systems evaluation', *Journal of Enterprise Information Management*, Vol 22 No. 5, pp. 492–503.

Piotrowicz, W. and Irani, Z. (2009), 'Analysing B2B electronic procurement benefits—information systems perspective' in: Proceedings of European and Mediterranean Conference on Information Systems 2009 (EMCIS 2009), Irani Z. and A. Ghoneim (ed.), Izmir, Turkey.

Riempp, G. and Gieffers-Ankel, S., (2007), 'Application Portfolio Management: A Decision-Oriented View of Enterprise Architecture', *Information Systems and E-Business Management*, 5(4), pp. 359–78.

Sayal, M., Casati, F., Dayal, U., and Shan, M.-C., (2001), 'Integrating Workflow Management Systems with Business- to-Business Interaction Standards', *Software Technology Laboratory*, HP Laboratories.

Serafeimidis, V. and Smithson, S., (1999), 'Rethinking the Approaches to Information Systems Evaluation', *Logistics Information Management*, 12(1/2), pp. 94–107.

Sherer, S.A., (2005), 'From Supply-Chain Management to Value Network Advocacy: Implications for e-Supply Chains', *Supply Chain Management: An International Journal*, 10(2), pp. 77–83.

Sherif, M.H., Egyedi, T.M., and Jakobs, K. (2005), 'Standards of Quality and Quality of Standards for Telecommunications and Information Technologies', *the 4th Conference on Standardization and Innovation in Information Technology, 2005 (SIIT2005)*, pp. 221–30.

Smith, S. and Johnson, J., (2005), *2004 Information Technology Annual Performance Report*, Intel Corporation, http://www.intel.com/it/pdf/2004-apr.pdf.

Smithson, S. and Hirschheim, R., (1998), 'Analysing Information Systems Evaluation: Another Look at an Old Problem', *European Journal of Information Systems*, 7(3)3, pp. 158–74.

Strohmaier, M. and Yu, E., (2006), 'Towards Autonomic Workflow Management Systems', in *IBM Centre for Advanced Studies Conference, Proceedings of the 2006 conference of the Center for Advanced Studies on Collaborative research*, IBM.

SUN, (2004), 'Assessing your SOA Readiness. A Technical White Paper', SUN.

SUN, (2006), 'The SOA Platform Guide: Evaluate, Extend, Embrace', SUN.

Turner, D. and Chung, S.H., (2005), 'Technological Factors Relevant to Continuity on ERP for E-Business Platform Integration, Modularity, and Flexibility', *Journal of internet Commerce*, 4(4), pp. 119–32.

Vickery, S.K., Jayaram, J., Droge, C., and Calantone, R., (2003), 'The Effects of an Integrative Supply Chain Strategy on Customer Service and Financial Performance: An Analysis of Direct Versus Indirect Relationships', *Journal of Operations Management*, 21(5), pp. 523–39.

Werle, R. and Iversen, E.J., (2006), 'Promoting Legitimacy in Technical Standardization', *Science, Technology & Innovation Studies*, 2, pp. 19–39.

Weske, M., van der Aalst, W.M.P., and Verbeek, H.M.W., (2004), 'Advances in Business Process Management', *Data & Knowledge Engineering*, 50(1), pp. 1–8.

Xia, M., Zhao, K., and Shaw, M.J., (2003), 'Open e-Business Standard Development and Adoption: An Integrated Perspective', in King, J.L. and Lyytinen, K. (eds), Proceedings of MISQ Special Issue Workshopon Standard Making: A Critical Frontier for Information Systems, *MIS Quarterly*, pp. 222–35.

Zhang, D., (2005), 'Web Services Composition for Process Management in E-Business', *Journal of Computer Information Systems*, 42(2), pp. 83–91.

## ⊘ Weblinks

Organization for the Advancement of Structured Information Standards. Works on the creation of open web standards: http://www.oasis-open.org.

Internet Security Alliance. Concentrates on information security issues: http://www.isalliance.org.

Bank Safe Online. Safety and security in online banking, run by APACS, the UK payments association: http://www.banksafeonline.org.uk.

Biometrics.org. Biometric-based personal identification/verification technology centre: http://www.biometrics.org.

World Wide Web Consortium (W3C). The W3C develops interoperable technologies, such as specifications, guidelines, software and tools: http://www.w3.org.

# Social and behavioural issues

## Introduction

Profound changes in social behaviour are being brought about though the introduction of e-business technologies. Such changes can be thought about at the individual level, and at the level of the organization, but also at the level of society itself. At the level of the individual, there is interest in the extent of adoption of e-business technologies as well as in their application. This chapter explores the changing nature of communication between individuals and groups facilitated by email and by the growth in virtual communities. It also sets out the effects of e-business technologies upon the decision-making behaviour of individuals as consumers. This includes consumer behaviour in relation to consumption of information or digitized products (such as downloadable music, video, and software), public information services, as well in relation to more conventional physical goods. The effects on the consumption of paid-for goods are of two kinds: the direct substitution effects of e-commerce upon retail sales through conventional channels of consumption, as well as the indirect effects upon the purchasing behaviour of consumers more broadly in relation to the consumer's decision-making process, for example in relation to search strategies.

Finally, the growth of e-business technologies has also generated a rich set of societal consequences, although whether these are beneficial or harmful is open to debate. From one perspective, the growth and widespread implementation of such technologies and their application is heralded as providing significant potential for social cohesion, through the enrichment of quality of life and the promotion of diversity and inclusiveness: heralding the emergence of a utopian 'e-society'. From another perspective, differential access to networked resources, evident even within the most richly endowed markets, has raised concern over the extent and implication of 'digital divides' and the risks arising from social exclusion, and has prompted fear of the undesirable consequences of mass participation, both nationally and internationally. So-called dystopian views of e-business technologies see their implementation within society having fatal flaws which undermine the original goals of their developers.

> **Social Exclusion** Being unable to access the things in life that most of society takes for granted. The UK government defines it as—the lack or denial of resources, rights, goods, and services, and the inability to participate in the normal relationships and activities available to the majority of people in society, whether in economic, social, cultural, or political arenas. It affects both the quality of life of individuals and the equity and cohesion of society as a whole.

# The effects of e-business technologies on individuals

In this section we describe changes in behaviour that have occurred amongst individuals and groups of consumers and citizens as a result of e-business technologies. We examine technology adoption rates of, barriers to, and global variations in technology adoption, and the impact on behaviours amongst individuals and groups in respect of the consumption of information as well as of physical goods.

## Access, adoption, and attitudes

Access to, adoption of, and attitudes towards e-business technologies by individuals exhibit significant differences. When thinking of levels of access and adoption, it is necessary to distinguish between access to the *technical infrastructure* and adoption and use of *applications* supported by that infrastructure. For example, in terms of household access, whilst on average only 57 per cent of European Union households owned a personal computer and 40 per cent had access to the Internet in 2008, with PC ownership ranging from 85 per cent in Denmark to as little as 27 per cent in Bulgaria (European Commission, 2008a). Of all the other infrastructure indicators, broadband access to the Internet appears the most significant in determining the extent to which individuals are able to make use of networked resources. 'Broadband' is an elusive term: definitions of what it constitutes differ.[1] Across Europe, domestic broadband connectivity (defined as connection via ADSL or cable) averaged 48 per cent of European households (EU27) in 2008, but varied more widely from 74 per cent of households in the Netherlands and Denmark to just 13 per cent in Romania, with a distinctive north-west/south-east bias.

---

1   The US Federal Communications Commission defines broadband as a connection of more than 200kbps (http://www.fcc.gov/cgb/consumerfacts/highspeedinternet.html); in the UK statistics, broadband is defined somewhat redundantly as being 'always on and providing a bandwidth greater than narrowband' (OFCOM, 2007); in Australia, broadband is interpreted as faster than 126kbps and the European Commission talks of 2Mbps as 'probably being the minimum speed for achieving good usage of services' and this is the bitrate target for the Lisbon 2010 agenda on information society: http://ec.europa.eu/information_society/eeurope/2005/doc/wg1_digi_divide_written_recs_290904.pdf.

But individuals of course have means of accessing Internet resources other than from their homes: access can occur in the workplace, in a public place (such as an Internet café), or via wireless or mobile technology. Whilst 31 per cent of UK adults said they had used their mobile phones to access the Internet in 2007–2008, the equivalent figure for Japan—where less online usage takes place at home—was apparently over 90 per cent as early as 2005 (OFCOM, 2008; A.T. Kearney, 2005). Explanations for this include higher usage of public transport for commuting (therefore generating more extensive opportunities to use mobile devices), and more innovative content provision by telecommunications companies. It is therefore important to employ a wider measure of Internet penetration that takes this assortment of access into account. Using a wider definition and examining worldwide penetration of Internet *usage* (as against ownership of particular hardware), higher levels can indeed be found, but significant variations in Internet penetration between countries within regions still persist (Table 4.1). Table 4.1 confirms that the

**Table 4.1  Internet penetration by region and selected countries within regions**

| World Regions | Countries | % Population (Penetration) | Usage % of World | Usage Growth 2000–2008 % |
|---|---|---|---|---|
| Africa | | 5.3 | 3.4 | 1,100 |
| | Reunion | 27.4 | | |
| | Sierra Leone | 0.2 | | |
| Asia | | 17.2 | 41.3 | 469 |
| | South Korea | 76.1 | | |
| | Myanmar | 0.1 | | |
| Europe | | 48.5 | 24.8 | 271 |
| | Iceland | 90.0 | | |
| | Ukraine | 14.6 | | |
| Middle East | | 23.3 | 2.9 | 1296 |
| | Israel | 74.0 | | |
| | Iraq | 1.0 | | |
| North America | | 73.1 | 15.7 | 128 |
| | Canada | 84.3 | | |
| | Bermuda | 72.1 | | |
| South/Central America | | 29.1 | 10.6 | 820.7 |
| | Chile | 44.9 | | |
| | Nicaragua | 2.7 | | |
| Oceania / Australia | | 59.9 | 1.3 | 170.2 |
| | New Zealand | 80.5 | | |
| | Solomon Islands | 1.4 | | |
| WORLD TOTAL | | 23.5 | 100.00% | 336 |

Note: Internet World Stats defines an Internet User as 'anyone currently with the capacity to use the Internet'. In particular: (1) the person must have available access to an Internet connection point, and (2) the person must have the basic knowledge required to use web technology.

largest proportion of world Internet usage (41 per cent) is now to be found in Asia, with over 650m users, rather than in North America or Europe. Asian markets are also growing faster than European and North American markets.

Whilst differences in both access and adoption are most often measured at the national level, this is not always meaningful in itself. European research shows a strong link between size of household and ownership of a personal computer. In Eastern Europe particularly, there is also a positive relationship between level of urbanization and PC ownership (European Commission, 2006). One of the reasons that South Korea has been able quickly to achieve high Internet penetration is that some 40 per cent of Korean households live in apartment buildings in urban areas, where the installation of fibreoptic cabling by government has been carried out much faster and more cheaply than would have been possible in separate dwellings.

It is also the case that individuals will differ in their receptiveness to e-business technologies. Several attempts have been made to classify consumers in terms of the differences in their likely attitudes. Table 4.2 provides one classification based upon a geo-demographic profiling of the UK population (at the personal rather than the household level) designed to produce a set of discrete market segments or behavioural clusters (Li et al., 2006). According to the research team responsible for this analysis, three predictors in particular can explain differences in awareness and use of e-business technologies:

- variations in household income: poorer individuals may have interest in becoming involved in e-business technologies, but not the means;

- variations in age: younger individuals may have grown up with the technology and have fewer inhibitions and more positive incentives to use it; and

- career stage: individuals with greater learning needs at a particular point in their career may be willing to invest more time in employing e-business technologies).

### Activity box 4.1

**What kind of e-society citizen are you ?**

Look at Table 4.2 and consider what type of e-society citizen you might be. Explore the associated website, http://www.spatial-literacy.org, which allows you to enter your residential postcode, and test your own assessment. How else might you classify individuals' attitudes towards e-society?

Classifications of this type are strongly influenced by age. Higher proportions of young people (aged between 16 and 25) are to be found amongst the 'e-experts'—those who use technologies for entertainment and shopping as well as those who are becoming increasingly engaged through the workplace. Across Europe, the average age of going online is 14 and users aged between 14 and 25 are up to 20 per cent more likely to email, use instant messaging, play games, and download music. Ownership of mobile phones

**Table 4.2  A classification of UK e-society**

| Group | Type | % population |
|---|---|---|
| A—E-unengaged | The 'E—unengaged' are typically groups that do not have access to electronic communications or technologies. Most are too old, too poor or too poorly educated to be able to access them, and instead traditionally rely upon personal contacts they trust for advice. | |
| | A01—Low technologists | 7.19 |
| | A02—Cable suffices | 8.08 |
| | A03—Technology as fantasy | 5.42 |
| | A04—Mobile's the limit | 10.29 |
| | A05—Too old to be bothered | 2.21 |
| | A06—Elderly marginalized | 5.13 |
| B—E-marginalized | The 'E—marginalized' are not necessarily averse to the use of electronic technologies but often lack the disposable income to equip themselves with them, or the training and education needed to understand how to make effective use of them. | |
| | B07—The Net—what's that? | 2.31 |
| | B08—Mobile explorers | 3.47 |
| | B09—Cable TV heartland | 2.93 |
| C—Becoming engaged | Members of this group often acquire their competence in the use of information technology at work, since many of them are young people working in junior white-collar occupations in modern offices. | |
| | C10—E-bookers and communicators | 2.98 |
| | C11—Peer group adopters | 2.47 |
| D—For entertainment and shopping | This group includes a number of moderately well paid blue-collar workers for whom the Internet and personal computing provide important leisure activities. | |
| | D12—Small time net shoppers | 8.05 |
| | D13—E for entertainment | 5.93 |
| E—E-independents | This group tends to take a rational and considered view of electronic communications and technologies. | |
| | E14—Rational utilitarians | 3.80 |
| | E15—Committed learners | 3.78 |
| | E16—Light users | 6.41 |
| F—Instrumental e-users | This group tends to use electronic technologies for purely instrumental purposes, because they provide a practical method of saving time or money. | |
| | F17—Computer magazine readers | 2.81 |
| | F18—E for financial management | 1.06 |
| | F19—Online apparel purchasers | 4.62 |
| | F20—Exploring for fun | 2.46 |
| G—E-business users | This group includes many people who use electronic technologies in order to run their business. These may be people working in a technology related business or in a small business that needs to keep in electronic contact with its suppliers or its customers. | |
| | G21—Electronic orderers | 5.48 |
| H—E-experts | Members of this group have every confidence in their abilities to undertake online transactions and to make full use of electronic technologies. | |
| | H22—E-committed | 2.62 |
| | H23—E-professionals | 0.51 |

with Internet capability is nearly twice as high as the overall average amongst 16 to 24-year-olds in the UK. Middle-aged groups tends to be more rational and utilitarian in their use of these technologies, whilst there are higher proportions of older people (over 65) to be found amongst the 'unengaged'.

These analyses also confirm that the geographical distribution of technologically literate individuals is not an even one. It is also only to be expected that urban areas with high population densities—particularly cosmopolitan metropolitan areas, with a legacy in terms of concentrations of wealthier, professional individuals, many of whom were early adopters of the technology—will offer significantly greater potential for Internet penetration and application adoption than rural areas. Figure 4.1 shows the very different distribution of 'e-experts' and 'e-unengaged' for the UK and makes it clear that national generalizations about access on their own can be unhelpful. For example, parts of London have ten times the number of 'e-experts' than elsewhere in the UK. Since evidence suggests that there tend to be more and better online options in larger markets,

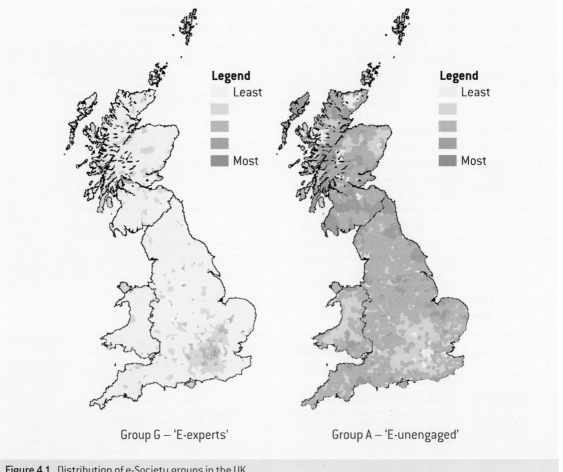

Group G – 'E-experts'            Group A – 'E-unengaged'

**Figure 4.1** Distribution of e-Society groups in the UK

these contrasts are likely to persist, although there is evidence that rural residents may have greater incentives to go online, other things being equal, to overcome isolation (Sinai and Waldfogel, 2004).

Factors other than age and location will of course also determine individual attitudes to e-business technologies. As early as 1998, Don Tappscott coined the term 'Net-generation' to encompass those people in the US who were accepting of diversity, curious, assertive, and self-reliant in their use of Internet resources (Tappscott, 1998). US studies have shown that a technologically oriented elite, which is not limited to a young demographic cohort, can be identified, consisting of three distinct segments all of whom are 'voracious consumers of information goods and services' (Horrigan, 2003). These include:

- the young 'tech elites', with an average age of 22 (20 per cent);
- the wired 'generation Xers' with an average age of 36 (60 per cent); and
- the older wired 'baby boomers' with an average age of 52 (20 per cent).

Louis Leung's analysis of a group of youngsters in Hong Kong seemed to suggest the particular characteristics of the 'net-geners' are not defined by age (or indeed perhaps by culture) alone even amongst the young, but rather by a combination of demographic cohort, values, life experiences, and behaviour (Leung, 2003). These users are he proposes strongly principled, with a belief in fundamental rights to information, emotionally open in their online communications, innovative and investigative, and independent, confident, and preoccupied with maturity. In South Korea, so-called 'netizens' have emerged who use the Internet to contribute towards social and political goals.

Gender and cultural differences will also affect attitudes to e-business technologies. For example, some of the interesting differences to emerge from a study of UK and Chinese students included the discovery that:

- men in both countries were more likely than women to use email or 'chat' rooms;
- men played more computer games than women, Chinese men being the most active games players;
- men in both countries were more self-confident about their computer skills than women, and were more likely to express the opinion that using computers was a male activity and skill than were women; and
- gender differences were more extreme in the British group than the Chinese group (Li and Kirkup, 2007).

There still exist real or perceived barriers to the adoption of e-business technologies amongst individuals. Inhibitors can include:

- the cost of accessing services (although competitive flat rate broadband services are starting to erode this barrier);
- the relevance of content (now being overcome for mainstream Internet access, but still in existence for mobile devices);
- accessibility (the growth of broadband, extensive wifi and portable devices are determining factors here); and

- security (an 'old' barrier but one which is still relevant in relation to the burgeoning range of new threats perceived by Internet users and reviewed in chapter 5).

## Communication and consumption

What use do individuals make of the networked resources to which they now have increasing access? A wide range of activities is habitually undertaken, with email followed by gathering information about products and services usually amongst the most popular (Figure 4.2). In this section, we distinguish between applications designed for communications (including email, instant messaging, and social networking), information and product search, and the use of the Internet for commercial transactions.

### Activity box 4.2

**You're as old as you feel**

Take a look at Figure 4.2. Identify and explain the reasons for the differences between online behaviours of 16–24-year-olds and those aged 65 or older.

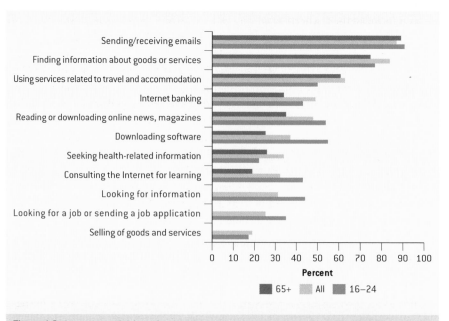

**Figure 4.2**  Internet activities of recent Internet users, by age groups, UK, 2008

## Communications

The first network email was sent in 1971 and email has become a strongly established form of communication and the most popular application of network resources.[2] The number of email inboxes is expected to grown from 253 million in 1998 to 1.3bn in 2008 to 1.8bn by 2012, according to the Radicati Group (http://www.radicati.com). During the same period, it is estimated (and it can be no more than an estimate) that the number of emails sent grew three times faster than the number of people emailing. By 2006 the email traffic from one person to another—excluding spam—already accounted for as much as 6 exabytes (6bn gigabytes)[3] (Ganz, 2007) with over 200bn emails being sent daily, one third of which are business-to-business.

> 'E-mail is a faster method of textual communication which combines aspects of letter writing with the informality of a phone-call.' *Leigh Clayton*

Is email really written communication? Some have suggested that it is in fact a verbal tool, permitting 'speech by other means' (Spinks et al., 1999). It has developed its own behavioural conventions, or *netiquette* such as *flaming*. Senders employ *emoticons* (graphical representations of facial expressions embedded in the message) and the medium has borrowed others (the *bcc*: box, the *sig*) as a signal to others and to assert the sender's personal identity. As we have become more comfortable with this communications medium, so we have started to use email informally as a substitute for face-to-face (F2F) or telephone conversations. As social networking sites such as Facebook and Twitter have emerged, so we feel that we can communicate in fewer than 140 characters. This has its risks. People tend to believe that they can communicate electronically more effectively than they actually can (Kruger et al., 2005). Research suggests, for example, that emotionally deficient emails (which are not sensitive to the needs of the recipient) can cause frustration and anger (Kato et al., 2007).

Blogs, have become a leading means of creating and expressing personal identity online. The typical blog is a form of personal journal, although blogs are also used to provide a running commentary on issues in politics, entertainment, sports, business, technology, culture and religion by individuals or small groups. The majority of blogs are personal in nature, but a growing proportion is corporate or professional. The first genuine weblogs appeared in 1994, although some earlier Usenet discussion groups had the characteristics of blogs. The size of the **blogosphere** is disputed. The Pew Internet & American Life project suggests that whilst only 8 per cent of US internet users keep a **blog** (7 per cent in the UK), 39 per cent of US Internet users read them (21 per cent in the UK), a ratio of 8:1 (Pew Internet & American Life Project, 2008; National Statistics, 2008). Blogs are therefore potentially influential. Internationally, it is estimated that over 133m blog records have been indexed since 2002 with bloggers posting over 900,000 updates per day, or over 37,500 updates an hour, during 2008 (Technorati.com, 2009[4]). We can even use them to track significant events (as the archive data in Figure 4.3 shows).

**Blogosphere** The collective community of all blogs. Since all blogs are on the Internet by definition, they may be seen as interconnected and socially networked. Discussions 'in the blogosphere' have been used by the media as a gauge of public opinion on various issues.

**Blog** A blog (a contraction of the term 'Web log') is a website, usually maintained by an individual with regular entries of commentary, descriptions of events, or other material such as graphics or video. Entries are commonly displayed in reverse chronological order. (Technorati definition)

---

2   By Ray Tomlinson, a programmer for what is now BBN Technologies, which developed some of the first packet switching systems: http://openmap.bbn.com/%7Etomlinso/ray/firstemailframe.html.

3   1 Exabyte = 1bn GB.

4   http://technorati.com/blogging/state-of-the-blogosphere/.

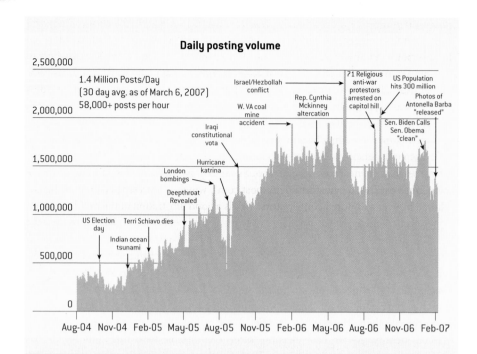

**Figure 4.3** Daily blog posting volume, 2004-2007

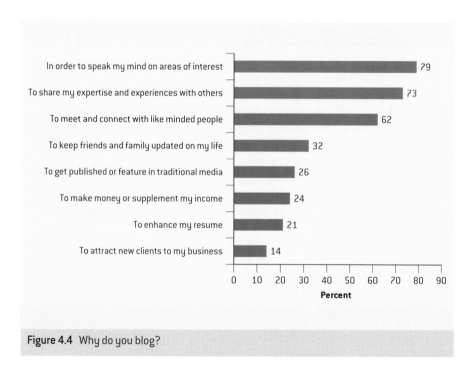

**Figure 4.4** Why do you blog?

Why do people blog? Often for personal reasons, as Figure 4.4 shows. However, whilst mundane personal journals are still the dominant manifestation of the blogging phenomenon (comprising some 79 per cent of all US blogs in 2008, according to Technorati), it is often distinctive, sometimes quirky, commentaries on other subjects than an individual's life and experience that achieve a higher profile amongst readers and win awards. For example, the winners of the 2006 Webby Awards for best personal blog was Rocketboom (http://www.rocketboom.com), a three-minute daily videoblog based in New York City, reporting a wide range of information and commentary from top news stories to quirky Internet culture. Political and news blogs can attract a particularly high readership. A consistent winner of political blog awards is the blog produced by the Huffington Post (http://www.huffingtonpost.com), which is scarcely personal, being co-authored by over a hundred contributors. This is a good illustration of the rapid evolution of online phenomena: when does a blog become a virtual community? Currently, the boundary can be related firstly to the extent of editorial control exerted by the owner of a blog (particularly in terms of authorizing new contributors and themes) and secondly to conventions determining the layout of a blog which makes it distinctive in terms of its journal style.

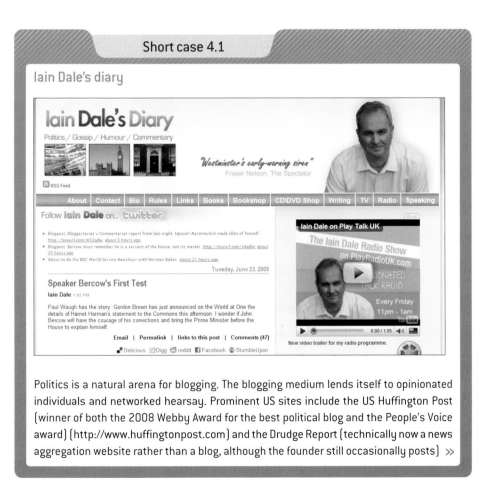

**Short case 4.1**

**Iain Dale's diary**

Politics is a natural arena for blogging. The blogging medium lends itself to opinionated individuals and networked hearsay. Prominent US sites include the US Huffington Post (winner of both the 2008 Webby Award for the best political blog and the People's Voice award) (http://www.huffingtonpost.com) and the Drudge Report (technically now a news aggregation website rather than a blog, although the founder still occasionally posts) » (http://www.drudgereport.com). But far more interesting are the kinds of 'samizdat' political blogs that presently sit below the popular radar, but that are required reading for those 'in the know'. In the UK, one of the most prominent of these is Iain Dale's diary (http://iaindale.blogspot.com/). Dale is an author and columnist for the UK *Daily Telegraph*. He has stood (unsuccessfully) for election as a Conservative party candidate. The blog was developed as a means for him to develop a connection back into mainstream journalism. Launched in 2006, it claims to offer a mix of political commentary, humour, and gossip, and attracts over 350,000 visitors a month (90,000 unique visitors) which is 'more hits than the Conservative, Labour and LibDem websites combined' (Iain Dale). Over the intervening five years, although initially only used as a platform to air his views, the Diary has begun to break stories ranging from fraud, the sexual peccadilloes of senior ministers and MPs' expenses. The blog has started to become influential in its own right, with conventional news agencies starting to pick up stories. Dale posts to the blog intensively, encourages commentary, has a Facebook group and can be followed on Twitter. Finally, Dale has himself been able to use his blog as a springboard into mainstream media, with broadcasting appearances and the launch of a new political magazine, *Total Politics*.

*Questions*

1. In what ways are political blogs influential?

2. Examine the links to other political blogs in Iain Dale's diary. Comment on your findings. What are the implications for political blog networks?

Perhaps the most significant behavioural phenomenon to have occurred as a result of the growth of e-business technologies has been the rise of group social behaviours.

'Community has become the "in-term" for almost any group of people who use Internet technologies to communicate with each other' *Preece and Maloney-Krichmar, 2005.*

Communities, and the associated terminology of user-generated content make up the building blocks of the Web 2.0 phenomenon. Historically, the term *community* has tended to refer to a small, relatively stable group of individuals, with a reciprocal bond of common interests and shared moral values, based in one geographic location, who engage in face-to-face interactions. The extension of this terminology to the Internet when describing online or virtual communities has created much speculation over whether or not these often 'ad hoc' groupings are genuinely communitarian, or may simply comprise unstable, superficial, and ephemeral associations between individuals in dispersed locations.

'Most web sites have less sense of community than a New York City subway car: at least people are going in the same direction on the subway.' *Jakob Nielsen, 1997*

Virtual communities have developed into significant social phenomena from their origins as simple discussion boards involving US academics on Usenet in the early 1980s. Today, there are a wide variety of virtual communities with a range of objectives. Some of the largest social networking sites by market share in the US are shown in Table 4.3. Porter provides a classification which distinguishes between the origins of the community on the one hand and the relationship orientation (social, professional, and commercial)

**Table 4.3  Top ten social networking sites, US, February 2007–2009**

| Rank 2009 | Rank 2007 | Name | Domain | Market share 2007 | Market share 2009 |
|---|---|---|---|---|---|
| 1 | 1 | MySpace | www.myspace.com | 80.74% | 34.40% |
| 2 | 2 | Facebook | www.facebook.com | 10.32% | 23.73% |
| 3 | – | YouTube | www.youtube.com | – | 9.62% |
| 4 | 10 | Tagged | www.tagged.com | 0.67% | 1.63% |
| 5 | – | Yahoo! Answers | answers.yahoo.com | – | 1.43% |
| 6 | 20 | myYearbook | www.myyearbooks.com | 0.11% | 1.07% |
| 7 | – | Yahoo! Groups | groups.yahoo.com | – | 1.06% |
| 8 | – | Meebo | www.meebo.com | – | 0.54% |
| 9 | 8 | Classmates | www.classmates.com | 0.72% | 0.54% |
| 10 | – | Yahoo! Profiles | profiles.yahoo.com | – | 0.52% |

Note: The Hitwise data featured is based on US market share of visits as defined by the Internet Advertising Bureau, which is the percentage of online traffic to the domain or category, from the Hitwise sample of 10 million US Internet users. Hitwise measures more than 1m unique websites on a daily basis, including sub-domains of larger websites. Hitwise categorizes websites into industries on the basis of subject matter and content, as well as market orientation and competitive context. The market share of visits percentage does not include traffic for all sub-domains of certain websites that could be reported on separately on the other. Member-initiated communities are those where the community was established by, and remains managed by, members. Organization-sponsored communities are communities that are sponsored by either commercial or non-commercial (for example, government, non-profit) organizations. At the second level of the typology, virtual communities are categorized based on the general relationship orientation of the community. Relationship orientation refers to the type of relationship fostered among members of the community:

- Member-initiated communities foster either social or professional relationships among members.
- Organization-sponsored communities foster relationships both among members (for example, customers, employees) and between individual members and the sponsoring organization, which might be for profit, non-profit or government activities (Porter, 2004).

We can also differentiate between 'top-down' community structures (including moderated discussion lists such as the BBC's 'Have Your Say'[5]) and 'bottom-up' social tools (including self-organizing social networks such as Facebook and Flickr) (Kim, 2000). This second category requires more effective user tools for organizing content and it is here that we have seen the biggest growth of *tagging*. At the end of 2006, 28 per cent of US Internet users had reported categorizing, or tagging, user-generated content online, including photographs, news stories, or blog posts. Amongst the most popular sites to benefit from this phenomenon are Del.icio.us (http://www.del.icio.us), Digg (http://www.digg.com) and Flickr (http://www.flickr.com) (see Short case 4.2), which derive much of their rationale from sophisticated self-organizing capabilities. For example, so-called 'tag clouds' provide a social dimension to tagging by demonstrating the content that was tagged by others (Rainie, 2007).

---

### Short case 4.2

#### Flickr

'For a whole generation, *Flickr* has become simply what you do with your pictures.' (Katz, 2006)

Flickr started by accident in 2002. Founders Caterina Fake and Stewart Butterfield had originally intended to develop an online gaming venture. On the way, some photograph-sharing software was developed by the programming team which formed the basis of a photo-streaming social network. »

---

5 http://news.bbc.co.uk/1/hi/talking_point/default.stm.

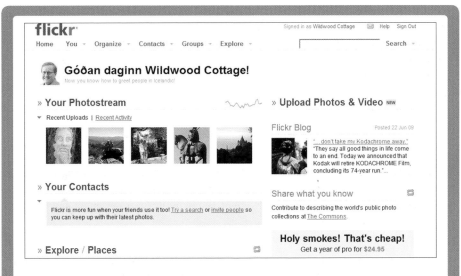

Flickr's goals are to:

- help people make their photos available to the people who matter to them; and to
- enable new ways of organizing photos.

Although Flickr did not invent the process of organizing digital photograph collections and photo-sharing, it took a different approach to more conventional sites. Rather than think of photographs in terms of 'albums', individual photos could be annotated, have captions added, and most importantly be tagged with words which described the photo's attributes. All the photos sharing a similar tag could then be grouped, into what became known as a 'folksonomy'. Fake and Butterfield were amazed to see that this feature was hijacked by members 'around fascinating subjects we would never have thought of'. Photos were shared between friends, newly acquired contacts, or published more widely. Adopting Creative Commons licensing standards (http://www.creativecommons.org) also meant that owners could set rules for re-use and re-distribution.

Successful social network sites grow more than exponentially (see 'Metcalfe's Law'). Today, Flickr's 2m users store and organize over 3bn photographs, amounting to 400TB of disk space. This is a drop in the ocean of digital images worldwide: those from digital cameras are estimated to have exceeded 150bn in 2006 and those from mobile phones over 100bn (Ganz, 2007).

The life cycle of social networking sites gets faster. Flickr was sold for $30m to Yahoo! just one year after its foundation and Yahoo! has enthusiastically integrated it into its other services and is investing in a wider networking strategy. For example, Flickr is now available on mobile phones. But the acquisition did not prove popular with some of the 'elders' of the Flickr community—early adopters known as the 'Old Skool'. For example, Yahoo!'s move to transition Flickr logins to Yahoo! IDs, and limit the number of contacts to whom Flickr users could link, reportedly caused a degree of backlash from the well-established members of the Flickr community (O'Hear, 2007). More recent commercial moves have included Flickr's 2009 alliance with Getty Images (http://www.gettyimages.com), a major commercial stock photography business, and that with the Qoop Group » (http://www.qoop.com), an organization dedicated to monetizing social networks. However, the two co-founders of Flickr left the business in 2008.

*Questions*

1. If Flickr's 'Old Skool' feels alienated, is this a problem for Yahoo!?

2. It is estimated that the number of digital images captured by cameras and other mobile devices worldwide by 2010 will double to in the order of 500bn images (Ganz, 2007). But does the world still need a dedicated image-sharing website when several multi-purpose social networking sites now exist?

How do virtual communities survive and grow? As chapter 2 discussed, the now-disputed Metcalfe's Law suggested the value of a network is proportional to the square of the number of users of the system, but for a more generalized social network to be useful for a single individual, a relatively high degree of saturation in the network may be required in order to ensure that prospective friends or acquaintances with common interests can be found. Note the way in which just two or three sites dominate the rankings shown in Table 4.3 in terms of their market share. In the case of more specialized social networks, such as a professional development forum, shared professional interests amongst a smaller group of individuals may substitute for social ties more quickly.

Even in these cases, however, generic obstacles to development can emerge which serve to hamper information sharing and lead to a forum's quick demise. These include:

- lack of familiarity among individuals;
- disparities in verbal skill;
- differing cultures;
- status differences; and
- the challenges associated with physical distance.

The role of cultural barriers is particularly important. One of the earliest open source news reporting communities was the South Korean service Ohmynews (http://www.ohmynews.com). Founded in 2000, it relied heavily on 'citizen journalism' to generate content, backed up by over 50 staff reporters. Some 42,000 citizen news reporters now write for the site. 'arguably the world's most domestically powerful news site' (Watts, 2003). The company sought to extend its operations to Japan in 2006, but the provocative contributions of a small number of Japanese citizen journalists have not been as welcome, and many Japanese tend not to want to express themselves as freely (Kambayashi, 2006):

'This is a society in which it is hard to demonstrate one's individuality. When one says something different from what many say, one feels isolated. One is also reluctant to do what others don't do.' *Ken Takeuchi, Japan Alternative News for Justice and New Culture, quoted in Kambayashi, 2006*

The growth of online communities may also be inhibited by government. In China, despite self-regulation by users (as is discussed in chapter 5), submissions by individuals are carefully scrutinized by video-clip social networking sites. The risks of not doing this are high: 'in the U.S. a naughty video might anger a few parents or religious groups; in China, a far tamer clip could spur censors to shut down your company' (Einhorn and Kharif, 2007). Responsible uploaders are rewarded and users themselves are keen to self-regulate—not wanting to see their communities closed down.

It is suggested that if some of these obstacles can be overcome:

'then a loose collection of professionals who share interest in a common topic but otherwise do not know one another or share task goals or incentives can develop a *rhythm of conversation* that allows them to develop sustainable interaction.' *Fayard and DeSanctis, 2005*

Irrespective of external barriers or obstacles, the reality is that *participation inequality* is an enduring characteristic of online communities. Kim suggested that those involved in online communities go through a journey with five key stages of involvement (Kim, 2000). They begin as visitors, become novices or 'newbies', then evolve into regulars, leaders, and finally elders. This is not an inevitable progression. So-called *lurkers* read but rarely participate in communities, although this may not be because of lack of experience: so-called 'constructive' lurkers only intervene with selective, well though-out comments. Nielsen proposes a 90:9:1 general rule: 90 per cent read, observe but do not participate; 9 per cent contribute from time to time; whilst just 1 per cent account for most contributions (Nielsen, 2006). More detailed analysis suggests that the proportion of lurkers may depend on the nature of the site. For example, health support distribution lists were found to have fewer (46 per cent) than software support lists (82 per cent) (Nonnecke and Preece, 2000). Nielsen reports that, in the (admittedly special) case of Wikipedia, as many as 99 per cent of users are simply observers: with just 1,000 people contributing two-thirds of the site's edits. The community socialization process tends to be moderated by self-appointed elders, a core group of motivated individuals who set the rules of engagement and will intervene to moderate what may be regarded as unacceptable or redundant postings. The evidence suggests that users prefer moderated communities of this kind to unmoderated ones (Wise et al., 2006).

### Activity box 4.3

**Tracking brand communities**

Identify two contrasting brands. Search for online communities or blogs which make mention of each brand. Categorize the kinds of feedback or commentary that you are able to find. Do the net results reflect broadly positive or negative attitudes?

The risk to firms who rely upon feedback from their online communities is that such feedback from the more voluble participants is likely to be wholly unrepresentative of their customer base as a whole. The ratio of response to non-response can be improved by:

- making it easier to contribute (clicking a rating, rather than contributing a message);
- allowing users to modify existing templates (such as Second Life avatars); and
- rewarding participants (through enhanced prestige such as reputation rankings).

Why might individuals wish to be involved in communities of this kind? According to Peter Kollock (Kollock, 1999) members of online communities may be motivated by three particular considerations, which are derived from *social exchange theory*. These range from:

- anticipated reciprocity (the willingness to draw upon the experience of others without feeling the need to immediately reciprocate); the potential for an

- enhanced reputation (allowing the provision of high quality information, prose, or technical details, or demonstrating a willingness to help others to contribute to one's prestige in the community); and a

- sense of efficacy (finding value and improved self-image in seeing the impact of one's actions).

For Rheingold, the opportunity to gain prestige or an enhanced reputation is one of the key motivators for contributors to discussion lists (Rheingold, 1993). For example, Amazon.com rewards its most prolific and highly regarded reviewers with 'top 100 reviewer' status. The top ranking position in 2009 was taken by Harriett Klausner, a former librarian from Pennsylvania with over 18,000 reviews to her credit who reads two books a day.[6]

A sense of efficacy can also be seen in the citizen activism which can result from online contributions. For example, South Korea's Ohmynews is said to have played a key role in the election of President Roh Moo-hyun in 2002. Similarly, reporting of an accident in which a US army tractor killed two Korean girls on the site by an eyewitness led to anti-US rioting (Watts, 2003).

## Information search and consumption

The use of electronic channels by consumers for information search and for transactional services has been long heralded. For example, commentators were predicting the arrival of electronic shopping as long ago as the 1960s (according to Burke, 1997). In 1980, Rosenberg and Hirschman presented some colourful scenarios of retailing without stores, although there were always caveats expressed about the real attractiveness of electronic channels to market for consumers:

> 'There is little reason to suspect that consumers will soon take to [new technologies] in large numbers and they offer marketers few, if any, tools for making their selling tasks easier. Nor do we believe that nonstore retailing will bring about the predicted revolution in retailing.' *Quelch and Takeuchi, 1981*

The kind of economic imperialism we reported in chapter 2 suggested that consumers would fundamentally change their behaviour in response to the opportunity presented by

---

6  http://amazon.com/gp/customer-reviews/top-reviewers.html/.

e-business technologies and that conventional intermediaries (notably retailers and other branch-based consumer service businesses) would no longer be necessary as a result. But does customer behaviour change when the Internet is used as a channel for commerce?

It is undoubtedly true that there has been a significant shift towards sales of goods and services through online channels in many developed markets, although the average penetration of conventional retail sales is still relatively small in most markets and the actual amount is hard to measure, since many multi-channel businesses will not keep accurate sales records by channel. Business-to-consumer e-commerce at $133bn is estimated to comprise only around 3.32 per cent of unadjusted US retail sales in 2008 (US Census Bureau, 2009). However, in the UK, estimates by analysts Forrester suggest that the equivalent figure for 2008 in the UK was £23.8bn, excluding travel, which is nearer 8.5 per cent of total retail sales (Bracewell-Lewis et al., 2009). As ever, averages can be misleading and it is important to understand the high degree of variability in the online penetration of retail sales between particular categories of goods. Categories which appeared most susceptible to online purchasing in the past have conventionally included electronic goods, computer hardware and software, but clothing/apparel and gifts have become important categories in recent years. (See for example the discussion of ASOS.com in Long case 6.1.)

New categories of digitized products have also emerged (notably audio, music, and video; but also information) capable of being directly downloaded, the introduction of which has transformed not just the economics of these product categories, as we discussed in Chapter 2, but also the attitudes and behaviour of consumers. For example, the early reaction of the music publishing industry in its legal pursuit of illicit downloading, argue Maltz and Chiapetta, transformed 'unauthorized copying' into 'fighting back' in the minds of many consumers (Maltz and Chiapetta, 2002).

Nevertheless, the current position is that whilst a number of changes have occurred in consumers' behaviour, extensive substitution of conventional means of shopping with online e-commerce, whilst significant in some sectors, has not so far become as widespread as commentators originally suggested at the height of the dot.com boom. What has changed is that consumers have become adept at deconstructing the buying process, using particular channels as appropriate to their needs. This has implications for retailers and other intermediaries who must seek to develop appropriate multi-channel strategies (Reynolds, 2003). Possible company strategies to address this emerging hybrid, multi-channel behaviour are discussed more fully in chapters 6 and 7.

The precise role of particular channels in a multi-channel environment is likely to be a result of the trade-off between the perceived negative aspects of conventional channels of consumption, which work to push consumers online, against the perceived attractions of the online experience:

- Push
  - poorer perceived accessibility and convenience of existing offline offers;
  - poorer perceived choice within conventional channels;
  - higher perceived prices within conventional channels;
  - safety concerns in offline environments (crime, terrorism).
- Pull
  - better perceived choice and prices online;
  - increased availability of digitalised products;

&ndash; Improved distribution and fulfilment services;

&ndash; cheaper costs of access—specifically broadband;

&ndash; increased consumer confidence in online transaction security;

&ndash; cumulative experience and word-of-mouth effects.

Just thinking of business-to-consumer e-commerce in terms of its direct effects on sales of products through conventional channels therefore gives an incomplete picture. Also, since statisticians have developed relatively narrow (and often different) definitions of what e-commerce entails, official data fail to capture the many indirect effects of the Internet on the buyer's decision-making process, ranging from the formation of attitudes about products pre-purchase, browsing as a search behaviour, formal product evaluations, and post-purchase experiences, all of which may differentially affect levels of customer satisfaction and future patronage.

> 'The actual value of transactions currently concluded online is dwarfed by the extraordinary influence the internet is exerting over purchases carried out in the offline world.' *Economist, 2004.*

### Online obstacles

The online environment itself still offers obstacles, or *need inhibitors*, which may act to deter consumers. Shoppers have a lifetime's experience of the offline world: they are comfortable with payment systems, they are aware of the risks of purchasing and are familiar, for example, with the process of returning unsatisfactory goods. For even the most experienced users, but particularly for new users, online environments can still be perceived as having higher risks. In 2004, popular concern was much more widespread than it is today:

> 'consumers sense there is a lack of respect for their rights and their safety online. Consumers are asked to pay for goods before they have seen them, and to hand over personal and financial details up front in an environment that they hear all the time harbours shady characters ...' *National Consumer Council, 2000*

In practice, whilst some consumer concerns have fallen from previously high levels, 63 per cent of US consumers (for example) remain 'very concerned' about identity theft and 53 per cent about loss of privacy (American Consumer Institute, 2009). And as chapter 5 will explore in more detail, some of the risks attached to the Internet for consumers are probably greater now than they were in 2004. Four particular types of risk can be identified amongst Internet consumers:

- *financial*: the risk of net loss of money to the customer;

- *product performance*: the risk that the product does not confirm to the customer's expectations, which is in turn linked to the problem that quality can often not be assessed online;

- *psychological*: concern over the disappointment, frustration, and shame that may result from an unfortunate purchase, and the lack of control some users perceive they have over the online environment; and the risk to

- *time and convenience*: which results from search and site navigation difficulties, as well as perceived or real delays in the fulfilment process.

Of these, financial risk is still the most significant factor (Forsythe and Shi, 2003).

As a result, online merchants must still take exceptional steps to reassure consumers over perceived risk and encourage their use of online resources. For example, auction site eBay has put into place a multi-layered system of checks and safeguards for its users, based around its Security and Resolution Center. (http://pages.ebay.com/securitycenter/) Here can be found tutorials (including interactive Q&A to test understanding), tips for buyers on how to 'buy safely', information on protection programmes, tools for stopping spoof emails and for reporting account theft. Key features of eBay's approach include:

- Seller Feedback: where buyers rate sellers and provide comments to other eBay users on their reliability and reputation;
- eBay Buyer Protection programme: policies protecting against items not received, or not corresponding to specifications;
- SafeHarbor programme: eBay staff actively monitoring the service for scams and fraud, supported by self-reporting by users;
- Escrow service partners: an escrow service for items typically of $500 or more, which involves collecting, holding, and sending a buyer's money to a seller once the buyer receives and approves the item from the seller;
- SquareTrade dispute resolution process: use of a commercial partner (http://www.squaretrade.com) to mediate disputes between buyers and sellers.

## Information search

At the information search stage of the buyer's decision-making process, the Internet plays an increasingly significant role even if, subsequently, the consumer chooses to buy offline. Consumers already have several ways of accessing information before making purchasing decisions:

- personal sources (friends, acquaintances and family);
- commercial sources (including conventional mass media and in-store browsing);
- third-party reports (for example, 'What Product?' or Consumers' Association buying guides);
- personal experience (from previous purchases).

In this context, online retailers' websites, manufacturer's websites, Internet-based search, price comparison, shopping comparison, and social shopping engines have emerged as important consumer decision support tools. In the US, 54 per cent of online users in 2006 classed themselves as 'informed consumers', reporting that they regularly researched online, especially for complex products, whilst subsequently purchasing offline. Technology consultancy Forrester found that as early as 2006 as many online Europeans used a retailer's website to browse for information on mobile phones, audio devices, and leisure travel as used regular branches (Forrester, 2007). For others, a store visit is still seen as being a necessary part of the information search process, but they may no longer find it necessary to make the purchase there: the so-called 'showroom effect'. Such free-riding behaviour poses a significant challenge to retailers without properly thought-through multi-channel strategies.

---

### Activity box 4.4

#### Channelling

Think about the last three discretionary purchases you made of contrasting goods and services. Sketch out the decision-making process you used to make your eventual purchases. What mix of channels and sources of information did you employ? Were these different from the last time you made this kind of purchase?

---

From the consumer's point of view, the best search engines at the information search stage of the buying decision-making process simplify the process of finding the right vendor and present product specifications, price, and a feedback rating. Rather like virtual communities, such engines benefit from scale. PriceGrabber.com claims to connect some 26m 'active, qualified and ready to buy shoppers on a monthly basis' with nearly 13,000 merchants (http://www.pricegrabber.com) offering these merchants access to an attractive younger, well educated, and affluent segment. The market is rapidly evolving and consolidating, but Table 4.4 provides a listing of selected services.

An overlap between commercial shopping search and social networking can be found in the form of social shopping sites such as Crowdstorm (http://www.crowdstorm.com), (which seeks to show the buzz around products), ShopWiki (http://www.shopwiki.com), and Zebo (http://www.zebo.com), which claims to be the world's largest repository of things people own. Users can ask friends for advice about products that they own, offer goods for sale, and talk about their product experiences. Comparison shopping engine Smarter.com (http://www.smarter.com) has introduced video reviews into its shopping search listings.

Peer-to-peer recommendation is an especially powerful mechanism in markets where products and services are of high economic or symbolic value or are infrequently purchased. Travel is a typical example, where independent travellers often want to visit new destinations but, by definition, have no experience of an area or its facilities and may have concerns over the objectivity of formal marketing material. In addition to over 5m formally structured traveller reviews, often with candid photographs of venues, Expedia's TripAdvisor service hosts a web forum, in which two-thirds of topics posted are replied to within 24 hours by fellow travellers. Respondents are often self-appointed experts or residents living within a particular area (http://www.tripadvisor.com).

Peer-to-peer communication is a form of so-called 'electronic word-of-mouth' or e-WOM. E-WOM can be defined as:

**Table 4.4  Categorizing shopping comparison sites**

| Rank Feb-09 | Rank Feb-07 | Web site | Online Since | Change |
|---|---|---|---|---|
| 1 | 3 | froogle.google.com(*) | 2001 | 2 |
| 2 | 1 | shopping.yahoo.com(*) | 1995 | −1 |
| 3 | new | live.com | 2008 | new |
| 4 | 2 | shopping.msn.com(*) | 1994 | −2 |
| 5 | 4 | shopping.aol.com(*) | 1995 | −1 |
| 6 | 5 | shopper.cnet.com(*) | 1996 | −1 |
| 7 | 6 | nextag.com | 1998 | −1 |
| 8 | 7 | shopping.com | 1997 | −1 |
| 9 | 8 | bizrate.com | 1996 | −1 |
| 10 | 11 | shoplocal.com | 1998 | 1 |
| 11 | 13 | shopzilla.com | 2002 | 2 |
| 12 | 27 | pronto.com | 2006 | 15 |
| 13 | 9 | pricegrabber.com | 1999 | −4 |
| 14 | 14 | smarter.com | 1998 | 0 |
| 15 | 12 | epinions.com | 1999 | −3 |
| 16 | 21 | thefind.com | 2006 | 5 |
| 17 | 10 | dealtime.com | 1998 | −7 |
| 18 | 28 | shopwiki.com | 2004 | 10 |
| 19 | 18 | become.com | 2004 | −1 |
| 20 | 15 | pricerunner.com | 1999 | −5 |

Note: (*) Note: traffic stats for these sites are aggregates of all traffic to the top domain (for example, Yahoo.com or Google.com) and thus cannot be used to judge how popular this particular price comparison service is.

'Any positive or negative statement made by potential, actual, or former customers about a product or company, which is made available to a multitude of people and institutions via the Internet.' *Hennig-Thurau et al., 2004*

**Figure 4.2**  On the Internet nobody knows you're a dog

**Table 4.5  Types of electronic word-of-mouth**

| Type of E-WOM | User characteristics |
|---|---|
| **1. Quasi-Spontaneous**<br>Initiated and/or carried out by individual consumers in web environments created by marketers (e.g., corporate websites) | **1. Opinion Leaders/Influencers**<br>Product evaluations are provided by self-designated experts on opinions web sites (e.g., www.epinions.com; www.crowdstorm.co.uk)<br><br>**2. Early Adopters**<br>Early adopters of books and music provide reviews and ratings of the books and music for other consumers to consider (e.g. Amazon reviews) |
| **2. Independent or Third Party-Sponsored**<br>Initiated and/or carried out by individual consumers in web environments created by special interest groups, professional associations, and/or organizations for purposes other than selling products. | **1. Opinion Leaders/Influencers**<br>http://www.ask.com provides access to a variety of 'experts' who provide answers to users' questions.<br><br>**2. Professional associations**<br>Unbiased information about a wide range of different online products and providers is available to consumers at http://www.consumerreports.org.<br><br>**3. Surrogate Consumers**<br>Input to consumer decision making is provided by other consumers who charge by the minute for their responses to users' questions on www.keen.com, or www.liveperson.com |
| **3. Corporate-Sponsored**<br>Initiated by marketers, but carried out by 'individuals' who are paid and/or otherwise motivated to 'spread the word' about a product or company for the purposes or selling its products or promoting the company. | **1. Co-browsing/'show and tell'**<br>A company sales representative, or virtual advisor tool, explicitly co-navigates the corporate web site with the customer or prospect via a shared browser. This may be achieved via a remote support session or call-back.software. Examples include http://www.gotoassist.com, www.intouch800.co.uk and http://www.pageshare.com.<br><br>**2. Buzz marketers**<br>Marketing representatives covertly assume an identity appropriate to their target audience within online environments and pitch their products and services. |

The categories of e-WOM appear relatively distinctive in Table 7.5, but sometimes it may be difficult for the end user to know whether the recommender is genuine, or masquerading as an independent customer or expert. This is because, as the famous cartoon suggests, 'on the Internet, nobody knows you're a dog'. Chapter 7 considers the ways in which marketers may exploit e-WOM through the use of, for example, viral marketing techniques.

### Product and service evaluation

Consumers currently use a range of factors in formally evaluating products and services, a ranked and weighted set of attributes often referred to as their *preference structure*. The availability of the Internet does not change the need for a preference structure, but it may serve to change the position of certain factors in the ranking, depending on the individual consumer, the type of purchase, and the context for that purchase. For example, Sinha (2000) suggested that increased cost transparency online would lead to a series of changed behaviours from consumers in relation to their perception of prices in other channels. It would, he suggested, make shoppers considerably more rational, by:

- eroding the consumer's risk premium (making it easier to take a chance on a product);

- making searches more efficient (through the growth of search engines);

- making the price floor more easily visible (through the activities of auction and *reverse auction* sites in educating consumers over what might be the 'lowest' acceptable price for a product or service of a certain quality);

- challenging companies' segmented pricing strategies (because they are more visible to consumers); and ultimately,

- changing consumers' perceptions of the cost of products and services (making them more reluctant to pay a price premium).

But regular surveys consistently tell us that behaviour in reality is not so rational and that non-price factors such as convenience, quick delivery, and more choice can remain important within preference structures. For example, convenience and ease of access may be as, or more, important than price for certain categories of goods and services:

> 'The time and browsing benefits of online shopping are likely to be manifested in more positive perceptions of convenience.' *Szymanski and Hise, 2000*

The early evidence on the importance of price had been unclear. Many researchers did see on average lower prices online than offline for identical goods, notably books and CDs (Brynjolfsson and Smith, 2000). But they also noted similar price ranges (dispersion between the highest and lowest prices) to those prevailing offline, contrary to what the *law of one price* might suggest. They blamed this dispersion on two main factors. Consumers were too lazy, impatient, or poorly informed to search beyond the first two or three sites. Secondly, consumers showed a lack of trust in new online retail brands offering the same products at lower prices. And this effect has persisted. For example, recent work has shown that high mark-ups online are, just as with store-based propositions, associated with higher quality (Rabinovich et al., 2008).

> 'Many economists expected online price comparisons to drive down prices, but retailers are deadlocked, resulting in fluctuating prices, which vary each day.' *Gatti et al., 2004*

More recent work has suggested that it is marketers themselves who have helped this process, by creating the obfuscation necessary to prevent a levelling down of prices, through line extension; re-packaging, and re-launches of products (Reynolds, 2003). Very few products are truly homogeneous (and even when they are, many companies bundle information or services to make comparison and evaluation more complex). Simply put, consumers find it difficult to find and compare like with like in many situations. It is not in most marketers' interest for this situation to change.

While habit and long-established brand preferences can also play a role in product and service evaluation, any kind of price awareness nevertheless puts pressure on retail brands. Whilst consumers' confidence in online buying has increased, what has also become clear from recent research is that online consumers still use brand as a proxy for supplier credibility in areas ranging from shipping reliability to after-sales service (Burt and Sparks, 2003; Reynolds, 2002; 2003).

## Satisfaction and loyalty

Satisfaction with the online experience has been described as the outcome of three factors: the *quality of products and services*, the *quality of the related information* and the *convenience of navigation within a website*—i.e., website design (Szymanski and Hise, 2000; Anderson and Srinivasan, 2003). A positive relationship exists between customers' willingness to revisit a website and their level of satisfaction online (Anderson and Srinivasan, 2003). When the customer makes a choice to buy through one of a number of competing marketing channels or indeed from between a range of alternative providers, then the decision over whether to change their behaviour from their last purchasing act will be influenced by their evaluation of their experience of that last purchasing act against their preferences. This difference between what was expected and what was felt after the purchase has been made has been called *post purchase dissonance* in the marketing literature. If the dissonance between what was expected and what was experienced is too great, the customer will be open to defect. A negligible or acceptable level of dissonance will result in a retained and potentially loyal customer.

But there is evidence that the Internet offers a much less robust medium for customer retention than that found in other channels. The web is perhaps more rational and less emotional than marketers might like. Some suggestion of this emerges from Figure 4.5,

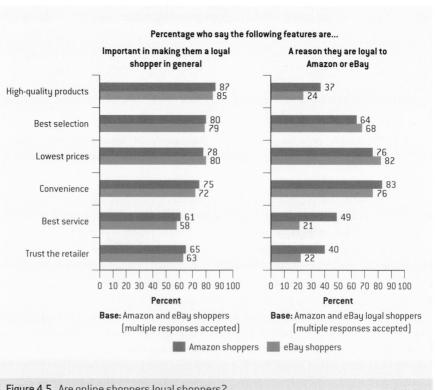

**Figure 4.5** Are online shoppers loyal shoppers?

which shows what constitutes the basis of loyalty amongst Amazon and eBay users, both in general terms and in respect of Amazon and eBay: a much narrower and arguably more vulnerable set of factors (mainly price and convenience) appear to determine customers' loyalty to these two online services.

## Short case 4.3

### Zlio: social commerce

Anyone can now become an online retailer. The Zlio service first appeared online in 2005 (http://www.zlio.com). Launched initially in France by an Israeli technical team, its goal is to create 'the largest salesforce in the world' by inviting signed-up members to create their own stores, stocked not with their own products but with those from the Zlio catalogue of over 6m items. One of Zlio's founders, Jeremie Berrebi, had early success with a news and information aggregator, Net2One, founded as early as 1997 but now sold to the Presse Plus Group (http://www.net2one.com). Leveraging the aggregation experience of Net2One, and working with co-founders David Levy and Jean Guetta made it possible to raise €4.2m in funding in 2007 to expand the business into Britain, France, Germany, and the US. By the beginning of 2009, Zlio hosted 330,000 stores, with members able to stock up to 1,000 branded products and open up to twenty different stores each. The business model used by Zlio is a mixture of CPA (commission per acquisition) and CPC (commission per click). Where a seller makes a sale, a commission can be paid which may vary up to 10 per cent. (For example, footwear retailer Yoox.com offers 4 per cent whilst health retailer Holland & Barrett offers 9 per cent.) Orders are fulfilled by the originating merchants. The social networking aspects of this service are of particular interest. In 2006, this site began allowing shops on its platforms to connect to one another, as 'partners', in a similar manner to friends on Facebook. Members can also vote for their favourite shops, which leads to those with most votes rising through the ranks. This sounds curious: surely, we might think, doing this simply favours competitors. Recent research has shown that linking shops in this way did increase revenue for the whole marketplace, but the benefit was quite small. In part, the research concluded, this was because many of those who were partnered did not reciprocate, leading to 'dead ends' and free-riders (Toubier and Stephen, 2009).

*Question*

Is there a conflict between social networking and commerce?

# The social consequences of e-business technologies

The concept of the 'digital divide' has come into common usage as policy-makers in particular have become concerned over differential access to e-business technologies amongst both citizens and between different types of firm. Even in markets as apparently developed as the US, the percentage of adults online appeared to have stabilized at around 75 per cent by 2008, suggesting that some 50m US adults did not have access to or choose not to use the Internet (see Figure 4.6). The Internet 'have-nots' tend to be concentrated within particular social, demographic, and economic groups: those in lowest income households, those over 65 (59 per cent) and those with less than a high school education (60 per cent) were much less likely to be online (Pew Internet & American Life Project, 2009; Madden, 2006). Across Europe, 25 per cent and 21 per cent of households without broadband Internet access claimed that this was because the cost of equipment or access costs were too high (European Commission, 2008b).

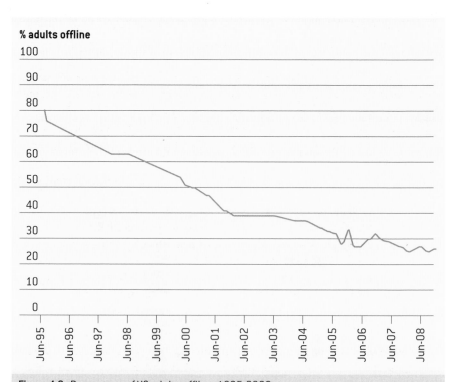

**Figure 4.6**  Percentage of US adults offline, 1995-2009

Note: Definition of 'online' changes during the period. See http://www.pewinternet.org/trends/Internet_Adoption_4.26.06.pdf

However, the concept of digital divide is not a straightforward one and has become contested. Recent attempts to measure its extent have shown that the position is much more complex and dynamic than simply thinking in terms of a split between 'haves' and 'have-nots'. At one level, the assumption that the simple dissemination of digital technology can bring about desirable social change (so-called **technological determinism**) is open to question, according to Warschauer (2003). An alternative paradigm sees technology as a 'site of struggle', where:

> 'Ultimately, the Internet is best understood as creating a new set of relationships and places, rather than as a high-technology tool. It is one more global arena in which struggles over the distribution of resources, power and information will be fought out.'
> *Wiseman, 1998*

In some respects, it is therefore not surprising to find that, other things being equal, it is those without economic and social power who are electronically disenfranchised within market economies. But in considering the contribution of e-business technologies to society, it is also important to distinguish between:

- improvements in the level of access to digital technology infrastructure; and
- increases in the ability of individuals to use such technologies to improve quality of life (for citizens) or contribute to firm performance (for companies).

Clearly, these are very different objectives and seeking to achieve one through the other may not be straightforward. Indeed, 'the worst failures occur when people attempt to address complex social problems with a narrow focus on the provision of equipment' (Warschauer, 2003).

A number of measures have been developed to assess the status of national economies in relation to e-business technologies. For example, the ICT-Development Index (IDI) is employed by the International Telecommunications Union. It is derived from ten indicators which seek to 'measure the overall ability of individuals in a country to access <u>and</u> use new ICTs' (ITU, 2009). The new ITU index is superior to other indices in its country coverage, measurement of ICT, and in its focus upon a richer mix of social as well as infrastructural indicators, including ICT access, use, and skills (Figure 4.7).

There are very different levels of performance between the 183 economies tracked by the Index. The Index's performance over time also challenges some of the preconceptions in this area: for example, that it is developed markets which are currently making the fastest progress in their use and application of e-business technologies. Whilst the divide persists between those economies that already had very high levels of ICT and the rest of the world, there has been some catching up by the so-called medium-to-low countries. Some of the countries with the highest growth rates are less developed—although, of course, starting from a low base. However, the survey suggests:

> 'While Western Europe and Eastern Asia have made significant gains on the IDI, Eastern Europe is the region that has improved the most its ICT levels between 2002 and 2007, with the most dynamic growth in the IDI of all regions.' *ITU, 2009*

**Technological Determinism** A view that technology determines behaviour. Attributed to sociologist and economist Thorstein Veblen in 1921. Critics suggest that it is technology working within a complex social structure which determines change in behaviour.

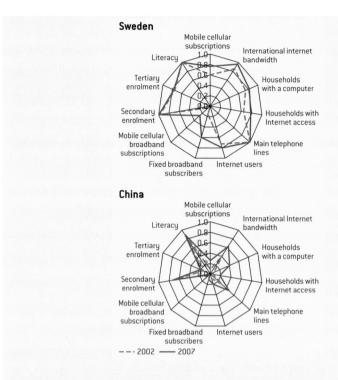

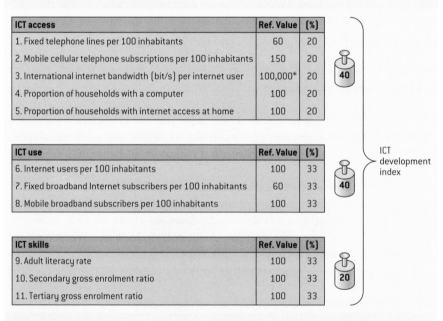

**Figure 4.7** ICT-Development Index, selected markets & index weighting, 2007. a. a. Selected markets showing IDI index component changes 2002–07. b. ICT Development Index: weighting of indicators

**Note:** *This corresponds to a log value of 5, which was used in the normalization step.

## Short case 4.4

### Romania

The ITU's ICT Development Index shows that Romania moved up 14 places from sixtieth position in 2002 to forty-sixth in 2007. Indeed, the Index put Romania into the second-highest ('upper') category of its list of economies by 2007. The period coincides with significant investments made by the country in the period prior and immediately following its accession to the EU in 2007. The country's telecoms sector has been deregulated, expanded, and modernized over the past eighteen years, building upon a substantial base of professionally skilled engineers and computer scientists. A positive change in GDP took place, which averaged some 6 per cent per annum over the period 2002–2007. The Romanian Ministry of Communications and Information Technology has demonstrated a strong commitment to e-business and e-government and has set out four objectives for the country's ICT strategy during this period:

- increasing the competitiveness of the Romanian economy;
- consolidating the ICT sector;
- increasing business and consumer motivation for using new technologies; and
- improving citizens' living conditions.[7]

For example, in 2004 the Romanian government started a 'Computers at Home' programme, targeted at the poorest households. Euro 200 vouchers are made available via schools, with household eligibility determined by regional inspectors. Computers come bundled with software and relevant curriculum material to encourage e-learning. Over 150,000 households have benefited from the programme. Four ITU Index components in Romania experienced the most growth during the period:

»

7   Ministry of Communications and Information Technology, http://www.items.fr/IMG/pdf/Zsolt_Nagy-OD1.pdf.

- ICT access via computers in the home increased by 30 per cent.

- Mobile phone penetration increased from 23 to 107 per 100 inhabitants.

- International Internet bandwidth increased significantly.

- Tertiary educational enrolment nearly doubled during the period (with some 7,000 ICT graduates per year now being produced).

However, there has been recent concern that the Romanian economy's rapid growth, and continued public sector spending in the context of the economic downturn of 2008–2009, will lead to an unsustainably high current account deficit.

*Question*

What are the risks and benefits of governments actively intervening to encourage citizens to participate in the information society?

## The impact of e-business technologies on social relationships and communities

The Internet and other e-business technologies affect the ways in which people communicate. Because communication is the mechanism people use to develop and maintain social relationships, there has been considerable discussion over the extent to which Internet adoption has deleterious effects both in relation to people's daily lives as well as in the workplace. However, the evidence is not clear and the commentators are polarized in their views. On the one hand are those who propose that Internet users will become more isolated as a result of their time online displacing other activities, which are likely to have been social ones (Nie and Erbring, 2002). Particular concern has been expressed over a potential increase in social isolation as some survey respondents reported feeling that using the Internet had reduced their time with friends and family, or their ability or willingness to attend events outside the home, thus weakening local community participation.

> 'The more hours people use the Internet, the less time they spend in contact with real human beings … This is an early trend that, as a society, we really need to monitor carefully.' *Nie and Erbring, 2002*

In 1998, social psychologists at Carnegie-Mellon University established the HomeNet project, designed as a longitudinal study of the Internet's use at home (Shklovski et al., 2004). Even though interpersonal communication via email is the most important application of the Internet for most people, over the course of three studies, spanning eight years, they concluded that:

- greater use of the Internet was associated with declines in the size of participants' social networks, declines in communication within the family and, for teenagers, declines in social support; in particular that

- the links between communications media were asymmetric: that is to say, visits drove more email communication and phone calls drive more visits, but email drives neither phone calls nor visits; and that

- greater use of the Internet was associated with increases in loneliness and symptoms of depression.

In relation to work, too, there has been concern expressed over the self-reinforcing link between technology and workaholism (Porter and Kakabadse, 2006). The higher productivity environment facilitated by new information technologies puts pressure on employees, but equally can facilitate the development of behavioural addiction to technology. In the context of the workplace, so-called *technosis*, it is suggested, is a consequence of belief that technology such as email should always be available and is the only way of getting something done. When work activities spill over into home life, then addictive aspects of digital technology usage can have undesirable effects on families and relationships. For example, the growing dependence on smart phones and portable data assistants (PDAs), has led to similar concerns:

> 'Communications technology has always had the power to intrude into everyday life, leaving a person who is present but not part of the conversation feeling like an outsider. The BlackBerry takes this feeling of alienation to a new level: hidden under the desk but glanced at constantly, it sends a message that the user has his or her mind on more interesting things.' *Waters, 2005*

It might, of course, be argued that e-business technologies simply serve to accentuate existing pathologies: 'I was addicted to porn before there was an Internet' suggests the cartoon of one man talking to another in a bar (Vey, 2004 quoted in Wellman and Hogan, 2004.) This point of view is borne out in a wide-ranging review of the evidence of 'Internet addiction':

> 'There is no doubt that some Internet users develop problematic behavior. Most of these are probably premorbidly vulnerable people who often have a history of impulse control and addictive disorders, and whose abnormal behavior is a response to specific online content and activities. It is unlikely that "Internet addiction", as a disorder in its own right, exists.' *Yellowlees and Marks, 2007*

Others have argued that the impact of Internet usage on individuals' daily lives is more complex and much more fluid, and potentially significantly more positive. For example, *media substitution theory* suggests that Internet usage may simply displace other media, either in terms of overall or proportion of time allocated to an activity (because there are a finite number of hours in the day), or because of functional superiority of new media over old (where the displacement arises because the new media is superior in quality, cheaper, or easier to access than the old). According to some (but not all) studies, much of the initial increase in time spent online in the US—emailing, contributing to online discussion lists, or simply browsing the Internet—directly displaced time spent watching television (Kaye and Johnson, 2003). The official evidence in the US appears to confirm the growth in consumer Internet usage, but not a decline in TV viewing (although as Figure 4.8 shows, TV viewing hours in the US have been relatively stable since 2005, whilst overall media usage has continued to grow). But in every other country surveyed in a recent international study, broadband usage appears linked to a reported decline in time spent viewing conventional television. This is most apparent by age: for example, TV viewing by the 10 to 15 and 16 to 24 age groups in the UK has fallen by roughly 10 per cent from 2003–2008, partly offset by increases among older adults (DCMS, 2009). As ever, reality may be more complex than aggregate studies suggest. Whilst avid consumers of news may read newspapers less frequently because of the ready availability of online

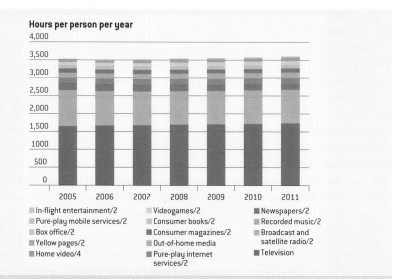

**Figure 4.8**  Trends in media consumption, US 2005-2011

Notes: 1. Can include concurrent use of media, such as watching television and reading e-mail simultaneously. Does not include media use at work.

2. Online and mobile use and spending on traditional media platforms, such as downloaded music, newspaper web sites, e-books, cable modems, online video of television programs and Internet radio were included in the traditional media segment, not in pure-play Internet services or pure-play mobile content. Pure-play Internet services and pure-play mobile content included telecommunications access, such as DSL, Internet-only Websites such as Yahoo!, GameSpy, eHarmony, and mobile-only services, such as MobiTV or text messaging services from telecommunication providers.

3. Telemundo and Univsion affiliates included in independent and public stations. Pay-per-view, video-on-demand, interactive channels home shopping and audio-only feeds included in premium cable, satellite & RBOC TV services.

4. Playback of prerecorded DVD discs and VHS casettes only.

news services such as CNN.com or Al-Jazeera.net, which may be functionally superior to a daily newspaper, they may still buy and read magazines for more leisurely analysis of current affairs. Some offline and online activities may also occur simultaneously: so-called 'stacking' involves between 70 per cent (Italy) and 83 per cent (Japan) of consumers claiming to access the Internet while watching TV. In the UK the figure is 74 per cent (OFCOM, 2008).

## Activity box 4.5

### What do you do with your time?

Professional market research firms spend millions tracking use of media usage time. Try this yourself to see to what extent your own experience matches national and international trends. Keep track of your media usage (TV, radio, online, newspapers, cinema, mobile, etc.). There are several software programmes around to do this, including http://www.rescuetime.com, http://www.dandelife.com, and life balance software, including Llama Graphics Life Balance (http://www.llamagraphics.com). Or you can simply use an Excel spreadsheet or a paper and pencil!

Some online activities may be differently related to the formation and maintenance of *social ties* than others. While some activities (for example, email and chat) seem positively correlated with the generation and maintenance of social ties, other activities (for example, web surfing) appear negatively associated with them (Zhao, 2006). We can also distinguish between the quality of these ties: between *core* social ties (those people who are 'very close' to the individual) and *significant* social ties those who are only 'somewhat close', but more than casual acquaintances). The evidence suggests that going online increases the number of significant ties and casual acquaintances more than core ties (Boase et al., 2006). It has also been suggested that young people will often prefer to use communication media such as the Internet and mobile phones to communicate because these give them more control over their interactions with others than they would have if, say, communicating via voice calls using the telephone or face-to-face (Madell and Muncer, 2007). The asynchronous nature of email, text messaging, and instant messaging in particular allowed them time to stop and think before giving a response.

Email has also proved a useful mechanism within societies where other forms of communication are not always available for particular groups. For example, more Qatari women now use email than men. As a result email is increasingly becoming an agency for cultural and social change: 'Arab women … are finding the internet serves as a convenient window on the world in an otherwise male-dominated society' (Al-Hail, 2005). Other groups within society may feel excluded by the increasing dominance of email as a preferred mechanism for written communication. Poor software design and inappropriate interfaces, combined with lack of experience and support can lead to older people being 'technologically alienated' (Morris, 1992).

As the range of possible activities that the Internet itself offers continues to evolve, it has been suggested that the use by individuals of social networks and the enormously varied opportunities they create for exchange makes it possible for a form of *social capital* to be created (Putnam, 2000). We can see how this kind of social capital works in practice in a number of instances. In the case of Wikipedia, for example, would-be administrators, or sysops, are regular users who have been able to establish trust amongst the existing group of editors through their responsible contributions to the online encyclopedia over a prolonged period. Consensus amongst the editors determines successful requests.[8] Members of discussion lists and chat rooms reward regular and highly regarded contributors with ranking status and especially valuable contributions to social networking sites such as YouTube (http://www.youtube.com) are starred. Expedia's TripAdvisor website (http://www.tripadvisor.com—'get the truth then go'), which operates in the US, UK and six other markets, includes 'goLists'—'insider' itineraries of where to stay and what to visit in particular places. The company summarizes the reasons for contributing a 'goList' as including:

- Access to millions of TripAdvisor travellers, 'people looking for the inside scoop, the whole story, the truth. Nobody wants to rely solely on a travel brochure'.

- Feature placement on TripAdvisor destination pages.

- Your name in lights! 'Other travellers can vote on your list; the best lists will continue to float to the top and we'll feature those best lists more broadly across the site.'

---

8  6 http://en.wikipedia.org/wiki/Wikipedia:Requests_for_adminship.

Wellman suggests that this leads to *networked individualism* where, he argues, rather than relying on a single conventional physical community for social capital, individuals are now able actively to seek out a variety of far-flung people and resources which are relevant to their needs at a particular time (Wellman, 2001). This is a beneficial process. Surveys undertaken by the Pew Internet & American Life Project conclude that seeking career advice, followed by helping another person with a major illness or medical condition, followed by advice on school choice for a child were the three most significant 'major moments' to prompt use of social networks (Boase et al., 2006). Contracting a rare, serious, or debilitating illness provides a powerful trigger to seek the support of others. Countless support fora have been established linked to both physical and psychological illness. Sometimes these are related to long-standing associations that have found electronic networks an ideal way of increasing their reach of affected individuals. For example, the Leukemia and Lymphoma Society, founded in 1949 and which is now the world's largest voluntary health organization dedicated to funding blood cancer research, education, and patient services, offers award-winning website services (http://www.lls.org). These include the extensive counselling and support bulletin board system, *First Connection*, which links newly diagnosed patients to a peer volunteer who has experienced a similar diagnosis; *Meet the Doctor* programmes; teleconferences and webcasts. Sometimes these are 'home-grown' grassroots websites which attract patronage and support through word of mouth.

Some have questioned whether social capital created in this way is as rich and as rewarding as that generated through face-to-face social activities. Putnam (2000) suggests that such virtual socialization is akin to 'bowling alone', with digital media displacing important civic and social institutions and creating 'pseudo communities'. Others argue that virtual communities and environments, such as Second Life (http://www.secondlife.com) discussed in Long case 4.2, can provide different but equivalent value. They employ the concept of the *third place*, originally developed to refer to the bricks-and-mortar places in which individuals can gather to socialize informally beyond the workplace and the home (hence a 'third place'). It is suggested that 'by providing spaces for social interaction and relationships … MMOs have the capacity to function as one form of a new "third place" for informal sociability' (Steinkuehler and Williams, 2006).

## Long case 4.1

### Twitter

The exponential growth of interest in real-time short messaging service Twitter over a two-year period shows the way in which a social networking e-business technology can capture the public imagination. What are you doing right now? Can you express yourself in 140 characters? The first prototype of Twitter was built by a US team led by Jack Dorsey in two weeks in March 2006 and was launched publicly in August of 2006. The company was incorporated in 2007. Dorsey was simply interested in learning what his friends were doing, and 'following' their activities. This very simple application commanded 7m unique » visitors at the beginning of 2009, from President Obama, with over 600,000 followers (http://twitter.com/BarackObama), to British comedian Stephen Fry, with 360,000, and is becoming part of the warp and weft of a networked society. During the terror attacks in Mumbai in 2008, some 80 tweets every 5 seconds were being posted from the city, providing eyewitness accounts, pleas for medical assistance and blood donors and updates on casualty numbers. 'Mumbai is not a city under attack as much as it is a social media experiment in action' (Busari, 2008). The Twitter name currently generates over 300m hits on Google. Some celebrities even employ a team of people to keep their tweets up to date.

By: Luc Legay. «My Social network 1st nov 2007» Work under Licence Creative Commons +Attribution-Share Alike 2.0 Generic

Twitter is 'device agnostic': that is to say it accepts input from SMS, web, mobile web, instant message, or from third party software projects suitably programmed. Sending and receiving Twitter status updates from a mobile device is clearly a very appealing feature: The Nielsen Company reported that 735,000 people accessed the website from their mobile phones at the beginning of 2009. Twitter is still in 'not-for-profit' mode, although a Japanese service is supported by advertising revenues:

> 'Twitter has many appealing opportunities for generating revenue but we are holding off on implementation for now because we don't want to distract ourselves from the more important work at hand which is to create a compelling service and great user experience for millions of people around the world. While our business model is in a research phase, we spend more money than we make.' *web site*    »

This means that the company is also listening to its users and constantly experimenting with new features. Recent innovations include the ability to send messages directly to members using the '@' feature (rather than broadcasting to the world), or to refer directly to members ('mentions'), a mobile site (m.twitter.com); and generating lists of 'suggested users' for members to follow.

The service itself has also been spawned into specialist interest areas. For example, an ExecTweets service (sponsored by Microsoft) allows participants to follow the commentary of top business executives (http://exectweets.com). A specialist site was developed (now closed) to focus on the 2008 US Presidential election. Nor are these applications limited to the end consumer or citizen: the enterprise cloud computing service Salesforce.com has developed Saleforce CRM for Twitter. The platform allows brand owners and companies to track their presence in the informal forum between Twitter participants, building upon the firm's 'Service Cloud' software-as-a-service proposition, which is an online 'customer community' package (http://www.salesforce.com/servicecloud). There are also a great many third-party organizations seeking to capitalize on the 'tweetstream', ranging from small-scale API projects to major brands. For example, Twitpic allows users to share photos (http://twitpic.com), whilst PespiCo has sponsored a visualization of the tweetstream emerging from the SXSW music, film, and media conference and festival in Texas: the PepsiCo SXSW Zeitgeist (http://pepsicozeitgeist.com/).

*Questions:*

1. 'Twitter is the new SMS.' Do you agree?

2. 'What we are losing is editing . . . Every person is his or her own publisher and/or her own editor or her own reporter. The discipline that should go with being able to communicate is gone' (Daniel Schorr, news analyst). Discuss.

3. How might the Twitter business model be monetized?

## Long case 4.2

### Second Life

During 2007, the virtual world Second Life experienced an explosion of interest as companies sought to understand and exploit innovative social networking and associated consumer behaviours. Leading Internet businesspeople at the Davos Economic Summit were interviewed virtually by the Reuters Second Life bureau chief. More recently, commentators have questioned the commercial potential of virtual worlds. Indeed, the Reuters virtual bureau closed its doors in March 2009. The virtual worlds phenomenon provides an excellent illustration of the extent of uncertainty which exists over the commercial potential of so-called Web 2.0 activities. Heralded as 'the next generation of the Internet' by IBM, recall that Second Life is not a role-playing game, but is rather at heart a graphical chatroom in which individuals interact as avatars:

'At first, I spent a lot of time in the water. I was not alone in my incompetence. Everyone was walking into walls, attempting to talk to you with their backs turned, and gesturing inappropriately.' *Moulds, 2007*

At the beginning of 2009, the world claimed 16.7m registered residents, although active visitors are more in the order of 1m (logged in during the previous month). Indeed, it is estimated that only 10 per cent of unique users have logged in for 40 hours or more and the highest recorded number of residents simultaneously online was 77,000 at the beginning of 2009. The average age on the adult grid is 33, and over half of the most active residents come from the US, France, and Germany. But a key differentiating feature of the Second Life environment is the monetization of the world. Residents may purchase virtual land with real money, create their own virtual goods and services (including clothes, works or art, buildings, and financial advice), and sell both. Land costs from approximately $117 (for 512 sq m) to $15,000 for a region, plus annual land tax. The LindeX exchange permits residents to buy and sell the Linden dollar and therefore realize real » economic benefits from their online activities. In 2009, residents spent $361m on virtual goods and services.[9]

One of the key attractions of virtual worlds such as Second Life to companies is clearly therefore the opportunity to research a new marketing platform, offering new possibilities for segmentation. In one of the early examples in 2006, Toyota's youth-friendly US brand, Scion, opened a dealership called 'Scion City', quickly followed by Pontiac and Nissan. At Scion City it is possible not only to buy one of the real and somewhat box-like Scions, but a virtual version to drive round in on the roads of Second Life. The Chicago motor show saw several product launches simultaneously at the show and in Second Life.

Second Life's big attraction to business is that it opens the door to a highly desirable young demographic—the cutting-edge pacesetters of Generation Y. They are affluent, computer-literate, media-aware—and for business that is both a draw and a dilemma. For these idiosyncratic consumers hate being talked down to. There is a premium on whatever is subversively creative and oddball. Any whiff of conventional corporate hard sell spells commercial death. Companies have to work that much more smartly to raise a smirk from the sophisticated young denizens of Second Life with their 'already been there, got the t-shirt' attitude.

Ploughmann (2006) suggests that companies buy space in Second Life for reasons other than to market their brand in a new environment (as have Dell, Adidas, and BBC amongst many others). They do it also:

- in order to be seen as innovative (politicians and political parties, such as the French Front National, and US members of congress);
- in order to connect with their alumni or with other communities (the Government of Sweden has an 'embassy' to Second Life, and the charity Save the Children offers residents the chance to buy a digitized yak);
- as a novel internal teleconferencing and social tool (IBM runs business meetings on its own island); or
- to experiment with products or environments that are difficult to replicate in 'real life' (Dutch reality TV show producers Endemol developed a virtual reality equivalent of their 'Big Brother' concept).

But companies and organizations don' have it all their own way. Residents have been generally unimpressed by presence of big brands which fail to think through the implications of a virtual presence, preferring home-grown 'in-world' brands. Some residents have also become vocal and demonstrative in the face of the growth of particular kinds of political presence (Burkeman, 2007).

After Second Life what will be the next big thing? Undoubtedly we will see more virtual worlds and even more corporate money pouring into them. This could lead to a devaluation of creative impact and street credibility, possible even a repetition of the current disillusionment facing users of niche Web 2.0 sites acquired by large corporate organizations. There might even be a backlash against commercial colonization—of  »

9   All the key economic data for Second Life in 2008 can be found here: http://tinyurl.com/n7hwpq.

the first stirrings of which there are already signs—and the founding of commerce-free virtual worlds by purist digerati. But how would they support themselves?

*Questions*

1.  To what extent is Second Life a legitimate 'third place' for social interactions to take place and relationships to develop?
2.  What does the backlash to the commercial colonization of Second Life suggest is the role for businesses and brands in this space?
3.  What is the future for virtual worlds and what are the social and societal implications of your conclusions?

# ⭐ Chapter Summary

The chapter began by seeking to understand the effects which e-business technologies had had on individuals and groups of users. It examined technology adoption rates as well as the barriers to and local and global variations in attitudes towards e-business technologies. It concluded that gender, age, and cultural and geographical distributions of most of the relevant variables were uneven. It then examined the motivations to use and the actual use made by individuals of networked resources—ranging from the growth in electronic communications of various kinds, through the consumption of information to that of more tangible products. It spent some time discussing the growth of group social behaviours which had arisen as a result of e-business technologies: their characteristics, stability, and benefits and risks to both individuals and organizations as well as to society at large in terms, for example, of a growth in citizen activism. Several worked examples were explored.

The chapter then considered the use of electronic channels by consumers for both information search and transactional services. It emphasized that the indirect effects of e-business technologies on consumer behaviour were probably more important than their direct effect on sales. It examined the remaining barriers to online purchase and described the different kinds of risks perceived by would-be customers. It reminded us that consumer behaviour, even in an online environment, may not be rational and that such factors as search costs and the perceived importance of price may not be quite as predictable as had been expected.

Finally, the chapter examined the broader social consequences of e-business technologies. It critically assessed the notion of the 'digital divide' before reviewing the measures that have been developed internationally to assess the ICT development potential of specific national markets. It considered the impact of e-business technologies on social relationships and communities both at home and at work—virtual socialization—and explored the notion of behavioural addiction to technology and the role such technology may play in creating new forms of social capital.

# ❓ Review questions

1. Why do we need to differentiate between users' access to technical infrastructure and their adoption and use of applications supported by that infrastructure?

2. What factors determine individual attitudes to e-business technologies?

3. What are the characteristics of virtual communities?

4. Review the advantages and disadvantages of email in the workplace.

5. In what ways can we categorize 'electronic word-of-mouth' (eWOM)?

6. Why is the concept of the 'digital divide' a contested one?

7. What are the effects of the use of the Internet on the size and characteristics of individuals' social networks?

8. How can individuals create social capital from e-business technologies?

# 💬 Discussion questions

1. Consider the effects of the Internet on your daily life and on that of an elderly friend or relative. What conclusions do you draw from your findings about the effects of the Internet on society?

2. 'Price is now overtaking convenience as the key factor for consumers in deciding whether or not to shop online.' Do you agree? Find examples to support your conclusions.

3. Seasoned Twitterers express concern about the likely effects of exponential growth of the service. (See

for example http://www.twine.com/item/123c9051b-g8/can-twitter-survive-what-is-about-to-happen-to-it.) What is your view?

4. Explore more fully the link between technology and workaholism.

5. Does the Internet simply displace the use of other media in people's lives?

# ➡ Suggestions for further reading

Department of Culture, Media and Sport, (2009), *Digital Britain: Annexe 1—Key Trends and Issues in UK Media and Telecoms to 2012*, Enders Analysis, http://www.culture.gov.uk/images/publications/digital_britain_interimreportjan09_annex1.pdf.
The UK Government's plan to ensure that the country is at the forefront of the global digital economy. The interim report contains more than twenty recommendations as well as a statistical review of the social and economic role of e-business and Internet technologies in the UK today.

European Commission, (2008a), 'E-Communications Household Survey', *Special Eurobarometer 293*, Eurostat, http://ec.europa.eu/public_opinion/archives/ebs/ebs_293_full_en.pdf.
One of the regular country-by-country analyses conducted by the European Commission of household adoption of and attitudes towards electronic communications networks and services.

International Telecommunications Union, (2009), *Measuring the Information Society: the ICT Development Index*, ITU, http://www.itu.int/ITU-D/ict/publications/idi/2009/material/IDI2009_w5.pdf.

The document which forms the basis for the ICT Development Index of the ITU for infrastructure development planning. Contains detailed methodology and country-by-country analyses.

Li, C., Webber, R., and Longley, P., (2006), *The UK Geography of the E-Society: a National Classification*, http://www.spatial-literacy.org/inc/resources/e_soc.pdf.
A report summarizing the results of the survey undertaken by University College London into the geography of e-society in the UK. The accompanying website contains the full analysis and a look-up search box to enable you to test your own e-society credentials (see Weblinks below).

OFCOM, (2008), *The International Communications Market 2008*, Office of Communications, http://www.ofcom.org.uk/research/cm/icmr08/icmr08.pdf.
The definitive guide to international communication markets undertaken by the UK's Office of Communications. Contains adoption and penetration information by country.

# → References

Al-Hail, A., (2005), 'Why Women Use Email Disproportionately in Qatar: An Exploratory Study', *Journal of Website Promotion*, 1(3), pp. 99–104.

Anderson, R.E. and Srinivasan, S.S., (2003) 'E-Satisfaction and E-Loyalty: A Contingency framework', *Psychology and Marketing*, 20(2), pp. 123–38.

American Consumer Institute, (2009), *Online Worries Remain High, ACI Survey Shows*, http://www.theamericanconsumer.org/2009/03/19/online-worries-remain-high-aci-survey-shows-consumers-most-concerned-about-identity-theft-viruses-privacy-and-spyware/.

A.T. Kearney, (2005), *Mobinet 2005: Raising the Stakes*, http://www.atkearney.com/index.php/Publications/mobinet-2005-raising-the-stakes.html.

BBC News, (2003), 'Bust Company Sacks Workers by Text Message', BBC News online, 30 May, http://news.bbc.co.uk/1/hi/business/2949578.stm.

Boase, J., Horrigan, J.B., Wellman, B., and Rainie, L., (2006), *The Strength of Internet Ties*, Pew Internet & American Life Project.

Bracewell-Lewis, V. et al., (2009), *UK Online Retail And Travel Forecast, 2008 to 2014*, Forrester.

Brynjolfsson, E. and Smith, M.D., (2000), 'Frictionless Commerce? A Comparison of Internet and Conventional Retailers', *Management Science*, April, pp. 563–85.

Burke, R.R., (1997), 'Do You See What I See? The Future of Virtual Shopping', *Journal of the Academy of Marketing Science*, 25(4), pp. 352–60.

Burkeman, O., (2007), 'Exploding Pigs and Volleys of Gunfire as Le Pen Opens HQ in Virtual World', *The Guardian*, 20 January, http://technology.guardian.co.uk/news/story/0,,1994883,00.html.

Burt, S., and Sparks, L., (2003), 'E-commerce and the Retail Process: a Review', *Journal of Retailing & Consumer Services*, Vol. 10, Issue 5, 275.

Busari, S., (2008), 'Tweeting the Terror: How Social Media Reacted to Mumbai', http://edition.cnn.com/2008/WORLD/asiapcf/11/27/mumbai.twitter/index.html.

Clayton, L., (1997), 'Are There Virtual Communities?', *Ends & Means*, 2(1), Autumn, http://www.abdn.ac.uk/philosophy/endsandmeans/vol2no1/clayton.shtml.

Department of Culture, Media and Sport, (2009), *Digital Britain: Annexe 1—Key Trends and Issues in UK Media and Telecoms to 2012*, Enders Analysis, http://www.culture.gov.uk/images/publications/digital_britain_interimreportjan09_annex1.pdf.

*Economist*, (2004), 'A Perfect Market', *The Economist*, 15 May, p. 371. (8375)

Einhorn, B. and Kharif, O., (2007), 'China: Falling Hard for Web 2.0', *Business Week*, 15 January, p. 66.

European Commission, (2006), 'E-communications Household Survey', *Special Eurobarometer 249*, European Commission, http://ec.europa.eu/public_opinion/archives/ebs/ebs_249_en.pdf.

European Commission, (2008a), 'E-Communications Household Survey', *Special Eurobarometer 293*, Eurostat.

European Commission, (2008b), 'Internet Usage in 2008—Households and Individuals', *Eurostat Data in Focus*, 46.

Fayard, A-L., and DeSanctis, G., (2005), 'Evolution of an Online Forum for Knowledge Management Professionals: A Language Game Analysis', *Journal of Computer-Mediated Communication*, 10(4), article 2, http://jcmc.indiana.edu/vol10/issue4/fayard.html.

Forrester, (2007), *Brands Should Embrace Search Engines and Comparison Web Sites*, Forrester.

Forsythe, S., and Shi, B., (2003), 'Consumer Patronage and Risk Perceptions in Internet Shopping', *Journal of Business Research*, 56(11), November, pp. 867–75.

Ganz, J.F., (2007), *The Expanding Digital Universe. A Forecast of Worldwide Information Growth through 2010*, IDC, for EMC[2], http://www.emc.com/about/destination/digital_universe/pdf/Expanding_Digital_Universe_IDC_WhitePaper_022507.pdf.

Gatti, R., Chirmiciu, A., Kattuman, P., and Morgan, J., (2004), 'Price vs. Location: Determinants of demand at an online price comparison site', *Trust and Triviality: Where is the Internet going?* Conference at University College London, London, UK, 12 November 2004.

Gordon, L.A., Loeb, M.P., Lucyshyn, W., and Richardson, R., (2006), *CSI/FBI Computer Crime and Security Survey*, Computer Security Institute, http://www.gocsi.com.

Hennig-Thurau, T., Gwinner, K.P., Walsh, G., and Gremler, D.D., (2004) 'Electronic Word-of-Mouth Via Consumer-Opinion Platforms: what Motivates Consumers to Articulate Themselves on the Internet?', *Journal of Interactive Marketing*, (18(1), Winter, pp. 38–52.

Horrigan, J.B., (2003), *Consumption of Information Goods and Services in the United States*, Pew Internet & the American Life Project, http://www.pewinternet.org/pdfs/PIP_Info_Consumption.pdf.

Hu, S.L.Y., and Leung, L., (2003), 'Effects of Expectancy-value, Attitudes, and Use of the Internet on Psychological Empowerment Experienced by Chinese Women at the Workplace', *Telematics & Informatics*, 20(4), pp. 365–82.

International Telecommunications Union, (2009), *Measuring the Information Society: the ICT Development Index*, ITU, http://www.itu.int/ITU-D/ict/publications/idi/2009/material/IDI2009_w5.pdf.

Kambayashi, T., (2006), 'OhmyNews to Put Down Roots in Japan', *Japan Media Review*, 30 March, http://www.japanmediareview.com/japan/stories/060329kambayashi/.

Kato, Y. Kato, S., and Akahori, K., (2007), 'Effects of Emotional Cues Transmitted in E-mail Communication on the Emotions Experienced by Senders and Receivers', *Computers in Human Behavior*, 23(4), July, pp. 1894–905.

Katz, I., (2006), 'Flickr, Caterina Fake and Stewart Butterfield', the *Guardian*, 4 November, http://technology.guardian.co.uk/news/story/0,,1939085,00.html.

Kaye, B.K. and Johnson, T.J., (2003), 'From Here to Obscurity? Media substituTion Theory and Traditional Media in an Online World', *Journal of the American Society for Information Science and Technology*, 54(3), pp. 260–73.

Kiecker, P. and Cowles, D.L., (2001), 'Interpersonal Communication and Personal Influence on the Internet: A Framework for Examining Online Word-of-Mouth,' *Journal of Euromarketing*, 11 (2), pp. 71–88.

Kim, A.J., (2000), *Community Building on the Web: Secret Strategies for Successful Online Communities* Addison-Wesley.

Kollock, P., (1999), 'The Economies of Online Cooperation: Gifts and Public Goods in Cyberspace', in Smith, M. and Kollock, P. (eds), *Communities in Cyberspace*, Routledge.

Kruger, J., Epley, N., Parker, J., and Ng, J.-W., (2005), 'Egocentrism over E-Mail: Can We Communicate as Well as We Think?', *Journal of Personality and Social Psychology*, 89(6), pp. 925–36.

Kuttner, R., (1998), 'The Net—a Market too Perfect for Profits', *Business Week*, 11 May.

Lenhart, A. and Fox, S., (2006), *Bloggers: A Portrait of the Internet's New Storytellers*, Pew Internet & American Life Project, http://www.pewinternet.org/pdfs/PIP%20Bloggers%20Report%20July%2019%20 2006.pdf.

Leung, L., (2003), 'Impacts of Net-generation Attributes, Seductive Properties of the Internet, and Gratifications-Obtained on Internet Use', *Telematics and Informatics*, 20(2), pp. 107–29.

Li, C., Webber, R., and Longley, P., (2006), *The UK Geography of the E-Society: a National Classification*, http://www.spatial-literacy.org/inc/resources/e_soc.pdf.

Li, N. and Kirkup, G., (2007), 'Gender and Cultural Differences in Internet Use: A Study of China and the UK', *Computers and Education*, 48(2), pp. 301–17.

Madden, M., (2006), *Internet Penetration and Impact*, Pew Internet & American Life Project.

Madell, D.E. and Muncer, S.J., (2007), 'Control over Social Interactions: An Important Reason for Young People's Use of the Internet and Mobile Phones for Communication?', *CyberPsychology & Behaviour*, 10(1), pp. 137–40.

Maltz, E. and Chiapetta, V., (2002), 'Maximizing Value in the Digital World', *MIT Sloan Management Review* Spring, 43 pp. 77–84.

Morris, J.M., (1992), 'The Effects of an Introductory Computer Course on the Attitudes of Older Adults towards Computers', *Proceedings of the 23rd SIGCSE Technical Symposium on Computer Science Education*, Kansas City, Missouri, USA, 5–6 March, pp. 72–5.

Moulds, J., (2007), 'Is Second Life the Next Generation?', *Daily Telegraph*, 16 February.

National Center for Missing and Exploited Children, (2006), *Teen Internet Survey*, May, http://www.missingkids.com/missingkids/servlet/NewsEventServlet?LanguageCountry=en_US&PageId=2383.

National Consumer Council, (2000), *Ecommerce and Consumer Protection*, NCC.

National Statistics, (2006), *Social Trends 2006 edition, 36*, Palgrave Macmillan, p. 59.

Nie, N.H. and Erbring, L., (2002), 'Internet and Society: A Preliminary Report', *IT & Society*, 1(1), pp. 275–83.

Nielsen, J., (1997), 'Community is Dead; Long Live Mega-Collaboration', *Jakob Nielsen's Alertbox*, 15 August, http://www.useit.com/alertbox/9708b.html.

Nielsen, J., (2006), 'Participation Inequality: Encouraging More Users to Contribute', *Jakob Nielsen's Alertbox*, 9 Octobe , http://www.useit.com/alertbox/participation_inequality.html.

Nonnecke, B. and Preece, J., (2000), 'Lurker Demographics. Counting the Silent', *Proceedings of the SIGCHI conference on Human Factors in Computing Systems*, The Hague, Netherlands.

OFCOM, (2006), *The International Communications Market, 2006*, UK Office of Communications, http://www.ofcom.org.uk/research/cm/icmr06/icmr.pdf.

OFCOM, (2007), *The Communications Market: Broadband. Digital Progress Report*, April, http://www.ofcom.org.uk/research/cm/broadband_rpt/broadband_rpt.pdf.

OFCOM, (2008), *The International Communications Market 2008*, Office of Communications, http://www.ofcom.org.uk/research/cm/icmr08/icmr08.pdf.

O'Hear, S., (2007), 'Flickr Abandons the "Old Skool"', *The Social Web*, 1 February, http://blogs.zdnet.com/social/?p=79.

Ploughmann, L., (2006), 'The Rush to Second Life is Like the Internet in the Mid-1990s', *Mind This* blog, http://www.mindthis.net/mindthis/2006/11/the_rush_to_sec.html.

Porter, C.E., (2004), 'A Typology of Virtual Communities: A Multi-Disciplinary Foundation for Future Research', *Journal of Computer-Mediated Communication*, 10(1), article 3, http://jcmc.indiana.edu/vol10/issue1/porter.html.

Porter, G. and Kakabadse, M.K., (2006), 'HRM Perspectives on Addiction to Technology and Work', *Journal of Management Development*, 25(6), pp. 535–60.

Preece, J. and Maloney-Krichmar, D. (2005). 'Online Communities: Design, Theory, and Practice', *Journal of Computer-Mediated Communication*, 10(4), article 1, http://jcmc.indiana.edu/vol10/issue4/preece.html.

Putnam, R.D., (2000), *Bowling Alone: The Collapse and Revival of American Community*, New York: Simon & Schuster.

Quelch, J. and Takeuchi, H., (1981), 'Non-Store Marketing: Fast Track or Slow?', *Harvard Business Review*, July–August, pp. 75–84.

Rabinovich, E., Maltz, A., and Sinha, R.A., (2008), 'Assessing Markups, Service Quality, and Product Attributes in Music CDs' Internet Retailing', *Production & Operations Management*, 17(3), p 320.

Rainie, L., (2007), 'Interview: Author David Weinberger Describes how Tagging Changes People's Relationship to Information and Each Other', *Online Activities and Pursuits*, Pew Internet and the American Life Project, http://www.pewinternet.org/PPF/r/201/report_display.asp

Reynolds, J., (2002), 'E-tail Marketing', in McGoldrick, P.J. (ed), *Retail Marketing*, McGraw-Hill.

Reynolds, J. (2003), 'Prospects for Electronic Commerce', in J. Reynolds and C. Cuthbertson (eds), *Retail Strategy: The View from the Bridge*, Butterworth-Heinemann.

Rheingold, H., (1993), *The Virtual Community: Homesteading on the Electronic Frontier*, Addison-Wesley.

Rosenberg, L.J. and Hirschman, E.C., (1980), 'Retailing Without Stores', *Harvard Business Review*, 58(4), pp. 103–12.

Shklovski, I., Kraut, R., and Rainie, L., (2004), 'The Internet and Social Participation: Contrasting Cross-Sectional and Longitudinal Analyses', *Journal of Computer-mediated Communication*, 10(1), http://jcmc.indiana.edu/vol10/issue1/shklovski_kraut.html.

Segalla, M., (2004), 'The Email Is Delivered Instantly So Why Do Responses Take So Long: A Study of Email Usage Attitudes Among European Managers', http://appli1.hec.fr/%7Eappliphp/hrm/papers/TheEmailIsDeliveredInstantlySoWhyDoResponsesTakeSoLong.doc.

Sinai, T. and Waldfogel, J., (2004), 'Geography and the Internet: Is the Internet a substitute or complement for cities?', *Journal of Urban Economics*, 56, pp. 1–24.

Sinha, I., (2000), 'The Net's Real Threat to Prices and Brands', *Harvard Business Review*, 78, March–April, pp. 43–8.

Spinks, N., Wells, B., and Meche, M., (1999), 'Netiquette: A Behavioural Guide to Electronic Business Communications', *Corporate Communications*. 4, pp. 145–55.

Steinkuehler, C., and Williams, D., (2006), Where Everybody Knows Your (Screen) Name: Online Games as "third places"', *Journal of Computer-Mediated Communication*, 11(4), article 1, http://jcmc.indiana.edu/vol11/issue4/steinkuehler.html.

Szymanski, D.M. and Hise, R.T. (2000), 'E-Satisfaction: an Initial Examination', Journal of Retailing, 76(3), pp. 309–22.

Tappscott, D., (1998), *Growing up Digital: The Rise of the Net-Generation*, McGraw-Hill.

Tiemann, R., (2007), 'At Work, at Rest, at Play', *Financial Times Digital Business Supplement*, 14 March, p. 1.

Toubier, O. and Stephen, A., (2009, forthcoming), 'Deriving Value from Social Commerce Networks', *Journal of Marketing Research*.

US Census Bureau, (2009), *Quarterly Retail E-commerce Sales*, 4th quarter, http://www.census.gov/mrts/www/data/pdf/08Q4.pdf.

Warschauer, M., (2003), 'Demystifying the Digital Divide', *Scientific American*, 289(2), pp. 42–7

Waters, R., (2005), 'The Cure for BlackBerry Addiction is in Your Own Hands', *Financial Times*, 3 December, p. 11.

Watts, J., (2003), 'World's first Internet President Logs on', *Guardian*, 24 February, http://www.guardian.co.uk/international/story/0,,901435,00.html.

Wellman, B., (2001), 'Physical Place and Cyber-Place: The Rise of Networked Individualism', *International Journal for Urban and Regional Research*, 25, pp. 227–52

Wellman, B. and Hogan, B., (2004), 'The Immanent Internet', in McKay, J. (ed.), *Netting Citizens*, St Andrews Press.

Wise, K., Hamman, B., and Thorson, K. (2006), 'Moderation, Response Rate, and Message Interactivity: Features of Online Communities and Their Effects on Intent to Participate, *Journal of Computer-Mediated Communication*, 12(1), article 2, http://jcmc.indiana.edu/vol12/issue1/wise.html.

Wiseman, J. 1998, *Global Nation: Australia and the Politics of Globalisation*, Cambridge University Press, Cambridge.

Yellowlees, P.M., and Marks, S., (2007), 'Problematic Internet Use or Internet Addiction?', *Computers in Human Behavior*, 23(3), pp. 1447–53.

Zhao, S., (2006), 'Do Internet Users Have More Social Ties? A Call for Differentiated Analyses of Internet Use, *Journal of Computer-Mediated Communication*, 11(3), article 8, http://jcmc.indiana.edu/vol11/issue3/zhao.html.

# ⚙ Weblinks

OFCOM Research. Repository of UK and international tracking research into the adoption of Internet and related e-business technologies: http://www.ofcom.org.uk/research.

Pew Internet and American Life Project. A wide-ranging set of surveys and analyses of the impact of the Internet in the US: http://www.pewinternet.org.

Search Engine Watch. News and analysis on the developments affecting search engines: http://searchenginewatch.com and http://blog.searchenginewatch.com/blog.

Spatial literacy. Location-based analysis of e-society characteristics: http://www.spatial-literacy.org.

Technorati.com. Indexing a tracking blogs and other user generated content sites: '71 million blogs: some of them have to be good': http://www.technorati.com.

# 5

# Ethical and regulatory issues

## Learning outcomes

Completing this chapter will enable you to:

- Understand the particular range of legal and ethical issues facing users, firms, and regulators in relation to privacy that have arisen from the growth of e-business

- Appreciate the increasing complexity of the intellectual property rights environment that has accompanied the growth of the Internet

- Realize the implications that e-business technologies bring with them for fraudulent and criminal activity; and

- Gain an insight into the evolving and contentious nature of Internet regulation

## Introduction

'There is a great danger that the web becomes a place where untruths start to spread more than truths, or it becomes a place which becomes increasingly unfair in some way.'
*Tim Berners-Lee, quoted in Johnson, 2006*

E-business technologies have created new and different forms of legal and ethical considerations for firms, regulators, and users—and these are not only to do with issues of truth or fairness, as the erstwhile inventor of the world wide web suggests, above. There is an increasingly delicate balance for firms to maintain between justifiable commercial activity and the rights of members of the e-business community, and this within an evolving regulatory environment. There may be no easy answers or trade-offs. Most e-business technologies, observe Nash and Peltu (2005) are 'double-edged', in that 'the same capability can be used for socially beneficial and destructive ends'. The only way these matters can be resolved, Wilson suggests, is through 'conflict and co-operation among the contending elites' who negotiate across four distinct societal sectors. Business is only one of these sectors: others include government, research and development, and civil society (Wilson, 2005), and managers need to be aware of the ways in which these issues are emerging being addressed. Behaviours that may seen as being unjustifiable often take place on the edge of and often wholly outside the control of the private sector, and shade into unscrupulous or illegal activities, which range from the harmless but irritating to the criminal. Internet users themselves remain concerned over a wide variety of issues connected with the privacy, safety, and security of networked information. Figure 5.1 summarizes the results of a worldwide survey by the International Telecommunications Union, in which 48 per cent of respondents felt that communications networks were unsafe in some way, and the same proportion felt that the resolution of security issues was important for safeguarding the future of the Internet. The figure demonstrates the extensive range of fears, from a variety of causes, expressed by respondents. This chapter focuses on three issues which have particular implications for business: those connected with privacy, those surrounding intellectual property rights, and finally those involving fraud or other criminal activities.

In terms of *privacy*, the same Internet capabilities which enhance personal freedoms online also make possible what may be seen as increasingly intrusive behaviours when undertaken by organizations. The consequences are differently perceived. Some types of activity by firms, such as the use of cookies and tracking software, are regarded with increasing suspicion by some users, but with increasing resignation by others. The tensions between firms and their customers are paralleled at the level of the nation-state: trends towards the removal of cross-border barriers for B2B (business-to-business) electronic business have gone hand in hand with the emergence of censorship, state licensing, and surveillance of online activity in some countries, as e-government has developed. For example, Human Rights Watch has documented the differential approach of countries

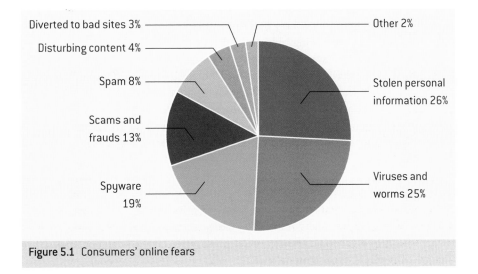

**Figure 5.1** Consumers' online fears

across the Middle East and North Africa to the reporting of news of expression of opinion on blogs or websites, where nevertheless:

> 'all of the countries surveyed continue to block Web sites for their political content or for other arbitrary reasons, and all retain and misuse vaguely worded and sweeping legal provisions to imprison Internet users for expressing unpopular or critical views.' *Human Rights Watch, 2005*

In part by their very nature, e-business technologies also invoke questions of *intellectual property rights*, where—for example—unprotected digitized products can be shared easily but illegally, and where copyright and trademark legislation lags behind technological development—and even where it is relevant and up-to-date may require (as in the case of recorded music piracy, for example) collective action by an entire business sector. Thirdly, the scope for deception and criminal activities such as payment fraud and identity theft, through such mechanisms as spamming and phishing, are of a new and different scale as a consequence of the dissemination and widespread availability of e-business technologies. Changes occurring in the regulatory environment affecting the Internet arising from some of these ethical and security concerns have direct implications for an organization's costs, processes, and procedures. These range from governance of the Internet itself, to changes in competition law, to regulations governing online transactions, intellectual property, information security, privacy and data protection.

**Phishing** Whereby thieves use deceptive emails to get users to divulge personal information, includes luring them to fake bank and credit card websites.

# Privacy

The concept of privacy is a complex and contentious one, rendered more problematic, it is suggested, by the potentially intrusive and rapidly evolving capabilities of e-business technologies:

> 'New technologies are radically advancing our freedoms, but they are also enabling unparalleled invasions of privacy.' *Electronic Frontier Foundation, http://www.eff.org*

It is suggested by others, however, that privacy is not only an elusive but, in practice, unrealistic concept in today's society. In a now infamous and often cited remark in 1999 at the launch of new networking technology, the then CEO of Sun Microsystems, Scott McNealy remarked: 'You have zero privacy anyway—get over it.' Such pragmatism may not be misplaced. Writer David Brin has also argued that the erosion of privacy is irreversible and that the real choice that users have is between the mere illusion of privacy—where, in response to contemporary concerns, surveillance is restricted to the authorities (itself an undesirable outcome)—or the destruction of that illusion with the recognition of access for all. Brin calls this sacrifice of privacy for freedom 'reciprocal transparency'.

## Definitions of privacy

A great deal has been written about the nature of privacy (see for example Margulis, 2003). US privacy expert Alan Westin (1967), suggests that privacy performs four roles for individuals in democratic societies, all of which focus on the limitation of access to themselves by others. These are in relation to:

- personal autonomy: allowing people to maintain their sense of individuality and to avoid being manipulated and dominated by others;

- emotional release: allowing people time in their lives when they can be 'off stage' and more at ease—with their families or other trusted groups, or anonymously;

- self-evaluation: allowing people to take time for personal reflection and review; and the concept of

- limited and protected communication: allowing people to engage in candid conversations with those they trust—be they family, friends, peer groups, or professional advisers, such as doctors, lawyers, or clergy.

The sense that people want to control, or at least be in a position significantly to influence, what is known about them by other people is often popularly termed *information privacy*. The kinds of data susceptible to information privacy concerns can be varied, as can their perceived sensitivity for users. These data can include:

- health and medical data;

- criminal records;

- personal financial data;

- genetic data;

- consumption data;

- locational data.

## Activity box 5.1

### 'Dataveillance'

How many different types of information are held about you by private businesses and public sector organizations? What kind of picture does this paint of you as an individual? How accurate do you think these data are?

## Information gathering by organizations

'We are all "glass consumers". Organizations know so much about us, they can almost see through us.' *Lace, 2005*

How are concepts of privacy influenced by the Internet and e-business technologies? Information gathering by organizations engaged in e-business has been referred to as the 'dark side of the information democracy' (Sotgiu and Ancarani, 2004). The legitimate collection and use of such data has the potential for radically improving the marketing and pricing performance of firms (with characteristics and consequences that are explored more fully in chapter 7). However, while these technologies can make users' lives more convenient, they can also be used for tracking the behaviour of users and, it is suggested, potentially making computers vulnerable to network attacks. Tracking techniques include the use of cookies, IP address storage, URL address embedding, and HTTP authentication. More recently, related technologies, such as radio-frequency identification (RFID) chips and global positioning systems in association with organizations' information-gathering capability have also raised concerns.

Cookies are the most popularly known form of information tracking employed by organizations. Likened to the ticket issued in the laundry shop or dry cleaners, the cookie is a string of text either stored in memory for the duration of a session, or saved as a file on a user's hard disk by a website (a 'persistent' cookie). In both cases, the cookie contains some kind of identification linking the user account to the site concerned. The text string is saved as a file if the site wishes to keep track of login or profile settings—necessary seamlessly to identify the user on a subsequent visit.[1] Cookies were initially developed for use in the Netscape Navigator browser at the end of 1994, but their use was not popularly appreciated until several years later, and their application is still not fully understood by a significant minority of users. Amongst potential areas of abuse are:

- inaccurate identification: potential for confusion between multiple users of a single computer;
- cookie theft: potential for an unauthorized entity to intercept a cookie, via monitoring of the network (so-called packet-sniffing or cross-site scripting)[2]; and
- cookie poisoning (potential for tampering with the value of a cookie).

Some of the difficulties perceived by users around cookies are linked to their application by advertisers or other third parties, on behalf of the original content provider. For example, most content providers outsource the distribution of online advertising content to third-party business service organizations, such as DoubleClick (acquired by Google in 2007), Right Media, or Adjuggler. In this case, a 'third-party' cookie is set when an ad is displayed or a paid listing is clicked on by the user. DoubleClick comment:

'the cookie helps marketers learn how well their Internet advertising campaigns or paid search listing perform … [this] includes the number of unique users their advertisers were displayed to, how many users clicked on their Internet ads or paid listings, and which ads or paid listing they clicked on.' *DoubleClick website*[3]

Cookies have in general received a bad press and indeed many consumers confuse cookies with malicious forms of spyware (dealt with later in this chapter). A company setting a third-party cookie can in principle track users across multiple sites, which would open up the possibility of creating a profile of users. DoubleClick itself had intended develop a product to link names from a financial information website with anonymous users' web profiles as early as 1999. However, cookies are seen by many as the price that has to be paid for a free Internet: 'instead of aiding privacy, the death of cookies might very well stifle it: many web sites would require more frequent registration' (Penenberg, 2005).

Cookies and related tracking techniques are not the only mechanisms of information gathering available to firms. It has been suggested, for example, that RFID will provide an enterprise-wide, cross-chain technology of the future. A study published by the

---

1   More information about cookies can be found at: http://www.cookiecentral.com and http://www.howstuffworks.com/cookie.htm,

2   Making the browser send cookies to servers that should not receive them.

3   http://www.doubleclick.com/us/about_doubleclick/privacy/faq.asp.

influential Advanced Practices Council of the Society for Information Management concluded that:

- RFID could represent a common standard for data storage and retrieval that could improve collaboration and data sharing.
- Inventories could be reduced, with accompanying cost savings, if e-tags were used to maximize information flow in the supply chain and minimize physical material flow.
- Ultimately, this could give rise to 'intelligent' products modifying transportation routes.

By making goods on the 'supply side' easier to trace, RFID could also cut waste, out-of-stocks and shrinkage. Procter and Gamble estimated that between 10–16 per cent of their products were out of stock at any one time. But in terms of the 'demand side'—in relation to product and marketing-related strategies—RFID and digital receipt technology could also offer some attractive applications, by:

- allowing manufacturers access to point of sale data to enable the integration of customer preferences into product and distribution processes; as well as
- offering through digital receipt technology locational and personalized merchandising opportunities.

Information on the location of customers and consumers—whether delivered by RFID chip or by GPS in mobile phones or other portable devices—have the potential further to impinge on information privacy. Long case 5.1 describes the growth of location-based services, and the ethical issues which the development of such services can bring about.

## Consumer awareness and concern

> 'Ask 100 people if they care about privacy and 85 will say yes. Ask those same 100 people if they'll give you a DNA sample just to get a free Big Mac, and 85 will say yes.' *Austin Hill (US entrepreneur) quoted in Weber, 2000*

Privacy is a popular subject for polling.

> 'In the past 25 years, references to public opinion have been used to frame the public as concerned, differentiated and, most recently, as willing to negotiate their privacy demands.' *Gandy, 2003*

Although there is generally rising awareness of threats to information and personal privacy, it is important to recognize that consumers express different levels of concern and that these attitudes are changing. One historical measure of concern about privacy was the Westin General Concern About Privacy Index, which sought to distinguish between three different types of US consumers:

- privacy fundamentalists: high concern—unwilling to disclose any information about themselves;
- privacy pragmatists: moderate concern—willing to trade information about themselves for something that they understand is of value, provided that they

can see the tangible benefits and are reassured over the safeguarding of that information; and

• privacy indifferents: low concern—willing to disclose almost anything about themselves.

---

### Activity box 5.2

#### What price privacy?

What attitudes do you have towards information privacy? Do your attitudes match one of the three Westin types? What evidence can you draw upon to support your conclusions? How, if at all, are your attitudes changing?

---

The Westin surveys are no longer published, but the historical data shows that attitudes to information privacy within the US do appear increasingly to have favoured the pragmatists—those holding a more balanced view—over the past decade. We might more properly see this in terms of a general growth in concern, since the way in which the Harris-Westin analysis configures 'pragmatists' is as representing those with a 'moderate' level of concern over information privacy (Figure 5.2) (Kumaraguru and Cranor, 2005b). Within Europe, the majority of citizens are concerned about information privacy, but only a minority (34 per cent in 2008) on average claimed to be 'very concerned'. However, those most actively concerned varied from 65–70 per cent in Austria and Germany to 5–8 per cent in Finland and the Netherlands (European Commission, 2008a). Attitudes

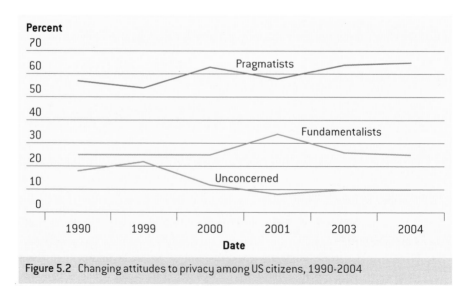

**Figure 5.2** Changing attitudes to privacy among US citizens, 1990-2004

towards information privacy are, of course, highly culturally dependent. Work by Dutch sociologist Geert Hofstede indicates that individuals living in societies characterized as more collectivist than individualist tend to have greater trust and faith in other people (Hoftstede and Hofstede, 2005). Recent studies suggest, for example, significantly less awareness and concern over privacy issues in India than in parts of the developed world although, here too, levels of both are rising (Kumaraguru and Cranor, 2005a).

## Short case 5.1

### Assessing children's use of the Internet

Amongst the most vulnerable groups within society to use the Internet and other digital technologies are children. The perception is that children are less aware of the need to safeguard their information privacy online than in more conventional settings and that the Internet and mobile phones can provide a mechanism for those wishing inappropriately to contact children—either for reasons of harassment or bullying, or for grooming. Assessing the extent to which children actually use the Internet is itself difficult. Estimates are normally made by asking parents—and in some cases, parents may be unaware of out-of-home use, or be poorly skilled themselves in either understanding the risks or in monitoring behaviour. Studies also consistently show that parents tend to underestimate adolescents' engagement in risky Internet behaviour as well as to overestimate the amount of parental monitoring in relation to Internet safety that actually occurs at home. One examination of adolescent Internet usage suggested that mothers have a better awareness of this than fathers (Liau et al., 2008).

»

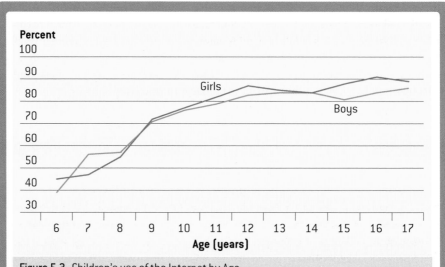

**Figure 5.3** Children's use of the Internet by Age

Note: Question – 'As far as you know, does your child use the Internet anywhere?' Base: EU 27

Online use starts early. Figure 5.3 shows that between 39 and 45 per cent of 6-year-old Europeans used the Internet in 2008. Thereafter, usage rates climbed to between 86 to 89 per cent at age 17. There is little difference between boys and girls at most ages—despite the stereotypes—although use by girls appears to exceed that by boys between 15 and 17 years of age. Some 75 per cent of European children between 6 and 17 years of age have access to a mobile phone, compared to 48 per cent three years previously (European Commission, 2008b). European parents are more worried about their children seeing explicitly violent or sexual content online than they are about 'cyberbullying', inappropriate contact, or the revealing of personal information. Fears in relation to violent content seem to be borne out by actual usage research which demonstrates the extent to which adolescent males prefer violent online games (see for example Tahiroglu et al., 2008). By contrast, other work has shown that despite relatively high levels of bullying online, parents underestimate their own children's bullying behaviour and don' really have a sense of how their children can become victims of online bullying. For example, 23 per cent of Dutch 11 to 12 year-olds reported having been bullied online (Dehue et al., 2008). However, all types of parental concern scored significantly higher for those parents who did not themselves have access to the Internet. As with other social indicators of e-business technologies, attitudes also vary across countries and cultures. Within Europe, there is greater overall parental concern in Portugal, France, and Greece than in Denmark, Sweden, and the UK.

What preventative methods do parents employ in seeking to regulate their children's Internet usage? Over 75 per cent of European parents claim to talk to their children about Internet usage; one-third even claimed 'co-use' (sitting next to their children whilst they were online). Of course, just as we have seen potential 'under-reporting' of actual usage, so we are likely to see 'over-claiming' as parents do not wish to be portrayed in a bad » light to interviewers. However, only 13 per cent claimed to always check their children's email messages or social networking behaviour.

*Question*

Some strategies employed by parents actively to monitor Internet usage by their children are identified above. Can you think of others? How relatively successful do you think these different strategies may be?

Paralleling (and in the eyes of some in practice fuelling) the growth of consumer concern over information privacy have been the growing number of public interest research groups, coalitions of consumer, civil liberties, educational, and other organizations and lobbying groups. The US Electronic Privacy Information Center (http://www.epic.org) lists seventeen organizations with interests in information privacy, twenty-one national and twenty-four international websites, and twenty-one mailing lists and electronic newsgroups. The scale of this activity inevitably raises the public profile of information privacy concerns, has a potential effect upon public policy formulation, and the actions of such organizations should be of legitimate interest to firms, since they themselves will often undertake surveillance and monitoring of business compliance in this area.

For example, we talked about RFID earlier. Its growth has led to organizations highlighting privacy concerns over individually tagged consumer products. Even the research conducted by the industry-sponsored Auto-ID Labs showed consumer hostility to product-level tagging.[4] Images of companies scanning tags from a distance post-purchase—even by satellite from orbit—circulate on some of the most vociferous websites (such as http://www.spychips.org). Of course, tags could be deactivated or 'killed' at the checkout—but this might negate some of the more innovative long-term applications, such as product 'intelligence' in the home (milk knowing it was past its sell-by date or clothes knowing what temperature wash to request, for example). The interest group CASPIAN (Consumers Against Supermarket Privacy Invasion and Numbering) is not convinced.[5] It comments: 'RFID chips, tiny tracking devices the size of a grain of dust, can be used to secretly identify you and the things you' carrying—right through your clothes, wallet, backpack, or purse. Have you already taken one home with you?' CASPIAN claims to have dissuaded firms from implementing RFID on consumer products until 2013 by means of threatened boycotts.

Company performance in relation to privacy compliance is regularly investigated by third-party organizations. For example, the privacy seal organization TRUSTe (http://www.truste.org) conducts an annual Most Trusted Company for Privacy award. American Express, eBay, IBM, and Amazon were recognized in 2008 as the top four, from a shortlist of twenty companies derived from over 700 suggested by 7,000 consumers. Table 5.1 highlights the significant variations in overall rankings by sector.

---

4  http://www.autoidlabs.org/.

5  http://www.spychips.com.

**Table 5.1  Top ranked companies for privacy by industry, USA, 2008**

| 2008 Ranking | Industry sectors | Top ranked company within industry | Average Rank |
|---|---|---|---|
| 1 | Consumer products | Johnson & Johnson | 45 |
| 2 | Healthcare | WebMD | 33 |
| 3 | Package & delivery | US Portal Service | 59 |
| 4 | Technology | IBM | 94 |
| 5 | Non-profit | National Rifle Association | 143 |
| 6 | Telecom | Verizon | 156 |
| 7 | Credit card & payments | American Express | 139 |
| 8 | Banking | US Bank | 72 |
| 9 | Investments | Charles Schwab | 90 |
| 10 | Pharmaceuticals | Schering-Plough | 102 |
| 11 | Financial services | ELoan | 110 |
| 12 | Insurance | Nationwide | 127 |
| 13 | Hospitality | Starwood | 148 |
| 14 | Retail | Amazon | 113 |
| 15 | Conglomerate | General Electric | 153 |
| 16 | Entertainment | Disney | 118 |
| 17 | Internet services | Yahoo | 135 |
| 18 | Health & beauty | Weight Watchers | 152 |
| 19 | Auto & transporation | Harley Davidson | 125 |
| 20 | Airlines | Southwest | 165 |
| 21 | Toy & gaming | Lego | 159 |
| 22 | Food service | Starbucks | 161 |
| | | | 111.03 |

Note: The table provides a listing of twenty-two different industry sectors in ascending average rank based on consumer trust ratings. Please note that these ratings were compiled from individual responses to a US national survey conducted in the October to November 2008 timeframe

But users often misunderstand the role and limitations of information tracking. For example, a US survey in 2005 demonstrated that consumers polled had little understanding of the limitations of cookies: whilst two-thirds of respondents erased cookies to 'protect their privacy', other reasons included 'to eliminate spam' and 'to prevent viruses' (Insight Express, 2005). Further, users often say one thing and do another: stated attitudes and actual behaviour vary. For example, despite rising concern over threats to information privacy, only 7 per cent of US citizens reported that they had changed their behaviour in response. Much user behaviour, particularly within developed markets, is increasingly pragmatic, and a 'new' economics of privacy has emerged which seeks to model this aspect of the privacy debate. Acquisiti (2004) and Chellappa and Sin (2005) suggest that the customers of e-businesses are willing to trade off their concern for privacy against some kind of economic value to them, provided that they can trust the organization offering that economic value. Culnan and Bies (2003) call this the 'privacy calculus', a weighing up of the costs and benefits. Jonathan Zittrain (2006) goes further, proposing that consumers are increasingly moving from seeing privacy as *defence* to privacy as *strategy*.

## Regulatory developments

'The question is whether consumers should have the right to make [the] choice and balance the trade-offs, or whether it will be pre-emptively denied to them by privacy fundamentalists out to deny consumers that choice.' *McCullagh, 2004*

Developing and implementing Internet privacy legislation is difficult for regulators, both domestically but even more so internationally. One of the societies most highly protective of information privacy is Germany. In 1983, the German federal courts identified 'informational self-determination' as a basic right of the German citizen, warranting 'the capacity of the individual to determine in principle the disclosure and use of his/her personal data'. But the nature of the Internet may make it difficult to arrive at responsibility for particular actions or activities by firms or by consumers in other jurisdictions. More importantly, however, activities that are regarded as not being breaches of privacy in one jurisdiction, but perhaps wholly admissible behaviour, may be inappropriate in another. Westin has suggested that his concept of privacy is only specifically applicable to Western democracies, for example. Sometimes states themselves are involved in the kinds of intrusion into individuals' information privacy that, in other countries, would be generally regarded as illegal, unethical, or otherwise unacceptable. Human rights group Privacy International has analysed what it calls 'the world's leading surveillance societies' in a ranking of national privacy (Figure 5.4). It noted in its most recent 2007 study that the position of most EU countries was deteriorating. In particular, it found that:

- The two lowest ranking countries overall in the survey were Malaysia and China. The highest-ranking countries were Greece and Canada (and even Greece was only 'adequate' in 2007).

- In terms of the strength of statutory protections and degree of privacy enforcement, the US was amongst the lowest ranking countries in the democratic world.

- The lowest ranking EU country was the United Kingdom, which fell into the 'black' category along with Russia and Singapore. (The black category defines countries demonstrating 'endemic surveillance'.)

- Despite having no comprehensive national privacy law, the United States scored slightly higher than the UK overall. South Africa, Romania, and India all scored higher than the UK.

Whilst bi-lateral and multi-lateral arrangements are being developed between countries, it may never be possible to arrive at truly global standards and legislation to

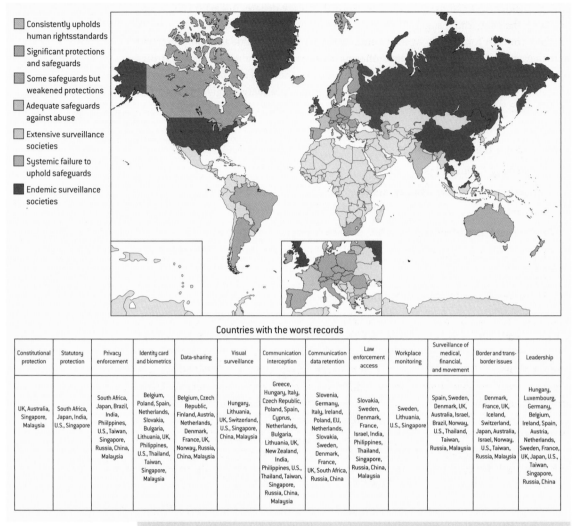

Consistently upholds human rightsstandards

Significant protections and safeguards

Some safeguards but weakened protections

Adequate safeguards against abuse

Extensive surveillance societies

Systemic failure to uphold safeguards

Endemic surveillance societies

Countries with the worst records

| Constitutional protection | Statutory protection | Privacy enforcement | Identity card and biometrics | Data-sharing | Visual surveillance | Communication interception | Communication data retention | Law enforcement access | Workplace monitoring | Surveillance of medical, financial, and movement | Border and trans-border issues | Leadership |
|---|---|---|---|---|---|---|---|---|---|---|---|---|
| UK, Australia, Singapore, Malaysia | South Africa, Japan, India, U.S, Singapore | South Africa, Japan, Brazil, India, Phiilppines, U.S., Taiwan, Singapore, Russia, China, Malaysia | Belgium, Poland, Spain, Netherlands, Slovakia, Bulgaria, Lithuania, UK, Philippines, U.S., Thailand, Taiwan, Singapore, Malaysia | Belgium, Czech Republic, Finland, Austria, Netherlands, Denmark, France, UK, Norway, Russia, China, Malaysia | Hungary, Lithuania, UK, Switzerland, U.S., Singapore, China, Malaysia | Greece, Hungary, Italy, Czech Republic, Poland, Spain, Cyprus, Netherlands, Bulgaria, Lithuania, UK, New Zealand, India, Philippines, U.S., Thailand, Taiwan, Singapore, Russia, China, Malaysia | Slovenia, Germany, Italy, Ireland, Poland, EU, Netherlands, Slovakia, Sweden, Denmark, France, UK, South Africa, Russia, China | Slovakia, Sweden, Denmark, France, Israel, India, Philippines, Thailand, Singapore, Russia, China, Malaysia | Sweden, Lithuania, U.S., Singapore | Spain, Sweden, Denmark, UK, Australia, Israel, Brazil, Norway, U.S., Thailand, Taiwan, Russia, Malaysia | Denmark, France, UK, Iceland, Switzerland, Japan, Australia, Israel, Norway, U.S., Taiwan, Russia, Malaysia | Hungary, Luxembourg, Germany, Belgium, Ireland, Spain, Austria, Netherlands, Sweden, France, UK, Japan, U.S., Taiwan, Singapore, Russia, China |

**Figure 5.4** Leading 'surveillance societies' in the world, 2007

ensure privacy. The OECD developed guidelines on the protection of privacy and trans-border flows of personal data for its member countries as early as 1980. The growth of cross-border activities since then has generated privacy laws in most member countries, in conformity with these guidelines. For example, the twenty-one members of the Asia Pacific Economic Co-operation group (http://www.apec.org) adopted a common Privacy Framework in 2004 which was compliant with the OECD guidelines. However, the growing volume of data flows and their changing nature has led to calls for a more global and systematic approach to cross-border privacy law cooperation. Whilst data exchange in the 1980s more often consisted of the physical exchange of recorded media, creation and growth of Internet bandwidth capacity is now the dominant feature of the communications landscape. Global bandwidth grew at a compounded annual rate of 57 per cent between 2002 and 2008, and by 62 per cent over 2007. However, since 2007, this capacity has outpaced global Internet traffic growth leading to lower utilization and falling prices for the use of that capacity.[6]

The European Union has sought to harmonize and strictly regulate data protection across the member states, recognizing that not to do so would hamper the development of cross-border flows of information within the single European market. Its 1995 Directive on the Protection of Personal Data requires a high level of data protection and identifies eight principles of good practice which are enforceable by law.[7] Data must be:

1) Fairly and lawfully processed.

2) Processed for limited purposes.

3) Adequate, relevant and not excessive.

4) Accurate.

5) Not kept longer than necessary.

6) Processed in accordance with the data subject's rights.

7) Secure.

8) Not transferred to countries without adequate protection.

And data may only be processed under certain sets of conditions, most notably only when the data subject has given his or her consent. In 2006, the European Commission, in response to the perceived terrorist threat posed by unmonitored electronic communications, introduced a Data Retention Directive (Directive 2006/24/E[8]). This requires member governments to introduce legislation compelling Internet service providers to retain details of users' emails, net phone calls, and other web traffic for a year. Content of emails will not be retained, but authorities will be able to obtain access with a warrant. Some countries have refused to implement the legislation. In April 2008, the Working Group on Data Retention, acting on behalf of 32 other organizations, submitted a brief to the European Court of Justice asking for the Directive to be annulled:

> 'While it threatens to inflict great damage on society, its potential benefit appears, overall, to be little. Data retention can support the protection of individual rights only in few and generally less important cases. A permanent, negative effect on crime levels is not to be expected ... [With data retention in place] citizens constantly need to fear that their communications data may at some point lead to false incrimination or governmental or private abuse of the data. Because of this, traffic data retention endangers open communication in the whole of society.' *Working Group on Data Retention, 2008*

In relation to cookies and other tracking techniques, Article 5(3) of the 2002 Telecommunications Privacy Directive states that users must have the opportunity to refuse their use or installation—although a recent report suggested that member states had not universally implemented this provision of the Directive. So-called 'safe harbour' legislation between the EU and US seeks to harmonize data privacy practices, since the US

---

6  According to TeleGeography research, http://www.telegeography.com/products/gig/samples08/gig.zip, © PriMetrica Inc, 2009.

7  http://www.europa.eu/scadplus/leg/en/lvb/l14012.htm.

8  http://eur-lex.europa.eu/LexUriServ/site/en/oj/2006/l_105/l_10520060413en00540063.pdf.

has—in the opinion of European lawmakers at least—a less rigorous IP regime. Samuelson (2005) suggests that the approach taken by the EU has several benefits. Unlike the regime prevailing in the US:

- It is coherent.

- Firms are aware of their responsibilities.

- The technical and system design considerations are clear.

- The public is reassured and therefore more willing to disclose data, given that misuse will be punished.

However, she also observes that the European legislation may be:

- over-broad and paternalistic in its reach;

- slowing down some socially beneficial uses of information;

- technically deficient in relation to the growth of more distributed computer environments (rather than mainframe data collection), which it was not designed to accommodate; and have the potential to

- create unnecessary transaction costs for firms.

During 2008, a number of agencies expressed criticism of the European legislation. The UK Information Commissioner commented: 'It is showing its age and failing to meet new challenges to privacy such as the transfer of personal details across international borders and the huge growth in personal information online. It is high time the law is reviewed and updated for the modern world.'[9] The Commission's own reviews highlight an apparently low level of knowledge of their rights amongst consumers. In 2008, only a quarter of those surveyed knew of all the rights to which they were entitled (European Commission, 2008a).

The US legislative environment was radically transformed with the passage of the USA Patriot Act in 2001, which introduced a raft of legislative measures to increase the surveillance and investigative powers of US law enforcement agencies. Critics suggest, however, that the act did not simultaneously put in place the kinds of checks and balances which would safeguard the civil liberties of the individual. The implications of the Act have had to be tested in the courts by firms affected. For example, a provision allowing the US Government to issue National Security letters to Internet service providers requiring them to release sensitive customer records without judicial review was struck down by the courts in 2004, requiring the Act to be amended. In 2006, the US Department of Justice sought to compel Google, AOL, Microsoft, and Yahoo! to release two months' worth of search queries, under the auspices of the Child Online Protection Act. Although these were to be anonymized, Google was concerned that a release on the scale demanded would substantially undermine users' confidence in the company's ability to keep information private. The subpoena was severely curtailed in the courts.

---

9  See: ICO Press Release, 'UK Privacy Watchdog Spearheads Debate on the Future of European Privacy Law', http://www.ico.gov.uk/upload/documents/pressreleases/2008/ico_leads_debate_070708.pdf.

## Organizational responses to privacy concerns

'In spite of a growing body of evidence that shows privacy's importance to marketing, and in spite of the obvious association between consumer privacy and brand trust, the data show that privacy is still regarded as an inconvenience to the marketing community.'
*Ponemon Institute, 2006*

What strategies have firms develop to address customer's concerns about privacy? Research by the Ponemon Institute amongst US marketers suggests that:

- Over half of US marketers reported 'never' asked for assistance from their corporate privacy offices.

- Over half of US marketers said that corporate privacy policies made their efforts more difficult.

- Fully 94 per cent of US marketers felt poorly informed on privacy laws and regulations.

- However, three-quarters felt that 'respecting consumer privacy preferences' was important to building trust.

Shah et al. (2007) suggest that multi-national companies have two alternative approaches available to them:

1) Implementing a restrictive 'one size fits all' privacy policy that is used across various countries.

2) Implementing different privacy policies that meet the privacy regulations of different countries and the expectations of those citizens.

Their survey of US-based employees of both domestic and international firms suggests that the majority of companies adopt the former route. Compliance with US privacy legislation can be costly for firms. Analysis across 44 US-based organizations in 2004 revealed total direct spending on privacy varied from $0.5mn to $22mn annually (IBM and Ponemon Institute, 2004). However, recent research across Europe put the figure for compliance with European Data Protection legislation as low as a one-off cost of Euro 2,100 with annual continuing costs of Euro 1,600. Large companies consulted did not see a financial burden in such compliance costs.

But the private sector, as represented by the International Chamber of Commerce, is concerned about the potential burden that future regulation might present to business efficiency and effectiveness (Hassan, 2006). It established the Business Action to Support the Information Society (BASIS) project in 2006 and recommended that governments:

- adopt a set of principles to ensure data protection which would not exceed those set out in the 1980 OECD Guidelines;

- adopt a flexible and responsive approach to the protection of personal information which favours self-regulation, and where specific laws are needed to protect consumers that these are enacted in a targeted way;

- educate the public about privacy protection;

- work to ensure a seamless environment for different privacy regimes; and
- avoid developing laws and policies that obstruct cross-border flows of personal data.

## Short case 5.2

### Who regulates the regulators?

Chapter 3 set out a list of recent significant international data theft and losses which generated major privacy breaches. In the UK, some of the most highly publicized data losses have not been experienced by UK companies, but by UK government departments and agencies. For example, in an especially notorious case in 2007, Her Majesty's Revenue and Customs (HMRC) lost two data discs containing all the agency's customer data in respect of the payment of Child Benefit—encompassing some 25m individuals and including addresses, bank account, and National Insurance numbers, as well as children's names and dates of birth. The value to criminals of this data was put at some £1.5bn, in terms of the average value of a stolen identity. In the UK, the Information Commissioner's Office (ICO) is responsible for regulating and enforcing the access to and use of personal information. In addition to dealing with over 100,000 phone calls and 25,000 written complaints in 2008, it reported 277 significant breaches of data protection in the year from November 2007, over 70 per cent of which were committed by public sector bodies (Information Commissioner's Office, 2008b). The office allows individuals to find out what personal information is held about them but is also responsible for enforcing the relevant legislation, including the Data Protection Act, the Privacy and Electronic Communications Regulations, and the Environmental Information Regulations. Its three roles are to:

- educate and influence users and organizations (by promoting good practice);
- resolve problems (by handling complaints against organizations or individuals who have breached the Data Protection Act in the way they hold and handle personal information); and
- enforce (by using legal sanctions against those who ignore or refuse to accept their obligations).

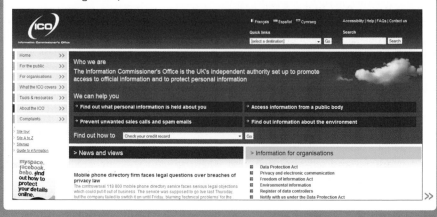

The ICO anticipates that increasing concern about data breaches by organizations will lead to it being greater regulatory powers, including the power to impose civil penalties and carry out spot checks and inspections without prior notice. The Poynter report into the HMRC data loss reported that there were institutional factors that created the environment in which the data loss could occur. It concluded that these were:

- weaknesses in specific information security policies;

- inadequate awareness, communication, and training in information security; and

- a lack of clarity around the governance and accountability for data guardianship.

*Question*
What factors might affect the level of importance attributed to data guardianship within organizations? How might the ICO (for example) seek to influence its priority?

## Intellectual Property

> 'Ideas are expensive to make, but cheap to copy. Ideas are becoming even cheaper to copy and distribute as digital technology and the Internet reduce the marginal cost of reproduction and distribution towards zero.' *HM Treasury, 2006*

The second distinctive area of relevance to firms in relation to the ethics and regulation of e-business is in respect of intellectual property rights (IPR)—the various legal entitlements which are associated with the production of information, ideas, and other intangibles. It is estimated that 70 per cent of an average company's value is vested in its intangible assets today, compared to only 40 per cent in the early 1980s. It is also of course inherently more difficult to protect ideas than it is to protect products. In part, this is because these sorts of entity are essentially non-rivalrous: that is, one person's possession of them cannot prevent their use and enjoyment by another. (So that I can listen to a radio programme—whether on my digital radio or over the Internet—but that does not stop my neighbour doing the same.) And rather like our discussion in relation to privacy, trade-offs therefore lie at the heart of intellectual property. Without legal protection, such innovations run the risk of becoming, in effect, public goods through copying and are susceptible to abuse by free riders, who may contribute less than their fair share of the costs of production. It is estimated by the Business Software Alliance, for example, that 38 per cent of software installed on personal computers worldwide in 2007 was illegal. On the other hand, it is all very well to reward innovation and creativity by granting exclusive rights to the innovators, but this may lead to monopoly pricing, the exclusion of other innovators and undesirable costs to consumers. Heald's (2006) study of so-called 'durable books' (those which continue to sell many copies) concluded that books still under copyright were not as accessible and were more expensive than titles in the public domain.

The way that IPR trade-offs are evolving in practice is therefore of particular interest to the private sector. For example, a study by Lau (2006) suggested that Asian consumers were 'pushed' into copying software illegally because the price of the original software was perceived to be too high. A balance has to be maintained, or the innovators have no economic incentive to innovate. But, as Benkler (2002) has argued, strong IPR may be actually less beneficial to society because it leads to 'commercialization, concentration and homogenization of information production'. The UK's Commission on Intellectual Property Rights (http://www.iprcommission.org) suggests that a weaker stance towards IPR may be in the best interests of developing countries wishing to develop their own capability for innovation.

The instruments available to regulate IPRs are of four types (Figure 5.5):

- Patents: a set of exclusive rights—designed to protect against unauthorized use by others—which is granted to commercially exploit a new, useful and non-obvious invention for a fixed period of time—usually twenty years. Such rights specifically exclude business methods, computer programs and

- Copyright: a set of rights prohibiting others from making copies or adaptations of creative or artistic works for a fixed period of time, including music, movies,

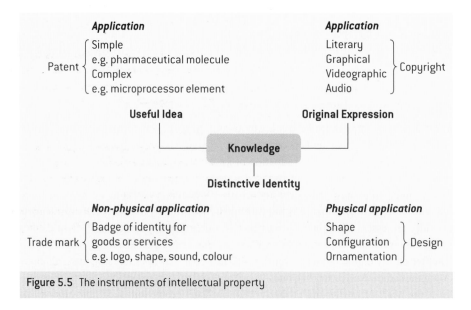

**Figure 5.5** The instruments of intellectual property

software, and radio and television broadcasts. Unlike patents, which must be applied for, copyright comes into force as soon as a work is composed.

- Trademarks: a 'distinctive sign' which is capable of distinguishing the products and services of different businesses and which may not be used by others once they have been registered. Once trademarks become synonymous with a particular category of product of service—for example 'biro' or 'hoover'—they become no longer enforceable.

- Registered designs: a right protecting the visual design of all or part of an object, provided that the object has a new or distinctive character.

The consequences of the Internet's growth have been not only to disrupt the conventional balance, but sometimes extend—or even call into question the relevance of—current IPR trade-offs. Applications of open source principles to collaborative software design (such as the Open Source Initiative, http://opensource.org) or the development of a notion of more flexible copyright which is more useful to innovators and users than the existing regulations (such as the licensing tools developed by Creative Commons Licensing (http://creativecommons.org), are two good examples. Gowers (2006) suggests that there are three main features of the Internet and its associated technologies which are of particular interest in relation to IPR:

- digitization and electronic storage of information (making it far easier to copy, distribute and reverse engineer products);

- growth in complex collaborative innovation processes (often requiring the combination of thousands of individual IP rights); and the emergence of

- new categories of technology (such as software and databases, which require IP protection, but which do not conform to conventional grouping).

## Digitization and its consequences

Many of the barriers to entry to unauthorized copying of digital products—cost, low bandwidth, and other technical limitations—have fallen away in recent years. With an estimated 1bn people having Internet access worldwide, there are now a variety of means by which unauthorized copying of digitized content can take place. These include:

- illegal websites: hosting large quantities of digitized content for free or low-costs distribution; usually located in markets where IPR is poorly enforced or developed;

- file-sharing systems
  - peer-to-peer (P2P) networks: conventional file sharing networks allowing individuals to share digitized content, such as Kazaa, Grokster, and Razorback[10];
  - BitTorrent: a file sharing protocol that uses network bandwidth more efficiently and is therefore more effective for larger files: see Short case 5.3, which discusses the Pirate Bay BitTorrent tracker;
  - LAN file sharing: within a local area network such as a university or business campus.

10 Both Grokster and Kazaa reached global out-of-court settlements with the record industry in 2003 and 2006 respectively.

- digital stream ripping: using software to convert and store music or video that is being digitally broadcast or webcast;

- mobile music piracy: using protocols such as Bluetooth to exchange music files between phones, or swapping memory cards.

Although all kinds of digitized content are susceptible to unauthorized copying, most attention has focused on music, movies, and TV programming and software—not least because of the risks perceived by established private sector interests in this area. In respect of music, the International Federation of the Phonographic Industry (IFPI) estimates that 20bn published songs were illegally downloaded or swapped in 2005 around the world. Pre-launch leakage is also a threat. The available evidence to date suggests that there is a net impact from file sharing systems on CD sales. Indeed, asks Liebowitz (2006), 'when given the choice of free and convenient high quality copies versus purchased originals, is it really a surprise that a significant number of individuals will choose to substitute the free copy for the purchase?' Estimates by Zentner (2006) from a survey of 15,000 European consumers suggest that P2P usage reduced the probability of buying music by 30 per cent. Of course, from another perspective, the extent of piracy reflects the potential for legitimate digital sales: worldwide revenue from such sales increased from $400m to $3.7bn between 2004 and 2008, comprising some 20 per cent of global recorded music sales (39 per cent of US sales), and the clear growth of a genuinely 'mixed economy' in format terms. Indeed, digital music sales themselves are presently split between the online and mobile channels at the global level, with mobile downloading as high as 91 per cent in Japan, where 140m mobile singles were sold in 2008, and 69 per cent in Italy: hence the industry's concern with growing mobile piracy. 21 per cent of US respondents to a survey conducted by MEF (Mobile Entertainment Federation), and 30 per cent globally, have purchased songs at least once on their mobile phones in the past twelve months. In the UK, one-third of 8 to 13-year-olds claimed to share music via their mobile phones in 2006.

The increasing penetration of high-speed broadband Internet connectivity also makes the unauthorized copying of movies and TV programming more practicable. Research commissioned for the US Motion Picture Association put the loss from illegal downloading and sharing in forty-two markets worldwide at $7.1bn in 2005, comprising 39 per cent of total revenues forgone through movie piracy (LEK, 2006).[11] Potential market shares lost to piracy by its US members were highest in China (90 per cent), Russia (79 per cent), and Thailand (79 per cent).

But some of the highest recorded financial losses from unauthorized copying are to be found in the software sector. According to the Business Software Alliance (http://www.bsa.org), the estimated retail value of unlicensed software was $53bn globally due to software piracy in 2008. Worldwide, for every $100 of software purchased legitimately, $69 worth was obtained illegally. In countries with a 75 per cent piracy rate or higher, for every one dollar spent on PC hardware, less than seven cents was spent on legitimate software (Business Software Alliance, 2009). The substantial financial loss incurred reflects the importance of consumer and business software to the world economy, in terms of its impact on job creation, tax revenues and overall economic growth. As with music and movies and TV programming, piracy rates are significantly higher in some countries than others. Figure 5.6 shows piracy rates in twenty countries worldwide, alongside the economic benefits of a ten-percentage-point fall in software piracy rates over the period 2008–2011.

---

11 Piracy rates are based on the value of legitimate movie tickets and DVDs that would have been purchased if pirated versions were not available.

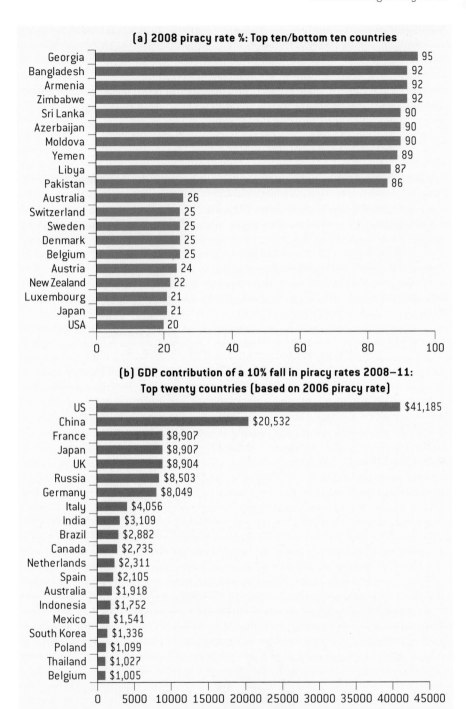

**Figure 5.6** Software piracy rates 2008 and potential economic benefits arising from a 10% reduction in piracy rate, 2008-11

Note: The piracy rate is the total number of units of pirated software deployed in 2008 divided by the total units of software installed.

## Activity box 5.3

### Piracy: where are the biggest problems?

Take a look at Figure 5.6. There seems to be a mismatch between those countries where software piracy is at its most extensive and the countries where a reduction would have the biggest impact on GDP. What might explain this discrepancy? What measures do you think commercial stakeholders might employ to reduce software piracy which would be proportionate to the scale of the problem?

## Short case 5.3

### The Pirate Bay: turning legit?

For some years, the Pirate Bay was the world's largest BitTorrent tracker, allowing users to download the means to connect with other users hosting data files including audio, video, applications, games, and other categories, including pornography. Based in Sweden, the organization has been operating publically since 2004 using as the basis for its activities that it is against censorship on the net and is understood to have some 25m 'peers' worldwide, sharing access to over 1.8m torrent files including pre-release movies. (For example, a 1GB early print of the X-Men movie, *X-Men Origins: Wolverine*, was uploaded in March 2009, one month before its official release, and had generated 75,000 illegal downloads within two days.) However, the Pirate Bay was not only funded by donations but also from advertising revenue, leading to accusations that it was commercially exploiting copyright-protected work. As a result, the site provided a constant target for litigation. Indeed, the organization uploaded lawyers' letters and its responses to its website (http://thepiratebay.org/legal). In summary: 'No action (except ridiculing the senders) has been taken by us because of these. :-).' The Pirate Bay was closed down for a short period in 2006 when police seized computers as part of a lawsuit with plaintiffs including Warner, Columbia, 20th Century Fox, Sony BMG, Universal, and EMI. The site was up again within three days and subsequently developed backup sites in Belgium and Russia. Countries from Denmark to Italy have forced ISPs to block the site. More seriously in 2008, four of the site's operators were charged with inciting others to breach copyright laws. The court found the operators guilty in April 2009 and handed down a one-year jail sentence and £2.4m in damages.

»

A more lasting challenge to the site's continued operation in Sweden was the introduction of the country's new Intellectual Property Rights Enforcement Directive (IPRED) in April 2009, which will, at least in principle, make it easier to identify illicit file sharers who use Pirate Bay's facilities. fifty-six per cent of Swedish men aged between 26 and 35 reportedly engage in active file sharing. The IPRED legislation will also increase financial penalties and will make any large-scale activity a criminal offence. In response, however, Pirate Bay has introduced IPREDator, an anonymity server using VPN which, in return for Euro 5 per month, keeps no records or logs of the end user. But is the Pirate Bay turning legit? In June 2009, it was announced that Global Gaming Factory would acquire the Pirate Bay for £4.7m, that 'files would be hosted legally', and that the company 'would pay users to share files'.

*Question*

Does the Pirate Bay have a future?

## Networked innovation

Protecting or even determining intellectual property rights is more challenging in a business environment increasingly characterized by networked innovation, involving a number of organizations or individuals working on a complex problem. We discuss this model of e-business strategy in chapter 6 and talk about innovation more generally in chapter 8. But networked innovation often involves:

- complex collaborative learning processes (in which individuals or organizations incrementally develop their understanding of an idea or concept);

- the tacit and dispersed character of ideas (where there may be the need to bring together specialists from a wide range of business to achieve a systematic vision of a new activity); and a reality in which

- ideas which are uncertainly held (the holder of an idea cannot articulate its roots or logic).

For example, the development of mobile Internet-based banking services required wide-ranging expertise in hardware, software, payment systems, database management, and financial services. IP rights within such networks either have to be flexibly demarcated and regulated, or those involved have to be willing to pursue a considerably more open model. The development of Bluetooth wireless technology is an excellent example of the former approach (http://www.bluetooth.com), and is discussed in Short case 6.3. The discussions and interactions of large multi-national corporations have resulted in a core specification for Bluetooth which is set about with formal contractual and licensing arrangements involving the assignment of IPRs. Somewhere in the middle, we can see the use of ideas such as 'patent pools', where the various providers of RFID technology have joined together to charge one royalty fee and to share royalty incomes according to the rights held. At the other extreme, we can see the way in which open source software has emerged as a substantially less centralized and essentially more creative model of software production and development. The open source philosophy encourages source code to be published and made available to the public, enabling anyone—from individuals to large companies—to copy, modify, and redistribute the code without paying royalties or fees. Mozilla Firefox, Open Office, and Linux are probably the most popularly known examples. (Short case 8.2 describes the experience of Mozilla Firefox in more detail.) Creative Commons licensing similarly takes a more open approach to innovation:

> 'An idea is not diminished when more people use it. Creative Commons aspires to cultivate a commons in which people can feel free to re-use not only ideas, but also words, images and music without asking permission—because permission has already been granted to everyone.' *http://creativecommons.org/about/legal*

## Activity box 5.4

### Protecting networked innovation

Examine either (1) the Apple Apps Store on iTunes or (2) Mozilla Firefox add-ins at https://addons.mozilla.org/en-US/firefox. For either apps or add-ins, where does the intellectual property reside and how are the rights of various stakeholders protected?

## New technologies

Finally, e-business permits the creation of new entities which have IP implications. In this way, for example, the collection of material into database structures—sometimes for the first time—has changed the specificity of that information. By information specificity, we mean the extent to which the value of information is restricted to its use or acquisition by specific individuals or during specific time periods. The development of full-text journal aggregation services for company researchers and universities is one illustration of this trend. Hitherto hard-copy journals available to registered users of a small number of university libraries are now increasingly stored as digitized content within large searchable databases developed by third-party firms who contract with journal publishers. Firms such as EBSCO Industries (http://www.ebscohost.com/) and ProQuest LLC (http://www.proquestcompany.com), owned by the Cambridge Information Group, make this information much more widely available online, requiring their clients to register legitimate users to access their services. Although the print material copyright principles still apply in the online version, the equivalent to the unauthorized copying that might have been undertaken by conventional photocopier has the potential to be much more widespread when electronic material is involved.

### Activity box 5.5

**Standing on the shoulders of giants**

Google Scholar provides a search of academic literature across many disciplines and sources, including theses, books, abstracts, and articles (http://scholar.google.com). How does Google make published material available? In particular, how does it address the IP and copyright issues that arise?

## Regulatory developments

The international governance framework for intellectual property has at its head the World Intellectual Property Organization (WIPO, http://www.wipo.int). An agency of the United Nations since 1974, WIPO seeks to develop 'a balanced and accessible international IP system' and administers treaties on behalf of its members, including the World Copyright Treaty (WCT). Ninety per cent of the world's nations are members. The World Trade Organization's 1994 Agreement on Trade-Related Aspects of Intellectual Property Rights (TRIPs) expanded the characteristics of what could constitute intellectual property—such as 'making patents available in all fields of technology' (Article 27)—and introduced IP law into the international trading system. However, there is some ambiguity in what is meant by 'all fields of technology', particularly in relation to e-business processes and computer-implemented inventions. Further, TRIPs has been criticized by advocates of trade liberalization as 'intellectual protectionism'.

Enforcement of IP rights is a matter for nation-states. In relation to patents, for example, whilst there is a comprehensive and unitary framework for patent enforcement within the US, within the European Union, there are thirty-one different legal jurisdictions, some of which have interpreted the patent laws in different ways, working under the European Patent Convention and the rules of practice of the European Patent Office (http://www.european-patent-office.org). Further, the European Parliament voted down a proposed Europe-wide directive on the patentability of computer-implemented inventions in 2005. According to Moetteli (2005), the result is currently a 'risky and complex legal environment'.

The conventional framework of protection of intellectual property rights has struggled to keep up with the IP consequences of the Internet's development. The Business Software Alliance has expressed its concern that unauthorizsed copying of software is not taken as seriously by governments and penalties are not as severe as in more conventional criminal cases. In the UK, for example, software theft carries with it a jail sentence of up to two years compared to up to ten years for theft of more tangible products. BSA proposes a five-step process for governments to reduce levels of software piracy:

1) Implement the WIPO Copyright Treaty.

2) Create strong and workable enforcement mechanisms (in conformity with the World Trade Organization's 'Trade-Related Aspects of Intellectual Property Rights Agreements', TRIPS).

3) Step up enforcement with dedicated resources:

   a. Create specialized IP enforcement units at the national level.

   b. Increase cross-border mutual collaboration.

   c. Support training of law enforcement professionals.

4) Increase public education and awareness.

5) Lead by example through active enforcement of IPR in the public sector.

Software-based digital rights management (DRM) tools have been developed by firms to control access to and use of digital data in an attempt to enforce compliance with copyright requirements. Whilst DRM has an unclear legal status in some jurisdictions, Europe and the US again stand out as legislatively sophisticated. The European Union's 2001 Copyright Directive (EUCD)[12] requires member states to implement legal protections for DRM, although the transposition of this requirement has not been even, with French transposition giving rise to the possibility that manufacturers might be required to share their proprietary DRMs. DRMs have also presented tempting targets for hacking. In the US, the passage of the 1998 Digital Millennium Copyright Act (DCMA) goes so far as to criminalize those seeking to circumvent measures taken to protect copyright, not merely infringing copyright itself.

The music publishing industry has been particularly assiduous at defending its IPR. In addition to legal action targeted initially at file sharing sites and subsequently through high-profile prosecutions of individual downloaders, it has achieved considerable success in raising public awareness of the problem. According to one case study, over 14,000 downloads of one album in the nine weeks before its official launch could have been supplemented by 450,000 further downloads—only prevented by intensive legal action by the publishers and industry associations. But at what cost? Evidence from elsewhere also suggests that legal challenges have not always been as effective as the industry has supposed:

'Individuals who share a substantial number of music files react to legal threats differently from those who share a lesser number of files … Even after legal threats and the resulting lowered levels of file sharing, the availability of music files on these networks remains substantial.' *Bhattacharjee et al., 2006*

12 Directive 2001/29/EC.

And as we discuss elsewhere, there is evidence in any case that the growth of social networking sites such as YouTube is changing the way in which users identify emerging music artistes—indeed redefining for many the ways in which popular culture evolves.

# Internet fraud

Fraud is of course not new. But the linking of fraud to emerging e-business technologies has created distinctive ethical and regulatory challenges. Rather like distinguishing between weeds and flowers, distinguishing between useful and harmful Internet activity is not as straightforward as it sounds and is often a subjective decision, dependent on the individual and upon the context in which the activity takes place. There are certain activities which are clearly fraudulent, such as identity theft; some activities (such as file sharing and unsanctioned digital downloading) in which users connive but which are also illegal in most jurisdictions; and still more activities which have nuisance value, but which are not inherently fraudulent.

## Spamming, spyware, and malware

Spamming involves the use of email or other systems to send unsolicited messages in bulk.[13] Internet folk myth has it that the term was first coined in 1993 by a Usenet administrator. The extent to which an email may be unsolicited is, of course, not clear-cut—particularly, for example, once we move beyond established commercial relationships between customers and organizations. In practice, there is no internationally agreed definition of what spam actually is. Whilst spamming is not always inherently malicious or fraudulent, it constitutes a significant nuisance and will affect the productivity of users and the efficiency of business systems. It is estimated that between 90 and 95 per cent of all raw email is spam. The costs of spamming[14] are borne by users, companies and Internet service providers. In addition to undermining trust in the Internet, effects include those which arise from:

- reductions in personal productivity (increasing time spent by the individual in opening and/or deleting unfiltered spam messages);
- increasing requirement to outsource anti-spam measures (from specialist third-party organizations such as MessageLabs, Sophos, and Symantec, because of increasing diversity of spam and inventiveness of spammers);
- reductions in systems efficiency and effectiveness (because of costs of installing additional server capacity; time spent by ICT staff managing the problem);
- loss of reputation amongst clients or customers (for example, amongst Internet Service Providers because of a perceived lack of ability to reduce levels of spam received by end users);
- increased potential for personal distress (for individuals from offensive promotional material, pornographic or otherwise).

13  A fuller definition can be found here: http://www.spamhaus.org/definition.html.
14  You can calculate the costs of spam for any organization on the 'ready reckoner' provided at http://www.praetor.net/marketing/spamcalc.htm.

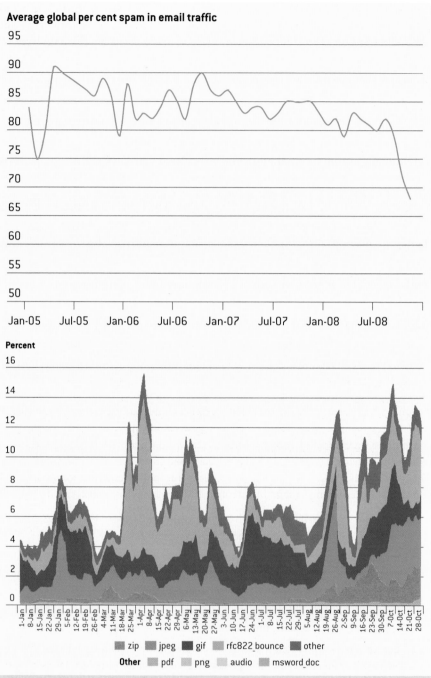

**Figure 5.7** (a) Spam rate (average % of emails intercepted as spam) 2005-08

(b) Spam by content type 2008 (omitting html and text only Spam)

The majority of spam email received by Internet users in North America and Europe during 2007 could be traced back (via aliases and addresses, redirects, hosting locations of sites and domains) to a small number of around 200 known spam operations (so-called 'spam gangs') according to the independent Spamhaus Project (see Short case 5.4).[15] Despite one major US hosting service sympathetic to spamming, McColo, being taken down in 2008, after which spam levels dropped by half, spam levels have been increasing again. Indeed, during the first part of 2009, it was reported by Google that spam levels were growing by 1.2 per cent per day.[16] Such operations specialize in particular kinds of scam, including pharmaceutical, pornographic, and stock promotion emails and their success relies upon a proportion of users responding to the blandishments of the sender. In fact, Böhme and Holz (2006) suggest that the stock spam business model actually works. They found that spam message campaigns were associated with an increase in the trading activity of the cited stock and positive abnormal returns shortly after the messages had been distributed. Fifty-five per cent of North American households report using spam-blocking technologies to avoid unwanted messages—increasing to 81 per cent amongst broadband households (Kim, 2006).

## Short case 5.4

### The Spamhaus Project

The Spamhaus Project, founded in 1998, is an independent, not-for-profit organization. Based in Geneva, but with servers in eighteen countries worldwide, its goal is fourfold: (1) to track spam activity on the Internet; (2) to provide dependable anti-spam protection for Internet networks; (3) to work with Law Enforcement agencies to identify and pursue spammers worldwide; and (4) to lobby governments for effective anti-spam legislation (http://www.spamhaus.org). Spamhaus estimates that its activities serve to protect over 1.4bn user mailboxes. The National Cyber Forensics and Training Alliance awarded The Spamhaus Project its Cyber Crime Fighter Award in 2008.

The Project maintains a list of the 100 worst known 'spam gangs' (ROKSO—Register of Known Spam Operations) that ISPs use to detect known spammers seeking to use their networks. Spam gangs consist on average of four to five spammers (giving a total of between 400 to 500 spammers in the ROKSO list). To be placed on the ROKSO list, spammers must first be terminated by three ISPs (the so-called 'three strikes' rule). The project also provides a series of open source 'blocking lists' (DNSBLs—Domain Name Server Blocking Lists) which are widely used by governments, ISPs, and businesses. A DNSBL is a database that can be queried in real time by Internet mail servers to obtain an opinion on the origin of incoming email. Every Internet network that chooses to implement spam filtering is, by doing so, making a policy decision governing acceptance and handling of inbound email. It is the ISP rather than Spamhaus which makes the decision on whether to use DNSBLs, which DNSBLs to use, and what to do with an incoming email if the email message's originating IP Address is 'listed' on the DNSBL. The DNSBL itself, like all spam filters, can only answer whether a condition has been met or not.    »

15  http://www.spamhaus.org.
16  http://googleenterprise.blogspot.com/2009/03/spam-data-and-trends-q1-2009.html.

**Table 5.2  Top ten ROKSO spammers, April 2009**

| Rank | Name | Spammer or spam gang | Country |
|------|------|----------------------|---------|
| 1 | Canadian Pharmacy | A long time running pharmacy spam operation. Uses botnet spam techniques to send tens-of-millions of spams per day. Probably uses many affiliates all over the world to spam but is probably based in Eastern Europe and hosts sites on botnets | USA |
| 2 | Leo Kuvayev / BadCow | Does 'OEM CD' pirated software spam, copy-cat pharmaceuticals, porn spam, porn payment collection, etc. Spams using virus-created botnets and seems to be involved in virus distribution. Partnered with Vlad—aka 'Mr Green' | Russian Federation |
| 3 | HerbalKing | Massive affiliate spam program for snakeoil Body Part Enhancement scams. Also does replica luxury goods, pharma, and porn. Spams via botnets, bulletproof hosting offshore and even sometimes uses fast flux hosting. | India |
| 4 | Vincent Chan / yoric.net | Mainly do pharmacy, and are able to send out huge amounts daily. The use a vast amount of compromised machines, for sending, hosting and proxy hijacking. | Hong Kong |
| 5 | Alex Blood/ Alexander Mosh/ AlekseyB/ Alex Polyakov | Massive botnet and child-porn spam ring, also pharma, mortgage, and more. May work with Kuvayev and Yambo. | Ukraine |
| 6 | Nikhil Kumar Pragji/ Dark-Mailer | Through the Dark-Mailer Windows based proxy-botnet based spamware, this spammer is responsible for and behind a large portion of the world's illegally sent spam | Australia |
| 7 | Peter Severa/ Peter Levashov | A spamming partner of Alan Ralsky and other spam gangs. | Russian Federation |
| 8 | Yambo Financials | Huge spamhaus tied into distribution and billing for child, animal, and incest-porn, pirated software, and pharmaceuticals. Run their own merchant services (credit-card 'collection' sites) set up as a fake 'bank' | Ukraine |
| 9 | Ruslan Ibragimov/ send-safe.com | Stealth spamware creator. One of the larger criminal spamming operations around. Runs a CGI mailer on machines in Russia and uses hijacked open proxies and virus infected PCs to flood the world with spam | Russian Federation |
| 10 | Sistemnet | Rogue Turkish network dedicated to hosting Eastern European botmasters and related cybercrime gang | Turkey |

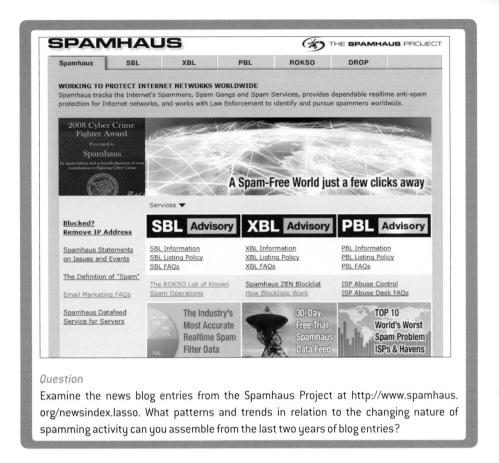

*Question*

Examine the news blog entries from the Spamhaus Project at http://www.spamhaus.org/newsindex.lasso. What patterns and trends in relation to the changing nature of spamming activity can you assemble from the last two years of blog entries?

More serious than promotional spam is more sophisticated phishing which is aimed at stealing personal information leading to identity theft, and involves programs seeking to take control of users' computers, or those seeking to damage or disrupt computer systems. Phishing[17] is a particular form of spam, often generated in combination with a fraudulent website, and, to date, targeted users of online financial services and auction sites. It uses both psychological, social engineering, and technical means to steal personal identity data and financial account information. Fraudulent emails, masquerading as genuine communications from financial institutions seek to persuade users to link to counterfeit websites where they may be led to disclose financial data. Phishing appears to be the fastest growing category of spam worldwide, although there are neither comprehensive figures on phishing incidence nor the financial loss incurred by users misled by the phishing attack. It was estimated in early 2009 that one in 300 emails were phishing emails and in the second half of 2008 between 15,000 to 27,000 unique phishing sites were in existence worldwide (an increase from 1,100 in 2004).

---

17  As early as 1996, stolen bank accounts were being referred to as 'phish'. The term phishing refers to the luring of customer account details from the 'sea' of Internet users.

A number of phishing variants have emerged. So-called 'spear-phishing' uses fraudulently obtained personal information to target specific users with an email which appears to be more trustworthy since it contains personal data. 'Vishing', or voice phishing, involves an email which requests the user to call a phone number, rather than clicking a weblink. A professional-sounding customer service line harvests the user's personal and financial data. Rather like spam attacks, phishing attacks originate from fewer than five networks of infected computers (so-called 'botnets'), the majority of which are based in the US, China, and Germany, according to the anti-phishing working group (http://www.antiphishing.org).

Phishing and malicious spam can also be used to download computer code (so-called malware or criminalware) on to users' computers. Anti-virus and anti-spam firm Sophos (http://www.sophos.com) identifies seven specific forms of spyware:

1) Password and information stealers: stealing sensitive personal information.

2) Keyloggers: monitoring keystrokes with the intention of stealing personal information.

3) Banking Trojans: monitoring information entered into banking applications and banking web forms.

4) Backdoor Trojans: containing any of the functionality of 1–3, but including the ability to allow hackers unrestricted remote access to a computer system when it is online.

5) Botnet worms: creating a network of infected computers, configured remotely to work together.

6) Browser hijackers: reducing browser security settings and/or modify browser settings with the intention of redirecting users to automatic download sites).

7) Downloaders: installing other, potentially malicious, programs without the user's knowledge.

The subsequent use of the data so harvested can result in identity theft/fraud or direct financial loss. Identity theft leading to financial loss is not, of course, a new phenomenon. But we might expect that the Internet lends itself, because of its inherent capabilities, to a growth in such occurrences. In practice, there is little reliable global data on the extent of and the costs associated with identity theft. In 2003, the US Federal Trade Commission estimated that more than 27 million people had been victims of identity theft or fraud during the previous five years, costing them $5bn and businesses and financial institutions almost $48bn. At the time, some 58 per cent of customers were contacted via email or through a website. Complaints about identity theft made up some 37 per cent of all consumer complaints to the FTC's ID Theft Clearing House service during 2005. Figure 5.8 shows the growth in ID theft complaints in the US from 2000 to 2007, which suggests an increasing trend over the long term. Commercial estimates suggest that online ID fraud (from phishing, spyware, or whilst making an online purchase—as against stolen wallets and the like) totalled 11 per cent of possible causes towards the end of 2008 in the US (Javelin, 2009). (It is worth observing that 65 per cent of US citizens reporting ID theft did not know how their information had been accessed.)

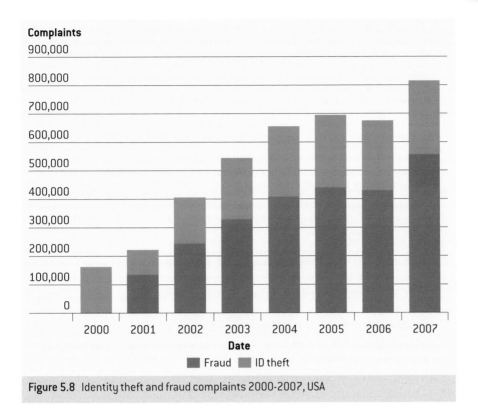

**Figure 5.8** Identity theft and fraud complaints 2000-2007, USA

## Regulatory developments

Many countries have passed new laws in relation to unsolicited commercial emails. Most European Union countries have transposed the Directive on Privacy and Electronic Communications 2002/58/EC, which came into effect in October 2003 and seeks to provide for a uniform legal solution to the issue of spam across jurisdictions. Article 13 of the Directive obliges member states to introduce legislation governing spam, requiring honest email headers and for businesses to gain prior consent ('opt-in') before sending unsolicited emails for direct marketing. This consent must be explicitly given, except where there is an existing customer relationship. The EU legislation is technology neutral in that it covers spam disseminated via SMS, MMS, VoIP, etc. Senders also have to indicate clearly the use of cookies or other tracking devices (including spyware).

In the US, the CAN-SPAM Act (Controlling the Assault of Non-Solicited Pornography and Marketing Act) of 2003 provides for federal legislation in relation to spam, including:

- a ban on false or misleading header information (any email's 'From', 'To', and routing information—including the originating domain name and email address—must be accurate and identify the person who initiated the email);
- a prohibition on deceptive subject lines (the subject line cannot mislead the recipient about the contents or subject matter of the message); and

- A requirement to give recipients an opt-out method (the marketer must provide a return email address or another Internet-based response mechanism that allows a recipient to ask not to be sent future email messages to that email address).

But the fact that European national legislative bodies have some discretion in the ways in which they introduce anti-spam regulations, it has been suggested, may cause some difficulty:

> 'The EU's conscious choice to allow diversity in spam legislation is the opposite of the US's standardization of divergent state spam law with CAN-SPAM. Though the policy reasoning around Europe is uniform (and in the Directive), varied implementation of these values could make a big difference in effectiveness. Differences in punishment, administration, cause of action, and simple investment in fighting spam could make European spam policy more uneven than the US policy once was, even with a uniform directive.' *Bolin, 2005*

At the international level, the proliferation of organizations seeking to co-ordinate a global response to the threat of spam has been almost as impressive as the growth of spam itself. Those claiming a role range from the Organization for Economic Cooperation and Development's Spam Task Force, the International Telecommunications Union's Global Cybersecurity Initiative (ITU), the European Union's Contact Network for Spam Enforcement Authorities (CNSA), the London Action Plan (LPA), the International Consumer Protection Enforcement Network (ICPEN), and the Asia-Pacific Economic Cooperation (APEC). Within several anti-spam organizations, expert and company focus groups have been created to defend their constituents' interests. In the US alone, these include the Anti-Phishing Working Group, (http://www.antiphishing.org), Phishtank (http://www.phishtank.com) and the National Consumers' League (http://www.phishinginfo.org).

The private sector again favours self-regulation in relation to unsolicited commercial email, whilst recognizing that governments need to legislate—or extend existing legislation—to focus on the prevention of illegitimate, fraudulent, or harmful messages. Measures within organizations to mitigate the effects of such activities would include:

- education: employees having to understand the need to be cautious when opening attachments and downloading and installing software;
- policy: ensuring that a robust, company-wide Internet policy is in place aimed at preventing unauthorized downloads; and
- technology: installing the latest browser and operating system patches, ensuring that browser security settings are set correctly, and deploying up-to-date security software.

## The regulation of the Internet

> 'The governance of issues related to the Internet is multi-layered, fragmented, complex and generally highly distributed.' *Dutton and Peltu, 2005*

Stability, consistency, and security in the way the Internet functions are critical to businesses and governance is therefore of legitimate interest to all kinds of organizations. Two broad issues dominate contemporary discussion of Internet governance. There is firstly the tension between the flexible (often absent) governance arrangements which facilitated the rapid early growth of the net, and subsequently that of the new digital businesses, and an ensuing tendency towards centralized control by governments and other institutions, which may risk choking off the kind of innovation that has characterized the Internet's growth to date. The plethora of institutional organizations and arrangements which seeks to regulate, co-ordinate or otherwise influence Internet governance is striking. The Internet itself, of course, comprises a network of hundreds and thousands of networks—not a single entity capable of being managed by a single organization.

The role of governments in Internet governance is a second important consideration, in which the distinction between Internet *government* and *governance* is a necessary one. Although the Internet is an increasingly international phenomenon, much of the original infrastructure was established and has developed within the US. This has left a legacy of US regulatory control, both real and perceived, which has been called into question by some commentators. For example, two key organizations managing issues in relation to the fundamental architecture of the Internet are working under contract from the US Department of Justice—ICANN and Verisign.

- The Internet Corporation for Assigned Names and Numbers (ICANN) http://www.icann.org has been responsible for 'maintaining the operation of the Internet' (specifically the global co-ordination of the Internet's domain names and addresses) since 1998, under contract with the US Department of Commerce. Its responsibilities are not just those of a 'technical caretaker', but also include the development of technical policy towards such issues as choosing top-level domains (TLDs) which may have broader policy implications (such as delisting). In late 2006, this contract was renewed to 2011, with ICANN reporting to the DoC and consulting with the Department on any material changes proposed. In the intervening period, however, ICANN has evolved from an organization where decisions could be quickly reached by a few people in one office, to one with a complex structure in which even simple decisions about the evolution of the Internet's architecture involve hundreds of working groups.

- Verisign's Internet Services Division, based in Mountain View, California, has run the .com domain registry since 1999 and .net since 2005. The .com domain is still the most popular of the net's addresses, with nearly 80m domains registered in 2008 (45 per cent of the 177m registered in that year). The company claims to handle 50bn domain name system inquiries daily. In 2006, the US Department of Commerce renewed Verisign's contract until 2012, subject to safeguards on the level of price increases.

Critics have questioned the continued dominance of US involvement with such fundamental aspects of Internet regulation including control over the delisting of top-level domains. They point to the fact that the US is no longer the country with the highest number of Internet users. The US commanded 220m Internet users—72 per cent of the population—in 2009 against 298m in China (22 per cent) and 297m in the European

**Table 5.3  Categories of Internet governance issues**

| Type | Key issues | Examples |
|---|---|---|
| I: Internet centric | Development of core technical Internet infrastructure and web standards and protocols. Sustains efficient, reliable Internet operations and timely adaptability to continuing and often rapid technological and other changes affecting the Internet | Standards setting for the Internet and World Wide Web |
| | | Assigning Internet addresses |
| | | Routing messages between senders and receivers |
| | | Smooth and secure Internet operations and development of core systems and services |
| II: Internet-user centric | How use or misuse of the Internet by individuals, groups and organizations—for legal or illegal, appropriate or inappropriate behaviour—is defined and policed. Deals with policies generally set by local, regional, and national jurisdictions, with international aspects developed through communication and negotiation among jurisdictions | Unsolicited 'spam' e-mail |
| | | Violations of users' privacy; data protection |
| | | Fraud and other cybercrimes |
| | | Malicious attacks on the stability or security of systems on the net |
| | | Employment of Internet 'chat rooms' by paedophiles to contact young people |
| | | Unwanted exposure to pornographic Web content |
| III: Non-Internet centric | Policy and practice anchored in bodies and jurisdictions not concerned primarily with Internet- related issues. Provides local and international policy contexts where developments in Internet infrastructure and use intersect with wider existing governance processes that shape more detailed Internet-related policies | Political expression, censorship |
| | | Copyright, intellectual property rights (IPR), trademarks |
| | | Closing digital divides, meeting UN MDGs |
| | | Human rights, cultural and linguistic diversity |
| | | Transmitting content through telecommunications carriers |

Union (61 per cent). They question whether US administration would be content (for example) to have a non-US government playing a similar role.

> 'When you concentrate power, whether it's the low-rent, measly power ICANN had, or full-blown global governmental power, that focus of power attracts the wrong people. People who are self-appointed to represent other people are there, governments are there, the private sector is there, but the world at large isn't.'
> *Dyson, 2004*

The concern here, from civic society stakeholders, is that in seeking to regulate for the perceived abuses which occur on the Internet, we may risk destroying its beneficial aspects by over-policing it, or by politicizing it. Nevertheless, it is likely that national governments will play an increasingly interventionist role in relation to the Internet. This trend may not be one which is inherently attractive to business either, if the effect is to suppress innovation and creativity, discourage investment or hamper the economic growth and development which has characterized the growth of the Internet over the past ten years. Further, we must note that there may be legitimately different views on how the Internet should be regulated—outside developed Western economies, for example. Long case 5.2 discusses the experience of Internet regulation in China.

When trying to categorize regulation, it is often helpful to think in terms of 'layers' of governance. In one early attempt, Benkler (1996) differentiates between three layers of communication: a 'physical infrastructure' layer, through which information travels, a 'logical' layer that controls the infrastructure, and a 'content' layer which contains the information which runs through the network. As a result, for example, the governance of IPR takes place at the content layer, while the question of universal access is really one for the infrastructure layer. Dutton and Peltu (2005) also find it helpful to distinguish between three broad types of Internet governance, but recognize that governance issues have not only gone well beyond the purely technical into the economic and the social, but that there are also many overlaps and interactions between layers (Table 5.3). They see the major challenge to be 'the devil in the detail' that emerges from the requirement to co-ordinate the different institutions, organizational forms, and processes. Internet governance is very much a 'work in progress'.

'There can be little doubt that the development of a global Information Society will require extraordinary co-operation, collaboration and co-ordination.' *Vinton Cerf, 2006*

---

## Long case 5.1

### Location-based services

The development of *location-based services* (LBS) driven by the growth in mobile communications and network services and powered by increasingly accurate locational tools and data, has prompted widespread concerns over both information and personal privacy.

> 'I used to be worried when my boyfriend didn't answer calls ... Now I can rest assured that he is at work or busy attending a seminar.' *Korean subscriber*

Technology analyst Gartner estimated that there would be up to 300m subscribers to LBS worldwide by 2011. The growth rate is dependent upon the roll-out of GPS-enabled mobile handsets and smartphones and, whilst the global recession which began in 2008 has slowed growth rates in the sales of these devices, the phenomenal success of Apple's iPhone (doubling its market share to 10.7 per cent between 2007 and 2008) has helped maintain the proportion of such phones sold as a percentage of all mobile devices to some 12 per cent. Several application areas have been suggested:                           »

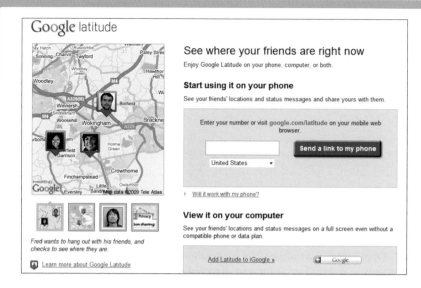

Fred wants to hang out with his friends, and
checks to see where they are.

Learn more about Google Latitude

- information and proximity services: local weather, news, tracking of people and assets, 'Find nearest store', concierge; find a friend, or a date;
- navigation: pedestrian and vehicle, congestion alerts;
- emergency response: disaster tracking, child tracking, 'astray alerts'.

Services such as 'Astray Alerts', in relation to the whereabouts of children, naturally resonate strongly with parental fears and concerns. Some 45 per cent of US parents surveyed with children under 13 in 2007 were 'interested in and willing to pay' for a child-tracking service. Examples include the US services Chaperone by Verizon Wireless and Teen Arrive Alive, which track family members' locations and driving habits: 'Basically, we feel like what we're offering are tools for parents to better protect their kids,' (Vice President of Marketing, Teen Arrive Alive). US telecoms company Sprint-Nextel offers a mobile locator service to allow employers to locate workers in real time. It is not hard to see, say critics, the potential for misuse of locational information about individuals, but in some markets the services have already proved attractive. In South Korea, where there are an average of 2.73 mobile handsets per household, mobile telecommunications carriers reported combined revenue of $5.1m from location-based services that utilized GPS-enabled handsets as early as 2003. Some 3.8m people have signed up for such services. The Information Ministry had planned to require local handset manufacturers to incorporate a GPS chip in all their products, but this move was successfully resisted by local human rights groups.

LBS went mainstream in 2009, with Google's launch of Google Latitude.

*Questions*

1. What do you think will prove to be the most successful types of location-based service? Why?

2. Does the growth in location-based services represent a major step forward in personal safety or a major threat to individuals' privacy?

3. To what extent will a country's privacy culture affect the take-up of location-based services?

## Long case 5.2

### Internet regulation in China

The Internet population of China was estimated to be some 298m in 2008 (China Internet Network Information Center, 2009), and now accounts for 46 per cent of users in Asia and nearly 19 per cent of Internet users worldwide. Chinese Internet users—of whom 67 per cent were under 30 years of age in 2008—log an estimated 5.5bn hours online each week, compared to only 3.7bn in the US.

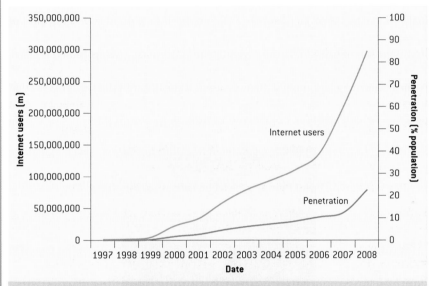

**Figure 5.9**  Internet growth in China, 1997-2008

Given the extent of this growth and the forecast that Internet usage in China will increase significantly, the nature of Internet activity regulation in China is clearly of some interest. The Chinese Government is estimated to have spent $121bn on e-government activity of various kinds in 2003, through a series of 'Golden projects', with the rate of spending growing at some 40 per cent per annum. However, the goal of such projects, it has been suggested, is not necessarily to improve the efficiency of government bureaucratic processes for the benefit of the citizen—a goal naturally assumed in other countries (West, 2003).

> 'Thus far... China's e-government project, both in purpose and in design, is oriented primarily towards strengthening central government control over other government entities, enterprises and citizens.' *Kluver, 2005*

The Ministry of Information Industry (MII) was established in 1998 to assume many of the responsibilities for telecommunications and Internet policy and regulation, although » there are still eleven other entities involved to varying degrees in Internet regulation. Internet information providers must be licensed by MII and must seek approval before establishing a joint venture with a foreign company. They are held legally responsible for content. MII also requires ISPs to retain records of log-on times, accounts, and originating phone numbers for 60 days, whilst content providers are required to monitor content and track users. Internet cafés must install blocking software and keep records of users and visits available for the Public Security Bureau. The OpenNet Initiative classes China's Internet filtering regime as the most pervasive of its kind in the world: 'the state employs a sophisticated infrastructure that filters content at multiple levels and that tolerates overblocking as the price of preventing access to prohibited sites' (Open Net Initiative, 2006). Some estimates suggest that 30,000 people are formally involved in filtering activity. In addition, self-censorship, through, for example, the 'Public Pledge of Self-Regulation and Professional Ethics' issued by the 150-member Internet Society of China, is a key component of regulation. Because the regulations on what is, and what is not, banned content are not specific (there is no list of banned sites, for example) Internet users tend to be reluctant to test the boundaries of what is permissible and content providers and ISPs tend to err on the side of caution.

China's 'self-censorship' approach has caused difficulties for foreign-owned digital businesses seeking to operate in the US. For example, Google claims that 'self censorship runs counter to Google's most basic values and commitments as a company' (Schrage, 2006). Despite this, the company launched Google.cn in 2006, a service which actively filtered content in response to Chinese laws and regulations. The company was not the only foreign business to act in this way, but was heavily criticized. In response, Google observed that it would:

- maintain its Chinese language Google.com unfiltered service alongside Google.cn;

- disclose to users where search results or links have been removed; and

- not introduce further services (such as Gmail or Blogger) until the privacy and security of users' information is sufficiently well protected.

This strategy, it claimed, would allow Google to make a meaningful contribution to the overall expansion of access to information in China. Such a contribution could be important. In addition to the sheer forecast growth in numbers, there are broader implications. A study conducted by the Chinese Academy of Social Sciences concluded that:

'the political impact of the Internet is more significant than it is in other countries. The impact can be seen not only in the relationship between government and citizens but also among people who share similar political interests. Thus, we can predict that as the Internet becomes more popular in China, the impact on politics will be stronger.' *Guo, 2005*

*Questions*

1. Was Google's decision over self-censorship of search results in China the correct one?

2. If the forecasts of Internet penetration in China are correct, 350m users will be working under the 'self-regulation' philosophy by 2010. What are the implications of this state of affairs, for (a) Internet users; (b) The Chinese government; and (c) Digital businesses outside China?

# ✪ Chapter Summary

The chapter began by considering the range of legal and ethical issues facing individuals, organizations, and regulators in respect of privacy and e-business. It noted that the same Internet capabilities which improved personal freedoms can also be seen as intrusive behaviours, leading to a growth in consumer awareness and concern. It distinguished between personal and information privacy, reviewed data gathering mechanisms employed by organizations and governments, and considered regulatory developments in Europe as against the US. The chapter also discussed the questions raised by intellectual property rights in the light of the growth of e-business technologies which had worked to increase the proportion of an organization's value vested in intangible assets. It examined the generic notion of IPR trade-offs, the instruments available to regulate IPRs, before reviewing the consequences for intellectual property of digitization for areas ranging from software to images and entertainment products. The IP issues surrounding networked innovation were seen to be especially complex, as were the implications for IP of the ways in which certain industries—such as music publishing—were evolving. Thirdly, in its consideration of Internet fraud, the chapter emphasized the elusive nature of the topic in its discussion of spamming and the growth of spyware and malware. It summarized the social and economic effects of Internet fraud on individuals and organizations and some of the unforeseen consequences of regulation in the area. Finally, the chapter examined Internet governance issues and sought to raise awareness of the distinction between the role of government and governance, the dominance of US agencies in fundamental aspects of Internet regulation, and the risks of destroying the beneficial aspects of the Internet by either over-policing it, or by politicizing it, thereby reducing the amount innovation and creativity characteristic of the Internet's growth over the past fifteen years.

# ❷ Review questions

1. How do the various general definitions of privacy relate to the Internet?

2. How do different kinds of users think about their privacy and how is this changing?

3. What challenges does the Internet pose for the creators and regulators of intellectual property?

4. What are the characteristics and incidence of piracy in either the (a) software or (b) music market?

5. Why is identifying, tracking, and regulating unsolicited email so difficult?

6. Compare and contrast the US and European regulatory mechanisms developed to combat spam and other forms of Internet fraud.

7. What are the issues which dominate contemporary discussion of Internet governance and how are they being resolved?

8. Why are the ways in which the Internet is governed of particular interest to businesses?

# ◑ Discussion questions

1. 'Our attitude towards Internet fraud should be a case of "let the buyer beware", rather than one which encourages intervention by the regulatory authorities.' Do you agree?

2. What kinds of information do you feel most or least concerned about seeing made available to firms? Why? What kinds of information would you be willing to trade strategically and for what?

3. Is it possible to develop effective strategies for Internet monitoring without impeding teenagers' freedom to interact with their peers online?

4. Examine the concept of Creative Commons (http://creativecommons.org). To what extent do you think that it provides a workable solution to intellectual property concerns for different stakeholders?

5. Is the Internet a force for good or evil? Review the two AOL advertisements to be found at http://www.youtube.com/watch?v=9JvVUUmQyBU and http://www.youtube.com/watch?v=pNXWbSNDT5Q. What does this tell you about the difficulty of reaching a conclusion?

# ➔ Suggestions for further reading

Dutton, W.H., and Peltu, M., (2005), 'The Emerging Internet Governance Mosaic: Connecting the Pieces', *Forum Discussion Paper* No. 5, Oxford Internet Institute.
An effective summary of the interlocking questions affecting choices to be made by governments and international agencies in the development of Internet governance.

European Commission, (2008a), 'Data Protection in the European Union: Citizens' Perceptions', *Flash Eurobarometer 225*, Eurostat, http://ec.europa.eu/public_opinion/flash/fl_225_en.pdf.
An example of the regular polling conducted by the European Commission of citizens in relation to the information society. In this case, attitudes towards data protection are being assessed.

HM Treasury, (2006), *The Gowers Review or Intellectual Property*, London: HMSO.
A definitive review of intellectual property in the digital age. Provides an accessible and insightful assessment of the conceptual and regulatory issues, together with a series of recommendations to the UK government.

IFPI, (2009), *Digital Music Report 2009. New Business Models for a Changing Environment*, http://www.ifpi.org/content/library/DMR2009.pdf.
The latest report from the International Federation of the Phonographic Industry (IFPI) reviews the rapidly changing ways in which music is being made available, alongside some of the intellectual property issues facing individual users, musicians, and organizations.

Lace, S., (2005), *The Glass Consumer: Life in a Surveillance Society*, Policy Press.
Suzanne Lace captures the contemporary concern about a surveillance society in this book. 'We are all "glass consumers". Organizations know so much about us, they can almost see through us. Governments and businesses collect and process our personal information on a massive scale. But is this in our interests?'

# → References

Acquisiti, A., (2004), 'Security of Personal Information and Privacy: Technological Solutions and Economic Incentives', In J. Camp and R. Lewis (eds), *The Economics of Information Security*, Kluwer.

Benkler, Y., (1996), *Rules of the Road for the Information Superhighway: Electronic Communications and the Law*, West Publishing.

Benkler, Y., (2002), 'Intellectual Property and the Organization of Information Production', *International Review of Law and Economics*, 22(1), July, pp. 81–107.

Bhattacharjee, S., Gopal, R.D., Lertwachara, K. and Marsden, J.R., (2006), 'Impact of legal threats on online music sharing activity: An analysis of music industry legal actions', *Journal of Law & Economics*, 49(1), pp. 91–114.

Böhme, R. and Holz, T., (2006), 'The Effect of Stock Spam on Financial Markets', *Working Paper*, Workshop on the Economics of Information Society, Cambridge.

Bolin, R., (2005), EU 'Demands Compliance with Spam Directive', *LawMeme*, 4 April, http://research.yale.edu/lawmeme/modules.php?name=News&file=article&sid=1415&mode=thread&order=0&thold=0.

Brin, D., (1998), *The Transparent Society*, New York: Perseus Books

Business Software Alliance, (2009), *Sixth Annual BSA and IDC Global Software Piracy Study*, http://www.bsa.org.

Cerf, V., (2006), 'Foreword' in Kapur, A., (ed) *Internet Governance*, Wikibooks, http://en.wikibooks.org/wiki/Internet_Governance.

Chellappa, R.K. and Sin, R.G., (2005), 'Personalization versus Privacy: An Empirical Examination of the Online Consumer's Dilemma', *Information Technology and Management*, 6, pp. 181–202.

China Internet Network Information Center, (2007), *20th Statistical Survey Report on the Internet Development in China*, http://www.cninc.net.cn/download/2006/18threport-en.pdf.

Commission of the European Communities, (2003), *First Report on the Implementation of the Data Protection Directive*, COM(2003)265, European Union.

Commission of the European Communities, (2005), *Annexe to the European Electronic Communications Regulations and Markets 2005 11th report*, COM(2006)68, European Union.

Culnan, M.J. and Bies, R.J., (2003), 'Consumer Privacy: Balancing Economic and Justice Considerations', *Journal of Social Issues*, 59(2), pp. 104–15

Dehue, F., Bolman, C., and Völlink, T., (2008), 'Cyberbullying: Youngsters' Experiences and Parental Perception', *CyberPsychology and Behavior*, 11(2), pp. 217–23.

Drake, W.J. (ed.), (2006), *Reforming Internet Governance: Perspectives from the Working Group on Internet Governance*, United Nations Information and Communication Technologies Task Force.

Dutton, W.H, and Peltu, M., (2005), 'The Emerging Internet Governance Mosaic: Connecting the Pieces', *Forum Discussion Paper* No. 5, Oxford Internet Institute.

Dyson, E., (2004), *The Debate on Internet Governance: What's at Stake?*, 24 September, Oxford Internet Institute.

EPIC Online Guide to Privacy Resources, http://www.epic.org/privacy/privacy_resources_faq.html.

European Commission, (1997), 'Information Technology and Data Privacy', *Eurobarometer*, 46(1), January.

European Commission, (2005), 'Social Values, Science and Technology', *Special Eurobarometer*, June.

European Commission, (2008a), 'Data Protection in the European Union: Citizens' Perceptions', *Flash Eurobarometer*, 225, Eurostat, http://ec.europa.eu/public_opinion/flash/fl_225_en.pdf.

European Commission, (2008b), 'Towards a Safer Use of the Internet for Children in the EU—a Parents' Perspective', *Flash Eurobarometer*, 248, Eurostat.

Fox, S., (2005), 'Online Threats and Fears are Changing Consumer Behavior', Pew Internet & American Life Project, http://www.pewinternet.org/PPF/r/49/presentation_display.asp.

Gandy, O.H., (2003), 'Public Opinion Surveys and the Formation of Privacy Policy', *Journal of Social Issues*, 59(2), pp. 283–99, June.

Guo, L., (2005), *Surveying Internet Usage and Impact in Five Chinese Cities*, Research Centre for Social Development, Chinese Academy of Social Sciences.

Hassan, A., (2006), 'Internet Governance: Strengths and Weaknesses from a Business Perspective', in Drake, W.J. (ed.), *Reforming Internet Governance: Perspectives from the Working Group on Internet Governance*, United Nations ICT Task Force.

Heald, P., (2006), 'Property Rights and the Efficient Exploitation of Copyrighted Works: An Empirical Analysis of Public Domain and Proprietary Fiction Bestsellers', paper presented at the *IP Scholars Conference 2006*, Berkeley, 10–11 August.

HM Treasury, (2006), *The Gowers Review on Intellectual Property*, London: HMSO.

Hofstede, G. and Hofstede, G.J., (2005), *Cultures and Organizations: Software of the Mind*, New York: McGraw-Hill, and http://www.cyborlink.com/besite/india.htm.

Human Rights Watch, (2005), *False Freedom: Online Censorship in the Middle East and North Africa*, http://www.hrw.org/reports/2005/mena1105/mena1105webwcover.pdf.

IBM and Ponemon Institute, (2004), *Cost of Privacy Study*, http://www.ponemon.org.

IFPI, (2006), *The Recording Industry 2006: Piracy Report. Protecting Creativity in Music*, http://www.ifpi.org.

IFPI, (2009), *Digital Music Report 2009. New Business Models for a Changing Environment*, http://www.ifpi.org/content/library/DMR2009.pdf.

Information Commissioner's Office, (2008a), 'ICO—Higher Profile? Stronger Powers? More Effective?', paper presented by Richard Thomas, Information Commissioner, *RSA Conference Europe 2008*, http://www.ico.gov.uk/upload/documents/library/corporate/notices/rsa_presentation_oct_08_final.pdf.

Information Commissioner's Office, (2008b), *Annual Report 2007/08*, http://www.ico.gov.uk/upload/documents/library/corporate/detailed_specialist_guides/annual_report_2007_08.pdf

Insight Express, (2005), 'New Research Reveals Significant Consumer Misunderstanding of Cookies', *Press Release*, http://www.insightexpress.com/release.asp?aid=248.

International Chamber of Commerce (2003), *Information Paper on Organizations Involved in Technical Co-ordination of the Internet*, http://www.iccwbo.org/policy/ebit.

International Telecommunications Union, (2006), *Online Cybersecurity Survey*, http://www.itu.int/newsroom/wtd/2006/survey/.

Javelin Strategy and Research, (2009), *2009 Identity Fraud Survey Report: Consumer Version*, http://www.idsafety.net/901.R IdentityFraudSurveyConsumerReport.pdf.

Johnson, B., (2006), 'Creator of Web Warns of Fraudsters and Cheats', *Guardian*, 3 November, http://media.guardian.co.uk/newmedia/story/0,,1938638,00.html.

Kim, P., (2006), *Consumers Love To Hate Advertising*, Consumer Advertising Profiles, Forrester Research, Inc.

Kluver, R., (2005), 'The Architecture of Control: A Chinese Strategy for e-Governance', *Journal of Public Policy*, 25(1), May, pp. 75–97.

Kumaraguru, P. and Cranor, L., (2005a), 'Privacy in India: Attitudes and Awareness' *Proceedings of a Workshop on Privacy Enhancing Technologies (PET2005)*, 30 May–1 June, Dubrovnik, Croatia.

Kumaraguru, L. and Cranor, L.F., (2005b), 'Privacy Indexes: A Survey of Westin's Studies', *Working Paper* CMU-ISRI-5-138, Institute for Software Research International, School of Computer Science, Carnegie Mellon University, December. http://reports-archive.adm.cs.cmu.edu/anon/isri2005/CMU-ISRI-05-138.pdf.

Lace, S., (2005), *The Glass Consumer: Living in a Surveillance Society*, Policy Press.

Lau, E.K., (2006), 'Factors Motivating People toward Pirated Software', *Qualitative Market Research*, 9(4), pp. 404–19.

LEK, (2006), *The Cost of Movie Piracy*, Motion Picture Association.

Liau, A., Khoo, A. and Ang, P., (2008), 'Parental Awareness and Monitoring of Adolescent Internet Use', *Current Psychology*, December, 27(4), pp. 217–33.

Liebowitz, S.J., (2006), 'File Sharing: Creative Destruction or Just Plain Destruction?', *Journal of Law and Economics*, 49(1), pp. 1–28.

McCullagh, D., (2004), 'Gmail and Its Discontents', CNET News.com, 26 April, http://news.com.com/2010-1032-5199224.html.

Margulis, S.T., (2003), 'Privacy as a Social Issue and Behavioural Concept', *Journal of Social Issues*, 59(2), pp. 243–61.

Margulis, S.T., Pope, J.A., and Lowen, A., (2006), 'The Harris-Westin's Index of General Concern About Privacy: An Attempted Conceptual Replication', summary of a presentation prepared for the *GPD International Survey Research Workshop*, Kingston Ontario, November, http://www.queensu.ca/sociology/Surveillance/files/Margulis_paper.pdf.

Moetelli, J., (2005), 'The Patentability of Software in the US and Europe', paper presented at the Institut für Europäisches und Internationalses Wirtschaftsrecht, EUR-HSG, St Gallen.

Nash, V. and Peltu, M., (2005), 'Rethinking Safety and Security in a Networked World: Reducing Harm by Increasing Co-operation', *Forum Discussion Paper No. 6*, Oxford Internet Institute.

OECD, (1980), *OECD Guidelines on the Protection of Privacy and Transborder Flows of Personal Data*, http://www.oecd.org/document/18/0,2340,en_2649_34255_1815186_1_1_1_1,00.html.

OpenNet Initiative, (2006), *Internet Filtering in China in 2004–05: A Country Study*, http://www.opennetinitiative.net/studies/china.

Penenberg, A.L., (2005), 'Cookie Monsters', *Slate*, 7 November, http://www.slate.com/id/2129656.

Ponemon Institute, (2006), *What Marketing Professional Think about the Value of Privacy to Consumers*, Ponemon Institute.

Rambøll Management, (2005), *Economic Evaluation of the Data Protection Directive 95/94/E*, May, Brussels: European Commission.

Richard Posner, (2005), 'Posner on Privacy," The Becker-Posner blog, http://www.becker-posner-blog.com.

Samuelson, P., (2005), 'Intellectual property arbitrage: how foreign rules can affect domestic protections', in Maskus, K.E. and Reichman, J.H., (2005), *International Public Goods and Transfer of Technology Under a Globalized Intellectual Property Regime*, Cambridge University Press.

Schrage, E., (2006), 'Testimony of Google Inc before the Subcommittee on Asia and the Pacific, US House of Representatives, 16 February, http://googleblog.blogspot.com/2006/02/testimony-internet-in-china.html.

Shah, Jaymeen R., White, Garry L., andCook, James R., (2007), 'Privacy Protection Overseas as Perceived by USA-Based IT Professionals', *Journal of Global Information Management*, 15(1), pp. 68–81.

Sotgiu F. and Ancarani, F., (2004), 'Exploiting the Opportunities of Internet and Multi-Channel Pricing: An Exploratory Research', *Journal of Product and Brand Management*, 13(2), pp. 125–36.

Sprenger, P., (1999), 'Sun on Privacy: "Get Over It"', *Wired News*, 26 January, http://www.wired.com/news/politics/0,1283,17538,00.html.

Tahiroglu, A., Celik, G., Uzel, M., Ozcan, N., and Avci, A., (2008), 'Internet Use Amongst Turkish Adolescents', *CyberPsychology and Behavior*, 11(5), pp. 537–43.

US Department of Justice, (2006), *Report on Phishing*, A report to the Attorney General of the United States, Bi-National Working Group on Cross-Border Mass Marketing Fraud, http://www.usdoj.gov/opa/report_on_phishing.pdf.

Weber, T.E., (2000), 'As Pendulum Swings, Protecting Privacy May Start to Pay Off', *The Wall Street Journal*, 12 June, p. B1.

West, D., (2003), *Global E-Government 2003*, Center for Public Policy, Brown University.

Westin, A., (1967), *Privacy and Freedom*, New York, Atheneum.

Wilson, E.J. (2005), 'What is Internet Governance and Where Does It Come from?', *Journal of Public Policy*, 25(1), pp. 29–50.#

Working Group on Data Retention, (2008), *Submission concerning the action brought on 6 July 2006. Ireland v Council of the European Communities, Case C-301/06*, http://www.vorratsdatenspeicherung.de/images/data_retention_brief_08-04-2008.pdf.

Yong, J.S.L., (2003), *E-government in Asia: Enabling Public Service Innovation in the Twenty-First Century*, Times Editions.

Zarwan, E., (2005), 'False Freedom: Online Censorship in the Middle East and North Africa', *Human Rights Watch*, 17(10E), http://hrw.org/reports/2005/mena1105/mena1105webwcover.pdf.

# ⊚ Weblinks

Zentner, A., (2006), 'Measuring the Effect of File Sharing on Music Purchases', *Journal of Law and Economics*, 49(1), pp. 63–90.

Zittrain, J., (2006), 'Private is the New Public', in Ofcom, *Communications—the Next Decade*, UK Office of Communications.

Cookie Central. More information about cookies: http://www.cookiecentral.com and http://www.howstuffworks.com/cookie.htm.

Information Society. The European Commission's Information Society website, including summaries of relevant legislation and directives: (http://www.europa.eu/scadplus/leg/en/s21012.htm).

The OpenNet Initiative. Investigating and challenging the filtering and information surveillance practices of states: http://www.opennetinitiative.org.

The Electronic Information Privacy Center. EPIC is a US public interest research centre which focuses public attention on emerging civil liberties and privacy issues: http://www.epic.org.

Spam cost calculator. You can calculate the costs of spam for any organization on the 'ready reckoner': http://www.praetor.net/marketing/spamcalc.htm.

# Part two

# The application of e-business technologies

# The strategy of e-business

## Introduction

'Far from making strategy less important, as some have argued, the Internet actually makes strategy more essential than ever.' *Porter, 2001*

The word 'strategy' has started to become a somewhat abused one in the context of business. Strategy has become the mantra of many organizations and, when misunderstood, used rhetorically, or just poorly applied, the downfall of some. Leading management academic Henry Mintzberg defines strategy in four ways: as a *pattern* of choices made over time, as a *plan* for possible future actions, as a *position* relating to choices about which products or services to offer, or as a *perspective*—presenting choices about how a business can be conceptualized (Mintzberg, 1994). Despite Michael Porter's words at the beginning of this chapter, in the context of e-business the term strategy has become even more rhetorical. In a chapter explicitly focusing on e-business strategy, we might be expected to gain exciting insights into the many ways in which new industrial sectors, new firms, and new forms of organization have arisen as a result of the Internet. Are there new rules of strategy to be learned? Perhaps. However, while there are indeed many interesting stories to tell, we must recall that the impact of the Internet can be seen in the context of established industries and firms. And, as we shall see, much of the evidence suggests that the old rules of the game are still pretty important for both new and incumbent firms.

We can consider the impact of e-business on strategy at the industry and at the firm levels. At the level of industry, the evidence seems to suggest that whilst the Internet has created some new kinds of activities (such as online search or social communities, about which we tend to hear a lot) much of our attention should be focused on the reconfiguration of existing industries. In manufacturing industries, for example, the precise nature and value contributed by e-business activities are largely (but not always) shaped by the character of existing production processes: think, for example, about the impact of e-business upon the automotive sector or the textile industry. Increasingly, manufacturers take the Internet into account when developing their strategies. For instance, cycle manufacturer Raleigh's manufacturing capability was outsourced to Asia, whilst its design and other functions remained in the UK. This would not have been conceivable in the absence of e-business technologies. (We focus specifically on business processes in chapter 9.) In services as well, e-business adoption patterns and impact will also vary enormously between, say, tourism and the newspaper industry.

At the firm level, the focus is upon the ways in which e-business can allow organizations to compete through, for example, operating at a lower cost; or through commanding a price premium through doing things differently. In the case of the public sector, e-business is also relevant at the level of the organization, where new kinds of services can be developed, or existing services may be able to be more efficiently developed. For example, the UK's Directgov service seeks to provide a new, one-stop shop for Government services: the same services, in many cases, but more efficiently delivered (http://www.direct.gov. uk). The impact of the Internet at the level of the organization has been analysed using a variety of conventional strategy tools, including the value chain framework and the resource-based view of the firm.

We can also see much preoccupation by commentators with 'business models' and, in particular, the search for new business models for firms previously unavailable to them. Indeed, this hunt for the 'holy grail' of business success characterized the period of dot. com boom and bust in the early 2000s. How is this different from industry- or firm-level analysis? Certainly, it has never been very clear what comprises a business model, although the sense is that it is much more than just a rational description of how a firm adds value—it may be as much about how everything works together.

## The effects of e-business on industry structure

The media are full of stories about industries that have been transformed by e-business technologies: from recorded music to auctions, from hotel bookings to postal services. Indeed, the news media themselves are undergoing radical change. On the one hand, the traditional news industry is having to transform itself into a digital news industry, characterized by the growth in electronic channels to readers and dealing with a consequent reorganization of conventional business structures. On the other hand, user-generated content is starting to play an important, but additionally disruptive, role in the way news-gathering and dissemination functions, with new sources and intermediaries competing for readers' attention. See, for example, news aggregator Reditt (http://www.reditt.com) and CNN's iReport (http://www.ireport.com), which contained over 300,000 reports at the beginning of 2009. Long case 6.2 examines the ways in which one organization, the UK's Guardian Media Group, is seeking to meet these challenges—but these are tests facing the whole industry and need to be examined at that level. But how can we assess the industry impact of e-business? There are several conventional ways to examine industry structure and evaluate the threats to existing organizations and, correspondingly, the opportunities presented to new entrants. Probably the most widely used is that developed by writer on management strategy Michael Porter: the so-called 'five forces' model, shown in Figure 6.1.

---

### Activity box 6.1

**Reading the News**

News organizations CNN and the BBC have both diversified the ways in which news is gathered and disseminated.

1   Compare and contrast the mechanisms that are used by each organization for both input and output, and how the two sets of mechanisms interrelate.

2   What conclusions can you reach about the changing structure of the news industry from this analysis?

3   Can you relate these conclusions to the 'Five Forces' model?

---

Porter's approach seeks to model the competitive intensity and therefore the relative attractiveness of a particular market both to incumbents and to new players. The framework is a useful starting point for the development of firm-level strategy and of course each industry under scrutiny will behave in a different way partly because of its own inherent characteristics, partly because of its circumstances at any one point in time. Helpfully, Porter provided a further iteration of this framework in 2001 in response to the growth of e-business technologies. It is this version that is presented in Figure 6.1.

Porter's five forces model had originally been criticized for its lack of applicability to the Internet economy. It was developed in the 1980s when, suggest some commentators, there were relatively more stable market structures than we find today. Critics have argued that the disruptive effect of e-business technologies has rendered such models less appropriate. However, think about the underlying basis for models like this, which is that every business necessarily operates in Porter's framework of buyers, suppliers, competitors, new entrants, and substitutes. These are fundamental concepts drawn from industrial economic theory. Such ideas remain valid for any economy based on the concept of free competition. The effects of e-business are simply to expose industries to greater scrutiny from all these sources than might have been the case in the 1980s, opening up new possibilities for competition more rapidly and unpredictably than once might have been the case.

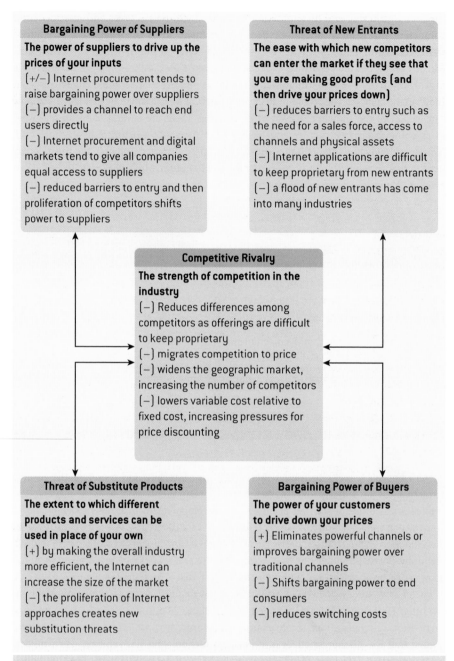

**Bargaining Power of Suppliers**

**The power of suppliers to drive up the prices of your inputs**

(+/−) Internet procurement tends to raise bargaining power over suppliers

(−) provides a channel to reach end users directly

(−) Internet procurement and digital markets tend to give all companies equal access to suppliers

(−) reduced barriers to entry and then proliferation of competitors shifts power to suppliers

**Threat of New Entrants**

**The ease with which new competitors can enter the market if they see that you are making good profits (and then drive your prices down)**

(−) reduces barriers to entry such as the need for a sales force, access to channels and physical assets

(−) Internet applications are difficult to keep proprietary from new entrants

(−) a flood of new entrants has come into many industries

**Competitive Rivalry**

**The strength of competition in the industry**

(−) Reduces differences among competitors as offerings are difficult to keep proprietary

(−) migrates competition to price

(−) widens the geographic market, increasing the number of competitors

(−) lowers variable cost relative to fixed cost, increasing pressures for price discounting

**Threat of Substitute Products**

**The extent to which different products and services can be used in place of your own**

(+) by making the overall industry more efficient, the Internet can increase the size of the market

(−) the proliferation of Internet approaches creates new substitution threats

**Bargaining Power of Buyers**

**The power of your customers to drive down your prices**

(+) Eliminates powerful channels or improves bargaining power over traditional channels

(−) Shifts bargaining power to end consumers

(−) reduces switching costs

**Figure 6.1** How the Internet influences industry structure

If we examine the component parts of the framework shown in Figure 6.1, we can see the way in which Porter has adapted it to an e-business context. For example, if we examine the 'Bargaining Power of Suppliers' component, we can see the ways in which e-business technologies might work positively or negatively to affect the structure of the industry. On the one hand, for organizations in a particular sector, Porter suggests that being able to buy online will—other things being equal—improve their bargaining power over suppliers. On the other hand, from the point of view of most industries, the Internet provides a potential channel for suppliers to reach end users directly—and possibly bypass an existing organization. Similarly, because buyers are more likely to be able to access a wider range of competitive suppliers, Porter proposes that their bargaining power is enhanced by e-business technologies and the cost of switching between competitors is reduced. Above all, e-business technologies have made it much easier for new competitors to enter the market by lowering the barriers to entry: e-business applications are often generic and their advantages open to all. Further, for many industries there may be a reducing rewquirement for the kinds of assets which used to make market entry for new firms so difficult: such as a sales force, a physical retail outlet, or some other form of physical asset. These considerations do seem to make sense when we relate them to what we see has happened in a number of industries. Take the example of the market for air travel, discussed in Short case 6.1. Take some time to work through some of the other boxes in Porter's framework for yourselves.

Another way of thinking about changes in industry structure with more direct resonance with the characteristics of e-business is that originally proposed by Malone et al. in 1987 and widely cited over the past twenty years. The so-called *electronic markets hypothesis* (EMH) suggests that e-business will cause a shift from hierarchical to more market-based forms of economic activity. Hierarchical markets represent conventional industry structures which involve purchasing from a sole supplier. Malone et al. suggested that as co-ordination costs fall, thanks to e-business technologies, more open and competitive mechanisms of economic behaviour would emerge. Further, product description and purchase would become less complex and asset specificity would be reduced. (You will note some similarities to some of the more optimistic economic hypotheses described in chapter 2.) The model suggests that firms are in a position to build an infrastructure that gives preference to existing arrangements and 'biases', before going on to become less biased as they seek new partners. The three stages of the EMH proposed that industries will move from:

1) *Hierarchical to biased electronic markets*: biased electronic markets provide for an intermediate stage in which firms use e-business technologies to put into place market mechanisms that bias information in their favour. Think of the way in which a search engine might put in place a weighting mechanism to favour prioritizing a particular company's products and services over others.

2) *Biased to non-biased electronic markets*: non-biased markets make all options for trading available and no supplier receives particular prominence, other than in response to buyer requirements. Think here of the case of Autobytel.com, which is a brand-neutral electronic platform for the dealers of thirty-four different motor vehicle firms (http://www.autobytel.com).

3) *Non-biased to personalized markets*: personalized electronic markets offer functionality that allows the buyer to filter the options available for trading in ways that shift the balance of power decisively to the end user. Think here of the way in which services such as iGoogle and My Yahoo! allow the user to create a personalized interface.

These shifts, suggest Malone et al., do not need to be (and are often not) made by industry incumbents; they can be made by new entrants to a market or industry. In many ways, we can see these three stages in the growth of the electronic airline travel market in the past thirty years, described in Short case 6.1, but the EMH is not without its critics, as we shall see below.

Indeed, whilst there have been an estimated 300 publications over the past twenty years based on the implicit endorsement of EMH, there is emerging evidence that there may be

## Short case 6.1

### Air travel reservations: last-minute expediency or sabre rattling?

Internet sites that can aggregate product and price information can now be found in a variety of markets. Nowhere more profound has been the industry outcome of this than in the case of the air travel reservations market. The European business to consumer online travel market has grown from 1.1 per cent of total sales in 2000 to an estimated 22.5 per cent in 2008. Air travel accounted for 57 per cent of this (see Figure 6.2)

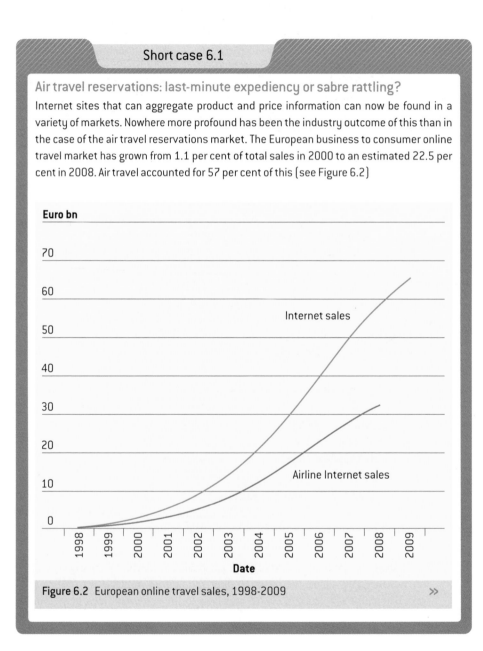

**Figure 6.2**　European online travel sales, 1998-2009　　　»

In fact, business-to-business (B2B) airline booking systems have been to hand for many years. Indeed, American Airlines' joint effort with IBM in the 1950s led to the development of SABRE (Semi-Automated Business Research Environment) in 1960, the second largest data processing system to that of the US government and a booking system which was made available to travel agents from 1964. As Sabre Holdings, it is still in existence, having been spun off by the airline in 2000 and subsequently acquired by two venture capital firms in 2007 (http://www.sabre-holdings.com). Today, the $1.63bn turnover Sabre Travel Network links 3m consumers with 400 airlines—as well as 76,000 hotels, twenty-eight car rental companies, thirteen cruise lines, thirty-five train companies, and 220 tour operators.

Despite Sabre's longevity, e-business technologies have transformed this market over the past twenty years. Indeed, Sabre has changed with it: moving through all three stages of the EMH model. The company was investigated in the 1980s for creating a biased electronic market in which competitors' discount fares were suppressed by the system. The then company president was unabashed: 'the preferential display of our flights, and the corresponding increase in our market share, is the competitive raison d'être for having created the system in the first place' (quoted in Copeland et al., 1995). Even with the biases removed, subsequent commentators reported a 'halo effect' resulting from American's identification with the system.

While the majority of individual airlines now offer online booking services, new independent entrants have found the airline travel market a challenging one. Conventional, non-biased consumer-facing intermediary websites include Travelocity (owned by Sabre http://www.travelocity.com), Expedia (originally a Microsoft company, http://www.expedia.com) and Orbitz/eBookers (http://www.orbitz.com). More recent sites include reverse auction site Priceline (http://www.priceline.com), and inventory clearance » specialist Lastminute.com (acquired by Sabre in 2005). The airlines themselves have reintermediated themselves back into the market through jointly owned subsidiaries such as Opodo (http://www.opodo.com), set up by nine European airlines and now co-owned by travel industry technology provider, Amadeus.

*Question*

Relate the development of the air travel reservation market to either (1) Porter's five forces model, or (2) Malone et al.'s electronic markets hypothesis. Examine some of the industry players identified in the case and consider how good a fit can be achieved.

some gaps and omissions in the theory which could have important strategic implications. Bonnie Glassberg and Jeffrey Merhout have assembled a list of several important issues, related to both B2B as well as business-to-consumer (B2C) markets (Glassberg and Merhout, 2007):

- *Business-to-business markets:* B2B markets have tended to be neglected in EMH research. But what is starting to be clear is that B2B markets appear not to place as much of a simple premium on lower transaction costs and may have other factors that they consider to be equally or more important. We can easily believe that firms in such markets may have good business reasons for establishing and maintaining links through long-term hierarchical relationships, in which short-term profitability is sacrificed for a longer term and more durable form of economic exchange. In some B2B marketing, for example, so-called 'domesticated' markets develop when firms build strong and enduring relationships with sole suppliers, often for reasons of trust and reliability, and to the extent that the costs of switching may be uneconomic (Arndt, 1979).

- *Business-to-consumer markets*: despite the high amount of academic attention on B2C markets, there may also be a series of refinements required for the EMH as it applies here. More recent research reported by Glassberg and Merhout suggests that EMH-compliant B2C markets are particularly likely to develop:

- where industries have highly variable pricing and product availability;
- where procurement is relatively less complex; and
- where standardized product ratings or formats become established.

Some industries have become adept at communicating product or service complexity in an unbiased way without reducing it (as the model suggested): for example, house-sale comparison sites across a variety of vendors have been able to use such techniques as Google Maps mashups to standardize and present complex residential property information (see, for example, http://www.zillow.com). In addition, asset specificity may not be as important as originally proposed: for example, sites such as eBay can offer highly sought after products with high product specificity, yet operate on the basis of an unbiased market. Finally, consumer behavioural factors (such as the need of consumers for trust in transactions, the importance of some non-price factors such as brand, and consumers' heightened perceptions of online transaction costs) as well as digital marketing strategies by firms may lead to consumer 'lock in' with particular suppliers, in the same way as for some B2B firms. Consumer behaviour and marketing strategies are explored in more detail in chapters 4 and 7.

Above all, therefore, the critiques of the EMH appear to stress the continuing importance of relationships, rather than just discrete transactions, as the basis for more accurate descriptions of the ways in which many kinds of market have developed in response to e-business technologies, be they B2B or B2C. This in turn may suggest that in certain sectors, successfully restructured electronic markets will be more cooperative in nature, or more network-based than purely hierarchical or transactional. The conclusion is that companies have a choice. Table 6.1 illustrates some of the criteria to affect this choice.

> **Asset Specificity** The extent to which products or services are designed to be attractive to a particular group of buyers.

---

**Table 6.1  EMH positioning choices**

**Choose Markets when:**

- Transaction cost is a primary concern
- Searching for brand-new suppliers
- Purchasing commodities
- The market is highly fragmented

**Choose Hierarchies when:**

- Proprietary issues are of high concern
- Asset specificity is very high
- Monitoring cost is high

**Choose Cooperative Ventures when:**

- Non-contractible issues (quality, timing, flexibility, customization, and responsiveness) are paramount
- To gain access to centres of excellence
- To build long term win-win relationships

For example, in an investigation of automotive industry 'e-hubs' (online collaborative marketplaces) Howard et al. (2006) demonstrated that the move from a supply hierarchy to an electronic market was much slower than the hype had suggested. The researchers proposed that a proper understanding was required of the motivations and barriers to the transition to an e-business strategy by different sectors. In this case, a vertically integrated mass production sector had thrown up a different mix of the benefits expected.

A final important reminder of the way e-business strategy works at the industry level is to recall that such activity takes place in the context of established ways of doing things, including regulation. As a result, 'the reality is that the old economic and business rules not only continue to be highly relevant but also favour established companies' (Finkelstein, 2001). This may work to distinguish what is practically possible from what is theoretically desirable according to an industry analysis. During periods of rapid technological change, the opposition of established interests and, to an extent, levels of political opposition, can increase rapidly. Further, it takes time for regulation to 'catch up' with market circumstances (as chapter 5 discussed).

For example, the early years of the introduction of e-commerce were marked by much defensive posturing by incumbents. For instance, the US Democratic Party lobby group, the Progressive Policy Institute (PPI, http://www.ppionline.org) suggested that in 2003 alone, US consumers paid $22bn more for goods and services as a result of what they called 'e-commerce protectionism' (Atkinson, 2003). Examples cited at the time included: de-listing threats by major US retailers to manufacturers seeking to develop their own, direct-to-consumer websites; lobbying to require online auction site developers to pass individual state auction licensing laws. In the state of Texas, at the behest of car dealers and their trade representatives, the Ford Motor Company was prevented from marketing used cars online, despite potentially huge savings to consumers.

Such strategies, either deliberately embarked upon or accidental in their nature, might derail the even the best planned e-business strategies. For example, the attempts by the BBC in 2008 to introduce an on-demand local news service with online video content were rejected by UK regulator OFCOM after newspaper publishers argued that it could damage their own local operations (BBC Trust/OFCOM, 2008). In fact, some commentators suggested that the service the BBC had proposed was technically superior to anything then available in the local news market. But the view that annual revenues at existing commercial providers would fall by 4 per cent nevertheless prevailed. Short case 6.2 on Internet radio provides a more detailed example of the effects of legal and regulatory changes within an established industry context upon the prospects of new market entrants.

---

### Activity box 6.2

#### EMH or not EMH?

Select four industry sectors (drawn from both B2B and B2B domains). To what extent do changes in their respective markets conform to or depart from the electronic markets hypothesis? Try to map your conclusions on to the categories of EMH positioning choices shown in Table 6.1. Are these mappings stable, or can you conceive of situations in which the categorization of your chosen examples might change?

## Short case 6.2

### Opening Pandora's Box: Internet Radio

Pandora was founded in 2000 by Tim Westergren, Will Glaser, and John Kraft as an outcome of the Music Genome Project, an ambitious attempt to reverse engineer and tag the characteristics of recorded music—so-called 'musical DNA' (http://www.pandora.com). Pandora is the largest of several Internet radio or webcasting services in existence which, between them, draw an estimated 72m listeners per month. But in early 2007 the whole future viability of Pandora, and of the IRS business model itself, was put at risk by changes in the charging regime for streamed music royalties.

The distinctive feature of Pandora's browser-based service is the ability it gives the listener to craft their own music channel, by telling the service which tracks they like and which they don't. Preferred tracks prompt further recommendations based on the detailed characteristics of the music, which may result in the listener discovering new artistes and genres: the listener's own personal radio station, but one which 'learns' the listener's preferences: 'Pandora has become one of the most important ways I find new music.' Other features include the ability to store listener profiles (a 'musical biography' that can be shared with others), undertake listener searches (to find other Pandora users who share your musical tastes) and 'Artists' Fans' (allowing the user to find other fans of specific artistes).

The company's strategy has been to derive revenues from three sources: advertising, subscriptions, and commerce. The free version of Pandora is supported by advertising revenues; a subscription-based version ($36 per year) gives access to an ad-free universal Pandora account. In terms of commerce, Pandora provides links to Amazon and iTunes. Variants on the subscription model provide the service via Sprint mobile phones or via Logitech and Sonos audio applications in the home (Pandora Everywhere).

> 'The big opportunity for us is advertising . . . it would be pretty much impossible for us to recover our bandwidth and licensing costs from commerce alone. Our costs are largely dominated by licensing and bandwidth. We are licensed through *SoundExchange, BMI, ASCAP, and SESAC.*' *Tom Conrad, CTO, Pandora*

Pandora's business model (like those of its competitors) relied upon a certain degree of stability in music markets—specifically in the royalties paid by Internet radio services to the US Copyright Royalty Board. Performance rights management is a complex area. >>

ASCAP  The American Society of Composers, Authors, and Publishers.

SESAC  Society of European Stage Authors and Composers.

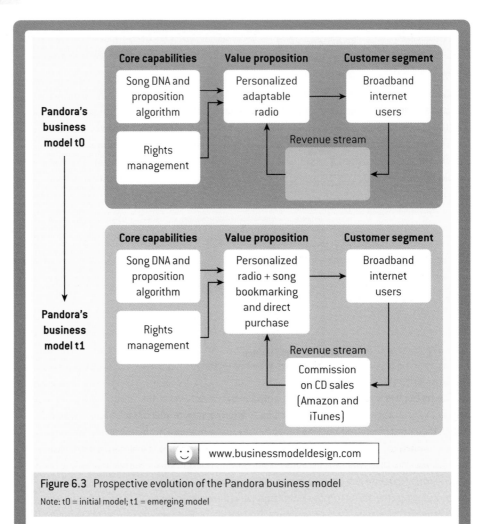

**Figure 6.3** Prospective evolution of the Pandora business model

Note: t0 = initial model; t1 = emerging model

Whenever a song is played, there are three parties involved: the songwriter who composed the song, the label that owns the recording itself, and the performing artist. Regular radio stations pay composer royalties, but don't pay performance royalties. Internet radio firms have to pay both, thanks to a clause in the US Digital Millennium Copyright Act. In March 2007, the CRB announced that royalties per streamed track would increase from 0.07¢ in 2005 to 0.19¢ by 2010. A separate agreement with small webcasters which had them making a contribution of 12 per cent of their revenues to artists and record labels would be scrapped. This might not sound much. But for some small webcasters, it risked increasing their royalty payments in excess of their total revenues. And for Pandora, it was estimated that 'such a royalty obligation might exceed the total proceeds of all their recent rounds of venture capital plus all their sales revenues to date' (McSwain, 2007).

During 2007, lobbying the US Congress produced the possibility of an Internet Radio Equality Act (IREA) to reset the royalty rules for non-commercial stations, and set the commercial royalty rate at the equivalent of that for satellite radio (7.5 per cent of  » revenues). In the meantime, the copyright holders are lobbying Congress to apply a sound recording performance royalty to terrestrial radio.

*Question*
'The Copyright Royalty Board can only be congratulated on their decision' (US blogger). What arguments would you use to defend the CRB's increase in charges?

# E-business, firms, and the value chain

'Those in the consumer value chain will need to understand under what conditions the consumer will prefer to purchase from single-source suppliers, brokered electronic markets and intelligent agent proxies for electronic markets.' *Benjamin and Wigand, 1995*

When we turn from notions or markets, or industry sectors, to firms, it is important to recognize that the concept of 'value' and how value can be added for the customer or consumer by the firm has become the focus of discussion. It has also become commonplace to use the concept of the value chain to structure discussions of the way in which firms can add value. The term, originally derived from Michael Porter's work on the competitive advantage of firms, has become part of the standard lexicon of strategic management (Porter, 1985). Resulting frameworks provide a useful mechanism for identifying particular kinds of activity from which an individual firm can seek to provide better value than its competitors. We can differentiate between primary activities (such as operations) and support activities (such as procurement) in thinking about the value chain. Figure 6.4 shows how early commentators used the value chain model to illustrate how e-business technologies might add value.

| Product/service development | Supply management | Manufacturing and assembly | Marketing | Sales and distribution | Customer service |
|---|---|---|---|---|---|
| **E-commerce economic levers** | | | | | |
| Improve product development by capturing customer input more effectively | Reduce sourcing costs through increased price transparency and competition | Lower transaction costs by reducing double handling of information | Strengthen customer relationships and improve cost effectiveness through targeting | Reduce sales and distribution costs through automation – e.g. sales tools, and printed material costs | Improve customer service |
| Enable collaborative development across companies and geographies | Reduce inventory costs through shorter procurement process and delivery times | Lower work in progress costs through improved forecasting | Research new user segments and geographies | Promote new products and services – e.g. cross-selling | Lower customer interaction costs |

**Figure 6.4** E-business technologies and the value chain: early thinking

In 1995 Robert Benjamin and Rolf Wigand were amongst the first to suggest that value chains would be transformed by the Internet and that firms adopting e-business technologies would benefit from this transformation. Chapter 2 discussed the concept of disintermediation in some detail and concluded that while the Internet increases the likelihood of disintermediation in value chains, at the same time, opportunities for new kinds of intermediaries to generate incremental value for other channel members are opened up. But is the notion of a value 'chain' as relevant to the ways in which today's firms may add value? More recently, writers have sought to extend the value chain framework beyond the individual firm, to firms linked together in a chain or network of interdependency. (This has some similarities with the ways in which the electronic markets hypothesis has been extended to include networked or co-operative structures). Extended value chains or value systems, may be local, national, or international in scope and can be quite complex. Think, for example, of the production of a motor vehicle and the way in which supplier firms are interrelated and how the decisions made by parts of the chain can have significant consequences both up and downstream. The global economic downturn had particularly devastating effects upon the motor vehicle components industry because of the interwoven nature of the relationships between firms and 'just-in-time' supply chain practices: so-called 'supplier shock'.

Arguably the first to challenge the notion of a 'chain' of value-creating activities were Richard Normann and Rafael Ramirez (1993). Writing as early as 1993, they argued that strategy should no longer be a matter of positioning a fixed set of activities along a value chain. According to them the focus for today's firms should be on the value creating system itself, 'within which different economic actors—suppliers, business partners, allies, customers—work together to co-produce value'. Successful firms are those which conceptualized strategy as 'systematic social innovation'. Normann and Ramirez called these systems 'value constellations'. They used the example of Swedish furniture chain IKEA (not, of course, itself an e-business exemplar) to illustrate the way in which a firm could achieve low costs and low prices not just through a conventional focus upon its own internal capabilities, but by creating an 'integrated business system' in which value is co-produced by all parties. 'We do our part, you do yours and together we save money' is the IKEA strapline, and this is achieved by activities ranging from the careful identification and cultivation of suppliers through to the education of customers to see flat-pack furniture as the trade-off for a lower price for equivalent quality.

Harvard Business School Professor Clayton Christensen has also considered the notion of the value network in the context of his work on disruptive innovation. He defined a value network as 'the collection of upstream suppliers, downstream channels to market, and ancillary providers that support a common business model within an industry' (Christensen, 1997). (We have already come across Christensen's work in chapter 1, where he specifically uses the Internet as an example of a disruptive technology, and we will examine it in more detail in chapter 8.) Others argue that the move towards a network perspective on value creation is one of the most fundamental shifts in this century.

Amongst the first to analyse the theoretical foundations of value creation in e-business in a more comprehensive way were business school academics Raphael Amit and Christoph Zott (2001). Drawing on an empirical analysis of fifty-nine US and European e-businesses, and relating this to a rich and well-established literature in economics, they suggested in 2001 that the value creation potential of such businesses was dependent upon four interdependent dimensions closely related to the ways in which transactions were enabled. These sources consisted of:

- *Transaction cost efficiency*: for e-business firms, chapter 2 established that transaction efficiency increases when the costs per transaction decrease. Efficiency gains are already a well-established characteristic of highly networked conventional industries—such as those found amongst Japanese firms. The greater the availability of widespread Internet connectivity, the greater the transaction cost efficiency gains that are possible for a particular e-business, the lower the costs and hence the more valuable it will be. Firms that are able to exploit this phenomenon will have a greater ability to create value than conventional competitors, through faster decision-making.

- *Complementarities*: The notion of complementarities refers to bringing a bundle of goods or services together that will provide more value than the sum total of providing each of the goods separately. In e-business, Amit and Zott (2001) distinguish between what they call *vertical* complementarities (such as after sales service) and *horizontal* complementarities (such as buying digital cameras as well as books on photography). Not all these complementarities need to be provided online. Indeed, the very notion of the multi-channel retailer is built upon the sense that some value can be added online (home delivery, extensive product range and competitive pricing) while another kind can be generated in store (such as browsing, immediate availability of some product and the more personal kind of customer service) that neither channel could offer in isolation. Complementarities leading to value can also arise between technologies (through, for example, the combination of video streaming technology and web browsers) and activities (such as supply chain integration).

- *Lock-in*: this is the way in which firms can enhance value generation by engaging customers in ways which actively discourage them from migrating to competitors: in other words, by building switching barriers. For example, firms may encourage customers to invest significant time in learning how to use their web service and in personalizing it for their own use. Customers may be unwilling to sacrifice this investment and switch to a competitor. For example, Google's Analytics service allows users to track where visitors come from and how they interact with a website. Advanced segmentation and customer reporting methods are relatively complex to learn and switching to an alternative provider would be time-consuming. Lock-in can also be a consequence of the network effects that the Internet facilitates. For example, large-scale virtual communities (such as those generated by e-collaboration platforms such as Exostar, discussed in chapter 3) create bonding effects, or network externalities, between participating firms. Even if there are no direct benefits to individuals or firms from interaction, there may be indirect network externalities that arise simply as a direct function of network size.

- *Novelty*: We deal in greater depth with innovation as a concept in relation to e-business in chapter 8. However, as a source of added value, e-business can give enormous potential for first-mover advantage, through the development of new transaction structures and content and the involvement of new kinds of business. Amit and Zott (2001) cite eBay as one of the most significant commercial beneficiaries of this principle.

Figure 6.5 shows how these elements can be seen to work together.

This framework, and the set of assumptions behind it, has inevitably been challenged as e-business technologies have evolved and as research has become more sophisticated. For example, Tse (2007) takes issue with Amit and Zott's (2001) conclusions and argues that many of these so-called distinctive capabilities are adversely affected by an excessive focus on technological or economic factors, at the expense of human and organizational considerations. Chapter 2 discussed the notion of economic imperialism and it is clear that the reality of contemporary experience weakens overly rational or deterministic attempts to conceptualize value creation in e-business. Tse notes that some 60 per cent of the 30 e-businesses which Amit and Zott praised for business excellence in 2001 have either stopped trading or have been acquired—and many of those that remain are significantly smaller than they once were. Tse provides comments in particular on three of Amit and Zott's dimensions of value by way of explanation:

- *Transaction cost efficiencies* can be adversely affected by any lack of context in the information being transmitted. For example, in an e-procurement exercise for chickens, a UK supermarket company was dissatisfied with the richness of the

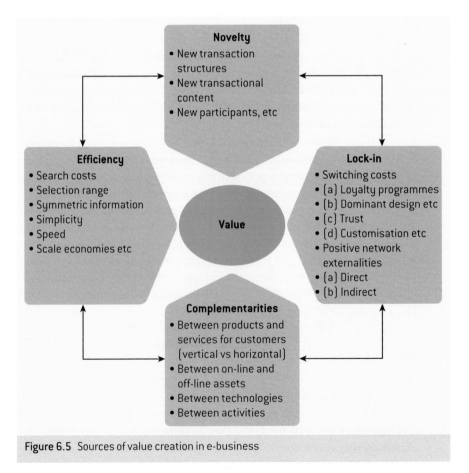

**Figure 6.5** Sources of value creation in e-business

information being transmitted by would-be suppliers—the data failed to establish track record, build trust, or create rapport—so-called 'thick description'. More work than had been expected was required to build the valued relationship between prospective buyer and supplier at a human level. Similarly, while retail customers of financial services firms are happy to engage with websites for relatively utilitarian transactions, they still value being able to visit a branch adviser for purchasing complex products which require trust and confidence-building.

- *Lock-in* may not always be as useful a method of retaining customers as originally believed. For example, Amazon is always cited as an excellent example of lock-in as a result of the added value it generates for customers through book reviews, recommendations and cross-selling opportunities which arise as a result of a customer's purchasing history. However, customers may still choose to 'freeride' on Amazon's information resources, whilst buying a book from a store-based retailer.

- Finally, Tse argues that there is a lack of empirical evidence to support the fact that *novelty* of itself, in the form of first-mover advantage, automatically brings sustainable competitive advantage. There are high costs to being a pioneer: pioneers can attract the unwelcome attention of legacy market incumbents as well as of regulators (see, for example, the discussion of Internet radio in Short case 6.2). It is often easier for subsequent entrants to learn from the mistakes of the first.

A further consideration driven by the way in which e-business technologies function is that, whilst Porter's value chain works well for physical products, it may be less appropriate for information flows. For Evans and Wurster (1997) it is the dissociation of the physical flow of products from the related information that offers strategic opportunities to all participants in the value system. Walters and Rainbird (2007) highlights three strategic directions open to firms which exploit the role of information and know-how in the value creation process and which could carve out a sustainable intermediary role within a value system:

- *Information richness*: using e-business technologies to acquire, distribute, and exploit information effectively. Walters and Rainbird cite the example of the Asian distributor Li and Fung, which in effect comprises an information hub, managing extensive external data collection and then distributing this information to relevant decision makers within the firm. It leverages advantage from deep, current knowledge of global sourcing and production networks and in-depth logistical expertise.

- *Relational exchange:* using e-business technologies to provide a basis to research and then to maintain external business relationships through the sharing of data, provided that compatible systems can be developed. (However environments created by e-business technologies are not as rich a medium for relational exchange as those for face-to-face interaction.)

- *Joint learning*: using e-business technologies as a means of achieving intra-organizational, cross-national learning.

The concept of strategic value nets that we introduced earlier is certainly a very timely and appropriate one for appreciating the opportunities for e-business strategies. In particular, recent work on value nets has highlighted the different logics which lead to new ways of creating value. Möller and Rajala's (2007) business net classification framework (shown in Figure 6.6) distinguishes between:

- current business nets (characterized by clearly-specified and relatively stable value systems);
- business renewal nets (which, while based on relatively stable value systems are embarked upon process improvements or new solutions for customers); and
- emerging business nets (characterized by 'dispersed and vaguely identifiable ideas about the future involving great uncertainty'),

based on their position along a continuum in terms of the level of determination of their value system logic and the value sets employed by the organizations involved. For example, 'current business nets' such as the airlines' Star Alliance are more about 'business as usual' than innovation, exploiting e-business technologies along the way. By contrast, the Bluetooth strategic value net (described in Short case 6.3) is about the long-term, strategic development of the concept, using an open system approach.

Although we can see e-business applications across the whole of this framework, some of the more interesting ones are the ones that the researchers characterize as emerging business nets. Here, Möller and Rajala's (2007) focus is upon:

- application nets: formed to support commercially viable applications from rapidly emerging technology;
- dominant design nets: coalitions of partially competing and partially collaborating firms jockeying for position in seeking to influence an emerging technological template); and
- innovation networks (loose science and technology-based research networks involving universities and the R&D functions of major corporations).

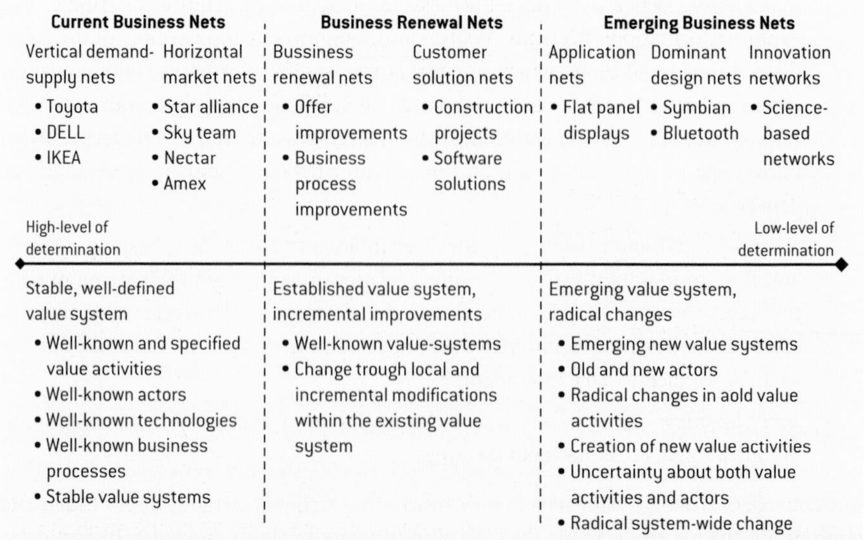

> **Open System** A management system that is capable of self-maintenance on the basis of throughput of resources from the environment.

| Current Business Nets | | Business Renewal Nets | | Emerging Business Nets | | |
|---|---|---|---|---|---|---|
| Vertical demand-supply nets | Horizontal market nets | Bussiness renewal nets | Customer solution nets | Application nets | Dominant design nets | Innovation networks |
| • Toyota<br>• DELL<br>• IKEA | • Star alliance<br>• Sky team<br>• Nectar<br>• Amex | • Offer improvements<br>• Business process improvements | • Construction projects<br>• Software solutions | • Flat panel displays | • Symbian<br>• Bluetooth | • Science-based networks |
| High-level of determination | | | | | | Low-level of determination |
| Stable, well-defined value system | | Established value system, incremental improvements | | Emerging value system, radical changes | | |
| • Well-known and specified value activities<br>• Well-known actors<br>• Well-known technologies<br>• Well-known business processes<br>• Stable value systems | | • Well-known value-systems<br>• Change trough local and incremental modifications within the existing value system | | • Emerging new value systems<br>• Old and new actors<br>• Radical changes in aold value activities<br>• Creation of new value activities<br>• Uncertainty about both value activities and actors<br>• Radical system-wide change | | |

**Figure 6.6** Business net classification framework

## Activity box 6.3

### Chains or nets?

Think of two different businesses in markets with which you are familiar. Can their value-creating activities best be characterized as being derived from chains or nets?

## Short case 6.3

### Bluetooth and the strategic value net

Founded in 1998, Bluetooth is a low-cost short-range wireless specification for connecting mobile devices and bringing mobile e-business applications to market, named after Harald Blatland, the tenth-century Danish king who unified the Danes and Norwegians (http://www.bluetooth.org). Similarly, Bluetooth was intended to unify different technologies, such as personal computers and mobile phones. The technology is now available in the fourth version of its core specification and continues to develop, building on some distinctive technical strengths, including its small-form factor radio, low power, low cost, built-in security, and ease-of-use. It is a key e-business technology and is very widely used. The 2008 market for mobile phones worldwide was close to 1.2bn handsets, with just over half having Bluetooth functionality—a figure likely to grow by 7.6 per cent annually to 2015. Major consumer applications of the technology include automotive applications (where Bluetooth speakerphones, GPS, and hands-free car kits are a feature of a majority of new vehicles) and gaming applications, where Bluetooth-operated gaming equipment (including the Nintendo Wii and Sony PS3) are now the second biggest Bluetooth device category by volume, after headsets. In B2B markets, the growth of chip-and-pin e-payment devices has been just one application of the growing number of mobile Internet devices used within business.

Bluetooth is also distinctive, however, for the strategic way in which the technology and its applications have been designed and developed by the businesses with a long-term interest in the success of the technology. Bluetooth technology is an open system and development is co-ordinated by a special interest group (SIG) founded in 1998. The Bluetooth SIG 'promoter' members include: Ericsson AB, Intel, Lenovo, Microsoft, Motorola, Nokia, and Toshiba and an additional 10,000 other member companies worldwide. Any company using Bluetooth must become a member, but promoter companies are highly engaged in the strategic and technical development of Bluetooth wireless technology. In addition to sitting on the SIG's Board of Directors, promoter members sit on the Bluetooth Qualification Review Board (BQRB), and nominate hundreds of employees to the Committees and Working Groups that guide the ongoing development and promotion of the technology, including the development of ultra low-power Bluetooth (Wibree).    »

*Question*

What are the advantages and disadvantages of this 'emerging business net'? Look online for recent stories on Bluetooth and its development to help with your answer.

## Business models, competition, and e-business

So far, we have talked about the way in which e-business technologies might alter the ways in which markets can be structured and we have discussed what such technologies can potentially do to the means by which firms, and networks or constellations of firms, might create value for their customers. By exploiting insight into the way in which consumers or customers perceive value, we have suggested, it may be possible for incumbent firms or new entrants to achieve profitability. But it's one thing to write about, or read about, conceptual models or to describe a successful company's achievements, even if we also seek to analyse the roots of that success. It's entirely another to set out a process by which others might build successful companies from scratch.

Amongst commentators and commercial practitioners seeking to explore the opportunities of e-business, there has been a frenzy to uncover new ways of doing business that will bring profitability to firms. As part of this activity, there has been much discussion of 'new business models'—although the phrase is not limited to the online environment. But what does the term 'business model' mean?

> 'Executives, reporters and analysts who use the term don' have a clear idea of what it means. They use it to describe everything from how a company earns revenue to how it structures its organization.' *Porter, 1985*

Indeed, Michael Porter once referred to the term as part of the Internet's 'destructive lexicon'. Most commentators propose that it refers to the way a company does business, a means by which it can sustain itself. The choice of model specifies a value chain or network position, in relation to other firms within an industry, and may be very simple or much more complex. To emphasize: a business model is not of itself a strategy; rather, it is reflective of strategic choices made by the firm. Shafer et al., writing in 2005, found twelve academic definitions and forty-two different building blocks of what a business model might be, none of which (they judged) had been accepted by the business community, although they also reported that some 27 per cent of Fortune 500 firms used the term in their annual reports. They concluded that the lack of consensus was because of the involvement of a wide range of disciplines with the viewpoints of each author driving the definition. Not to be outdone, they themselves developed a framework for these components (shown in Figure 6.7), focusing on four key organizing terms, and defined a business model as 'a representation of a firm's underlying core logic and strategic choices for creating and capturing value within a value network.'

In practice, this way or organizing the key components of a business model is extremely helpful. One the one hand, a business model requires a logic that articulates

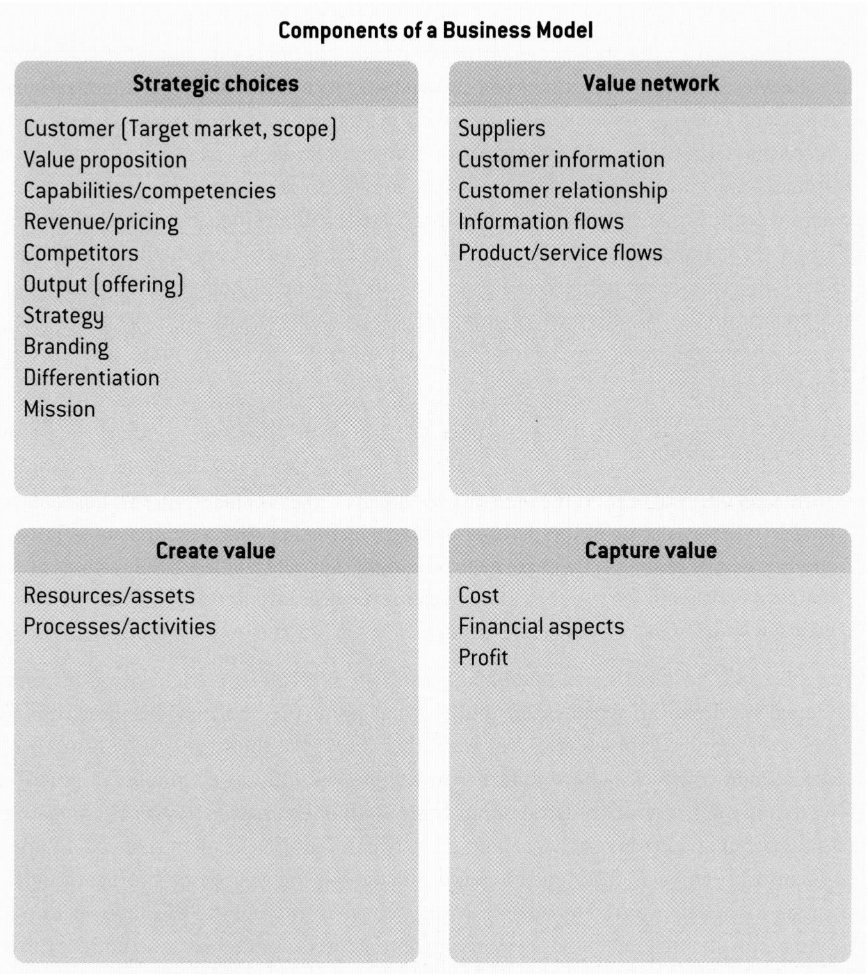

**Components of a Business Model**

| Strategic choices | Value network |
|---|---|
| Customer (Target market, scope)<br>Value proposition<br>Capabilities/competencies<br>Revenue/pricing<br>Competitors<br>Output (offering)<br>Strategy<br>Branding<br>Differentiation<br>Mission | Suppliers<br>Customer information<br>Customer relationship<br>Information flows<br>Product/service flows |
| **Create value** | **Capture value** |
| Resources/assets<br>Processes/activities | Cost<br>Financial aspects<br>Profit |

**Figure 6.7** Components of a business model affinity diagram

the assumptions and consistency of the strategic choices made by firms. On the other, firms can only compete if they are able to create and capture value in ways that are relevant to the customer. For example, this may be through operating at a lower cost, improving operational effectiveness through the use of better technologies, superior inputs, better trained people, more effective management structure, or by commanding a price premium as a result of some form of strategic positioning, employing a different set of features, different array of services or different logistical arrangements from the competition. Porter suggested that 'the Internet makes it harder for companies to sustain operational advantages, but opens up new opportunities for achieving or strengthening a distinctive strategic positioning'.

In earlier work, consultants Accenture suggested that business models are more 'mindsets than methodology':

> 'in practice, a business model is much more than a rational description of how an organization creates value. It's a rich, tacit understanding about how all the pieces work together to make money.' *Linder and Cantrell, 2000*

We are interested in the strategic elements of business models throughout this chapter, but there will clearly be implications of a chosen business model for a firm's organizational structure and culture—issues that we deal with in chapter 11. Increasingly, we have seen both conceptualizations and taxonomies of e-business models emerging as academics, consultants, and commentators seek to provide some kind of rigour and formality to what up until recently has been fairly 'loose talk'. But there is still no single, accepted, taxonomy although that proposed by Shafer et al. does provide a useful organizing framework. Further, whilst business models and processes are capable of being protected through patenting within the US, this form of protection is not available within other jurisdictions, such as within the European Union. This may work to prevent greater formality in business model logic.

But it may also be unrealistic to expect to be able to develop a sense of what is the 'winning' business model within an e-business context. Not least:

> 'there is an intrinsic irony in the mad rush to "discover" the dominant Internet business model. What awaits us is the perhaps deflating realisation that e-commerce is just another kind of business. There are countless "right" answers, endless combinations of business models and infinite permutations of key themes and approaches. There will be no magic bullet.' *Rayport, 1999*

In practice, we have seen a considerable variety of strategic approaches to e-business developed by firms. To what extent and at what point they become business models in their own right is problematic. Not least, this is because the typologies advanced by academics and consultants have difficulty in keeping up with developments in practice. However, another way of thinking about business models is to look not at competing definitions, but at what is out there in practice. North Carolina academic Michael Rappa has spent over ten years distinguishing and cataloguing the web-based business models operating in the real world. His open learning website is listed in the Weblinks section at the end of this chapter, but Table 6.2 summarizes the forty models he has so far identified, giving contemporary examples of their usage.

This is an enormously useful exercise but, as Rappa himself makes clear, it is not a definitive or static list of 'ways to do business': the universe of business models seems

## Table 6.2  Categories of e-business models

| Model category | Model | Description | Example |
|---|---|---|---|
| **BROKERAGE** | | | |
| *Market makers, bringing buyers and sellers together* | Marketplace Exchange | Independent or consortium-backed, offering transaction process services | *Orbitz, ChemConnect* |
| | Buy/Sell Fulfillment | Takes customer orders to buy or sell a product or service | *CarsDirect* |
| | Demand Collection System | The 'name your price' model | *Priceline.com* |
| | Auction broker | Conducts auctions for sellers | *eBay* |
| | Transaction broker | Provides third party payment mechanism | *Paypal* |
| | Distributor | Catalog operation connecting manufacturers with retail buyers | *Screwfix.com* |
| | Search agent | Software agent to search out price and availability information | |
| | Virtual marketplace | Hosted environment for online merchants | *Amazon Marketplace* |
| **ADVERTISING** | | | |
| *Extension of the traditional media broadcast model* | Portal | A search engine including varied content or services | *Yahoo!* |
| | Classifieds | A list of items for sale or wanted | *Craigslist* |
| | User registration | Content-based sites requiring registration of marketing-relevant data | |
| | Query-based paid placement | Sells link positioning or advertising related to particular search term | *Google* |
| | Contextual advertising/ behavioural marketing | Freeware developers who bundle adware with their product | |
| | Content-targeted advertising | Delivery of relevant ads to each visited web page | *Google* |
| | Intromercials | Ads placed at the entry to a site | *CBS Marketwatch* |
| | Ultramercials | Interactive online ads, intertwined with content | *Salon/Mercedes-Benz* |
| **INFOMEDIARY** | | | |
| *Information intermediaries, assisting buyers/sellers understand a given market* | Advertising networks | Feed banner ads to a network of member sites | *DoubleClick* |
| | Audience measurement services | Online audience market research agencies | *Nielsen Online* |
| | Incentive marketing | Programme providing points or coupons for making purchases; data sold for targeted advertising | *Q Interactive* |
| | Metamediary | Facilitates transactions between buyers and sellers | *Edmunds.com* |

»

**Table 6.2** Continued

| Model category | Model | Description | Example |
|---|---|---|---|
| **MERCHANT** | | | |
| *Wholesalers and retailers of goods and services* | Virtual merchant | Retail merchant operating solely over the web | *Amazon.com* |
| | Catalog merchant | Mail order business with web-based catalogue | *Land's End* |
| | Click and mortar | Traditional retail firm with online presence | *Tesco* |
| | Bit vendor | Vendor of digital products | *Apple iTunes Music Store* |
| **MANUFACTURER (DIRECT)** | | | |
| *Vendor reaching buyers directly* | Purchase | Direct sale of product | *Dell Computer* |
| | Lease | Direct leasing | |
| | License | Direct licensing (transfer of usage rights) | *Software licensing* |
| | Brand intergrated content | Created by the brand manufacturer for product placement | |
| **AFFILIATE** | | | |
| *Offers financial incentives to affiliate sites on a pay-for-performance basis* | Banner Exchange | Trades banner placement amongst a network of affiliated sites | |
| | Pay-per-click | Site that pays affiliates for a user click-through | |
| | Revenue sharing | Offers percent of sales commission for a click-through | |
| **COMMUNITY** | | | |
| *Viability based on user loyalty, with revenues derived from a range of ancillary activities* | Open Content | Content developed collaboratively | *Wikipedia* |
| | Public broadcasting | User-supported PBS model extended online | *PBS* |
| | Social networking services | Connection to other individuals based on common interests | *Flickr* |
| **SUBSCRIPTION** | Content services | Text, audio or video content | *Netflix* |
| *Fee charged to subscribe to a service* | Person to person Networking | Intermediaries for distribution of user-submitted information | *Friends Reunited* |
| | Trust services | Membership associations | *TRUSTe* |
| | Internet service providers | Offer network connecttivity | *BT.com* |
| **UTILITY** | Metered usage | Invoices users based on actual content consumed | |
| *Based on a 'pay-as-you-go' metered approach* | Metered subscriptions | Invoices users based on pre-paid content | *Slashdot* |

constantly to evolve beyond the simple 'merchant' or 'brokerage' models which were at the heart of much of the early thinking on how e-businesses might operate. (Long case 6.1 nevertheless illustrates how successful such models can be.) Secondly, just because a particular way of doing business has been developed, this does not of course automatically lead to sustainably profitable performance. Coltman et al. (2007) suggest that a successful e-business strategy may be determined either by successful strategy *content*, or *process*, or both. From the point of view of strategy content, economic, technological, political, and competitive forces will comprise external conditions affecting success. Internally, the firm's core competences (the things it does well and which competitors may find difficult to emulate) and its dynamic capabilities (its ability to integrate, build, and reconfigure internal and external competences to address rapidly changing environments) will correspondingly determine successful strategy content. Strategy *process* deals with the explanation of *how* e-business strategy should be implemented, rather than being particularly concerned with its content. For example, chapter 10 focuses upon e-business project management giving particular attention to process. Because both strategy content and process (but particularly content) are so firm-specific, both these concepts have been used to explain variation in e-business-related performance.

A firm's implementation of a business model may also fail because it may be that some of the assumptions behind the business model (some of the strategic choices, in other words) are flawed. Shafer et al. (2005) suggest that there may be four common problems, linked back to the four components of their definition:

- flawed assumptions underlying the core logic;
- limitations in the strategic choices considered;
- misunderstandings about value creation or value capture; and
- flawed assumptions about the value network.

For example, the recent extensive growth of social networking sites clearly represents a different and distinctive way of doing business. But many social networking firms have yet to demonstrate that their sites are actually profitable in the longer run. Whilst Facebook had 150m active users in 2009 and was recently valued at $15bn, the logic for its profitability is not as clear as, say, for a telecoms firm or an airline. (Although if Facebook were a country, it would now be the eighth most populated in the world.) In part, Facebook's profitability relies upon marketers and advertisers developing new and effective mechanisms for capturing the attention of people who are looking for each other rather than for goods and services. We address these so-called 'second-generation' marketing tools in greater depth in chapter 7. But these new mechanisms in turn may require some changes in users' mindsets so that they are willing to accept commercial messages in this context:

> 'Although you've provided the infrastructure, the network and all the interactions belong to the members … they feel like the space and the networks are theirs, and are very uncomfortable with you, as a company, taking too much advantage of it.' *Gary Stein, Ammo Marketing, quoted in Lamb, 2008*

Further, many business-to-consumer e-business services (particularly those in Rappa's *Infomediary* or *Community* categories) are often free (at least monetarily) at the point

**Activity box 6.4**

### A Commercial Face

Think about your own use of Facebook or its equivalents, or examine a social networking site of your choice. Develop a typology of the different ways in which your chosen site demonstrates its commercial credentials. To what extent might you recognize and respond to these?

of use. How does the profit and strategic logic of such services stack up? Have a look at Short case 6.4, which reviews the LinkedIn business social network and poses some hard questions. Journalist and commentator Chris Anderson, responsible for bringing the Pareto principle and the long tail concept to public attention, has developed thinking about what he calls the 'Four Kinds of Free' in which he suggests that there may be new kinds of profit logic, even if they are not visible to the end user. Figure 6.8 depicts Anderson's models.

Moving from strategic choices, to business model, to implementation requires that organizations develop a well-thought-out process. Start-up organizations will face a different mix of implementation issues from existing organizations. But,

> 'the challenge of the Internet is less how to respond to a completely different channel structure than how to manage a more complex one in which a new Internet channel sits beside pre-existing channels and in which Internet technology alters how the existing ones function.' *Saloner and Spence, 2002*

Initially, for both start-ups and existing firms, some of the recommendations on implementation were a little thin on detail and on financial rigour. For example, Follitt (2000) suggested that for existing organizations, the only requirements of the implementations process included:

- a champion;
- a vision;
- a plan to achieve the e-transformation;
- a rigorous communications strategy; and
- a healthy company culture.

More recently, and perhaps with the benefit of hindsight, requirements have been more detailed and scrupulous. So-called 'road-mapping' of implementation has been an increasingly common approach. For example, IBM's Institute for Business Value has produced a multi-stage roadmap for retail firms seeking to develop a multi-channel presence (Figure 6.9). The roadmap also stresses that the impetus must come from the top of the organization, treating (in this instance) multi-channel retailing as a strategic issue across the business. Internal objectives and incentives have to be aligned, suggests the research, and the performance and costs of specific activities in each channel will also need to be measured to identify the most promising opportunities for optimization.

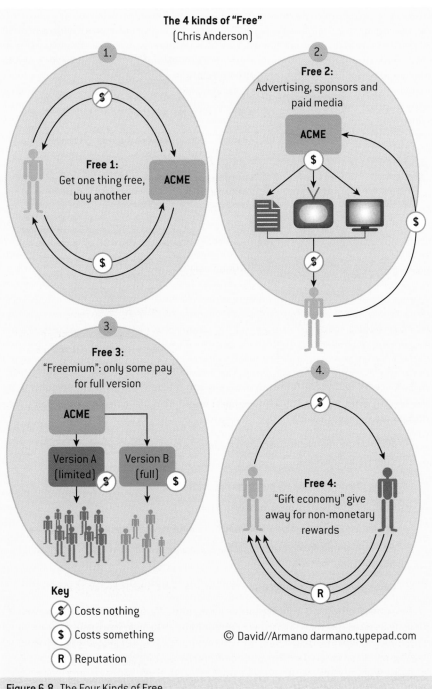

**The 4 kinds of "Free"**
(Chris Anderson)

**1.**

**Free 1:**
Get one thing free, buy another

ACME

**2.**

**Free 2:**
Advertising, sponsors and paid media

ACME

**3.**

**Free 3:**
"Freemium": only some pay for full version

ACME

Version A (limited)        Version B (full)

**4.**

**Free 4:**
"Gift economy" give away for non-monetary rewards

**Key**

$ Costs nothing

$ Costs something

R Reputation

© David//Armano darmano.typepad.com

**Figure 6.8** The Four Kinds of Free

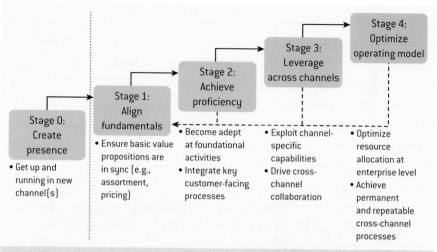

**Figure 6.9** Stages of multi-channel retail evolution

## Short case 6.4

### LinkedIn

LinkedIn is a social networking site oriented towards business professionals (http://www.linkedin.com). Founded by former Oxford philosophy student and serial entrepreneur Reid Hoffman in 2002, the site has 41m members drawn from 150 different professions. The benefits to members include:

- finding potential clients, service providers, subject experts, and partners who come recommended;

- being able to be found for business opportunities;

- searching for new job opportunities;

- finding 'inside connections' that may be helpful in obtaining new jobs or contracts;

- finding high-quality so-called 'passive' candidates (who are not actively in the job market); and

- getting introduced to other professionals through contacts known to the member.

The justification to join is evidence that respondents are thirty times more likely to respond to another LinkedIn member than to a conventional email. Revenue comes from three sources. Advertising accounts for some 30 per cent of income and averages between $75–$100m per annum. The company also offers corporate recruitment services, including job postings, which comprise a further 30 per cent. Finally, a balance of subscription income is generated from those users who want more extensive involvement with the site. Whilst LinkedIn is free to join and use to a limited extent, paid premium accounts are also available which allow increasingly greater numbers of Requests for Introduction and InMails to be sent and search results to be displayed. Subscriptions vary between $24.95 and $499.95 per month. In late 2008, the service was enhanced with a series of free applications allowing members to share files, presentations and blogs, and providing access to the Huddle.net secure online workspace.  »

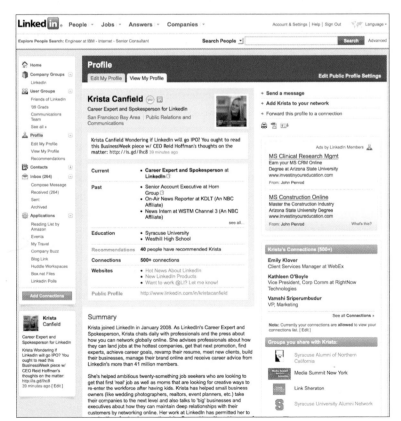

How robust is the company's profit logic against an economic downturn? Not yet publicly listed, LinkedIn claims to be profitable and its founder believes that the site is well suited to recessionary conditions. 'Essentially, every individual is a small business', he argues and in difficult times, employees look outside their organizations to build a prospective safety net of contacts and to reinforce their professional credentials. The site is also less reliant on advertising income than other social networking businesses. It also had the benefit of an injection of new capital at the end of 2008 from Goldman Sachs, SAP, and McGraw-Hill—surely an indicator of confidence in this particular social network's future—which value the company at more than $1bn.

*Question*

What 'kind of free' is LinkedIn? What are the chief characteristics of its business model and what are the biggest threats to its continued profitability?

Somewhat less diplomatically, when writing about the practical challenges of implementing a business opportunity arising out of the long tail hypothesis, which we discussed in chapter 2, venture capitalist Guy Kawasaki delivers what he calls a 'cynic's checklist' of issues which outlines the tactical items required for firms to succeed (Kawasaki, 2006). These range from: the importance of strategic singleness of purpose through to assumptions about production, inventory, and distribution costs.

## Public-sector e-business strategies

Why do we devote a separate section to understanding what e-business strategy means for public sector organizations? Should we expect public sector experience to be any different from that of the commercial sector? In practice, there are likely to be a great many similarities in public sector experience of e-business, but also some significant differences. E-business strategies in public services and government are much less well researched than in the commercial sector. Clearly, from the point of view of the customer, most public services exist in an essentially non-competitive environment. (It may be difficult to find an alternative provider of taxation or land-use planning services, for example, but areas such as postal services or education are open to competition in many markets.) Commercial motives for moving to e-business, such as gaining market share or improving profitability, are not generally relevant to public sector organizations.

There are nevertheless many similarities. Paul Beynon-Davies proposes a model of the e-government agenda which looks remarkably comparable to a value chain approach (Figure 6.10). He distinguishes between two dimensions of e-government—vertical (central, regional, and local)—and horizontal (in terms of the external and internal processes of government). As a result, he sees several, interrelated, value chains. The increasing involvement of government agencies and outsourced suppliers mimics the B2B aspects of commercial e-business models ('supply chain'), whilst the provision of services between government and citizen mimics the B2C model ('customer chain'). Finally, the internal value chain of internal

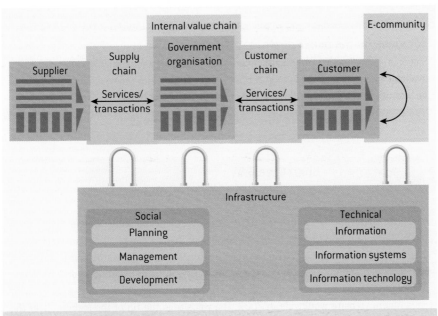

**Figure 6.10** The public services value chain

governmental processes is seen to be similar to 'intra-business e-business'. Beynon-Davies defines an e-government strategy as 'the use of information and communications technology to change the structure and processes of government organizations'.

The focus of public service organizations tends instead to be on achieving greater efficiency and accessibility of services within the context of Government policy objectives. E-business strategies tend to be target-driven. Short case 6.5 develops the example of Transport for London as it seeks to respond to targets set by the Greater London Authority. Similarly, unlike profit-driven corporations, there will naturally be less of an entrepreneurial and competitive environment, which may in turn suppress the motivation to innovate and also mean that the core competences and dynamic capabilities of commercial organizations may not to be found in sufficient quantity to deliver world-class e-business applications. Certainly, the experience of ICT within government generally is one with 'a history of resource wastage and underperforming information systems' (Waring and Maddocks, 2005). Are we to expect e-business experience to be any different?

Interestingly, one of the external pressures to innovate comes not from other firms or from end users, but from other governments. Beynon-Davies's study of the UK Inland Revenue strategy of developing electronic service delivery to a mass customer base showed that one aim was to improve the status of the UK as an information society by comparison with other nations, as part of a 'modernization' agenda. Recall the table showing levels of national e-readiness in chapter 1. This can often lead to unrealistic targets being set that are incapable of being delivered in practice. In a highly critical assessment, Fuat Alican writes of the Information Society Strategy in Turkey, which he describes as the outcome of 'experts without expertise' attempting to deliver a project design for a developed market into an emerging economy: 'the end result is an unworkable project and a grand risk of failure' (Alican, 2007).

## Activity box 6.5

### Solutions for the public sector?

Select a public sector organization or government agency. By exploring publically available material online, investigate and document the extent to which it has developed an Internet-based strategy. Critique the strategy and its outcomes.

## Short Case 6.5

### Transport for London

It seems somewhat unlikely for a UK transport utility company, whose business is the underground and buses, to be the winner of such a prestigious and fashionable international prize as a Webby Award (http://www.webbyawards.com). However, Transport for London (TfL), the London Assembly's arm for implementing and managing transport strategy across the capital, won the People's Voice Webby Award for the best government website worldwide in 2008. The website is the tip of the iceberg. Over the past ten years, TfL has employed e-business technologies to implement new information communications and payment systems using e-government principles to improve access to the streets and public transport system. Amongst the mayor's ten strands of transport strategy is:

- reducing traffic congestion;
- increasing capacity, reduce overcrowding, and increase both reliability and frequency of services;
- making radical improvements to bus services across London, including increasing the bus system's capacity, improving reliability, and increasing frequency of services; and, most particularly,
- bringing forward new integration initiatives to ensure that taxis and private hire vehicles are improved and fully incorporated into London's transport system; and provide much better information and waiting environments benefiting from one of the most advanced integrated transport ticketing services in the world, together with state of the art, multi-channel, multi-modal transport and travel information.

E-government principles are at the heart of delivering this strategy. TfL relaunched its website in March 2008 last year and is achieving nearly 5.8 million visits to its site each month with a range of travel tools covering planning, mobile, and safety issues. For example, Journey Planner service delivers integrated travel planning information to users on the site and by text; free mobile travel alerts warn of tube delays to pre-stored journeys; the Cabwise text service allows vulnerable travellers to get the numbers of one taxi and two licensed minicab firms in the area they are texting from—100,000 texts were sent in 2007.

≫

The second major innovation is in multi-mode payment systems. Its Oyster stored-value contactless smart card was introduced in July 2003 and today more than 75 per cent of all tube and bus journeys are paid for by Oyster, with over 10m cards issued, around half of which are in regular use. Ticket renewals and pay-as-you-go top-ups can be made online. Insights from analysis of card data are used to improve TfL's ability to enhance the integration of different transport modes and understand the impact of fare »

changes. It is planned to replace the current ticketing system with contactless bank cards provided by Visa and Mastercard, as well as to use mobile phones enabled with near-field communications technology.

*Question*

Examine the recent policy announcements of the current Mayor of London on transport issues and consider the implications for the Transport for London e-business strategy. You can find them here: http://www.london.gov.uk/mayor/. In what ways are public service e-business strategies vulnerable to political pressures?

Beynon-Davies' value chain model is underpinned by the requirement for effective social and technical infrastructures. One of the key findings of ICT research in public services is that both of these tend to be more deficient than in commercial firms. For example, thinking can often be short-termist and resistant to change. Bureaucratic models of organizations, of which public services are typical examples, are characteristically hierarchical, and do not lend themselves to the agility required of e-business implementation. Chapter 11 investigates some of the cultural implications of e-business technologies at both corporate and country levels.

## Long case 6.1

### ASOS: the online fashion store

'The Clothing sector is now the Internet's third largest, so "ya boo sucks" to those who said fashion would never sell online.' *Blogger*

Founded in 2000 by Nick Robertson, ASOS was originally called 'As Seen On Screen' and had a very different business model to the one according to which it operates today. The company sold celebrity-inspired products: either scarce items designed to attract high bids (such as the Big Brother Diary Room chairs) or copies of desirable ephemera, such as the picture frame from Rachel's front door in Friends. Clothing only accounted for 10 per cent of sales. Nine years later, the company is the number two company in the UK online clothing market (see Table 6.3), with over 14,000 lines for sale at any one time. ASOS was seventeenth in terms of traffic generated of all UK shopping websites in 2008. More than 4.5m individual customers visit the company's site every month (more than twice the level of a year previously) and ASOS has astounded the fashion retailing sector by bucking the downwards trend in store-based sales. Indeed, in 2008, sales were up by 90 per cent to £81.0m, and the company reported record profits (before tax), up 117 per cent to £7.3m.[1]

1   ASOS plc, (2008), Annual Report and Accounts, http://www.asosannualreport2008.com/Doc/pdf/AnnualReport2008.pdf.    »

Table 6.3  Top 10 online clothing retailers, July 2008 (% market share)

| Rank | Firm | 2008 | 2009 | Change |
|------|------|------|------|--------|
| 1 | Next | 8.96 | 10.71 | −175bps |
| 2 | **ASOS** | **4.74** | **3.04** | **+170bps** |
| 3 | Topshop.co.uk | 2.75 | 2.46 | +29bps |
| 4 | River Island | 2.61 | 1.85 | +76bps |
| 5 | New Look | 1.83 | 0.59 | +124bps |
| 6 | M&M Direct | 1.45 | 1.62 | −17bps |
| 7 | Mothercare | 1.41 | 1.40 | +1bps |
| 8 | Mosoon | 1.34 | 1.21 | +13bps |
| 9 | Dorothy Perkins | 1.31 | 1.28 | +3bps |
| 10 | Boden | 1.22 | 1.71 | −49bps |

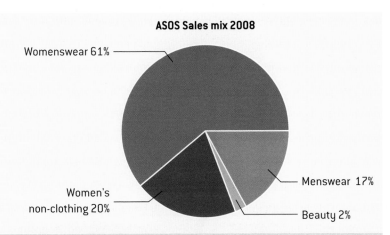

**ASOS Sales mix 2008**

Womenswear 61%
Women's non-clothing 20%
Menswear 17%
Beauty 2%

**Figure 6.11**  Disruptive innovation

It has often been suggested that clothing would never sell online. In 2000, retail analysts Verdict estimated that as little as 0.01 per cent of clothing sales were being made online in the UK. The then chief executive of Marks & Spencer, Sir Richard Greenbury, stressed the 'importance of fit and feel, and the personal input of a salesperson, which can' be offset by even the best electronic service.'[2] He was willing to concede that commodities 'like white knickers' might sell online—but not other products. He was wrong. Thirty per cent of UK women now report that they have brought clothes online.[3] ASOS's average basket size is some £61: more than the average pair of knickers. The company's strategy is based on three elements: choice, presentation,

2  Quoted in Daniel, C., (2000), 'From cradle to grave', *Financial Times*, 13 September. http://specials.ft.com/lifeonthenet/FT318WDR2DC.html.
3  According to the Interactive Media in Retail Group.

»

and service. ASOS offers not only 600 clothing brands, but also 5,000 own label styles, including styles commissioned from sixteen independent designers, and collaboration with the London College of Fashion. Three to five thousand new lines a month are launched on the site. A staff of just over 300 design, source, photograph, film, and upload high-quality product images to the website from a single building in north London. The firm's productivity is exceptionally high, with eighty video clips a day being produced, every day of the week. Its lean profile means that it is well placed to move from concept to sale much faster than its competitors. Stock turns over every ten weeks and 95 per cent of orders placed before 4.00pm now leave the warehouse the same day, meaning that the firm's delivery terms have shortened from three to four to one to two days. Investments in customer service mean that 85 per cent of orders can now be tracked and the average response time for email enquiries is now 30 minutes, 24 hours a day 7 days a week.

ASOS has also been able to seize on emerging trends and respond to them faster. And it can turn off supply which no longer matches fickle fashion demand. For example, the maxi dress was heralded as a likely success in the summer of 2008. With constant rainfall, this turned out not to be the case and whilst ASOS was able to re-purpose much of the stock, competitors were left with unsold stock in store.

The cost profile of an online shopping business is considerably different from a store-based retailer. Property costs normally figure largely for store-based businesses, closely followed by staff costs. In the case of ASOS, total operating costs comprised 36.3 per cent of sales in 2008 and staff costs were nearly one-third of these. Marketing and IT costs for online firms tend to be generally higher than those for offline, and in the case of ASOS make up 13 per cent and 10 per cent of operating costs respectively. Moreover, the company planned to spend £4m keeping its IT up to date in 2009. Returns, often a significant and unanticipated hidden cost in an online shopping business, were »

26.1 per cent by value in 2007–2008. This might seem high, but is only two-thirds of the sector's average.

ASOS supports its online activity with a 200-page hard copy and digital edition monthly magazine, voted Customer Magazine of the Year in 2008, which now commands a circulation of half a million and generates £1/3m in advertising revenue. Two major strategic developments will characterize ASOS' future growth. The first is the launch of a series of themed strands within the site. The first is ASOSRed, a branded clearance section (http://www.asos.com/red) with up to 70 per cent of branded lines drawn from fifty brands and presented using the main site's look and feel. Other streams include Kids and Designer & Luxury Store. The second is a plan to develop a consumer-to-consumer marketplace for customers to trade with one another.

*Questions*

1. Why has ASOS been so successful when the sales of most conventional store-based clothing retailers have stalled or declined during the past two years?

2. 'It's as big as we want to make it' (Nick Robertson, ASOS). Is it? Are there limits to ASOS's growth?

## Long case 6.2

### Guardian Media Group

The *Guardian* has a distinguished history as an independent UK newspaper. As the *Manchester Guardian*, it was founded as a weekly paper by John Edward Taylor in 1821. Taylor intended that the paper should promote liberal interests in the aftermath of the Peterloo Massacre and the growing campaign to repeal the Corn Laws that grew strongly in Manchester during the early part of the nineteenth century. The abolition of Stamp Duty allowed the paper to be published daily from 1855. The newspaper was handed over to the Scott Trust in 1936 to ensure its continuing independence. The *Observer* was acquired in 1993. The Trust now wholly owns the Guardian Media Group and it is this Group (which also owns the *Observer*, the *Manchester Evening News*, *Auto Trader* magazine and radio, and TV interests) that has pioneered the newspaper's involvement in electronic channels to market. As 'Guardian Unlimited' (now guardian. co.uk), the Group first launched a series of websites in January 1999 and by March of the following year commanded 2.4m unique users—the most popular UK newspaper website at that time. In 2004, digital editions of the new main newspapers were made available as online replicas, and in 2007 a digital archive was launched to make its paper archive available online. By 2008, Guardian News and Media was making £261m in sales but making an operating loss of £24.9m (although the Group itself was profitable).

In some senses, however, the reproduction of the hard-copy paper in digital form (either as a replica or on a web page) can be seen as an 'old economy' response: perpetuating traditional models of journalism and forms of communication. Traditional media models, driven by advertising income, may no longer to be sustainable within an Internet economy (Águila-Obra et al., 2007). Of far greater interest in terms of this chapter therefore is the way in which the Group has sought to transform the *Guardian* from a UK newspaper operation to a 24/7 international print and digital publisher. Indeed, much of the loss in 2008 came from the investment and restructuring costs incurred during this process. Such investment was made more straightforward by the fact that the newspaper is not publicly owned, but is still owned by trustees. There have been several strands to this transformation process.

During the year, the Guardian Unlimited website was relaunched as guardian. co.uk, supported by a £19m investment programme in the site improving its design, functionality, and usability. The online audience continued to grow strongly during the year. In August 2008, guardian.co.uk set a new record by attracting 23m unique users and serving over 200m pages, year-on-year increases of 46 per cent and 36 per cent respectively. At the same time, the company launched or enhanced several services:

- a series of fourteen separate email alerts, providing appropriately timed daily summaries or weekly syntheses of especially popular news themes, such as media, football, higher education, or the best of the Northern press (http://www. guardian.co.uk/emailservices);

- fifty blogs ranging from news and business, to sports, lifestyle, culture, and science & technology (http://www.guardian.co.uk/tone/blog);

- embedded video (http://www.guardian.co.uk/video);

- user personalization, with readers able to collect 'clippings' and assemble 'collections' of their own stories;

- distributed RSS (Rich Site Summary) feeds providing full text of stories for Internet news readers.                                                                    »

RSS (Rich Site Summary) a web feed standard for the dissemination of regularly changing web content (blog page entries, news headlines).

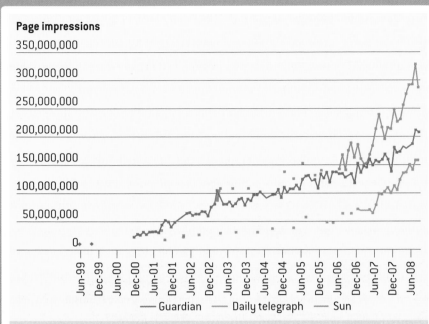

**Page impressions**

**Figure 6.12** Online page impressions, selected UK newspapers, 1999–2008.

Newspaper display advertising revenues grew by 6.6 per cent and digital display by 49 per cent. By the end of the 2007–2008 financial year, the decline in print recruitment advertising revenues had been offset by a 49 per cent increase in digital recruitment revenues. As a result of this and of the launch of Guardian America, two-thirds of the Guardian's reach is now outside the UK. The *Guardian* won a Webby award for the third year in succession in 2008. And yet there are still questions and challenges as the market for news evolves.

*Questions*

1. While the *Guardian*'s growth in page impressions has been impressive since the beginning of the decade, the growth in those of its rivals (for example, the *Daily Telegraph* and the *Sun*) appears to have been faster, especially in the last two years. Why?

2. 'Over the next few years, traditional newspaper companies will be falling like trees in the rain forest' (commentator). Do you agree?

## ❷ Chapter Summary

This chapter began by defining strategy and discussing the term's use and abuse. It talked of the need to distinguish between strategy at the industry and at the firm level. While at the industry level, e-business technologies have enabled the creation of wholly new kinds of activity, far more interesting in many respects have been their effects in reconfiguring existing industries and markets. At the firm level, on the other hand, the interest lies in understanding how organizations can employ e-business technologies to compete more efficiently or more effectively. The chapter also pointed out the importance of these goals for public sector organizations.

The chapter then proceeded to set out some of the conventional ways in which industry and market structure could be analysed in order to evaluate the nature of the threats to existing organizations and the opportunities available for prospective new entrants. It considered the extent to which the characteristics of e-business technologies might change the usefulness of these analytical tools and how they might need to be adapted. It introduced and illustrated the electronic markets hypothesis, which, commentators had suggested, would cause a shift to more market-based forms of economic activity. It considered some of the later evidence to challenge the merits of this framework in relation to both B2B and B2C markets.

Similarly, the chapter reviewed frameworks and concepts relevant to understanding the ways in which e-business technologies might allow firms to create and capture value for customers and consumers. Again, conventional thinking on value 'chains' had been challenged by the growth of the value network or constellation concept as a new means of generating value-creating activities. This included notions of the co-creation of value. This shift in focus appears to have proved especially helpful in the consideration of e-business technologies. The chapter reviewed evolving thinking on the sources of the value creation potential of e-business technologies, as the technologies themselves had evolved and as research had become more sophisticated. It noted that markets for information behaved in somewhat different ways than expected and than markets for products.

The chapter then turned to the question of business models: their definition as well as their misuse. It focused on their key role as representations of a firm's underlying core logic and the strategic choices available to it for creating and capturing value within a value network. It provided a number of useful taxonomies and frameworks of available models and emphasized that these were neither definitive nor static, within a fast-moving business environment. It then dwelt on and illustrated some of the reasons for the potential failure of a firm's business model before discussing some of the practical challenges in implementing a business opportunity arising out of an e-business technology.

Finally, the chapter considered whether the design, development, and implementation of e-business strategy within the public sector could be expected to be different from wholly commercial experience. It pointed out many of the similarities between the two sectors, but also highlighted significant differences, including the inherent lack of competition, a politically oriented, target-driven backdrop to strategy development, and challenges arising out of the social and technical infrastructure of public sector organizations.

## ❷ Review questions

1. Describe the most widely used framework for evaluating industry structure. How has this had to evolve to accommodate e-business considerations?

2. Critique the 'electronic markets hypothesis', giving examples to illustrate your conclusions.

3. Account for and illustrate some of the institutional barriers to industry or market change by e-business that can be generated by existing incumbents.

4. What are the merits and demerits of thinking of organizations in terms of value nets rather than value chains?

5. Describe the four dimensions of value creation potential developed by Amit and Zott. How have they been subsequently modified?

6. Why is the term 'business model' problematic?

7. Why does the implementation of a particular business model not automatically lead to sustainably profitable performance for a firm?

8. What are the similarities and differences between public and commercial sector approaches to the development of e-business strategy?

## Discussion questions

**1.** Are there any industries incapable of being transformed by e-business technologies?

**2.** Have the disruptive effects of e-business technologies rendered models such as Porter's Five Forces less appropriate for analysing industry structure?

**3.** Which of Michael Rappa's business model categories offer the most potential for sustainable profitability? Why?

**4.** 'The reality of contemporary experience weakens overly rational or deterministic attempts to conceptualize value creation in e-business.' Discuss.

**5.** Do you think that public sector organizations' attempts to emulate commercial firm development and implementation of e-business technologies are inherently more likely to fail? If so, why? If not, why not? Illustrate your answer.

## Suggestions for further reading

Amit, R. and Zott, C., (2001), 'Value Creation in e-Business', *Strategic Management Journal*, 22, pp. 493–520.
This classic article sets out for the first time some distinguishing features of e-business technology's value creation potential. Although later criticized, its logic and analytical rigour are compelling.

Glassberg, B.C. and Merhout, J.W., (2007), 'Electronic Markets Hypothesis Redux: Where Are We Now?', *Communications of the ACM*, 50(2), pp. 51–5.
Glassberg and Merhout's article re-evaluates the electronic markets hypothesis and provides some thoughtful and well-illustrated examples of ways in which some aspects of reality do not appear to conform to the rhetoric, conclusions which have some important strategic implications for organizations.

Porter, M.E., (2001), 'Strategy and the Internet', *Harvard Business Review*, March, pp. 63–78.
Michael Porter's classic reinterpretation and partial defence of the frameworks he has developed in strategic management in the light of the growth of e-business technologies. Written at the height of the dot.com boom.

Rappa, M., (2009), *Business Models on the Web*, http://digitalenterprise.org/models/models.html.
Michael Rappa's extensive site on Managing the Digital Enterprise is well worth a visit for other aspects of thinking on e-business, but this specific listing refers to the section of the site specifically addressing business models.

Shafer, S.M., Smith, H.J., and Linder, J.C., (2005), 'The Power of Business Models', *Business Horizons*, 48, pp. 199–207.
This article is a later, more reflective, version of work undertaken by consultants Accenture into the nature of business models online. As well as some helpful synthesis of prevailing definitions, the article usefully captures distinctions between business models and strategy, and provides some thoughtful illustrations.

## References

Águila-Obra, A.R. del, Padilla-Meléndez, A., and Serarols-Tarrés, C., (2007), 'Value Creation and New Intermediaries on Internet. An Exploratory Analysis of the Online News Industry and the Web Content Aggregators' *International Journal of Information Management*, 27(3), pp. 187–99.

Alican, F., (2007), 'Experts without Expertise: E-society Projects in Developing Countries—the Case of Turkey', *Information Polity*, 12, pp. 255–63.

Amit, R. and Zott, C., (2001), 'Value Creation in e-Business', *Strategic Management Journal*, 22, pp. 493–520.

Arndt, J., (1979), 'Towards a Concept of Domesticated Markets', *Journal of Marketing*, 43(4), pp. 69–75.

Atkinson, R.D., (2003), 'The Revenge of the Disintermediated: How the Middleman is Fighting E-Commerce and Hurting American Consumers', *PPI Policy Report*, http://www.ppionline.org/ppi_ci.cfm?contentid=251838&knlgAreaID=140&subsecid=900055

BBC Trust/OFCOM, (2008), *Local Video Public Value Test: Description of Service*, http://www.bbc.co.uk/bbctrust/assets/files/pdf/consult/local_video_service_des.pdf.

Benjamin, R. and Wigand, R., (1995), 'Electronic Markets and Virtual Value Chains on the Information Superhighway', *Sloan Management Review*, 36(2), pp. 62–72.

Beynon-Davies, P., (2005), 'Constructing Electronic Government: The Case Of the UK Inland Revenue', *International Journal of Information Management*, 25, pp. 3–20.

Christensen, C.M., (1997), *The Innovator's Dilemma: When New Technologies Cause Great Firms to Fail*, Harvard Business School Press.

Coltman, T.R., Devinney, T.M., and Midgley, D.F., (2007), 'e-Business Strategy and Firm Performance: A Latent Class Assessment of the Drivers and Impediments to Success', *Journal of Information Technology*, 22(2), pp. 87–101.

Copeland, D.G., Mason, R.O., and McKenney, J.L., (1995), 'Sabre: The Development of Information-Based Competence and Execution of Information-Based Competition', *IEEE Annals of the History of Computing*, 17(3), pp. 30–57.

Evans, P.B. and Wurster, T.S., (1997), 'Strategy and the New Economics of Information, *Harvard Business Review*, September–October, pp. 71–82.

Finkelstein, S., (2001), 'Internet start-Ups: so why can't they win?' *Journal of Business Strategy*, 22, pp. 16–21.

Follitt, E., (2000), 'The Keys to e-Transformation—You Need All Five of These Critical Factors to Deliver Sustainable Growth to your Company', *Information Week*, 28, pp. 145–6.

Fry, J., (2007), 'Anxious Times for Net Radio', *Wall Street Journal*, 12 March, http://online.wsj.com/article/SB117338580828931370.html?mod=Real-Time.

Glassberg, B.C. and Merhout, J.W., (2007), 'Electronic Markets Hypothesis Redux: Where Are We Now?', *Communications of the ACM*, 50(2), pp. 51–5.

Howard, M., Vidgen, R., and Powell, P., (2006), 'Automotive e-Hubs: Exploring Motivations and Barriers to Collaboration and Interaction', *Journal of Strategic Information Systems*, 15, pp. 51–75.

IBM, (2005), *Cross Channel Optimization: A Strategic Roadmap for Multi-Channel Retailers*, IBM Institute for Business Value, http://www-935.ibm.com/services/us/imc/pdf/g510-6186-cross-channel-retailer.pdf.

Kawasaki, G., (2006), 'The Wrong Tale: A Checklist for Long-Tail Implementations', *How to Change the World: A Practical Blog for Impractical People*, http://blog.guykawasaki.com/2006/07/the_wrong_tale_.html.

Lamb, G.M., (2008), 'Many New "Friends" to be Made Online, But What About Dollars?' *ABC News*, 3 August, http://abcnews.go.com/Technology/AheadoftheCurve/story?id=5498194&page=1.

Linder, J. and Cantrell, S., (2000), *Carved in Water: Changing Business Models Fluidly*, Institute for Strategic Change, Accenture.

McSwain, D., (2007), 'Webcast royalty decision announced', *Radio & Internet Newsletter*, 2 March, http://www.kurthanson.com/archive/news/030207/index.shtml.

Malone, T.W., Yates, J., and Benjamin, R.I., (1987) 'Electronic Markets and Electronic Hierarchies', *Communications of the ACM*, 30(6), pp. 484–97.

Marcussen, C.H., (2008), Trends in European Internet Distribution—of Travel and Tourism Services, http://www.crt.dk/UK/staff/chm/trends.htm.

Mintzberg, H., (1994), *The Rise and Fall of Strategic Planning*, Free Press.

Möller, K. and Rajala, A., (2007), 'Rise of Strategic Nets—New Modes of Value Creation', *Industrial Marketing Management*, 36, pp. 895–908.

Normann, R. and Ramirez, R., (1993), 'From Value Chain to Value Constellation: Designing Interactive Strategy', *Harvard Business Review*, 71(4), pp. 65–77.

Porter, M.E., (1985), *Competitive Advantage: Creating and Sustaining Superior Performance*, The Free Press.

Porter, M.E., (2001), 'Strategy and the Internet', *Harvard Business Review*, March, pp. 63–78.

Rappa, M., (2009), *Business Models on the Web*, http://digitalenterprise.org/models/models.html.

Rayport, J., (1999), 'The truth about Internet business models', *Strategy+Business*, 3rd quarter, http://www.strategy-business.com/press/16635507/19334.

Saloner, G. and Spence, A., (2002), *Creating and Capturing Value: Perspectives and Cases on Electronic Commerce*, Wiley & Sons, New York.

Shafer, S.M., Smith, H.J., and Linder, J.C., (2005), 'The Power of Business Models', *Business Horizons*, 48, pp. 199–207.

Tse, T., (2007), 'Reconsidering the Source of Value of e-Business Strategies', *Strategic Change*, 16, pp. 117–26.

Walters, D. and Rainbird, M., (2007), 'Cooperative innovation: A value chain approach', *Journal of Enterprise Information Management*, 20(5), pp. 595–607.

Waring, T. and Maddocks, P., (2005), 'Open Source Software Implementation in the Public Sector: Evidence from the Field and Implications for the Future', *International Journal of Information Management*, 25, pp. 411–28.

# 🔗 Weblinks

Eric Long's e-Business blog. Eric is an online marketer, information architect, web strategist, and social media enthusiast. In real life, he is a practitioner working in IT application and development for a major US consumer goods company: http://www.ebusinessblog.org/.

Mashable. All that's new on the web. Mashable, founded in 2005, is the world's largest blog focused exclusively on Web 2.0 and Social Networking news: http://mashable.com.

Save Net Radio. Founded in 2007, the Save Net Radio lobbying group is an excellent example of the way in which new entrants to an industry can seek to take on established interests: http://www.savenetradio.org.

TechCrunch. Founded in 2005, TechCrunch is a weblog dedicated to profiling and reviewing new Internet products and companies. In addition to covering new companies, it profiles existing companies that are making an impact (commercial and/or cultural) within e-business: http://www.techcrunch.com/.

The Forrester Blog for e-Business and Channel Strategy Professionals. Does what it says on the tin. A way of keeping in touch with this technology consultancy's thinking on e-business issues. http://blogs.forrester.com/ebusiness_strategy/.

# Digital marketing

## Learning outcomes

Completing this chapter will enable you to:

- Understand the broad role and scope of marketing
- Review the extent to which digital marketing both complements and changes contemporary marketing practice
- Understand attitudes towards and adoption of digital marketing techniques by firms
- Appreciate the challenges for organizations in developing an integrated multi-channel marketing strategy
- Distinguish between first- and second-generation digital marketing techniques
- Consider the characteristics, strengths, and weaknesses of a selection of digital marketing techniques

## Introduction

E-business technologies are opening up an extraordinary new range of possibilities for firms in terms of marketing products and services to consumers and business customers, and in creating and managing relationships with those customers. However, as we have already suggested in chapter 4, these technologies have at the same time given greater power to many end users over their buying decisions at every stage in the buying process. This may no longer therefore be a process of which firms are necessarily fully in control. For example, the ready availability of product reviews online, the development of price comparison engines such as Kelkoo and Pricegrabber, as well as of bespoke e-procurement services and exchanges permit customers to compare prices and other data for otherwise similar products. The ease with which customers can provide readily accessible feedback online presents real challenges for firms, and the growth of Web 2.0 social networking tools exacerbates this challenge. The consequence for organizations is that, in order to maintain a brand's awareness and its perceived usefulness in the customer's mind through their marketing strategies and tactics, they must become considerably more customer-centric, focused, indeed, increasingly on the individual consumer rather than on large customer segments. In practice, and as we have done in earlier chapters of this book, this means that they need more effectively to understand the contemporary 'customer journey' in gaining awareness of a brand—the way in which customers evaluate alternative products and services, including such factors as the importance of price, and how they make their final purchases. Only then can appropriate marketing techniques be developed and employed.

However, digital marketing techniques are evolving at such a rapid pace that trial and error and experimentation is the order of the day as much as is well-understood and measured application. Few of the digital marketing techniques that we will describe below are yet proven over the long term and will take time to be properly evaluated. For example, sixty leading consumer and Internet brands participated in the launch of a new advertising system on the social networking site Facebook in 2007.[1] But there is little evidence on how such a presence might work, how consumers will relate to these brands in this context, or even if they work at all in increasing brand awareness and stimulating sales revenues.

Further, in many cases, it may be that digital marketing techniques will not always replace existing ways of reaching customers, but will serve to complement conventional mechanisms. As a result, the marketing strategies that managers seek to develop must be more integrated if they are not to avoid increasing marketing's cost base without achieving a commensurate growth in revenue. For example, research suggests that in fewer than 50 per cent of cases does increased marketing expenditure generally lead to a growth in sales (Abraham and Lodish, 1990).

Companies therefore need to have a better understanding of the 'touchpoints' that customers employ in their browsing and buying behaviour. For example, some research shows that the decline in conventional TV consumption in developed economies is directly proportional to the rise of web use: but this does not necessarily mean that firms should switch their advertising expenditures wholesale from one medium to another (Woods, 2006). Other research suggests that unconventional TV consumption (via time-shifting, downloading, or streaming video) is rising rapidly and that many, especially younger, media consumers multi-task—watching TV whilst emailing or messaging or simply browsing Internet content (Nielsen Media Research, 2008). For example, heavy Internet users in the US watch more TV than light Internet users. As a result, it may mean that marketers need to target each medium more carefully and perhaps even use each for different purposes.

After considering the broad role and scope of marketing, this chapter examines the extent to which digital marketing techniques might complement or change firms' marketing strategies. It then explores organizations' attitudes towards and adoption of the emerging range of digital marketing techniques. The chapter reviews selected developments in more detail, ranging from first-generation tools such as email, search, and affiliate marketing to second-generation tools including electronic word of mouth (EWOM) marketing using social networks and viral marketing. The chapter concludes by considering challenges facing firms in the development of integrated marketing strategies.

**Touchpoint** An interaction that a customer will have with the resources of the firm at a particular stage in the buying process. This may be human and physical, or virtual. The term is most commonly used in the context of the growth of multi-channel marketing, where we have witnessed a proliferation of potential touchpoints.

---

[1] Press Release, (2007) 'Facebook Unveils Facebook Ads', 6 November, http://www.facebook.com/press/releases.php?p=9176.

# What do marketers do?

A necessary preliminary to a discussion of digital marketing is of course to understand the nature and characteristics of marketing as a discipline. It's not unreasonable to assume that, while the Internet will have provided new tools and techniques and may possibly even have changed the balance of power within marketing channels, many of the fundamental principles of marketing still remain in place. There are two ways of thinking about marketing: as *what marketers do* and as *a way of thinking about customers*. Marketing departments within organizations will be carrying out many of the kinds of functional task that we will discuss below alongside the work conventionally undertaken by them. However, a marketing mindset is not just restricted to an organization's marketing professionals, but should ideally be shared by others in the firm and is best characterized as a customer orientation. Think about the last time you experienced exceptional levels of customer service, or when a member of the sales team really understood your needs as a customer.

Conventionally, therefore, you will often hear talk about organizations being *market-oriented*. By this is meant that they look outwards, rather than inwards, recognize and seek to respond to customers' needs more effectively than the competition, and ensure that it is market factors (rather than purely internal concerns) that will drive business decisions. Most organizations—including even some public-sector organizations—will claim to be market-oriented. We need therefore to think about marketing as more of a state of mind for organizations than simply in terms of functions or a body of knowledge.

In developing a marketing strategy, organizations focus on the ways in which they can create and capture value for their customers. This requires them to (1) undertake some form of market analysis, better to understand the situation within which customers' needs can be met and what customers value can be understood; (2) identify a specific target market based on some kind of segmentation process leading to the identification of groups of consumer in relation to whom the product or service's value proposition can be developed and positioned; and (3) carry out a programme of actions in the market to ensure the sale of the product or service, which might include the way in which it is designed, promoted, and distributed, with a price designed to signal value—actions often collectively referred to as the 'marketing mix'. Finally, organizations have to put mechanisms in place to retain existing customers, once acquired. Figure 7.1 summarizes this process. In this chapter, we are particularly focusing on some of the segmentation and targeting undertaken by firms where digital marketing techniques have provided some greater insight, but we are also interested in those marketing actions—especially that of marketing communications—where new e-business tools have transformed the marketer's role.

In a rapidly evolving market environment, it may be that organizations have to take more risks than simply listening to what their customers want. Customers may not know what they want, or may not be able to express their needs effectively, and organizations may have to work to anticipate latent needs. It is important therefore to distinguish between organizations which are *market-driven* and those which *drive markets*.

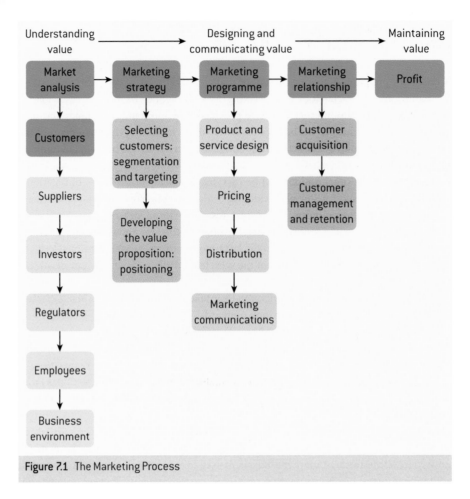

**Figure 7.1** The Marketing Process

- Market-driven firms seek to learn, understand, and respond to customers within a given market structure. Their focus is on customer satisfaction (often over the short term).

- Firms which drive markets are those which seek to change the composition, roles and/or the behaviour of players in a market, often focusing on customers' latent needs. They do this by focusing on customer value, over the long term, by observing customers, by experimenting and through partnerships with other organizations.

Table 7.1 summarizes the main differences between the two approaches.

From Table 7.1 we can begin to understand that the evolving e-business environment is going to favour market-driving firms and that the most successful marketing strategies will be developed by those firms who are driving markets: those who experiment, understand who their lead customers are, and who work with them rather than market at them, and are focused upon creating and maintaining customer value rather than simply customer satisfaction.

**Table 7.1  Two different approaches to marketing**

| Characteristic | Market driven | Driving markets |
| --- | --- | --- |
| Marketing Objective | Obtaining customer satisfaction | Creating and maintaining customer value |
| Consumer orientation | Expressed wants of consumers | Expressed wants and latent needs of consumers |
| Organizational adjustment style | Responsive to market | Anticipating market |
| Timescale | Short-term | Long-term |
| Organizational learning process | Customer focus<br>Key account relationships<br>Focus groups<br>Concept testing | Customer observation<br>Lead-user relationships<br>Continuous experimentation<br>Selective partnering |

---

### Activity box 7.1

**Is your favourite company market-driving or market-driven?**

Consider a market-facing company that you admire. Are they market-driving or market-driven? What evidence of their behaviour towards you would you use to support your choice?

---

# The effects of e-business technologies on marketing strategy

It is clear from this that while the fundamental objectives of marketing have not changed with the advent of e-business technologies, such technologies have the potential to change the ways in which many kinds of products may be marketed. This is of course most obvious for products which have themselves become digital, such as recorded music and videos. You may recall that in chapter 2 we talked about the concept of the long tail. This theory, we agreed, was particularly applicable to digitized products, but the phenomenon also carries with it a set of implications for the marketing of such goods. For example, consider the ways in which we now become aware of digitized music from our friends rather than necessarily directly from marketers. It is unreasonable to expect—and uneconomic for firms to incur—marketing expenditure to promote the slowest-selling items. Instead they may rely on the marketing efforts of others—through social networks such as MySpace (http://www.myspace.com), or through 'electronic word of mouth' from friends. This may be supplemented by commercial promotion on email, in addition to more conventional means such as radio and concerts. Other aspects of the marketing mix will also be affected, ranging from the ways in which an online track is 'packaged' (as a digital download with a.jpg album cover); the ways in which it is priced (by track rather than just as an album or compilation); and the ways in which it can now be distributed (via platforms such as iTunes (http://www.itunes.com) and online retailers such as Wal-Mart (http://musicdownloads.walmart.com)). Less obvious to the casual observer might be the ways in which paid keyword search prioritizes particular products and services in search engine results, but this is such an important and growing aspect of digital marketing that we devote a separate section to it in this chapter.

What is the digital marketing toolkit that is available to organizations? Table 7.2 sets out the most often reported digital techniques that are capable of being employed for commercial purposes. It distinguishes between first- and second-generation techniques.

> ## Activity box 7.2
>
> ### Understanding the personal impact of digital marketing
> Using your favourite recording artist, identify and categorize some of the ways in which the artist's work is featured online in websites, blogs, and social communities. Can you identify which of these are commercially sponsored?

The former category includes tools where we can already see some degree of commercial experience and sophistication and where we are getting a sense of how such tools may be appropriately used in a marketing context. These include email marketing and search marketing. Second generation tools, whilst in use, are to a greater extent unproven and in evolution. Note that we have avoided using the term 'Web 2.0' to describe the second category: this term tends to be associated with purely social media. Not all second-generation tools have social connotations. We also need to be careful in conflating digital marketing tools and digital marketing channels—and for this reason, for example, 'mobile marketing' is not so much a tool in its own right, but a channel through which (for example) email, display advertising, and search can be communicated.

How are customers likely to relate to digital marketing techniques? In turn, where do marketing objectives fit into the customer buying process? (Figure 7.2). *Brand building* helps customers to become aware of new products and services and keeps that awareness in customers' minds. *Consideration* makes sure that—at the information search and price comparison stage—both rational and emotional features of a firm's products and services are effectively communicated to customers. *Direct response* ensures that the mechanisms are in place that will allow customers to make purchases. And *customer retention* means moving beyond simply satisfying consumers to ensuring that the organization's behaviour will increase the likelihood that customers will re-purchase and that loyalty will be subsequently be generated. For a diverse range of consumer-facing businesses, the expectation is that the major areas of customer take-up of digital technologies will be not so much in relation to direct selling (although this is of course important) as in relation to pre-purchase activities, such as becoming aware of new products, information search, and price comparison, as well as in post-purchase customer service. Nor is this simply a consumer marketing phenomenon: manufacturing firms surveyed expect a majority

**Table 7.2  The digital marketing toolkit**

| Tool | Description | Commercial application examples |
|---|---|---|
| **First-generation digital marketing tools** | | |
| Email marketing | Targeted communications composed and transmitted from a computer network | Email marketing service providers www.e-dialog.com |
| Online advertising | Commercial messages placed on third-party web sites | Ad serving businesses www.doubleclick.com |
| Podcasts/video podcasts/webcasts | Digital media files distributed via electronic networks and (in the case of podcast) listened to on an .MP3 player | Podcast aggregator www.podcast.com |
| Referrals and affiliate marketing | Revenue sharing between online advertisers/ merchants and other online publishers | Commission Junction www.cj.com |
| Search marketing | Website promotion through optimization of search engine results pages | Google AdWords www.google.com/adwords |
| **Second-generation digital marketing tools** | | |
| Blogs | Online journals or weblogs | www.shinyshiny.tv |
| Online gaming | Massive multi-player games or networked games consoles | World of Warcraft www.worldofwarcraft.com |
| Mashups | Integration of data from more than one source into a single application | Mapdango www.mapdango.com |
| RSS/Atom | A standard for web feed subscription to frequently updated content from blogs, news sites etc. | |
| Social networks and fora | Online aggregations of common interests, talents, or knowledge created and maintained by end users; commercially these can be manifested as brand communities | Harley Davidson user forums www.hdforums.com |
| Virtual worlds | Holistic online environments | Second Life www.secondlife.com |
| Widgets | Programmes allowing immediate access to specific web-based content | Clearspring widget network www.clearspring.com |
| Wikis | Collaborative publishing vehicles, outsourcing content to end users | Enterprise wiki business service firm www.atlassian.com/software/confluence/ |

of customers to be using digital techniques to become aware of new products as well as searching for information, even if the majority then use more conventional techniques for price comparison and purchasing (such as face-to-face negotiation with sales teams). These perceptions will naturally determine how firms allocate their marketing budgets in future and will have a particular impact on tools related to marketing communications.

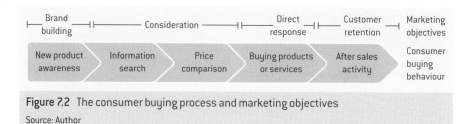

**Figure 7.2** The consumer buying process and marketing objectives
Source: Author

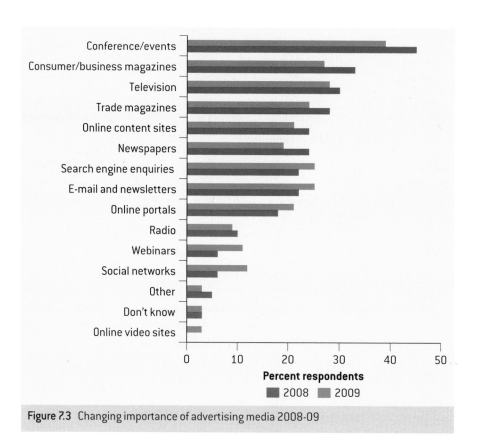

**Figure 7.3** Changing importance of advertising media 2008-09

Figure 7.3 shows how companies surveyed in 2008 felt that the relative importance of digital marketing communications tools would shift within just a twelve-month period.

But incorporating digital tools and techniques into the development and execution of an overall marketing strategy can be complex. How do organizations see the link between digital marketing tools and their marketing objectives? Whilst such understandings are constantly evolving, we can relate elements of the digital marketing toolkit to the four broad marketing objectives that we defined earlier (brand building, consideration, direct response, and customer retention). A survey of US marketers generated five specific conclusions:

- *Brand sponsorship and display advertising* are thought to be best for attaining brand building objectives.

- *Search marketing* appears to be most popular at the two pre-purchase stages— (including information search and price comparison).

- *Referral via affiliates* works best against consideration and direct response objectives.

- *Email marketing* is strongly associated with both direct response and customer retention, whilst podcasts also seem to be particularly popular in relation to the objective of retention.

- So-called *emerging vehicles* (which include blogs, virtual worlds, widgets, and wikis) generated the highest number of 'don' knows' amongst respondents (Court et al., 2000).

This research also suggested that the number of firms using digital marketing tools in practice is significantly lower than the number of firms saying it is important to them. We should not be surprised by this: many market research surveys of this kind tend to reveal a more optimistic view amongst respondents of their interests and intentions than actually make it through to practice. This is another reason for being cautious when interpreting the results of commercial surveys which seek to present very optimistic views of the development of e-business and e-commerce: a theme we have tried to develop throughout this book. In this case, it is important to understand what barriers might prevent users' aspirations being borne out in practice. Three major barriers can be recognized:

- *lack of measurement mechanisms*: firms are often unwilling to adopt marketing techniques without a corresponding mechanism for measuring their effectiveness;

- *lack of internal capabilities*: whilst firms may be interested in principle in adopting a wide range of digital marketing techniques, the relative lack of skills and capabilities within the organization may slow down or prevent such adoption; and

- *problems convincing management*: fast-moving developments in digital marketing mean that, while there may be relatively well-informed individuals aware of such techniques within marketing departments, they have difficulty convincing less aware and more risk averse senior managers of the appropriateness of such techniques for particular firms.

A final, significant, barrier to adoption is the difficulties that organizations have in integrating conventional and digital marketing activities. Business-to-business (B2B) marketers particularly struggle to integrate online and traditional marketing tactics, partly because even conventional marketing activities are often not as well embedded in firms that rely upon their sales forces and key account management to build brand awareness and generate leads.

"The data flows are very complex and marketers are struggling to figure out how to manage them. Multiple streams of data, from advertising servers, search engines, websites, and offline activity, rarely measured in the same way, are bombarding marketing organizations.' *Edelman, 2007*

The kind of digital marketing tools we describe in this chapter, it is worth repeating, are not necessarily substitutes for more conventional forms of marketing activity. In many cases, the tools provide additional choices for marketers in determining how they may work with consumers or customers. But as a result they provide technical and organizational challenges to firms in trying to achieve fully integrated marketing strategies and plans.

## Customer retention and e-CRM

Having targeted and communicated with customers to acquire them, marketers need to invest in the creation and maintenance of a relationship with those customers if the effort and cost incurred in acquisition is not to be wasted. Customer relationship management is conventionally defined as:

> 'Using the appropriate mix of marketing tools to create and manage relationships with customers' *Chartered Institute of Marketing, 2001.*

But according to the Chartered Institute of Marketing, e-CRM (CRM using electronic channels) makes all kinds of interactions between all the parties involved possible, not just between firms and customers, but also with intermediaries and other business partners. It does this because it is:

- more consistent;
- more trackable and measurable;
- faster;
- cheaper; and
- more customer-controlled.

Think about the ways in which, as a consumer, you receive emails or SMS messages from commercial firms after you have made an initial purchase. For B2B firms, too, e-CRM plays an important role. Sales force automation is a critical part of achieving consistency and efficiency in communications with existing clients. The firm's intention is to keep in touch with you—even if you do not plan an immediate repurchase from that organization—to keep you aware of new products and services and to have you keep the brand in mind. At the same time, the firm can at least in principle track the proportion of people who open the email and who act upon its contents by clicking on a link. It is the 'E' in e-CRM that provides the technology to allow these relationships to be real-time and personalized, as a means to an end. Two consequences arise from this: that it is the customer who decides on the nature and depth of the relationship that they require; and that as a result customer expectations may well run ahead of the ability of the firm to deliver in practice.

How effective is e-CRM for organizations? One piece of research tracked 650 million visitors to eight different kinds of website, and found a strong association between measures taken to increase customer retention and loyalty, and profitability (Agrawal et al., 2001). The best-performing sites achieved a customer conversion rate of 12 per cent (against an average of 2.5 per cent) and a repeat-purchase rate of 60 per cent (against an average of 18 per cent)—far better than poorer performers. The researchers explained this superior performance as a direct consequence of superior underlying operational skills in acquiring, converting, and retaining customers. Long case 7.1 provides a working example of e-CRM in practice and chapter 9 will talk in more detail about some of the business processes that organizations can put into place to support customer service.

## Measuring the extent of digital marketing activity

So firms say that digital marketing is increasingly important to their markets, but at the same time highlight a number of difficulties in adopting digital marketing techniques. How much digital marketing activity is actually underway in aggregate and how fast is it growing by comparison with more conventional marketing mechanisms? There are no fully internationally comparable data available, although individual markets reports their own estimates and there are also estimates for some of the component elements of marketing expenditure. For example, Figure 7.4 shows the extent to which Internet *advertising* featured in the total per capita *advertising spend* of seven OECD economies in 2006 (the latest date for which comparative figures are available). The absolute figures, however, disguise substantial variations in expenditure by market and do not reflect other online-related marketing spend. In proportional terms, the figures vary between 2 per cent for Italy to over 15 per cent for the UK.

This picture can change quickly, however, and it is important to be aware of the very rapid growth of new media promotional channels. Figure 7.5 demonstrates the transformational change to have affected advertising revenues in the UK over a longer-term period particularly clear, and provides an estimated 2008 figure for Internet advertising revenues which now matches that of TV advertising—nearly half of which comes from one firm: Google (*Guardian*, 2008). Worldwide, the Internet is forecast to double its share of global advertising spend between 2007 and 2011, increasing to 13.6 per cent of total spend, or $106bn, 45 per cent of which will be in the US (IDC, 2008).

What of other expenditures? The UK's Institute of Practitioners in Advertising (IPA) publishes a more broadly based Bellwether Report into marketing expenditure every quarter, which is based on a survey of 250 companies representative of the economy as a whole. By the end of 2007, this source reported that the web now accounted for over 6 per cent of all marketing spend. Over 40 per cent of companies were allocating at least 5 per cent of their total marketing spend to the Internet, with an average of 8.7 per cent across the sample, equivalent to some £2.5bn of marketing spend per annum in 2007. There also appears willingness to sustain growth in digital marketing spend within an otherwise difficult economic period, especially that on Internet search, whilst cutting back on other more traditional or 'below-the-line' marketing expenditures, such as TV and press spending, as well as market research and public relations.

But there are several other ways of understanding the scale and measuring the extent of potential interest in digital marketing activity. We can use the Internet itself to measure a variety of surrogates. The Google Trends service allows the tracking and analysis of search strings and website access which gives us a sense of brand awareness

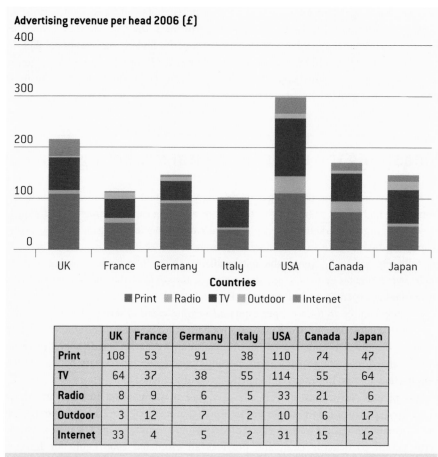

**Advertising revenue per head 2006 (£)**

|          | UK  | France | Germany | Italy | USA | Canada | Japan |
|----------|-----|--------|---------|-------|-----|--------|-------|
| **Print**   | 108 | 53     | 91      | 38    | 110 | 74     | 47    |
| **TV**      | 64  | 37     | 38      | 55    | 114 | 55     | 64    |
| **Radio**   | 8   | 9      | 6       | 5     | 33  | 21     | 6     |
| **Outdoor** | 3   | 12     | 7       | 2     | 10  | 6      | 17    |
| **Internet**| 33  | 4      | 5       | 2     | 31  | 15     | 12    |

**Figure 7.4** Advertising revenue per head, selected OECD countries, 2006

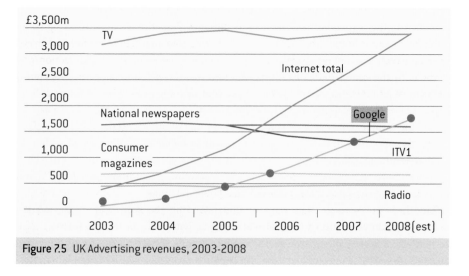

**Figure 7.5** UK Advertising revenues, 2003-2008

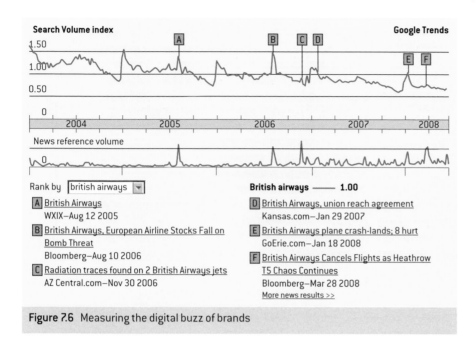

**Figure 7.6** Measuring the digital buzz of brands

(http://www.google.com/trends). Figure 7.6 shows shifting levels of interest by users in the airline BA's website over a five-year period, with accompanying news stories. The 'buzz' around BA is based not just on those news stories, but also exhibits a degree of seasonality linked to holiday planning in the UK.

---

### Activity box 7.3

**Digital buzz**

Identify a distinctive brand of your choice which has its own website. Use Google Trends to examine the 'buzz' associated with both the brand and its website. What might account for differences between the search term results, the news reference volume, and website hit results? How might the brand's marketers make use of these insights?

---

Finally, we can examine the likely impact of digital marketing techniques by considering how effective marketers themselves think they may be individually and how they think this will change by 2010. Figure 7.7 ranks marketing techniques in terms of their perceived effectiveness in a recent survey of US marketers. There is a clear divide between those techniques that are considered to be becoming less effective, and those more so. Perceived casualties include newspapers, telemarketing and Yellow

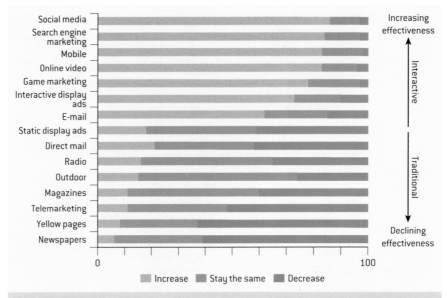

**Figure 7.7** Perceived effectiveness of marketing communications channels, US

Note: Base 235 interactive marketers, interviewed in 2007. Question: "In the next three years, do you think marketing's effectiveness will increase, stay the same or decrease in each of the following media?"

Pages companies; indeed, all those tools thought to be static or in decline are classed as 'traditional' marketing techniques, with the exception of static online display advertising. By contrast, two-thirds or more of all respondents back more 'interactive' marketing tools to increase in effectiveness. It is these attitudes that are likely to dictate future expenditures.

## Market analysis

Before firms can properly consider the adoption of digital marketing tools, they need to better understand consumer attitudes to them. In chapter 4, we showed a number of examples of how we might categorize the consumer or customer in order to better identify those more or less positively disposed towards e-business technology in general. In thinking about market analysis, however, some consumer-facing firms have begun purposefully to segment digital audiences using more explicit behavioural segmentation—in ways which can help them identify early adopters and influencers who may be more susceptible to innovative marketing techniques. Short case 7.1 describes one example.

## Short case 7.1

### The 'virtual hide'

The UK trends research firm the Future Laboratory established a 'virtual hide' on the social networking site http://www.myspace.com in 2007. Project: Creative Lab was a ten week search in 2007 'to define who will be the next generation of MySpace stars for 2008'. The organization also used the exercise to observe and segment the MySpace audience and to identify opinion leaders and influencers, interviewing over 1,000 MySpace users who explained how they defined themselves. The types of individual the project identified included:

- *netrepreneurs* (4 per cent): people who used social networking sites for making money and for little else.
- *scene breakers* (5 per cent): individuals who kept up with new talent on the social networks—bands, writers, actors, models—and shared it with others in their circle.
- *collaborators* (5 per cent): these people would be known as event planners in the work world.
- *connectors* (10 per cent): viral agents that passed on interesting links and information to their contacts.
- *transumers* (TRANSient consUMERS) (28 per cent): 'followers' who joined groups that other people started and which connected with their hobbies and interests; and
- *essentialists* (38 per cent): individuals who tended to use the network as a basic communication utility, or for staying in touch with friends or family.

The project's researchers also identified ten individuals for more detailed case study work. They were asked to answer a series of questions via email and take part in a short telephone interview with a project researcher. In return for submitting examples of their photography, music, or video files, case study candidates received £200.

MySpace itself continues to evolve, with a re-launch in 2008 which sought to ensure that it is 'more organized around people, content and culture', according to Sales and Marketing President, Jeff Berman. But this has involved more interventionist digital marketing activity, including so-called 'brand takeovers', when major consumer brands such as Taco Bell and Nestea bid to occupy the MySpace home splash page for a period.

*Question*

How ethical was Future Lab's presence on YouTube? How useful will their findings be over the longer term?

---

The kind of segmentation which digital marketing techniques make possible is potentially more intrusive than conventional mechanisms. Chapter 5 has already established the extent of concern over the privacy issues attached to the transmission of consumer data to Internet companies and chapter 3 has explored some of the technical processes that make this possible. From the point of view of the digital marketer, however,

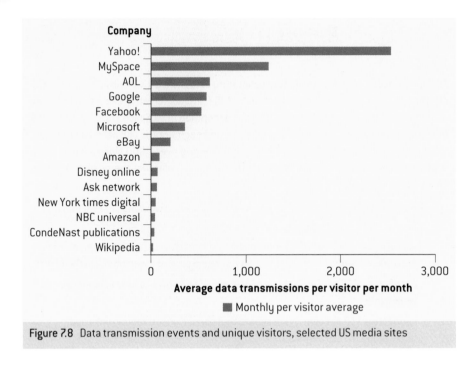

**Figure 7.8** Data transmission events and unique visitors, selected US media sites

capturing customer information is a critical part of the digital marketing process. Their argument is that there are policies in place to protect consumers' names and personal information, and that polling such data is extremely helpful in ensuring the right consumers are targeted with the right kinds of marketing communication. Such polling is already very extensive. Research commissioned by the *New York Times* in 2007 provides one estimate of its extent. Figure 7.8 shows the potential that the top fifteen major media companies had to collect online data in December 2007: so-called 'data transmission events'. The top five firms alone recorded over 336bn transmission events during the reporting period. These might not be just the number and type of searches conducted, but display ads, videos, and page views which might have occurred on their sites.

# First-generation marketing tools

## Email marketing

One of the earliest marketing applications of e-business technologies has been through growth in the use of email. As chapter 4 established, reading or sending email is still the most popular use of the Internet. The chapter described the characteristics of email usage from a social perspective, for both consumers and employees. Here, we are interested in the ways in which marketers can make use of the estimated 1.6bn email inboxes worldwide, of which approximately 500m are corporate inboxes.[2] These inboxes receive some 183bn emails each day worldwide. Some 70 per cent of these messages are thought to be unsolicited commercial ones.

There are five main advantages to email marketing for organizations:

- *Email campaigns can be conducted at a lower cost*: compared to other direct marketing channels, email marketing is considerably less expensive. Most costs are incurred up front and there are then very low incremental costs in emailing target lists once established.

- *Email entails faster delivery and response*: emails arrive in a few seconds; responses can be equally quick. The success, or otherwise, of a campaign can be demonstrated much faster than is the case through conventional media.

- *Email is a 'push' rather than 'pull' promotional tool*: it lets the advertiser push the message to its audience, as opposed to a website that waits passively for customers to arrive.

- *Email is more appropriate for niche markets*: for small audiences, traditional channels can be prohibitively expensive.

- *The performance and contribution of email campaigns can be more easily tracked*: an exact return on investment can be calculated and detailed insights can be gained into the proportion of prospects who take specific actions from opening the email through to responding or unsubscribing.

B2B organizations place particular reliance upon email amongst other digital marketing mechanisms available. Analysis by Forrester Research suggests that 85 per cent of US B2B companies employed email as a lead generation tool in 2008 (Ramos, 2008). However, this often appears to be a one-way process. The same analysis suggests that fewer than 30 per cent of the same companies found these tactics effective since, as we shall see, cultivation of new business may require much greater interactivity.

You may recall that we reviewed the growth of unsolicited emails (spam) and the counter-productive nature of such marketing activity in chapter 5. Spam also has consequential effects on the impact of legitimate commercial email. However, recall that defining what users consider spam and what legitimate commercial email is essentially subjective and therefore virtually impossible—almost like defining a weed (just a plant in the wrong place). Nevertheless, the growth of spam has served to erode some of the early advantages of email as a marketing medium and converted them into distinct disadvantages. These include:

- *Information overload*: the sheer number of emails now in circulation makes it increasingly difficult for a legitimate marketing message to stand out.

- *Deliverability*: email is increasingly filtered by recipients and intermediaries. Seventy-one per cent of US Internet users employed spam filters in 2007. Business users reported a decline in their receipt of unsolicited messages in 2007 thanks to more effective corporate filters as well as greater sensitivity amongst Internet service providers to customer complaints. a consequence of this is the incidence of so-called 'false positives'—emails mistakenly classified as spam by filters—where ISPs err on the side of caution.

---

2  http://www.radicati.com/news/market_stats/vol_5-1.asp.

- *Impact on brand reputation*: the implications of potentially unwelcome, irrelevant, or unsolicited email on consumer attitudes towards an organization. According to the Pew Internet & the American Life project, 55 per cent of US Internet users said that spam email had made them less trusting of email in general, and only 4 per cent claimed to have ordered a product or service that was offered in an unsolicited email, although nearly a quarter had clicked on a link.

- *Legal considerations*: many jurisdictions have introduced legislation regulating unsolicited email, such as the CAN-spam Act of 2003 in the US, and national marketing associations frequently issue guidelines on appropriate email use by firms.

The combination of these factors means that the effectiveness of email marketing may have been eroded in recent years. The need to increase consumers' trust in email marketing and their receptiveness to email marketing messages has led to a growth in the popularity of so-called *opt-in*, or *permission-based* email marketing. As the name suggests, opt-in email marketing requires the end user's agreement to be included in a marketing campaign. The assumption is that such recipients will be more likely to open, take notice of, and potentially act upon the contents of an opt-in email since it is more likely, other things being equal, to be aligned to their needs.

How is the effectiveness of email marketing measured? In addition to tracking when emails are most likely to be opened, the most commonly used metrics for measuring the effectiveness of email marketing are the *open rate* and the *click-through* rate. Sometimes these can be combined as a *click-to-open* rate. Table 7.3 shows an example of rates of opening and click-through for a variety of Internet service providers.

**Open Rate** The proportion of emails opened at a particular time.

**Click-through rate** The proportion of emails where an embedded web link is clicked by a recipient.

**Click-to-open rate** The ratio of unique clicks as a percentage of unique opens.

**Table 7.3  Indicative statistics for comparative email marketing campaigns**

| Email Sample | B2B Newsletter | | | Ecommerce Email | | |
|---|---|---|---|---|---|---|
| ISP/Domain | Open | CTR | CTOR | Open | CTR | CTOR |
| AOL | 12.0% | 3.2% | 26.7% | 14.4% | 8.2% | 56.9% |
| Earthlink | 42.1% | 2.6% | 6.2% | 47.4% | 14.6% | 30.8% |
| Hotmail | 30.0% | 7.5% | 25.0% | 24.8% | 8.9% | 35.9% |
| Yahoo! | 21.2% | 5.8% | 27.4% | 23.5% | 9.2% | 39.1% |
| All Other Domains | 42.5% | 10.6% | 24.9% | 40.9% | 11.2% | 27.4% |
| Total | 39.6% | 9.9% | 25.0% | 33.6% | 10.9% | 32.4% |
| Variance: Low-High | 30.5% | 8.0% | 21.2% | 33.0% | 6.4% | 29.5% |

In isolation, these figures look relatively unimpressive—especially the click-through rates. But it is important to see them in comparison with paper-based methods. The US Direct Marketing Association's most recent surveys suggest that electronic marketing mechanisms are consistently more successful and less costly than paper-based ones, although rates will vary by sector and objective (Direct Marketing Association, 2009). For example:

- *direct order and fundraising*: direct marketers with the main objective of attracting direct-order sales or motivating customers to make a contribution achieved the highest response rates: catalogue (2.24 per cent) and direct mail (2.15 per cent).
- *lead generation*: email (4.09 per cent) produced the highest absolute response rates for those whose main objective was to generate sales leads.

The growing sophistication of email marketing has led to a proliferation of bulk mailing and response analysis software as well as to the development of third-party email service provider firms (ESPs). The benefits of outsourcing in this way are that the sender can create and transmit a more professional message to a more segmented target audience, and can receive tracking reports on bounce rates, the number of un-subscribers, and opening and click-through rates as a result of any particular campaign (see Short case 7.2).

## Short case 7.2

### e-Dialog, the innovative ESP

Based in Lexington, Massachusetts since its establishment in 1997, e-Dialog provides email marketing services and solutions and is a leading (but by no means the largest) email service provider (http://www.e-dialog.com). Now owned by GSI Commerce, a US firm offering transactional e-commerce services, e-Dialog has offices in London as well as Boston, Seattle, and New York. In its final year of independent operation, e-Dialog recorded net revenues of $33.9m (+59 per cent) and income from operations of $5.2mn (+151 per cent). The company is distinguished by its entrepreneurial outlook, its product innovation and customer service as well as its increasingly international reach.

»

What does e-Dialog do? The company provides web-based software that helps clients implement and manage email marketing campaign functions such as reporting, message deployment, segmentation, and analysis. The company's service offerings include dynamically printed direct mail, RSS, and mobile messaging. e-Dialog offers campaign management services for clients needing a 'full-service' option. Typical of this approach is the partnership with BA, for whom the firm provides advice, service, and support for the airline's communications with Executive Club members and registered users of its website, http://www.ba.com.

> 'Email is becoming our principal customer communications channel and e-Dialog brings strategic and technological expertise that will allow us to make our communications more effective and talk to our customers on an individual basis.' *Jayne O'Brien, BA, quoted in e-dialog, 2006*

Precision Central is the name of e-Dialog's 'self-service' platform, which allows clients to build and measure the return on investiment (ROI) of their own email campaigns. Analysts Jupiter Research named e-Dialog the top performing email marketing service provider among service-oriented ESPs for the third year in a row in 2008, and Forrester Research also rates the business as one of its 'leading' ESPs:

> 'Functionally, this vendor has one of the best platforms in the market because it takes into account how users interact with the tool and focuses on message relevance.' *Forrester Research, 2007*

An important aspect of the self-service operation is quality control. For example, automated tests ensure that any outgoing emails are checked to ensure that they have an 'unsubscribe' link and comply with local legislation. Tests also check that users have not omitted obvious fields, such as a subject line. Predefined templates, which can be locked down by senior management, provide for a high degree of consistency and security in mailing.

e-Dialog's global client portfolio currently supports email campaigns that are sent in twenty-two languages to nineteen countries and delivered to more than 500 global Internet Service Providers. Clients appear enthusiastic about e-Dialog's levels of customer service and its ability to provide relevant innovation. The small size of the firm and its intensive customer focus appears important in facilitating a close working relationship between itself and clients. The firm has also developed an innovative and well-received process for improving the relevance of email communications, which it calls its 'Relevance Trajectory'. A relevant email communication, suggests the firm, is:

- customized through content-driven audience segmentation to individual customer attributes and behaviour;
- timed using triggered messaging to coincide with certain customer behaviours or milestones; and
- used to encourage customer interactivity and flexible enough to recognize and adjust to measured customer interest and response.

## Question
What are the contemporary challenges facing firms like e-Dialog?

# Online advertising

'It seems as though we are at the point where online advertising is an obsolete term. The best marketing initiatives are rarely limited to online channels, and the best ideas marketers are exploring are really not advertising at all.' *Edelman, 2007*

One of the biggest transformations in marketing expenditure in economies in which e-business is playing a leading part has been in the area of online advertising. Online advertising has been defined as:

'commercial messages placed on third party web sites, including search engines and directories available through Internet access.' *Ha, 2008*

How can we classify online advertising? Although the genre is in constant evolution, we can identify five broad types of online advertising, classified in terms of the how they appear on websites:

- *Standard image/text link*: Advertisements that are comprised of many components, typically both image and text beneath the images, all of which link to the same destination URL.

- *Standard image*: Animated or static image ads; GIF or JPEG file format-based ads. HTML ads are also classified under this category.

- *Flash (generic)*: Macromedia's vector-based authoring tool that outputs file formats used to display interactive elements. To see these, the end user requires a plug-in (Flash Player).

- *Rich media*: a method of communication that incorporates animation, sound, video, and/or interactivity via a proprietary ad platform. Specialist vendors include Bluestreak, Eyeblaster, Klipmart, PointRoll, and Viewpoint Unicast.

- *Sponsored links*: text-based ads that often appear as a result of a keyword search either on a search engine or associated site. These ads are often displayed alongside natural search results but identified under specified headers (e.g., 'Paid Sponsor', 'Sponsored Link', 'Sponsored Sites' or 'Sponsored Results').

Does the form of online advertisement matter? How do users relate to advertising online and how can organizations measure the effectiveness of their campaigns? Web design guru Jakob Nielsen pinned his colours to the mast very early on in this process by observing as early as 1997 that 'web ads don't work' (Nielsen, 1997). More recently, he coined the term 'banner blindness' in confirming that users 'almost never look at anything that looks like an advertisement' (Nielsen, 2007). Heat maps from eye-tracking studies seem to confirm that users actively avoid advertising banners—and even areas which appear to be advertising banners. Figure 7.9 shows an example of such a study. In the figure, green boxes (drawn after the study) show the location of advertising images, whilst the coloured areas show where users focused more of their attention. However, academic research published from a laboratory study also in 2007 suggests that just incidental exposure to banner advertising may actually have a positive effect on consumer attitudes, even if people could not recall the content of the ad, as a result of what is called the 'mere exposure effect' (Fang et al., 2007).

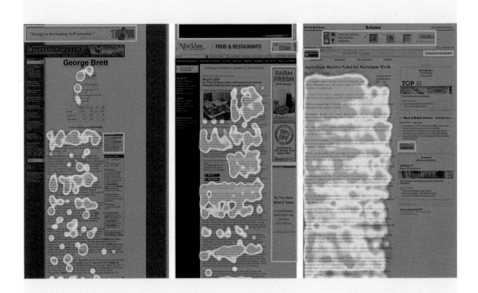

**Figure 7.9** Heatmaps from eye-tracking studies of web page usage.

Jupiter Media Metrix has estimated that an average US Internet user was exposed to around 950 banner ads in 2005. This compares relatively favourably in the context of conventional promotions where, for example, the average American child is exposed to some 40,000 television commercials every year (Strasburger, 2001). Clearly, there is also considerably more experience amongst advertisers in placing conventional campaigns than is making use of existing media. For example, it has been suggested that engaging in more sophisticated placement strategies and increasing repetition rates targeting more content-relevant websites can improve click-through rates (Yaveroglu and Donthu, 2008).

What evidence is beginning to emerge in relation to consumer attitudes to more intrusive advertising is that it can be actively resisted by users. In a recent survey of US Internet users, more than 50 per cent reported that a pop-up ad affected their opinion of the advertiser very negatively and nearly 40 per cent reported that it affected their opinion of the website very negatively. Research by Jakob Nielsen again suggests that users have started to defend themselves against pop-ups. One of the leading ad-blocking software companies, Adblock Plus, estimated that there were 2.5m users of its product worldwide in 2007, with new users being accepted at a rate of between 300,000–400,000 per month.[3]

So what is the good practice that online advertisers should adopt when seeking to gain end users' interest and trust? We can identify four main considerations:

- *clarity*: the advert should clearly identify itself as such;
- *relevance*: online advertising should relate to the user's reason for being on a particular site;

---

3  http://www.nytimes.com/2007/09/03/technology/03link.html.

- *content* : the advert should contain sufficient information for the reader on which to base a judgement without having to leave the page;

- *intention*: the advert should indicate what will happen if clicked on.

But if 'banner blindness' does exist, it appears not to extend to search engine results pages (SERPs): text and classified adverts do appear to get viewed, and it is to this form of interactive marketing that we now turn.

## Search marketing

Targeting online advertising more effectively is one of the 'holy grails' of digital marketing. This is a separate challenge from developing appropriate and effective vehicles and content for such advertising. Advertisers employing traditional channels, such as TV, consumer magazines, or cinema have had the benefit of decades of experience in being able to better target communications to the right audience, but still have to rely upon approximate demographics or other segmentation information derived from sample populations of prospective users. In the case of online advertising, mechanisms are rapidly evolving in their incidence and sophistication. Search marketing provides the biggest opportunity in this field at present. Forrester Research expects corporate investment in search marketing within the US to increase from $8bn in 2007 to $25bn in 2012, and in Europe to double from its level in 2007 to Euro8.1bn by 2012 (Kemp, 2007). Google dominates this market, as you can see shown in Figure 7.10.

The pioneer of paid search is Google, which introduced its keyword-targeted advertising AdWords system in 2000 to provide a mechanism for monetizing advert placement on

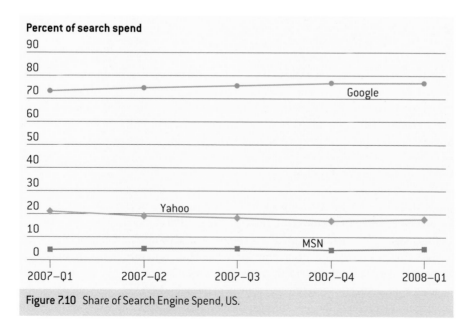

**Figure 7.10** Share of Search Engine Spend, US.

| Advertiser | CPC bid | Quality score | Rank # | Position | CPC |
|:---:|:---:|:---:|:---:|:---:|:---:|
| A | $0.40 | 1.8 | $0.40 x 1.8 = .72 | 1 | $0.37 |
| B | $0.65 | 1 | $0.65 x 1 = .65 | 2 | $0.39 |
| C | $0.25 | 1.5 | $0.25 x 1.5 = .38 | 3 | $0.01 |

**Figure 7.11** How Google Calculates a Rank Position for Advertisers

its search results pages and on the pages of partner sites. Google's system accommodates keyword targeting and placement-targeting approaches.

In keyword targeting, the aim for the advertiser is to achieve a high ranking for its advert by entering an appropriate bid for the keyword. Figure 7.11 shows the case of three advertisers using the same keyword. What determines the order in which companies bidding for the same keyword are ranked? In effect, Google auctions the position on the page. In the example, each advertiser has made a different bid for the use of a chosen keyword, and each has been given a different quality score by Google, based on the keyword's click-through rate (CTR) on the site, the relevance of the advert text and the quality of the click-through site (for which advertisers are, in effect, rewarded). Quality scores are not visible to the user, however. Google then calculates a rank number by multiplying the cost-per-click (CPC) bid by the quality score. But how much should each advertiser be charged for each click? The eventual cost per click is the minimum amount needed to maintain a rank number higher than the next lower advert: one cent more than the amount that would result in a rank number that would cause the ad to appear in the next lower position. So for advertiser A, Google divides advertiser B's rank number of 0.65 by advertiser A's quality score, giving 36¢, to which it adds 1¢. The process continues for advertiser B. Interestingly, advertiser A ends up paying less per click than advertiser B, because of its higher quality score.

An alternative approach is for the advertiser to adopt a placement-targeted strategy, in which a bid is made for the cost of the advert appearing in a search result 1,000 times (without the user necessarily clicking through). This is known as CPM or cost per 1000 impressions.

The Google search network system was complemented by the development of AdSense in 2002. AdSense provides a mechanism for web publishers to earn money from Google by hosting AdWords adverts on their own websites. Google ads can be contextually targeted by analysing the structure and content of the publisher's web pages, alongside the geographical location of the user through their IP address. Alternatively, advertisers can themselves choose specific web placements.

**Publishers** Independent parties that promote the products or services of an advertiser on their website by means of links or other mechanisms.

Activity box 7.4

## Googlewhacking

Can you Googlewhack? Googlewhacking (http://www.googlewhacking.com) refers to the challenge of securing a single search result from entering two words, without quotation marks, into the Google search box. This is more difficult than it sounds! What does this tell you about digital marketing?

This makes it sound very simple. However, Figure 7.12 provides an approximate schematic of the AdWords and related AdSense systems which demonstrates both their complexity, but also the extent to which there are relative unknowns in the way both systems function. The boxes marked 'algo' refer to proprietary algorithms created, maintained, and consistently retuned by Google to optimize returns and reflect changes in the bidding environment.

The benefits of Google's AdWords system are claimed to be fourfold:

- *Reach*: over 80 per cent of US Internet users are reached by the Google Network.

- *Cost*: there is no minimum spend. A user can set a maximum spend or budget, or pay only for impressions or click-throughs.

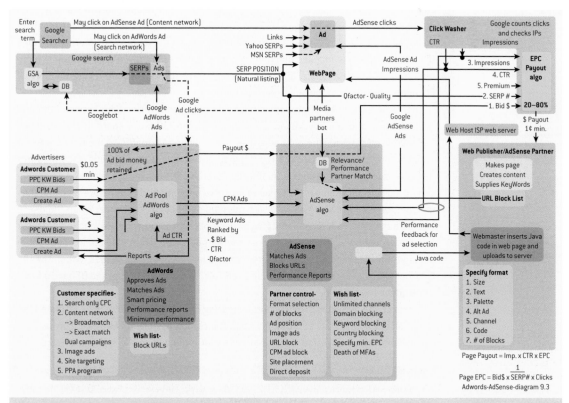

**Figure 7.12**  How the Google AdWords/AdSense programmes work

- *Timing*: AdWords continuously matches and targets advertisements with users, meaning that advertisements are served at the same time as buying decisions are made.

- *Flexibility*: The advertisement is available to see within 15 minutes of its creation and can be changed whenever required. It can be targeted at multiple locations and in multiple languages.

A number of other such analysis and targeting systems are now commercially available, but are not without their critics. Short case 7.3 discusses the example of Phorm.

## Short case 7.3

### Phorm

'Behavioural targeting-firms are doing the rounds in Europe and America offering the prospect of working out what web surfers are thinking, perhaps even before they know it themselves.' *The Economist, 7 June 2008*

A need for better behavioural targeting of marketing communications led to the growth of business service companies such as NebuAd (http://www.nebuad.com), FrontPorch (http://www.frontporch.com), and Phorm (http://www.phorm.com), which all claim to help companies deliver more relevant advertising to end users. Founded as 121media. com in 2002 (it was renamed Phorm in 2007), Phorm has developed software as part of its open internet exchange platform (OIX) to intercept and analyse users' web page requests on behalf of ISPs and advertisers whilst maintaining users' data privacy. Phorm maintains that 'our company is focused on creating a new "gold standard" for user privacy, a more relevant Internet experience, and more value for advertisers, publishers, Internet Service Providers and others in the online ecosystem'.

The company's business model is based on being an intermediary between the end user, the ISP, and the advertiser. The benefits to the ISP are a share in the revenues and increased attractiveness to advertisers. The claimed benefits to the user are fewer irrelevant adverts, alongside the red-flagging of fraudulent or malicious sites. Phorm's *Webwise* service sets a cookie in the user's browser, assigning a unique, randomly-generated number to a user's browser to preserve anonymity. The software then matches the categories of browsing activity with advertising-relevant keywords. When the user's interests match an advertiser category and a threshold of keywords is reached, the user can see a relevant ad in place of a generic, untargeted ad.[4] Users may opt in or opt out of the system—depending on ISP preferences and local regulatory regimes. Within the UK, ISPs including the Carphone Warehouse's TalkTalk, Virgin Media Group, and BT have sought to introduce the system.

However, the activities of behavioural targeting firms such as Phorm have attracted the attention of privacy activists, who question the company's claims to privacy protection, despite their technical efforts. Phorm argues that it has set a new, higher standard    »

**Behavioural Targeting** Customer targeting employing software which intercepts and analyses web page requests, which generate profiles against which advertising can be more accurately delivered.

---

4  An independent technical assessment of Phorm's Webwise service can be seen at Clayton, R., (2008), The Phorm 'Webwise' system, http://www.cl.cam.ac.uk/~rnc1/080518-phorm.pdf.

for privacy and anonymity. For example, behaviours contributing to a customer profile are deleted once a match has been made and no IP address, name, email, or digits longer than three characters are intercepted by the software. The company's share price suffered significantly from adverse news stories during 2008.

*Question*
How far is it ethical for firms to go in developing behavioural targeting mechanisms?

## Affiliate marketing

Affiliate marketing is a form of online promotion similar to a conventional 'finder's fee' model, where individuals who introduce new clients to a business are compensated for their efforts. In a digital marketing application, online merchants or advertisers that sell products or services pay publishers only for results, such as a visitor making a purchase or filling out a form, rather than paying simply to reach a particular audience. This is often described as a 'pay-for-performance' model, rather than the alternative of simply paying in the expectation of reaching a particular audience. When an end user clicks on a merchant's link provided by an affiliated publisher, a cookie is set that identifies the merchant, the publisher, and the specific link and commission rates. When the visitor makes an actual purchase online or fills out a form, that transaction is tracked and recorded and the publisher rewarded according to a pre-planned commission structure including, for example, the number of days in the cookie period. Affiliate marketing has several advantages to the parties concerned:

- *Improved brand awareness*: affiliates increase exposure to the merchant's brand as well as providing market insight.
- *Improved conversion*: affiliates provide an efficient way of generating sales or leads, and reduce some of the costs and risks associated with sales.
- *Improved metrics*: affiliation marketing provides a better structure for accounting for referred sales.
- *Improved cost base*: affiliation reduces any duplication of commission payments that might arise from more conventional business referral.

However, affiliate marketing can also carry with it a number of significant risks:

- *Earnings risk*: firms can end up paying commission on sales that they would be perfectly able to generate themselves, leading to lower margins on those sales, or paying commission on sales which lead to fraudulent returns.
- *Cost risk*: search costs can be driven up if not controlled properly.
- *Reputational risk*: the brand can potentially be misrepresented on the affiliate's website. The incidence of so-called 'thin' affiliates (websites made up entirely of affiliate links) is also increasing, which might again damage the affiliated brand.

Some firms have abandoned affiliate marketing because of the cost and effort required to police affiliates to mitigate unethical practices, ensure appropriate representation and amongst concerns that affiliates simply cannibalize direct sales.

Nevertheless, so-called next-generation affiliate marketing is providing new promotional mechanisms for firms. Over and above simple links, merchants can provide video and audio podcasts and RSS to affiliates, or new technology like web services and click-to-call.[5] Increasingly, affiliate programmes are outsourced to specialist business service firms, such as Commission Junction (http://www.cj.com) or DoubleClick Performics (now owned by Google).

**Click-to-call** A service which lets users click a button on a website in order to speak to a service representative of the company.

---

### Short case 7.4

#### Hotel Chocolat

*'Your site visitors will discover our exclusive brand of chocolate, and experience the excitement and mystique that only chocolate made with premium ingredients, passion and flair can provide.'* Hotel Chocolat website

A particularly tasty example of an effective affiliate programme is to be found in the multi-channel Hotel Chocolat business (http://www.hotelchocolat.co.uk). Founded in the UK as a catalogue operation in 1993, the business now generates £39m in sales from twenty-two outlets, a tasting club with 100,000 members and a website. In 2007, sales in Hotel Chocolat's Internet business grew by 30 per cent over the previous year and the firm has attributed much of this sales growth to a successful affiliates programme, with over 25 per cent of direct sales now being generated by affiliate marketing.

Affiliate Chocolate Easter egg Give-away 2008

»

---

5   Chris Bishop's blog on affiliate marketing: http://chris-bishop.blogspot.com/.

The programme allows affiliates to earn unlimited commission. When a visitor is referred to Hotel Chocolat from an affiliate link, and that visitor places an order, the affiliate earns a standard 7 per cent commission. Even if visitors don't make a purchase on the first visit, any made within 45 days will earn commission, courtesy of a cookie. Affiliates can access online sales reports and understand and optimize how specific links are working thanks to a toolkit provided by the firm. Supportive copy and bespoke banners are also provided and product training, instore activities, and other social events are made available.

Publishers are encouraged to 'deeplink' into over 200 specific pages on the Hotel Chocolat website, promoting individual products such as Kir Royale Truffles and Macadamia Turtles, seasonal products such as Easter Eggs or Christmas chocolate products, or Tasting Club gift membership and Club vouchers. The Hotel Chocolat affiliates team are also adept at offering incentives at peak seasonal sales periods, increasing commission up to 10–12 per cent and adding a bonus element linked to specific sales targets. The extension of Hotel Chocolat's activities to the US has also allowed them to offer a US affiliates programme, which can be cross-linked to the UK service.

Whilst Hotel Chocolat has encountered a number of the risks associated with affiliate marketing, (for example, it has had to deal with affiliates who abuse the rules in relation to paid search promotion by using trademarked keywords), the company's enthusiasm for this online promotional channel remains undiminished.

*Question*
What are the pros and cons of affiliate marketing?

## Second-generation digital marketing tools

We have already suggested that marketers may not be wholly in control of communications with customers over products and services within a digital marketing environment. There are often informal interactions between marketers, third parties and customers, and between customers themselves. Commercial blog publishing networks such as Gawker are one way in which marketers can seek more formally to build new product awareness. Short case 7.5 examines one such network. But these interactions are particularly characteristic of what we may call second-generation digital marketing tools and occur on blogs and other social media, as well as in virtual worlds. This is another area where the terminology of e-business is less than helpful to firms. The marketing-inspired activities which take place through the variety of second-generation tools described in Table 7.2 are interchangeably referred to as consumer-generated media (CGM), viral marketing, electronic word-of-mouth (eWOM), or buzz marketing. We should recognize that three of the four terms pre-date digital marketing, but have been re-introduced in electronic guise. Chapter 4 has already provided an introduction to eWOM. We consider some of the marketing implications of eWOM below, alongside a discussion of viral marketing.

One problem which the growth in eWOM that we identified in chapter 4 can create is the potential need for marketers to correct misperceptions generated by third parties: perhaps innocently, or potentially deliberately by malicious commentators. This is particularly the case with blogs and discussion forums. For example, the period prior to the launch of the Apple iPhone in 2007 was characterized by much heavily negative publicity in blogs. One, entitled, 'We Predict the iPhone Will Bomb', suggested: 'when the iPhone comes, Digg will likely be full of horror stories from the poor saps who camped out at their local AT&T store, only to find their purchase was buggier than a camp cabin', before outlining seven distinct sets of problems that it thought would beset the product's launch.[6] Later commentators were critical of these:

> 'Based on nothing but a fertile imagination, [the author] predicts the iPhone's touch-screen might easily crack, that the on-screen keyboard "will be about as useful for tapping out emails and text messages as a rotary phone," and that the battery life will prove dismal.'

A heavy-handed response by an affected firm's lawyers in such circumstances might be counterproductive. Similarly, ignoring the posting may result in readers assuming that there is some truth in the allegation or criticism. But it is logistically challenging for marketing or customer service teams to monitor and respond to all instances of criticism. Computer company Dell (http://www.dell.com) has a highly developed approach to eWOM, and has invested significantly in brand 'self-awareness'. A team of forty-two employees are engaged to work in social media such as Facebook (http://www.facebook.com) and Twitter (http://www.twitter.com), monitoring and seeking to respond in a positive and helpful manner to concerns raised by posters. By setting up its own blogs and discussion boards, the company has also attempted to bring 'in house' criticisms and questions about the brand. Founder Michael Dell suggested:

> 'If we don't do that at Dell.com, it's going to be on CNET or somewhere. I'd rather have that conversation in my living room than in somebody else's.' *Fortt, 2008*

---

### Short case 7.5

#### Shiny Shiny

Shiny Media was founded by three UK journalists—Katie Lee, Ashley Norris, and Chris Price—in 2003. It started life as just one of a growing number of technology information blog with its 'TechDigest' blog, but has since developed into the UK's most innovative commercial blog publishing network, offering forty blogs in five categories (fashion, technology, lifestyle, sport, and gaming), which include two lifestyle blogs launched in the US in 2007, and a YouTube channel (http://www.youtube.com/user/shinymedia). Together the blogs attract over 4m visitors a month. (The leading blogs are shown in Table 7.4.) Commercial blog publishers play a potentially powerful role in creating new product buzz for marketers, but must tread a careful line between blatant product endorsement and spirited independence if they are to retain both the trust of their audience and the support of brand manufacturers in making available new products.

The blogs themselves also attract commercial advertising in addition to featuring new products and services. Brands who have recently advertised on Shiny Media blogs include Marks & Spencer, LG, Nokia, Sony, Philips, Dyson, Gillette, the 3 phone network,  ≫

---

6  http://www.crunchgear.com/2007/06/07/the-futurist-we-predict-the-iphone-will-bomb/.

### Table 7.4  Shiny media: characteristics of selected blogs

| Blog | Positioning | Visitors per month |
|------|-------------|--------------------|
| TechDigest | Europe's leading site for consumer technology, news, view and opinions | 440,000 |
| ShinyShiny | A girl's guide to gadgets | 312,000 |
| Catwalk Queen | Your very own personal stylist | 246,000 |
| Shoewawa | Every girl's favourite obession: shoes | 230,000 |
| The BagLady | Handbag and accessory blog | 165,000 |
| Bridalwave | Frocks, shoes, food and booze - helping you to stay 'I do' | 180,000 |
| CorrieBlog | Blog dedicated to UK TV soap Coronation Street | 102,000 |

Electronic Arts, and Sky Networks. It is suggested that 'potential advertisers are drawn to blog networks because they want to be perceived as hipper and more forward-thinking'.

The Shiny Shiny blog (http://www.shinyshiny.tv) is one of the company's most distinctive and is typical of its approach to creating new product buzz. The site takes a female standpoint on the consumer technology world, with news, reviews, and opinion produced using freelance writers and journalists. But this is a challenging position to adopt in the face of the growing sensitivity of this consumer audience.

> 'When we launched Shiny Shiny about three years ago, we made the masthead pink because manufacturers were starting to launch pink gadgets and we thought it was exciting—finally they were recognising that women wanted to use technology, too. In the past year, it's become a bit naff—it's patronising and lazy. Girls are still being ghettoised, and it's amazing we're not seeing any advance.' *Susi Weaser, Editor, quoted in Llewellyn-Smith, 2007*

*Question*

How can commercial blog publishers make their products stand out, given the size of the blogosphere?

# Viral marketing

Explicit use of electronic word-of-mouth mechanisms by firms (rather than by genuine end users) shades into viral marketing. Viral marketing can be defined as:

*'A mechanism that facilitates and encourages people to pass along a marketing message voluntarily.'*

Efficient viral marketing campaigns seek to identify highly socially networked individuals who are capable and willing to pass a message along. Again, rather like word of mouth, there is nothing new about this process: it takes advantage of a fundamental aspect of human nature. Indeed, the term viral marketing was attributed to Professor Jeffrey Rayport of Harvard Business School as early as 1995.[7] Rayport suggested six rules for effective viral marketing which are still relevant today. We list these below alongside examples of contemporary usage within the Internet environment.

- *Stealth is the essence of market entry*: viral marketing campaigns tend to use less obvious ways of bringing brands to customers' attention, such as unusual product placement or contexts. For example, the US mixer company Blendtec operates a channel on YouTube[8] demonstrating the power of its products to blend unusual items, ranging from a Chuck Norris doll to the Apple iPhone.

- *What's up front is free—payment comes later*: most viral marketing programmes give away products or services to attract attention. For example, free software programs are made available; they perform a limited range of functions which can be upgraded in the 'pro' version.

- *Let the behaviours of the target community carry the message*: this suggests that effective viral campaigns should be designed in ways that maximize their transmissibility. For example, Sporting Clube de Portugal employed a viral feature in a marketing campaign to sell season tickets. A video on the website requested the user's name and phone number. The coach then 'called' the user back to encourage them to buy the season ticket. 200,000 page view phone calls were triggered within 24 hours.

- *Look like a host, not a message*: by becoming part of the everyday experience, viral campaigns can be especially successful. For example, components of some viral marketing have become memes. Memes can take the form of popular catch phrases: such as Nike's 'Just Do It', or Budweiser's 'Whassup?' of the early 1990s.

- *Exploit the strength of weak ties*: the most efficient way of spreading a message is via those individuals with extensive, but perhaps weaker, social connections. Conventional examples of this include the now legendary 'Tupperware parties', where members of a suburban neighbourhood would assemble to buy plastic containers under the auspices of a social gathering. Today, we can see Facebook groups providing a similar opportunity.

- *Invest to reach the tipping point*: finally, Rayport concluded that conventional viral marketing might take a long time to reach a commercial threshold of visibility and

**Meme** A piece of cultural information which is transmitted from the mind to another, self-replicating. See http://www.thedailymeme.com

---

7  http://www.netzkobold.com/uploads/rayport_the_virus_of_marketing.pdf.
8  http://www.youtube.com/user/Blendtec.

scale. He cited the slow initial growth of rolling news broadcaster CNN before it became the channel of choice for politicians and citizens alike. Today, as chapter 2 made clear in its discussion of network effects, e-business technologies allow these to grow much faster and commercial messages to reach an audience of millions in a very short period. Half of the most popular content on YouTube is commercial in nature.[9]

Of particular interest to marketers is the propensity of email readers to forward their messages to others. A study by Chiu et al. in 2007 confirmed that the likelihood of messages being forwarded is a function of the message *source* (family, friends, or someone known to the recipient), its *content* (whether it contains useful or entertaining information), and of the *personality* of the recipient (more emotionally responsive, open and curious individuals will tend to forward messages). Other studies have shown that—89 per cent have no adverse feelings towards brand sponsorship, but a hard core 5 per cent will refuse to share content that contains a clear brand message. Figure 7.13 shows a breakdown of what users say they share (or at least admit to sharing) by type of content.

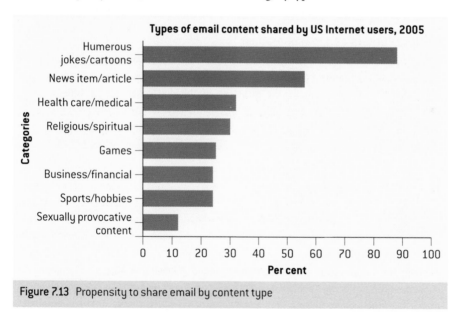

**Figure 7.13** Propensity to share email by content type

Online magazine Beer.com's *Virtual Bartender* is a classic example of the exploitation of effective forwarding criteria. Just ten emails sent to friends of beer.com, with no other marketing activity, resulted in a significant amount of forwarding. The email contained a link to a mock webcam of a scantily clad virtual bartender who would respond to questions posed by the user. The target market was young American men aged between 18 and 26. The original ten emails led to 15,000 click-throughs the following day and achieved no fewer than 10m user sessions by the end of the month. 205,000 people signed up for the Virtual Bartender fan club:

---

9  http://no-mans-blog.com/2007/08/youtube-trends-report-5-series-finale-double-bill/.

'There is no way to predict how an audience is going to react to a given piece. We believed strongly that Virtual Bartender was going to get millions of visitors, but this exceeded our wildest expectations.' *Founder, beer.com)*

It is also easy to see how the growth of social networking sites, discussed in chapter 4, will have facilitated the use and appropriateness of online viral marketing techniques, although it is equally important to identify the right online target audience for viral communications. Long case 7.2 provides a more comprehensive example of the ingenuity of viral marketing employing social networks. How effective are such campaigns? What metrics should be used to measure effectiveness? Research by Jupiter Research in 2007 suggested that just 15 per cent of viral campaigns in the US during that year succeeded in prompting consumers to promote the marketer's message (Jupiter Research, 2007).

---

### Activity box 7.5

#### Posters, lurkers and masquerades

Identify a discussion forum of your choice which focuses upon commercial products or services as well providing summary detail on the posters themselves. Choose a well populated thread and examine the structure of the discussion in the thread. What characterizes 'expert' posters? What language do they use? How are they identified and rewarded? What other aspects of electronic word-of-mouth can you distinguish?

---

### Long case 7.1

#### HP Technology @ Work

Keeping the organization in the customer's mind following a sale, and ensuring a consistent reputation for adding value for those customers, is nowhere more challenging than in high-technology B2B markets. But it is a process which has benefited enormously from the application of digital marketing techniques. One of the earliest proponents was HP, one of the world's largest IT companies with revenue of over $104bn and with a portfolio of products ranging from printing and personal computing to software, services and IT infrastructure. The merger with Compaq in 2001 meant that there were two organizations with disparate and often contradictory marketing communication strategies and a confusing range of electronic routes to market. With over 1bn customers in 170 countries worldwide across retail and enterprise markets, the challenge of keeping in touch in a relevant way with the customer base in a fast-moving market for the new HP business was and is enormous.[10]

10   http://www.hp.com/hpinfo/newsroom/facts.html.                    ≫

HP's more integrated engagement with digital marketing techniques, begun in 2001, now stretches in a variety of guises across its after-sales 'Technology at Work' email marketing processes, blogs and discussion fora, technology showcase conferences, customized portals and newsletters, and has continued to evolve as new digital marketing technologies have become available. The company started by creating a rich contact database to be used for permission-based email marketing of after-sales and product and software driver updates. A customizable series of newsletters followed for enterprise clients, with over fifty possible permutations of content, including the ability to determine how technical the communications from the firm will be. Broad content and product preferences can also be selected. For enterprise clients, personalized portals can also be designed in areas such as health care, financial services and retail and distribution, containing customizable information on products, solutions, support, and driver updates. Alerts can also be requested of new product developments or software updates. These user choices are supplemented by behavioural targeting based upon actual levels of click-through and response, which may lead to additional information being included or the triggering of email enquiries suggesting users update their profiles.

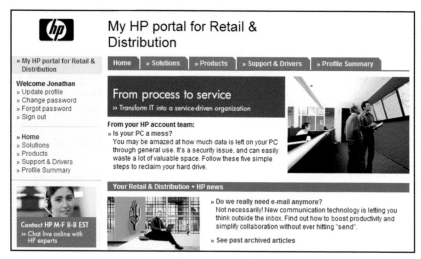

HP Communities support blogs and discussion fora in areas as diverse as business, services and technology, global citizenship, and knowledge management.[11] Although not formally part of the email and newsletter marketing programme, the company's annual showcase conference series for enterprise customers is also badged 'Technology @ Work'. The series 'presents an annual opportunity for HP enterprise customers to discover, discuss and decide upon actions that will deliver better business outcomes', and distributes the outputs of its meetings via webcast.

Outbound marketing activity of this kind generates a number of benefits to the organization, beyond the obvious maintenance of relevant aspects of the HP brand in the minds of existing customers, including a reduction in inbound service calls to

11   http://www.communities.hp.com/online/blogs/Bloggers.aspx.                    »

contact centres, the better ability to track additional sales arising from post-sales communications, and the internal benefits arising from sharing programme results across the organization. How effective have such activities proved? In 2006, HP estimated that the Technology at Work email marketing initiative alone was already influencing $100m in sales.

*Questions*

1. What other benefits accrue to HP from this integrated digital marketing activity? Are there any hidden costs to the business of engaging in this form of post-sales communication with customers?

2. Check out the HP Communities site at http://www.communities.hp.com/online/blogs/Bloggers.aspx. Which types of discussion fora appear to be attracting most attention and why? How should HP's marketers react to your findings?

## Long case 7.2

### Cream eggs, gorillas, and murder mysteries

Reaching 16- to 24-year-old audiences has proved an increasingly elusive goal for brand owners, not least for confectionary manufacturers such as Cadbury. By its own admission until recently, Cadbury's had been a very traditional marketing organization with little experience of digital marketing. Creme Egg, a seasonal confectionery product, available only between January and April, provided the first product focus for its experiments in the digital arena.

»

So-called 'live brand integration' may be an answer. This new digital marketing genre had its inception in a set of 3–4-minute YouTube video blogs created in 2006. The videos purported to tell the story of Bree, a teenager involved in a mysterious cult. It was soon established that the main character was actually played by a 19-year-old actor. Despite being revealed as a fictional character, 'LonelyGirl15'[12] attracted a massive following: some 70m combined views by the end of 2007. The show is now in its third 'series' (http://www.lg15.com) in what has become known as the *Breeniverse*. The international commercial potential of the genre through product placement became apparent with the launch of a UK spinoff series in June 2007, on social networking site Bebo, called KateModern.[13] Set in the East End of London KateModern shares many similarities with the original: a teenage girl with a dark secret—so dark that the main character is killed off at the end of the first series. The second series in 2008 (dedicated to uncovering who killed Kate) received 4m views per week. Microsoft, Procter & Gamble, and Orange were among brands that paid up to £250,000 each to embed their products into the story. Strict rules on product placement in the UK do not apply online. Among the advertisers also signed up for the new series are Toyota and Cadbury's. Scenes involved characters playing 'Touch the Toyota' and one actor, playing the role of a PR executive, attempts to organize a stunt with Cadbury's Creme Eggs in Leicester Square, which goes wrong.

In its second year of interactive marketing, Cadbury's used live brand integration as just one component of its interactive marketing. The 'Here Today, Goo Tomorrow' campaign for the Creme Egg brand (http://www.cremeegg.co.uk/) was again designed to raise awareness of the brand with teenage consumers in the critical sales period. The website included games and quizzes. Importantly, the interactive campaign was integrated with more conventional communications, including several very short 10-second TV adverts featuring 'suicidal' eggs. 'In many respects', suggests the UK Marketing Director

12   http://www.youtube.com/profile?user=lonelygirl15.
13   http://www.bebo.com/Profile.jsp?MemberId=4337221200.

>>

of Cadbury's, 'the clip length of the ads really has an online ethos at its heart. The target market is 16- to 24-year-olds and we need to be about interest and variety, rather than just creating one or two ads that you keep banging.' Other promotional channels included email marketing, bus-side posters showing eggs diving and splatting, and six-sheet billboard posters where the eggs have jumped off a building.

How effective has the campaign been? The absence of historical benchmarks against which to judge performance proved especially challenging for the firm. It generated a database of 150,000 new customers, who received a product sample, in a matter of days. As a result, the firm is now much more confident in its use of digital marketing techniques. Its subsequent campaign for the mainstream Dairy Milk chocolate product on YouTube and Sky, 'Gorilla'[14], attracted over 5m views aand was 'one of the most successful and talked about campaigns of the year'. Cadbury's has attributed the 5 per cent increase in chocolate sales during the period to the success of live brand integration, although subsequent commentators have questioned its effectiveness in converting 'buzz' into sales.

*Questions*

1. Are live brand integration campaigns only suitable for 16- to 24-year-old audiences? What are the implications of your conclusions for the ways in which marketers should engage with other consumer segments?

2. Cadbury's has extended its viral campaign from Creme Egg to its traditional Dairy Milk chocolate tablet. What factors do you think might affect the success of this extension?

14   http://www.youtube.com/watch?v=CbLr2NEV_7o.

## ⭐ Chapter Summary

This chapter began by reviewing the role and scope of marketing and differentiated between thinking about marketing as 'what marketers do' as against 'a way of thinking about customers' within the organization. It set out the characteristic processes of marketing before considering the distinction between firms that are market-driven in terms of their approach to customers, and those that—by contrast—drive markets more proactively and experimentally. Suggesting that the challenge presented by e-business favoured the latter, the chapter explored the effects of e-business technologies on marketing strategy. These included the ways in which both customers and firms would relate to the adoption of digital marketing techniques, which would both have an impact upon the make-up of marketing budgets in the future. The chapter distinguished between first- and second-generation digital marketing techniques and set out the toolkit available to firms, considering how organizations might relate these tools to four broad sets of objectives in developing their overall marketing strategies, recognizing that there might be currently powerful barriers preventing firms' ambitions being realized, not least difficulties in achieving a fully integrated approach to any marketing strategy.

We then examined the extent of digital marketing activity and noted the fast, but variable, growth in many indicators between countries, notably in terms of online advertising spend, and the increasing levels of interest expressed in digital marketing communications by users and firms—as well as firms' perceptions of the likely future effectiveness of particular techniques. Consideration of the kinds of market analysis conducted by organizations to segment digital audiences led us to wonder to what extent these methods were more intrusive than conventional segmentation approaches.

This led to a detailed discussion of the characteristics, strengths, and weaknesses of a range of digital marketing techniques adopted by organizations. Although email marketing applications were amongst the earliest of these, barriers had emerged to erode some of the first-mover advantages of this tool. Turning to online advertising, the chapter examined some of the evidence over effectiveness and perceived intrusiveness of particular forms, and concluded that there was still much work to do. Search marketing and its monetization, on the other hand, was proving a sophisticated method of targeting marketing communications, although affiliate marketing was not without its risks. Exploring the ways in which second-generation tools might be embraced to achieve greater involvement of customers themselves allowed us critically to review the growth of electronic word of mouth and more explicit viral marketing techniques. We concluded that many of these techniques appeared attractive, but there was no real way to predict customer reaction to them and that, consequently, many organizations were still engaging in widespread experimentation.

## ? Review questions

1. What are the main features distinguishing *market-led* from *market-leading* organizations?

2. Set out the main ways in which digital marketing techniques fit into either (a) the buying process or (b) the marketing objectives of firms.

3. What are the main barriers to the adoption of digital marketing techniques?

4. What are the advantages and disadvantages of email marketing for firms? How and why are these changing?

5. What are the main types of online advertising and what can be said about consumers' attitudes towards them?

6. What are the costs and benefits of the Google AdWords system?

7. Several firms have abandoned affiliate marketing. Is this a short-sighted decision?

8. What is the difference (if any) between buzz marketing, electronic word of mouth, and viral marketing? Give examples to illustrate your answer.

## O Discussion questions

1. What might explain why the number of firms using digital marketing tools is reportedly significantly lower than the number of firms saying that the use of these tools is 'very' or 'extremely' important?

2. To what extent do Rayport's 'six rules' of viral marketing still apply to their use in a digital marketing context? Can you think of any viral campaigns to which you have been exposed which employ other or different rules?

3. Is 'behavioural targeting' of online advertising based on intercepting anonymized customer web search results a good or a bad idea?

**4.** Look back at Figure 7.1, which shows the role and functions of marketing in creating and maintaining value for customers. Having read the chapter, within which activities do you think the most impact of digital marketing has been felt most?

**5.** What do the seven principles of Google marketing mean? Can you identify ways in which these principles have been put into practice?

# → Suggestions for further reading

Abraham, M.M. & Lodish, L.M., (1990), 'Getting the Most out of Advertising and Promotion', *Harvard Business Review*, 68(3), pp. 50–60.
This article is now nearly twenty years old, but still retains its place on my bookshelf. It provides a salutary reminder of the importance of measuring marketing and promotional effectiveness: the incremental sales of a product over and above those that would happen without the advertising and promotion. It provides a useful backdrop to the rhetoric of Internet marketing.

Clifton, B., (2008), *Advanced Web Metrics with Google Analytics,* John Wiley.
This is a useful guide to getting the most out of Google's web analytics system. As well as providing a useful overview of features, the book contains guidance on analysis of data and tips on how to create meaningful key performance indicators (KPIs) from the marketer's perspective.

Cooke, M. and Buckley, N., (2008), 'Web 2.0, Social Networks and the futUre of Market Research', *International Journal of Market Research,* 50(2), pp. 267–92.
An exploration of the potential of the collaborative tools and platforms available within social media for market researchers. The article examines the role of 'participatory panels' and 'research communities'.

Edelman, D.C., (2007), 'From the Periphery to the Core: As Online Strategy Becomes Overall Strategy, Marketing Organizations and Agencies Will Never Be the Same', *Journal of Advertising Research*, 47(2), pp. 130–34.
The article argues that consumers today are spending more time online than with any other marketing channel. This fundamental shift is driving both how consumers engage with brands and how marketers understand and cater to their consumers. This author explores the shifting foundations of the media landscape and poses some specific strategies that will permit marketers to cope with, and even exploit, this changing environment

Hennig-Thurau, F., Gwinner, K.P., Walsh, G., and Gremler, D.D., (2004), 'Electronic Word-of-Mouth via Consumer-Opinion Platforms: What Motivates Consumers to Articulate Themselves on the Internet?', *Journal of Interactive Marketing*, 18(1), pp. 38–52.
The authors draw on findings from research on virtual communities and traditional word-of-mouth literature, and develop a typology of motives for consumers to make contributions to online fora. Analysing a large online sample leads to the suggestion that (1) consumers' desire for social interaction, (2) their desire for economic incentives, (3) their concern for other consumers, and (4) the potential to enhance their own self-worth are the primary factors leading to then engaging in electronic word of mouth.

# → References

Abraham, M.M. and Lodish, L.M., (1990), 'Getting the Most out of Advertising and Promotion', *Harvard Business Review*, 68(3), pp. 50–60.

Agrawal, V., Arjona, L.D., and R. Lemmens, (2001), 'E-Performance: The Path to Rational Exuberance', *The McKinsey Quarterly*, 1.

Chartered Institute of Marketing (2001)

Chin et al. 2007

Clayton, R., (2008), *The Phorm 'Webwise' System*, http://www.cl.cam. ac.uk/ffrnc1/080518-phorm.pdf.

Court, D., McLaughlin, K., and Halsall, C., (2000), *Marketing Spending Effectiveness. How to Win in a Complex Environment*, McKinsey Marketing Practice, http://www.mckinsey.com/practices/marketing/ourknowledge/pdf/WhitePaper_MSE_HowtoWininaComplex.pdf.

Direct Marketing Association (2009)

e-dialog (2006)

Edelman, D.C., (2007), 'From the Periphery to the Core: As Online Strategy Becomes Overall Strategy, Marketing Organizations and Agencies Will Never Be the Same', *Journal of Advertising Research*, 47(2), pp. 130–34.

Fang, X., Singh, S. and Ahluwalia, R., (2007), 'An Examination of Different Explanations for the Mere Exposure Effect.', *Journal of Consumer Research*, 34(1), pp. 97–103.

Forrester Research, (2007), 'The Forrester Wave™: Email Marketing Service Providers, Q4 2007', http://www.forrester.com.

Fortt (2008)

*Guardian*, (2008), 'UK Advertising Revenues, 2003–2008', http://www.guardian.co.uk/uk/interactive/2008/apr/18/googlerevenue.

Ha, L., 'Online Advertising Research in Advertising Journals: A Review', *Journal of Current Issues and Research in Advertising*, 30(1), pp. 31–48.

Hennig-Thurau, F., Gwinner, K. P., Walsh, and G., Gremler, D.D., (2004), 'Electronic Word-of-Mouth via Consumer-Opinion Platforms: What Motivates Consumers to Articulate Themselves on the Internet?'. *Journal of Interactive Marketing*, 18(1), pp. 38–52.

Jaworski, B., Kohli, A.K. & Sahay, A., (2000), 'Market-Driven Versus Driving Markets,' Journal of the Academy of Marketing Science, 28(1), pp.45-54.

IDC, (2008), 'Worldwide Internet Advertising Spending to Surpass $106 Billion in 2011', Digital Marketplace Model.

Jupiter Research, (2007), Viral Marketing: Bringing the Message to the Masses, Jupiter Research.

Kemp, M. B., (2007), 'Europe's Search Engine Marketing Investment', Forrester Research.

Kiecker, P. and Cowles, D., (2001), 'Interpersonal Communication and Personal Influence on the Internet: A Framework for Examining Online Word-of-Mouth', Journal of Euromarketing, 11(2), pp. 71–88.

Llewellyn-Smith, J., (2007), 'The Pink Pages', Daily Telegraph, 26 December.

Nielsen Media Research, (2008), 'Nielsen Reports DVR Playback is Adding to TV Viewing Levels', Press Release, February.

Nielsen, J., (1997), 'Why Advertising Doesn' Work on the Web', http://www.useit.com/alertbox/9709a.html

Nielsen, J., (2007), 'Banner Blindness: Old and New Findings', http://www.useit.com/alertbox/banner-blindness.html

Ramos, L., (2008), 'B2B Marketers Fail the Community Marketing Test', Forrester Research.

Strasburger, V.C., (2001), 'Children and TV Advertising: Nowhere to Run, Nowhere to Hide', Journal of Developmental and Behavioural Pediatrics, 22, p. 185.

Woods, S., (2006), 'Internet Use Outstrips TV Viewing for the First Time', Brand Republic, 8 March, http://www.brandrepublic.com/bulletins/digital/article/545047/internet-use-outstrips-tv-viewing-first-time/.

Yaveroglu, I. and Donthu, N., (2008), 'Advertising Repetition and Placement Issues in On-Line Environments', Journal of Advertising, 37(2), pp. 31–43.

# Weblinks

**Affiliates 4 U.** Founded in 1999, Affiliates 4 U is an online community for affiliate marketers: http://www.affiliates4u.com/.

**Interactive Advertising Bureau.** IAB members are responsible for selling over 86 per cent of online advertising in the United States: http://www.iab.net/. The UK equivalent is the Internet Advertising Bureaue: http://www.iabuk.net.

**Marketing Vox.** An aggregator for online marketing news, 'designed to keep marketers and media professionals abreast of industry news, trends and culture': http://www.marketingvox.com.

**Search Engine Watch.** Provides tips and information about search and search marketing and analysis of the search engine industry: http://www.searchenginewatch.com.

**Seth Godin's blog.** Seth Godin is the author and popularizer of the term 'permission marketing'. His blog is one of the most widely read marketing blogs: http://sethgodin.typepad.com/.

# 8

# Product and service innovation

*by Malobi Kar*

## Learning outcomes

Completing this chapter will enable you to:

- Develop an insight into the theoretical foundations of innovation
- Identify different types of innovation involving e-business, including e-product innovation, e-service innovation, and open innovation
- Consider the role of users and user communities in open innovation for e-businesses
- Identify the distinguishing features of the stages associated with new e-product and e-service development
- Consider the characteristics and challenges of e-business innovation in the public sector.

## Introduction

Chapter 7 highlighted how e-business has essentially become customer-centric and illustrated the resultant control that customers can now exercise over various business processes and the level of their involvement with the firm. In such a business environment, companies not only have to tailor products and services to meet customer needs and wants but have to do so in tandem with frequently changing consumer requirements, if they are to avoid losing those customers.

Product and service innovation in such an environment therefore needs to be customer focused and in real time from the very beginning: from the idea generation stage through to concept validation, product and market testing. At a macro level, there is also a greater requirement for efficiency, effectiveness, and competitiveness based on innovation and knowledge. In order to increase productivity and quality and facilitate exploitation of resources, firms also need to scan the technological environment and assess investment decisions in implementing e-business technologies. As chapter 6 suggested, e-business represents a new way for firms to manage relationships with trading partners and reflects a firm's strategic intention to use the Internet to share information, facilitate transactions, improve customer service, and strengthen back-office integration. Innovative activities have to take these factors into consideration.

Given the many technological opportunities from which firms can potentially choose, they need to identify those that are most clearly associated with improved competitiveness and growth. For example, in recent years there has been a lot of media hype and excitement around virtual worlds. You will recall from the case study of Second Life in chapter 4 that virtual worlds are computer-generated environments where people, using 'avatars', emulate real-world phenomena whilet participating in online communities. Many strategy professionals view virtual worlds as one of the applications which may fit into future e-business toolkits for communications, media ecosystem support, and (perhaps) direct revenue generation. However, while the creation of virtual worlds means that firms can seek to create business opportunities in this space, from the point of view of innovation, they also need to know the tipping point between novelty and viability. This judgement is by no means straightforward.

After defining the concept of innovation and discussing both macroeconomic and organizational perspectives on innovation, together with emerging models of innovation, this chapter examines innovation in the context of e-business. It then explores the various stages associated with new product and service development, seeking to identify some of the nuances which characterize innovation derived from e-businesses technologies. The chapter then focuses on some of the key characteristics of public-sector innovation, elaborating on e-government services, and concludes with a discussion on the challenges of e-innovation in the public realm.

## The concept of innovation

The Oxford dictionary defines innovation as:

> 'The action of introducing a new product into the market; the bringing of an invention into widespread, practical use.' *OED online definition 5.*

Conceptualizing innovation is not a straightforward task as it embodies a number of different traditions and can be approached from a wide variety of perspectives. Indeed, individual disciplines have had the effect of restricting the conceptualization of innovation into superficial silos. A richer understanding of the concept can be had from combining the fundamentals of the different schools of thought. The innovation literature can essentially be divided into that which takes a macroeconomic perspective and that which takes an organizational perspective.

### A macroeconomic perspective on innovation

Economists see innovation from a primarily macroeconomic point of view and are especially interested in the link between innovation and economic growth and development. This view is especially relevant in understanding the external drivers, barriers and different cycles of innovation (Zaltman and Dunken, 1973). According to Schumpeter (1912), economic development occurs as a result of drastic external and internal changes to existing routines and is primarily caused by innovation. He sees innovation as a disruption consciously driven by organizations and individuals, which is characterized by new combinations of economic resources. (This is familiar: we have already come across the 'disruptive' role of e-business technologies in affecting the structure of markets for goods and services in chapter 2.) Schumpeter was also one of the first to provide a fuller definition of innovation. According to him, innovation could comprise a number of activities, including:

'(1) The introduction of a new good that is one with which consumers are not yet familiar or a new quality of a good. (2) The introduction of a new method of production, that is one not yet tested by experience in the branch of manufacture concerned, which needs by no means be founded upon a discovery scientifically new, and can also exist in a new way of handling a commodity commercially. (3) The opening of a new market that is a market into which the particular branch of manufacture of the country in question has not previously entered, whether or not this market has existed before. (4) The conquest of a new source of supply of raw materials or half-manufactured goods, again irrespective of whether this source already exists or whether it has first to be created. (5) The carrying out of new organisation of any industry, like the creation of a monopoly position (for example trustification) or breaking up of a monopoly position.' *Zaltman and Dunken, 1973; Schumpeter, 1934*

Schumpeter's five different types of innovation distinguish between:

- new products;
- new methods of production;
- new sources of supply;
- exploration of new markets; and
- new ways to organize a business.

Note that these types of innovation do not explicitly mention services or technology although clearly these may be a feature of innovation in terms of new product and methods of production, and may facilitate new sources of supply, finding new markets, or in assisting firms to organize in more productive ways. The technological dimension of innovation was first acknowledged by Solow (1956, 1957), who proposed technological change as the single most important contemporary component of long-term economic growth. More specifically, he suggested that a steady state rate of growth depends on the rate of technological progress and the rate of investment in technology. According to Solow, in purely economic terms, innovation comprises the ability to *extract greater economic value from advances in science and technology*.

Later, endogenous views of innovation extended Solow's analysis (Romer, 1990; Grossman and Helpman, 1991). At the heart of an 'endogenous' approach is the view that the acquisition of technology on its own is not sufficient to explain why economies and industries grow at different rates. The endogenous view of innovation proposes that institutional intermediation (acts by institutions such as governments, agencies, and firms) takes place in the process of technological change. These might include government policies on investment in education, subsidies, or incentives to encourage research and

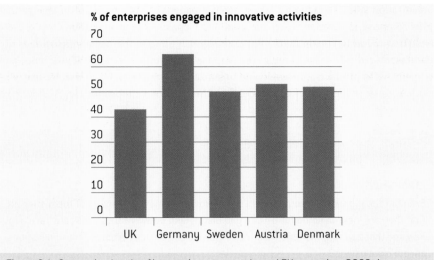

**Figure 8.1**  Comparing levels of innovation across selected EU countries, 2002-4

development (R&D), or the choices that sectors make in relation to their own investment, R&D, or training needs.) The result is that technological progress, and the resultant effect on innovation, is not just an economic but also a social phenomenon. This endogenous view therefore accentuates the importance to the 'production process' of new technologies and the role of human capital in that.

The endogenous theory of innovation is extended further by Nelson and Winter (1997) who emphasize the crucial role of institutions such as governments in delivering the necessary resources for innovation. For example, there is considerable concern that the UK has been identified as one of the poorest performers in innovation according to traditional innovation indicators such as private- and public-sector investment in formal research and development as well as the number of patents registered (NESTA, 2007). Figure 8.1 shows a comparison of innovativeness across five EU markets. According to the fourth Community Innovation Survey (CIS 4), 43 per cent of UK enterprises were engaged in innovation activities; two points below the EU-15 average and well below levels in Germany (65 per cent), Sweden (50 per cent), Austria (53 per cent), and Denmark (52 per cent).

## Organizational perspectives on innovation

An organizational perspective on innovation extends the concept of innovation from economics into broader social science. Researchers are as interested in how innovation occurs as with its consequences. According to Penrose (1961), it is the team effort of managers and entrepreneurs within the organization, coupled with bundles of organizational resources, which account for the way firms innovate and grow. Contrast this view with the macroeconomic perspective above. You may also see some links with the discussion we had on the nature of value creation in chapter 6. Sociologists and organization studies academics take a much broader view of the extent of change that may comprise innovation. (See, for example, Gopalakrishnan and Damanpour, 1997 and Hristov and Reynolds, 2007.) For example, they suggest that most innovation is not particularly radical—it tends rather to comprise minor improvements, adjustments, and refinements to products, processes, and organizational practices. Of course, we may well ask how we draw the line between 'radical' and 'incremental' innovation (see Activity 8.1).

---

**Activity box 8.1**

Innovation or not?

Examine the products in your kitchen or bathroom cabinet. How many of them suggest that they are 'new' in some form? Can you distinguish between those that are 'radically' new and those simply 'incrementally' new? How do you decide? What are the implications of your conclusions?

---

The organizational literature on innovation focuses on the innovation decision process in a firm, looking specifically into how innovation occurs within the organization, the process of innovation and the diffusion of innovation within the firm. It has a number of important components. Diffusion researchers focus on the study of innovation from the point of view of dispersion of an idea, product, process, or practice. The process theory of innovation investigates the nature of the innovation process, namely: 'how' and 'why' innovations emerge, develop, grow, and terminate from the perspectives of generation, adoption, and organizational structure. A cognitive dimension of innovation is associated mainly with managerial sense-making, cognitions, and the absorptive capacity of organizations and industries for actually undertaking innovation activity.

## Models of innovation

The varied ways in which innovation is conceptualized has resulted in the identification of distinct types of innovation which help to explain the link between technology cycles and organizational innovation. These models can be characterized either as static—which are mainly concerned with the types of innovation and their strategic impact on firms—or dynamic—which adopt a more longitudinal approach to innovation in broader technology cycles (Afuah, 2003).

Rebecca Henderson and Kim Clark have identified four types of innovation as a result (Abernathy and Clark, 1985; Henderson and Clark, 1990). Figure 8.2 classifies innovation along two dimensions: the horizontal captures an innovation's impact on a firm's component capabilities; the vertical an innovation's impact on the linkages between components. Let's illustrate each in turn, using Henderson and Clark's example of a room air fan.

- *Incremental innovation*: this is about minor changes to a product or service. This type of innovation capitalizes on the existing capabilities of the firm, refining and extending an established design. Whilst this design improves, the underlying concepts and the links between them remain the same. In the case of the room air fan, improvements in blade design or the power of the motor would be incremental innovations.

- *Radical innovation* is at the opposite end of the spectrum from incremental innovation. Radical innovation establishes a new dominant design which may represent a step change in both the components and indeed for the whole system. Such change would call for a new set of competences to replace the existing ones (Abernathy and Clark, 1985; Tushman and Anderson, 1986). In the case of the room air fan, a move to central air conditioning would be a radical innovation. The need for compressors, refrigerants, and so on would require wholly new capabilities and technical skills.

- *Modular innovation* suggests changes only to designs of the component technology as in the case of transition from analogue to digital telephone technology—the core design concept has changed, but the architecture has not.

- *Architectural innovation* is the most radical and perhaps subtle departure from an incumbent technology and existing market linkages. It involves the introduction of new technology which in turn opens up a new market as was the case with xerography (the technical basis for most modern photocopiers) or the radio—or perhaps is now the case with applications such as online auctions. In the case of our room air fan, the introduction of the *portable* fan would be an architectural innovation: 'while the primary components would be the same, the architecture of the product would be quite different', suggest Henderson and Clark: for example, 'the smaller size of the apparatus would probably introduce new interactions between the performance of the blade and the weight of the housing' Abernathy and Clark (1985), who initially proposed this type of innovation, suggest that architectural innovation is most likely to occur in an entrepreneurial organization which is free of bureaucratic constraints, since they are less likely to be constrained by established ways of doing things. Again, we can start to see how new e-business firms may be in a position to innovate differently.

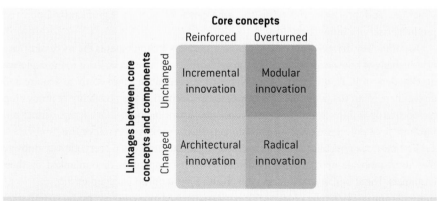

**Figure 8.2** A framework for defining innovation

## The context for innovation

A fundamental conclusion to emerge from the previous discussion is that the potential of an innovation cannot be grasped without a prior understanding of the context in which it occurs. Innovation is a complex process sequence of decisions made by many people in different situations. Tornatzky and Fleischer (1990) identify three key elements of a firm's context that influence the way in which it will innovate:

- *The environmental context* represents the business and regulatory arena in which the firm operates.
- *The technological context* comprises external and internal technologies relevant to the firm.
- *The organizational context* is typically defined in terms of size, operating processes, managerial structure, the extent of underutilized human capital and other resources.

# Innovation in the context of e-business

From the second half of the twentieth century, academics researching the field of innovation have been increasingly in agreement that technological change (a term which they have tended to use synonymously with innovation) is the single most powerful force for economic growth. Economic globalization has significantly increased the competitive pressure on enterprises in many sectors. This comes as a result of, among other factors, the emergence of new, lower-cost producers, fast-changing demand patterns, increased market fragmentation, and shortened product life cycles. In such an environment, innovation (either in terms of business processes or of final products and services) becomes crucial for the lon- term competitiveness and survival of enterprises.

Very often, organizations adopt ICT systems during the course of the enterprise's overall development within a specific technological, commercial, and business environment. From such a point of view, the use of ICT in a firm's operations would not be considered fundamentally different from the purchase of other up-to-date machinery. The full potential of e-business technology is realized in an organization when it is understood and implemented as an integral part of a much broader process of transformation of business structures and processes involving the emergence of new or significantly improved product or service innovation.

One of the key drivers of innovation using e-business technologies is the increasing ease of availability of knowledge required to trigger the innovation process. Prior to the explosive development of ICTs, information and knowledge were much more costly to acquire and disseminate. With the fall in the cost of accessing information the possibility of innovation has opened up to a much wider range of economic actors, including, for example, small and medium-sized enterprises, as well as customers themselves. As a result of this, innovation has become not a possibility but a necessity for organizations—when everyone can innovate they must innovate or risk being undercut by their competitors or outflanked by their customers. The abundance of information creates a *pro-innovation environment*.

Another precursor for the adoption of e-business-enabled innovation within an organization is the increasing flattening of organizational hierarchies. As organizations become more aware of the importance of innovation for their competitiveness, alongside the need to be proactive innovators, interactions among different categories of employees and managers evolve. Information has to be shared much more widely than in the past and ICT-enabled e-business processes tend to generate information flows that ignore formal hierarchies. The process of innovation therefore no longer remains the formal remit of the research and development units within the organization: it can happen anywhere by involving other departments, especially those which interact with customers and are in a position to gauge customer trends, needs and wants, and thereby collaborate in the innovation process.

In an information-rich business environment the Internet also serves as a platform for enabling collaborative innovation with customers. Widespread deployment of the Internet has greatly enhanced the ability of firms to engage with customers in the product innovation process. The Internet is a two-way conduit and e-product designers can take advantage of this two-way mechanism and create environments in which customer knowledge can be acquired through an ongoing dialogue. Much more relevant and personalized product offerings can then be developed.

Given the significance of real-time interactions between consumers and between the firms and consumers, e-business innovation can only thrive in an environment that moves at the speed of Internet and 'real time'. Firms which cannot keep up with the required pace of change will be unsuccessful in their e-innovation endeavours. Hence a culture that encourages adaptability is more likely to be successful in the arena of innovation, and more specifically e-business innovation in this case, an aspect which we discuss in more detail in chapter 11.

ICT and latterly e-business technologies have therefore profoundly changed the techno-economic context within which innovation takes place today. Previously, innovation revolved around the concepts of mass production, economies of scale, and corporate-dominated R&D. In the last three decades of the twentieth century this was replaced to a large extent by an emphasis on economies of scope, exploiting the benefits of interconnected, flexible production facilities and greater flexibility and decentralization of R&D and development. Flexibility, interconnectedness and collaboration are therefore the distinguishing characteristics of innovation using ICT.[1]

In developing digital economies, government involvement also represents a critical driver of the diffusion of technological advancements as well as the implementation of such technologies, as the discussion of macroeconomic perspectives on innovation suggested earlier. Government influence is not only about implementing guidelines and policies regarding the use of e-business, but also about removing any structural barriers that might impede the diffusion of e-business initiatives.

## Activity box 8.2

### Mapping e-business onto the innovation framework

Identify an example of innovation through e-business technologies for each quadrant of Henderson and Clark's innovation framework. Justify your choices.

---

1  See United Nations Conference on Trade and Development (UNCTAD) Information Economy Report 2007–2008, *Science and Technology for Development: The New Paradigm of ICT.*

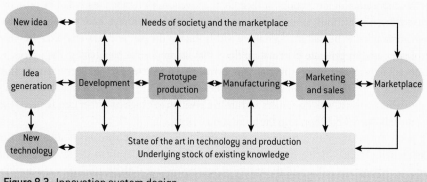

**Figure 8.3** Innovation system design

Figure 8.3 above presents the basic model of the interactions between markets, science and technology, and innovation in the context of the operation of markets. E-business technologies can be introduced at any point in the model in order to stimulate innovation—at the product level or in processes. They can also be applied in marketing or communication, supply chain management, knowledge management, recombining existing technologies, and product development.

While Figure 8.3 draws upon an example from the manufacturing sector, Figure 8.4 highlights how customer-focused service organizations take the outside-in approach and use their customers as an integral part of idea generation for innovation.

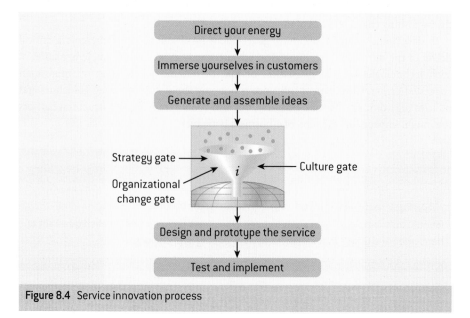

**Figure 8.4** Service innovation process

# Types of e-business innovation

## E-product innovation

*E-product innovation* occurs when a company adopts new technology to offer products to customers in a way that is new to the enterprise. E-product innovation corresponds to the generation of a new product function where technology is the primary enabler. One product characteristic fundamental to e-product innovation is that of *modularity* or *transmutability* (Arakji and Lang, 2007; Gershenson et al., 2003). Modular products are those which consist of distinct, relatively independent building blocks among which the interactions are determined by standardized interfaces. Modular design in products allows the pairing of common units with different modules to create product variants. In other words, unlike integrated product design, modular product designs enable alteration of a specific module that is usually assigned for a specific function without necessarily requiring an entire redesign of the product. It is this specific feature of modular products that facilitates e-product innovation.

The major advantage of modular products is the ease with which the functionality of the product can be changed. Recall that the characteristic of modularity enables alteration of a functional element of the product by changing the corresponding component, leaving the other components alone. Firms can therefore respond to changing markets and consumer demand rapidly and inexpensively by developing new products derived from existing modular products. Much e-product innovation can therefore be categorized as 'modular' and/or 'incremental' innovation rather than radical or architectural innovation.

Good examples of modular products in e-business are digital products. Modular digital goods such as video games and online games lend themselves to innovation. Video games also allow for collaborative forms of innovation by allowing the user to modify the game or add new functionalities. Such modifications can vary from changing the visual environment of the game to partial or complete modification of the game. (Partial conversion might entail adding characters and objects or adding extra playing levels to the game. Total conversion might constitute complete departures from the original game theme.) Once the modification is complete the product can then be delivered through the Internet, either through the game's website or through websites run by the gamers themselves. Another market where e-product innovation is common is that for recorded music. Here, customers regularly engage in ripping, mixing, and burning music files on sites such as http://www.mixunit.com.

## E-service innovation

*E-service innovation* refers to new or significantly changed service concepts or service delivery processes that deliver added value to the customer by means of new or improved solutions to a problem, or improvement of performance. Van Ark et al. define service innovation as:

> 'A considerably changed service concept, client interaction channel, service delivery system or technological concept that individually, but most likely in combination, leads to one or more (re)new(ed) service functions that are new to the firm, change the service/good offered on the market and do require structurally new technological, human or organisational capabilities from the service organisation.' *Van Ark et al., 2003*

Technology is considered one of the key components of contemporary service innovation. Commercial analysts Gartner have defined e-service as including processes, policies, procedures, people, tools, and technologies that enable enterprises to provide assisted and unassisted customer service using the Internet as its platform.

The term 'net-based customer service system' is also used to denote a concept of e-service. According to Brohman et al. (2003), 'a net-based customer service system delivers service to customers either directly or indirectly'. We can also distinguish between *direct* delivery of service—through a browser, PDA, or cell phone—and *indirect* service delivery which occurs via a customer service representative. The definitions above emphasize the interactive and multidimensional nature of e-service innovation. These definitions also recognize that service innovations are often incremental improvements rather than radical innovations. Table 8.1 captures several dimensions of service innovation and the proliferation of technology across all these dimensions is evident.

## Open Innovation

As technological change accelerates, competitive pressures force companies to augment their knowledge and capabilities. An increasingly important way to do this is to use

**Table 8.1  Examples of the Dimensions of e-Service Innovation**

| Dimension of Service Innovation | Examples of Innovative Service Concepts |
| --- | --- |
| New network, business model and value chain configurations | Financing, insurance and phone services offered by supermarkets, e.g Tesco Finance<br>Open source software development and distribution |
| Delivery System innovation | ATMs, telephone and Internet banking<br>Amazon.com Internet bookshop offering electronic customer interface, new delivery system, and extensive customer profile data |
| Organizational innovation | First Direct's purpose built organization,<br>office buildings, and location facilitating call centre functions of telephone and online banking |
| Customer interface innovation | Global tracking of deliveries via purpose-built Internet site. Followed by introduction of eShipping Tools for automated shipping process, eCommerce Solutions enabling online trading integrated with FedEx shipping capabilities<br>eSupply Chain Solutions enabling improvements in global supply chain performance |
| Technology and product-based innovation | Mobile phone based tracking<br>GPS location identification services<br>Radio Frequency Identification (RFID)<br>Nanotechnology-based developments |

## Short case 8.1

### Coke Studios

Launched in 2002 by Coca-Cola North America, Cokemusic.com features streaming radio, music demo creation, music downloads, and personalized V-ego avatar characters. V-egos are online, virtual personas individually created by every new registrant to the site. Registrants choose everything about their V-ego's physicality, from skin tone and hair-do to the colour and style of clothing, shoes, and shades. From a virtual disco party in Tokyo to a virtual New York subway station, V-egos can talk or shout amongst each other in Coke Studios, the interactive area of cokemusic.com in which users can visit virtual venues around the globe and other user studios using the V-ego character that they created during registration. Once inside Coke Studios, V-egos can move around, interact with each other, play music demos that they' created at Create Your Demo mixing stations, dance, and drink virtual Coca-Cola. V-egos and visitors alike can test their ability to create personalized music demos by blending the sounds of guitar, drums, and other instruments, and later sample their mixes in Coke Studios for their V-ego friends. V-egos can also design and create their own studio for hanging out, playing music and talking with other V-egos. Cokemusic.com is believed to be the first webSite to combine avatar technology and music demo sampling within an interactive, online community.

Coca Cola has also partnered with online music leader, AOL Music, to feature eight to ten fresh new bands and solo artists each month on the site. Based in Dulles, Virginia, America Online is the world's leader in interactive services, web brands, Internet technologies, and e-commerce services. AOL Music, a division of America Online, Inc., reaches the largest audience of online music fans in the world through a rich array of programming products and services that make it easy to discover, experience, listen to, and buy music online.

In December 2007, Coca-Cola said it will migrate Coke Studios, the virtual world it has run within its MyCoke.com Web site for almost five years, to a new continent in the There.com virtual universe owned and operated by Makena Technologies. Coke's new 3D world will be called CC Metro. 'Coke Studios has been very successful, but it's really a 2-D, old-style avatar world,' Coke spokeswoman Sue Stribling said. Coca-Cola looked at the various virtual platforms available and opted for a long-term exclusive agreement with »

Makena's There.com, a moderated PG-13 world that offers a richer 3D experience than Coke could devise in-house.

*Question*
What dimensions of e-service innovation does Coke Studios exploit?

*open innovation*—a term that describes how companies that are leaders in their field work to complement their in-house R&D efforts with technologies developed by others and open up their own technological knowledge to outsiders (Chesbrough, 2003). In the case of open innovation, traditional inward-oriented technological capacity-building efforts tend to be complemented or even replaced with more outward-looking strategies which rely on the output of networks of universities, joint ventures, starts-ups, suppliers, competitors, and customers. The resultant technological alliances become instruments of learning. This concept bears many similarities with the notion of value nets and constellations introduced in chapter 6. Open innovation is related to the idea that users of any component should be integrated into the innovation process. Von Hippel (2005) refers to this as 'democratising innovation'. This gives users (enterprises or customers) the opportunity to become involved with innovation of requisite products and services which they can then freely release, unlike in traditional innovation where the manufacturers will identify users' needs, develops the products and then profits from selling them. In cases of open innovation, users tend to innovate collaboratively in communities. We discuss some of the particular considerations of working with online communities below.

One of the most successful examples of open innovation is that of open source software (OSS), which consists of collaborative projects involving people around the world who use the Internet to pool their collective knowledge. Free and open source software (FOSS) provides the most visible model of that trend. FOSS enables software developers to enhance their skills and to improve more easily on software-based business models. Participation in FOSS projects facilitates the creation and consolidation of local pools of expertise in ICT and, given the low barriers to access to that software, enables the emergence of new ICT-related business activities. This very often results in the launching of new products and services geared to the specific needs of local demand which may not have been possible with proprietary software. Short case 8.2 discusses the example of Mozilla Firefox.[2]

New kinds of intermediary may be able to take advantage of these sorts of open innovation processes. InnoCentive is an e-business venture set up by US-based pharmaceutical company Eli Lilly (http://www.innocentive.com). InnoCentive uses the Internet to help firms find scientific and technical expertise that they can use to meet innovation challenges. So-called 'seeker' companies (including large transnational firms) post their queries on InnoCentive and any participant in the network can then attempt

---

2   See UNCTAD 2007–2008 for more information on OSS and FOSS.

to resolve the issue. InnoCentive is active in a number of developing countries including China, India, and Russia. In China, InnoCentive has established partnerships with twenty-six academic institutions. Chinese scientists participate in a lot of InnoCentive's global efforts at problem solving via open innovation. The advantages of participation of Chinese scientists in schemes such as these are not merely financial, since it allows them to gain access to and understand the problems and methodologies of international companies in a wide range of industries.

---

### Short case 8.2

#### Mozilla Firefox

The Mozilla project is an offshoot of the Netscape browser. Mozilla was released as an open source version of Netscape in January 1998. Since that time, Mozilla has released many versions of its browsers. Netscape and AOL use its browsers. Firefox is the latest version of the Mozilla browser.

The Mozilla Firefox story is one where the individual user becomes a marketing agent and exploits the power of the Internet to meet marketing goals. The 63,000 volunteers who have made this possible have used the Internet as a marketing forum to organize to maximize downloads. Volunteers have spread the word by linking to the main download site, blogging about Firefox, adding a link in their email signature file, putting up buttons on their website, collecting testimonials, and visiting technical sites to vote for their favourite browser.

The result of these myriad, seemingly small, marketing activities has seen the establishment of Mozilla Firefox as a credible competitor in a tough marketplace dominated by corporations. The central tenet of community-led marketing is that consumers exert their power in the marketplace through collective action. The new idea is that a user community produces, markets, and services a product that competes favourably with corporate products in the marketplace. Making the source code open to all is a deliberate business strategy. Providing open access creates an environment where any interested party can innovate. Open source products build a community of interested individuals around themselves. These individuals help test the product, provide customer service to others, provide feature requests and also, help market it. While some of the developers may be involved in the marketing, a new group of individuals may get involved in the marketing of the product.

One of the main features of the Firefox marketing campaign was that the community organized many distinct web sites.

- Download site: this was the site that everybody had to visit to download the browser.
- Browser switching site: the volunteer community was focused on one action—getting consumers to switch from IE to Firefox.                                    »

- The marketing site: the main purpose of this site was to organize all the volunteers. Affiliates who provided the most traffic were recognized on this site. Regular updates about the number of downloads were provided.
- Incompatible site list (http://www.defendthefox.com) was devoted to focusing and bringing pressure on sites that were incompatible with Firefox. Users could visit this site and provide names.

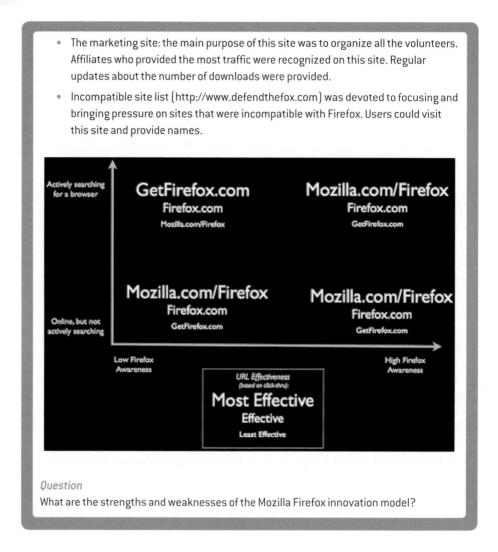

**Question**

What are the strengths and weaknesses of the Mozilla Firefox innovation model?

# Open innovation and new product and service development

Despite the discussion of open innovation, the actual stages of new product and service development in e-business are not totally dissimilar to those of new product development in traditional firms. However, there are some technical and customer-specific nuances of product and service development in an e-business environment that merit attention, particularly in the context of open innovation.

## Idea generation

At the idea generation stage in e-business, firms usually emphasize richness over reach in their collaborative arrangements with customers. (In other words, fewer, higher quality, customers are the order of the day.) The next section discusses in more detail some of the available mechanisms for harnessing customers in this way.

Contributions from customers may then be added to suggestions created by employees. Employees are a valuable source of ideas and information sharing across the organization. They need to be provided with the appropriate tools to encourage group communication. Blogs and wikis are the typical examples of informal and free flow of thought within the firm. These provide an integrated, organization-wide social network which can cross national boundaries. Intel is a good example of an organization that uses such mechanisms to generate ideas from their employees. We discussed Intel as a good practice example of an integrated e-business in chapter 3. There are some 1,700 blogs maintained across the Intel businesses. With around 86,000 employees in sixty different countries, Intel has identified blogs and wikis as a valuable way of capturing intra-organizational discussion on innovation. Conversations between Intel engineers based in different corners of the world enable the organization to keep abreast of new technological development. Blogs allow ideas to be vetted before they are introduced thereby refining and strengthening an idea through peer feedback. Such vetted ideas are usually much stronger ideas. Intra-organizational blogs allow collaborations between employees which would not otherwise have been possible.

## Concept validation at the front end

Once a tenable idea has been generated, it is necessary to take it forward and develop it into a comprehensive concept that can be further tailored to meet the needs and preferences of customers. This is followed by the formal identification of the target market. In order to gain an accurate insight into customers' needs and preferences, firms very often create online labs to test customer reactions to products and services currently under development. A good example of this is Volvo's Volvo Concept Lab (http://www.conceptlabvolvo.com). Firms very often use online market intelligence services to monitor blogs, websites, and bulletin boards to identify trends in customer behaviour. (We discussed the case of Dell in relation to electronic word-of-mouth in chapter 7.) At the concept testing stage, customers are given the option to make trade-offs among attributes of new product concepts using different web-based implementations. General Motors has created a web-based tool that helps customers to choose the right automobiles for themselves based on their preferences. As a result of this initiative, General Motors is able to collect quantitative data on customer preferences from all its customers on an ongoing basis at very low incremental cost.

## Designing the new ideas

In order to allow customers to participate directly in the product design stage, firms create various toolkits to facilitate user-driven innovation. These methods allow user participation in a much more active and in depth way. One such method is called User Design (UD). This tool enables users to design their own products according to their wants and needs. Design and feature options, engineering constraints, and price impacts are all displayed to prospective users in real time. The users can use a web-based drag and drop option to create the ideal product. Firms also use interactive toolkits which give customers the capability for trial-and-error learning by doing. Such toolkits give customers the option to make design-related changes including price, performance, and appearance. Once the changes have been effected, the visual prototypes of the products are immediately visible on the screen and further changes can then be made to adjust the designs according to the customers' personal preferences.

Such an approach to product design is novel as it does not only aim to identify customer needs and wants during the idea-generation stage but encourages customers to evaluate, elaborate, and challenge detailed product concepts. This exercise gives them the opportunity to discuss and improve optional solutions thereby making the most of their creative and problem-solving skills. For example, Peugeot initiated an Internet-based design contest where almost 3,000 enthusiasts from 90 different countries were registered with their proposed car designs on the theme of 'Retrofuturism' (http://www.peugeot-avenue.com).

Online toolkits are not just useful in generating ideas directly from customers. They can also be used by communities of customers to build upon designs created by other customers. As a result, new product development is not just limited to individual customer ideas, but the concept of peer-to-peer customer collaboration is also given expression in such online forums.

## Product and market testing

Firms have a number of options to engage customers in the product and market testing stage, especially in the virtual environment. For example, Nike simply uses the mass-customization approach in its website wherein customers are able to purchase personalized trainers from the website.

At the test and launch stage, members of the virtual community can take on the role of buyers and end users and give the firm feedback on the product after virtual presentations and simulations. Internet-based stock markets or experimental markets for product concepts are other opportunities to integrate community members in the product launch and test stage.

Google has recently started to rely on user experience groups to figure out what web surfers like and the aim is to determine what changes make the service easier to use. The company has recently launched this strategy in Japan where it has introduced the Google Mobile Marketing strategy to gauge real-time feedback on service experience from customers.

---

### Short case 8.3

#### Google mobile marketing in Japan

A relative newcomer to Japan's mobile market, Google is in the unfamiliar position of being the underdog in everything from maps to videos to blogs. But not for long. Google is working with the two leading Japanese wifi operators, which have a combined subscriber base of 82m. In January the firm announced a partnership in mobile ads, search, email, photos, and YouTube videos with NTT DoCoMo, the number one Japanese telecoms carrier. And since 2006, Google and the number two carrier KDDI have cooperated on text » ads and on developing a better mobile search engine. 'Our fundamental strategy is to take ideas from Japan and apply them to other markets,' says Emmanuel Sauquet, who oversees Google's relations with mobile carriers in Asia.

To determine what mobile web surfers like, the company relies on user experience groups, or 'UX' in Google-ese. Dozens of participants are given phones with Internet access and asked to complete simple tasks, either in a company lab or out on the streets of Tokyo. 'We'll tell them: find me a restaurant for tonight in Shibuya, and we just watch,' says Sauquet. At other times, Google conducts what it calls '1 per cent tests', in which a small portion of users see different layouts, fonts, and other features on Google pages.

The aim is to determine what changes make the service easier to use. For instance, Google has found that letting users choose a default neighbourhood can make their search queries faster. And while Americans raved when Google launched a mobile version of maps last August, the Japanese criticized it for being too slow and hard to navigate. So maps now load faster and feature arrows along each side that make it easier to change the map view. Software engineer Ken Wakasa observed: 'People's expectations are very high here compared to other regions. That's why we get good feedback.' Another lesson is that the information people are looking for can change with the season or news events. Last July, the mobile search site was flooded with queries immediately after strong earthquakes shook northern Japan, so the company now automatically posts links to news sites when quakes strike. And during the end-of-year holidays, when Japanese send New Year's greeting cards, Google makes postal code data easy to find.

*Question*

What role are the customers playing in the innovation process here—are they idea generators, concept validators, or final product/market testers? How generalizable will any ideas generated in Japan likely be in delivering innovation to other markets?

# Utilizing user communities for open innovation

As we have seen, e-business innovation is characterized by a growing reliance on 'user-generated content', where the Internet is used to involve interested individuals in the definition and development of new products. This results, as we have suggested, in the democratization of the innovation process. ICT grants individuals with the right skills freer access to the innovation process within the organization. Users tend to innovate collaboratively in communities and the Internet makes this process even more effective.

Community-based open innovation offers a deeper understanding of how customers can be integrated into new product development within an e-business environment. But in order for community-based innovation to be effective, the firm needs to identify the key consumer attributes which will support the innovative company, identify the online community where such customers will be found, design the appropriate interaction pattern with the targeted community in order to gain insights and learn from the development task, and also find appropriate mechanisms to contact the community members.

## Activity box 8.3

### Safeguarding organizations and customers

What are the risks to organizations and customers of open innovation? In particular, given privacy concerns, how can organizations ensure that data generated from online communities represent genuine needs and wants?

## Determining user indicators

In selecting the appropriate customers for virtual innovation, firms need to consider the development task which is to be assigned to the customer community and then aim to find the optimal fit between consumer abilities, their characteristics and the developmental task.

Kozinets (2001, 2002) identifies different kinds of user within the online community and that they vary depending on the types of social ties they keep and their level of involvement within the community. He characterizes them as: 'tourists', lacking strong ties but with short-lived contemporary interest in the topic; 'minglers' who maintain strong social ties but are not that involved with the topic; 'devotees' who are highly involved with the topic but not related to the community; and 'insiders' who are both strongly associated with the community and highly involved in the topic. The users particularly well suited to virtual new product development are those who are devoted, enthusiastic, actively involved, and sophisticated in their interaction within the online community. They typically exhibit what is known as 'lead user' characteristics, their needs are usually ahead of the others in the community, and they also possess in-depth technical knowledge and a general understanding of product functionalities. They share many of the characteristics of the 'early adopters' of the innovation diffusion model.

This was the case with 'Threadless', a community-centred online apparel store run by skinnyCorp, Chicago (http://www.threadless.com). The founder, Jake Nickell, invited his online friends from a web design site called Dreamless.org, where he used to spend hours at a time cruising the forum—talking to his online friends and engaging in a pastime called Photoshop tennis. Photoshop tennis involved designers passing digital photographs back and forth and challenging one another to manipulate images in the most outrageous ways possible. Within the Dreamless.org community, Jake Nickell had a ready base of actively involved dedicated designers when he decided to run the first design competition for Threadless. An innovating company would typically benefit from the insights of such users at the idea generation and concepts stage as well as in designing and engineering. In order to stimulate ideas from the virtual community, firms organize online idea contests and in some cases virtual stock markets to identify qualified community members. For example, members of the Threadless community submit t-shirt designs online; the designs are then put to a public vote. A small percentage of submitted designs are selected for printing and sold through an online store. Creators of the winning designs receive a prize of cash and store credit.

## Identifying the community

Having identified the appropriate user characteristics, firms need to progress to the next step of identifying the appropriate online community with users bearing resemblance to those characteristics. Companies use various mechanisms to identify the appropriate community:

- Companies themselves operate communities which then become the source of potential ideas. For example in Threadless, participation is not just about voting for designs that customers want to buy. It is also an exploration of new ideas. Designers upload their t-shirt designs to the website, where visitors and members of the community score them on a scale of 0 to 5. On average, around 1,500 designs compete in any given week.

- Staff members who are in close contact with relevant communities are also used as a source for identifying the appropriate community. In the case of Threadless, 75 per cent of the company's fifty employees were community members before they were hired.

- Powerful search engines on the Internet are also useful for identifying communities. With the appropriate keywords, search engines can become very useful means of locating newsgroups, chat rooms, bulletin boards, or web portals of topic-related magazines, societies, and clubs.

- To ensure relevance of the community, a careful evaluation of the exchanged content, the degree of professionalism, information regarding traffic, and the total number of participants also need to be evaluated.

- Firms also need to gain sufficient familiarity with the members of the community, the individual community members, their behaviour, and skill level. Members of communities can react very differently to external inquiries—some are pleased to offer their support, others are willing to support subject to certain terms and conditions whilst some may refuse to participate all together. In cases where

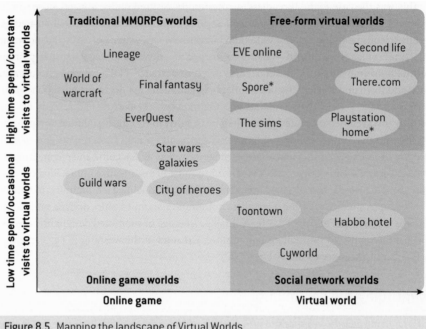

**Figure 8.5** Mapping the landscape of Virtual Worlds

netiquette is available, firms can gauge the extent to which the communities will be receptive to external queries.

For example, Figure 8.5 shows that an understanding of the relationship between different types of virtual world and the amount of time users spend online will be a key determinant of identifying and recruiting a particular community.

## Virtual interaction design

Design of the appropriate virtual interaction is completely contextual. Every virtual interaction needs to be tailored to the participant and the development task transferred to them. A number of design parameters need to be considered in aligning the virtual interaction with the objectives of consumers and producers. These parameters are as follows:

- the intensity of interaction (number of participants, frequency, and duration);
- the level of multimedia richness (animations, virtual product presentations);
- the communication style (formal/informal; one or bi-directional, anonymity of the interacting parties);
- the offered incentives (notation as co-inventor, monetary compensation, fun factor); and
- the applied tools (toolkits, virtual concept testing, idea competitions or discussion forums) (Fuller et al., 2006).

While involving consumers in the virtual design process, firms needs to understand that customers have to be sufficiently motivated to participate. In cases where the motivation is intrinsic and driven by factors like demand for new and better products, curiosity and exploratory search behaviour, acknowledgement and support from the community, or the possibility of getting exclusive information on innovations, users are likely to be more motivated and thereby have a greater impact on new product development. To assume that users can be motivated to participate only by monetary incentives like awarding of bonus points, drawing prizes, or sharing product is unwise. In Threadless, while the winners of the design receive cash awards, other customers are also given credit for referring new buyers and for submitting photos of themselves wearing Threadless shirts.

## User access and participation

Users' awareness needs to be raised well before the onset of the innovation process. Companies often make announcements and share details about impending innovation projects through pop-up windows and banners on relevant websites. Provision also needs to be made for prompt response to queries from users. More importantly, innovators need feedback on their input for the status of their developmental activities and their contributions can be analysed from the first set of results, following which modifications can also be suggested. When community members are integrated virtually into new product development for the first time, it is useful to gather information about their experiences, their willingness to participate again, and their expectations regarding further virtual product development projects. Threadless designers labour mightily on their submissions: they typically spend weeks tinkering with their designs and soliciting advice from other members. Threadless also helps with this—it sends out artists digital submission kits that include HTML code and graphics to help them create professional looking advertisements for their design.

---

### Activity box 8.4

**Online guinea pigs**

Have you or has anyone you know ever participated in online community chats as part of an innovation exercise? How useful were your ideas to the company concerned? Did you enjoy the experience? Were you given feedback on your contributions?

---

# E-business innovation and the distribution of economic activities

The increasing influence of the open innovation paradigm has affected the geographical distribution of innovative activities and centres of excellence. Companies that fully understand and implement e-business-enabled strategies have developed the ability to participate in geographically complex international networks as a result of a combination of activities whose centres of excellence may be sited in distant locations.

Since the early 1990s, multinational companies from developed countries and increasingly some advanced developing countries have increased their cross border investments in the field of R&D, including R&D in developing countries. Table 8.2 lists the top ten global companies by R&D expenditure in 2004 and shows how practically all of them have established research facilities in developing countries. These research facilities have become the focus of technology development for local, regional, and increasingly global markets. Since ICT enables faster cross-border knowledge, dissemination particularly within transnational corporations, it helps to improve their capacity to combine disparate technologies in new applications.

# E-innovation in public-sector organizations

Innovation in public services is essential for meeting the economic and social challenges of the twenty-first century. In line with endogenous innovation theory, education, health, and transport provide the underpinning for all innovative activity. There is also a growing demand amongst public service users for more efficient services as well as for services that are personalized to their needs. According to the UK's Department for Business Enterprise and Regulatory Reform (BERR), meeting the challenges of the twenty-first century will depend increasingly on innovative solutions that raise standards, meet new objectives,

**Table 8.2  Geographical distribution of R&D facilities of the top ten R&D companies in 2004**

| Company | Home Country | Locations of R&D facilities | Newest locations |
|---|---|---|---|
| Microsoft | United States | US (3), China, India, UK | India |
| Pfizer | United States | US (5), Canada, China, France, Japan | China |
| Ford | United States | US, Germany | Germany |
| Daimler Chrysler | Germany | Germany (4), US(4), China, India, Japan | China, Japan |
| Toyota | Japan | US(2), Europe (2), Australia, Thailand | Thailand |
| General Motors | United States | 11 centres including in Australia, Brazil, China, Germany, Korea, Mexico, Sweden and US | Germany, Sweden |
| Siemens | Germany | 150 centres in 30 countries | China, India, Russian Federation |
| Matsushita Electric | Japan | 10 sites in the US and centres in Canada, China, Europe and Malaysia | China |
| IBM | United States | US(4), China, India, Israel, Japan, Switzerland | India |
| Johnson & Johnson | United States | Australia, Belgium, Brazil, Canada, China, France, Spain, Switzerland, UK and US | United States |

and improve efficiency. A better service for citizens and businesses and a better return for the taxpayer will require innovation across a range of activities, including incremental innovation to improve existing services by using new technologies to improve access and responsiveness, as well as 'self directed' services that will give users much greater control in shaping services to their needs.

Privacy issues are a particular challenge for the successful implementation of e-government services. Unless safeguards are put in place, adoption of e-technologies may result in citizens' rights being compromised—such as the right to individual liberty and privacy; the right to influence governmental decision-making—and the loss of control over politicians' decision-making agendas (Zuurmond, 1988; Perri, 2000). Technology is only a tool and the impact of e-technologies cannot be viewed in isolation from social and political decision making.

Innovation in the public sector generally reflects the import of technological solutions provided by private firms and commercial technology providers into public services. Irrespective of the public service to which the innovation is transferred, the basic principles of service delivery such as processes, cooperation, trust, and social acceptance continue to apply in e-service delivery in public services. The basic principles of e-service include processes, cooperation, trust, and social acceptance. These principles apply whether the service is delivered electronically or not.

Halvorsen and Hauknes's five concepts of public-sector innovation incorporate the dimensions of concept, delivery/organization, and products and production processes, all of which are enabled by the adoption of e-business technology (Halvorsen, 2005; Hauknes, 2005):

- Innovation involving *changes in the characteristics and design of service products and production processes*, including development, use, and adaptation of relevant technologies. An example here is the UK's. NHS Direct, a telephone and Internet helpline for health services (http://www.nhsdirect.nhs.uk).

- *Delivery innovations* involving new or altered ways of solving tasks, delivering services, or otherwise interacting with clients for the purpose of supplying specific services. For example, e-government is a new mechanism of delivering government services since it uses websites, PDAs, and other technological artefacts as new customer interfaces for service delivery.

- *Administrative and organizational innovations* involve new or altered ways of organizing activities within the supplier organization. For example, the provision of online tax filing resulted in different ways of organizing the US Internal Revenue Service.

- *Conceptual innovations* involve introducing new missions, new world views, objects, strategies, and rationales. Private–public partnerships between commercial firms and public-sector organizations would be an example of conceptual innovation.

- *System interaction innovation* includes new and improved ways of interacting with other organizations and knowledge bases.

## Short case 8.4

### Activeworlds in education

One of the most innovative public sectors in relation to the adoption of e-business technologies has been education. The University of Colorado has made use of virtual reality provider Activeworlds to deliver *Business Computing Skills 1000,* which is an entry-level, three-credit-hour course required for undergraduate business administration students at the University of Colorado–Boulder (http://www.activeworlds.com). The goal of the course is to foster business computing skills within a business-related context. By using an innovative 3D environment as a context for learning, the designers have created a *place* in which distributed learning is anchored in an environment that is both familiar and engaging. Visual cues such as buildings representing applications afford distance learners an intuitive interface for course structure as well as provide the necessary resources for learning.

The Active Worlds Educational Universe (AWEDU, http://www.activeworlds.com/edu/awedu.asp) is an educational community that makes the Active Worlds technology available to educational institutions, teachers, students, and individual programmes in a focused setting. Via this community, educators are able to explore new concepts, learning theories, creative curriculum design, and discover new paradigms in social learning. In addition to the over eighty educational worlds available in the AWEDU, there are a number of educational worlds in the main Active Worlds Universe where classes are taught, experiments performed, and meetings are held. Activeworlds offers educational pricing packages for institutions interested in hosting virtual worlds in the Active Worlds Universe or within their own intranet servers.

>>

The University of Colorado's curriculum covers a wide range of business-related concepts, such as computer security, information systems, and communication. These concepts are presented in tandem with such program applications as Microsoft Word, Excel, Access, and PowerPoint. Student assignments consist of weekly individual exercises designed to provide students with basic business-computing skills ranging from résumé writing to creating relational databases. In addition to these weekly assignments, students are required to participate in four collaborative group projects in which they apply and integrate their newly acquired skills into various projects that address several of the concepts covered in the curriculum. Although the course design for the university is primarily asynchronous for the individual assignments, group assignments require students to meet and interact synchronously to collaborate. For the individual assignments, the virtual world provides the interface and context for the course. Students move from building to building to complete the assignments. They are able to submit assignments, review grades, and send and receive feedback online by way of the Active Worlds integrated web browser. Students collaborate on group projects by meeting in arranged meeting areas (patios) and by using the chat tool for communication.

*Question*
What kind of public sector innovation is Activeworld's 'e-learning ecosystem'?

## E-government initiatives

Government bodies—whether local or national—increasingly portray themselves as 'enlightened providers' of public services, using information technology to market themselves to their community base in a new climate that has been termed 'citizen-centric'. (See, for example, Long case 1.1 on Canada in chapter 1.) More than ever before, citizens are aware of their rights as customers of government. They demand best value services, which is convenient, accessible, and responsive to their needs. The challenge for government in meeting such demands is to achieve integration between front-office service delivery and back-office fulfilment efficiently and effectively to connect citizens to government services. E-business technologies have begun to transform the nature of service delivery and resulted in many innovations.

The adoption of e-business technology by governments is therefore not primarily a technical exercise, but a fundamental attempt to improve the political and social environment in which they operate, as chapter 6 also suggested. The main purpose of adopting such technologies in governmental service delivery is to provide alternative forms of citizenship, different patterns and trends of relationship and power, and alternative approaches for connecting people to the political process.

E-government services have a number of objectives including prompt, accurate service, improved quality of service, removing barriers to access, and tackling social exclusion. Typical examples of national and local government e-business initiatives include the following:

- providing access: making information accessible to citizens;
- connection to a process or service: providing information or access to government ICT-based systems, information management solutions, and web-based services;

- raising awareness: providing information on the political process, services, and options that are available for the decision-making process;
- facilitating consultation or communication: initiating and developing the means of capacity building, exchanging prior gained experiences, access to experts, and other information and knowledge of mutual interest;
- encouraging active citizen involvement: in some cases e-government services also encourage citizens to become involved in government decision making, problem solving, and the election process.

---

### Activity box 8.5

**Fit for purpose?**

Examine the website of the UK Home Office at http://www.homeoffice.gov.uk/. How far does the site meet the objectives identified above?

---

Innovative e-government services are largely delivered via websites. Three categories of site can be identified:

- *Portals*: primarily designed as an information repository. Customers have access to information about products and services. Portals are static sources of information with no interactive element.
- *Market makers*: act as a platform and delegated delivery agent through a pan-governmental service utility. They facilitate the transactions that occur between the citizens and the governmental agencies while not providing any services themselves. In providing this service, they guarantee security and trust in the business transaction.
- *Product/service providers*: they feature owner delivery or shared delivery through integration. They deal with the customers directly and take responsibility for the delivery standards and the resultant impact on the brand name of the governmental agency.

## Measuring the effectiveness of e-government initiatives

Unlike the commercial sector, where the success of innovation can be measured through increased market share, profitability, or efficiency gains, measuring the effectiveness of e-government initiatives is rather less straightforward. The effectiveness of e-government initiatives is assessed largely by the extent to which they serve the needs of the customers. Targets are often employed to minimize such issues as social exclusion, but the acceptance of citizen-users is usually a more reliable measure of success.

Citizens are usually more receptive to e-government services which relate to matters affecting their rights or duties, failure to comply with which results in punitive actions. For example, research into the effectiveness of e-government services of Taiwan examined the case of e-tax-filing, where the government put in place an innovative 'declaration-free' tax-payment system, while also making available to the public systems for database queries and calculations (Wen and Cheng, 2007). As a result, citizens no longer had to declare their taxes—the government simply used appropriate technologies to assist the public in calculating payments. This was an e-service which not only provided static information to citizens about the declaration of taxes but assisted them in going through the entire process of calculating and paying the taxes as well, and was well received.

By contrast, when the e-government service was limited to downloading formerly hard copy forms for completion, the service was only partially beneficial as it failed to make complete use of the special nature of the Internet to satisfy user needs and provide genuine practical convenience to the citizens. However, just like firms, the public sector has to be careful not to get too far ahead of its users. The Taiwanese government also introduced the provision of e-tuitions for university students in Taipei. The uptake of this service was not high and the conclusion was that citizens were not ready to give up their habits in favour of this new integrated service delivery channel. Further, taking e-tuitions was not obligatory on the part of citizens: it was simply a new delivery channel and unlike the e-tax-filing system there were no punitive actions associated with failure to use it.

E-government initiatives are generally more effective when they relate to services that customers are legally obliged to fulfil, and when the e-service provides an integrated platform from which the citizens can access successfully all the stages related to completion of the service. Local government and front line delivery bodies are a rich source of innovation in public services. Newham Council in East London is an example of local government leading the development of a new, single, and integrated approach to support and review innovation at a local level.

## Short case 8.5

### Newham Council: an innovator and leader in local government

Newham is a borough in East London, which has an annual budget of £261 million, and delivers around 500 services to a population approaching 250,000 people. With over eighty main information systems in place, dealing with around 50m paper records and over 30m images, the borough's mayor has identified integrated information management as a key factor in the cost-effective delivery of services. As a result, the council is seeking to develop a more corporate digitized approach to records management with a comprehensive information asset list, managed by a unified back office in Docklands. Newham's goal is to be 'the leading UK centre for information and communication technologies in terms of both its commercial exploitation and its use to benefit the local community'.

»

Residents of the council can access a variety of council and non-council services online: pay their Council Tax or apply for secondary school admissions, request a bulk waste collection, check planning permissions. A very comprehensive set of information can also be accessed from the Newham Council website, including a list of primary and secondary schools where residents can seek to admit their children and information on job opportunities within the council. Residents of the council also have the opportunity to report a wide range of issues such as street problems or missed domestic waste collections online with the 'Report It' forms available to be downloaded from the Council's website.

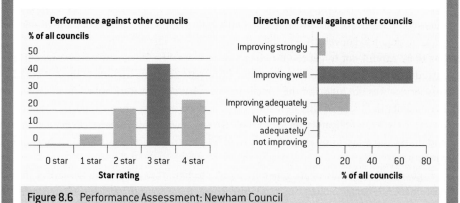

**Figure 8.6**  Performance Assessment: Newham Council

In addition, Newham has introduced a number of new services, including a service, delivered by text, which alerts users to high levels of air pollution in the borough. This enables those at risk of, for example, asthma, to manage their exposure to poor-quality air. The council also runs Newham Neighbourhood Information Management System (NIMS), an online central data repository that enables local strategic partners (LSP) to share data. NIMS partners include the the London Borough of Newham, the Metropolitan Police, the London Fire Brigade, Newham University Hospital NHS Trust, and Newham Primary Care Trust, amongst others. Various users such as partnership agencies, voluntary groups, students, and businesses have also been using NIMS in their research reports and for general interest.

*Question*
Is Newham Council's website classified as portal, market creator, or product-service provider?

## Long case 8.1

### Habbo Hotel

The game development company Sulake Labs launched the first Habbo Hotel in Finland in August 2000. By 2007, Habbo Hotel had 70 million registered accounts. Habbo is an audiovisual chat environment on the web that can be accessed with a web browser with the Shockwave plug-in. Others talk about it as a virtual hotel where one can hang out and make new friends. The unique selling point of Habbo, compared with other virtual worlds, is that it is intended for teenagers, since one's avatar is a boy or a girl—not a grown-up. Habbo is fairly easy to start, since it is not a separate program, but works within the web browser. Also, one does not have to choose lots of character capabilities or attributes for one's avatar, just gender and clothes. Habbo has no subscription fee, which is usually difficult for teenagers to pay; it is free to chat, but some extra hotel services cost money. Users have to follow the 'Habbo Way', which basically means being nice and polite, and not swearing nor cheating, which is far from the 'anything goes' attitude of other virtual environments. Once a member, each Habbo character has access to a Habbo Console. This enables them to keep track of other friends using the service and to communicate through an instant message, WAP browser, SMS, or email.

All of this is done without sharing e-mail addresses or mobile phone numbers. In addition to the furniture graphics, users can also buy logos for their mobile phones, which are sent as SMS text messages to the phones. Users can earn Habbo credits worth 10p each, by designing mobile phone logos which other users subsequently buy. But the virtual cheese plants and mobile phone logos are not the site's only form of revenue. It also earns money from advertising, sponsorship, and from market research, allowing brands to access its user base to conduct ad hoc research projects. In a recent project, Heinz used the site to »

help it decide between two alternative names for a new pizza brand, soliciting thousands of responses in the space of just a few days.

When checking in to the virtual hotel one creates one's own cartoon-like Habbo avatar that can walk, dance, eat, drink, and chat in the cafés, restaurants, swimming pools, and games rooms. The virtual hotel allows users to create their own private rooms and kit them out with funky furniture, socialize with friends old and new, swap gossip, send SMS messages to friends, and design and buy mobile logos.

Habbo Hotel's official fansite suggests that the Habbo characters can be divided into four groups—they are furniture-traders, competitive players, VIPs, and chatters. One of the most popular activities on the website is that users can design their guest room to imitate anything. They enjoy designing to rooms to imitate, for instance, popular TV shows like 'Who wants to be a Millionaire', or just arranging a quiz, or bingo. Other popular events have been Miss Habbo beauty contests. Some just do it for fun, others participate in or create games to get more furniture.

In 2008, Habbo generated about $100m in revenue, 75 per cent of which came from teenage users buying virtual furniture to fit out their private rooms in the Habbo Hotel. The remainder came from advertisers. Big-name advertisers such as Nike, Adidas, Nintendo, Kraft, Sony, Wrigley, and Johnson & Johnson have been spending to reach Habbo users with marketing efforts. Habbo is looking to expand its global teen reach—it has about 9m users—to older audiences although it is acutely aware of start-ups looking to poach its users. According to Jeff Brookes, Sulake's Asia-Pacific regional director 'It's the brightest star in the online sector in terms of development and where people see the future.' According to him, 'for Habbo, once the users hit 17 they pretty much drop off. It's why there are 200 virtual worlds in development . . . everyone is trying to get another one going that will catch them at 17 and catch them again after that.'    »

*Questions*

1. What are the unique characteristics of Habbo Hotel? How is it different from Second Life?

2. To what extent does Habbo Hotel encourage collaborative customer innovation? How can marketers utilize the insights gained from Habbo Hotel?

## Long case 8.2

### Microsoft Live Anywhere

Gaming has become an integral part of the computer and consumer electronics economy. In keeping with the ever-rising popularity of the gaming industry, Bill Gates introduced the Microsoft Live Anywhere project at the E3 2006 game industry convention at Los Angeles. As part of the Vista upgrade to Windows, this platform would be seen to extend the Xbox 360 Live gaming community across web and wireless. Mobile users would be able to access game-accounts data and manipulate characters or vehicles and weapons at play in a user's console game. They could even play mini-games attached to a game they play in their living rooms. Microsoft's plans were that within the launch window of Windows Vista, players would be able to have a common identity between the two platforms.

According to Chris Early, studio manager for Microsoft Casual Games:

'we have 25 to 30 million people playing monthly on all of Microsoft's different game services. What Live Anywhere is doing is bringing them all together so that there is one common identity for you as a gamer across all of those different platforms. That is the "Anywhere" portion. That is why mobile is an important part of the announcement, because it is about how we extend the gaming experience of those 25–30 million people out into the mobile environment.'

»

Early brought out a mobile phone, and upon starting up the Live Anywhere interface it showed what games were available on the phone, as well as information about those games that the user might find important, such as high score, unlocked achievements, the player's Gamerscore, and the next person on the player's list of friends to beat at that particular game, regardless of platform. That last portion is the key to what Microsoft is attempting to do with Live Anywhere—to build and extend a player's community so that it is not restricted to a given platform. 'What is important to me is the people I play with on a regular basis,' said Early. 'Where do I stack up compared to them?' He also commented that Microsoft is working on a way for users to download a game once and have access to it on just one platform, or across all platforms, with a different download fee assigned depending on the choice made by the user.

Early then showed an example of pulling up a potential download of the popular puzzle game Luxor on the mobile phone. However, using Live Anywhere another set of download options appeared on the screen.

> 'We could download this to our phone, or we could turn around and download the demo version of Luxor to our Xbox 360 or to our Vista machine as well. This is essentially turning your phone into a remote control device, giving you contact with other platforms as well.'

Another feature of Live Anywhere is what is called an Alert, which allows a player to be informed once content for a specific game is available for download. Once a download is available, the user is notified on their mobile phone, prompting them to download the new content, such as a new map, for example. Live Anywhere is smart enough not to download the content to the phone, however, but rather to the places where it knows the user has the game installed. Early did note that if, for example, the user's Xbox 360 or Vista PC is not turned on at the time, the download will simply be scheduled, and will commence once the machine is powered on and connected to Live Anywhere.

The benefits of Live Anywhere were shown for the casual user, as well as the more traditional, or hardcore type of game player. For example, Early's daughter was demonstrated to be having trouble completing a crossword puzzle game on the PC, and she sent a message to her father for help. Early responded by completing the word she was having trouble with in her game, and sending that information back to her using his mobile phone. Another example was shown again with Shadowrun, wherein a member of Early's clan unlocked an achievement, and upon being notified on his mobile phone, he was able to watch a video of the achievement being earned.

'This is a capability we give the developers to allow players to stay connected,' said Early. 'Additionally, if you have a video-capable phone, and the game supporting it, you    » can actually spectate that game from your phone as well.' He also commented: 'I think the most interesting side of this is going to come from the game creators. We' giving them the platform to be creative with, and that's what I really want to see.'

*Questions*

1. Relate the value created from a product like Microsoft Live Anywhere to the concepts of innovation introduced in the chapter.

2. Over three years after Bill Gates' announcement, Live Anywhere has yet to really make its mark. Why?

## ⭐ Chapter Summary

The chapter began by highlighting macroeconomic and organizational perspectives on innovation with the aim of developing a comprehensive view of the concept. The next section of the chapter placed product and service innovation in e-business into context. The aim was to highlight the external and internal environmental factors which make e-product and e-service innovation more tenable in some cases than others. Modular products such as digital products and video games which allow partial or complete conversion were identified as ideal for e-innovation. Customer collaboration was discussed as a key component of e-innovation—real-time customer innovation and elicitation of social knowledge from customers were identified as integral aspects of customer collaboration. Another distinguishing feature of e-product and e-service innovation was community-based open innovation. The key attributes required for creating an online social space which would then become a repository of customer centric information were outlined. The various stages associated with determining user indicators, identifying the community and designing virtual interaction were discussed in detail.

The chapter then examined the various dimensions of public-sector e-innovation. A typology of e-business innovation in the public sector was developed and the nature of e-government initiatives explored. The chapter pointed out that e-government initiatives are most effective in the case of services which the citizens are legally obliged to fulfil.

## ❓ Review questions

1. What are the differences between the macroeconomic and organizational perspectives on innovation?

2. What is the context for e-product and e-service innovation?

3. What are the stages associated with e-product and e-service innovation?

4. Discuss the distinguishing features of e-product and e-service innovation. Elaborate your answer with examples.

5. Identify the distinguishing features of open innovation.

6. What are the stages associated with open innovation?

7. What are the possible objectives of public-sector engagement with e-business technologies?

8. What are the challenges associated with the measurement of public-sector innovation effectiveness?

## Ｏ Discussion questions

1. 'User driven' innovation is becoming the norm in e-business innovation. How will companies derive and sustain competitive advantage if they all begin to use the likes of Habbo Hotel and Coke Studio to gain consumer insight?

2. Traditional marketing uses data collected from market research to assist in the innovation process. E-innovation uses community websites to gain insights into consumer behaviour—what is the difference (if any at all) in these two methods of data collection for new product and new service development.

3. The resource-led view of the firm suggests that companies should be inward looking during the innovation process and align organizational resources closely to new product and service development. Do you think such a view of innovation would be relevant in e-businesses?

4. How would companies adapt collaborative customer-led innovation to a global business environment and capture the cultural nuances in e-product and e-service innovation? Discuss with examples.

5. Given the varied levels of e-readiness and the digital divide identified in chapters 1 and 4, what would be the most appropriate ways of advancing public sector innovation?

## ➔ Suggestions for further reading

Arakji, R.Y. and K.R. Lang, (2007), 'Digital Consumer Networks and Producer-Consumer Collaboration: Innovation and Product Development in the Digital Entertainment Industry', in *Proceedings of the 40th Hawaii International Conference on Systems Sciences*.
This paper examines new forms of collaboration between producers and consumers that are emerging in the digital entertainment space. Taking the case of the video-game industry, the authors demonstrate how firms have successfully engaged in outsourcing parts of their game design and development process to digital consumer networks. It is a good paper for an insight into the nuances of open innovation

BERR, *Innovation Nation* (March 2008) Department for Innovation, Universities and Skills—Report presented by the Secretary of State for BERR.
This paper presents the case for a much closer relationship between policies to promote innovation and policies to facilitate the adoption and use of ICT by enterprises. It highlights that innovation policy frameworks that fully take into consideration the changes generated by ICT must give prominence to open approaches to innovation. The paper suggests how policies can support open innovation and discusses the general environmental conditions that are necessary for the development of open innovation.

Chafkin, M., (2008), 'The Customer is the Company', http://www.inc.com/magazine/20080601/the-customer-is-the-company.html.

This article is an overview of the inception, growth and development of Threadless, a community-centred online apparel store run by Skinny Corporation of Chicago, Illinois. Threadless churns out dozens of new items every month with no advertising, professional designers, sales force, or distribution.

Von Hippel, E., (2005) 'Democratizing Innovation', http://web.mit.edu/evhippel/www/democ1.htm
Democratizing Innovation's main message is that 'lead users' are a great source of innovations', 'Lead users' are the users with the most advanced needs. The logic behind this phenomenon is that lead users will innovate because they cannot find the products or services that meet their advanced needs. Therefore, they themselves will develop the tools they need, as it would be too time-consuming to convince suppliers to develop them. Also, since they only intend to use these innovations, not to sell them, they have an incentive to share their solutions with other users, especially if they think others may share similar innovations with them. This book is an interesting insight into the 'niche' aspects of user-driven innovation.

Wen, J. and Cheng, L., (2007), 'Innovation in e-Government Initiatives: New Website Service Interfaces and Market Creation—The Taiwan Experience', *Management of Engineering and Technology*, 5–9 August, pp. 2799–806.

This paper applies the principles of innovation studies to the Taiwan government's use of the Internet. Taiwan has employed the Internet as an enabler to speed up public services online and has earned a top ranking worldwide for its achievements. This paper identifies Taiwan's major e-government projects, which include e-tax-filing, e-housekeeping, etc., and stakeholders in these e-initiatives, including technology providers, heads of project, IT staff, and domain experts. This paper contributes to innovation studies by describing the proactive potential of service innovation in e-government initiatives.

# → References

Abernathy, W.J., and Clark, K.B., (1985), 'Innovation: Mapping the Winds of Creative Destruction', *Research Policy*, 14, pp. 3–22.

Afuah, A., (2003), *Innovation Management: Strategies, Implementations and Profits*, OUP.

Arakji, R.Y. and K.R. Lang, (2007), 'Digital Consumer Networks and Producer–Consumer Collaboration: Innovation and Product Development in the Digital Entertainment Industry', *Proceedings of the 40th Hawaii International Conference on Systems Sciences*.

Asgarkhani, M., (2002), 'e-Governance in Asia Pacific', *Proceedings of the International Conference on Governance in Asia*, Hong Kong.

BERR, (2008), 'Innovation Nation', Department for Innovation, Universities and Skills—*Report* presented by the Secretary of State for BERR

Booz Allen Hamilton, (2005), *The Booz Allen Hamilton Global Innovation 1000: Money Isn' Everything*, by Barry Jaruzelsky, Kevin Dehoff, and Rakesh Bordia, http://www.boozallen.com/media/file/151786.pdf.

Brohman, M.K., Watson, R.T., Piccoli, G., and Parasuraman, A., (2003), 'Data Completeness: A Key to Effective Net-Based Customer Service Systems,' *Commun, ACM*, 46(6), pp. 47–51.

Chafkin, M., (2008), 'The Customer is the Company', http://www.inc.com/magazine/20080601/the-customer-is-the-company.html.

Chesbrough, H., (2003), *Open Innovation: The New Imperative for Creating and Profiting from Technology* Harvard Business School Press.

Füller, J., Bartl, M., Ernst, H. and Mühlbacher, H., (2006), 'Community Based Innovation: How to Integrate Members of Virtual Communities into New Product Development', *Electronic Commerce Research*, 6, pp. 57–73.

Gershenson, J.K., Prasad, G.J. and Zhang, Y., (2003), 'Product Modularity: Definitions and Benefits', *Journal of Engineering Design*, 14(3), pp. 295–313.

Gopalakrishnan, S. and Damanpour, F., (1997), 'A Review of Innovation Research in economics, Sociology and Technology', *Omega*, 25(1), pp. 15–28.

Grossman, G.M. and Helpman, E., (1991), 'Quality Ladders and Product Cycles', *Quarterly Journal of Economics*, 106, pp. 557–86.

Gustafsson, A. & Johnson, D., (2003), Competing in a service Economy: how to create a competitive advantage through service development and Innovation. San Francisco: Jossey-Bass.

Halvorsen, T., (2005), 'On Innovation in the Public Sector, in T. Halvorsen, J. Haulnes, I. Miles, and R. Roste (eds), *Innovation in the Public Sector: On the difference between Public and Private Sector Innovation*, Publin Report No. D9.

Hauknes, J., (2005), 'Some Thoughts about Innovation in the Public and Private Sector Compared, in T. Halvorsen, J. Haulnes, I. Miles, and R. Roste (eds), *Innovation in the Public Sector: On the difference between Public and Private Sector Innovation*, Publin, Publin Report No. D9.

Henderson, R.M. and Clark, J., (1990), 'Architectural Innovation', *Administrative Science Quarterly*, 35, pp. 9–30.

Hristov, L. and Reynolds, J., (2007), *Innovation in the UK Retail Sector*, University of Oxford.

Kozinets, R., (2001), 'Utopian Enterprise: Articulating the Meanings of Star Trek's Culture of Consumption,' *Journal of Consumer Research*, 28, pp. 67–88.

Kozinets, R., (2002), 'The Field behind the Screen: Using Netnography for Marketing Research in Online Communications', *Journal of Marketing Research*, 39(1), pp. 61–72.

Mowery, D. and Rosenberg, N., (1978), 'The Influence of market Demand upon Innovation: A Critical Review of Some Recent Empirical Studies', *Research Policy*, 8 (2), pp. 102–53.

Nelson, R.R. and Winter, S.G., (1977), 'In Search of Useful Theory of Innovation', *Research Policy*, 6(1), pp. 36–76.

NESTA, (2007), *Hidden Innovation: How Innovation Happens in Six 'Low Innovation' Sectors*, Research Report, June, NESTA.

Penrose, E., (1961), *The Theory of the Growth of the Firm*, Blackwell.

Perri, A., (2000), 'E-governance: Weber's Revenge?', *Proceedings of the Annual Conference of the Political Studies Association*, LSE, 10–13 April, p. 5.

PICMET, (2007), 'Interfaces and Market Creation—The Taiwan Experience', *PICMET 2007 Proceedings*, 5–9 August, Portland, Oregon.

Romer, P.M., (1990), 'Endogenous Technological Change', *Journal of Political Economy*, 98(5), pp. S71–S102.

Schumpeter, J.A., (1912), *Theorie der Wirtschaftlichen Entwicklung*, Duncker & Humboldt.

Schumpeter, J.A., (1934), *The Theory of Economic Development: An Inquiry into Profits, Capital, Credit, Interest and the Business Cycle*, Harvard University Press.

Schumpeter, J.A., (1939), *Business Cycles: a Theoretical, Historical and Statistical Analysis of the Capitalist Process*, McGraw-Hill.

Solow, R.M., (1956), 'A Contribution to the Theory of Economic Growth', *Quarterly Journal of Economics*, 70(1), pp. 65–94.

Tidd, J. and Hull, F. (eds), (2003), *Service Innovation: Organisational Responses to Technological Opportunities and Market Imperatives*, Imperial College Press.

Tornatzky, L.G. and Fleischer, M., (1990), *The Process of Technological Innovation*, Lexington Books.

Tushman, M.L. and Anderson, P., (1986), 'Technological Discontinuities and Organizational Environments', *Administrative Science Quarterly*, 31, pp. 439–65.

UNCTAD (2008) Information Economy Report 2007–2008, *Science and Technology for Development: The New Paradigm of ICT*, UNCTAD.

Van Ark, B., Broersma, L., and den Hertog, P., (2003), 'On the Soft Side of Innovation: Services Innovation, Performance and Its Policy Implications' *De Economist*, 151, pp. 433–52.

Von Hippel, E,. (2005), 'Democratizing Innovation', http://web.mit.edu/evhippel/www/democ1.htm.

Wen, J. and Cheng, L., (2007), 'Innovation in e-Government Initiatives: New Website Service Interfaces and Market Creation—The Taiwan Experience', *PICMET 2007 Proceedings*, 5–9 August, Portland.

Zaltman, G. and Dunken, R., (1973), *Innovation and Organizations*, John Wiley.

Zhang, X. and V.R. Prybutok, (2005), 'A Consumer Perspective of E-Service Quality,' *IEEE Transactions on engineering management*, 52(4), pp. 461–77.

Zuurmond, A., (1988), 'From Bureaucracy to Infocracy: Are Democratic Institutions Lagging Behind?', *Public Administration in an Information Age: A Handbook*, IOS Press, pp. 259–72.

## 🔗 Weblinks

Fluevog. This company is based in Vancouver, British Columbia, and has shops in nine major cities in the world. The designer, Mr Fluevog, solicits ideas on shoes and their style from customers, encouraging brand enthusiasts to submit their own sketches for weather boots, high-heeled dress shoes, even sneakers with flair. He posts the submissions on his company's website (http://www.fluevog.com/files 2/os-1.html), invites visitors to vote for their favourites and manufactures and sells the most promising designs: http://www.fluevog.com.

Forum Nokia. Forum Nokia offers a wealth of resources to help design, build, test, certify, market, and sell or promote your applications, content, services, or website to mobile users. Community members can develop mobile applications, mobilize websites, get design ideas, find out about testing, signing, and technical support and also go to the market with the applications they develop: http://www.forum.nokia.com.

Jonessoda. A fast-growing soft-drink company based in Seattle, which does not rely on customers to invent new drinks or to reinvent existing lines, but instead relies on them to infuse the company's brand image and retail presence and exercise their voice in shaping a message in the marketplace. Its website displays a selection of images that have been sent by mail or email to Seattle: http://www.jonessoda.com.

**Tech Café.** To support knowledge sharing, the motorcycle company Ducati has created the 'Tech Café','a forum for exchanging technical knowledge. In this virtual environment, fans can share their projects for customizing motorcycles, provide suggestions for improving Ducati's next-generation products, and even post their own mechanical and technical designs: http://www.ducati.com/bikes/techcafe.jhtml.

# Reshaping business processes

## Learning outcomes

Completing this chapter will enable you to:

- Understand the main principles underlying efficient operational processes, supply chains and networks and their relevance to an organization's overall business performance

- Appreciate the ways in which such processes can be supported, developed and restructured by the Internet

- Gain specific insights into the features of electronic procurement and trends in the sourcing of goods and services by firms

- Understand the growing importance of information sharing and collaboration as a means of driving supply chain integration

- Appreciate the characteristics and consequences of both outsourcing and off-shoring of business processes by firms.

## Introduction

'Technology has an impact of some sort in almost every area of operations management.'
*Slack et al., 2006*

Unlike new or improved products and customer-facing services, new or improved operational business processes within and between firms are less visible to the casual observer. They are nevertheless critical to successful business performance. Sometimes it is only when processes fail that they become an issue—for example when supermarket on-shelf product availability falls below acceptable levels. Or when measures aimed at improving the efficiency of business processes result in a reduction of perceived effectiveness by customers, as for example has emerged in the extensive use of overseas call centres by some organizations. Or where their introduction raises wider social issues—in terms for example of de-skilling, or the loss of jobs through the development of new technology—that business processes themselves attract scrutiny. As market environments become increasingly turbulent and dynamic, the particular contributions that Internet technologies can make to business processes become more and more important to firms, but similarly their impact on the way the organization functions can also be more significant.

Process improvements can take place between firms as well as within firms. Whilst successful application of e-business thinking takes place through the effective integration of digital technologies into the business processes and systems within firms, the nature of the Internet means that it is process restructuring within the networks of suppliers, customers, and other collaborators in the value chain upstream of buying firms which have the greatest consequences and the biggest potential gains. However, whether organizations are using e-business to improve internal or inter-firm processes, doing either successfully also presents incumbent firms with some of their biggest challenges. This is because the integration of e-business processes alongside established systems and processes within firms may often require their significant modification or even complete replacement. Processes between firms may be even more difficult to change because they have often been based on custom and practice and the development of bespoke relationships between buyers and sellers. Figure 9.1 summarizes the importance of e-business processes to firms and its impact. By contrast, pure-play firms that are new to markets have no such inhibitions derived from legacy processes and are able to develop the kinds of strategy we have already seen discussed in chapter 7.

This chapter complements the learning in chapters 7 and 8 by identifying the areas in which process improvements through e-business technologies can be achieved, looking at their impact on existing operations management activities, supply chains, and networks. It focuses particularly upon the evolving role of e-procurement and e-collaboration and undertakes a detailed examination of the way in which Internet technologies have facilitated the growth of off-shoring and outsourcing of business processes of many kinds. In part three of the book, some of the specific organizational implications that arise from these developments are explored more directly. Organizational challenges can be found in areas such as project management, in securing appropriately skilled employees, or in creating the right kind of business culture to allow the successful implantation or evolution of business processes.

# E-business and operations management principles

The business processes with which we are concerned are those which convert various kinds of input (whether these are tangible or intangible) into outputs (products or

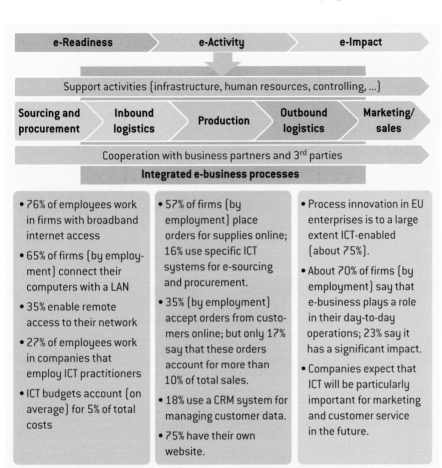

**Figure 9.1** The impact of e-business on European supply chains

services, or a mixture of the two). The overall management of this activity by an individual firm is referred to as **operations management**, whilst its co-ordination between firms is often referred to as **supply chain management**. Look at Figure 9.2 which outlines the principles of operations management and the ways in which processes convert input to outputs. Think about how this transformation might be different for particular kinds of organizations.

The transformation of tangible inputs can conventionally refer to material goods or components, but can also include customers, especially in service organizations. For example, airlines 'process' passengers (sometimes using not dissimilar mechanisms to those used for airfreight). Processes can also transform intangible inputs, such as information. For example, the market research company Ipsos-MORI (http://www.ipsos-mori.com) has used Internet technologies in several ways to transform information: a trade-marked computer-assisted process enhances the conversion of conventional interview data into insight and analysis, a wide range of online data collection is

**Operations Management** Management of the processes which transform inputs such as raw material, information, and labour into outputs in the form of finished goods and services.

**SCM** Supply Chain Management: the co-ordination of business processes between firms.

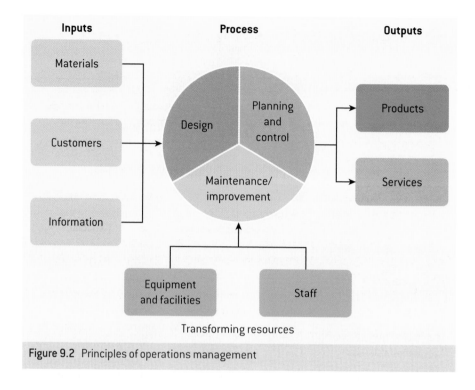

**Figure 9.2** Principles of operations management

undertaken, and the use of mobile phone SMS surveys to achieve a quick survey response for a client has been successfully explored.

Operations management processes themselves can involve three kinds of activity:

- *process design*: designing the layout of the process and the equipment and human resources required to deliver the process;

- *planning and control*: ensuring that business processes run efficiently and effectively in practice;

- *maintenance and improvement*: preventing or reducing failure and continually improving business processes.

A business process will make use of available resources within the organization to transform these inputs into products or services (or some combination of the two). These resources comprise not just the people involved in the process (including the application of their physical labour, alongside their skills and know-how) but also the plant, equipment, technology, or other physical resources that are required for the transformation itself. For example, business consulting firms will use the know-how and expertise of their partners to create value-adding consulting services for their clients through consistent approaches to knowledge management in just the same way as a confectionery manufacturer will employ and refine a particular kind of equipment to ensure the consistency of liquid chocolate delivered to the moulding department.

### Activity box 9.1

What do consultants do?

Access the websites of one or more of the leading management consulting firms. Is it possible to identify some of the business processes used by these firms to offer value to their clients? How are they described? Why might it be difficult to find very detailed descriptions of a consulting firm's business processes published? Are there any similarities between one firm and another in relation to the claims they make about their business processes?

As Figure 9.3 shows, some types of organization tend to focus on processing one kind of input over another and this will of course affect the scale and nature of the process and the capability for that process to be transformed by Internet technologies.

Effective and efficient operations management can deliver competitive advantage to an organization in five ways:

- *quality advantage*: delivering defect free output;
- *cost advantage*: delivering cost efficiency;
- *adaptability advantage*: delivering flexibility in response to changing demand;
- *reliability advantage*: delivering consistency in products and services; and
- *service advantage*: delivering continuous improvement.

Even before the Internet, of course, these processes sought to convert the inputs into goods or services with the aim of satisfying customers' needs in an efficient and effective manner, in line with the advantages described above. But Internet technologies can play their part as transforming resources for operations management processes. Internet technologies used as equipment and facilities can improve the efficiency or even replace the way in which members of staff deal with operations management inputs, transforming existing business processes but also potentially permitting the development of wholly

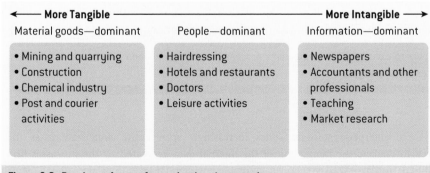

**Figure 9.3** Dominant focus of organizational processing

new ones in support of new products and services For example, airlines have taken advantage of Internet technologies to develop remote check-in processes which work to improve customers' experience of air travel, to provide efficiency gains in the processing of information, as well as to allow the better utilization of customer service staff. Similarly, Internet technologies can permit a retail bank to achieve greater efficiency in the flow of information between its branches, while at the same time allowing it to develop an entirely new process of engaging in secure transactions directly with the retail customer, through the development of Internet banking.

> 'The intensity, focus and impact of e-business depend upon the business activities of companies and on the configuration of the value system in which these companies operate.' *European Commission, 2007*

Applying Internet technologies to business processes is a form of innovation. It has been suggested that the objectives of such innovation can be of three kinds:

- improving the *flexibility* of product or service provision;
- increasing the *capacity* for production or service provision; and
- reducing *costs* per unit produced or provided.

Compare this list with the list above and observe the way in which these three specific objectives relate to the five kinds of competitive advantage that can be delivered by means of efficient and effective operations management.

But the adoption of innovative business processes will not be consistent by size and type of organization. Look at Figure 9.4. This illustrates the extent of process-related innovation amongst selected European firms, organized by sector, in 2005. It also distinguishes between small and large companies processes. Of course, not all process innovation by any means will have been linked to the growth of the Internet. But according to the European Commission's e-Business W@tch research unit, more than 75 per cent of European business process innovation was reported to be ICT-enabled at this time. Larger firms (of 250+ employees) were more likely to have engaged in Internet-related process innovation than smaller. But the figure does give us an indication of which sectors appear to have engaged most in new forms of process innovation.

---

### Activity box 9.2

Contrasts in business process innovation

Look at the data distribution in Figure 9.4. Can you explain some of the differences that appear to exist in terms of business process innovation between different sectors and sizes of company?

---

Large enterprise software suites increasingly span entire organizations as they seek to manage the integration of the internal data generated by the processes firms employ into a unified system, encouraging the standardization of procedures for the input, transformation, and dissemination of data. In addition to customer relationship

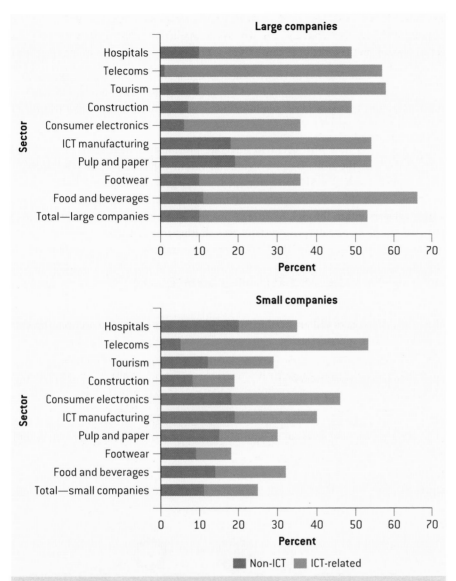

**Figure 9.4** Process-related innovation amongst European firms, 2005.

Question posed to respondents: "In the past twelve months, has your company/organization introduced any new or significantly improved processes, for example for producing or supplying goods and services?" (If so: "Have any of these process innovations been directly related to or enabled by information or communication technology?")

Note: Enterprises using computers. Total includes enterprises from 10 sectors and 10 European countries.

management (CRM) and supply chain management (SCM) applications, so-called enterprise resource planning (ERP) systems encompass at least two or more previously separate systems (such as payroll, inventory, or procurement). From an e-business perspective, ERP systems predate the Internet and have their origins in manufacturing. Indeed, by the late 1990s, it was estimated that some 60 per cent of large companies and 40 per cent of small- and medium-sized companies in the US already had ERP systems in place (Cissna, 1998). Firms have spent significant amounts of time and money in customizing their ERP systems. The worldwide market for ERP systems in 2007 was estimated to be in the order of $32bn.

> 'ERP systems are believed by many to deliver significant cost savings and increased profit to organizations based on reduced procurement costs, smaller inventories, more effective sales strategies, lower administration costs and reduced direct and indirect labour costs.' *Grant et al., 2006*

Figure 9.5 shows how ERP seeks to integrate previously independent systems and processes within the firm. Despite significant recent consolidation activity amongst ERP suppliers (with over $150bn being spent on mergers and acquisitions of over 500 companies from 2003-07), the global ERP market is expected to grow at an estimated 7 per cent per annum through to 2011. A major conclusion of a 2004 industry study was that the focus of enterprise systems was shifting from an internal to an external orientation (Daniel & White, 2005). For many organizations, it is these systems which will provide the context for e-Business investments and it is therefore important to understand the challenges that organizations face in exploiting ERP systems. These are fourfold:

- the rising cost of ERP ownership (the combined costs of fees and licences, together with that of specialist staff);
- the difficulties of use often associated with ERP systems (requiring skilled users to manage complex interfaces);
- A proliferation of business process requirements (the need for greater process flexibility leading to high potential customization costs); and
- the difficulties of integration with other systems (particularly as interoperability becomes more necessary).

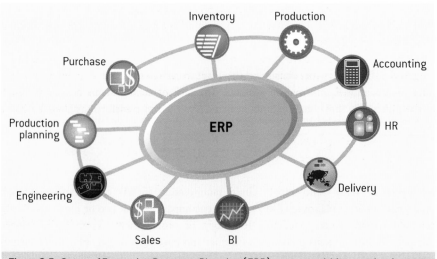

**Figure 9.5** Scope of Enterprise Resource Planning (ERP) systems within organizations

These last two challenges have accelerated with the growth of e-business technologies and we pick up some of the implications of this shift in our later discussion of e-collaboration.

# E-business in supply chains and networks

The growth of the Internet has had a profound effect on the study of supply chains. In looking outside the boundaries of their organizations, managers have always been encouraged to think in a more structured way about how they collaborate with supplier organizations in order to improve the efficiency, effectiveness, and competitiveness of their commercial activities. But the notion of the supply and value chains that date from the work of Michael Porter in the 1980s have come under scrutiny as the business environmental pressures on firms have increased and the pace of change has quickened. No longer can such 'chains' be considered as semi-permanent fixtures for organizations, although the term continues in popular usage. As early as 1990, Walter Powell developed the concept of the extended enterprise, which began the move away from static, hierarchical models of supply activities towards more dynamic, network-based arrangements (Powell, 1990). But in order for such arrangements not to descend into chaos, effective co-ordination and communication is still required.

> **Extended Enterprise** The notion that a company is made up not just of its employees, its board members, and managers, but also its business partners, its suppliers, and even its customers.

Secondly, the hierarchical models that were employed by early thinkers about supply chains (and even the terminology itself) also tended to presuppose the development of tightly coupled relationships between organizations. These were sometimes expensive and time-consuming to establish and maintain, and although they were beneficial in building trust and commitment between the partners, they could also be counter-productive in leading to the growth of what have been called 'domesticated markets' in which all the parties show a reluctance to change 'comfortable' arrangements (Arndt, 1979). The information systems developed to support such relationships tended to be very bespoke—perhaps constructed specifically to meet the needs of this one supply chain. These might well have been satisfactory within stable, slow-changing markets. Firms now need to be able to manage increasingly flexible and agile relationships. More dynamic business environments mean that the links between firms need to be reviewed on a more frequent basis and this leads in turn to the need for more agile, open inter-organizational information systems. The lack of such systems has contributed to the difficulties that some incumbent firms have had in transforming their business processes.

Johnson and Whang (2002) suggest three ways in which the Internet can transform supply chain or network processes:

- *e-commerce*: in helping networks of supply chain partners identify and respond quickly to changing customer demand;
- *e-procurement*: in allowing firms to procure materials and value-added services; and
- *e-collaboration*: in facilitating the co-ordination of activities between the supply chain partners beyond transactions—most notably in terms of information.

Figure 9.6 shows how these three components relate together in what Johnson and Whang call the 'e-enabled firm'.

A further significant shift in the way we think about supply chains has been in relation to their orientation. The traditional supply chain concept has been based on the source of production. Manufacturers procured the raw materials necessary to manufacture a product that had been designed to meet a perceived end user need: a so-called *push supply chain*. The driving force of manufacturing was production efficiency. In a production oriented supply chain, production determined availability and usually equalled sales. In a retail value chain, for example, the manufacturer sold to wholesalers, who in turn supplied independent retailers. A contemporary supply chain, on the other hand, is consumer-oriented. A so-called *pull supply chain* uses the volume of consumer purchases as a surrogate measure of consumption. The two types of supply chain are shown in Figure 9.7. Notice how the direction of flow is different and that there are different characteristics and requirements for the organizations at each stage in the process.

The example Figure 9.7 also suggests that, in order to function, a pull supply chain will have a number of fundamental pre-conditions:

POS  Point-of-sale refers to the location where a transaction occurs, but the technology now conventionally employed to capture a sale can also enable sales management, forecasting, and customer analysis activity to be undertaken.

- point of sale (POS) or reliable and comprehensive user sales data: this provides the 'fuel' driving the whole supply chain and for retail supply chains has only been possible since the widespread introduction of barcode scanning equipment;

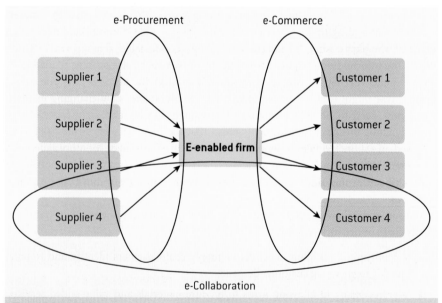

**Figure 9.6**  The impact of e-business on the supply chain

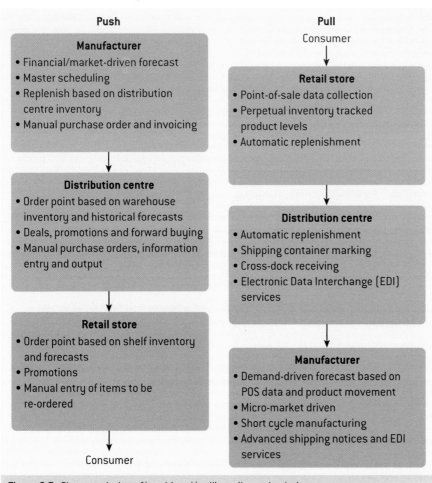

**Figure 9.7** Characteristics of 'push' and 'pull' retail supply chains

- ICT integration of operations: the linking of individual components of distribution and supply;
- data synchronization between the partners: a 'single streamlined gateway' for standardized and constantly synchronized product data;
- visibility: with the level of retail sales visible to all entities within the supply chain.

One of the key technologies to the further development of 'pull' supply chains is radio frequency identification (RFID), using e-tags at the palette or, more usefully, product level. Short case 9.1 outlines the ways in which this might happen, alongside some of the technical and behavioural challenges.

## Short case 9.1

### RFID

It has been suggested that radio frequency identification (RFID) will provide the future enterprise-wide, cross-supply chain technology of the future. The technology can be used to tag palettes or individual products. RFID is being used upstream even if consumer privacy issues have slowed developments downstream. A study published by the influential Advanced Practices Council of the Society for Information Management concluded that RFID and its associated applications provided both process and product improvements, as well as some potentially innovative marketing applications. In terms of process, they concluded that:

- RFID could represent a common standard for data storage and retrieval that could improve collaboration and data sharing.
- Inventories could be reduced, with accompanying cost savings, if electronic tags were used to maximize information flow in the supply chain and minimize physical material flow.
- ultimately, this could give rise to 'intelligent' products modifying transportation routes.

By making goods easier to trace, RFID could also cut waste, out-of-stocks, and shrinkage. Procter and Gamble estimated that between 10 and 16 per cent of its products were out of stock at any one time. In terms of product- and marketing-related advantages, RFID and digital receipt technology could:

- allow manufacturers access to point of sale data to enable the integration of customer preferences into product and distribution processes; and
- through digital receipt technology offer locational and personalized merchandizing opportunities.

But there are also several barriers to be overcome. The APC report cautioned that RFID systems would need to operate across the regulatory boundaries of countries and regions to be effective. Costs have also provided a significant barrier to extending RFID beyond such applications as animal-tracking and road-toll collection. Nor is the technology,  »

as ever, proving completely foolproof. Palette read-rates of 80 per cent or less have been reported because of electromagnetic interference.

*Question*

Do the benefits of RFID outweigh the costs? What is the balance of the argument for palette-level as against product-level tagging?

## E-procurement

'Much of the hype surrounding B2B e-commerce is based on a naïve view of corporate procurement.' *New et al., 2002*

We have already established that the e-business concept goes beyond the *sell-side*, or *downstream* e-commerce that takes place between businesses and consumers (the right-hand side of the diagram in Figure 9.4). In Western Europe alone, the *buy-side* or *upstream* e-commerce market was valued at Euro 1,269bn in 2006: seven times the value of the sell-side market. Even by 2010, this ratio is still forecast to be more than 3.5 times as large.

One of the most widely discussed application areas of Internet technologies for business processes has therefore been in the field of procurement of goods and services by firms—inter-organizational buying and selling. Formerly a 'lowly back-end process', effective procurement is now seen as critical to successful business performance (Hawking et al., 2004). E-procurement is defined by the UK Chartered Institute of Purchasing and Supply as 'using the Internet to operate the transactional aspects of requisitioning, authorizing, ordering, receipting and payment processes for the required services or products'. The benefits of e-procurement over the manual or bespoke handling of buying for organizations include:

- a greater simplification, standardization, and transparency of procurement procedures (leading to a potential reduction in purchasing cycle time or order times)'
- a reduction in duplication of procurement functions and offices (leading to a reduction in costs of operation);
- greater transparency and accountability of decision-making; and the
- potential benefits of scale from consolidation of procurement processes (including a reduction in the number of suppliers, an increase in the number of products supplied by main suppliers, inventory savings, and potential reductions in purchasing price to the end user).

The benefits of e-procurement will also be different for different forms of buying. Whilst organizations buy an enormous range of products, there is an important distinction between the procurement which takes place for raw materials and parts—termed manufacturing or direct input—and that for non-production goods, such as office supplies—termed operational, MRO (maintenance, repair, and overhaul) or indirect input. There is also a distinction to be drawn between sourcing which is systematic and long term, with buyers negotiating contracts with suppliers, and spot sourcing, where companies seek to buy to meet an immediate need, perhaps at the lowest possible cost.

But there are also significant barriers to the development and application of e-procurement processes, not all of which are technical. These include:

- a lack of awareness of and capability to implement e-procurement technologies within the firm;

- a lack of suppliers within a particular marketplace; and

- a resistance to change from traditional purchasing methods. For many firms procurement can be based on strong, well-established relationships between buyers and suppliers. Even after integrating key suppliers, companies may still struggle with low user adoption and costly non-catalogue and off-contract purchases.

Surveys suggest that the barriers we described are still effective in preventing companies engaging in the widespread adoption of integrated e-procurement systems. For example, a survey of thirty-eight major Australian organizations showed that direct procurement was still heavily dependent upon traditional practices whilst indirect procurement was more likely to use e-procurement practices. Small- to medium-sized organizations were also found to be more agile at adopting e-procurement practices. Technical issues dominated e-procurement barriers in Australia, with cost factors dominating e-procurement drivers. Similarly, a relatively small proportion of companies in Europe— some 10 per cent—reportedly used software or Internet-based services as an integral part of their procurement processes in 2006, likely again to be as a result of one or more of these barriers. However, nearly 50 per cent of firms placed at least some orders online, most probably by using the extranets and websites of their suppliers. By running poorly integrated, hybrid procurement processes, of course, such firms would be much less likely to obtain the kinds of benefit outlines above. Nevertheless, the low adoption figures conceal significant variation between sectors (Figure 9.8). The likelihood of placing orders online ranged from over 70 per cent for telecommunications companies to less than 30 per cent for footwear businesses. But there are some sectors—notably shipbuilding and repair and hospital activities—where a high proportion of firms place 25 per cent of more orders online. Adoption of specialist e-procurement software or systems is also a function of company size. Larger companies are much more likely to have deployed such systems than smaller, with as many as 30 per cent of European firms with over 250 employees using a specific e-procurement solution.

## Activity box 9.3

### Patterns of e-procurement

Look at the data in Figure 9.8. Can you explain some of the reasons behind the significant differences between sectors in their likelihood of placing orders online?

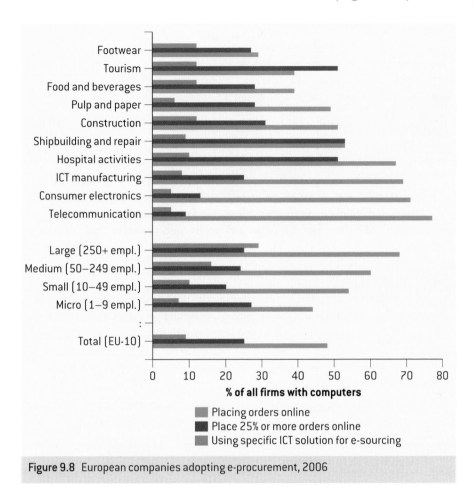

**Figure 9.8** European companies adopting e-procurement, 2006

E-procurement is not a unitary concept, as the definition we have used at the beginning of this section suggests. We can consider e-procurement as having a number of component parts. In practice, these divisions can blur within organizations, but they provide a useful framework within which we can see how the various elements of e-procurement fit together. Figure 9.9 provides one way of dividing up the e-procurement system and we consider each element in turn below.

## E-tendering

Manual tendering is a long and often unwieldy process which can be costly for both buying and selling organizations. E-tendering involves automating a range of activities, from the buyer's preparation of a tender specification, to advertising, to undertaking tender aggregation, to the evaluation and placing of the contract, including the exchange of all relevant documents in electronic format. The e-tendering process is similar to issuing a request for tender (RFT) and can also involve a preliminary request for quotation (RFQ).

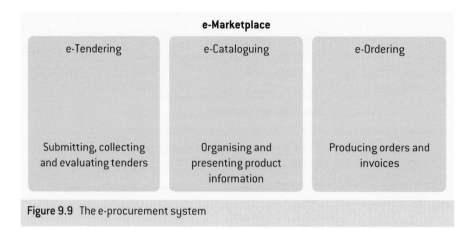

**Figure 9.9** The e-procurement system

E-tendering solutions are usually web-based, which are either hosted on the buyer's own servers (Internet or intranet) or by third-party service providers. Interested parties download the invitation to tender (ITT) and respond with their bids to the buyer, which are then evaluated in a systematic way.

There are five specific sets of benefits to e-tendering over more conventional routes to seeking offers from suppliers:

- *faster* tender process cycle times, including faster responses to questions during the tender period;
- *more accurate* pre-qualification of tenders leading to the early rejection of those not complying with specifications;
- *more efficient* receipting, recording, and distribution of tender submissions; and
- *higher quality and consistency* of tender specification, supplier response, and audit trail of management information.

For example, the London 2012 Olympic Delivery Authority acquired an e-tendering service from BravoSolution (a leading international provider of e-sourcing solutions) to facilitate the efficient procurement of all goods and services to be supplied to the exceptionally complex and challenging London 2012 Olympic Games programme (https://tenders.london2012.com). The e-tendering system allows suppliers to register their interest in supplying the London 2012 programme, permits them to view existing and forthcoming opportunities, and take part in the tender process online.

The effort and cost involved in implementing an e-tendering solution on its own is relatively low, especially in comparison to some more holistic e-ordering systems. For this reason, many e-procurement business service providers see e-tendering as an entry=level application.

## E-cataloguing

Electronic catalogues provide the basis for buyers to search out product information in a more structured manner. They serve to aggregate products in one place and are especially useful for buyers who tend to make small, infrequent, but perhaps also important purchases. By way of illustration, think of industries such as the pharmaceutical industry, where chemists working in research and development (R&D) often need small amounts of reagents, but often need them quite quickly. Price may not be the most important criterion for purchasing under such circumstances, although a supplier which can provide ready availability combined with a good price may win the order.

We can distinguish between two types of e-catalogue:

- a *private, buyer-specific* e-catalogue: a bespoke range of products is made available by a supplier for a buyer on the supplier's externally-facing website, or the buyer's intranet, perhaps offering pre-negotiated prices and terms, or a more specific range of products;

- a *public, buyer-neutral* e-catalogue: where buyers' search costs are high, price volatility is low, and purchase times are critical, it can often be worthwhile for a supplier to establish an extensive online catalogue of its products and services available to all potential buyers.

Consider the example of pharmaceutical company GlaxoSmithKline (GSK), which employs a private e-cataloguing service purchased from SciQuest, a strategic e-procurement services company (http://www.sciquest.com). Seventy R&D supplier catalogues were initially aggregated to provide a total of 720,000 products with price levels set specifically for GSK and real-time product availability for the most important suppliers. Within a year, GSK had increased users' 'contract compliance' (ensuring that users bought from approved suppliers at approved prices, rather than using non-contracted sources) by 35 per cent, and 92 per cent of searches were successful. For a more detailed example look at Short case 9.2 which describes the success of Electrocomponents, an organization able to develop both public and private e-catalogues for its customers.

## Short case 9.2

### E-cataloguing: the case of Electrocomponents

Electrocomponents (http://www.electrocomponents.com) is a leading international high-service distributor of electronic and electromechanical supplies offering a vast range of 350,000 products to 1.5m customers in twenty-seven countries and with revenues of £877m in 2006. The traditional channel to market for the firm is its catalogue, designed for the typical customer: an engineer requiring a wide range of components at short notice and with rapid delivery. The size and frequency of distribution varies from market to market, but in the UK its catalogue comprises five volumes and is issued every six months. Yet the average order value is less than £100. This single channel had proven a costly and complex operation. E-cataloguing in the context of the development of an overall e-Commerce offer allows the company considerably greater flexibility to introduce new products and quickly change prices to match the competitive conditions in the markets » within which it trades. Electrocomponents now offers seventy websites in seventeen languages operating around the world (the UK website is shown in the adjacent image).

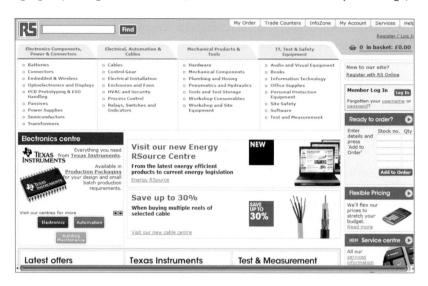

Its website front end plug-in, PurchasingManager™ launched in 2002 is provided free to customers. The service was designed to allow employees to place low-value orders from their own computers, using the process described in the diagram above. Purchasing managers at the individual company level can set allowable spending levels for employees and receive email notification if an employee exceeded his or her spending limit. A more fully-fledged e-procurement service can be integrated with a customer's own e-procurement system. The level of sales via e-commerce varies from market to market (ranging from 57 per cent in Japan to 10 per cent in the US) but averages around 28 per cent of the Group's sales.

*Question*
What are the weaknesses of e-cataloguing systems?

## E-ordering and e-invoicing

E-ordering and e-invoicing systems are employed to allow customers to place orders, for them to be notified electronically of order and shipment status, and for payments and customer management to be undertaken. For example, oil company BP sends electronic invoices to customers using the industry-wide platform called Elemica (discussed below). The payment aspects of this activity are often referred to as the financial supply chain. More than 30bn invoices are issued every year across Europe by organizations. The average processing cost of a paper invoice across Europe is in the region of €30, and it is estimated that by using e-invoicing an 80 per cent cost saving is possible. E-ordering benefits include:

- simplified, standardized, and more user-friendly forms;
- pre-filled forms to reduce the data-entry burden;
- intelligent validation which can reduce errors and rejected orders;
- 24/7 availability allowing orders to be processed more quickly.

There are three specific obstacles in relation to e-invoicing, which have held up its widespread implementation:

- *Legal obstacles*: e-invoicing lies at the intersection of several areas of legislation, including that regulating VAT, accounting, payment, authentication, company transparency, and data retention, which adds to the complexity of any solution.
- *Trust and operational obstacles*: whether an invoice is sent in paper form or via electronic means has no bearing upon the level of trust between the trading partners involved, but rejection of an invoice—perhaps because of more stringent controls—may be seen as an opportunity for the buyer to delay payment.
- *Standardization obstacles*: there are many specifications of e-invoicing standards worldwide, including those promulgated by the ISO and the UN as well as proprietary accounting, industry, and company specifications.

No more fragmented, complex, and costly e-invoicing situation can be found than in Europe. Regulations on e-invoicing differ substantially across Europe and are not always clear in their operational implications for firms. The European Union is involved in a project to lift barriers to mass adoption of electronic invoicing (European Commission, 2007). The creation of the Single Euro Payments Area from January 2008 has prompted the development of an open and interoperable European Electronic Invoicing Framework.[1] The Commission believes that realizing electronic invoicing could significantly reduce supply chain costs by €243bn across Europe, as well as helping to streamline business processes and drive innovation. However, its introduction will not be a straightforward process.

## E-marketplaces

Business-to-business e-marketplaces provide a final potentially integrating component of e-procurement. They can be defined as:

> 'electronic inter-organizational platforms through which multiple buyers and suppliers conduct transactions and interact with each other' *Holzmuller and Schluchter, 2002*

---

1 SEPA is the area where citizens, companies and other economic actors will be able to make and receive payments in euro, within Europe, whether between or within national boundaries under the same basic conditions, rights and obligations, regardless of their location.

This definition provides for a more comprehensive interaction between buyers and sellers than e-tendering, e-cataloguing, or e-ordering, but still in the context of buying rather than in terms of other forms of collaboration, such as information sharing. But integrated e-marketplaces are not new. In what is now a well-known example, proprietary networks led to the development of the SABRE flight-planning system by American Airlines and IBM in the early 1960s, which was second only in size to the US government's own systems. Initially developed as a purely internal database, American began marketing SABRE as a booking tool to travel agencies in the US in the mid-1970s (Gasson, 2003) In 2000, business-to-business (B2B) e-marketplaces, particularly those involving auctioning activity, were heralded in much the same way as business-to-consumer (B2C) e-commerce as having the potential significantly to transform established ways of doing business. In this case, the transformation was in respect of inter-organizational procurement processes. Early forecasts of e-marketplace growth were at a similar level of optimism as those for business-to-consumer applications. Analysts IDC predicted in 2001 that by 2004, $1.2trn of business-to-business revenue would come from e-marketplaces. Although we don' have data on e-marketplace startups over a prolonged period, Figure 9.10 illustrates the intensity of firm announcements in the area from 1998 to 2002, including the period immediately prior to and following the dot.com bust.

> 'Let's see, you want me to put all my products and prices online so my customers can beat me about the head and shoulders. Then I can commoditize myself even more to take my razor-thin margins down to microscopic levels. Finally, I get to pay transactions fees for this privilege … What am I missing?' *Un-named supplier, quoted in Henig, 2000*

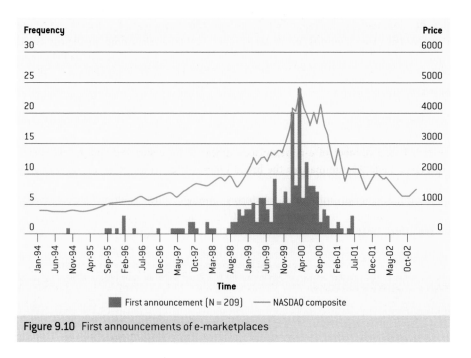

Figure 9.10  First announcements of e-marketplaces

Analysts Forrester subsequently reported that 2001 revenues of 40 per cent of the e-marketplaces that they surveyed were less than $10mn—whilst 40 per cent of firms refused to respond at all to the market researchers. Look at Figure 9.10, which shows the rapid rise and fall of new e-marketplace announcements between 1999 and 2001. Why were the early forecasts so misguided? What is the present extent and characteristics of e-marketplace activities and what have proved to be the criteria for—and barriers to—success?

The un-named supplier in the quotation above may have correctly identified suppliers' concerns about such e-marketplaces, but Steve New suggests that there are four main reasons behind the widespread early failures of e-marketplaces:

- *a naive view of the buying process*: with participants failing to understand the importance of trust and personal relationships in the procurement process, particularly for certain kinds of goods and services;

- *the wrong products*: a failure correctly to identify the kinds of product which might form the basis of a successful e-marketplace (for example, commodities with differentiation based purely on price rather than goods and services differentiated in terms of quality or other non-price factors);

- *a single-minded focus on cost-cutting*: a temptation to use e-marketplaces by buyers simply to cut procurement costs—leading to some suppliers making excessively low bids but then clawing back savings through charges post contract, so-called 'low-balling';

- *poor performance measurement*: failing to develop appropriate metrics to judge the performance and effectiveness of e-marketplaces.

### Activity box 9.4

**The secrets of success**

Identify three contrasting markets where you might expect e-marketplaces to have very different chances of success. Justify and explain your choices.

Nevertheless, a number of e-marketplaces appear to have survived and, to an extent, prospered. Table 9.1 summarizes the broad types that can now be found operating in international markets.

One example of an independent network is that of Elemica (http://www.elemica.com) which was developed in 1999 by twenty-two of the leading chemical companies in the world for the benefit of the whole industry and its related markets. By 2007, some $50bn-worth of transactions were handled through Elemica. Its network is designed as an open one, embracing all industry buyers and sellers looking for a robust infrastructure, and network and e-commerce solutions to improve their core business processes. Elemica is not an 'aggregator' of material purchasing, nor a 'buyer', 'seller', or 'owner' of products—it is a facilitator of transactions. Compare this with Short case 9.3, which describes the experience of Tejari, a regional horizontal e-marketplace

**Table 9.1  Types of e-marketplace**

| Type | Description |
| --- | --- |
| Buyer-oriented | Run by a consortium of buyers in order to establish an efficient purchasing environment and to exploit buyer power |
| Supplier-oriented | Set up and operated by a number of suppliers who are seeking to establish an efficient sales channel via the Internet to a large number of buyers |
| Independent | Operated by a third party which is open to buyers or sellers in a particular industry |
| Private | Established by single big companies to facilitate their own purchasing and/or selling activities |
| Vertical | Providing online access to businesses vertically up and down every segment of a particular industry sector |
| Horizontal | Connecting buyers and sellers across different industries or regions |

based in the Middle East. Another good example is agribusiness. Clasen and Muller (2006) studied 233 agribusiness e-marketplaces. Key success factors were market liquidity, an international orientation, and concentration on providing exchange services.

Some genuine cost benefits can be achieved from the contemporary use of e-marketplaces. These include:

- easier ordering processes;
- a more transparent supplier base;
- the possibility of reduced inventories; alongside
- product price reductions; and a
- reduction in purchase order costs

Early work by Kaplan and Sawhney (2000) sought to provide a framework within which the particular role of different e-marketplaces could be understood. It drew upon the differences between what businesses buy (manufacturing and operational inputs) alongside how they buy—systematic and spot. Figure 9.11 shows how this combination led to four possible types of e-marketplace emerging. (Beware that some of the terminology that Kaplan and Sawhney employ in describing 'e-hubs' and 'cataloguing hubs' is not necessarily consistent with contemporary usage.) You may recall that it chapter 2 we discussed the extent to which the Internet caused disintermediation and created more efficient markets. In the context of e-procurement, migrating a market to an electronic setting has traditionally been viewed as suggesting a movement towards purely price competition amongst suppliers.

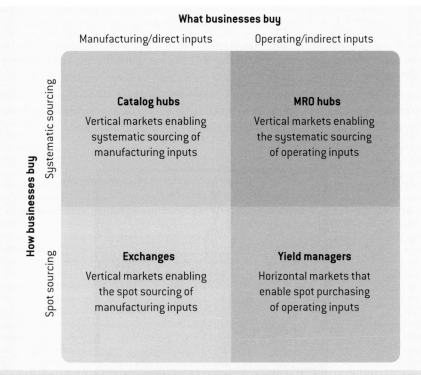

**Figure 9.11** A B2B Matrix of e-procurement options

---

### Tejari—the Middle East e-marketplace

Tejari (http://www.tejari.com) is an e-marketplace service originally dedicated to buyers and suppliers in the Middle East, launched in 2000 and owned by Dubai World, an investment company for the Dubai government (http://www.tejari.com). Over $5bn billion worth of business was transacted through spot purchases and online auctions in 2008, amongst the 200,000 businesses registered as members (an increase of 31 per cent over the previous year), with government and private sector both aggressively adopting e-procurement. The government sector accounts for some 60 per cent of the value of transactions through Tejari, with 40 per cent from the private sector. The government sector has been one of the leaders in adopting e-procurement in the Middle East, with more than 41,000 government requests for quotation (RFQs) and auctions carried out through Tejari in the period from 2004 to 2006. Recent major government  » transactions through the Tejari Marketplace include its largest ever auction: the UAE Road Transport Authorities purchase of new buses worth Dhs 2bn, and major deals for the Dubai Department of Nationalization and Residency, and Dubai Transport. Seventy per cent of the UAE health service's pharmaceutical products, medical goods, and consumables are bought online and the department has been involved in over 6,000 auctions. Tejari China was launched in December 2007: 'Te Jia Ye' meaning 'wonderfully beneficial deal'. In 2009, a specialized online transaction platform was announced in association with the US Export Council.

*Question*

What are the pros and cons of a regionally based e-marketplace such as Tejari? Listen to the interview with Tejari's CEO Omar Hijazi: http://www.ameinfo.com/192685.html.

It is also clear that a certain level of operations and information systems sophistication is initially required for firms successfully to participate in e-marketplaces. However, those firms which are in a position to make best use of such e-business technologies may be the ones who have already made considerable investments in technologies such as EDI (electronic data interchange) and in strategies for procurement (for example, in the form of supplier development programmes). It may therefore be much harder for e-marketplaces to demonstrate real advantages in terms of cost or effectiveness over the current practice in such firms. For example, in a study of the use of electronic marketplaces in the airline industry, Wagner (2006) found that whilst both full service and low-cost airlines were likely make use of e-marketplaces, adoption was linked to airline size (less subject to knowledge and technology barriers) and to those airlines involved in partnerships (such as code-sharing alliances) where the use of ICT systems was already likely to be sophisticated. Cost savings were to be found in standard spares and repairs and office supplies. Such products and services (unlike, for example, engines and accessories, which would be linked to service contracts or require complex repair procedures) were more likely to be fragmented.

B2B e-marketplaces continue to face challenges. These include:

- complex internal politics, particularly when the largest buyers and suppliers are present and the e-marketplace company itself may be new, or quite small;

- competition from other B2B initiatives, where opportunities may be seen in this still fast-moving area for market entry by new players;

- competition from internal developments within participating organizations, (where established procurement professionals within the firm seek to develop their own internal platforms, or are resistant to the introduction of third-party platforms);

- the heavy financial and human resources investment requirements of e-marketplaces: for example, the US consumer products e-marketplace—now a 'data pool'— Transora received over $250mn from over 50 supplier companies, when it was originally established); and

- the continued requirement to build trust or relational capital despite the apparently mechanistic nature of e-marketplaces.

However, we should not always assume that a firm's prime motivation for introducing e-procurement is to achieve lower prices from suppliers through discrete, anonymous transactions (as the Kaplan and Sawhney model presupposed). Strategic sourcing and multi-attribute sourcing (where there are factors such as higher product quality and faster delivery) may bring more effective improvements in company performance, and e-procurement now forms a component in the strategic sourcing mix:

> 'Sourcing in the strategic sense no longer refers to getting materials at desired prices, but a decision incorporated into the operating strategy of the firm, allowing purchasing to support or even improve the firm's competitive advantage.' *Fairchild et al., 2007*

Figure 9.12 shows how we can now assemble a richer and more interactive approach to procurement intelligence, with which e-business capabilities will need to align.

**Strategic Sourcing** A buying process that includes definition of product and service requirements, identification of qualified suppliers, negotiation of pricing, service, delivery, and payment terms, and supplier selection (Fairchild, 2006).

# E-collaboration

> 'While e-Commerce and e-Procurement have captured most of the business press headlines ... the promise of e-Collaboration may be far greater.' *Johnson and Whang, 2002*

As the recognition has grown that narrowly defined transactional exchanges fail to meet the more complex needs of organizations, within procurement let alone beyond, we

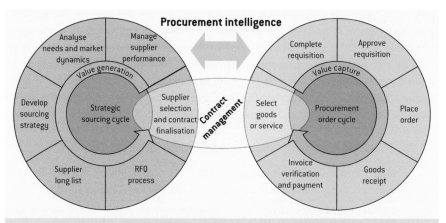

**Figure 9.12** Developing Procurement Intelligence

have seen the development of broader mechanisms of e-collaboration. These comprise a wide range of activities: from information sharing and integration to decision, process, and resource sharing. Inter-organizational information systems provide the key to this broader collaboration between firms. However, there are competing technical routes to achieving e-collaboration objectives, all of which are in the process of rapid evolution, and whilst there are some useful examples of industries and sectors achieving effective collaboration, there have also been practical challenges.

Daniel and White (2005) identified four kinds of inter-organizational information system which might form the basis of more broadly based e-collaboration:

- enterprise Resource Planning (ERP) systems (discussed earlier in this chapter);
- web services based on open systems: a set of interrelated technologies allowing systems to be assembled from a standard set of components;
- enterprise portals or enterprise information portals (EIP): increasingly seen as replacements for extranets, enterprise portals provide a platform for linking disparate sources of information together and permitting the customization of that information for particular individuals or work groups;
- electronic hubs: 'web-based systems which enable automated transactions, trading or collaboration between multiple business partners' (White and Daniel, 2004).

It has been suggested that ERP systems may be reaching a structural limit in relation to their capabilities to provide support for more broadly collaborative activities between organizations. We have already noted their particular complexity. Further, the bespoke development route followed by many ERP systems within firms can make collaboration difficult.

One of the most pervasive aspects of inefficient supply chains is the so-called bullwhip effect (BWE). It describes the phenomenon according to which order variability increases as orders move upstream along the supply chain. The variance in production then exceeds the variance in sales. Such an amplification effect can lead to excess inventory, increases in operating costs, and deterioration in customer service levels. Hitherto, so-called 'order-up-to' (OUT) procurement strategies might be expected to reduce variance amplification, but not eliminate it. In practice, information sharing is seen as the most direct way of reducing the BWE (Chatfield et al., 2004). The Internet (and in particular extranets) can allow appropriate information to be shared in a more timely and useful manner. In particular, if high-quality information on customer demand can be shared with the upper echelons of the supply chain before orders are generated, the nervousness generated within supply chains which lead to uncertainty can be reduced and the kinds of failure cascades which occur under the BWE can be avoided. Cachon et al. (2006) has drawn attention to the role of retailers in smoothing BWEs. But Short Case 9.4 shows how challenging this can be.

Moving from established technologies with clear common standards to evolving technologies can also create problems in terms of business processes. As buyers installed their own extranets or enterprise portals, for example, they started to put pressure on suppliers to replace older EDI connections with exclusive use of their own services to place orders and share forecasts (Levinson, 2006). Chapter 1 talked about EDI as 'an invisible technology' and one which some companies have been using for decades to exchange information between themselves. Replacing or even supplementing EDI with a range of extranets or enterprise portals will not always be an efficient solution for the supplier, particularly if several buyers introduce incompatible portals, and indeed may lead to an increase in headcount within supplier firms.

**OUT** order-up-to procurement.

**Failure Cascade** A failure in one part of a system which leads to sequential failures in successive parts of the system.

## Short case 9.4

### Wal-Mart's Retail Link

One of the biggest e-collaboration projects in existence is Wal-Mart's Retail Link data sharing system. Established in the early 1990s—when it was reliant upon dial-up connections—the system has now grown to accommodate over 100,000 registered users, 40,000 companies, and a 600 terabyte database containing 104 weeks' worth of POS information. Suppliers can download sales and inventory data which can be analysed in a variety of ways and, in particular, used to assist in forecasting demand. Retail Link is therefore more than just an e-procurement system for Wal-Mart and its suppliers internationally (see for example its Chinese presence at http://www.wal-martchina.com/english/service/rl/rl.htm). Indeed, a whole industry has grown up around best practice in the use of this phenomenally powerful e-collaboration tool. Training programmes on how to use Retail Link effectively and add-on analytical software are available from third-party suppliers, and over fifty user groups around the US share insight and expertise. As the supply chain environment has evolved, Retail Link has been customized and extended. For example, log-in screens now present users performing different roles with different views of their data. Similarly, following Wal-Mart's aggressive approach to the roll-out of RFI technology, with a mandate issued to suppliers, at the carton and palette level, Retail Link also now provides information from all the RFID 'read points' which generates near-live tracking status on goods in transit and inventory levels.                    »

But Retail Link is not without its challenges. Suppliers have equated the current information supplied through Retail Link as being rather like 'drinking water from a fire hydrant'. Managers admit that the system is too complex and have been pursuing a simplification strategy since 2006. User groups also help in providing feedback to Wal-Mart on suggested improvements to the system. As a result, for example, reformatted reports on sales, margins, inventory, and goods in transit now allow users to focus on analysis and exceptions rather than bespoke report design. Similarly, the time taken to synchronize new product introductions has been reduced from twelve days to one or two. Retail Link also forms a basis for suppliers to present new products for consideration to the company's buyers who were otherwise difficult to access.

*Question*

In what ways and for which business activities is Wal-Mart's Retail Link a more or less effective substitute for face-to-face encounters between retail buyers and suppliers?

## Outsourcing and off-shoring

'When sound became a feature of the movies, thousands of piano players asked: Who will employ us now? You know, we could have kept all those piano players. Does anybody think that would have been a step forward?' *Scott McNealy, CEO of Sun Microsystems*

Two particular types of reorganization of business processes have become particularly common amongst firms in the last twenty years: the delegation of control over activities

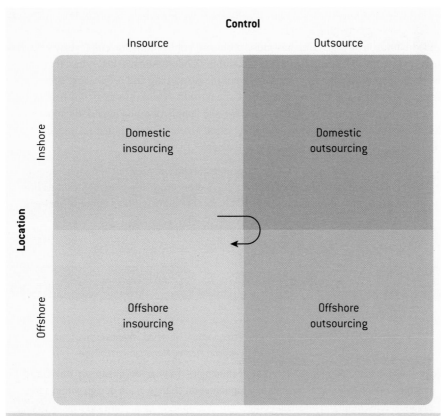

**Figure 9.13** Reorganisation of occupations, tasks and processes

to third-party business service companies (outsourcing) and the movement of activities to non-domestic geographical locations (off-shoring or multi-shoring). These decisions are interrelated, as Figure 9.13 shows. The development of e-business technologies has both increased the scale and changed the character of restructuring in sourcing. Choices made by firms over outsourcing tend either to be specifically related to information technology activities (ITO) or may involve other business process activities more generally (BPO). Worldwide revenues from BPO outsourcing (including human resources, procurement, accounting, administration, and customer services such as call centres) exceeded $140bn in 2007. BPO outsourcing growth rates of between 7 and 10 per cent per annum are forecast between 2007 and 2012 and the BPO market may exceed that for ITO in size by 2011.

These kinds of restructuring decision have implications not just for tasks, but for employees within particular occupations. Many of those involved in e-business will find themselves, as a result, working for business service intermediary firms on behalf of one

**Outsourcing** The delegation of control over certain activities to third party business service companies

**Off-shoring** The movement of certain business activities to a non-domestic geographical location.

or more client companies. Off-shoring, on the other hand, has tended to take advantage of fast-growing emerging markets in which labour costs in particular are lower, using so-called labour arbitrage. This has more profound implications for employees, since this may involve the disappearance of the job within the domestic market, rather than simply working for a different employer. The extent of outsourcing and off-shoring decisions by firms—and especially the combination of them, often referred to as rightsourcing—has a significant implication for the demand for and supply of e-business skills in particular locations. But the growth of digitzation has itself accelerated the potential impact of such decisions upon firms' efficiency and effectiveness.

> 'It is estimated that some 20% of all people employed carry out the kinds of tasks and functions that could potentially be carried out from any geographical location owing to technological advances in ICTs and the increased tradability of services.'
> OECD, 2006

**Labour Arbitrage** the tendency of jobs to flow towards whichever country has the lowest wages per unit output at the time and has reached the minimum required level of political and economic development to support a particular activity.

**Rightsourcing** The determination of an appropriate combination of locational and sourcing control decisions for a particular organization.

---

### Activity box 9.5

#### Dream commuters cross borders

'The technology is there that allows people to work from wherever, whenever they want to if they're doing information work.' *Peter Thompson, Henley Management College*

The increase in adoption of Internet technologies (alongside cheap air travel and flexible working practices) has led to a fundamental change in job design within some organizations. Read the television programme synopsis at http://news.bbc.co.uk/1/hi/business/6385851.stm and consider (1) which kinds of organizations can take best advantage of this trend; and (2) what the advantages and disadvantages of this may be for the business processes of the firms concerned.

---

Investment in outsourcing and off-shoring has been driven by a number of factors:

1. *Networking and software ubiquity*, notably increasingly global access to low-cost, high-bandwidth networks, the availability of standardized operating systems, software platforms, and business software applications.

2. *Business process re-engineering*, notably the consequences of work process digitization leading to a greater ease in outsourcing increasingly commoditized tasks to a wide variety of locations.

3. *Cost pressure*, derived from investor concern over cost inflation, changing form of ownership (particularly the growth of venture capital), off-shoring 'good practice' by market leaders, and the growth of business service companies able to facilitate the process.

4. *Regulatory change*, including improved lowering of trade barriers (as for example in India and China), tax breaks in developing markets, and growing regulatory encouragement for trading in business services.

5. *Improvements in educational provision in developing markets*, including investment by governments in business schools and technology colleges.

6. *Labour force mobility*, including increased movement of students and workers across national borders, and the repatriation of professional ICT talent to developing markets.

With companies originally expecting between 20 and 30 per cent cost savings from outsourcing according to Apte et al. (1997), and increasingly concerned about the risks of 'going it alone', questions of outsourcing have become increasingly important, despite popular concerns over the deleterious effects of what can be seen under some circumstances as 'exporting jobs'. However, leaving particular business functions in-house may constrain a firm's ability to exploit economies of scale, limits its access to skills and new technology, and can lead to complacency, with no incentive to benchmark against peers or to introduce best practices.

---

### Short case 9.5

#### Outsourcing at the BBC

The British Broadcasting Corporation has put in place an increasingly wide-ranging set of outsourcing contracts, ranging from technology to HR and accounting and finance, as it seeks to reduce the cost of support services in order that more money raised from public licence fee income can be directed towards programme-making. Its £1.5bn ITO outsourcing deal was with Siemens Business Services, which acquired BBC Technology in 2004, designed to generate an estimated £275m in savings over a ten-year period. As »

well as support of 'ICT commodities' (PCs and telephony) and transferring 1,400 staff, the contract covers specialist technology projects and strategic areas of investment ranging from digital content development to programme uplinking to satellite. This has extended to BPO, with Capita (http://www.capita.com) providing human resource outsourcing under a ten-year contract, whilst Groupe Steria (http://www.steria.com) operates a similar arrangement for the corporation's finance and accounting functions. The Steria contract, worth £85m over ten years, seeks to save the BBC £200m over the period, partly by off-shoring transaction processing to Chennai in India: a sum equivalent to the cost of funding Radio 1 for a year, or to 1.5m licence fees.

*Question*

The broadcasting union BECTU protested against the BBC's technology outsourcing deal, suggesting that it was 'not just the BBC selling off one of its Crown Jewels, it's a case of handing its central nervous system over to the private sector'. What are the advantages and disadvantages of a strategic technology outsourcing deal for the BBC?

To help you answer this question, see:

BBC Outreach, (2006), *Outsourcing*, http://www.bbc.co.uk/outreach/2006_review/business/outsourcing.shtml, and

BBC Trust, (2006), *BBC Outsourcing*, review conducted by the National Audit Office, http://www.bbcgovernorsarchive.co.uk/docs/reviews/vfm_outsourcingreport.pdf.

Companies have three main choices when it comes to the control they choose to exercise over business functions of various kinds.

1. *Employ or acquire in-house specialists* as an integral part of the business, on- or off-shore.

2. *Use in-source resources* to manage tasks in-house, using sub-contractors or freelance specialists, on- or off-shore.

3. *Outsource tasks* which are managed externally, through

   a. *prime contractor outsourcing*, where a single intermediary business services firm will co-ordinate all aspects of the activity, with a range of sub-contractors, under a master services agreement;

   b. *multi-sourcing*, where a range of intermediary business service firms will share responsibility for different aspects of the outsourced activity;

   c. *co-sourcing*, where several firms requiring outsourcing will share resources and facilities, or

   d. *combining strengths*, where over and above a purely contractual arrangement, customer and supplier develop a closer relationship to engage in joint product or service development.

Outsourcing can be an attractive means of achieving efficiency improvements in the provision of existing services and support as well as for new product and service development. In the case of services and support, which are often increasingly commoditized, economies of scale can be achieved and clients can often obtain access to people, best practice, and new technology that would otherwise be unavailable in-house. Even for product development, where there might be some risk to a firm's competitive differentiation, outsourcing can still provide access to specialist skills; development can usually be undertaken faster and at lower risk than within an individual firm.

However, whilst outsourcing has become an attractive option for firms, Barthelemy (2001) suggests that there are a number of hidden financial costs to the practice. These include vendor search and contracting costs; the costs associated with the transition of in-house to outsourced (including costs of redundancy and potential disruption to the business); the costs of managing the outsourcing effort, including unanticipated variations on contract and back-end loading by the contractor; and subsequent potential costs if the outsourcing deal fails for whatever reason and the activity has to be reintegrated with the rest of the business. For example, UK grocery retailer J Sainsbury (http://www.j-sainsbury.co.uk) embarked on a £1.7bn ITO with Accenture (http://www.accenture.com) in 2000, in a deal involving over 800 staff. The company's justification was that heavy investment in systems was required to sustain its competitiveness. In 2005, the company was forced to terminate the arrangement, declare £550m in exceptional costs (of which direct termination costs comprised £65m) (BBC News, 2004) and rebuild its internal capability. The company commented that: 'IT systems have … failed to deliver the anticipated increase in productivity and the costs today are a greater proportion of sales than they were four years ago.'

Partly for that reason, the relative attractions of particular sourcing control models have shifted over the last twenty years: in particular, so-called 'megadeals' (defined as ITOs of more than $1bn) have become less attractive. If we look at just one company—General Motors—we can see the way in which different models have been dominant at different times in the company's history. Initially, General Motors (http://www.gm.com) acquired in-house expertise to manage its ICT requirements, through its purchase of EDS (http://www.eds.com), then a 22-year-old company, in 1984. EDS worked as a wholly owned subsidiary for twelve years, simultaneously developing its business with other clients, over and above its obligations to its new parent company, before being spun-off by GM in 1996. The two companies then signed a ten-year master service contract, with EDS acting as prime contractor. In 2006, at the end of the contract period, GM opted for multi-sourcing by signing three further ICT outsourcing contracts worth in total over $1.5bn (with HP, IBM, and Capgemini). Nevertheless, EDS itself still received $3.8bn in a new five-year contract for global system integration services. Multi-sourcing like this—as well as at a smaller scale—has gained popularity since 2003, with a 2006 Gartner survey estimating that clients will contract with an average of four ICT business service organizations.

It is clear that some occupations are more capable than others of being carried out independent of location, whether by the firm itself, or by a business service intermediary. According to OECD (2004), so-called 'offshorability attributes' might include those occupations where:

- there is intensive use of ICT, or where
- output can be traded or transmitted with the help of ICTs, or where
- work comprises highly codifiable information or 'knowledge' content, or finally where
- work does not necessarily require face-to-face contact.

Many e-business occupations score highly against most of these criteria in principle. Indeed, on this basis, up to 20 per cent of people employed in OECD countries are potentially at risk because they undertake tasks with these sorts of characteristic to varying degrees. In 2006, 73 per cent of US Forbes 2000 companies said that off-shoring was an important part of their overall growth strategy (although 'achieving cost reductions' was still the most important reason cited, according to Duke University, 2005). Gartner predicted worldwide off-shore spending would reach $50 billion in 2007.

However, it is important to make a distinction between the off-shoring of clerical and of more professional ICT occupations, in which we may find a higher proportion of e-business skills. Companies tend to move through a series of stages in their use of off-shoring. Initially, off-shoring purely for cost-cutting reasons, led to firms substituting cheaper off-shore labour for lower skilled personnel in the home market on a one-to-one basis. Call and data centre occupations were a prime target for this stage. Even today, ICT engineering costs in India are still 60 per cent less then those in the US, despite Indian salary inflation running at 14 per cent. More recently, companies have been using off-shoring to leverage more efficient growth strategies by accessing more highly qualified personnel unavailable in the home market—in occupations such as product development, R&D, and software engineering. The net effects of this stage is of an increase in employment overall: a ratio of up to thirteen jobs created off-shore for every job eliminated in the US, for example, according to the Off-shoring Research Network in 2006. There is growing competition for these kinds of workers.

Popular attention is often focused upon south-east Asian countries as beneficiaries of off-shoring, particularly China and India. Although absolute numbers of skilled occupations in these markets is proportionally low, the overall stock of workers is large in absolute terms because of the size of their overall working population.

Just like outsourcing, off-shoring carries risks for firms. These include concerns over:

- the maintenance of appropriate service quality levels;
- the extent of the cultural fit between domestic and off-shore activities;
- the extent of employee turnover;
- the potential loss of control over the business;
- the degree of infrastructural instability, including data security and IP issues; and
- the extent of political stability.

Some companies have begun to revise their view of the real benefits of off-shore outsourcing and some of the largest firms are turning to off-shore insourcing as a successful compromise. For example, 50 per cent of global bank HSBC's software development work is conducted off-shore, with 4,000 engineers in India, 1,000 in China, and an operation in Brazil that employs 200 programmers. This is managed in-house, with six business units, regularly benchmarked against external providers, selling business services to the main business. HSBC works to reduce cultural barriers and organizational fragmentation by incentivizing domestic team leaders for successfully integrating the bank's multi-cultural, multi-national teams across locations. The cost base for IT programming in HSBC has been reduced by 2 per cent through off-shoring.

Choices over sourcing are, of course, just one response to perceived skill shortages, but also have implications for the nature, growth (or decline), and distribution of e-business skills in different parts of the world. Indeed, the practicalities of securing sufficiently skilled individuals has led to a growing enthusiasm for 'corporate virtualization' through a diverse outsourcing of business processes to locations where such employees can be found.

## Long case 9.1

### E-Procurement and e-marketplaces in China: the case of Alibaba

Procurement in China by overseas business has historically faced challenges, driven by perceived concerns over quality, reliability, and intellectual property issues. There were some 42m SMEs in China in 2006. Small and medium-sized Enterprises (SMEs) in emerging markets face three particular challenges in developing trading activities:

- difficulty in finding and developing customer and supplier relationships beyond their local markets;
- limited resources for sales and marketing activity; and
- problems in working out who to trust.

But the combination of rapid economic growth in China alongside the growth of the Internet has led to real opportunities for the expansion of B2B marketplaces. One of the primary initiatives for the development of e-commerce here has been for the state to encourage such firms to use third-party e-commerce platforms as a way of reaching export markets. Such mechanisms can provide a trusted intermediary for foreign firms. Penetration of such platforms is high and expected to grow fast over the next five years (see chart). But non-Chinese marketplaces, such as eBay, have not played a major role in this growth.

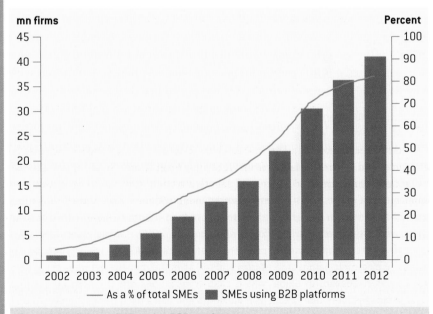

**Figure 9.14** Chinese SMEs using B2B platforms

Alibaba.com is an e-commerce business founded in Hangzhou in 1999 by Internet entrepreneur Jack Ma originally to provide sales leads from China and overseas to small buyers and suppliers for online trading.

> 'What customers wanted was a place where they can meet in a very simple way. So, we chose a model that's free for buyers to use, suppliers advertise and it's more like a dating site for buyers and sellers to buy and sell in volume'. *Porter Erisman, Alibaba*

Yahoo! acquired a 40 per cent economic stake in 2005. The company's flotation on the Hong Kong Stock Exchange in October 2007 generated $1.7bn and was oversubscribed 250 times. Its online marketplaces have 40m registered members in 240 countries, 481,000 of whom were paying members in the first quarter of 2009. In 2008, the Alibaba Group achieved revenues of $438m (+38 per cent on the previous year). Alibaba.com is now the world's most visited B2B e-commerce site, according to Alexa.com (a subsidiary of Amazon.com that measures global Internet traffic).

In 2003, Alibaba started a fixed-price B2C website with no transaction fees, Taobao.com. At the time of writing it is Asia's largest retail marketplace in terms of gross merchandise volume (GMV). The Taobao Chinese consumer marketplace business is extraordinarily dynamic and innovative. Well before eBay bought Skype, Taobao allowed instant messaging between buyers and sellers, making the trading environment less anonymous. It serves about 120m registered users and more than 1.5m sellers have opened up stores on the service. Taobao was ranked the thirty-eighth most popular global website in terms of traffic by Alexa.com in 2009. Taobao incorporates an innovative, escrow-based online payment system, called Alipay. The system, which holds the electronic payment in escrow and releases the money only when the goods arrive, was necessary in China, where cash transactions are the norm. Presently, Alipay manages more than 150m user accounts and had a daily transaction volume of RMB700m ($102m) at the beginning of 2009. Although it began as an online payment »

solution for Taobao, Alipay has become the de facto standard for online payment by consumers and small business in China. EBay China's share slid to 7.2 per cent in 2007 from 79 per cent in 2003, despite dropping transaction fees and merging with local Internet firm TOM Online in December 2006. By contrast, Taobao now accounts for nearly 1 per cent of China's total retail trade.

But challenges remain for the B2B site. International buyers have to do a lot of offline work to satisfy themselves that a supplier is capable and trustworthy. As a result, once buyers have found a supplier they like, they tend to stick with them, rather than searching again when they have a new order to place. Counterfeiting is still perceived to be a problem. However, the company is diligent in its pursuit of such activity. Goldman Sachs reports that the company takes down nearly 100 listings every month in response to patent and copyright complaints.

> 'We have a form online that people can use to report postings of products that violate intellectual property rights (IPR). Suppliers suspected of violating IPR are given a chance to respond to the complaint. If they can't respond satisfactorily, then we go ahead and take down their posting. If they repeat the violation, then we close their account.' *Alibaba*

The company has also worked hard to help its customers weather the storm of the economic downturn through such initiatives as the Gold Supplier Starter Pack, which allows premium storefronts to be established for less than $3,000.

*Questions*

1. Why do domestic e-marketplaces, such as Alibaba, appear to have been more successful in China than foreign entrants such as eBay? What are the implications of your conclusions for the growth of truly international e-marketplaces?

2. What should Alibaba.com do next?

## Long case 9.2

### Outsourcing to India: from contact centres to remote infrastructure management

> 'With Anglicized names and feigned Western accents, Indians handle credit card problems and troubleshoot computers, collect debts and conduct customer satisfaction surveys.'
> *Time Magazine, 16 October, 2007*

The popular perception of business process and IT outsourcing to India is one dominated by the call, or contact, centre industry. Certainly, that industry employs over 350,000 people and the economic arguments of the pursuit of economies of scale and access to specialist resources have long supported the case for the outsourcing of customer-service activities, amongst others, to third-party specialist business service operations. Increasingly, also, the development of intensively networked organizations has provided a persuasive argument for the off-shoring of these ≫

activities to so-called low-cost countries (LCC) such as India. UK telecommunications firm British Telecom (BT) outsourced its customer interaction services to India as early as 2003.

But Indian BPO is more than just contact handling: this is just the tip of the iceberg. India now leads the world in off-shore outsourcing which was valued in 2008 at an estimated $47.8bn (£24bn), ten times the value in 1998. Over this period, from a focus on basic data-entry tasks, Indian BPO firms certainly moved extensively into voice-based services and back office. But in the last five years e-business technology has enabled businesses to take on more complex processes, involving rule-based decision-making and even research services requiring informed individual judgement: the attractiveness of 'off-shorability' has been enhanced. The fastest growing application areas have included: advanced data management (ADM), software development and R&D, and remote infrastructure management (RIM).

RIM is an unsexy, but business-critical area of ICT support services that has benefited significantly from the application of e-business technologies. RIM includes:

- remote desktop support services;
- server management;
- wide- and local-area network support; and
- corporate help desk services

Leading Indian firms Infosys, Wipro, HCL and Tata Consulting Services are not yet generating the kinds of revenue in this area commanded by market leaders »

Accenture and HP/EDS, but are no longer seen as regional 'low-cost' providers. On the contrary, they now offer increasingly high-value global support services and achieve high client scores for quality of execution and support. Nor is such outsouring/off-shoring support based solely within India. Consider Wipro Technologies, a leading Indian BPO services firm (http://www.wipro.com) with revenues from IT services alone of over $1bn in 2008. It employs 95,000 people in thirty-five countries and, in a practice becoming known as 'reverse off-shoring', runs its remote monitoring and management services through three 'global command centres' in California (USA), London (UK), and Dubai.

These moves into higher value services by Indian business service firms come at the same time that increasing customer disenchantment with simple voice-based overseas call centres is leading to some re-focusing of off-shoring by client firms. For example, UK bank Lloyds TSB decided in 2007 to reduce its reliance on Indian call centres for consumer-facing support as a result of customer complaints. The Lloyds TSB Mumbai call centre opened in 2004 and at its peak employed 700 staff. When it was first opened, the bank shut a call centre in the UK with the loss of 968 jobs. Instead, this time, it introduced interactive voice recognition software and the ability for customers to call branches directly (Treanor, 2007). Shortly after moving customer-facing contact back to the UK, however, Lloyds TSB announced that it would begin off-shoring back office ICT staff roles to India (Mari, 2008). In response to these kinds of pressures, Indian contact centres have become more 'multi-channel', migrating to provide more complex and higher quality customer interaction services (CIS) which exploit a range of capabilities including voice-over IP, email response, and SMS handling.

But more broadly based Indian BPO firms face challenges, too. Shortage of appropriate talent, alongside international competition from lower cost economies such as Vietnam, Morocco, and Mexico has led to leading BPO firms facing high attrition rates amongst middle management and technical staff. Wage inflation in India has experienced five consecutive years of growth over 10 per cent. For BPO firms irrespective of geographical base, a combination of increasingly experienced client firms and technical change also means that clients are becoming more discriminating in their selection of outsourcing and off-shoring partners. Outsourcing may be expanding, but contracts are becoming smaller, are spread amongst a larger mix of providers, and are more frequently renegotiated.

*Questions*

1. What will determine whether banking customers continue to prefer speaking to their branches on the phone (whether locally or off-shore) or will take advantage of e-business interaction mechanisms, such as email or SMS?

2. What do you think are the biggest challenges facing the leading Indian BP outsourcing firms in developing their businesses, and how might these be overcome?

# ✪ Chapter Summary

This chapter began by setting out the main principles underlying efficient operational processes, supply chains, and networks, distinguishing between operations management and supply chain management. It examined the ways in which improvements in the efficiency and effectiveness with which business processes function can contribute to an organization's overall performance and deliver competitive advantage. This chapter also sought to provide an appreciation of the ways in which such processes can be supported, developed and restructured by the Internet by improving the flexibility of product or service provision; by increasing the capacity for such provision, or by reducing the costs of production. In doing so, we demonstrated that conventional concepts of value and supply chains might be more usefully reconfigured in terms of the extended enterprise, and the networked, or even virtual, organization. We then sought to gain specific insights into the characteristics, strengths, and weaknesses of e-procurement and e-collaboration in transforming supply chains or networks and creating the 'e-enabled' firm. In a detailed discussion of the major component parts of the inter-organizational buying and selling process (including e-tendering, e-cataloguing, e-ordering, and e-invoicing), we demonstrated that the benefits would be different for different forms of buying (such as between long-term contracts and spot sourcing). We also showed that there exist a number of barriers—many of which are essentially non-technical—which might prevent the proper development and application of such processes within and between organizations, especially in relation to the development of integrated e-marketplaces. This led us to a discussion of the growing importance of information sharing and collaboration between organizations as interrelationships become more complex. But it also allowed us to explore the difficulties of moving from established technologies with clear, common standards to e-business technologies with evolving standards. Finally, we concluded by analysing the characteristics and consequences of the growth of outsourcing and off-shoring of business processes by firms, facilitated by the integration of e-business technologies. In distinguishing between the two phenomena, we also considered some of the implications for tasks and for employees within particular occupations and what this meant for the relative advantage of both firms and nations.

# ❓ Review questions

1. Describe and give examples of the different ways in which business processes turn inputs into outputs.

2. What are the differences between 'push' and 'pull' supply chains?

3. What are the challenges facing organizations which seek to introduce enterprise resource planning (ERP) systems?

4. What are the main opportunities and challenges of e-procurement processes?

5. What explains the early rise and fall in popularity of e-marketplaces?

6. Why do inter-organizational information systems 'provide the key to broader collaboration between firms'?

7. Why are firms' attitudes towards outsourcing changing?

8. What are the costs and benefits of off-shoring?

# ○ Discussion questions

1. How can effective and efficient operations management deliver competitive advantage to organizations? Think of two examples of firms or sectors for which the advent of the Internet has altered operational processes.

2. Some of the most successful e-marketplaces appear to be regional rather than international in their focus. Why might this be the case?

3. Are there any markets for products or services for which e-procurement might be inappropriate? Why?

4. Are there limits to the business processes and activities that can be outsourced? Might this vary by type and size of organization?

5. Which professional occupations are most at risk from off-shoring? How and why might this change?

# → Suggestions for further reading

Christopher, M., (2004), *Logistics and Supply Chain Management: Creating Value—Adding Networks*, FT/Prentice-Hall.
Although now a little old, this book is still selling well. This is partly because author Martin Christopher has been able to write a superb summary of issues in supply chain management and logistics, from a business (rather than a technical) perspective. He outlines the role of logistics in using service levels to segment markets, and explores the ways in which organizations can assess logistics productivity and service performance. The book provides information on auditing logistics systems and describes how greater responsiveness in the supply chain can be achieved through lead time reduction.

Daniel, E.M. and White, A., (2005), 'The Future of Inter-Organizational System Linkages: Findings of an International Delphi Study', *European Journal of Information Systems*, 14, pp. 188–203.
The article suggests that information systems linkages with partners are increasingly critical to the success of organizations. The authors review the available developments in information systems and technology which might provide the basis for such linkages and consider the relative strengths and weaknesses of electronic hubs, web services, enterprise resource management systems, and enterprise portals.

Goel, A.K. et al., (2008), 'Time to Rethink Offshoring?', *McKinsey Quarterly*, 4, pp. 108–11.
This article discusses the economic efficiencies associated with the off-shore outsourcing of high-tech manufacturing, including that of products such as televisions and computer servers. The authors describe issues relating to supply chain management and the logistics of managing off-shore production. Rising oil prices, wage inflation, and the weakening of the US dollar are presented as disincentives to moving production to emerging Asian markets.

Johnson, P.F., & Klassen, R.D., (2005), 'E-procurement', *MIT Sloan Management Review*, 46(2), pp. 7–10.
This is a useful contextual article on e-procurement which looks at recent research analysing the benefits and pitfalls of what the authors identify as the three most visible forms of e-procurement—e-sourcing, e-coordination, and e-communities (we have used slightly different wording in this chapter). They argue that whilst the strategic use of these technologies can have positive effects, including improving the information flow along the supply chain and strengthening the strategic relationships that exist with other companies, each has drawbacks that must be carefully managed.

Weeks, M.R. and Feeny, D., (2008), 'Outsourcing: From Cost Management to Innovation and Business Value', *California Management Review*, 50(4), pp. 127–46.
The article discusses whether outsourcing information technology (IT) is incompatible with innovation. Many large organizations have significant experience of extensive IT out-sourcing. Such relationships have conventionally been used to deliver high-quality services at low cost. The article also explores the extent to which the right outsourcing partner can deliver innovation and added value to the client.

# → References

Apte et al. (1997)

Arndt, J., (1979), 'Towards a Concept of Domesticated Markets', *Journal of Marketing*, 43, pp. 69–75.

Barthelemy (2001)

Cachon, G.P., Randall, T. and Schmidt, G.M., (2006), 'In Search of the Bullwhip Effect', *Manufacturing and Service Operations Management*, 9(4), Fall, pp. 457–79.

Chatfield et al (2004)

Cissna, T., (1998), 'ERP Software Implementation Brings Pain with its Gains', *Electric Light and Power*, 76(11), pp. 43–4.

Clasen et al (2006)

Daniel, E.M. and White, A., (2005), 'The Future of Inter-Organizational Systems Linkages', *European Journal of Information Systems*, 14, pp. 188–203.

Duke University (2005)

European Commission, (2007), *European Electronic Invoicing Final Report*, Informal Task Force on e-Invoicing, http://ec.europa.eu/information_society/eeurope/i2010/docs/studies/eei-3.2-e-invoicing_final_report.pdf.

Fairchild, A., O'Reilly, P., Finnegan, P., and Ribbers, P.M., (2007), 'Multi-Criteria Markets: An Exploratory Study of Market Process Design', *Electronic Markets*, 17(4), pp. 286–97.

Gasson, S., (2003), 'The Impact of e-Commerce on the Air Travel Industry', in M. Kosrow-Pour (ed.), *Annual Cases on Information Technology*, Idea Group Inc.

Grant, D., Hall, R., Wailes, N., and Wright, C., (2006), 'The False Promise of Technological Determinism: The Case of Enterprise Resource Planning Systems', *New Technology, Work & Employment*, 21(1), pp. 2–15.

Hawking, P., Stein, A., Wyld, C.D., and Foster, S., (2004), 'E-procurement: Is the Ugly Duckling Actually a Swan Down Under?', *Asia Pacific Journal of Marketing and Logistics*, 16(1), pp. 3–26.

Henig, P., (2000), 'Revenge of the Bricks', *Red Herring*, August.

Holzmuller & Schluchter (2002)

Johnson, M.E. and Whang, S., (2002), 'E-Business and Supply Chain Management: an Overview and Framework', *Production & Operations Management*, 11(4), pp. 413–23.

Kaplan, S. and Sawhney, M., (2000), 'E-hubs: The New B2B Marketplaces', *Harvard Business Review*, May–June, pp. 97–103.

Levinson, M., (2006), 'B2B Ecommerce: How to Stop the Web from Becoming a Trap', CIO, 1 May, http://www.cio.com/article/20528/B_B_E_Commerce_How_to_Keep_the_Web_from_Becoming_a_Trap_.

Mari (2008)

New, S., Meakin T., and Southworth, R., (2002), *Understanding the E-marketspace: Making Sense of B2B*, Saïd Business School, University of Oxford.

OECD (2006)

OECD (2004)

Powell, W.W., (1990), 'Neither Market nor Hierarchy: Network Forms of Organization', *Research in Organizational Behavior*, 12, p. 295.

Short, J.E. & Venkatraman, N., (1992), 'Beyond Business Process Redesign: Redefining Baxter's Business Network', *MIT Sloan Management Review*, 34 pp. 7-21.

Slack, Chambers & Johnston (2006)

Treanor (2007)

Wagner et al. (2005)

White, A. and Daniel, E.M., (2004), 'The Impact of e-Marketplaces on Dyadic Buyer–Supplier Relationships: Evidence from the Healthcare Sector', *Journal of Enterprise Information Management*, 17(6), pp. 441–53.

# ⊘ Weblinks

Business Link's guide to E-marketplaces, online auctions, and exchanges. Business Link is the UK government's online service offering practical advice for business: http://www.businesslink.gov.uk/bdotg/action/layer?topicId=1075387398.

Globalwise. An off-shoring and outsourcing blog: http://coreadvisor.com/globalwise/.

Institute for Supply Chain Management. The ISM is the largest supply management association in the world and undertakes surveys and research as well as representing the interests of its 40,000 members: http://www.ism.ws/index.cfm.

NASSCOM is the leading trade body and the chamber of commerce of the IT-BPO industry in India: http://www.nasscom.in.

Strategic Sourcing Europe. A blog on e-sourcing run by Jean-Philippe Massin, Vice President of Capgemini Business and Technology Consulting: http://www.massin.nl/eSourcing/.

# Part three

# The organization of e-business

# E-business project management

*by Christine Cuthbertson*

**Learning outcomes**

Completing this chapter will enable you to:

- Be aware of the environmental context for project management
- Understand the general principles of project management as they apply to established e-businesses
- Differentiate between project management and systems development
- Understand the environment of the entrepreneurial or start-up e-business and how that relates to the development of a project management approach
- Appreciate the variety and uses of the various tools, techniques, and methodologies available to an e-business project manager

## Introduction

Projects take place in every sector and in every environment—from health, education, and defence to construction, pharmaceuticals, and financial services. A project is a series of linked activities that aims to design and implement a process, procedure, product, service, or system to solve a problem or realize a vision. Widely differing examples of projects might include building a bridge, introducing congestion charging for vehicles in a city centre, or manufacturing an affordable PC for families in developing countries.

A project has a set time period, which may be firmly fixed—like the building of the athletes' village for an Olympic Games—or less obviously time critical, such as a loyalty

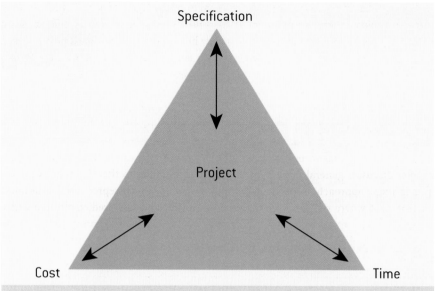

**Figure 10.1** The balancing act of time, cost and specification

card programme for a chain of bookstores. Strictly speaking, a project is unique, a 'one-off', and having a predetermined time period is one of the characteristics that sets a project apart from the ongoing business activities in the main functional areas of the business.

A second characteristic separating a project from regular business activities is that a project has its own financial constraints and targets for return on investment, so that estimates of cost are made beforehand and reviewed throughout to ensure both that funds are available and that the final benefits will outweigh the costs over an acceptable time period.

A third characteristic is that a project has aims and objectives that specify the problem and what constitutes its solution or provides the means of articulating the vision of what would be a successful outcome. This specification serves to delimit the project in terms of scope and quality.

In summary then, as Figure 10.1 suggests, projects are desired changes that can be isolated from the ongoing activities surrounding them by giving them a specific timeframe, a number of financial constraints and a well-defined business rationale. All projects are measured on the extent to which they satisfy this balancing act of time, cost, and specification.

## The environment for project management

Some firms are almost entirely project-based. And this might be true for an advertising agency as much as for a construction company. Other firms find that most of their activities are operations-based, such as a parcel delivery service or a firm of solicitors. However, in practice most companies have a mixture of project-based activities and day-to-day business activities.

A project-based approach may require a firm to realign some of its activities, meaning that a conscious choice must be made to consider some activities as different from others, and separate them from the day-to-day business. Implementing a project-based business environment may therefore require a cultural change for any company that adopts one. Despite this, project-based approaches are increasingly popular. But such an approach may require a reorganization of human resources, accounting procedures, and methods of working. In this way, a project-based organization and approach is more closely aligned with ideas of open systems and human relations models of management. A project approach to e-business is naturally adopted in established firms that are familiar with projects in other areas of the business. The first part of this chapter discusses general project management as it applies to this situation. A project management approach is particularly well suited to an entrepreneurial e-business environment where risks may be perceived as higher and less predictable, and where we might expect to find a culture where creativity, commitment, and involvement are highly valued. The second part of this chapter is focused on this situation. Chapter 11 examines questions of e-business culture in more detail, but to get a flavour of how project management can be manifested in an e-business context, take a look at the very distinctive project-based approach taken by movie production company CoProducer in Short case 10.1.

> **Human Relations** A model of management that focuses on the social processes

It is useful firstly to consider the ways in which project management in an e-business environment is similar to project management in any other environment. Software engineer Fred Brooks says, in the preface to his updated seminal work on software engineering projects, the Mythical Man-Month:

> 'in many ways, managing a large computer programming project is like managing any other large undertaking—in more ways than most programmers believe. But in many other ways it is different—in more ways than professional managers expect.' *Brooks, 1995*

His suggestion is that there are some underlying principles associated with project management and some aspects that are related to the character of the project—and that the distinction isn't always very clear to anyone involved. And it is not just a one-way street: in IT project management, extensive research by both practitioners and academics has created a rich vein of research, case studies, and best practice from which to draw, and Moran and Youngdahl (2008), for example, suggest borrowing IT project management techniques in global projects of any type, particularly where there is a great deal of uncertainty.

Project management for e-business is most likely to be almost synonymous with IT project management. Of course, e-business firms may also have projects relating to the recruiting and deployment of staff, location of sites and offices, and so on but at their core they are concerned with the development and use of information technology-based systems, products, and processes. And in any case, Sauer and Cuthbertson's (2003) survey of 1,500 UK IT project managers in all sectors revealed that over half of all project time was spent communicating with clients and other stakeholders, planning, monitoring, and controlling the project—very much general project management skills.

In summary, there are some general project management principles that e-business firms can adopt, extensive experience in IT project management to be exploited, and some particular aspects of e-business project management that need to be considered in context.

## Short case 10.1

### Collaboration master class at CoProducer

CoProducer is a collaborative project that aims to produce a world-class film (http://coproducer.yougov.com). The project platform is hosted by UK research and consulting firm YouGov and led by Chief Innovation Officer of YouGov and executive producer of CoProducer, Stephan Shakespeare. An online panel of self-selected co-producers are be involved in all aspects of the movie, from pitch through to post-production. Co-producers will receive a share of any profits from the film.

Although there is a core membership of paid 'nerds' (their description), unlike most e-business projects, when project team membership is a part of the job, the success of CoProducer depends on its ability to capture and retain a group of interested co-producers from the general public. Participation is open to all, and co-producers have been attracted by YouGov polling, referrals from registered co-producers, word of mouth, and viral marketing.

The CoProducer project was separated into phases, with the possibility of new co-producers joining as each new stage opened. Each subsequent stage was effectively specified by the co-producers themselves, with guidance from the executive producer. Co-producers were used to test the platform and online process and the results fed in to the first stage. In the first phase, over 6,000 ideas were pitched in a single line. For example, 'Man chosen to serve on jury of murder trial of which he is the killer.' These were gradually whittled down through surveys, CoRating, and CoDiscussion to a top ten, based mostly on the ratings but also on the amount of discussion that they had engendered and with one or two editor's choices. The top ten pitches were expanded in response to the discussions, with two or more versions of the same storyline for co-producers to choose from in the second phase. The aims and process of the later phases were all developed within the » co-producer forum. Co-producer decisions for the second stage included the involvement of professional scriptwriters, the number of scripts to develop, the process of interviews and auditions for jobs and roles, and the involvement of CoProducer in other projects.

Communication between team members is enthusiastic, knowledgeable, and intelligent. A CoDiscussion board gives the opportunity for co-producers to discuss issues in more depth. Co-producers' comments are in turn rated by other co-producers so that a consensus is reached. Some co-producers have been retained as moderators on the basis of their contributions to discussions. A team blog allows various permanent team members to document their side of the process of refining and moderation as each new phase gets under way. A further blog by Stephan Shakespeare keeps co-producers informed on a strategic level.

*Question*

What might be the advantages and the disadvantages, from a project management perspective, of having so many co-producers on a movie?

# What is project management?

Project management is considered a discipline, independent of the industry in which the projects take place. Like all management disciplines, project management has its own tools and techniques, professional membership bodies with qualifications and accreditation, conferences, and academies. The principles of project management are general and applicable in any project environment. Therefore e-business project management *is* project management. It is project management with a strong emphasis on speed, flexibility, adaptability, user interaction, and security—but that may be true of the command and control systems in theatres of war or the staging of an exhibition of the works of Picasso, and many of the principles of project management remain as valid in e-business as in other environments. In established firms that add an e-business element to their business activities, such as Tesco.com, Boots.com, and Johnlewis.com, these principles are already well established. Large, successful e-businesses such as Amazon.com and eBay.com also have the general project management principles at the heart of their online activities. We begin, therefore, in outlining the fundamental principles of project management.

Projects have a beginning, a middle, and an end. Although they may vary in terms of the phrases used, and the degree of concurrency, iteration, and formalization, all approaches have phases that include envisioning and set-up, planning and scheduling, executing, monitoring, and controlling, implementing and evaluating. A project will have a project leader or manager and a number of project team members depending on the size of the project. The originator of the project may serve as a champion or sponsor. Various members from the group of final beneficiaries of the project may also be involved, particularly in documenting the project requirements and in testing the results. The management of the project entails the key processes of initiation, planning, executing,

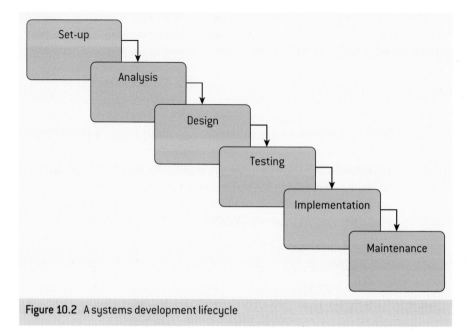

**Figure 10.2** A systems development lifecycle

monitoring and controlling, and closing, while the project team members proceed through what might be a more linear systems development lifecycle of set-up, analysis, design, testing, implementation, and maintenance. As we will see later, alternative systems development lifecycles to this traditional 'waterfall' approach may be more appropriate in an e-business environment, such as lifecycles based on prototyping or rapid development. For the moment it is important only to differentiate between the processes of project management and systems development.

A project-based approach as so far described seems to suggest that a project leader is responsible for one project and has a number of team workers dedicated to that one project throughout the lifecycle. Seeing through a project from inception to evaluation would be extremely advantageous for communication, and a sense of ownership and job satisfaction. However, reality is often different. For very good reasons, different specialists are required in different phases of the project and requirements and priorities may change as a project progresses. Personnel changes may be caused by sickness and vacations, key team members leave, project sponsors change their role within the business or disappear altogether. All these changes create difficulties in handover and communication, in maintaining a strategic perspective, and in organizational learning. In addition, projects can take place in parallel so that one project manager may be leading two projects, acting as a specialist on a third and a sponsor of a fourth with functional responsibilities in the ongoing activities of the firm. Project team members may have roles on several projects and functional responsibilities as well as moving between teams, as programme managers with a more strategic perspective allocate resources between competing projects. In the e-business world characterized by great change and development, project disturbances may be even more likely than in other environments and cause extra complications in a business that already relies heavily on emerging technologies and innovation. Short case 10.2 gives an example of how one particular e-business firm addresses such an environment, by harnessing the creativity of the workforce.

## Short case 10.2

### A passion for books at AbeBooks.com

AbeBooks is the world's largest online marketplace for new, secondhand, rare and out-of-print books. AbeBooks is gaining a reputation for making hard-to-find books easy to find. There are more than 110 million books listed for sale on Abebooks.com sites from 13,500 booksellers in over fifty countries. In 2007, AbeBooks sold books worth $190m. Several million people visit the AbeBooks sites each month and up to 30,000 books are sold each day.

AbeBooks was founded in 1995, went live in 1996 and was bought by Amazon.com in December 2008. There are 135 employees worldwide, over 100 at the Headquarters in Victoria, BC, Canada, where the company was founded. There is also a European office in Düsseldorf, Germany. Low-cost websites, with reduced subscription rates and trading under the subsidiary Gojaba.com brand, have been established in Brazil, Sweden, and Russia.

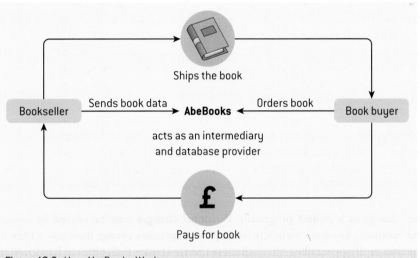

**Figure 10.3** How AbeBooks Works

AbeBooks has a relaxed working culture with a flat management structure. Although the number of employees has continued to grow, Leith Painter, Manager of Development at AbeBooks says:

>>

'the company has always been a relaxed place to work. Macleans magazine, Canada's version of Newsweek, has listed AbeBooks as one of Canada's top 100 employers for the past five years. Anyone can make a suggestion for a site improvement and the senior management team are always open to new ideas.'

AbeBooks is constantly evolving and new 'products' are always being developed or planned. First, a 'product council' gives the green light to new ideas to be developed. They work from a constantly evolving list of possibilities. The product is put into the hands of a product manager who breaks the project into 'stories'—essentially a way of making sense of everything that is needed. Development builds the product and Quality Assurance tests the product. Finally, Operations places the new product into 'production' at scheduled intervals where changes to the site are introduced.

*Question*

How do AbeBooks balance the needs of creativity and structure in project management? To what extent do they succeed?

## The project management process

It has become popular to synthesize best practice and relevant research within particular functions and activities into formalized so-called 'bodies of knowledge'. The project management body of knowledge (PMBOK®) is held by the Project Management Institute to be best practice in general project management principles, independent of context, and PMBOK is an international standard for project management (http://www.pmi.org). PMBOK divides the process of project management into over forty processes that fall

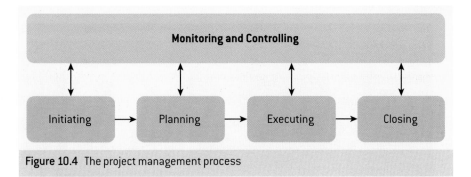

**Figure 10.4** The project management process

into five activities common to all projects: initiate, plan, execute, monitor and control, and close. A 'rival' body of knowledge is the APM body of knowledge (APMBOK), which similarly has over fifty project management processes that fall into the phases of concept, definition, implementation, handover, and closeout (http://www.apm.org.uk). Figure 10.4 shows these activities in graphical form.

Directly relevant to e-business project management are the nine areas of knowledge set out in the third edition of PMBOK: the *standard* project requirements related to cost, time, scope, and quality, as well as the *focus areas* of integration, risk, procurement, human resources, and communication, which generally differentiate one type of project from another and highlight the ways in which e-business project management can be considered different from project management in some other areas of business. Each of these areas of knowledge is explained in more detail below. Short case 10.3 provides an example of how many of these factors interact in an e-business context.

## Short case 10.3

### Get connected in a whole new way at Youniverse.com

Youniverse, powered by Imagini™, is a free social network based on images. Users discover their own 'VisualDNA' by selecting images that describe their personal sense of art, freedom, love, and so on. Once users have discovered their VisualDNA, they can make new friends, create groups, and chat live with video and instant messaging. As well as general Youniverse modules, such 'light my fire' and 'test your personality', Imagini develops relationships with firms such as lastminute.com, eHarmony, and hotels.com to suggest products to Youniverse members based on the same VisualDNA techniques. The results should be much more accurate than selecting a date and a destination (which may not be the customer's own critical criteria) and trawling through hundreds of possibilities.                                                                 »

The appeal of Youniverse is in delighting its many members. The quizzes are engaging and interesting, and Youniverse can have up to 70,000 unique visits a day. New projects are constantly emerging to increase the length of time users spend on the site and the frequency of their visits by adding fresh modules, images, and functionality.

The culture at Imagini is young, energetic, and fast-moving. While the business is sales-driven and with a networking focus, the IT group is geeky and intellectual—mostly young men who play as they work. They work closely with the creative group, which is artistic, young and largely female.

Anthony Powell at Imagini says:

> 'Over time the IT culture has become more relaxed and mature and less inclined to trip over itself as we have become less focused on individuals and more team-oriented. In that sense, in the past we were more task-based than project based, which often led to projects being reprioritized.'

There are three key units involved in projects at Imagini:

- core infrastructure team to provide abstraction and generalization;
- B2C (business-to-consumer) team to focus on keeping Youniverse.com fresh and alive;
- B2B (business-to-business) team to deliver bespoke applications for clients.

It's a fairly flat structure, but each team leader stays leading their team with contractors moving between the teams, depending on the overall requirements. This is a development from the individual, task-based approach based on skill-sets of the early development period at Imagini. Powell continues:

> 'our core members in all the teams are young so we don't have years and years of experience. What we do have are team leaders with the ability to learn quickly, great technical skills and superb communication skills. The ideal Imagini project manager is someone who is open to new ideas, capable of independent thought and ownership and really clear about how to achieve results based on how Imagini operates and what we are trying to achieve. When things aren't moving fast enough, an outside view might be to put in more man-hours but that certainly doesn't work in this environment. Here our response has to come from an understanding of our methods and our aims. For example, a project might begin as a few paragraphs from the client that we can work with but to turn it into something I can give to a contractor can take three further days. We would create a project bottleneck if we had to explain our approach and aspirations at every twist and turn of a project.'    »

## Cost, time, scope, and quality

During the setting up of a project, costs are inevitably estimates. As the project proceeds, estimates get better until eventually the full cost of the project is known. The longer the project lasts, the more difficult it can be accurately to estimate costs at the beginning. Estimates are more difficult where there is uncertainty, and uncertainty may be very familiar in an e-business environment. Here, team members will take time to learn and employ new methods and technology. Staff changes may be more common as staff gain new, highly valued experience in the latest tools, techniques, and methods and move on or move around the organization. Emerging technologies may be employed or integrated for the first time, or used in innovative ways, making some e-business projects largely exploratory and difficult to estimate.

There are many estimating techniques. Verzuh (2008) highlights four categories of estimating technique:

- *phased* estimating, where estimates are made only for the next phase;
- *apportioning* or top-down estimating, where a proportion of the total cost of the project is assigned to each phase and task;
- *parametric* estimating that uses past data to devise a basic unit of work that can be multiplied to estimate the tasks and phases; and
- *bottom-up* estimating, which begins with the detailed tasks and build that up into an estimate for the whole project.

Verzuh (2008) goes on to claim that bottom-up estimating is the most accurate. However, particularly in an e-business environment, the time that bottom-up estimating takes and the impossibility of specifying each task accurately enough make it among the least likely methods to be used by e-businesses. Both apportioning and parametric estimates rely on historical data. Whilst projects are by definition unique, there are likely to be great similarities between some projects in some environments, and enough data and experience exists to make apportioning and parametric estimates accurate enough. In e-business project management, however, for all the reasons already highlighted, both data and experience may be less readily available. Phased estimating is therefore more likely to be the most effective method for e-business. Phased estimating suits a learning environment and is associated with risk management, as only the costs for the next phase are committed. And, as we will see later on, phased estimating also fits in well with an agile systems development lifecycle.

Time estimates are also more difficult the longer and more complex the project. Realistic scheduling comes from accurate activity definition, sequencing, and duration estimates based on the resources available for the project. These are used to develop a schedule of project activities that are monitored and controlled throughout the project lifecycle.

The longer the project, usually, the greater the cost and so the elements of cost and time are often tightly associated. In more general terms, time and costs constitute the resources of the project. As with cost, the time required to complete the project may be an estimate at the beginning—to be refined as more is known. On some projects, a time contingency is built in up front. However, some projects do have fixed deadlines. It is of no use to have a Christmas campaign deadline slip to 3 January or the timing systems for the track and field events at the Olympic Games a couple of weeks overdue. More modern methods of project development in use in e-business today deliberately impose strict deadlines to give greater emphasis to delivery, forcing decisions to be made with regard to the scope and quality rather than lose the timing. These time boxes may be very short, to place the emphasis on deliverables and to get the maximum benefit from the effort made available.

Projects can be large and complex, such as a new European air traffic control centre, or small and well-defined, such as finding the most efficient way of marking car-parking bays in a car park. This is generally known as *project scope*. Large projects are often separated into a number of smaller projects, and the series of interdependent projects is sometimes known as a programme, with a programme manager as leader. It is as important to complete only what is required of the project as it is to satisfy the project requirements. Changes to scope, which often occur after agreements have been made regarding time, cost, and quality, have a knock-on effect. This needs to be approved, well managed, and documented.

Quality planning, quality assurance, and quality control ensure that what is finally implemented is satisfactory in terms of the aims and objectives of the project, and also the process of project management itself. Scope and quality are often also, like cost and time, strongly associated, as they constitute the requirements of the project.

Issues of cost, time, scope, and quality are common to all projects from mapping the human genome to staging a new production of Shakespeare's *Hamlet*. The Pareto principle, which states that 80 per cent of the effect derives from 20 per cent of the effort, holds true for many management situations including the management of projects (see Figure 10.5). In the 1960s, software engineer Fred Brooks was working on a new operating system for IBM when he first observed the phenomenon as the project ran out of control. Brooks (1995) coined the term 'mythical man-month' to describe the hopelessness of increasing resources to complete a project.

The decisions made by the project leadership around the balance between the project requirements and the resources that are available to meet those requirements are among the most important decisions taken throughout the lifetime of any project.

## Integration, risk, procurement, human resources, and communication

Integration management ensures that the various elements that make up a project are co-ordinated, and this is a key project management technique. Without co-ordination, schedules and costs become increasingly difficult to estimate, scope becomes shapeless, and quality suffers. Changes to its scope are likely to occur during the course of the project as elements of the project are completed and new requirements are added. Integration

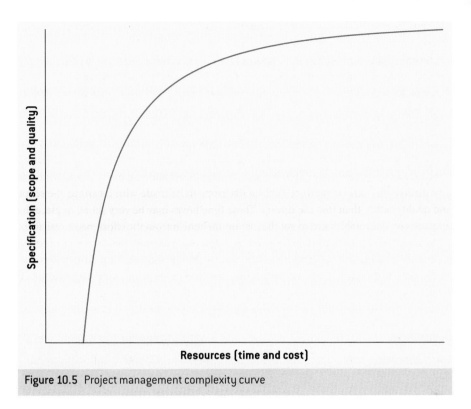

**Figure 10.5** Project management complexity curve

management identifies how changes affect the project as a whole. In projects where there is a great deal of uncertainty, changes can alter the very nature of the project as a whole and without the strategic view of the project leader there is a danger that the final results will prove difficult to assess against any meaningful criteria.

Integration management is also necessary to ensure that the project has the right links to other projects. At one time, it was the headache of the IT Project Manager to ensure that links with other projects and systems around the business were maintained and enhanced. The advent of enterprise resource planning systems such as SAP and Oracle (discussed in more detail in chapter 9) in the early 1990s went some way towards integrating 'islands of information', which had meant that firms were very often maintaining many different versions of the same data. A firm may consider it is selling walking boots in the UK but as soon as new projects to add a forum, link up with a walking holiday provider, or create a boot-selection module are implemented, new links are formed. In an e-business environment, as soon as a project goes live, dynamic links between systems can quickly, silently, and invisibly be forged that serve to innovate business processes, create links between divergent systems, or identify new stakeholders.

As Donald Rumsfeld famously said when he was US Secretary of Defense:

'there are known knowns; they are things we know we know. We also know there are known unknowns; that is to say we know there are some things we do not know. But there are also unknown unknowns—the ones we don't know we don't know.'

The same is true for projects, and identifying and responding to both the opportunities and risks continue throughout the lifetime of the project.

Some risks are internal and very much under the influence of the project leader: for example, staff changes and location issues. Other risks are external and entirely outside the control of the project: for example, economic variations and changes in legislation. Risks are categorized by their likelihood and can be expressed in terms of their impact on the key project processes of time, cost, scope, and quality of the project.

Assessing risks may be more difficult in an e-business environment. One reason is that many methods of assessing risks rely on experience. Assessing risks is about predicting the future. There can be a reliance on historical data, which may not be available to an e-business. This can be more of an issue in an e-business project environment where one project may be quite different from anything else ever attempted and staff may in any case have less general experience to call on. Another reason is the platform itself, as the use of new technologies is more unpredictable than using tried and tested techniques in an established environment. The documentation of the identification and response to opportunities and threats is important to provide historical data for future projects.

---

### Activity box 10.1

**Risk**

A world-class business school has a vision of providing high-quality, part-time education to senior executives around the world in an e-learning environment. Identify the major stakeholders. How many risks can you identify? Which risks can be avoided, mitigated, or transferred? Does this project seem too risky?

---

It may be that everything needed to complete the project is available to the project team throughout the whole of the project lifecycle, and this can happen on small projects. However, it is more likely that there will be some specialisms not present in the team, new software and training to acquire, or new equipment needed (see the discussion in Short case 10.2, for example). The procurement process is about acquiring the appropriate goods and services. Usually the focus is on procuring from outside the organization, but formal agreements may be entered into within the organization, depending on how the project is funded and accounted for. The procurement process includes the decision on whether and what to procure, as well as sourcing and contracting people and equipment. For an e-business, there may be a reluctance to share strategies, plans, and developments with outside contractors or suppliers due to the exploratory or innovative nature of the project. Conversely, lack of experience may make the use of specialists desirable at certain times in the lifecycle. Some external repositories of expertise may be available: the European Union developed the Information Services Procurement Library (ISPL) to offer 'a best practice library for the management of acquisition processes related to Information Technology'.

Human resources management ensures that the best use is made of staff skills and experience. In theory, the temporary nature of a project and the coming together of various team members and stakeholders from around and outside the organization lead to project team relationships that are newly forged for the purposes of the project. In addition, the human resources necessary for a project vary throughout its lifecycle, so that members come and go. In many ways, then, a project team is not like a team in an operational environment. Roles and responsibilities are allocated early on in the project, and include:

- a *project manager* or leader who will maintain a strategic view of the project as a whole and be responsible for the major decisions;
- a *business sponsor* or champion who initiates the project;
- a *beneficiary* or user, or more likely a group who will provide information to help scope the project and may be involved in testing;
- project *team members* responsible for the bulk of activities in the systems development lifecycle from set-up to maintenance;
- one or more technical or business *specialists*, needed at different times throughout the development lifecycle depending on the project requirements.

It is not always easy to identify the customer of a project. The person or role or unit funding the project is not necessarily the group who will benefit, or at whom the project is aimed. Better, then, to identify stakeholders who have varying levels of influence over the project at the beginning and as it progresses. With the multiple and varied stakeholders outlined above, it is well established that project management is largely about communication. Effective communication needs to take place within the project team, between project teams, and between the team and the various stakeholders (see Table 10.1). Moreover, in many cases, an e-business has additional, more diverse and sometimes more widely dispersed stakeholders and less predictable impacts, making issues such as the make-up of the project team and the required communication skills potentially more important than in some other environments. Very often, communication management is concerned with documenting and disseminating project progression.

**Table 10.1  Potential stakeholders**

| Internal | Micro environment | Macro environment |
| --- | --- | --- |
| Project leader | Business sponsor | Communities |
| Team members | Business representatives | National and local governments |
| Specialists | Beneficiaries | Government agencies |
| | Suppliers | Campaigners |
| | | Causes |

---

**Activity box 10.2**

Stakeholders

http://www.turnto.com, http://www.about.com and http://www.threadless.com are three very different e-businesses. Visit the sites and identify the stakeholders for each e-business. To what extent would each stakeholder be involved in a project to create greater community interaction?

---

**Activity box 10.3**

Culture and project management

A social network with a great deal of success in the English-speaking world is initiating a project to make itself more attractive to the countries of Asia-Pacific. What are the cultural and logistical difficulties that the geographical boundaries present? How will this affect the make-up of the project team?

---

# Project management techniques, tools, and methodologies

In Tom DeMarco's novel, *The Deadline*, the main protagonist is a project manager of a software development project with an impossible deadline on which his life literally depends. With almost unlimited resources at his disposal, he sets up multiple teams working on the same problems using a variety of approaches, techniques, tools, and methods. In real life, every project is a one-off, resources are limited and there is often little or no time available for reflection, consolidation, and organizational learning. However, in common with all areas of business management, project management practitioners and researchers have developed and refined techniques, tools, and methodologies better to ensure success. There is confusion relating to the use of these terms and so for the purposes of this book:

- An individual *technique* is, for example, a document to complete or a model to populate that addresses a specific project management step, such as a Gantt chart to schedule tasks and a risk log to monitor risk.

- A *tool* is a (usually automated) collection of techniques aimed at one of more of the areas of project management knowledge, such as time and cost. Microsoft Project is a project management tool.

- A *methodology* is an integrated set of techniques with support for the whole of the project management process from initiation to close and which includes an overarching philosophy. PRINCE2 and VersionOne are both project management methodologies.

In addition, there are tools, techniques, and methodologies associated with the systems development lifecycle. These include techniques such as entity relationship modelling or scrum meetings, tools such as HP's QuickTest Professional (QTP) for testing, and methodologies such as SSADM and DSDM. Short case 10.4 develops the AbeBooks example discussed earlier through a discussion of the project management tools and techniques employed by the firm.

---

### Short case 10.4

### Change at Abebooks.com

AbeBooks reviews direction and goals on a monthly basis, which leads to new ideas and proposed changes via the product council group. Customer feedback is also received either via surveys, forums, or almost immediately through the customer support department. In addition, system and business metrics are captured to reflect any trends. Response to change can be very rapid depending on the requirements. It can be almost immediate as, in common with all e-businesses, AbeBooks is a 24-hours-a-day, seven-days-a-week operation.

Site changes at AbeBooks are released into production every three weeks—that three-week period is the sprint-release cycle. Typically, a blend of changes is released at each iteration, comprising projects (large features), quick hits (small features), and infrastructure improvements. The mix depends on priorities and the risks associated with each one. »

Once a product has been placed into production and goes live, it is constantly monitored. AbeBooks must remain an efficient platform for selling and buying books at all times so usability, capacity, accuracy, and speed are vital.

With each product change request it is measured against what service level it requires: Gold (highest level), Silver (medium level), and Bronze (lowest level). These levels help determine quality of service expectations. Real-time system metrics are captured to verify and maintain these service levels.

AbeBooks is a global business and transactions occur every day of the year. They cannot shut up shop for maintenance like a 'bricks-and-mortar' business. Implementation of products is a vital part of the process as an e-business is always open.

*Question*

The balance between business initiatives and infrastructure initiative planning is a fine line for a 24x7 e-business site, knowing that continually adding business product site changes may show signs of infrastructure instability and scalability difficulties if the infrastructure changes are not planned in parallel. To what extent is this a project management problem and to what extent a business function problem? Is the balance between development of new products and maintenance of established business activities more difficult because it is in an e-business environment, or can you find parallels in other businesses?

There are many varied techniques to support every knowledge area in the project management process. As we have already discussed, techniques for estimating can be categorized as phasing, apportioning, parametric or bottom-up, and for e-business, a phased approach that does not rely on historical data is most useful. Phased estimating requires the project to be broken into a series of mini-projects. Using a waterfall lifecycle, a phase might be a stage of development, such as analysis or design. Using a prototyping or spiral approach to development creates a natural decision point at the end of each prototype, sprint, or cycle. An overall ball-park figure is given for the project as a whole to begin with and a detailed estimate of the first phase. At each phase, experience is gained as to the real cost of the on-going project. This revises the overall cost estimate and feeds into the detailed estimate for the next phase. The project team is committed only to the cost of the next phase, with the overall estimate gradually becoming more accurate. Phased estimating meets the needs of project management, especially where there is uncertainty, as it provides a more realistic time horizon and motivates the team with attainable, short-term goals. However, it may not be as attractive to whoever is funding the project. Once again, communication with stakeholders is important to set expectations and make clear that the advantages of reducing risk and increasing the number of decision points is of benefit to everyone involved.

All cost estimates rely on realistic work breakdown and scheduling. The work breakdown structure (WBS) can be a hierarchical diagram or simply a task list that takes the initial project concept and divides it into its stages, tasks, and steps. The depth of detail required will depend on the type of project and the desired level of certainty, but the end point should be a brief description of each and every meaningful unit of work.

It is the work breakdown structure on which work schedules that allocate resources, cost estimates, and progress monitoring and control are based. Effective scheduling based on the work breakdown structure ensures that tasks are completed by the right combination of team members and other resources in the right order to meet time and cost constraints. Tried and tested techniques such as network analysis and the identification of the critical path, Gantt charts, and time-scaled networks are all very familiar in a project environment.

Risk management is about identifying the risks associated with a particular project, analysing and prioritizing those risks, and developing planned responses. Techniques for risk assessment are very familiar to any management discipline, and work well in a project management environment. Techniques such as SWOT (strengths, weaknesses, opportunities, and threats) analyses, Porter's 5 forces (discussed in chapter 6), and PESTEL (political, economic, social, technological, environmental, and legal) analyses create a picture of the macro environment. Forecasting and sensitivity analyses based on historical data allow trend identification and 'what if?' explorations. Scenario planning takes a qualitative approach to explore different possible futures to see what can be avoided, overcome, or mitigated. All these techniques can be as much use to e-business as they can to the construction or pharmaceutical industries. Risk management continues throughout the life of the project, as new risks are identified and appropriate measures are taken and monitored.

Kolltveit et al. acknowledge that:

> 'project management has to deal with an enormously broad range of issues: technology, organization, strategy, finance, contracts, culture, planning, control, communication, environment, teamwork, etc.' *Koltveit et al., 2007*

In the project management literature the authors identified a move away from the earlier perspective of tasks in project management to the perspective of leadership as the critical success factor. While their warning is that researchers and practitioners may be focusing on leadership issues to the detriment of other important factors in project management success, it remains that the softer issues of leadership, communication, and teamwork are as much in need of tools and techniques as the other areas of project management.

Communication between team members and other stakeholders takes place through documents and meetings, both formally and informally. Some of the techniques already mentioned in this section facilitate communication by ensuring that it is clear who does what and when throughout the development lifecycle. Authorities and responsibilities should be clear and reinforced by the monitoring and control of the project leader: in past times, letters and memos added to the telephone conversations, meeting minutes to keep everyone informed. More latterly, time and place discontinuity has made emails popular but Lynch (2008) warns that projects can get lost in a storm 'of "reply-all" e-mails that overwhelm users trying to manage projects or collaborate on new business opportunities'. The author goes on to explain, 'E-mail, used by itself, just doesn't cut it anymore for project management and interoffice communication'. The author uses experiences at Bell Canada as an example of enterprise blogs to facilitate communication in the management of projects, and it seems that blogs and wikis really can aid communication in a way that other communication methods have failed to do. In e-business particularly, with many highly technical stakeholders, the attraction of such methods of communication across location and time barriers is very attractive. Recall that Short case 10.1 described CoProducer, a project which used blogs and discussion forums as well as emails to generate interest and keep in touch with the many co-producers involved.

## Activity box 10.4

### Structure

An innovative online fashion retailer involves its customers and wider community in the design of the clothes that it sells. This e-business start-up is led by a hard-working, skilled, and charismatic entrepreneur who has collected around her a well-motivated and highly creative workforce. They take a project approach and projects are never late and always surprise, if not amaze, the stakeholders, and even in a difficult economic outlook, potential investors continue to show an interest. However, the costs are often higher than expected and the average team member is working seventy hours a week during peak periods. What are the potential risks and rewards of introducing more structure and formalism to the process of project management?

Microsoft Project is a project management tool that supports the general project management principles already discussed. It can be used on any project in any industry, including large projects. Project incorporates many of the tried and tested techniques on the desktop for task identification and breakdown, budget creation, resource allocation, and task scheduling. The use of such tools allows project team communication with multiple and variable type access, exploration of different scenarios, and speedy identification of critical tasks and potential bottlenecks. Microsoft Project is a popular choice, but other open source and proprietary solutions exist for individual tools and for integrated methods, either on the desktop or web-based. For example, TenStep's cOrdin8 is their portfolio and project management office system that uses the TenStep® approach to project management.

Many organizations use a variety of tools and techniques as appropriate for their project management needs—sometimes leaving the choice of tools as a decision for the project manager. However, integrated methodologies for project management do exist. Methodologies have tended to fall into one of two categories, *prescriptive* or *dynamic*. An example of a prescriptive proprietary methodology used widely in Europe is the UK Office of Government Commerce's PRINCE2 (PRojects IN Controlled Environments) (http://www.prince2.com). An example of a dynamic methodology is that created and marketed by VersionOne (http://www.versionone.com).

For a long time, the choice of project management approach was settled by using a prescriptive method for large, complex, and safety-critical systems and a more dynamic approach for smaller, less-critical, but more time-constrained projects. As the benefits of the more agile methods for project management were seen to be more user-oriented, the prescriptive approaches incorporated dynamic elements, blurring the boundaries somewhat—but the general principle holds.

However, many e-businesses present the IT project management professional with large, complex, safety-critical requirements for projects that are required quickly. Combined with a high required level of usability, a whole new generation of approaches, methodologies, tools, and techniques is being developed. In discussing leading projects 'at the edge of chaos', Moran and Youngdahl (2008) state that 'the highly systematic approaches of project management can break down when we apply pressures of uncertainty, complexity and stretched resources'.

Pollack (2007) sees this in project management terms in a paradigm shift from 'hard' to 'soft'. The author contends that a hard approach to project management, as typified by the PMBOK, gives a false impression of control, and that softer techniques and methodologies could usefully be applied in some circumstances—particularly where many people are involved in highly stressful situations. One response to this shift may have been that rather than use integrated methodologies, successful e-business projects tend to employ a collection of techniques that suit the team members and the working environment as well as the project type—and the case studies that we have used in this chapter seem to demonstrate the point.

It was Takeuchi and Noneka (1986) who first suggested shifting away from using the metaphor of a relay race in product development, as one stage passes the baton to another, to the metaphor of a game of rugby where the project proceeds with 'the constant interaction of a hand-picked, multidisciplinary team whose members work together from start to finish'. Their approach neatly demonstrates the difference between the traditional waterfall lifecycle first outlined in Figure 10.2 above. Adopting this metaphor as more appropriate for an emphasis on speed and efficiency, Schwaber and Beedle developed Scrum as a software development method. Schwaber (2004) later went on further to explain the role of the ScrumMaster with case studies from a variety of perspectives. Scrum is a set of practices and roles that fulfil the development lifecycle with the minimum prescription. Usable increments are known as 'sprints', and sprints are no longer than one month. During a sprint, changes are not allowed and any required changes must wait for the next sprint. While Scrum accepts that changes are to be expected, it makes it much more obvious to all stakeholders that the decision about what can and cannot be achieved is a team decision. Stakeholders are divided into committed 'pigs' (product owner, scrummaster, and team member) and involved 'chickens' (users, stakeholders, and managers). A scrum meeting takes place at the same time each day during a sprint, lasting fifteen minutes, and with set objectives. Like all agile approaches, Scrum is focused on timeboxing, usable deliverables, and involvement.

Timeboxing A time-management technique in which a schedule is divided into a number of separate time periods with each part having its own independent deliverables, deadlines, and budgets.

## Activity box 10.5

### Exploring metaphors

Takeuchi and Noneka (1986) talked about product development as either a relay race or a game of rugby and this metaphor has been used to describe Scrum. Developing a project metaphor forms an intrinsic part of eXtreme Programming. Explore some other metaphors for e-business project management. Try pole vaulting, Formula One motor racing and basketball. Move on to using the metaphor of a car, a horse, a bee colony and a court case. Think of some others and then select the metaphor you consider to be most appropriate.

eXtreme Programming (XP) is not entirely focused on 'programming' as its name suggests but is a software development method that covers the whole of the development process. XP takes the form of a series of rules and practices derived from experience and 'taken to the extreme'. An underlying belief is that changes to requirements are natural and necessary throughout the project development process and that adaptability is the critical success factor in managing a project.

Like XP, Feature-driven development (FDD) has at its core a belief in agile principles. FDD is organized into five stages or activities: develop overall model, build feature list, plan by feature, design by feature, build by feature. Once again, the focus is on small tasks (called 'features') arranged into a series of milestones with many decision points.

The emphasis on the more agile methodologies is in providing a framework rather than a rigid structure, and on presenting an underlying philosophy rather than a series of detailed stages, tasks, and steps. The lifecycle, as an alternative to the waterfall approach of early and more prescriptive methodologies, is iterative and incremental. Agile methodologies are very much about providing the greatest gain with the least amount of fuss, and force a constant consideration of the differing priorities of time, cost, scope, and quality. There is a greater focus on issues of customer involvement, team work, and communication. All these factors make agile methodologies, or a collection of tools and techniques borrowed from the methodologies, very attractive in an e-business project environment.

## Long case 10.1

### Imagini's project management process

Imagini is the London-based creator of the VisualDNA concept, as used by Youniverse, described in Short case 10.3 above. Imagini's B2B team employ VisualDNA methods to work with clients such as Pepsi and the British Army on bespoke projects to fit their e-business requirements.

Imagini does not have a formalized project development process but is developing a flexible model tailored to Imagini culture and work practices. Imagini's project management and development process might be considered typical for a start-up and, in the words of Imagini's Anthony Powell 'is a million miles away from formalized project management techniques or software design techniques'.

It starts with a vision. The process is initiated in a conversation with an agency, client, or the Imagini marketing team. What follows is the creative-led, highly visual, and very tailored conception of requirements. This stage is very fast—maybe a single meeting with the client. The handover to technical staff involves a series of meetings in which the vision is thrashed out. Powell says that this can be 'a painful process because the visions are often very ambitious and unconnected to reality' during which a common understanding is eventually reached. Although this can take up to one-third of the project time available depending on the similarity of the projects to other projects completed, it is crucial to the overall success of the project and cannot be skimped. This might mean four  » weeks out of a 'meaty' three-month project. The output is a product specification and a technical specification, which is then signed off by the originator. The level of detail in the original vision and the sign-off are crucial. Otherwise there is every likelihood that the final product will look nothing like the original idea. A key initiative at Imagini in recent times is greatly improved specifications to provide a library of projects. Finally, implementation takes place.

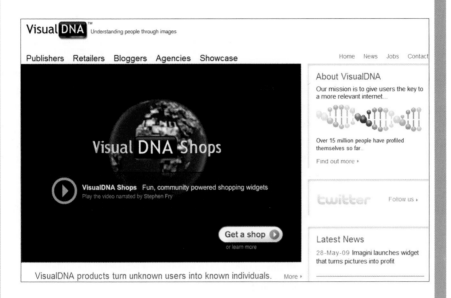

There are some interesting projects that have come entirely from the technical side of the business and that have taken some time to get a sponsor from outside the IT group. An example is an infrastructure project that led to a move to service-oriented architecture: the project had no obvious benefit to the customer but is now a core asset for Imagini. Another example is the development of an analytics tool and tracking technologies. In that sense, the vision for a new project can come from anywhere.

For project development, Imagini experimented in the past with close adherence to an agile approach but found that used strictly, the agile philosophy demands extremely strong product direction and can be ineffective if used in Imagini's more exploratory environment. Agile methods require very focused specifications to reap all the benefits and in this way, even agile methods may be seen to stifle innovation or limit creativity. Instead, Imagini use some aspects of agile development to get 'quick turnaround without chaos'. For example, there is a minimum atomicity of a two-week development period—nothing shorter. The specifications are very stable to begin with and it is clear that finishing a sprint isn' the end of the technical input. The technical team go on to make sure that results are deployable and have been QA tested, compatibility tested, and upgrade tested with what is already live.

Powell continues:

> 'We've also disassociated finishing a product increment, i.e. a sprint, from the deploy cycle. What happened in the past was that micro changes were regularly requested and »

we could be doing up to five deployments a day, which is unacceptable. There must be a balance between responsiveness and structure, and so now we have turned deploying into a calendar with fixed slots, like airport landing slots. If you miss your slot, that's it until the next one becomes available. We have a number of deploys per week for each product—slots that may or may not be used. There is a lead time of two days during which the product must be quality tested. The fundamental driver is volume of data because it is essential to test products with real data and refreshing a test environment that mirrors the live environment takes time. So it's not full-on agile. We might have a Scrum team of eight or nine people and then work in smaller groups of maybe three people but we don't have ten minute, strictly managed meetings every day and there isn't a person managing a separate pipeline for each. These guys are doing it for themselves.'

With regard to time, Powell admits that it has been a steep learning curve:

'Most projects now are on time but we have had to learn from past mistakes. As we have sharpened the specifications and improved the whole process we have seen all subsequent projects fall into line on time, to specification and within budget. Without well-defined specifications that outline the vision there is the possibility of huge disappointments when projects are complete. This just doesn't happen now.'

*Question*

Is the process of project management at Imagini, as Powell says, 'a million miles away from formalized project management techniques or software design techniques'? To what extent can the PMBOK project management activities and knowledge areas be seen in Imagini project management? How much of what happens at Imagini is particular to:

1. an IT development environment
2. an e-business project environment and
3. Imagini?

## Long case 10.2

### Take the lottery out of discovery

Snagsta is a recommendation engine based around lists. If you are looking for a traditional English restaurant in Oxford, check out the list of possibilities offered by the friend who studied there last year. If you are trying to find the best e-business conference to attend this year, see what others in the industry recommend. Snagsta users can also add their own lists of, for example, objects of desire, books to read, or most relaxing holiday destinations, and share lists with friends. At the time of writing, Snagsta is in the private beta phase.

As Alex Moore, one of three co-founders of Snagsta explains:

'Snagsta was born from a spreadsheet I used to keep on my desktop at work and created back in 2001 when I was running my own website development company in Hong Kong. The spreadsheet started life as a list of my favourite books and book recommendations from  » friends but soon grew to include films, hotels, beaches, mountain biking trails, restaurants, pubs, music and even quotes.'

Moore initially created the spreadsheet to overcome the frustration brought on by the overwhelming amount of information sifting necessary to find recommendations that 'fitted'. And he wanted a repository for all the trusted recommendations he had received. Moore continues:

> 'By about 2003 it had grown to sizable document. I started sharing more and more of its content with friends and family, and found it more and more useful. The more I shared it with people the more it grew. This is when I first started to think that I might be able to turn lists of people's favourite things into a successful online business.'

All three co-founders contribute ideas that are implemented on Snagsta in a fairly equal contribution, born of an equal passion for the site. Phil Hofmeyr, Snagsta co-founder explains the process:

> 'First we debate. Decision by committee can be time-consuming but we've found that nine times out of ten, 1 + 1 + 1 = 5 (and the most project management focused one of us sometimes has to call us to order and say: "That's enough!"). We are very different and occasionally have heated debates. Ordinarily, differences can so often deteriorate into conflict. However, our mutual respect for one another and recognition of our strengths and weaknesses means that we've worked it in our favour'.

»

With such a small team of three directing developments, any new features or ideas are 'fleshed-out' in an initial specification by whoever feels most closely associated with the project. The specification comprises screenshots and an explanation. The other two team members then review the specs and recommend changes if necessary.

Hofmeyr says:

'I think if we keep the team small we can continue in the same way, although we might have to more clearly distinguish between the roles and do less by committee once we're fully operational.'

After an initial period during which Snagsta employed a single developer to realize the founders' ideas, the group went back to basics with a new team, found through the recommendation of Snagsta's main investor. This first painful period is recounted by Hofmeyr:

'Our first developer simply couldn't build the site as we wanted it. The code didn't work, the site was slow, and so on. We managed him very badly and simply trusted he knew what he was doing. When he failed to deliver, he somehow convinced us he was just about to crack it. Embarrassingly enough, this went on for months. That could have something to do with the fact that he was a friend of ours.'

New developments and site maintenance are taken care of by the new team of ten very smart graduates led by a senior programmer. Hofmeyr says 'they have needed *very* little project management'.

*Questions*

1. Identify the elements of Snagsta's development environment that conform to the general principles of project management, as adopted by more established e-businesses.

2. To what extent have the founders of Snagsta provided a firm platform from which to develop project management principles that enable future expansion?

## ⭐ Chapter Summary

The conclusion might be that there are no substantial differences between project management in general, specialist IT project management, and e-business project management in particular. However, as we have seen, the emphasis on some aspects such as speed and flexibility in design and management might be far greater in an e-business environment than, say, in a new patients' records system for a health service, where specification and cost might be higher priorities. There is a greater acceptance in the type of project management that is typical in an e-business environment of the importance of human resources and communication. In addition, some social and political elements of e-business project management are likely to become so important that the planned response of such elements overrides all other considerations, giving a whole new meaning to 'disaster recovery' in project management—which might now, whether intentionally or not, be about opposing or bowing to government censure, providing evidence in the divorce court of a distant land, affecting elections, selling firearms, human organs for transplant, or babies, facilitating suicide pacts, stalkers, and organized terrorism, and fighting libel cases. Much of what can be observed as different in project management in an e-business environment as against any other sector or industry is to be found in the make-up of the project teams and in the systems development methods used.

## ❓ Review questions

1. What are the characteristics of a project?

2. What are the main processes of project management?

3. Outline the PMBOK knowledge areas for project management

4. Distinguish between the process of project management and the project development lifecycle.

5. What techniques, tools, and methodologies are most appropriate for e-business project management?

6. What techniques, tools, and methodologies are most appropriate for e-business systems development?

7. Distinguish between the terms 'tool', 'technique', and 'methodology', with an example of each.

8. What separates the traditional approach to project management from the agile approach favoured in an e-business environment?

## ⭕ Discussion questions

1. Jelassi and Enders (2008) claim that 'it's too early for e-business to drop its "e"': is it, then, too early for e-business project management to do the same?

2. To what extent do you consider e-business project management to be different from general project management and IT project management?

3. What role can organized bodies of knowledge play in e-business project management?

4. To what extent is the balancing act between time, cost, and specification affected by the size, complexity and uniqueness of the e-business project?

5. How can an e-business ensure that future projects incorporate learning from the achievements and difficulties of past projects?

## ➡ Recommended reading

Bocij, P., Greasley, A., and Hickie, S., (2008), *Business Information Systems: Technology, Development and Management for the e-Business*, Prentice-Hall
This popular and accessible general book on business information systems provides some useful case studies and examples.

Mulcahy, R., (2005), *PMP Exam Prep: Accelerated Learning To Pass PMI's PMP Exam—On Your First Try!* RMC Publications Inc.
There are many study aids including flashcards, practice examinations, and simulations to support those wishing to become Project

Management Professionals, accredited by the Project Management Institute. Together with the PMBOK guide, this book provides a thorough grounding.

Newton, R., (2005), *Project Manager: Mastering the Art of Delivery in Project Management*, Prentice Hall.
Taking a communication-oriented view of project management, this book also outlines the most popular tools and techniques.

PMBOK Guides, (2004), *A Guide to the Project Management Body of Knowledge: PMBOK Guide*, 3rd edn, Project Management Institute.

For the general principles of project management in any industry, the PMBOK guide is the definitive resource. A new edition (fourth) is due in 2009.

Wysocki, R.K., (2006), *Effective Software Project Management*, John Wiley & Sons

This book gives a great description of all the lifecycles and phases of a software development, including many case studies and examples from this experienced author.

# ➜ References

Brooks, F.P., Jr., (1995), *The Mythical Man-Month: Essays on Software Engineering*, 20th anniversary edition, Addison-Wesley.

DeMarco, T., (1997), *Deadline*, Dorset House Publishing

Jelassi, T. and Enders, A., (2008), *Strategies for e-Business: Creating Value through Electronic and Mobile Commerce*, 2nd edn, Pearson Education.

Kolltveit, B.J., Karlsen, J.T., and Grønhaug, K., (2007), 'Perspectives on Project Management', *International Journal of Project Management*, 25, pp. 3–9.

Lynch, C.G., (2008), 'Blogs Clean Up Project Management Messes', *CIO Magazine* January.

Moran, R.T. and Youngdahl, W.E., (2008), *Leading Global Projects: For Professional and Accidental Leaders*, Butterworth Heinemann.

Pollack, J., (2007), 'The Changing Paradigms of Project Management', *International Journal of Project Management*, 25, pp. 266–74.

Sampson, G., (2008), *Electronic Business*, 2nd edn, British Computer Society.

Sauer, C. and Cuthbertson, C., (2003), *The State of IT Project Management in the UK*, Templeton College.

Schwaber, K.. (2004). *Agile Project Management with SCRUM*, Microsoft Press.

Takeuchi, H. and Noneka, I., (1986), 'The New New Product Development Game', *Harvard Business Review*, 64, pp. 137–46.

Verzuh, E., (2008), *The Fast Forward MBA in Project Management*, 3rd edn, John Wiley & Sons.

# ➜ Weblinks

**Association for Project Management.** The aim of the Association for Project Management (APM) is to aim is to develop and promote project management across all sectors of industry in Europe: http://www.apm.org.uk/. APM is the repository for the APM body of knowledge (APMBOK): http://www.apm.org.uk/BOK.asp.

**British Computer Society.** The British Computer Society is a professional body to promote the study and practice of computing and to advance knowledge of and education in IT for the benefit of the public: http://www.bcs.org. The British Computer Society runs several specialist groups, including one for project management: http://www.bcs.org/server.php?show=conWebDoc.1239.

**Information Services Procurement Library.** The Information Services Procurement Library (ISPL) is a European best practice library for the management of acquisition processes related to Information Technology: http://projekte.fast.de/ISPL/.

**International Project Management Association.** The International Project Management Association (IPMA) IPMA promotes project management to businesses and organizations around the world. They certify project managers, award successful project teams and researchers, and publish in the area of project management: http://www.ipma.ch/Pages/default.aspx.

**Office of Government Commerce.** Prince2 is developed and promoted by the UK's Office of Government Commerce as a general project management methodology: http://www.ogc.gov.uk/.

**Project Management Institute.** The Project Management Institute is a worldwide membership association for project management professionals: http://www.pmi.org/. it has members in over 170 countries, including a UK chapter: http://www.pmi.org.uk/. The Project Management Institute is also the repository of the project management body of knowledge (PMBOK®): http://www.pmi.org/Resources/Pages/Library-of-PMI-Global-Standards.aspx.

**Standish Group.** The Standish Group undertakes research and consultancy in the area of IT project management. The group conducts the CHAOS survey on project management: http://www.standishgroup.com/.

# E-business skills and culture

## Learning outcomes

Completing this chapter will enable you to:

- Understand the changing human resource implications of e-business
- Distinguish between the different categories of skills and different kinds of skills shortage
- Identify the trends in demand for e-business skills worldwide
- Improve your awareness of the recruitment practices of e-businesses
- Recognize the behavioural consequences of the introduction of e-business technologies in the workplace
- Appreciate selected cultural dimensions of e-business organization and entrepreneurship

## Introduction

'There is a shortage of IT skills on a worldwide basis. Anybody who can get those skills will have a lot of opportunity.' *Bill Gates,* quoted in Dawson, 2006.

Concern about a shortage of 'e-skills' is commonly expressed by businesses around the world and comprises an important element of policy at all levels of many governments worldwide, but this—along with the cultural dimensions of e-business—is often a neglected aspect of books on e-business and e-commerce, which tend to treat e-business as a rational and normative set of activities. This chapter therefore focuses on the changing human resource requirements of e-business. It defines what is meant by e-business skills, as distinct from more general ICT skills, distinguishing between skills shortages, gaps, and mismatches, and summarizing trends in demand for and supply of such skills. It reviews initiatives in certification and in curriculum development, and examines the importance of training and development within businesses. It examines the recruitment practices of e-business firms and concludes with a discussion of some of the cultural issues affecting e-business organizations. For organizations as well as for individuals, while access to and application and use of e-business technologies has provided new opportunities for improvement in productivity and working practices, it has also posed new kinds of challenges, for both employees and managers. These include changes in communications practice in the workplace and the psychological consequences that arise from the blurring of boundaries between home and work, as well as the implications for social control which the abuse of e-business technologies can bring about.

Concerns about a skills shortage in relation to e-business have arisen for a number of reasons. The increasing tradability of services worldwide, driven by technological change, has had the effect of rapidly increasing the importance of particular skills to a country's prosperity, since activities can increasingly be located according to the mix and comparative advantage of a country's skills-set. Technology is also substituting not only for lower skilled activities but also some intermediate skill jobs, such as craft jobs (eSkills UK, 2006). Finally, e-business and more broadly-based ICT investment are seen as major drivers of economic growth in most developed and, increasingly, developing economies. Up to 5 per cent of total employment in OECD countries is in ICT specialist occupations and around 20 per cent in ICT-using occupations.

'Employment in the IT industry is forecast to grow at 5 to 8 times the UK average over the next ten years. For the IT professional workforce that means 180,000 new people for new and replacement jobs every year. Yet in 2002 only 8,800 new graduates entered this sector within six months of graduation, and only 20% of these were women. In the general workforce 90% of new jobs require IT user skills, a quarter of businesses lack employees with the right IT skills now, and 7.6 million employees need to increase their skills to meet growing demand over the next three years.' *e-skills UK, 2006*

Governments feel that it is a particular responsibility to ensure the provision of people with e-business or 'e-skills' because of their growing importance to the success of a modern economy. In March 2000, for example, the EU Heads of States and Governments agreed to make the EU 'the most competitive and dynamic knowledge-driven economy by 2010' (BBC News, 2005) but the agenda has failed so far to deliver the number of jobs required to generate the growth that was anticipated. Surveys and anecdotal evidence suggests that the supply of 'properly qualified' people is seen as lagging behind demand within developed economies:

'Already today, millions of vacancies in Europe are unfilled because there are not enough people with the right skills to fill them … We cannot let this situation get worse.' *Barroso, 2008*

While the growth of offshore outsourcing[1] is seen as providing evidence for skills shortage in domestic markets, even in emerging markets there is concern about a shortfall in appropriately skilled workers. In India, for example, the main software industry body NASSCOM (http://www.nasscom.in) estimated in 2007 that the country's ICT industry, where the business process outsourcing industry has been growing at 30 per cent per annum, requires some 350,000 engineers per annum, but that only 150,000 are available. We discussed e-business outsourcing in detail in chapter 9.

---

[1] Outsourcing refers to the sending of work to another organization to be done. Off-shoring refers to where the work is done. The 'off-shorability' of tasks are defined as those tasks that could potentially be carried out from any geographical location, particularly in low-wage economies.

# What do we mean by e-business skills?

Part of the problem in addressing the question of 'e-business skills' is that defining what they are is quite difficult—let alone forecasting the likely levels of demand for and supply of them. This is for three reasons:

1) *Rapid and unpredictable change in ICT.* The volatile and changing character of developments in e-business means that such skills need to be redefined, re-acquired, or renewed on a more frequent but less predictable basis than in many other occupations. Partly as a result, there are

2) *Problems in measurement of demand.* The measurement of ICT professional and e-business skills suffers from a lack of agreed definitions and ambiguity in assessing true levels of demand by governments, companies, and sectors. As a result, we can see

3) *Lag effects in supply.* The educational system lags in its ability to provide appropriately qualified entrants to the job market.

Nowhere could these factors be seen coming together more clearly than at the height of the dot.com boom. The kinds of estimate made then in relation to the demand for ICT and e-business skills turned out to be over-optimistic:

'The estimated shortage of European ICT professionals in 2003 [is thought to be] 1.7 million persons. Adding to this the categories of e-business professionals and call centre professionals leads to a total estimated skills gap of 3.8 million persons. The shortage of e-business professionals is expected to increase particularly rapidly, reflecting the more than threefold increase in the demand for e-business skills over the forecast period 1999–2003.' *European Commission*, 2000

But even today, over a fifth of UK IT and telecoms companies reported difficulties in recruiting people with the right skills (e-Skills, 2008). 'E-skills' are often thought of as being skills equivalent to those entirely to be found within the field of information, communication and technology. This is incorrect. Most commentators are agreed that e-business skills go beyond the purely technical, but that there have been few attempts to qualify or quantify a particular skill-set. One way of classifying ICT skills is in terms of their level of sophistication. The OECD originally differentiated between *basic, advanced,* and *professional* ICT skills.

- *Basic skills* referred to competent users of generic tools needed for functioning with a knowledge economy and society (such as word processing, spreadsheet, and email software).

- *Advanced skills* referred to competent users of more sophisticated and often sector-specific software tools (such as enterprise-wide software, customer relationship management systems (CRM), or geographic information systems (GIS)). In both these cases, ICT is seen as a tool, a means to an end, rather than the main job.

- In the case of *professional skills*, however, we tend to think in terms of ICT specialists exercising specific roles in relation to the development, operation, or maintenance of the ICT systems themselves (but this may vary from software programmers to cable fitters).

Another way of classifying ICT skills is to distinguish between users (which corresponds broadly to advanced skills) and *practitioners* (which corresponds to professional skills). Increasingly, professional or practitioner skills alone are seen as being no longer sufficient; particularly as basic tasks in developed economies have been automated, digitised, or off-shored by companies. Specialist job definitions are evolving which extend the boundary of ICT skills into, amongst other areas, business.

E-business skills can be seen as *strategic* in nature, in that they address longer-term developmental needs of firms, rather than providing solutions to more immediate technical or *tactical* questions. As Figure 11.1 also suggests, they are a subset of more general business skills and comprise the mixed set of competences which are required to exploit business opportunities provided by ICTs, at all three levels—basic, advanced, and professional. Appropriately related business skills might involve, for example, project management, marketing or sales management, and inter-personal skills—each of which might now require a different mix of ICT skills to demonstrate competence.

But the logic for a hybrid skills set can be seen as contributing to the development of new products and services, as well as enabling business efficiency improvements. They intersect with ICT skills at all levels, but are particularly powerful where the combination will add the most value: amongst ICT professionals and practitioners. It has been suggested that these *cross-disciplinary* skills can comprise business, creative, and technical skills partially learned in: 'business studies, commerce, multimedia, multimedia, information systems, fine art, librarianship, journalism, film studies, photography ...' (Expert Group on Future Skills Needs, 2001). More specifically, e-business skills can also be seen as those required by 'internet business strategists or internet-dependent professionals' (EITO, 2001). The organizational impact of combined professional ICT and e-business skills can go far beyond providing purely technical solutions and may contribute to broader improvements in the efficiency and effectiveness of organizational structures. For example, looking at the firm- level evidence on the impact of ICT investment suggests that:

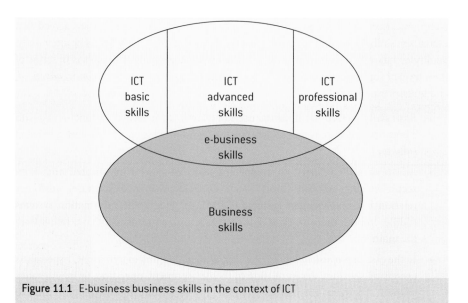

**Figure 11.1**  E-business business skills in the context of ICT

'ICT use is [not only] correlated with increases in the demand for human capital skills, but also with more decentralised decision--making and greater use of teams.' *Bresnahan et al., 1999.*

E-business skills are also differentially distributed geographically. There is a high degree of correlation between the extent to which a country is 'e-ready' (see chapter 1 for a discussion of e-readiness) and its e-business skills readiness, according to work carried out by INSEAD's e-lab for the European Commission (Figure 11.2). The analysis recognises recognizes three sub-groups of countries, where the Nordic markets, the USA, Singapore, Switzerland, and South Korea dominate the top of both rankings, whilst while Poland, Romania, and Greece feature at the bottom. Thirty-nine per cent of the German workforce considers that they have 'a strong and broad range of digital skills', compared to only 13 per cent in Poland.

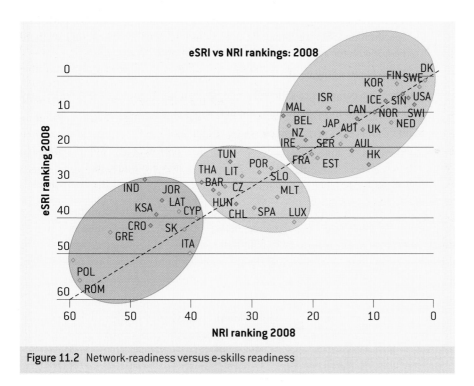

**Figure 11.2** Network-readiness versus e-skills readiness

---

### Activity box 11.1

#### Sectors in need?

There are 25 UK sector skills councils responsible for boosting the skills of the sector workforces. Choose a UK sector skills council of your choice and investigate the extent to which (1) the sector faces a skills shortage and (2) it has developed a strategic response to that shortage. How active is the council? Critically examine the skills council response to any shortage. You can find a listing of sector skills councils here: http://www.sscalliance.org/Sectors/SectorSkillsCouncils/SectorSkillsCouncils.asp.

# Understanding skills shortages

Discussion of skills 'shortages', especially in economically important occupations or business sectors, is often politically sensitive and open to debate (Ghosh, 2006). The concept of 'shortage' is itself an ambiguous one. For example, what may be described as a skills shortage by a firm or sector—leading to a call for more investment in external training and education—may be seen as poor recruitment and internal training practice by outside commentators. What we can say is that there is often poor alignment between the demand for e-business skills and their availability (whether from existing employees or from prospective recruits). Research undertaken by RAND Europe for the European Commission (2005) suggests that this lack of alignment can be of three kinds:

- Skills shortage (a recruitment need)
  - There are not enough people to fill the number of jobs available of a particular specification. Shortages may be overcome through the recruitment of more people with the appropriate skill-set.
- Skills gap (a retraining need)
  - There is a competence shortfall amongst existing ICT professionals, which may be overcome through training and development of existing staff.
- Skills mismatch (a curriculum need)
  - There is a difference between observed and expected ICT professional competences. This can only be overcome through dialogue between organizations education, and training institutions.

Figure 11.3 shows the ways in which education, training, and the workforce interact in practice for e-business. The dynamic nature of digital business means that new developments inevitably require new skills, there will need to be frequent changes to the e-business curriculum to remedy mismatches, and continuing professional development

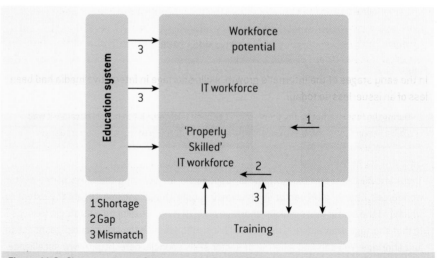

**Figure 11.3** Shortages, gaps & mismatches in the ICT labour market

## Short case 11.1

### Skills and training in the UK interactive media industry

Analysing demand by sector shows that ICT and e-business-related jobs in media and publishing exhibited the biggest growth of any sector in the UK during the middle of the current decade, driven by the particular exposure of the sector to the effects of digital technological innovation (*Computer Weekly, 2006*). In newspaper publishing, for example, firms have been moving towards the creation of integrated newsrooms and multi-media hubs (see picture) (*Guardian, 2006*).

Long case 6.2 discussed the case of the Guardian Media Group in more detail. Not only has a chronic shortage of skilled people been identified, but many of those already in post feel underequipped to deal with the changing requirements of their posts. In the interactive media industries (comprising computer games, Internet, and web design occupations), two-thirds of the employment base is under 35 (compared with 36 per cent of the UK workforce as a whole). Despite 80 per cent of the workforce comprising graduates (compared to 16 per cent in the UK as a whole), two-thirds reported a training need, primarily in order to stay up to date with or improve their ability to address current work requirements and to develop new technical skills (Sector Skills Council for the Audio-Visual Industries, 2005).

> 'Continually improving and adding to your portfolio of skills is an absolute necessity for people working in this industry. The speed of change—technically, editorially, commercially—is breathtaking, and to achieve career longevity people have to keep their skills up to date.' *Dinah Caine, CEO, skillset* [2]

In the early stages of the Internet's growth, skills shortage in interactive media had been less of an issue; less so today:

> 'During the first Internet boom, there weren't enough talented, skilled people because it was such a new industry, but then the reality was that clients knew nothing anyway. You could put someone with one or two years' experience in front of them; interactive was easy to blag. Clients now have six, seven or eight years' experience in interactive media, so if you put a junior person in front of them, then the skills gap becomes clear very quickly.' *Tribal DDB*

The skills-set required for interactive media is often referred to as T-skills: that is, a combination of a broad set of general skills (the bar of the 'T') together with a set of deep, specialist skills (the vertical bar). Specialist skills (whether transient or enduring) range

[2]  http://http://www.skillset.org.      »

from software programming principles to HCI design and digital rights management; whilst transferable general skills include client and end user empathy as well as business, financial, and sales and marketing capabilities. Increasingly, senior practitioners are also expected to demonstrate cross-disciplinary awareness of the interactive media industry and its processes, particularly in production management and publishing.[3]

Question

Relate the 'skills shortage' identified by the interactive and media industries in the UK to the frameworks used earlier in the chapter. What solutions are practically available to employers?

[3] A good example of how computer gaming is attracting women into the workforce with transferable skills can be seen in this profile of Paulina Bozek, Senior Producer, Sony Playstation: http://www.skillset.org/games/careers/article_4356_1.asp.

(CPD) is needed to mitigate the widening skills gaps of existing employees. Short case 11.1 discusses the specific experience of the UK interactive media industry, where in addition to the considerations above, the early days of the industry witnessed a mismatch between the skills of the sector's clients and those of supplier companies.

### Activity box 11.2

#### Assessing evolving journalistic skills

The mix of skills required by journalists is significantly affected by e-business technologies. Read the reflections on the BBC's Future of Journalism conference at the Online Journalism Blog at http://onlinejournalismblog.com/2008/12/01/bbc-future-of-journalism-day-1-some-reflections/. Focus particularly on the skills-related comments and on the concept of a 'News Diamond'. What are the implications for the future skills mix?

## Changes in demand for e-business skills

Jobs involving technology are likely to be amongst the fastest growing and most highly rewarded occupations in many countries. Those additionally involving e-business skills are particularly prone to high rates of growth in demand. Forrester Research suggested in 2005 that companies would require more individuals skilled as enterprise architects, business analysts and relationship managers, web services, business intelligence/web-enabled analysts, and business process modellers (Symons, 2005). They noted that many of these roles involved a mixture of professional ICT and business skills.

In the US some categories of jobs involving technology are projected to grow at more than twice the national average for all occupations from 2006 to 2016, according to the US Department of Labor (2005). Conversely, the analysis in Figure 11.4, which illustrates the absolute change in job numbers, also shows that whilst some occupations—particularly those concerned with business intelligence and applications—are likely to increase significantly, some hitherto specialized areas of ICT (such as computer operating and word processing and typing) will be in decline. This is a classic illustration of the downward cascade of increasingly pervasive ICT skills to many more categories of occupation. Indeed, many of these skills may be increasingly and more appropriately configured as digital literacy, or life skills, rather than tied to particular occupations. Three types of digital literacy skill have been identified by Gareis (2006):

- operational skills: needed to operate ICTs—fixed and mobile hardware, operating and applications software, Internet access;
- information skills: needed to search, identify, and manipulate online information; and
- strategic skills: such as the kind of 'environmental scanning' skills needed to achieve improvements in social and economic status of the individual.

In 2006, commentators were very gloomy about fulfilling demand for posts:

'We do have a glass that is full, and you cannot get any more into it. There is a finite number of IT people in the UK, and the education system produces a limited number each year. The demand is far greater than that, so there will always be full IT employment in the UK, in terms of volume, though the type of demand will change.' *Paul Smith, Harvey Nash Group*

But forecasts of demand in this area are inherently unreliable: actual demand can be very volatile, even in the short term. Looking back at the employment characteristics of the Internet boom and bust, it is clear that there was an overestimation of US e-business skills needs in 2000, given the volatility in the following three years:

- Some 175,000 workers in Internet-related businesses were laid off in the US between 2000 and 2003—according to outplacement company Challenger, Gray & Christmas (2004).

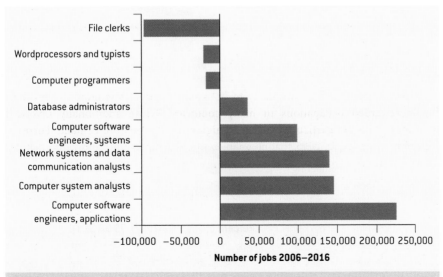

**Figure 11.4** Projected growth in selected US ICT-related occupations 2006-2016

- The Internet directly or indirectly supported 3m workers in the US in 2000.
- Thirty-one million Americans were estimated to have been affected in some way by the dot.com downturn, according to analyst Webmergers.com (which itself was acquired by the 451Group).

One way of validating current forecasts is to examine the recent growth and decline of vacancies for particular types of job advertised on recruitment websites. On this basis, it appears that once again many countries are entering a recession in terms of IT job demand. For example, in the third quarter of 2008, ICT jobs advertised on the web fell by 7 per cent over the same period in 2007—but they still stood at nearly four times the level of the low point reached in 2003. Figure 11.5 breaks down that change in demand by job category and shows that it is web specialists, management, and PC support categories which continue to show strong growth, although the present recession in many markets will likely have a depressing effect on overall demand.[4]

Finally, the reality in most modern economies is of a 'two-speed' market for specialist ICT and e-business skills. This is reflected in a widening wage gap between more experienced senior and less experienced junior ICT professionals, with demand for basic ICT skills declining and those for higher-quality hybrid skills increasing.

## Responses to e-business skills shortages

The uncertainties surrounding the scale and character of growth in professional ICT and digital business occupations has resulted in significant leads and lags in the supply of prospective recruits and in the skill-set of the available workforce. Demand goes where the skills are.

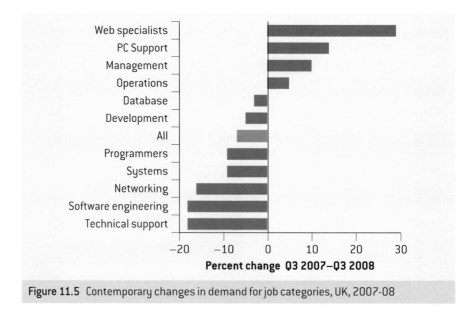

**Figure 11.5**  Contemporary changes in demand for job categories, UK, 2007-08

[4] The latest commentary on the UK ICT recruitment market can be read here: http://www.salaryservices.co.uk/commentary.

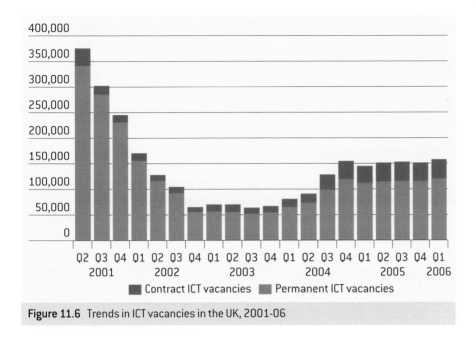

**Figure 11.6** Trends in ICT vacancies in the UK, 2001-06

'In discipline areas such as information technology and e-business, technology advances so rapidly that the issue of developing student skills, and capabilities adequate to the demands of the industry, becomes a moving target.' *Petrova and Claxton*, 2005)

For example, by the time the education system was geared up to produce graduates for the burgeoning Internet sector, the dot.com bust was well on the way. In the UK, graduate entry into the ICT workforce fell by 36 per cent between 2000 and 2002. As Figure 11.6 shows, recovery in terms of the number of vacancies was gradual. Although the slowdown affected computer science less than other subjects, the recruitment of graduates into professional roles is still higher for non computer science subjects than for computer science itself. Similarly, with sectors involved in e-business today increasing their demand for employees, particularly graduates, the supply of such graduates has not kept pace. This is not just a problem for a few markets, nor indeed just for developed markets, as the figure shows.

'Worldwide, a lot of the developed countries are not graduating as many IT students as they were in the past, which is kind of ironic as it does mean it does increase the opportunities.' *Bill Gates, 2006*[5]

As Table 11.1 suggests, response to perceived skill shortages can occur over the short or long term, can be undertaken by firms and organizations themselves, or by governments and their agencies, and may be different depending upon the level of skill. The most immediate consequences can be seen in the short-term actions of firms and organizations in reconfiguring tasks and business processes, but there are also medium-term strategies to be considered, including outsourcing and off-shoring, as well as longer-term investment in education, training, and development.

---

[5] Speaking at the 2006 Microsoft Business Forum in Moscow..

**Table 11.1  Actions in response to ICT skills shortages**

| Area of Shortage | Short-term demand | Long-term demand |
|---|---|---|
| Highly-skilled personnel | Immigration<br>Outsourcing to countries with a highly qualified labour force | Increased output of tertiary education |
| Medium-skilled personnel | Immigration<br>Outsourcing to countries with a qualified labour force<br>e-Learning<br>Training and retraining activities | Increased output of secondary education |
| Low-skilled personnel | Training and re-qualification activities | Increased computer and Internet literacy in primary and secondary education |

## Short-term recruitment practices

Despite the corporate investments in training and development described above, the reality often is that because of the immediacy of business needs, many firms find it is easier to recruit as needed within the labour market, rather than recruiting and training for the task (to 'buy' rather than to 'make'), particularly given the speed of change within those sectors highly exposed to the effects of digitization and technological innovation. Sometimes, so-called *spot demand* is created: arising out of the combination of variety and complexity in software and hardware products, together with the unique circumstances of a particular company. As a result, 'the right person with the right skill at the right time' is recruited. Such an opportunistic hiring strategy may be practical, but risks being short-sighted. It may lead to:

- inflation in salaries and employment costs;
- the emergence of potential differentials in terms and conditions between new hires and existing employees, leading to dissatisfaction and low morale; and
- the risk of developing a culture within which there is headhunting and defection of a firms' employees as a matter of course.

A growing lack of alignment between supply and demand can lead to undesirable consequences for businesses. For new, young industries, such as computer gaming, where there is heavy reliance on rapidly evolving skill-sets, in areas such as animation, programming, production, quality assurance, brand development, and marketing, the company's success and even very survival will depend upon the ability to recruit and retain the right employees. For larger, more established, firms and public-sector organizations, there will be different challenges, as they seek to accommodate a digital skill-set within an established workforce. These may include a:

- misunderstanding of the nature, role, and contribution of e-business skills to the firm;
- inadequately designed job specifications;
- potential mismatches in salary levels between new and established employees;
- inadequate training and development;

- retraining requirements for existing staff;

- development of an 'us and them' culture which makes organizational change more difficult.

# Education, training, and development

As Table 11.1 showed, it is through effective investment in training and development that countries and organizations will find longer-term solutions to the supply of suitably skilled employees. However, concerns over the nature and relevance of existing training and development in relation to ICT and e-business skills have been expressed. For example, there is substantial variation between European countries in terms of access to ICT training (Figure 11.7). According to the European Centre for the Development of Vocational Training, the four particular concerns are:

- the lack of a common definition of skills and skill levels relevant for employment;

- the lack of qualification definitions/levels relevant to ICT;

- few common approaches exist to skill and training standards and assessment/certification; and

- there is no way to validate training (CEDEFOP, 2004).

This has led to the establishment of a European e-Skills Forum, to co-ordinate activity at the European level to ensure adequate e-skills for the future across both workforce and population. Within the UK, an action plan in the form of an E-Skills Sector Skills Agreement was put into place in 2006 in an attempt to ensure that businesses have access to the IT skills they need over the next ten years (http://www.e-skills.com/ssa). The plan recognizes that as basic IT functions are moved off-shore, the UK's IT professionals will increasingly need business and management skills. Redesigned courses combine business, IT, and communications skills to create larger numbers of prospective recruits. A network of IT academies will provide opportunities for existing employees to obtain certificated re-skilling and re-training. (Certification is an important consideration: a study commissioned by Microsoft in 2006 of European human resources (HR) managers concluded that firms would be willing to pay an average of 6.9 per cent more salary for those with certified skills.) In late 2006, the UK government-commissioned Leitch Review of Skills concluded that government attention should focus on economically valuable skills in a demand-led system, rather than being centrally planned. It also recognized that for ICT skills in particular, it was difficult to predict future demand and that the framework created should be flexible and adaptive (HM Treasury, 2006). Public sector e-business skills are also of concern. Similarly, in Australia, the federal government has announced the establishment of a taskforce to combat threatened shortfalls in some ICT skills within the Australian Public Service (APS). The taskforce will work with educational institutions and industry bodies like the Australian Information Industry Association and the Australian Computer Society to address an emerging imbalance in the supply and demand of specialist ICT professionals within the public sector.

In developing markets, too, training and development are seen as high priorities but are not seen as being adequate for e-business needs. For example, the OECD concluded that Indian economic growth potential may well be constrained by the country's capacity to produce ICT professionals. The Indian Institutes of Technology (IITs) were first established

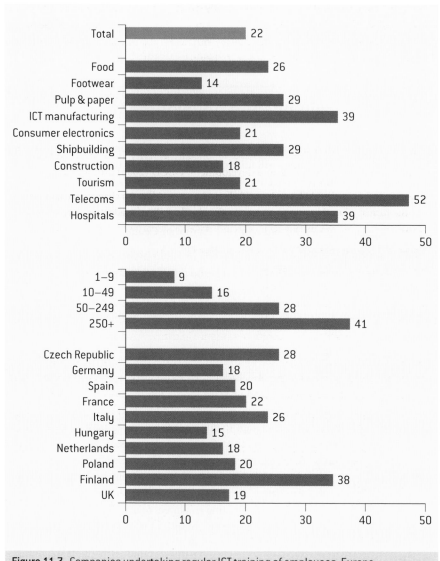

**Figure 11.7** Companies undertaking regular ICT training of employees, Europe.

in the 1950s to train scientists and engineers for the professionalizing Indian workforce. There are now seven, with a current capacity for 15,500 undergraduate and 12,000 graduate students. Certainly, the Indian IITs were ranked third-best worldwide for technology, after MIT and Caltech by The Times Higher Educational Supplement's World University Rankings (http://www.thes.co.uk/worldrankings/). Overall, however, the two best IITs could still only rank 154th (Delhi) and 174th (Bombay) in 2008. IITs were criticized in their early days for contributing to a brain drain in the Indian economy, with many graduates emigrating to more lucrative jobs in the west. However, the combination of economic liberalization and the growth of off-shoring by western companies in India has led to increased talent repatriation. The Institutes have also developed specialized graduate programmes in areas such as business administration, technology management, and intellectual property. While in both India and China there are proportionally small numbers of resident ICT and digital skills specialists, the absolute stock of these workers is relatively large because of the overall size of the workforce in these markets. But, as with developed markets, it will take time for the educational initiatives in both countries to begin to pay off:

> 'Whether or not India can pull off this trick in the next five years, I don't know—I don't think they will have solved the world-class excellence issue, and I know for a fact that they won't have solved their widening-participation issue in that time frame.' *William Lawton, quoted in Gill, 2008*

Finally, companies themselves have had to become actively involved in longer-term strategies for education, training, and development. OECD (2006) propose that:

> 'because ICT specialist skills needs are likely to change rapidly with changes in technology … the formal education system may not offer the flexibility for adapting curricula that private sector schemes, usually set up as multi-stakeholder partnerships, can offer.'

Multi-national ICT businesses, such as HP and Microsoft, have opened research facilities in India, China, and elsewhere which have not only proved attractive recruitment destinations for local talent but have also secured the services of some of those students returning home from education overseas. But longer term, it also makes sense for the largest such businesses to invest resources which will work to embed ICT skills awareness within communities. For example, Microsoft's community initiatives include:

- an IT Academies Programme: currently supporting 2,000 academic institutions across the EU25 with support for academic education tracks, Microsoft certification, and training for IT-related career opportunities;

- a Partners in Learning Programme: working with primary and secondary schools by providing software, refurbished PCs, and supporting expanded teacher training. The company has signed Partners in Learning agreements with over 100 countries engaging 90m students, teachers, and educational policymakers; and

- an Unlimited Potential Programme: which has supported over 37,000 Community Technology Centres in over 100 countries with software, curriculum, refurbished PCs and training grants in a move to provide IT skills training for the unemployed, the elderly, and those with disabilities.

Ultimately, whilst there is clearly a role for government in the funding and provision of an educational infrastructure for e-business skills, the private sector itself has to play a major role in ensuring the right climate for the provision of an appropriately skilled workforce. Efforts to date have been overly supply driven, with the consequence that skills shortages, gaps and mismatches have emerged. A demand-led approach requires employers to articulate their needs and then for them to work, perhaps within trade associations, with governments and other education providers in planning supply to meet those needs. Businesses are, after all, best placed to understand the sector's volatility and rapidly changing future requirements. At the same time, an overly demand-driven approach results in short-termism and opportunistic hiring strategies, whilst even more strategic sourcing practices—from outside the business or offshore—can have undesirable market consequences. But even the leading companies face recruitment and training challenges. By way of conclusion, Long case 11.1 (p. 404) presents a short case on the issues faced—and largely overcome—by one of the world's leading e-businesses, Google.

## The effects of e-business technologies on employees in the workplace

In general, businesses tend to have a more positive attitude towards the potential for change through the introduction of e-business technologies and e-business processes than do their employees, which suggests that something of a communications gap may exist (DTI, 2005). The gap varies in size, however. It is substantial in Japan, for example, where research has shown that Japanese companies tend to push technology onto their staff often 'without adequate training and support': 19 per cent of staff reported feeling 'resistant' to new technologies and only 4 per cent reported a willingness to 'embrace new technologies enthusiastically. Conversely, in Italy, employees are generally more positive towards change through e-business technologies than are their employers. However, only 22 per cent of European firms reported 'regularly sending their employees on ICT training programmes' (European Commission, 2006).

## The effects of email on productivity and behaviour

Organizations have traditionally utilized face-to-face (F2F) communication as their means of interacting and of creating and sustaining relationships with their employees and other stakeholders. The growth of computer-mediated communication (CMC), it is suggested, causes a complex interplay between email and more conventional means of interaction (O'Kane and Hargie, 2007). Within the workplace, email communication can of course be used by employees in ways that are enormously useful to the firm, both economically and socio-culturally. Economically, email is conventionally considered to have a beneficial effect on employees' productivity.

However, the evidence is that the productivity effect can be negative if systems are inappropriately designed, or if inefficient coping behaviours develop or are employed by users. In an exploratory study, some employees reported wasting on average over

40 per cent of a typical five-hour session on their computers due to frustrating experiences. The largest number of these experiences occurred while using word processing, email, and web browsing software (Lazar et al., 2006). In the case of email, this is often seen to be the result of continual interruption, despite the fact that this is a form of interruption that can generally be controlled: 'although an email alert may intrude upon consciousness, people have decision latitude to negotiate when, whether and how to respond to the interruption' (Russell et al., 2006).

Uncontrolled email interruption can lead to inefficient information processing. Drawing on psychologist Stanley Milgram's work in the 1970s, Denning suggests that there are six coping behaviours adopted by employees when faced with information overload of this kind:

- spending less time on each input (skimming emails);
- disregarding inputs (reading fewer emails);
- shifting the burden to others (forwarding emails);
- blocking reception (setting up blocking services);
- filtering; and
- creating institutions to share the burden (employing others to set up blocking services).

None of these behaviours are necessarily conducive to improved productivity: such users become 'overwhelmed, frustrated and detached' (Denning, 2006). It is also clear that these behaviours vary by national culture. A European survey of business email attitudes suggested that:

- 49 per cent of the Spanish respondents (as opposed to a survey average of 65 per cent) felt the need promptly to respond to email;
- Italians reported that, on average, they have to chase after 60 per cent of the emails they send, compared to 13 per cent in the UK; but that
- 25 per cent of the British sample reported dreading returning to a mountain of email, compared to 11 per cent on average (Segalla, 2004).

Over and above any implications for productivity, there may be positive cultural benefits from email communication. For example, the extent to which emails are copied to other recipients—or not—has the positive effect of building up a common information pool. It can also be used to build personal identity and alliances between individuals. Hu and Leung (2003) suggest that empowered workers generally feel that they have significant control and influence in the organization when they use email frequently, and perceive that email can help them expand their social network and build closer relationships with others.

On the other hand, email to third parties 'may also be used for reasons of social control, for instance in order to gain compliance or to put pressure on the addressee to conform to social norms of conduct' (Skovholt & Svennevig, 2006). Inappropriate use of email by managers could also result in internal harassment and discrimination claims by employees involuntarily subjected to offensive content by colleagues. An email is in many jurisdictions treated as a published document, which can be produced in a court of law. But corporate responses to email abuse vary by country. In a 2008 survey of large (more than 1,000 employee) firms in the US and the UK, 51 per cent of US companies claimed to have disciplined workers for violating email policies (78 per cent in the UK), and 26 per cent to have fired someone in the previous six months (44 per cent in the UK). Twenty-nine per cent of US firms had hired staff to read or analyse outbound email (38 per cent in the UK). These figures are higher for larger firms (Proofpoint, 2008). Violations included posting emails to a social networking, media sharing site, blog, or discussion forum. Some of the ethical issues that this kind of surveillance raises were discussed in chapter 5.

## Abuse of online resources

Abuse of work-based online resources by employees has been a long-standing issue for organizations. As early as 1999, it was estimated that so-called 'recreational web surfing' cost US firms $5.3bn (Bronikoswki, 2000). But the proportion of US companies reporting insider abuse of Internet access (which includes such abuses as downloading pornography and inappropriate chatroom usage, as well as personal Internet use) has fallen from 95 per cent in 1999 to 44 per cent in 2008, according to a series of surveys by professional body the Computer Security Institute (but still the second highest kind of incident reported after virus incidence (CSI, 2008). Undoubtedly, part of this decline is the consequence of the growth of Internet access outside the workplace, but much is also due to changing organization policies on what constitutes 'abuse', a clearer understanding by users of these policies, and the development of sophisticated monitoring systems designed to detect abuse or filter site access. Early targets were the so-called 'sinful six': pornography, gambling, illegal activities, hate sites, tasteless material, and violent content. Today, a leading web-filtering business services firm such as Websense has 42m seats under subscription with 50,000 organizations worldwide and filters 20m websites in fifty different languages classified into ninety categories (http://www.websense.com). Managers can also use e-business technologies themselves in overtly deleterious and socially undesirable ways. For example, one UK insurance claims company made 2,400 employees redundant by text message in 2003.

Getting the balance right is therefore important. For example, some companies are more positively accommodating employees' personal activities online:

> 'Work has been imported into personal lives and personal lives are migrating into the office. Cisco hugely embraces the idea that employees can also do personal business in work hours, because so many employees are doing work in their personal hours. Provided their work objectives are met, their personal and work lives will be more harmonious.' *John Stewart, chief security officer at Cisco Systems* quoted in Tieman, 2007.

## Teleworking

*Teleworking*, defined as 'the use of information and communications technologies to enable remote working from the office', has become increasingly possible and popular in developed economies. The number of teleworkers in the UK rose from 0.9mn to 2.4mn between 1997 and 2005—representing a more than doubling as a percentage of people in employment, from 3.5 per cent to 8.5 per cent, over the period (National Statistics, 2006). It is estimated that 82m employees seek secure access to corporate networks from off-site locations in the US and western Europe (Neil, 2007). Teleworking appears to be of most interest to those who are married, those with a high proportion of work that can be done at home, those with supervisors or colleagues who are supportive, and those who have long or frustrating journeys to work. (Average commuting times in Europe range from 25 minutes in Italy to 45 minutes in the UK.) The economic, management, and security implications of teleworking are dealt with elsewhere, but in behavioural terms, e-business technologies have served to accelerate the growth of individuals who have chosen or who are increasingly required to work away from the office. Mobile teleworking is more frequently used for sales, research, and customer service. Mobile devices and personal digital assistants enhance productivity: a 2007 study showed that the typical BlackBerry users converted 60 minutes of downtime into productive time per day.

Illegems et al. (2001) suggest that employees are more likely to find themselves teleworking if they are employed by organizations where one or several of the following conditions are satisfied:

- the organization is active in a knowledge-based sector; and is
- located in a congested area;
- characterized by a high level of electronic communication;
- driven mainly by output-oriented coordination and control systems;
- focused on non-routine decision making;
- built upon team organization;
- already experienced in the use of flexible work hours;
- already experienced in outsourcing;
- characterized by a high number of employees; or is
- characterized by a high proportion of white-collar workers and a high proportion of employees with a high education level.

Finally, this also hints at the emergence of fundamentally different ways of working. This is especially the case for young people entering work for the first time. Rainie suggests that such new entrants are 'digital natives'—individuals who start their jobs fully experienced in the use of e-business technologies (unlike so-called existing employees, termed 'digital immigrants', because of their greater unease with technology) (Rainie, 2006). Continuous, partial attention is one distinctive characteristics of these individuals' working styles:

'I'm the one who works all the time with two monitors on, listening to a digital radio station, with multiple IM screens on, or having online phone conversations simultaneously.' *David Cintz, 22, cited in Rainie, 2006*

## Understanding the culture of e-business

Particular kinds of corporate culture have been associated with the success of certain types of e-business innovation.[6] Adoption of e-business technologies can also have an

[6] For example http://www.google.com/intl/en/corporate/culture.html.

effect upon the cultures of existing businesses and it is important for firms to understand the organizational change and change management issues implicit in the adoption of e-business technologies. Indeed, some commentators have argued that appropriate cultural transformation is a prerequisite of success (see, for example, Schein, 1985). Here we draw together some of the available thinking on e-business and organizational culture. Cultural change is often seen as a particular challenge for small- and medium-sized business but, as we shall discover, large firms appear to have bigger difficulties in terms of cultural evolution.

What is an organizational culture? It represents the basic beliefs and assumptions held in common by the employees and other stakeholders in a firm or other organization. It may reflect the history and development of the organization, the nature of past and present leaders, as well as any relevant elements of the locational and sectoral context of the organization's activities. It may be influenced by technology, by the size of the organization, or by the ownership of the business. Often referred to as 'the way we do things here', organizational culture is fuzzy and ambiguous and has rituals and rules that may be opaque to the outsider. Yet at the same time the culture may be surprisingly vulnerable to external change. A more formal definition might be:

> 'a pattern of basic assumptions—invented, discovered, or developed by a given group as it learns to cope with its problems of external adaptation and internal integration— that has worked well enough to be considered valid and, therefore, to be taught to new members as the correct way to perceive, think, and feel in relation to those problems.' *Schein, 1985*

Think for example of the way in which IBM's organizational culture even led to a required style of dress:

> 'Big Blue had a very strong culture: one where the legendary IBM uniform of white shirt, dark suit (no blazers) and sincere tie was only the tip of the iceberg.' *Gib Akin, 2003*

We can see this now in the informal, almost anti-establishment way in which e-business start-ups behave and the rules and rituals they adopt, in part to differentiate themselves from incumbent firms:

> 'We've created a fun and inspiring workspace you'd be glad to be a part of, including on-site doctor and dentist; massage and yoga; professional development opportunities; shoreline running trails; and plenty of snacks to get you through the day.' *Google, 2009*

There are a number of ways of categorizing organizational cultures. Figure 11.8 shows that developed originally by Harrison and reported by Charles Handy. His 'culture quadrants' differentiate between organizations in terms of the extent of their *centralization and formalization*. This produces four distinctive types of culture. Table 11.2 provides greater detail on each of these.

Academic Gareth Morgan suggests that we can also use metaphors to make sense of organizational cultures:

> 'By using different metaphors to understand the complex and paradoxical character of organizational life, we are able to manage and design organizations in ways that we may not have thought possible before.' *Morgan, 1986*

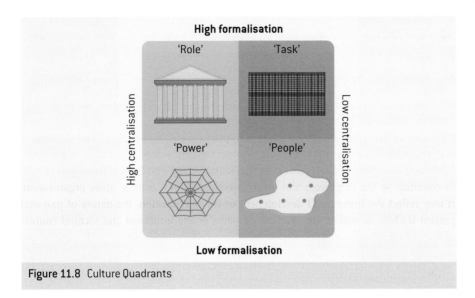

**Figure 11.8** Culture Quadrants

He distinguishes between eight 'images' of organization:

- *machines*: organizations as rational enterprises, designed and structured to achieve predetermined ends as efficiently as possible, using the 'one best way' to organize and linear notions of cause and effect;

- *organisms*: organizations as living organisms, seeking to adapt and survive in a changing environment;

- *brains*: organizations as brains, which are flexible, resilient and inventive. Here, the capacity for intelligence and control is seen as being distributed throughout the enterprise, enabling the system as a whole to self-organize and evolve along with the emerging challenges;

- *cultures*: organizations as mini-societies, with their own distinctive values, rituals, ideologies. and beliefs. An ongoing process of reality construction, which allows people to see and understand particular events, actions, objects, comments, and situations in distinctive ways;

- *political systems*: organizations as systems of political activity, with patterns of competing interests, conflict, and power;

- *psychic prisons*: organizations as systems that get trapped in their own thoughts and actions; and in which obsessions, mind traps, narcissism, strong emotions, illusions of control, anxieties, and defence mechanisms become the focus of attention;

- *flux and transformation*: organizations as expressions of deeper processes of transformation, and change;

- *instruments of domination:* organizations as systems that exploit their employees, the natural environment, and the global economy for their own ends; exposing the ethical and social dimensions as important points of focus.

In any organization, the particular role of managers is critical. For the purposes of our discussion, this is not just for existing organizations contemplating an e-business investment but for start-ups. In chapter 1, when describing the events surrounding the

**Table 11.2 Culture quadrants**

| Quadrant | Description |
|---|---|
| Power | Rays of power and influence spread out from a central figure or group. There may be a specialist or functional strucure but central control is exercised largely through appointing, loyal key individuals and interventionist behaviour from centre.whim and personal influence rather than on procedures or purely logical factors |
| Role | Often referred to as a bureaucracy, it works by logic and rationality. Its pillars represent functions and specialisms. Departmental functions are delineated and empowered with their role e.g. the finance dept., the design dept etc. Work within and between departments (pillars) is controlled by procedures, role descriptions and authority definitions. |
| Task | The emphasis is on results and getting things done. Resources are given to the right people at whatever level who are brought together and given decision making power to get on with the task. Individuals empowered with discretion and control over their work. The task and results and the main focus and team composition and working relationships are founded on capabiltiy rather than status. |
| Person | The individual is the central point. If there is a strucure it exists only to serve the individuals within it. If a group of individuals decide to band together to do their own thing and an office or secretary would help—it is a person culture. The culture only exists for the people concerned; it has no super-ordinate objective. |

## Activity box 11.4

### Quadrants and technology

How might attitudes towards the development and management of technology be different for firms in each of Handy's cultural quadrants? Which quadrants are particularly appropriate for e-business start-ups? Compare this framework with the metaphors used in Morgan's 'images' of organization. Which is the most persuasive way of thinking about organizational culture for e-business?

dot.com boom and bust, we referred several times to the poor quality of, and decisions taken by, managers in e-business firms being a contributory factor in their failure.

> 'In a competitive economy, above all, the quality and performance of managers determine the success of a business, indeed they determine its survival. For the quality and performance of its managers is the only effective advantage an enterprise in a competitive economy can have.' *Drucker, 1967*

But what do managers actually do? Military analogies have often proved popular. For example, nineteenth-century French engineer Henri Fayol saw managers 'planning, organising, commanding, coordinating and controlling'. An American engineer of the same period preferred a more scientific approach. Frederick Taylor defined 'scientific management' as the science of work. He introduced ideas ranging from time and motion studies to the scientific selection and development of workers. Academic Rosemary Stewart studied what managers actually did (rather than what theorists thought they did). Seeing managers occupying a 'superordinate position within an employment hierarchy', she distinguished between those who were 'machined decision-takers' and

## Short case 11.2

### Who ya gonna call? Geek Squad

The Geek Squad provides 24-hour technology support for both residential and commercial customers of US electrical retailer Best Buy (http://www.geeksquad.com). Founded in Minnesota in 1994 by Robert Stephens, the business uses a 'law enforcement' analogy to structure and deliver its support services through 18,000 field agents in the US, UK, Canada, and China. The firm was acquired in 2002 by Best Buy as part of its 'customer-centric' business strategy. Four million service calls are made annually in the US. With the average call-out costing $50, this is clearly a revenue-rich business model, although its primary reason for existence is to provide after-sales service to Best Buy products and stores.

In addition to benefiting directly from the adoption of e-business technologies in the home (which inevitably require support) such technologies provide a key way of involving customers, employees ('agents') in developing the business. Indeed, key to the division's success is the way it has become adept at harnessing the natural passion and enthusiasm of technology 'geeks':

> 'Do all things technology fire you up? Can you swap a motherboard or hook up a home theater system blindfolded? Does the thought of installing an LCD in an SUV—and getting paid for it—make you salivate? If you answered yes to any of these questions, congratulations. Your dream career might be waiting for you at Geek Squad®.'

Geek Squad is a networked culture which seeks to differentiate its employees from 'civilians' on the basis of their technical knowledge:

> 'Geek Squad technicians have morphed beyond their origins as PC pros to become the resource that civilians depend on for making the most of their computing, home theater and car electronics gear.'

In addition to offering 'precincts' in all Best Buy stores, there is a 24-hour Internet- and phone-based support service, as well as a dedicated PC repair facility in Kentucky.

Agents keep each other in touch with latest problems and fixes but also share these with customers through a variety of social media, including:

- live geekonomics chat sessions on upstream TV;
- free instructional videos on YouTube for solutions to common technical problems;
- blog commentary from geek squad contributors nationwide;
- a Facebook group; and
- a dedicated wiki.

The Wiki is split into two main sections: a Top Secret area which only allows Agent access, and a 'Technical Knowledgebase'. The knowledgebase has been opened up for anyone who wishes to visit.

### Question

The Geek Squad has been developed independently of the recruitment process and culture of the Best Buy retail chain. What kind of issues might this generate?

those who were what she called 'reactive socialisers' (Stewart, 1967). It is at this point that the importance of an organization's social network and the way in which the manager cultivates and operates that network starts to be seen as being important. Finally, academic Professor Henry Mintzberg set out seven major contemporary roles that the manager might take on:

- entrepreneur;
- resource allocator;
- figurehead/leader;
- liaisor/disseminator;
- monitor;
- spokesman/negotiator;
- disturbance handler.

It is no accident that Mintzberg sees entrepreneurship as one of the key roles of the manager—even within an established business. It is also clear that an entrepreneurial approach has tended to be particularly associated with the growth of new e-business organizations and that it appears to be an important skill-set. But this is a word, rather like strategy, which has been subject to much abuse. We need to ask: what is entrepreneurship? The term has its origins in the writings of the seventeenth-century French economist Richard Cantillon, who wrote of: 'one who bears risks by buying at certain prices and selling at uncertain prices'. This is quite a narrow description but contains a number of important words, such as 'risk' and 'uncertainty', both considerations which we may safely say are characteristics of many e-business ventures. We heard about economist and political scientist Joseph Schumpeter in chapter 8, in relation to innovation. Writing in the last century, Schumpeter linked the notions of entrepreneurship with innovation: 'an entrepreneur is an innovator who implements change within markets through the carrying out of new combinations of goods, methods of production or markets'. Schumpeter saw an entrepreneur operating a new enterprise or venture for the risks and outcome of which he or she assumed full responsibility. In practice, empirical research now tells us that successful entrepreneurs actually have quite complex attitudes to risk: they are more passionate experts than gamblers, and can overestimate their own abilities whilst in practice making quite cautious assumptions about demand (Caliendo et al., 2009; Wu and Knott, 2006). They are successful because their passion for an outcome leads them to organize available resources in the new and more valuable ways that Schumpeter described. Israel Kirzner's entrepreneurs are able to 'demonstrate alertness to exploit profit opportunities' (Kirzner, 1967). Entrepreneurs have not always been as highly regarded as they are in some markets today: prior to modernization in China, being an entrepreneur was perceived to be the result of not being able to hold down a good government job!

It is clear that an entrepreneurial organizational culture has a close association with e-business start-ups. The case studies on Geek Squad and Google in this chapter demonstrate this, but the discussion of two online education social networking sites in Long case 11.2 is most expressive of the way in which an entrepreneurial culture may affect the nature of e-business growth and change in different geographical locations. (Recall that chapter 2 discussed some of the economic considerations which had led to distinct clusters of e-business activity developing in particular parts of the world.) But

## Short case 11.3

### The man behind Craigslist

Craig Newmark learned most of what he knows about computer programming from thirty years' ICT experience at companies such as Bank of America Schwab and IBM. What he didn't transfer from these firms to his new commercial start-up in 1999 was the culture.

Craigslist offers local classified ads and forums for more than 550 cities and over fifty countries worldwide. It actually started as a hobby, hosting a list of local science fiction events in 1995. The hobby-in-the-living-room story is a familiar one, but this service now generates more than 12bn page views per month—the eighth largest global site in terms of views—and is used by more than 50m people each month, who publish more than 30m new ads—largely for free. But it's still run by twenty-five people from a small Victorian house in San Francisco. eBay acquired a minority stake in 2004.

Now 55, he's somewhat older than most e-business entrepreneurs, but Newmark leaves the running of the business to CEO Jim Buckmaster, whilst still working in 'customer service'. He's acquired something of a reputation as a 'geek savant' during his time in the Bay Area. Whilst continuing to 'embrace his inner nerd', his resumé (still online on his regularly updated personal blog), however, is compellingly modest:

> 'my focus includes Web oriented architecture, design and implementation, including
> legacy integration, and security. I use a combination of strong organizational and people
> skills, fitting easily into work environments ranging from traditional MIS to new media
> culture. My efforts complete on or ahead of schedule, while leading others to do the same.'
> http://cnewmark.typepad.com/resume.html

A little long for an epitaph, but refreshingly unpretentious.

### Question

Take a look at Craig's blog (http://www.cnewmark.com) along with Craigslist itself. What conclusions can you reach about Newmark's values and pre-occupations and how this may have affected the organizations with which Craig is involved? What does this tell you about the nature of e-business entrepreneurship?

### Activity box 11.5

#### This is Your Life

Identify an acknowledged e-business entrepreneur of your choice. What makes him/her tick? What evidence can you find of the influence of your chosen entrepreneur on (1) the culture of their own organization or (2) other e-business organizations with which they have become involved?

it is also clear that the different ways in which individuals choose to exercise their social capital have a strong influence on the manner in which innovative e-business firms have developed. For example, attitudes to achievement and extravagant wealth will affect differing levels of innovation performance. One frustrated US entrepreneur wondered why she could not enthuse her Dutch colleagues with her passion for entrepreneurial activity. The response: 'I can't be American because I'm Dutch.' Geographical differences, reflected in national cultural differences, as well as organizational differences are also therefore an important consideration. For example, Freytag and Thurik demonstrate the ways in which cultural aspects of upbringing may constrain the behaviour and preferences of would-be entrepreneurs in different nations (Freytag and Thurik, 2007). In this context, Short case 11.3 examines one particular individual to have made a significant contribution to the development of e-business: Craig Newmark, the founder of Craigslist.

### Long case 11.1

#### Google's recruitment process: can one conversation change the world?

In the war for talent between digital businesses, Google, with revenues of $16.5bn in 2007 and a market-leading position in the information search industry, is a hard destination to beat for those with the right skills.

> 'We nurture an invigorating, positive environment by hiring talented, local people who share our commitment to creating search perfection and want to have a great time doing it.' *Google*, 2009

The company's recruitment site offered 387 openings within the US in January 2009, the highest number of which was in software engineering (http://www.google.com/jobs/). The compelling message from Google is that 'our strategy is simple: we hire great people and encourage them to make their dreams a reality'. But it is also clear that Google has necessarily become a recruiting machine to support its ambitions. The company's full-time employee headcount increased significantly over the three years to September 2008, growing from 4,989 to 20,123, an increase of over 400 per cent Leaving aside temporary hires, therefore, Google recruited at least ninety-seven people a week, every week, during this period. Nor is the recruitment process simple:

> 'We have . . . maintained a rigorous, highly selective and time-consuming hiring process. We believe that our approach to hiring has significantly contributed to our success to date.' *Google*, 2006.

≫

Virtually every person hired by Google has at least four interviews, drawn from management and from a pool of potential colleagues, starting with a 40-minute telephone interview and, if successful, a complex on-site interview process. Consensus-based hiring decisions can take up to two weeks. Despite this, although it claims to be having difficulty in recruiting good-quality developers and engineers, Google still inspires envy amongst other recruiters. One recruiter for Amazon.com comments: 'Google has managed to turn the process around. Smart people now make the pilgrimage to Google, and Google spends the bulk of their time turning great people away.'[7] This is not just an effect limited to developed markets. Google overtook Microsoft India as the most preferred employer amongst the leading seventy-three Indian Technology School graduates in 2007.[8] Graduates' perception is based on some of the distinctive attributes of the Google business.

> 'Our employees are everything. We are focused on providing an environment where talented, hard working people are rewarded for contributions to Google and for making the world a better place.' *Larry Page, Google Co-founder*

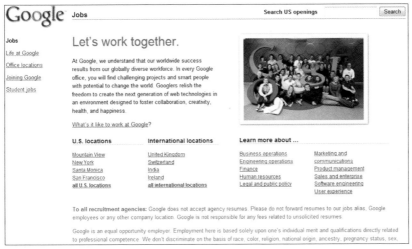

In particular, the company offers:

- a distinctive recruiting culture, including:
- a high ratio of recruiters to applicants;
- programming competitions to attract and reward the most talented young people;
- innovative job marketing activity;
- a reputation for technological innovativeness in every function of the firm;
- a distinctive business culture, including the notion of 20 per cent time for personal projects; and
- high-profile training opportunities once in post.

Background investment in building awareness of the Google brand as an employer, as well as identifying prospective recruits, takes many forms. For example, 'Code Jams'

---

[7] 'Google's secret weapon', http://www.cabochon.com/~stevey/blog-rants/google-secret-weapon.htm.
[8] According to ACNielsen's Campus Track T-Schools 2006 survey, http://www.acnielsen.co.in/news/20060510.shtml.    »

have been held in the main world regions since 2005, offering participants the chance to solve challenging mathematical and programming problems. For the 2008 Code Jam 11,000 participated in online rounds, 500 semi-finalists reached the regional stage, and 100 finalists from twenty-three different countries competed at Google's headquarters for a $10,000 prize. Half the top twenty winners came from emerging Asian markets. The motives for these exercises are not wholly to do with recruitment of software developers, although, as Google commented, 'we're especially delighted that over half the finalists expressed their interest in working for Google'.

The picture is not wholly rosy. These features combine to increase the company's attractiveness to prospective hires to such an extent that Google has been called a 'disruptive recruiter' (Sullivan, 2005). The need to recruit in a market of scarcity has also led to some legal disputes between the leading firms—most recently when Microsoft's head of search research was headhunted by Google (US Securities & Exchange Commission, 2006). Further, Google says that it is having to pay employees more and offer variable bonus and other incentive arrangements in order to retain as well as attract employees, and that this may produce perceived or real inequities within the business between new hires and existing employees. Indeed, such is the wealth of many of its earliest employees that financial incentives alone may be insufficient to retain them. Finally, Google itself is not immune either to economic conditions or to the attractions of newer, up-and-coming firms. In the early part of 2009, the firm cut back its reliance on external recruitment agencies as the recession took hold around the world. It has also been recently affected by departures of senior personnel attracted by start-up opportunities elsewhere.

*Questions*

1. Think about the final paragraph of this case. How sustainable is the 'Google effect'? Is there a 'Facebook' effect on recruitment? Or a 'Twitter' effect?

2. What hiring strategies might Google's competitors employ to counter the 'Google effect'?

## Long case 11.2

### Learn something new: two ways of building an e-business

Do underlying differences in values and, in particular, different cultural attitudes and approaches to entrepreneurship explain how e-business firms might develop around the world? Take the example of online education, which seems an obvious candidate for a social community networking application because of its highly fragmented nature. (Teachers tended to have to rely upon small ads on sites like Craigslist or even posters in the local coffee shop.) Two start-up businesses launched almost simultaneously in 2008—one in the US, one in the UK—have taken contrasting approaches to this new market.

TeachStreet is the idea of Seattle-based Dave Schappell (http://www.teachstreet.com). Formerly a Director of Product Development at Amazon.com and Director of Marketing » at viral digital media firm JibJab, Schappell had been brought up in an environment where start-ups were the order of the day amongst his friends: he longed to start his own. 'Dave noticed how hard it was to find a cool class in his area and figured there must be an easier way' (company website). The idea was to bring students and teachers together, creating a marketplace in which teachers from all areas could market themselves to potential clients. No subjects are off limits. For example, there are sixty-seven results for 'fly fishing' in the Seattle area alone. Schappell found it relatively easy to raise money, and although he needed to invest $100,000 of his own, he was also able to obtain $2.25m in a first round of business angel financing. A second round of funding included a contribution from Esther Dyson, a founding member of the US West Coast 'digerati' and serial entrepreneur

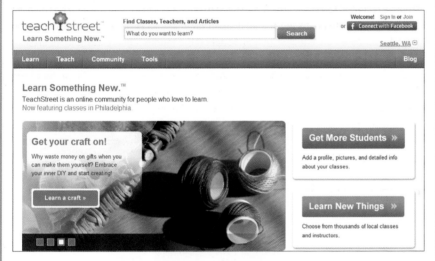

in her own right. The business model is based on contextual advertising revenues, with a plan to evolve into premium services for teachers commanding a subscription fee.

By contrast, the UK-based School of Everything, launched in September 2008, was actually founded two years previously by Paul Miller and four other friends (http://schoolofeverything.com). Miller, a former analyst at the political think-tank Demos, held strong views about developing web-based projects that would achieve social goals. In the case of online education, he saw School of Everything as a means of democratizing the education process: commercial considerations were secondary. Nevertheless, the team needed money to launch the site. Rather than go the conventional venture-capital route, Miller successfully approached the Young Foundation, a London-based social innovation charity set up in 2005 to fund initiatives addressing unmet social needs, for a £25,000 loan. UK broadcaster Channel 4 also invested. Whilst second-round funding of £350,000 attracted more conventional resourcing (including, coincidentally, Esther Dyson), Miller claims that the initial funding gave a much clearer steer to the firm's social goals: 'none of us had the mindset of being entrepreneurs . . . we're still not quite sure how we ended up running a business' (company website and Moules, 2008).[9]

[9] Quoted in Moules, J., (2008), 'Two Lessons in Education', Financial Times, 21st October.

»

The site works in a not dissimilar way to TeachStreet: after registering for free, users set up a learning or teaching profile. Those looking for learning opportunities are asked to list subjects that are of interest and indicate whether they want one-to-one personal or online tuition (which determines the geographical scope of the search). In doing so, the user is shown how many teachers and similarly minded learners are also registered, with a Google mashup map showing their locations. Clicking on a teacher profile will tell you more about them and where they are based. Teachers' fees are listed on the site. The business model is predicated on a small transaction fee levied on people who arrange payment through the service.

What have been the outcomes of these different kinds of motivations and investments? TeachStreet now operates in Seattle, Portland, and San Francisco, with 9,000 teachers and 60,000 classes. Having generated 89,000 visits in December, it has plans to expand elsewhere in the US once it has fully understood the market dynamic within its existing markets. [10] By contrast, School of Everything, with 2,000 teachers, plans its expansion into Europe by translating the website into five languages. Growth to date has been through viral marketing.

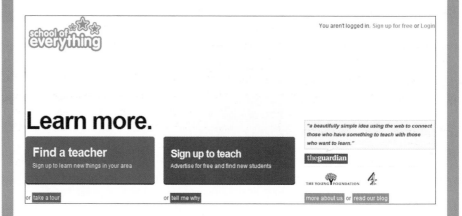

*Questions*

1. Was School of Everything naive in its approach to developing a sustainable commercial social networking site?

2. Which site stands the biggest chance of success nationally and internationally?

[10] TeachStreet's 'accomplishments of 2008' can be found here: http://blog.teachstreet.com/homepage/teachstreets-2008-accomplishments/.

# ✪ Chapter Summary

The chapter began by suggesting that skills and cultural considerations in e-business were often neglected aspects of e-business and e-commerce books, despite the importance of skills issues, in particular to both businesses and governments. It then outlined some of the reasons why it might be difficult to arrive at a meaningful definition of e-business skills and described some of the volatility in demand for particular skill-sets which has accompanied booms and busts in the Internet economy. E-business skills are seen as fundamentally strategic and often cross-disciplinary in nature, addressing the longer-term developmental needs of firms. Skills shortages represent a lack of alignment between demand for skills and their availability, but it is important to differentiate between skills shortages, gaps and mismatches, which lead to different solutions.

The chapter then reviewed the contemporary changes in demand for e-business skills, focusing on the occupational impact. It drew attention to the 'downward cascade' of increasingly pervasive ICT skills to many more categories of occupation and a 'two-speed' market for both ICT and e-business skills. However, it also noted that forecasts of demand are inherently unreliable and this led to a discussion of the leads and lags this produced in the education and training system of nations. It examined the short-, medium-, and long-term mechanisms available to firms and governments in response to skills shortages, contrasting responses in developed markets with those in emerging economies.

Finally, the chapter sought to develop an understanding of the cultural aspects of e-business. Cultural considerations are important not just for start-up businesses, but also for existing organizations seeking to adopt e-business practices and may play a role in affecting the success of both kinds of organization. The chapter reviewed definitions of organizational culture, of managers as well as of entrepreneurs, and related these definitions to the experience of e-businesses. It concluded that different aspects of an individual's upbringing might affect the propensity of particular countries to produce entrepreneurs.

# ❓ Review questions

1. Why is the demand for e-business skills so difficult to assess?

2. Review and compare the different ways of defining skills in relation to e-business.

3. What are the differences between skills shortages, gaps, and mismatches?

4. What is the relationship between digital literacy skills and e-business skills?

5. What are the barriers to effective training and development in e-business?

6. Give examples of the kinds of response that can be developed to short- and long-term demand for e-business skills.

7. Compare and contrast Handy's and Morgan's mechanisms for distinguishing organizational cultures.

8. What are the distinguishing features of entre-preneurs?

## Q Discussion questions

1. Why are there so many different ways of defining e-business skills?

2. E-business skills appear to be hybrid and multi-disciplinary. What challenges does this pose to (a) recruiters and (b) training and educational organizations? Illustrate your answer with reference to a sector of your choice.

3. Why is the demand for e-business skills so volatile?

4. What might a company like Amazon do to counter the 'Google effect' in recruitment?

5. Why might attitudes to e-business entrepreneurship vary between country?

## → Suggestions for further reading

E-skills UK, (2008), 'Technology Counts', *IT & Telecoms Insights 2008*, January.
Summarizes a series of documents providing an in-depth understanding of the existing IT and telecoms landscape and forecasting the future based on input from over 4,000 employers in the UK. The report forms the basis of a series of strategic plans for ICT and e-business skills.

HM Treasury, (2006), *Leitch Review of Skills. Prosperity for All in the Global Economy—World Class Skills*, HMSO.
The UK's Lord Leitch was commissioned with a remit to 'identify the UK's optimal skills mix in 2020 to maximize economic growth, productivity and social justice, and to consider the policy implications of achieving the level of change required'. His report recommends that the UK should aim to be a world leader on skills by 2020, in the upper quartile of OECD countries: http://www.dfes.gov.uk/furthereducation/uploads/documents/2006-12%20LeitchReview1.pdf.

Hofstede, G., and Hoftstede, G.J., (2004), Cultures and Organizations: Software for the Mind: Software for the Mind, McGraw-Hill.
An atlas of cultural values, based on cross-cultural research conducted by the authors in seventy countries over more than thirty

years. This book reveals the unexamined rules by which people in different cultures think, feel, and act in business and in other forms of organization.

INSEAD, (2008), E-Skills, Competitiveness and Employability, paper presented at the European E-Skills 2008 Conference, Greece, elab@INSEAD.
A white paper that reports on INSEAD's research on e-skills and employability. It reviews the prospects for e-business skills in Europe in 2025, from both the demand and supply perspectives. Supported by an online database of statistical resources: http://www.insead.edu/elab/eskills.

Liu, S., & Avery, M., (2009), Alibaba: The Inside Story Behind Jack Ma and the Creation of the World's Biggest Online Marketplace, HarperCollins
He is often described as 'China's Bill Gates' and Jack Ma's story is a fascinating one—based on his upbringing during the cultural revolution and his development of keen entrepreneurial instincts which led to the establishment of an e-business now worth over $26bn. Alibaba features in Long case 9.1

## → References

Akin, G., (2003), 'In Search of Virtual Teams', Unpublished article.

Barroso, M., (2008), *Lisbon: A Strategy for All Seasons*, speech delivered by the President of the European Commission at the Lisbon Council Growth and Jobs Summit, Brussels, http://uk.youtube.com/watch?v=7OFGh3Hgb4U.

BBC News (2006), 'Universities Challenged', 21st March, http://news.bbc.co.uk/1/hi/business/4816236.stm

Bresnahan, T.F., Brynjolfsson, E. &, and Hitt, L.M., (1999), 'Technology, Workplace Organization, and the Demand for Skilled Labor: Firm-Level Evidence', *Working Paper 7136*, National Bureau for Economic Research, Cambridge, MA.

Bronikowski, L., (2000), 'Esniff.com sniffs out cyberslacking', *ColoradoBiz*, 27, p. 46.

Caliendo, M., Fossen, F., and Kritkos, A., (2009), 'Risk Attitudes of Nascent Entrepreneurs—New Evidence from an Experimentally Validated Survey', *Small Business Economics*, 32(2), pp. 153–67.

CEDEFOP, (2004), Towards a comprehensive European e-skills reference framework: ICT and e-business skills and training in Europe, http://www.cedefop.europa.eu.

Computer Security Institute, (2008), *2008 CSI Computer Crime & Security Survey*, CSI, http://i.cmpnet.com/v2.gocsi.com/pdf/CSIsurvey2008.pdf (requires registration).

*Computer Weekly*, (2006), 'Skills on the Rise as Market Shifts', 31 October 2006.

Dawson, C., (2006), 'Gates: As US IT grad slow, Russia fills the gap', *ZDNet Education*, November 13th, http://education.zdnet.com/?p=653

Denning, P.J., (2006), 'Infoglut', *Communications of the ACM*, 49(7), pp. 15ff.

Department of Trade and Industry (DTI), (2005), *Business in the Information Age: The International Benchmarking Study*, http://www.businesslink.gov.uk/Growth_and_Innovation_files/ibs2004.pdf.

Drucker, P., (1967), The Effective Executive, Harper & Collins.

EITO (2001), EITO report 2001, European Information Technology Observatory, Frankfurt.

Enticknap, N., (2006), 'Skills on the rise as market shifts'. *Computer Weekly*, 1st August, http://www.computerweekly.com/Articles/2006/08/01/217247/skills-on-the-rise-as-market-shifts.htm

E-Skills UK, (2006), IT Insights: Trends and UK Skills Implications, E-Skills UK/Gartner Consulting.

European Commission, (2000), 'European Skills Shortages in ICT and Policy Responses', *European Competitiveness Report* 2001, Annexe III.1, http://ec.europa.eu/enterprise/enterprise_policy/competitiveness/doc/competitiveness_report_2001/.

European Commission, (2004), E-Skills for *Europe: Towards 2010 and Beyond*, The European E-Skills Forum, http://ec.europa.eu/enterprise/ict/policy/doc/e-skills-forum-2004-09-fsr.pdf.

European Commission, (2006), *Report on the Supply and Demand of e-Skills in Europe*, Rand Europe.

Expert Group on Future Skills Needs, (2001), Responding to Ireland's *Skills Needs: Third Report on Future Skills Needs*, Forfás.

Freytag, A. and Thurik, R., (2007), 'Entrepreneurship and Its Determinants in a Cross-Country Setting', *Journal of Evolutionary Economics*, 17, pp. 117–31.

Gareis, K., (2006), 'Lifelong Learning, Digital Literacy and eLearning: Some Results from a European Population Survey', *Towards a Long Term e-Skills Strategy*, European e-Skills 2006 Conference, http://eskills.cedefop.europa.eu/conference2006/presentations.asp.

Ghosh, P., (2006), 'Computer Industry "Faces Crisis"', BBC News, 17 November, http://news.bbc.co.uk/1/hi/technology/6155998.stm.

Gilbert, A., (2005), 'Tech industry sheds fewer jobs in 2004', CNet News, January 12th, http://news.cnet.com/Tech-industry-sheds-fewer-jobs-in-2004/2100-1022 3-5533981.html?

Gill, J., (2008), 'Access Drive Could Hamper India's Push for Excellence', *Times Higher Education Supplement*, 30 October, http://www.timeshighereducation.co.uk/story.asp?sectioncode=26&storyco de=404136.

Google, (2006), *Annual Report*, http://investor.google.com

Google, (2009), 'Top 10 Reasons to Work at Google', http://www.google.com/intl/en/jobs/lifeatgoogle/toptenreasons.html

*Guardian*, (2006), 'MEN Builds Multimedia Hub', http://media.guardian.co.uk/newmedia/story/0,,1935947,00.html.

Harrison, R., (1972), 'Understanding Your Organisation's Character', *Harvard Business Review*, 50(3), pp. 119–28.

Hu, S.L.Y. & Leung, I., (2003), 'Effects of expectancy-value, attitudes, and use of the Internet on psychological empowerment experienced by Chinese women at the workplace', Telematics & Informatics, 20(4), pp. 365–382.

Illegems, V., Verbeke, A. and S'Jegers, R., (2001), 'The Organizational Context of Teleworking Implementation', *Technological Forecasting and Social Change*, 68(3), pp. 275–91

Kirzner, I., (1967), *Competition and Entrepreneurship*, Chicago University Press.

Lazar, J., Jones, A., and Schneiderman, B., (2006), 'Workplace User Frustration with Computers: An Exploratory Investigation of the Causes and Severity', *Behaviour & Information Technology*, 25(3), pp. 239–51.

Morgan, G., (1986), *Images of Organization*, Sage Publications.

Moules, J., (2008), 'Two Lessons in Education', *Financial Times*, 21 October.

Neil, R., (2007), 'Dream Commuters Cross Borders', *BBC News*, 23 February, http://news.bbc.co.uk/1/hi/business/6385851.stm.

OECD, (2006), *Information Technology Outlook* 2006, http://www.oecd.org/dataoecd/27/59/37487604.pdf

O'Kane, P. and Hargie, O., (2007), 'Intentional and Unintentional Consequences of Substituting Face-to-Face Interaction with E-mail: An Employee-Based Perspective', *Interacting with Computers*, (19)1, pp. 20–31.

Orlowski, A., (2005), 'MS Nixes Google Hire', *The Register*, 28 July, http://www.theregister.co.uk/2005/07/29/ms_google_phoney_war/.

Petrova, K. and Claxton, G., (2005), 'Building Student Skills and Capabilities in Information Technology and eBusiness: A Moving Target', *Journal of Information Systems Education* 16(1), pp. 27–41.

Proofpoint, (2008), *Outbound Email and Data Loss Prevention in Today's Enterprise, 2008*, Proofpoint Inc., http://www.proofpoint.com/downloads/Proofpoint-Outbound-Email-and-Data-Loss-Prevention-in-Today%27s-Enterprise-2008.pdf (requires registration).

Rainie, L., (2006), *Digital 'Natives' Invade the Workplace*, Pew Internet & the American Life Project, http://www.pewinternet.org/ppt/New%20Workers%20--%20pewresearch.org%20version%20_final_.pdf.

Ruiz, Y. & Walling, A., (2005), 'Home-based working using communication technologies', *Labour Market Trends*, vol 113, no 10, pp 417–426

Russell, E., Purvis, L.M., and Banks, A., (2007), 'Describing the Strategies Used for Dealing with Emailnext Term Interruptions According to Different Situational Parameters', *Computers in Human Behavior*, 23(4), pp. 1820–37.

Schein, E.H., (1985), *Organizational Culture and Leadership: A Dynamic View*, Jossey Bass.

Sector Skills Council for the Audio-visual Industries, (2005), *Survey of the Audio-Visual Industries' Workforce*, Skillset,

Segalla, M., (2004), 'The Email is Delivered Instantly So Why Do Responses Take So Long: A Study of Email Usage Attitudes Among European Managers', *Working Paper*, HEC School of Management.

Skovholt, K. and Svennevig, J. (2006). 'Email Copies in Workplace Interaction', *Journal of Computer-Mediated Communication*, 12(1), article 3 http://jcmc.indiana.edu/vol12/issue1/skovholt.html

Stewart, R., (1967), *Managers and Their Jobs*, Macmillan.

Sullivan, J., (2005), 'A Case Study of Google Recruiting', http://www.ere.net/articles/db/06465389A59D4E0FAA6F0EFFD 4A78126.asp.

Symons, C., (2005), 'IT Skills Shortages on the Horizon—the IT Skills That Will Be in Demand in 2005 and Beyond', Forrester Research.

US Securities and Exchange Commission, (2006), Google Inc., Form 10-Q, 30 September.

US Department of Labor, (2007). Economic and Employment Projections, 2006–2016, Bureau of Labor Statistics, http://www.bls.gov/news.release/ecopro.toc.htm

Tieman, R., (2007), 'At work, at rest, at play', Financial Times, 14th March, Page 1.

Wu, B. and Knott, A.M., (2006), 'Entrepreneurial Risk and Market Entry', *Management Science*, 52(9), September, pp. 1315–30.

## ⊗ Weblinks

*E-skills UK*. The voice of employers on IT and Telecoms founded to create an appropriate skills environment in the UK: http://www.e-skills.com.

*European Centre for the Development of Vocational Training*. Established in 1975 to help promote and develop vocational training across the European Union: http://www.cedefop.europa.eu.

European e-Skills 2008 Conference. Papers from the most recent high level conference on e-skills: http://eskills.cedefop.europa.eu/conference2008/.

Google Jobs. Information on life at Google and a list of openings at Google sites around the world: http://www.google.com/int/en/jobs/index.html. (Other recruiter sites include: http://www.microsoft.com/careers, http://www.ebaycareers.com, and http://careers.yahoo.com).

US Department of Labor. Collects statistics via the Bureau of Labor Statistics (http://www.bls.gov) and publishes the annual Occupational Outlook Handbook: http://www.bls.gov.oco.

# Part four

# Conclusions

# Future challenges and opportunities

## Introduction

In this text, we have tried to achieve something of a balancing act. There is still a great deal of rhetoric and hyperbole surrounding e-business technologies (such as that to involve so-called 'web 2.0' technologies) and levels of interest in reading about emerging trends and applications is still extensive. The book has sought to assess the merits of this material dispassionately. But stable analytical and conceptual frameworks, together with the robust evidence base needed to support such frameworks, are developing relatively slowly and academic insight is still comparatively limited. This is in part, of course, a direct consequence of the rapid change characterizing e-business. It's also a consequence of the fact that the speed of this change is largely out of synchronization with the academic publishing cycle, in which it can take up to two years for an article to appear in a reputable journal. When taking into account that any fieldwork may have been conducted in the year before article submission, this may result in a three-year gap between initial enquiry and publication—by which time, e-business and the real world will have moved on.

This final chapter, however, seeks to be a little less constrained in its structure and focus. It takes as the basis for its content the first section of the book: dealing with the various environments which provide the context for e-business. For each aspect of the section, the chapter explores the kinds of future challenge and opportunity that will face organizations and other stakeholders, as e-business continues to evolve.

While the adoption of e-business technologies continues briskly in many sectors and countries, and its future is anticipated to be significant (see Figure 12.1) it is still possible to identify sectors and types of organization which have not taken full advantage of their potential. In addition, the nature of product and service innovation and of strategy development in e-business means that while extraordinarily imaginative and creative ideas continue to be generated, their longer-term commercial viability is still often in question. In particular, in order to understand the future potential of—for example—new mobile, social and business collaborative e-business applications, we may need to think about the kind of analytical tools that we employ. The chapter therefore concludes with a critical review of the utility of forecasting and scenario planning techniques in relation to e-business.

Finally, there is another tightrope to be walked. This book is published in late 2009, at the end of one of the most difficult and intractable years for the global economy, for organizations and for individuals around the world. It is unlikely that e-business will have remained unscathed, but the precise impact remains poorly understood—not least because the explanations for and evolution of prevailing economic conditions themselves remain poorly understood.

## Challenges and opportunities in the environment for e-business

Four chapters in the text reviewed the interrelated series of drivers which provide the context for the application of e-business technologies by firms. These four elements also constitute the basis of the conditions that will affect the adoption of e-business technologies in the future. Looking forward, each of these is likely to provide both constraints and incentives. The interaction between the four elements will also provide tensions and ambiguities for individuals and organizations involved in e-business.

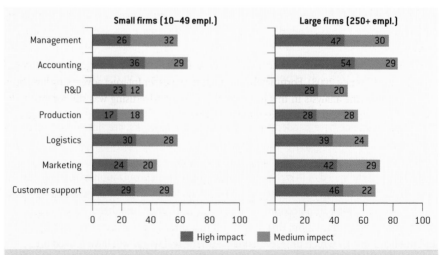

**Figure 12.1** Percentage of companies anticipating a high/medium impact of ICT on specific activities in the future

# Economic considerations

Chapter 2 argued that e-business technologies made significant contributions to the growth and productivity of markets and nations. Are those businesses which rely more heavily on e-business technologies more or less vulnerable to changing economic conditions than more conventional businesses? This is a hard question to answer and will of course likely be different between sectors as well as for business-to-business (B2B) as against business-to-consumer (B2C) markets. There are certainly macroeconomic factors, such as changing commodity prices, currency exchange, and interest rates and the availability of credit which will differentially affect e-business firms.

We might argue that because B2B organizations have improved their efficiency of operation through the application of e-business technologies to obtain lower transaction costs, then they will be leaner and fitter and more resilient as a consequence than their more traditional competitors. We might also argue that those firms to have, for example, used the capabilities of e-business technologies such as e-procurement marketplaces to expand outside their home markets, or who have reduced infrastructure management or service costs through off-shore outsourcing will be able better to weather domestic economic difficulties. However, we might also suggest that start-up businesses employing e-business technologies will be particularly vulnerable in the early stages of their development to the availability of capital to fund their growth. Any generally increased difficulty in attracting capital is more likely to hurt them than it will established businesses with a strong track record for performance. Even established firms may be at risk if the efficiencies gained by some in the value net through e-procurement (such as motor vehicle manufacturers in relation to low supplier inventory levels) lead to a lack of flexibility during a more general downturn in demand. But capital deepening for all kinds of organizations will be challenging if credit is less available. One clear indicator of all this will be, for example, to watch the revenues of the off-shore outsourcers. Some predictions were that these firms (including Accenture, IBM, Infosys, and Wipro) would be beneficiaries of any economic downturn (Kaushik, 2008).

Similarly, B2C e-business firms with business models predicated on revenue generated from sources which are themselves under economic pressure may also discover operating difficulties. Figure 12.2 shows the forecasts made for 2009 in respect of US advertising revenues—the basis of many such firms' profitability. In recent years, advertising revenue generally has tended to track the economy, even before any secular changes in promotional channel mix (Sweney, 2008). Fortunately, although revenues for Internet advertising have been downgraded by the analysts in this instance, this form of advertising was still forecast to be the most resilient during 2009 (indeed, the only form to experience growth) and to undergo a rebound in 2010. Long Case 12.2 (p. 438) reviews an example where the prospect of increased advertising revenue provided the motive for a firm's strategic development into a new domain.

Other things being equal, B2C firms which employ e-business technologies to reach customers will be just as exposed to the vicissitudes of the consumer economy as conventional firms. However, as chapter 2 demonstrated, the lower transaction costs that e-business firms are more easily able to generate may favour them with consumers who will be more price-sensitive during a downturn. (See, for example, the discussion of Moneysupermarket.com in Short case 2.4.) On the other hand, market research company Comscore reports that US online spending fell between Black Friday (Thanksgiving: the day in the year when most US retailers go into the black, or into profit) and Christmas Eve in

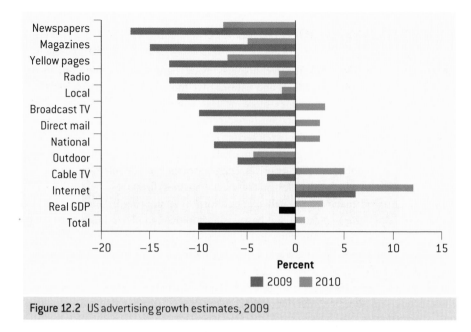

**Figure 12.2** US advertising growth estimates, 2009

2008, compared with a 20–25 per cent growth in the equivalent period of 2007. Why might this be? Two possible explanations are that firstly much online shopping is dominated by discretionary purchases and that secondly most purchases are made by credit card—both kinds of consumer spending that tend to come under significant pressure during economically difficult times. Similarly, current research is showing that users are seeking to trim their overall telecommunications costs, along with other discretionary expenditure.

## Short case 12.1

### E-business as an economic stimulus

As part of the efforts to revive the US economy in early 2009, the then incoming US administration proposed a five-year plan to modernize all healthcare record-keeping, by making them standardized and electronic. The lay onlooker might be struck by two surprising observations: firstly, that US healthcare records are not already standardizsed and electronic; secondly, that the scale of the challenge is such that it could cost between $75–100bn over five years and require a significant amount of specialized labour to achieve, creating nearly 250,000 jobs in the process—hence the interest in this project as an economic stimulus.

It is important to understand the scale of US healthcare. A $2 trillion industry, it is second only to the manufacturing sector in size. Indeed, the US healthcare system is equivalent to the world's eighth largest economy—larger than the total economy of Italy (Sultz and Young, 2008). Yet it is phenomenally complex, in terms of cost base, infrastructure, labour intensity, and medical ethics: over 47m Americans remain uninsured. Yet in practice, only some 8 per cent of over 5,000 US hospitals and around 17 per cent of over 800,000 » medical professionals use any kind of common computerized record-keeping system. US Health Secretary Tom Daschle commented: 'it is an embarrassment that the United States lacks an interoperable system for electronic health records.' 'Your grocery store automatically knows what brand of chips you bought last year, but your cardiologist doesn't automatically know what prescriptions your family doctor prescribed for you yesterday,' said a US Democrat Representative. But modernizing this system would be a formidable technical and organizational challenge, as experience in the UK has shown (Doward, 2008).

The Obama plan for complete modernization builds on the previous administration's call for 'most' health records to be stored electronically by 2014. A bill was passed in July 2008 by the US Congress calling for a national Health Information Technology (HIT) infrastructure to be established. But the scheme has technical, privacy-related and financial challenges.

- Technically, the project requires more specialist staff to implement than are presently available in the US.
- From a privacy perspective, whilst information-keepers are required to notify patients in the event of security or privacy breaches, information privacy lobbyists are concerned over possible hacking as well as the potentially invasive nature of a national system.
- Financially, it is estimated that the system would save the healthcare industry between $200–300m annually in administrative costs, which could in turn reduce Americans' healthcare costs (themselves growing at around 9 per cent annually). However, the $100bn cost would comprise an eighth of the Obama administration's overall stimulus plan.

But, in the context of a $2trillion industry, $100bn is a drop in the ocean.

## Question

What lessons could the US learn from the UK's Connecting for Health initiative? Review the UK Parliament Committee of Public Accounts investigation into the use of IT in the National Health Service: (http://www.publications.parliament.uk/pa/cm200607/cmselect/cmpubacc/390/390.pdf).

# Technological considerations

In chapter 3 we identified technology as both a driver of change as well as an enabler to support new business concepts. We also expressed caution in seeking to place bets on which e-business technologies would be critical for future business success, but recommending rather that we think in a more measured way about how we might classify e-business technologies, how they have developed over time, and to provide an outline of some of the main issues affecting their application within organizations. But in looking forward, it is clearly important to identify some technological themes which may be important in influencing the nature and scope of e-business futures. In this section, we focus on three concepts: broadband ubiquity, technology mobility, and security.

The availability of broadband access[1] to end users (whether individuals or organizations) is seen as a critical future facilitator of economic activity and a key component of developments in information society, including 'new possibilities for communication and lifestyle' (Cawley and Preston, 2007). Indeed, the link between broadband in use and enhanced economic performance is now unambiguous: as Table 12.1 suggests, in markets where mass-market broadband is introduced, there is more rapid growth in employment, in the number of businesses overall, and in businesses in IT-intensive sectors, relative to comparable communities without broadband technology (Gillett et al., 2006). Current estimates suggest that the total number of broadband lines in the world passed 400m during 2009. Commentators forecast that the total in the forty biggest broadband countries in the world will grow from 393 million by the end of 2008 to 635 million by 2013. Elsewhere, an additional 32m lines will be added, to reach 683m in total.[2]

**Table 12.1  The effects of broadband on economic development**

| Economic Indicator | Results |
| --- | --- |
| Employment (Jobs) | Broadband added about 1–1.4% to growth rate, 1998-2002 |
| Business Establishments (Proxy for Numbers of Firms) | Broadband added about 0.5–1.2 to growth rate, 1998-2002 |
| Housing Rents (Proxy for property values) | More than 6% higher in 2000 in Zip codes where broadband avaliable by 1999 |
| Industry Mix | Broadband added about 0.3–0.6% to share of establishment in IT-intensive sectors, 1998–2002 |
|  | Boardband redused share of small(<10 employees) establishments by about 1.3–1.6%, 1998–2002 |

[1] Recall that the definition of 'broadband' has historically varied from country to country. Whilst it is generally accepted as comprising a high-speed, 'always on' Internet connection, minimum download speeds vary from 128Kpbs to 2Mbps or higher. The definition used in this text is from the ITU.

[2] http://www.itu.int/ITU-D/ict/newslog/680+Million+Broadband+Lines+In+2013.aspx.

However, the distribution of broadband in a region like Europe is in practice very uneven. Recall from chapter 4 that the definition of broadband has evolved over time but that there is now an accepted definition The European regulatory model is designed to increase competition in the telecommunications market and whilst broadband penetration in the EU rose from 16.2 per cent in 2006 to 20.0 per cent in 2007 and, on average, 52,000 broadband lines were added per day during 2007, only three European countries (Denmark, Finland, and the Netherlands) were then world leaders in broadband penetration, surpassing the US, Japan, and South Korea, but there were also some countries significantly behind the curve, including Ireland, Greece, and Slovakia. Cawley and Preston argue that the European Union agenda for broadband has been focused in the main upon infrastructure rollout and bandwidth (and even here, the Lisbon 2010 objectives have not been met), with the view that innovative applications and services will simply follow the provision.

> 'As the broadband experience in Europe shows, this has not been the case, particularly with regard to innovative content services, but also in terms of the online transaction of e-government and e-business services.' *Cawley and Preston*, 2007

The growing importance of location-based services (perhaps a more fashionable term for what was once 'm-commerce') was highlighted in Short case 5.1. This is a change which is taking place in the context of the greater mobility of e-business technologies themselves. One of the consequences of mobility for organizations is the extent to which it may potentially work to free up the geographical dimension in the ways companies compete and succeed. (Although we should be wary of indulging in technological determinism: recall out discussion in chapter 2.) The notion of location-aware task managers adjusting work schedules or even shopping lists based on locational information from the GPS unit in the mobile device becomes a real possibility.[3] For example, social mapping services like Loopt transform the mobile phone into a form of 'social compass' that shows users where friends are located and what they are doing via detailed, interactive maps, in addition to helping them connect with friends and navigate their social lives by providing a geographical orientation to people, places, and events (http://www.loopt.com). Users can also share location updates, geo-tagged photos and comments with friends in their mobile address book or on online social networks, communities, and blogs. Services like Dopplr—initially aimed at corporate users as an internal tool—and Tripit offer travel and visit planning with the added incentive of sharing trips privately with colleagues and friends (http://www.dopplr.com, http://www.tripit.com). Alongside location-based services has been the more general growth in the quality and availability of the mobile web, given revolutionary impetus by the development of the iPhone and the mobile web browser (also see Long case 12.2).

One possible future for the telecoms industry during the current economic slowdown is that fixed-to-mobile substitution (FMS) will be accelerated as consumers reduce their communications bill by cutting their fixed line in favour of mobile services. With mobile broadband deals now more readily available and affordable, there is a potential 'double whammy' to this in that fixed-line operators could not only lose further fixed-voice revenues but valuable broadband revenues as well.

---

[3] However, see the interesting discussion in Clear and Dickson (2005).

Finally, technology security will continue to require attention in an increasingly interconnected e-business world. The growth of open systems and of such concepts as cloud computing means that the typical organization is much less inward-looking than it used to be and information, payments, software. and services are received and transmitted across networks in increasing quantity and commercial confidentiality. This has significant security implications.

'Information has become the new currency of business—and its portability, accessibility and mobility back and forth across international, corporate and organizational boundaries are crucial components of a collaborative, globally connected business world. At the same time, however, protecting corporate information assets is equally critical—especially as mobile devices proliferate, open use of the Internet surges, new business models shake out, and strategic sourcing initiatives stretch "long reach" supply chains further and across more countries and companies than ever before.' *PWC, 2008*

According to Table 12.2, commercial organizations appear to be becoming more adept at safeguarding their information resources and e-business networks, although the

**Table 12.2  Implementation of security technologies by firms, 2007–2008**

| Implementation | 2008% | 2007% |
|---|---|---|
| Encryption, Laptops | 50 | 40 |
| Encryption Databases | 55 | 45 |
| Encryption, File share | 48 | 37 |
| Encryption, Backup tabes | 47 | 37 |
| Encryption, Removable media | 40 | 28 |
| Web/Internet, Content filters | 69 | 51 |
| Web/Internet, Website security/accreditation | 58 | 48 |
| Web/Internet, Secure browsers | 66 | 55 |
| Web/Internet, Web services security | 58 | 48 |
| Detection, Tools to discover unauthorised devices | 51 | 40 |
| Prevention, Tools to prevent intrusions | 62 | 52 |
| Prevention, Secure remote acces via VPN | 68 | 59 |
| Prevention, Wireless handheld devices security technologies | 42 | 33 |

protection of removable media and wifi devices appears to be less well practised. Chapter 3 has already highlighted the significant lapses of security amongst public-sector agencies which largely centre around removable media being misplaced or stolen. PWC's survey showed that the most promising opportunities to safeguard sensitive information are concentrated in five areas:

- improving privacy protections;
- getting better control over access;
- strengthening the security that enables sourcing, alliances, and other collaborative networks;
- using people and process to take full advantage of data loss prevention (DLP) technologies; and
- taking a risk-based approach to compliance with regulations and standards ranging from Sarbanes Oxley and the European Union Data Protection Directive to the global payment card industry's (PCI) data security standards.

## Social considerations

Chapter 4 considered the range of social and behavioural changes which the development and adoption of e-business had brought about, at the individual level, the level of the organization, and the level of society itself. As we look forward in this chapter, it is clear that such changes will continue to provide a source of both challenge and opportunity. At the individual level, the productivity and efficiency gains to be obtained from the use of e-business technologies are likely to remain extremely varied, in part because of the different educational and socio-economic circumstances of the individuals concerned, but also because of the different levels of access to such technologies. The general predictors of individual adopters of e-business technology will remain: level of income and education, age, and career stage (Li et al., 2006), together with a particular set of values, lifestyle, and experience.

But some of the greatest changes will be seen as the more technologically literate, so-called net generation, enters the mainstream. For example, research by telecoms and software consulting firm Ovum in 2008 reinforces the findings from our discussion from the technological environment in relation to the switch to mobile. The study concluded that younger people are more likely to want to shift their personal communications profile from fixed line to mobile in the future. Ten per cent of 16–25-year-olds were likely to drop their fixed-line connection altogether, whilst 28 per cent would keep a fixed connection but rely more on their mobile phone for calls (Philpott, 2008). The propensity to switch from fixed line to mobile appears higher in markets where mobile phones are already a significant part of the culture, including South Korea and Italy; and is correspondingly lower in some western European markets such as Germany and France.

The social consequences of e-business technology adoption will not always be clear-cut however. Chapter 4 drew particular attention to the blurring of the work–life divide arising from the seamless use of devices outside formally scheduled work time. Some argue that this blurring is to the detriment of an individual's well-being and the well-being of family and friends around them. This phenomenon is not likely to diminish, as companies make use of more technologies which encourage more productive and inexpensive working from their employees.

Amongst these technologies are those services which permit online collaboration, allowing people in different geographical locations work on projects. Services which allow the creation and sharing of presentations or to look at the work that others have conducted and download them are growing fast as cloud-computing applications become increasingly attractive. For example, Slideshare is the world's largest community for sharing presentations online (http://www.slideshare.net). Founded by Rashmi Sinha, Jonathan Boutelle, and Amit Rajan, the company itself is based between San Francisco and New Delhi. Using it, individuals and organizations can upload presentations to share their ideas, connect with others, and generate leads for their businesses. Similarly, anyone can find presentations on topics that interest them. They can then tag, download, or embed presentations into their own blogs and websites. The company uses Amazon.com to sustain its near exponential demand for storage space. Meanwhile, new start-up http://www.280.com allows users to create their own presentations from scratch.

## Activity box 12.2

### Racheting up roaming

What are the implications for B2C e-business firms of a shift from fixed to mobile telecoms amongst customers?

Group social behaviours are seen as the most significant behavioural phenomena to have arisen from the growth of e-business technologies. We are the point where many of these behaviours have reached a sufficiently large critical mass to be important in influencing the behaviour of e-businesses and indeed of societies (see Short case 12.2)

## Short case 12.2

### Kiva: loans that change lives

'Kiva mixes the entrepreneurial daring of Google with the do-gooder ethos of Bono, lead singer of the rock band U2.' *Forbes Magazine*, 2008

The story of Bangladeshi banker and economist Muhammad Yunus, and the development of his Grameen (Village) Bank, has become well known for demonstrating the role that micro-finance can play in helping those who don't already have financial assets, by providing loans and other financial services (http://www.grameen-info.org/). By the end of 2007, the bank had made loans totalling $6.6bn; $731m in 2007 alone. As the financial services    » of micro-finance usually involve small amounts of money—both loans and savings—the term 'micro-finance' helps to differentiate these services from those which formal banks provide, but also shows how far the $6.6bn has been spread—over 80,000 villages.

Combining social networks and micro-finance generates the concept behind Kiva.org. Kiva was founded in 2004 as a hobby by Matt and Jessica Flannery. (Matt was formerly a programmer with digital video recorder business TiVO.) The e-business is now the world's first person-to-person micro-lending website, allowing individuals to lend directly to individual entrepreneurs in emerging markets. Users browse the site, choose an entrepreneur to whom they wish to lend and offer a micro-loan of between six to twelve months' duration. Qualified entrepreneurs have identified 100 professional micro-finance partners for inclusion on the site. Micro-loans, processed through the professional partners, do not disappear into the ether: the site allows lenders to track the way the money flows through the entire cycle and the effects it has on the individuals borrowing and using the money through email journal updates. In future, it plans to track the social and economic impact of its loans more formally. When the loan is repaid, the lender can find another potential recipient for their support.

Kiva.org has nearly 500,000 lenders and, with the typical loan of $25, has helped 95,000 borrowers in over forty countries with a total of $66.3m in micro-loans by the middle of 2009: a current average loan size of $423. The default rate is just over 2 per cent.[4] While Kiva's micro-finance partner institutions charge a modest interest rate on the loans, Kiva relies upon voluntary contributions. By comparison with Grameen, Kiva might seem small beer with only a one-thirtieth of Grameen's annual disbursements, but at one point in 2007, Kiva actually briefly ran out of prospective individuals to assist because of the numbers of lenders registering.

Question

In what ways do you think social networking technologies might allow Kiva.org to develop in the future?

---

[4]  http://www.kiva.org/about/facts/.

# Regulatory and ethical considerations

Two issues will dominate the future regulatory and ethical environment for e-business: information rights and issues of environmental sustainability. Chapter 5 discussed some of the implications for privacy and commercial confidentiality arising out of increased surveillance of electronic communications, and we saw earlier that information security is already a key technological issue for firms. From the regulatory point of view, it is clear that tensions between protection of intellectual property and promotion of innovation as well as between national security and human rights (including information rights) will become ever more significant. Further, as users become more reliant upon e-business technologies, so the scope for industrial espionage and anti-competitive practices such as denial of service activity increases. Those working to regulate and enforce intellectual property law and copyright protection are, in effect, in an arms race with data criminals seeking to find ways to copy and share content without payment.

However, at the governmental level there is considerable pressure to introduce the monitoring of electronic communications not just for reasons of national security but for reasons of legal compliance over copyright. Chapter 5 has already addressed many of the ethical concerns raised by lobby groups over surveillance and intrusion. For example, vested interests such as the Motion Picture Association of America (MPAA) have been lobbying the new US Administration to introduce automated-detection technology and a 'three strikes' policy for banning those users who download illegally. Similar attempts have been rejected within Europe, but the likely cost and implications of this kind of intervention presents significant potential challenges for organizations.

The EU Data Retention Directive, which is currently being transposed into UK law, requires that communications service providers (CSPs) store communications traffic data for between six months and two years. During 2008 and 2009, the UK government, through the Home Office, undertook consultation and has been preparing plans, which have not yet taken the form of proposed legislation, known as the Interception Modernisation Programme. This could include the creation of a single database which will automatically gather and retain all communications data generated in the UK—data including the billing records of all calls made, as well as emails sent, and web pages visited, although not their contents. It is suggested that citizens are already suspicious of organizations' abilities to manage information securely, as we discussed in chapter 5. An average of only 8 per cent of Americans said they were 'very confident' in the ability of US retailers, government, and banks to protect their personal information, according to a national telephone survey commissioned by an IT software management company in 2008 (although we might ask what the other respondents thought!).[5] Chapter 3 outlined the many mistakes made by UK public agencies in the handling of data in 2008 alone.

As they grow in significance, understanding the environmental impact of e-business activities will be a further important ethical consideration for regulators seeking to implement sustainability policies. Superficially, we would anticipate e-business to have a positive environmental impact, but most commentators distinguish between three order-effects of ICT and e-business technologies on the environment:

---

[5] http://www.businesswire.com/portal/site/google/?ndmViewId=news_view&newsId=20080716005159&newsLang=en.

- *first order* (direct): the impacts and opportunities created by the physical presence of technology and the infrastructure and processes involved (largely negative and, for example, including carbon emissions during manufacture or disposal of hardware);

- *second order* (indirect): the impacts and opportunities created by the ongoing use and application of technologies (largely positive and, for example, including teleconferencing as a substitute for long-haul air travel);

- *third order (indirect):* the impacts and opportunities created by large numbers of people using technology over an extended period of time (largely un-researched and, for example, including the likelihood of increased consumption of lower priced online goods) (Yi and Thomas, 2007).

But the net impacts are not completely clear-cut. For example, B2C e-businesses could contribute positively to sustainable consumption in three ways:

- *Energy consumption:* this can be achieved, for example, through more centralized and optimized delivery networks (by both retail and logistics firms); through the centralized management of carbon emissions; and by the storage of goods at higher densities than can be achieved by retail stores (although some decentralized models can also be energy efficient).

- *Sustainable consumption:* the development of digital products which can be intangibly distributed to customers makes a contribution to sustainable consumption by drastically reducing resources in production.

- *packaging and waste:* delivering goods directly to homes means that there is the potential to reduce the level and complexity of individual product packaging.

Similarly, from the point of view of the consumer, e-commerce can entail a significant reduction in consumers' time and capital, by substituting a home delivery for a personal shopping trip. In particular, there can be substitution of freight for personal transportation. And finally, e-commerce generally favours planned over impulse purchasing (although the growth of location-based services might prompt more spontaneous buying behaviour).

However, the jury is still out on a number of these issues because there may be a whole range of hitherto hidden costs. For example:

- *Energy consumption:* the impact on the infrastructure of the increased number of freight vehicles delivering to homes has not been calculated; multi-channel customers may visit stores to undertake research and shopping online leaves consumers with more time to engage in other activities—including more store-based shopping.

- *sustainable consumption:* all activities have some impact on the environment, even consuming digital products. Even searching on Google has a carbon footprint. US physicist Alex Wissner-Gross claimed that a typical Google search on a desktop computer produces about 7g of $CO_2$—about half the cost of boiling a kettle—not least because of the high-energy intensity of server farms. (Google suggests that in practice a typical search generates 0.2g of $CO_2$, equivalent to the energy burned by the body in ten seconds (Google, 2009).) Putting this into context, however, analysts Gartner estimate that the global IT industry generated as much $CO_2$ as the airline industry in 2008.

**Carbon Footprint** The total amount of greenhouse/gases produced by an individual, organization, or society at large, usually expressed in equivalent tons of carbon dioxide ($CO_2$).

## Short case 12.3

### Ocado: the green grocer

Oneline grocery retailer Ocado (http://www.ocado.com) was founded in 2002 by three former Goldman Sachs bankers. Now partly owned by the John Lewis Partnership, operators of the upmarket Waitrose grocery stores, with which it has a five-year supply deal, it now commands a £1bn turnover and has a 20 per cent UK market share of online grocery goods, delivering Waitrose branded goods to the south-east, midlands, and north-west of England: a potential market of around 13.5m households. Food manufacturer Procter & Gamble took a notional 1 per cent stake in the firm in 2008 and Jörn Rausing, investor and son of the founder of packaging firm Tetra Pak (now Tetra Laval) invested £15m in 2003. Ocado was expected to be profitable by the end of 2008, having made £76.8m in reported losses since its foundation. Christmas 2008 sales were double the same period in 2007. But the company has made green principles a means for its differentiation. This is based on several distinctive features arising out of the firm's e-business credentials, in addition to conventional procurement and traceability policies.

- *Warehouse-based fulfilment system:* the company has no stores, distributing goods instead from a single warehouse in Hatfield. This allows it to undertake careful inventory management and to avoid the high environmental costs of building and running a conventional network of stores. Energy management includes an energy-efficient refrigeration plant and a combined heat and power (CHP) plant, providing half the carbon footprint of a conventional installation.

- *'Green' delivery slots:* customers are incentivized to book a delivery slot when the van is already in their area, to minimize the carbon impact of distribution.

- *Bio-diesel-fuelled delivery vans:* each journey made by an Ocado delivery van, converted to biodiesel in 2006, is equivalent to twenty return grocery shopping journeys by car, as it holds space for twenty orders. The company calculates that twenty-seven items would need to be bought on a dedicated shopping trip to achieve the same level of energy efficiency as van delivery. Zero emission electric and palm oil fuelled vans are being trialled.

- *Closed-loop recycling of plastic bags:* plastic bags are 100 per cent biodegradable and are collected by the driver, recycled, and reused.

- *Waste reduction:* Ocado prints expiry dates for products on its till receipts.

Environmental technology consultant Greenstone Carbon Management made recommendations for improvements in energy operations and transport that reduced Ocado's carbon footprint by 21 per cent in six months (http://www.greenstonecarbon.com). The firm's carbon audit suggests that Ocado is now 'as green as walking to the supermarket' (although it draws the line at car-borne shopping). Ocado won the Online Green Awards (OLGA) in 2008.

### Question

Relate Ocado's operations and environmental achievements to the three 'levels' of environmental impact of e-business.

# Tools to manage complex and ambiguous e-business futures

How do firms and public-sector agencies come to terms with the possibilities of e-business futures? Too often, conventional forecasting has proved inaccurate or downright dangerous as decision-makers seek to make sense out of a plethora of new or imperfectly understood phenomena. The track record on this is not good. It is instructive, for example, to look back at the evidence of the quality of past insights. The insights in Table 12.3 were derived from a conference on 'Fifty Years of Business Computing' held in London at the end of 2001 (Ellis, 2002). Helpfully, they try to summarize both 'what we have learned in the past 50 years' as well as reporting on some crystal ball gazing for the next fifty (some quite imaginative and possibly unrealistic), based on a prize-winning paper by Professor Chandra Amaravadi.

Interestingly, the business trends to 2051 focus significantly upon the impact of e-business technologies on human resources: those discarded by and required by the firm of 2051. Another way of thinking about the future might be to ask users how they feel e-business will affect them in the future. Figure 12.3 does just this as part of an investigation into the kinds of consumer technologies customers believe will be in use by 2015. The research investigates the appeal of particular technologies, how likely customers are to use them, how new they feel they are—and finally whether they believe these technologies will be in use by 2015. It is instructive to explore which technologies

**Table 12.3 Lessons from the past; forecasts of the future**

**(a) What we have learned in the past 50 years**
- We are not good at programming
- We are still bad at estimating and managing software projects
- The paperless office has still not happened
- Information overload—search engines are often months behind web content
- Not enough attention is paid to the human an element in business computing
- Security,trust and standardisation are of increasing importance
- Senior managers are not enthusiastic about e-commerce or e-business

**(b) Key business trends 2001–2051**
- The Mega Corporation will be a reality.Scale economies,technological complexity and capital requirements drive out most medium and small-sized businesses
- Automation results in tremendous job displacement
- Most clerical, admin and middle management jobs replaced by robots or standardised programmes
- Tremendous labout shortages for mathematicians, engineers, physicists,bio-physicits and pharmacists
- Limitless power generation will re-shape most industries, especially the transportation industry
- The utilities will be the greatest users of computing resources as they will include grocery,transportation, power and communications facilities
- Companies will compete for customers based on the size of their yearly business
- Companies have done away with physical bulidings

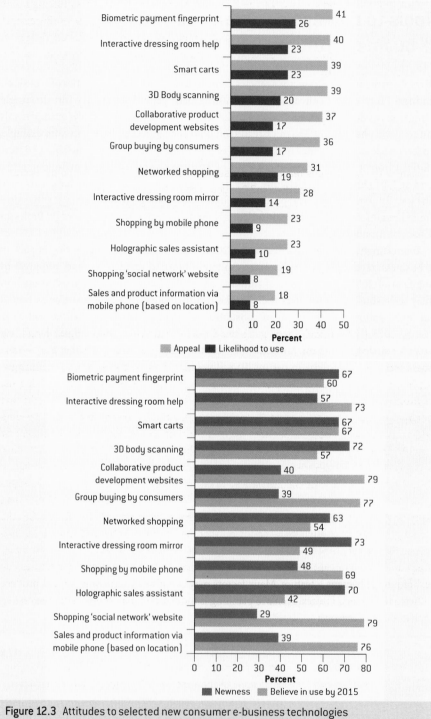

**Figure 12.3** Attitudes to selected new consumer e-business technologies

are both attractive and seen as likely to be in use, such as the 'interactive dressing room' (a changing room provided with a touchscreen mirror which can display clothing against the customer's reflection) and compare this with others which appear to have little appeal, but about which customers feel there is a certain inevitability, such as shopping from a social shopping website.

---

### Activity box 12.3

Future perfect?

Examine the conclusions reached by consumers from Figure 12.3. Where do the scores converge and where do they diverge? Can you account for your findings?

---

# E-business scenarios

The making of more flexible long-term plans for organizations, however, cannot simply rely upon linear forecasting mechanisms—particularly during especially uncertain economic times, or when the futures that are being considered involve other unstable, hard-to-predict, or closely interrelated phenomena. Even this chapter has been considering the environmental drivers for e-business in a degree of isolation, when the reality is that they are often closely interrelated: for example, evolving social attitudes towards digital downloading will affect regulatory approaches adopted by governments and the technology sought by organizations to limit piracy. One alternative approach to simple trend extrapolation to have been developed by strategists is that of scenario planning. The technique involves developing plausible, internally consistent alternative world views drawn from the interrelated insights generated from the environment in which the decision-maker operates (Figure 12.4). When scenario planning was used in a military context, this might have included the weather, the terrain, the motives of the opposing forces, and the attitudes of the planners' own armed forces. In business, where scenario planning was first used in the 1970s by analyst Pierre Wack at the oil company Royal Dutch/Shell for investigating its own strategic futures, the technique has become a feature. Many factors may combine in surprising ways to produce hitherto unforeseen futures. Scenario planning is more useful than simple trend forecasting for a number of reasons:

- It encourages exploration of the real drivers behind change.
- It challenges the assumptions we make about what may be happening.
- It discourages the notion that future situations are either predictable or inevitable.
- It builds a proactive awareness within an organization about possible futures and a willingness to accept multiple possible views.
- It permits the development of 'organizational resilience' in response to 'off-trend' developments and prepared alternatives for some of these situations.

But there will be some events that even scenario planning cannot prepare an organization for and an important component of the scenario planning process is to distinguish between events or trends that we believe we know something about and events and trends that we might consider uncertain or unknowable (see Activity 12.4).

---

### Activity box 12.4

**E-business imponderables**

Scenario planning focuses as much on elements we regard as unknown or unknowable as it does on things we believe we know something about. Is it possible to discuss the extent to which there are 'unknowns' in e-business futures? In which areas might we find them?

---

Not surprisingly, e-business has attracted probably more than its fair share of scenario planners. The European Commission's BEACON project is a good example of flexible thinking by governments over e-business futures. The main objective of this project was to conduct a socio-economic impact assessment of broadband access and use, in the context of electronic services and related issues in the European networked, knowledge-based economy. Undertaken during 2005–2006, it sought to develop meaningful scenarios which represented potential outcomes of the progress of the European Union towards a workable 'i-networked society' in 2012. (Interestingly, the authors thought that this goal could not be achieved by the original target date of 2010.) In particular, the work explored the interaction between broadband penetration and economic growth rate. Figure 12.5 shows the four possible scenarios that resulted.

The Consortium set thresholds of fixed and 3G penetration for each scenario and sought rich descriptions of the conditions which explain these outcomes. Table 12.4 shows some of these descriptions and provides some insight into the consequences for e-business of each scenario. The outcomes generated by this process are interesting, not least since with the rapid scaling back of economic growth forecasts with the current recession, the economic growth rate for the EU15 (the original basis for the study) is running at around -0.1 per cent and the forecast for 2010 is 0.8 per cent, while broadband penetration was running at 25 per cent by the beginning of 2008—putting the EU15 well within the 'Doldrums' scenario at one level, but sharing many of the characteristics of the 'Economy Stupid' scenario. This does not call into question the correctness of a scenario approach, but does indicate that such scenarios need to be regularly revisited.

A survey undertaken by the Pew Internet & American Life Project about the effect of the Internet on social, political, and economic life in the year 2020 was published at the end of 2008. It provides more quantified and focused (and of course more recent) results than the BEACON work and seeks to evaluate eight specific Internet-oriented scenarios. By canvassing nearly 600 Internet specialists and analysts, and over 600 other interested stakeholders, the research team may have emerged with somewhat more rhetorical and optimistic futures than might have been achieved by asking a random sample of consumers or non-technical business people, for example. Nevertheless, the

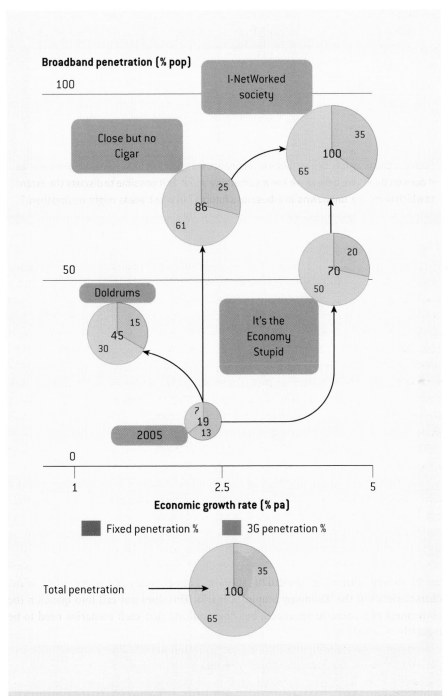

**Figure 12.5** Project BEACON scenario structure

**Table 12.4 Comparison of scenario factors and e-business implications**

| The Doldrums | It's the Economy Stupid | Close, But No Cigar | iNetWorked Society |
|---|---|---|---|
| *EU broadband penetration 12%* | *EU broadbrand penetration 25% by 2010* | *EU broadband penetration 35%* | *EU broadband penetration 45% or higher* |
| *Economic growth 1.5%*<br>Growth EU-15 below 2005 levels. Business investment and consumption is down | *Economic growth 3%*<br>Growth is driven by consumption, business investment levels and world trade | *Economic growth 2.5%*<br>Growth is moderately higher than in 2005. EU-wide competitiveness has improved, regulatory barriers have decreased | *Economic growth 3.5%*<br>Growth is driven by consumption, business investment, world trade. Virtuous cycle in which broadband stimulates the economy and vice versa. |
| Low levels of value chain integration | Moderate additional value chain integration, outsourcing and new business models. | Value chain integration accelerating | High levels of value chain integration |
| Lack of compelling content services on broadband | Slow progress in digital and interactive content | Innovative new content services emerging at a reasonable pace | Innovative new content services |
| E-government services fragmented and more likely to be informational than transactional services | Slow progress in e-government, e.g. solutions per governmental organization and focus on online information | E-government services focus on online participation and transaction | Fully integrated e-government services |
| E-work activities revolve around collaboration, teleworking and homeworking | Moderate progress in e-work | Rates of successful e-work range considerably from highly successful and fully supported in some member states, to states where there has been no change in e-work take-up | Ambient digital ICTs enable high levels of e-work |
| Advertising slow to support digital media | Advertising sector devoting more attention to digital media | Advertising sector devoting more attention to digital media | Business and advertising models now highly profitable and consumers very comfortable with paying for online content |

Pew survey, the third in the series, very much represents the 'state of the art' in thinking about an Internet future. Table 12.5 summarizes the balance of views surrounding each scenario.

The most interesting features of this exercise lie in contrasting the areas where there is a high degree of consensus with areas where there is much less clarity (recall the  important distinction between these two in our definition of the scenario-planning process). For example, the highest degree of consensus is to be found for Scenario 7. The vast majority of respondents strongly felt that we are unlikely to see a radical replacement for the underlying Internet technology that we have by 2020. Improvements would be incremental and would build on the existing infrastructure. Similarly, a significant majority of respondents disagreed with the notion that copyright protection technology would regulate content control by 2020. Many felt that a 'Pandora's Box' had already been opened and that unless there was unanimity on regulation, users would continue to circumvent established rules. By contrast, respondents were much more evenly balanced in the case of Scenario 4, which set out the case for the positive aspects of data sharing: presupposing a change in the public's notion of privacy, in which the benefits of sharing information, personal opinions, and emotions outweighed the risks. The even-handed judgement by respondents reflected genuine uncertainty over whether the impacts from greater transparency were positive or negative.

Of course, the scenario-planning technique has its weaknesses within organizations. Even within Royal Dutch Shell, there was often a lack of follow-through to take the right  important distinction between these two in our definition of the scenario-planning process). For example, the highest degree of consensus is to be found for Scenario 7. The vast majority of respondents strongly felt that we are unlikely to see a radical replacement for the underlying Internet technology that we have by 2020. Improvements would be incremental and would build on the existing infrastructure. Similarly, a significant majority of respondents disagreed with the notion that copyright protection technology would regulate content control by 2020. Many felt that a 'Pandora's Box' had already been opened and that unless there was unanimity on regulation, users would continue to circumvent established rules. By contrast, respondents were much more evenly balanced in the case of Scenario 4, which set out the case for the positive aspects of data sharing: presupposing a change in the public's notion of privacy, in which the benefits of sharing information, personal opinions, and emotions outweighed the risks. The even-handed judgement by respondents reflected genuine uncertainty over whether the impacts from greater transparency were positive or negative.

Of course, the scenario-planning technique has its weaknesses within organizations. Even within Royal Dutch Shell, there was often a lack of follow-through to take the right decisions, even though the scenarios themselves were rigorous and effective. Following an audit of the Shell approach, one insider commented:

> 'the scenario team were bright and their work was of a very high intellectual level. However neither the high level "Group scenarios" nor the country level scenarios produced with operating companies really made much difference when key decisions were being taken.' *Briggs, 2008*

**Table 12.5 Internet scenarios for 2020**

| Scenario | Description | Experts mostly agree (%) | Experts mostly disagree (%) | All respondents mostly agree (%) | All respondents mostly disagre e (%) |
|---|---|---|---|---|---|
| 1 | The mobile phone is the primary connection tool for most people in the world in 2020 | 77 | 22 | 81 | 19 |
| 2 | Social tolerance has advanced significantly due in great part to the internet. | 32 | 56 | 33 | 55 |
| 3 | Content control through copyright-protection technology dominates | 31 | 60 | 31 | 61 |
| 4 | Transparency heightens individual integrity and forgiveness. In 2020, people are even more open to sharing personal information, opinions, and emotions than they are now. | 45 | 44 | 44 | 45 |
| 5 | Many lives are touched by the use of augmented reality or spent interacting in artificial spaces | 55 | 30 | 56 | 31 |
| 6 | In 2020, the most commonly used communications appliances prominently feature built-in voice recognition. | 64 | 21 | 67 | 19 |
| 7 | Next-generation research will be used to improve the current internet; it won't replace it | 78 | 6 | 80 | 6 |
| 8 | Few lines divide professional time from personal time, and that's OK. | 56 | 29 | 57 | 29 |

Note: Where percentages fail to add to 100, the residual represents non-responses. Experts' responses included in 'all responses'

---

## Long case 12.1

### Virtual gifts for virtual worlds

Five years ago, the practice of selling intangibles was probably limited to financial services firms and mobile phone ring tones. But just because a product is virtual, rather than physical, does not mean that it cannot now be profitably sold and marketed in any arena. Indeed it is estimated that some $1.5bn annually is spent on virtual goods in e-commerce environments, comprising hundreds and thousands of so-called 'micropayments'—and the global recession which began in 2008 appears, if anything, to have accelerated the growth, as consumers stay at home and look for more modest ways of expressing themselves. Corporations are also keen to explore the use of branded virtual products to extend their marketing activity into social media. Jeremy Liew of venture capital firm Lightspeed identifies three typical purposes for digital goods: (1) increased functionality; (2) self expression; and (3) communication (Liew, 2008). »

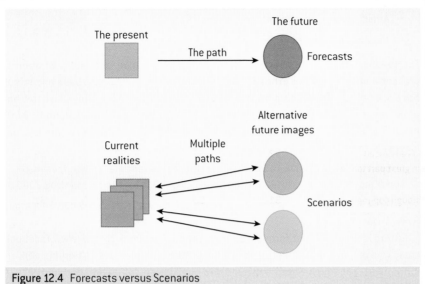

The present

The future

The path → Forecasts

Alternative
future images

Current
realities

Multiple
paths

Scenarios

**Figure 12.4** Forecasts versus Scenarios

We can see examples of functional goods in the e-books offered by Amazon.com and music files sold by iTunes and others, as well as in plug-ins, widgets, and other productivity-related accessories acquired by users. It is the acquisition of virtual goods for self-expression which probably has the most interesting potential for increasing online consumption. For example, users in the Second Life virtual world live in the world as avatars: virtual representations of themselves. And just like in the real world, not only do residents need to have something to wear, but they also want to use clothing to express their personalities. While basic membership provides some off-the-shelf wear, no-one wants to wander around in the poorly rendered discount jeans and t-shirts that are freely available. Fashionable clothing therefore increasingly carries the same kind of cachet as in the real world, as well as offering other interesting parallels, and there has been a proliferation of virtual designers and retailers. Amongst the most talked about fashion retailers 'in-world' are Nicole David, Loa Marquez, and Liam Oliver. David (pictured in her Second Life persona)—a real-world furniture designer—and her partners initially established a store called Elephant Outfitters in 2006. The store specialized in virtual casual wear, which is displayed and sold from a relatively conventional store environment. Residents 'touch' the display items to add a piece of clothing to their avatar's inventory. After buying their own Second Life island in 2006, they spent over a year developing a shopping village. In addition to a branch of Elephant Outfitters, the village contained five other brands:

- Armidi (leisurewear and beachwear);
- Gisaci (upscale clothing);
- Armidi Gisaci (upscale accessories);

»

- Armidi Beauty (hair, beauty, and cosmetics products);
- Intermizzo (lingerie).

The feedback from residents has been uniformly positive and the aspiration to present a more European ethos for the predominantly US shopper base appears to have been effective. Building traffic to brands in Second Life has proved elusive and problematic for many retailers. Traffic to the Armidi island averages around 30,000 residents a week. Suggesting that she would 'give her right arm for Armidi', one blogger wrote:

> 'There's clothing, accessories and hair, with each found in a separate building. The sim is so well put together, it really feels like you're shopping in Rome :).' *Dream Style blog, 2007*

Most recently, Armidi has launched a website selling virtual fashionwear: Shoparmidi (www.shoparmidi.com).

Gifting is the dominant form of communication. Facebook (http://www.facebook.com) was one of the first social networking sites to implement gifting in February 2007. 'With Facebook Gifts', suggests the application, 'you can send and receive Facebook's limited edition virtual gifts, small tokens of appreciation that are the perfect way to say "Happy Birthday", "Congratulations", or just "I'm thinking of you..."'. Most gifts cost $1 and are designed by Susan Kare, responsible for the original icon set on the Apple computer. A personalized message can be attached to each gift. An artificial notion of scarcity is created by producing gifts in a 'limited' run, particularly during holiday periods: of between 15,000 and 10m. When the number of a particular gift available falls below a minimum threshold, the number remaining is shown. In addition, advertisers can sponsor gifts which then become free to the sender. This aspect of e-business might seem trivial, but Jeremy Liew's analysis in 2007–2008 suggested that up to 470,000 a week of particular gifts might be given and that, in total, such sales could amount to $35m annually for Facebook.

Monetizing copyrighted material in electronic environments presents legal and licensing challenges and has led to new kinds of e-business service firms being created. Virtual Greats is a leading virtual goods sales and distribution system, which seeks to connect celebrities, artists, and content creators with prospective buyers through the online trade of likenesses, fashion, catchphrases, and other virtual representations of real-world talent (http://www.virtualgreats.com).

Questions
1. How sustainable is the gifting business model?
2. What other e-business markets lend themselves to the gifting model?

## Long case 12.2

### Google Android: the motives for mobile collaboration

Android is not a handset, nor an application, but an open software platform developed by information and search company Google for mobile devices. Recognizing the growing importance of mobile technology and the need to remain in touch with advertising revenues as routes to Internet access diversified, Google purchased a small company making software for mobile phones called Android, Inc. in 2005. Two years later, the Android platform was launched, at the same time as the Open Handset Alliance, a group of forty-seven handset manufacturers, mobile operators, semiconductor, and software companies including China Mobile, eBay, Intel, LG, Motorola, Nvidea, NTT DoCoMo, Sony Ericsson, and Telefónica 'who have come together to accelerate innovation in mobile and offer consumers a richer, less expensive and better mobile experience' (http://www.openhandsetalliance.com/).

All parts of the 'mobile ecosystem' or value constellation are represented in the Alliance. Some companies have contributed significant intellectual property that will be released under the Apache v2 Open Source licence. Others are working to make sure their chipsets support the platform. Handset manufacturers and mobile operators are working to develop handsets based on the platform. Commercialization partners are working with the industry to support the platform via a professional services model. The early models of the devices supporting Android have not generally been as sophisticated as the Apple iPhone, but this is in line with Google's ambitions for an 'affordable' device. However, Sony Ericsson released a more upmarket series of devices in summer 2009 and a full touch-screen version is also likely. Indeed, the nature of an open source platform is that it is flexible and capable of rapid evolution. For example, just three months after the launch of the first commercial HTC device in 2008, plans were announced to add video capture and stereo Bluetooth support to the next release of the platform.

What are Google's motives for taking the lead in this area? Advertising on mobile devices is seen as a major future revenue earner and can be twice as profitable as a conventional online ad because it has the potential to be more personal, increasing conversion rates. Google has already had experience in delivering its applications in mobile form to handset operators, but the development of a bespoke platform goes

>>

**Table 12.6 US mobile advertising revenue forecasts, 2007-2012 ($m)**

| Vehicle | 2007 | 2008 | 2009 | 2010 | 2011 | 2012 |
|---|---|---|---|---|---|---|
| Mobile message advertising | 810 | 1470 | 2380 | 3060 | 3830 | 4500 |
| Mobile display advertising | 34 | 85 | 186 | 327 | 453 | 541 |
| Mobile search advertising | 35 | 107 | 242 | 531 | 910 | 1484 |
| TOTAL | 879 | 1662 | 2808 | 3918 | 5193 | 6525 |

Note: 'Message' includes SMS texts and campaign costs; 'display' includes banners,links, or icons; 'search' includes sponsored display ads, text links alongside search results, and spending on audio ads

beyond this. Indeed, the company even envisages a free mobile device and service, funded entirely from advertising revenue. By way of context, global spending on mobile phone advertising in 2007 (which includes placing ads in text messages, on web pages, and in videos) was only $1.5bn, according to market analyst eMarketer. But the firm projects that this figure will grow to $14bn by 2011 (see Table 12.6 for information on the US market). Presently, the majority of revenues come from text message ads—but the mix will shift as display and search advertising revenues increase. A number of Asian markets, already leading in terms of mobile application usage, are seen as growing this mix even faster.

For mobile phone operators such as Vodafone, T-Mobile, and Telefónica, the plans are a double-edged sword. Google's powerful brand and its popular web-based services could, on the one hand, help operators sign up more subscribers to data packages, on which they increasingly rely as voice revenue declines. The competition in the mobile device/PDA market is significant, with Symbian, Apple, Windows Mobile, Research in Motion's BlackBerry, and now Google jockeying for position. However, on the other hand, incumbent operators will need to be wary about losing control over the mobile advertising market to a dominant industry player.

Questions

1. Is Google Android's 'mobile advertising revenue model' a new business model, or simply an extension of an existing one?

2. What can you tell about the motives and nature of e-collaboration in the Open Handset Alliance by who is, and perhaps more importantly, who is not a member (http://www.openhandsetalliance.com/oha_members.html)?

# ⭐ Chapter Summary

The chapter began by looking forward at the four elements in the business environment most likely to affect the scale and nature of e-business adoption by organizations and individuals: economic, technological, social, and ethical and regulatory. It stressed that the interaction between these elements would provide tensions and ambiguities for those involved. In terms of economic considerations, the chapter discussed the future links between e-business and economic performance, particularly in the context of an economic downturn. It examined the extent to which those firms adopting e-business might be more or less protected from difficult economic conditions. It then turned to technological considerations and identified three technological themes that would be important in influencing the nature and scope of e-business futures: broadband ubiquity, technology mobility, and security. It reiterated that caution was required in placing any bet on which e-business technologies would be critical to future business success. Thirdly, in examining social considerations, the chapter reviewed a selection of features of individual, organizational, and societal themes that would provide a source of both challenge and opportunity. Generational adoption of mobile telephony, the social consequences of the blurring of the work–life balance (picking up on issues raised in chapter 4), and the growth of services permitting online collaboration were reviewed. Finally, the chapter explored some elements affecting the future of ethical and regulatory matters, building upon discussions in chapter 5. It judged that the issues surrounding information rights and environmental sustainability would come to dominate the business environment.

The chapter then turned to the tools required to manage complex and potentially ambiguous e-business futures. It critically reviewed conventional trend forecasting techniques before examining the usefulness of scenario planning techniques in developing more flexible and longer-term plans for organizations. The chapter concluded with a discussion of two particular examples of scenario planning for e-business.

# ❓ Review questions

1. Are organizations which rely more heavily on e-business technologies more or less vulnerable to changing economic conditions than more conventional businesses?

2. What are the links between the introduction of broadband and economic development?

3. What are the consequences of greater future mobility of e-business technologies for either (a) firms or (b) individuals?

4. Why will the social consequences of e-business usage within organizations remain less than clear-cut?

5. What are the arguments for and against strengthening the monitoring of electronic communications?

6. Describe and illustrate the three 'order effects' of the environment on e-business.

7. What are the weaknesses of trend forecasting and extrapolation?

8. Why is scenario planning more useful than trend forecasting? Illustrate your answer with examples from e-business-relevant scenarios.

## Discussion questions

1. Google *'will be able to keep tabs on us all'* (Mostrous and Evans, 2006). Do you agree? Discuss the tensions that exist between information transparency and information privacy. The original article on which this question is based can be found here: http://technology.guardian.co.uk/news/story/0,,1938475,00.html?gusrc=rss&feed=20.

2. Look at Table 12.3a and reflect upon the extent to which 'what we have learned in the past 50 years' in 2001 might apply today.

3. Under what circumstances might the second-order positive effects of e-business outweigh the first order negative effects?

4. Trend analysis suggests that a higher proportion of young people are keen to move from fixed to mobile Internet access. And yet Figure 12.3 suggests that neither shopping nor receiving sales and product information via mobile phone has much appeal amongst consumers. Discuss and explain this apparent contradiction.

5. Which kinds of e-businesses will be most at risk if there is a significant downturn in advertising revenue?

## Suggestions for further reading

Anderson, J.Q., and Rainie, L., (2008), *The Future of the Internet III*, Pew Internet & American Life Project, http://pewinternet.org/pdfs/PIP_FutureInternet3.pdf.
Technology stakeholders and critics were asked in an online survey to assess scenarios about the future social, political, and economic impact of the Internet. This report analyses their views and commentary.

Doctorow, C., (2008), *Content: Selected Essays on Technology, Creativity, Copyright and the Future of the Future*, Tachyon Publications. Cory Doctorow is a Canadian blogger, journalist, and science fiction writer. Content is a book of short, though-provoking personal essays about the future, focusing upon web and e-business-related issues.

TNS Market Research, (2008), *New Future in Store. How Will Shopping Change by 2015?*, Research Report.
There are many forward-looking pieces of research seeking to understand consumers' preferences in relation to e-business. This report by TNS Market Research is a particularly good example.

Van de Heijden, K., (2005), *Scenarios: The Art of Strategic Conversation*, John Wiley.
Thinking about scenarios—the different plausible future environments that can be imagined—is a dynamic process. This book deals first with the principles of organizational learning and then moves on to describe practical and down-to-earth ways in which the organization can develop its skill in conducting a scenario-based strategy process.

Yi, L. and Thomas, H.R., (2007), 'A Review on the Environmental Impact of e-Business and ICT', *Environment International*, 33, pp. 841–9. This useful review article draws together existing academic work on the environmental impact of e-business technologies. In addition to distinguishing the three 'levels' of impact, the paper concludes that traditional assessment techniques are insufficient to measure impacts on sustainability and that new measures are needed.

## References

Amaravadi, C. S., (2003), 'World and Business Computing 2051', *Journal of Strategic Information Systems*, 12(4), pp. 373–86.

Anderson, J.Q., and Rainie, L., (2008), *The Future of the Internet III*, Pew Internet & American Life Project, http://pewinternet.org/pdfs/PIP_FutureInternet3.pdf.

Anon, (2008), 'Barclays Ad Forecast: Bullish on Online Search, Bearish on Newspapers', *Seeking Alpha*, 18 December, http://seekingalpha.com/article/111461-barclays-ad-forecast-bullish-on-online-search-bearish-on-newspapers.

Beacon Consortium, (2006), 'The BEACON Broadband Future Planning Guide', *Deliverable D3.1*, European Commission 6th Framework Programme, http://www.ovum.com/beacon/pdf/plan.pdf.

Briggs, P., (2008), 'The Phony Hype from Shell on Scenarios', Paddy's Writing on *Brand and Reputation*, http://shellbrand.blogspot.com/2008/01/phoney-hype-from-shell-on-scenarios.html.

Cawley, A., and Preston, P., (2007), 'Broadband and Digital "content" in the EU-25: recent trends and challenges', *Telematics and Informatics*, 24, pp. 259–71.

Clear, F., and Dickson, K., (2005), 'Teleworking Practice in Small and Medium-Sized Firms: Management Style and Worker Autonomy', *New Technology, Work and Employment*, 29(3), pp. 218–33.

Doward, J., (2008), 'Chaos as £13bn NHS Computer System Falters', *Guardian*, 10 August, http://www.guardian.co.uk/society/2008/aug/10/nhs.computersystem.

Ellis, P., (2002), '"Reading the Tea-Leaves" from 50 Years of Business Computing', *Futures*, 34, pp. 873–81.

eMarketer, (2008), 'Mobile Advertising Spending to Surpass $6.5 billion in 2012', http://www.marketingcharts.com/direct/mobile-advertising-spending-to-surpass-65-billion-in-2012-4097/.

Forbes Magazine (2008)

Gillett, S., Lehr, W.H., Osorio, C.A., and Sirbu, M.A., (2006), *Measuring the Economic Impact of Broadband Deployment, Final Report, National Technical Assistance, Training, Research, and Evaluation Project #99-07-13829, US* Department of Commerce, http://www.eda.gov/ImageCache/EDAPublic/documents/pdfdocs2006/mitcmubbimpactreport_2epdf/v1/mitcmubbimpactreport.pdf.

Google, (2009), 'Powering a Google Search', *The Official Google Blog*, 11 January, http://googleblog.blogspot.com/2009/01/powering-google-search.html.

Kaushik, A., (2008), 'Offshoring and Recession: Impact on Outsourcers', *CIO*, 8 December, http://www.cio.com.au/article/269888/offshoring_recession_impact_outsourcers?pp=1.

Li, Webber and Longley (2006)

Liew, J., (2008), 'Facebook Digital Gifts Worth around $15m/year', http://lsvp.wordpress.com/2008/01/23/facebook-digital-gifts-worth-around-15myear/.

Mostrous, A. and Evans, R., (2006), 'Google "will be able to keep tabs on us all"', *Guardian*, 3 November 2006, http://technology.guardian.co.uk/news/story/0,,1938475,00.html?gusrc=rss&feed=20.

Philpott, M., (2008), 'Broadband Remains a Sticky Service', *Cellular News*, 8 December, http://www.cellular-news.com/story/35044.php?source=newsletter.

Preston, P. and Cawley, A., (2008), 'Broadband Development in the European Union to 2012—A Virtuous Circle Scenario', *Futures*, 40, pp. 812–21.

PWC, (2008), *Safeguarding the New Currency of Business: Findings from the 2008 Global State of Information Security Study*, http://www.pwc.com/extweb/home.nsf/docid/C1CD6CC69C2676D4852574DA00785949.

Sweney, M., (2008), 'UK Newspaper Ad Revenues "will fall by 21 per cent in 2009"', *Guardian*, 21 November, http://www.guardian.co.uk/media/2008/nov/21/advertising-pressandpublishing.

Sultz, H.A. and Young, K.M., (2008), *Health Care USA: Understanding Its Organization and Delivery*, 6th edn, Jones & Bartlett.

Yi, L. and Thomas, H.R., (2007), 'A Review on the Environmental Impact of e-Business and ICT', *Environment International*, 33, pp. 841–9.

# Weblinks

ClickZ Stats. The ClickZ Network is the largest resource of interactive marketing news, information, commentary, advice, opinion, research, and reference in the world, online or off. ClickZ Stats is source for interactive and Internet research. The site provides facts, figures, research, and data on every facet of the online industry, domestic and worldwide: http:// http://www.clickz.com/stats.

FuturePerfect. Jan Chipchase is Principal Researcher in Nokia's Design Centre in Tokyo. His blog is about the collision of people, society, and technology, drawing on issues related to the design research that he conducts: http://www.janchipchase.com.

Rolf Skyberg—*Pattern Hound*. Rolf Skyberg is a Platform Product Manager for eBay, who doubles up as an Internet evangelist. His blog always contains thought-provoking comments on the present and future of the net, and his presentations provide good insight into emerging practice: http://rolfskyberg.wordpress.com/.

*Trendwatching*. One of the world's leading trend firms, trendwatching.com and its 8,000+ trend spotters scan the globe for emerging consumer trends. There are often free or sample reports to be downloaded: http://trendwatching.com/.

The Register. The Register is the one of the world's biggest online tech publications, with more than 5m unique users worldwide. The US and the UK account for more than 1.5m readers each month. Its Technical Panel provides useful insights into emerging trends: http://www.theregister.com.

# Glossary of terms

**AP** Application Portfolio—the integrated management of all company IT applications.

**ASCAP** The American Society of Composers, Authors, and Publishers.

**asset specificity** The extent to which products or services are designed to be attractive to a particular group of buyers.

**B2B marketplace/exchange** Web-based systems that link multiple businesses together for the purposes of trading or collaboration.

**BAM** Business Activity Monitoring.

**behavioural targeting** customer targeting employing software which intercepts and analyses web page requests, which generate profiles against which advertising can be more accurately delivered.

**blog** A blog (a contraction of the term 'Web log') is a website, usually maintained by an individual with regular entries of commentary, descriptions of events, or other material such as graphics or video. Entries are commonly displayed in reverse chronological order. (Technorati definition)

**blogosphere** The collective community of all blogs. Since all blogs are on the Internet by definition, they may be seen as interconnected and socially networked. Discussions 'in the blogosphere' have been used by the media as a gauge of public opinion on various issues.

**BMI** Broadcast Music Inc.

**BPEL** Business Process Execution Language.

**BPEL4WS** Business Process Execution Language for Web Services.

**BPM (1)** Business Process Management systems

**BPM (2)** Business Process Modelling

**BPML** Business Process Modelling Language—a meta-language for modelling business processes.

**capital deepening** An increase in the intensity of capital employed by an economy.

**carbon footprint** The total amount of greenhouse gases produced by an individual, organization or society at large, usually expressed in equivalent tons of carbon dioxide ($CO_2$).

**CEN/ISSS** European Committee for Standardization (Comité Européen de Normalisation in French).

**click-to-open rate** The ratio of unique clicks as a percentage of unique opens.

**click-through rate** The proportion of emails where an embedded web link is clicked by a recipient.

**click-to-call** A service which lets users click a button on a website in order to speak to a service representative of the company.

**co-ordination costs** The costs of doing business with a variety of suppliers, including the assembly of product and price information, negotiation, tracking delivery and payment.

**CRM** Customer Relationship Management.

**crowdsourcing**  the outsourcing of a task or activity to an unspecified, but generally large, group of people.

**DES**  Data Encryption Standard.

**digital natives**  A term applied to individuals who have grown up immersed in digital technologies. Attributed to US writer and game designer Marc Prensky.

**disintermediation**  Occurs when an intermediary is ejected from a conventional market niche between buyer and seller by a change in market conditions leading to buyer and seller dealing directly.

**disruptive innovation**  A technological innovation, product, or service that eventually overturns the prevailing status quo in the market. Attributed to Christensen (1997).

**EAI**  Enterprise Application Integration. Systems used to integrate various IT applications.

**ebXML**  E-business XML, undertaking electronic business using eXtensible Markup Language. XML-based infrastructure.

**economic imperialism**  The extension of economics to go beyond the classical scope of the subject. Some economists claim to be able to explain all social behaviour by using the tools of economics.

**EDI**  Electronic Data Interchange—a pre-Internet set of standards defining the electronic exchange of information relevant to business.

**e-government**  'The use of technology to enhance the access to and delivery of government services to benefit citizens, business partners and employees' (Deloitte and Touche, 2003).

**emergent strategy**  A situation where companies' strategies emerge, rather than being deliberately planned. Attributed to Mintzberg (1992).

**ERP**  Enterprise Resource-based Planning. Software packages providing a suite of systems to manage and co-ordinate operational processes across a wide range of internal business activities.

**extended enterprise**  The notion that a company is made up not just of its employees, its board members, and managers, but also its business partners, its suppliers, and even its customers.

**failure cascade**  A failure in one part of a system which leads to sequential failures in successive parts of the system.

**GPS**  Global Positioning System—satellite system to determine location of the GPS device.

**HaaS**  Hardware as a Service

**HTTP**  HyperText Transfer Protocol—a standard governing the transfer of hypertext between servers and browsers.

**human relations**  A model of management that focuses on the social processes

**hype cycle**  A concept seeking to describe the stages in the maturity, adoption, and business application of specific technologies. Attributed to technology consultancy Gartner, Inc. in 1995.

**information asymmetry**  A situation (negotiation or transaction) where one party has more, or higher-quality, information than the other.

**ISO**  International Standards Organization.

**JIT**  Just in Time—a concept developed in manufacturing which aims at reducing inventory levels.

**labour arbitrage**  the tendency of jobs to flow towards whichever country has the lowest wages per unit output at the time and has reached the minimum required level of political and economic development to support a particular activity.

**logical incrementalism** An approach to strategy formulation which involves a non-linear mixture of strategic planning and spontaneous change. Attributed to James Quinn (1978).

**long tail** An interpretation of the Pareto law applied to the stimulation of consumer demand possible in electronic markets, developed by journalist Chris Anderson. Refers to the ability of firms to obtain significant profits from the sale of small amounts of previously hard-to-find items to many customers, rather than selling only large amounts of a smaller number of popular items.

**mashup** A web application which combines data from more than one source.

**meme** A piece of cultural information which is transmitted from one mind to another, self-replicating. See http://www.thedailymeme.com.

**MRP** Materials Requirements Planning—a software-based production planning and inventory control system.

**multi-shoring** The movement of certain business activities to several non-domestic geographical locations.

**network effect** The idea that a service becomes more valuable as more people utilize it, thereby encouraging increasing numbers of users. Classic examples can be found in the communications market and include the telephone, fax machine, email, and of course the Internet itself.

**NPV** Net Present Value.

**OASIS** Organization for the Advancement of Structured Information Systems.

**off-shoring** The movement of certain business activities to a non-domestic geographical location.

**open rate** The proportion of emails opened at a particular time.

**open system** A management system that is capable of self-maintenance on the basis of throughput of resources from the environment.

**operations management** Management of the processes which transform inputs such as raw material, information, and labour into outputs in the form of finished goods and services.

**OUT** order-up-to procurement.

**outsourcing** The delegation of control over certain activities to third party business service companies

**P2P** Person-to-Person.

**pharming** Using deceptive email messages to redirect users from an authentic website to a fraudulent one, which replicates the original in appearance.

**phishing** Whereby thieves use deceptive emails to get users to divulge personal information, includes luring them to fake bank and credit card websites.

**PIP** Partner Interface Processes.

**PKI** Public Key Infrastructure.

**POS** Point-of-sale refers to the location where a transaction occurs, but the technology now conventionally employed to capture a sale can also enable sales management, forecasting, and customer analysis activity to be undertaken.

**publishers** Independent parties that promote the products or services of an advertiser on their website by means of links or other mechanisms.

**radical innovation** High-risk innovation involving significant change 'at a stroke' in markets, products, or services, with a higher degree of uncertainty over likely outcomes.

**rightsourcing** The determination of an appropriate combination of locational and sourcing control decisions for a particular organization.

**RNIF**  RosettaNet Implementation Framework.

**ROI**  Return on Investment.

**RSA**  Algorithm for public-key cryptography.

**RSS**  Rich Site Summary—a web feed standard for the dissemination of regularly changing web content (blog page entries, news headlines).

**SaaS**  Software as a Service.

**SCM**  Supply Chain Management.

**SESAC**  Society of European Stage Authors and Composers.

**SMiShing**  Sending text messages ('SMS') to cell phone users that trick them into going to a website operated by the thieves. Messages typically say that unless users go to the website and cancel, they will be charged for services they never actually ordered.

**SMM**  Standards Maturity Model.

**SOA**  Service-Oriented Architecture. Concept of flexible IT architecture design.

**SOAP**  Protocol for exchanging structured information in web services.

**SOC**  Service-Oriented Computing. See SOA.

**social exclusion**  Being unable to access the things in life that most of society takes for granted. The UK government defines it as—the lack or denial of resources, rights, goods, and services, and the inability to participate in the normal relationships and activities available to the majority of people in society, whether in economic, social, cultural, or political arenas. It affects both the quality of life of individuals and the equity and cohesion of society as a whole.

**SoundExchange**  A performing rights management organization established by the RIAA (Recording Industry Association of America).

**spear-phishing**  Impersonating a company employee/employer via email in order to steal colleagues' passwords/usernames and gain access the company's computer system.

**SRM**  Supplier Relationship Management.

**SSL**  Secure Sockets Layer—a secure communications protocol.

**strategic sourcing**  A buying process that includes definition of product and service requirements, identification of qualified suppliers, negotiation of pricing, service, delivery, and payment terms, and supplier selection (Fairchild, 2006).

**supply chain management**  The management of the network of manufacturers, wholesalers, distributors, and retailers, who turn raw materials into finished goods and services, and deliver them to consumers.

**sustaining innovation**  Incremental investments in products and services involving more conventional technology. Attributed to Christensen (1997).

**TCP/IP**  Transmission Control Protocol (TCP) and the Internet Protocol (IP).

**technological determinism**  A view that technology determines behaviour. Attributed to sociologist and economist Thorstein Veblen in 1921. Critics suggest that it is technology working within a complex social structure which determines change in behaviour.

**timeboxing** A time-management technique in which a schedule is divided into a number of separate time periods with each part having its own independent deliverables, deadlines, and budgets.

**touchpoint** An interaction that a customer will have with the resources of the firm at a particular stage in the buying process. This may be human and physical, or virtual. The term is most commonly used in the context of the growth of multi-channel marketing, where we have witnessed a proliferation of potential touchpoints.

**UBL** Universal Business Language—a library of XML documents.

**UDDI** Universal Description, Discovery and Integration.

**UPS** Uninterruptible Power Supply.

**W3C** World Wide Web Consortium.

**Web 2.0 (or Web 2)** An elusive term which seeks to differentiate current Internet behaviours from those which characterized 'Web 1.0'. These centre around social networking, user-created content and other forms of collaboration between end users. Attributed to O' Media in 2003.

**WEEE** Waste Electrical and Electronic Equipment directive—legislation which requires the reuse and recycling of certain types of electrical waste.

**WfMS** Workflow Management Systems used to visualize and model processes

**WSDL** Web Services Description Language.

**WSRP** Web Services for Remote Portlets.

**XML** eXtensible Markup Language, data interchange standard.

**Zeitgeist** The intellectual, moral, and cultural characteristics of a particular period of time.

# Artwork acknowledgements

## Figures

Figure 1.1  Reproduced by permission of Charles Peattie and Russell Taylor. www.alexcartoon.com

Figure 1.3  Reproduced from Gartner, 2008. www.gartner.com

Figure 1.4  Reproduced from European Commission, 2008. © European Communities, 1995–2009.

Figure 1.5  Reproduced from European Commission, 2007. © European Communities, 1995–2009.

Figure 1.6  Reproduced from Accenture, (2005). Leadership In Customer Services: New Expectations, New Experiences.

Figure 1.7  Reproduced from Oxfam, Oxfam GB, 2008.

Figure 2.1  Reproduced from the Office of National Statistics, 2008. (c) Crown Copyright.

Figure 2.2  Reproduced from OECD, (2008), Investment Data and Shares of ICT Investment in GDP and Total Non-residential GFCF.

Figure 2.3  Reproduced from Criscuolo, C. and Waldron, K., (2003), 'E-commerce and Productivity', *Economic Trends*, 600, pp. 52–7

Figure 2.4  Reproduced from Alamy, 2008

Figure 2.5  Reproduced with permission from Alina M. Chircu; Robert J. Kauffman, Strategies for Internet Middlemen in the Intermediation/ Disintermediation/Reintermediation Cycle in: Electronic Markets, Vol. 9 (2), 1999, Taylor & Francis.

Figure 2.6  Reproduced from OECD, 2008

Figure 2.8  Reproduced from http://nyanyan.to/skype/40hr_chart.php 2008

Figure 2.9  Reproduced from Barton, 2009. www.glimfeather.com/borderless

Figure 3.1  Reproduced from Microsoft Corporation, 2007.

Figure 3.2  Reproduced from www.sapdesignguild.org

Figure 3.3  Reproduced from Riempp, G. and Gieffers-Ankel, S., (2007), 'Application Portfolio Management: A Decision-Oriented View of Enterprise Architecture', Information Systems and E-Business Management, 5(4), pp. 359–78.

Figure 3.4  Reprinted Courtesy of International Business Machines Corporation, copyright 2006 © International Business Machines Corporation.

Figure 3.5  Reproduced from www.m2sys.com.

Figure 4.1  Reproduced from www.spatial-literacy.org 2007

Figure 4.2  Reproduced with permission from National Statistics website: www.statistics.gov.uk. Crown Copyright.

Figure 4.3  Reproduced from Technorati.com, 2007. www.sifry.com/alerts/archives/000493.html. Licensed under Creative Commons.

Figure 4.4  Reproduced from Technorati.com, 2008. http://technorati.com/blogging/state-of-the-blogosphere/the-what-and-why-of-blogging/ Licensed under Creative Commons.

Figure 4.5  Reproduced from Forrester Research, Inc., 2004.

Figure 4.6  Reproduced from Pew Internet and American Life Surveys, March 2000–March 2009.

Figure 4.7  Reproduced from International Telecommunications Union, 2009. www.itu.int/ITU-D/ict/publications/idi/2009/material/IDI2009_w5.pdf

Figure 4.8  Reproduced with permission from US Census Bureau 2009.

Figure 5.1  Reproduced from ITU online cyber security survey 2006.

Figure 5.2  Reproduced from Harris Interactive. Calculated from the Harris-Westin General Concern about Privacy Index 1990–2004 www.harrisinteractive.com

Figure 5.3  Reproduced from European Commission, 2008b. © European Communities, 1995–2009.

**Figure 5.4**  Reproduced from Privacy International, 2009. www.privacyinternational.org

**Figure 5.5**  Reproduced from HM Treasury, 2006. (c) Crown Copyright.

**Figure 5.6**  Reproduced with permission from IDC Global Software Piracy Study and IDC Piracy Reduction Impact Study, Business Software Alliance, 2009

**Figure 5.7**  Reproduced from Symantec 2009.

**Figure 5.8**  Reproduced from Federal Trade Commission, 2008. www.ftc.gov/sentinel/reports/sentinel-annual-reports/sentinetl-cy2007.pdf

**Figure 5.9**  Reproduced from United Nations, China Network Information Centre.

**Figure 6.1**  Reprinted by permission of Harvard Business Review. Adapted from "Strategy and the Internet", by Michael E. Porter, March 2001. Copyright © 2001 by the Harvard Business School Publishing Corporation.

**Figure 6.2**  Reproduced from www.crt.dk/trends 23rd March 2009

**Figure 6.3**  Reproduced from Osterwalder A, http://business-model-design.blogspot.com

**Figure 6.4**  Reproduced from European Commission, 2000. © European Communities, 1995–2009.

**Figure 6.5**  Reproduced from Amit, R., & Zott, C., (2001), 'Value Creation in e-business', Strategic Management Journal, 22, pp.493–520.

**Figure 6.6**  Reproduced from Möller, K. and Rajala, A., (2007), 'Rise of Strategic Nets—New Modes of Value Creation', Industrial Marketing Management, 36, pp. 895–908.

**Figure 6.7**  Reproduced from Shafer, S.M., Smith, H.J., and Linder, J.C., (2005), 'The Power of Business Models', Business Horizons, 48, pp. 199–207.

**Figure 6.8**  Reproduced with permission from © David//Armano 2009. http://darmano.typepad.com

**Figure 6.9**  Reprint courtesy of International Business Machines Corporation, copyright 2005 (c) International Business Machines Corporation.

**Figure 6.10**  Reproduced from Beynon-Davies, P., (2005), 'Constructing Electronic Government: The Case Of the UK Inland Revenue', International Journal of Information Management, 25, pp. 3–20.

**Figure 6.11**  Reproduced from ASOS website, 2009; www.asos.com

**Figure 6.12**  Reproduced from © ABCe, 2009; www.abce.org.uk

**Figure 7.3**  Reproduced from Ecomomist Intelligence Unit, 2008

**Figure 7.4**  Reproduced from Advertising Association, 2007

**Figure 7.5**  Reproduced from The Guardian, 18th April 2008. www.guardian.co.uk/uk/interactive/2008/apr/18/googlerevenue

**Figure 7.6**  Reproduced from Google Trends, 2008.

**Figure 7.7**  Reproduced from VanBoskirk, S., (2007), 'US Interactive Marketing Forecast, 2007 To 2012', Forrester Research, Inc.

**Figure 7.8**  Reproduced from Forrester Research 2008.

**Figure 7.9**  Reproduced from www.useit.com

**Figure 7.10**  Reproduced from Efficient Frontier, 2008. www.efrontier.com

**Figure 7.11**  Portions of this page are reproduced from work created and shared by Google and used according to terms described in the Creative Commons 2.5 Attribution License.

**Figure 7.12**  Reproduced from Vaughan's 1-page summaries, 2007. www.vaughans-1-pagers.com/internet/adwords-adsense-diagram.htm

**Figure 7.13**  Reproduced from eMarketer, 2006.

**Figure 8.1**  Reproduced from European Commission, Community Innovation Survey 4, 2006. © European Communities, 1995–2009.

**Figure 8.2**  Reproduced from Henderson, R.M. and Clark, J., (1990), 'Architectural Innovation', Administrative Science Quarterly, 35, pp. 9–30.

**Figure 8.3**  Reproduced from Mowery, D. and Rosenberg, N., (1978), 'The Influence of market Demand upon Innovation: A Critical Review of Some Recent Empirical Studies', Research Policy, 8 (2), pp. 102–53.

**Figure 8.4**  Reproduced from Gustafsson, A. & Johnson, D., (2003), Competing in a service Economy: how to create a competitive advantage through service development and Innovation. San Francisco: Jossey-Bass.

**Figure 8.5**  Reproduced from Forrester Research, Inc., 2007. "The Real Business Of Virtual Worlds, by Paul Jackson, March 23 2007 http://www.forrester.com/Research/Document/0,7211,40701,00.html

**Figure 8.6**  Reproduced from the Audit Commission 2006.

**Figure 9.1**  Reproduced from E-business w@tch, 2007. © European Communities, 1995–2009.

**Figure 9.4** Reproduced from E-business W@tch, 2006. © European Communities, 1995–2009.

**Figure 9.5** Reproduced from Intercept Software Labs.

**Figure 9.6** Reproduced from Johnson & Whang, 2002.

**Figure 9.8** Reproduced with permission from E-business W@tch, 2006. © European Communities, 1995–2009.

**Figure 9.10** Reproduced from New, S., Meakin T., and Southworth, R., (2002), Understanding the E-marketspace: Making Sense of B2B, Saïd Business School, University of Oxford.

**Figure 9.11** Reprinted by permission of Harvard Business Review. Adapted from "E-Hubs: the new B2B marketplaces" by Kaplan, S. & Sawhney, M., May–June 2000. Copyright © 2000 by the Harvard Business School Publishing Corporation.

**Figure 9.12** Reproduced from Capgemini, www.capgemini.com

**Figure 9.14** Reproduced from Alibaba.com.

**Figure 10.3** Reproduced from AbeBooks. www.abebooks.co.uk/docs/Sell

**Figure 11.1** Reproduced from European Commission/ RAND Europe, 2005. © European Communities, 1995–2009.

**Figure 11.2** Reproduced from eLab@INSEAD, based on GITR data, 2008.

**Figure 11.3** Reproduced from European Commission/ RAND Europe, 2005. © European Communities, 1995–2009

**Figure 11.4** Reproduced with permission from US Department of Labor, 2007.

**Figure 11.5** Reproduced from Computer Weekly, 2008.

**Figure 11.6** Reproduced from Computer Weekly/ Salary Services Ltd.

**Figure 11.7** Reproduced from E-business W@tch, 2006. © European Communities, 1995–2009.

**Figure 11.8** Adapted from Harrison, R., (1972), 'Understanding Your Organisation's Character', Harvard Business Review, 50(3), pp. 119–28.

**Figure 12.1** Reproduced from E-business w@tch, 2006. © European Communities, 1995–2009.

**Figure 12.2** Reproduced from Barclays Capital, 2008.

**Figure 12.3** Reproduced from TNS Market Research, · 2008.

**Figure 12.5** Reproduced from BEACON Consortium, 2006. © European Communities, 1995–2009.

## Images

**Image 1.1** Reprinted from Ian Muttoo, 2006. Licensed under Creative Commons, www.flickr.com/ photos/imuttoo/2628589070. p21

**Image 1.2** Reproduced with permission from the Government of Canada. p21

**Image 1.3** Reproduced from Oxfam, Oxfam GB, 2009. p24

**Image 1.4** Reprinted from net_efekt, 2008. Licensed under Creative Commons, www.flickr.com/photos/ wheatfields/2624415403/sizes/o. p24

**Image 1.5** Reprinted from net_efekt, 2008. Licensed under Creative Commons, www.flickr.com/photos/wheatfields/ 2625195092. p24

**Image 2.1** Reproduced from Andy Welsh, 2007. Licensed under Creative Commons. www.flickr.com/photos/wallrevolution. p37

**Image 2.2** Reproduced from Alamy. p41

**Image 2.3** Reproduced with permission from MoneySupermarket Group PLC, 2009. www.moneysupermarket.com. p51

**Image 2.5** Reproduced from Skype, 2009. p54

**Image 2.6** Reproduced from Ryan Fanshaw Photography, 2007. Licensed under Creative Commons, www.flickr.com/photos/002

**Image 2.7** Reproduced from eBay, 2009. p57

**Image 2.8** Reproduced from eBay, 2009. p57

**Image 3.1** Reproduced from William Hook, 2008. Licensed under Creative Commons. www.flickr.com/ photos/williamhook/2830319467. p65

**Image 3.2** Reproduced courtesy of Intel Corporation. p73

**Image 3.3** Reproduced with permission from RosettaNet. www.rosettanet.org . p77

**Image 3.4** Reproduced with permission from Barclays plc. p79

**Image 3.5** Reproduced with permission from Exostar, 2009. p86

**Image 3.6** Reproduced with permission from PayPal, 2009. p88

**Image 3.7** Reproduced with permission from PayPal, 2009. p89

**Image 4.1** Reproduced from Iain Dale's Diary, with permission. p103

Image 4.2   Reproduced from Steve Punter, 2008. Licensed under Creative Commons, www.flickr.com/photos/spunter. p104

Image 4.4   Reproduced from Walter Rumsby. Licensed under Creative Commons, www.flickr.com/photos/wrumsby/2098806069. p115

Image 4.5   Reproduced from Zlio, 2009. p119

Image 4.6   Reproduced from Dan Nevill, 2008. Licensed under Creative Commons, www.flickr.com/photos/dnevill/2327838667. p123

Image 4.7   Reproduced from Luc Legay, 2007. Licensed under Creative Commons, www.flickr.com/photos/luc/1824234195. p129

Image 4.8   Reproduced from Twitter. p130

Image 4.9   Reproduced from http://twitter.com/BarackObama. p130

Image 4.10   Reproduced from Linden Research Inc. Second Life is a trademark of Linden Research, Inc. p131

Image 5.1   Reproduced with permission from Wired Kids, Inc and Parry Aftab. p145

Image 5.2   Reproduced from Net Nanny. p145

Image 5.4   Reproduced from Don Hankins, 2007. Licensed under Creative Commons, www.flickr.com/photos/23905174@N00/1594411528. p154

Image 5.5   Reproduced from The Pirate Bay. p160

Image 5.6   Reproduced from The Pirate Bay.

Image 5.7   Reproduced from: The Spamhaus Project. p169

Image 5.9   Reproduced from Robert Scoble, 2008. Licensed under Creative Commons, www.flickr.com/photos/scobleizer/3024192707. p178

Image 6.1   Reproduced from Rene Ehrhardt, Licensed under Creative Commons www.flickr.com/photos/rene_ehrhardt/2391114010. p193

Image 6.2   Reproduced from Mike Zara, Licensed under Creative Commons, www.flickr.com/photos/brachiator/477994281. p194

Image 6.3   Reproduced from SqueegyX, Licensed under Creative Commons, www.flickr.com/photos/squeegy/2178926436. p197

Image 6.4   Reproduced from Bluetooth SIG Inc., 2009. p205

Image 6.5   Reproduced from William Hook, 2008, Licensed under Creative Commons, www.flickr.com/photos/williamhook/2220450293. p206

Image 6.6   Reproduced from Mario Sundar, 2007, Licensed under Creative Commons, www.flickr.com/photos/mariosundar/467945281. p215

Image 6.7   Reproduced from LinkedIn Corporation, 2009. p215

Image 6.8   Reproduced from Jasmic, 2006. Licensed under Creative Commons, www.flickr.com/photos/jasmic/162465222. p219

Image 6.9   Reproduced from John Millar, 2008. Licensed under Creative Commons, www.flickr.com/photos/hermes-/2173737710. p219

Image 6.10   Reproduced from www.asos.com/PRShots. p222

Image 6.11   Reproduced from Everydaylifemodern, 2007. Licensed under Creative Commons, www.flickr.com/photos/everydaylifemodern/455975707. p224

Image 7.1   Reproduced with permission from British Airways, plc. p247

Image 7.2   Reproduced with permission from Hotel Chocolat. p256

Image 7.3   Reproduced with permission from Shiny Media. p259

Image 7.4   Reproduced with permission from HP. p263

Image 7.5   Reproduced from www.eqal.com. p264

Image 7.6   Reproduced from Svadilfari, 2008. Licensed under Creative Commons, www.flickr.com/photos/22280677@N07/2312526351. p265

Image 8.1   Reproduced from Kıvanç Niş, 2006. Licensed under Creative Commons, www.flickr.com/photos/kiwanc/238383298. p281

Image 8.2   Reproduced with courtesy of David Rolnitzky, from his blog giantspatula.com. p284

Image 8.3   Reproduced from Omid Tavallai, 2007. Licensed under Creative Commons, www.flickr.com/photos/tavallai/2084954580. p287

Image 8.4   Reproduced from Nathans Pictures, 2007. Licensed under Creative Commons, www.flickr.com/photos/8768779@N03/1181820113. p294

Image 8.5   Reprinted courtesy of the Sulake Corporation. p299

Image 8.6   Reprinted courtesy of the Sulake Corporation. p300

Image 8.7   Reprinted from www.zunevideoconvertor.com

Image 8.8   Reproduced from www.Endgadget.com. p301

Image 9.1    Reproduced from Midnightcomm, 2006. Licensed under Creative Commons, www.flickr.com/photos/midnightcomm/171587228. p318

Image 9.2    Courtesy of RS Components Ltd© RS Components Ltd. p324

Image 9.3    Reproduced from Fady Habib, 2008. Licensed through Creative Commons, www.flickr.com/photos/untitlism/2623288733. p330

Image 9.4    Reproduced from: Daniel Ng, 2006. Licensed by Creative Commons, www.flickr.com/photos/galaygobi/114527025. p334

Image 9.5    Reproduced from MonkeyMyshkin, 2009. Licensed by Creative Commons, www.flickr.com/photos/monkeymyshkin/3623191672. p337

Image 9.6    Reproduced from www.Alibaba.com. p342

Image 9.7    Reproduced from Fraboof, 2007. Licensed by Creative Commons, www.flickr.com/photos/fraboof/2125693213. p334

Image 10.1    Reproduced from AbeBooks. www.abebooks.co.uk. p358

Image 10.2    Reproduced from AbeBooks. www.abebooks.co.uk. p367

Image 10.3    Reprinted courtesy of Imagini Holdings Ltd. p360

Image 10.4    Reproduced from Snagsta, 2009. p375

Image 10.5    Reprinted courtesy of Imagini Holdings Ltd. p373

Image 10.6    Reproduced from www.coproducer.org. p354

Image 11.1    Reproduced from David Sim, 2006. Licensed under Creative Commons, www.flickr.com/photos/victoriapeckham/261126130. p385

Image 11.2    Reproduced with permission from Media Bistro. p403

Image 11.3    Reproduced with permission from Google, Inc. p405

Image 11.4    Reproduced with permission from www.teachstreet.com. p407

Image 11.5    Reproduced with permission from 'School of Everything'. p408

Image 12.1    Reproduced from the Center for American Progress Action Fund. Licensed under Creative Commons, www.flickr.com/photos/americanprogressaction/452460042. p419

Image 12.2    Reproduced with permission from www.kiva.org. p425

Image 12.4    Reproduced from Asim Bharwani, 2008. Licensed under Creative Commons, www.flickr.com/photos/modenadude/3299052814. p439

## Tables

Table 1.1    Reproduced with permission from www.ifpi.org ITU, OECD.

Table 1.2    Reproduced with permission from Pew Internet & the American Life Project, 2001.

Table 2.1    Reproduced from e-Business W@tch, 2008. © European Communities, 1995–2009.

Table 3.1    Reproduced from Sun Microsystems, 2006. www.sun.com/software/whitepapers/webservices/soa_sysdev.pdf

Table 3.2    Reproduced from Piotrowicz, W., (2008), 'Electronic Procurement Evaluation'. unpublished PhD theses, Brunel University.

Table 3.3    Reproduced from Piotrowicz and Irani 2009.

Table 4.1    Reproduced from www.internetworldstats.com 2009. Steve Punter, Flikr © Miniwatts Marketing Group. All Rights Reserved.

Table 4.2    Reproduced from www.spatial-literacy.org 2007

Table 4.3    Reproduced from Hitwise, an Experian Company 2007, 2009.

Table 4.4    Reproduced with permission from ProBargainHunter.com, derived from Alexa Data 2009.

Table 4.5    Adapted from Kiecker, P. and Cowles, D.L., (2001), 'Interpersonal Communication and Personal Influence on the Internet: A Framework for Examining Online Word-of-Mouth,' *Journal of Euromarketing*, 11 (2), pp. 71–88.

Table 5.1    Reproduced from Ponemon Institute, (2009), *What Marketing Professional Think about the Value of Privacy to Consumers*, Ponemon Institute.

Table 5.2    Reproduced from The Spamhaus Project 2009.

Table 5.3    Reproduced from Dutton, W.H, and Peltu, M., (2005), 'The Emerging Internet Governance Mosaic: Connecting the Pieces', *Forum Discussion Paper* No. 5, Oxford Internet Institute.

**Table 6.1**  Reproduced from L Glassberg & Merhout, 2007. Copyright © 2007, Association for Computing Machinery, Inc.

**Table 6.2**  Reproduced from Michael Rappa© 1998–2009, Managing the Digital Enterprise® http://digitalenterprise.org

**Table 6.3**  Reproduced from Hitwise UK, 2009. www.hitwise.co.uk

**Table 7.1**  Reproduced from Jaworski, B., Kohli, A.K. & Sahay, A., (2000), 'Market-Driven Versus Driving Markets,' Journal of the Academy of Marketing Science, 28(1), pp.45–54.

**Table 7.3**  Reproduced from Lyris ffl EmailLabs, 2004. www.emaillabs.com/email_marketing_articles/article_click_to_open_rate.html

**Table 8.2**  Reproduced from Booz Allen Hamilton, (2005), The Booz Allen Hamilton Global Innovation 1000: Money Isn' Everything, by Barry Jaruzelsky, Kevin Dehoff, and Rakesh Bordia, http://www.boozallen.com/media/file/151786.pdf.

**Table 11.1**  Adapted from European Commission, 2000. © European Communities, 1995–2009.

**Table 11.2**  Adapted from Harrison, R., (1972), 'Understanding Your Organisation's Character', Harvard Business Review, 50(3), pp. 119–28.

**Table 12.1**  Reproduced from Gillett, S., Lehr, W.H., Osorio, C.A., and Sirbu, M.A., (2006), *Measuring the Economic Impact of Broadband Deployment, Final Report, National Technical Assistance, Training, Research, and Evaluation Project #99-07-13829*, US Department of Commerce.

**Table 12.2**  Reproduced from PWC, (2008), Safeguarding the New Currency of Business: Findings from the 2008 Global State of Information Security Study, www.pwc.com/extweb/home.nsf/docid/C1CD6CC69C2676D4852574DA00785949

**Table 12.3a**  Adapted from (a) Amaravadi, C. S., (2003), 'World and Business Computing 2051', Journal of Strategic Information Systems, 12(4), pp. 373–86 (b) Ellis, P., (2002), '"Reading the Tea-Leaves" from 50 Years of Business Computing', *Futures*, 34, pp. 873–81.

**Table 12.3b**  Adapted from (a) Amaravadi, C. S., (2003), 'World and Business Computing 2051', Journal of Strategic Information Systems, 12(4), pp. 373–86 (b) Ellis, P., (2002), '"Reading the Tea-Leaves" from 50 Years of Business Computing', *Futures*, 34, pp. 873–81.

**Table 12.4**  Reproduced from Preston, P. and Cawley, A., (2008), 'Broadband Development in the European Union to 2012—A Virtuous Circle Scenario', Futures, 40, pp. 812–21.

**Table 12.5**  Reproduced from Anderson, J.Q., and Rainie, L., (2008), The Future of the Internet III, Pew Internet & American Life Project, http://pewinternet.org/pdfs/PIP_FutureInternet3.pdf

**Table 12.6**  Reproduced from eMarketer, (2008), 'Mobile Advertising Spending to Surpass $6.5 billion in 2012', http://www.marketingcharts.com/direct/mobile-adver-tising-spending-to-surpass-65-billion-in-2012-4097/

# Index